SURVEY OF INVESTMENTS

HOLT, RINEHART AND WINSTON SERIES IN FINANCE

William Beranek, Advisor

Pennsylvania State University

Alexander A. Robichek and Alan B. Coleman

Management of Financial Institutions: Notes and Cases

Donald E. Vaughn

Survey of Investments

SURVEY OF
INVESTMENTS

Donald E. Vaughn
LOUISIANA STATE UNIVERSITY

HOLT, RINEHART AND WINSTON, INC.
New York / Chicago / San Francisco / Atlanta
Dallas / Montreal / Toronto / London

preface

This broad study of investment principles is intended as a textbook in a basic course in investments. Those seeking to learn investment methods and how the stock market operates will benefit from reading the book. Students are assumed to have completed one year in accounting, one year in economics, and one semester each in money and banking and corporate finance.

A variety of investment media are covered, and the student should find in this book the tools that will enable him to increase his return and control his investment risks. The text is divided into five parts: (1) "Investment Media and Priorities," (2) "Security Market Operations," (3) "The Fundamental Approach to Security Analysis," (4) "The Technical Approach to Timing Security Transactions," and (5) "Portfolio Management."

Before a student formulates his investment goals, he should be aware of the various types and classes of security media. Chapters 2 and 3 describe the numerous types of fixed- and variable-return securities available to the investor. On a fixed-return security, such as a bond, savings account, or preferred stock, the rate of return is limited to a specified annual amount, but with common stocks or rental property, the returns are variable, being neither assured nor limited to a specified rate.

The risks associated with these investments are treated in Chapter 4, while Chapters 5 and 6 consider the amount of emergency liquid funds and insurance that one should carry, home ownership, provision for education of children, supplementary income, retirement income, and building and preserving an estate.

Part Two deals with security markets and their development, the mechanics and regulation of security trading, the marketing of security issues, and sources of investment information.

An investment text is not complete without a section dealing with investment fundamentals. Chapter 12, therefore, analyzes financial statements, including the more important footnote items that are often an integral part of such statements, and describes the key ratios that are of value to the financial analyst. Chapters 13, 14, and 15 consider methods for analying industrial, utility, and transportation issues, respectively. Security-valuation methods, which are used to detect underpriced and overpriced issues, are treated in Chapter 16, while effects of special situations on market values are analyzed in Chapter 17.

From 1950 to 1965 the individual who sought capital appreciation was, on balance, successful, as evidenced by the fact that an investment in Standard and Poor's Average of 500 Stocks over this period appreciated at an annual rate of about 12 percent. It is one thing to invest successfully in a popular average, such as the Dow Jones Industrial Average or Standard and Poor's 500 stocks, and another to achieve success with a few issues. The individual with limited means normally invests in a few stocks, and he may wish to employ tools that will permit him to determine the time and price at which a given security is to be purchased or sold. One such device, described in Part Four, is the use of price and/or volume of trading information, commonly referred to as the technical approach. Chapter 18 describes the bar chart method and illustrates chart patterns that frequently precede price rises or declines. Chapter 19 illustrates the point-and-figure method for detecting accumulation and distribution of security holdings in individual issues, while technical indicators of the strength of the over-all market as well as of particular industries are described in Chapter 20. Chapter 21 presents some suggestions for locating bearish and bullish issues.

Part Five of the book, deals with portfolio management by the individual, the mutual fund, and other institutions such as endowment funds, pension funds, insurance companies, and common trust funds. Not only are individuals investing indirectly in common equities through financial intermediaries, such as mutual funds, but because of the impact that financial institutions exert upon the stock market through their security transactions, the alert investor may be able to profit from knowing what issues these institutions are buying and selling.

This book offers numerous advantages over other basic investment texts. The coverage is much more extensive than that of the typical investment textbook, which is often limited to one, two, or three of the five major areas presented in this volume. The book emphasizes the use of current literature in the study of investments, and many of the end-of-chapter problems require the student to consult the basic investment services and periodicals. It is believed that a student who works problems, does outside research, and develops a habit of reading current literature has a more lasting learning experience than one who is taught by the lecture method. Numerous investment schemes and techniques currently being followed by individual and institutional investors are described, illustrated, and evaluated with empirical data.

It is recommended that before reading a chapter the student first thumb through it, scanning the topical headings to gain some idea of the material covered. It may also be useful to read the chapter summary before reading the text itself. After the student has read the chapter, he should answer the "Questions for Review," which are based upon the text and which can usually be answered without reference to outside sources. The "Problems" are largely designed to acquaint the student with financial literature and to permit him to apply the principles illustrated within the chapter.

No one individual can learn or remember everything about stock market operations. He must, therefore, learn to gather relevant financial data from whatever sources are available, analyze these facts, and make a decision leading to the attainment of his investment objectives.

Sincere appreciation is expressed to Dr. William Beranek, advisory editor; to Mr. William L. Jiler and Mr. Kenneth W. Lutz, both of Trendline Corporation, who devoted some time to locating the Trendline charts illustrated; and to the numerous reviewers of the manuscript. The valuable assistance rendered by security brokers and dealers, investment services, librarians, and typing assistants is also appreciated.

Donald E. Vaughn

BATON ROUGE, LOUISIANA
AUGUST 1967

contents

part one | Investment Media and Priorities

The first step in the study of investments is to become acquainted with the characteristics of the most common types of securities. Chapter 2 describes fixed-return securities, Chapter 3 presents variable-return securities, and Chapter 4 indicates the nature of the risks associated with each of these types of securities.

Chapters 5 and 6 illustrate how the individual can formulate for himself concrete investment priorities that will provide adequate liquidity, protection of his family in the event of his early death, protection against inflation and deflation, and permit him to accumulate wealth to be used, among other things, as a source of income.

Part I is designed to accomplish four objectives: (1) to acquaint the reader with the various types of security media; (2) to develop a vocabulary of investment terms; (3) to evaluate the risks associated with each type of investment; and (4) to assist in outlining a personal program of investment priorities.

chapter 1   Introduction|

Every family should have a financial plan or set of investment goals, such as the accumulation of a savings account for meeting emergency situations, the acquisition of insurance on the life of the wage earner, the purchase of a home, the provision for adequate retirement income, or the building of an estate. In order to develop goals and realistic plans for their attainment, the individual should have a knowledge of the various security types, their advantages and disadvantages (including their associated risks), and the ability to estimate their potential returns.

Knowledge of the general features of each type of security is necessary in order for the investor to choose those with characteristics that are most attractive to him. It is important to know the risks associated with each medium, so that in the selection of securities the individual can make a more informed choice of balancing risks against the return. Ordinarily, the higher the risk on a security, the greater will be the expected return required by an investor.

Risks that should be considered by the investor are *inflation, deflation, financial failure,* and *changes in security prices.* The inflationary risk refers to the probability or chance of a loss in purchasing power of interest income and principal repayment from a fixed-return security, such as a bond, savings account, or life insurance contract, as the general price level rises. In this context the general price level is usually measured by a "cost of living" index. The deflationary risk is the probability or chance of a decline in prices of real property and common stocks. The safety of investments in government and corporate securities is dependent upon, among other things, the financial success of the issuer, since financial failures usually impose losses upon security holders. Bond prices fluctuate over the business cycle, and the possible decline in market values of fixed-return securities is referred to as the *interest rate risk.*

At the outset, the individual should decide whether he plans to be an *investor*—that is, whether he intends to invest in a given security for the long-term—or a *speculator* and commit his funds on a short-term basis. An investor, as defined in this sense, will select securities by a different technique than the speculator. The investor tries to locate stocks that will grow or appreciate in price in the long run, say over several years, and/or securities that provide an assured interest or divided return. (Stocks that have substantial potential for price appreciation are often said to be undervalued.) During the holding period, the investor disregards short-term fluctuations in the market value of his stocks. The speculator, however, wishes to invest his funds for a short-term capital gain, and in order to forecast security price movements may make use of so-called *technical aids*, for example, bar charts and point-and-figure charts.

Some writers, particularly economists, distinguish between a speculator and an investor on the basis of motive: the investor is said to seek *current income*, that is, interest or dividends, while the speculator desires *capital appreciation*, that is, a price increase in his investment.

Some individuals elect to commit a portion of their securities, or investment portfolio, to long-term investments—disregarding short-term market fluctuations—and place the balance of their common stock fund in speculative issues that are faster moving and that have wider price movements. The latter are traded at frequent intervals when the desired level of capital gain, such as 10 to 20 percent, can be achieved. The proceeds are then reinvested in other "reasonably priced" issues or held in cash until the previously held issues have declined to an attractive buying level.

Many individuals who wish to invest in common stocks because of their potential growth in value but who wish to be free from the mental anguish frequently accompanying a direct investment in stocks elect to buy the shares of investment companies, permitting the professional management of the latter to make the decision as to what and when to buy and sell. Some 300 investment companies in the United States offer a broad diversity of investment policies, some investing almost exclusively in so-called *growth stocks*, that is, stocks that grow in sales and profits more rapidly than their industry and the U.S. economy, while others invest heavily in fixed-return securities. The holders of investment company shares receive diversification in their security portfolios, since the typical investment company commits its funds in from 75 to 150 different stocks that represent from 15 to 25 industries. The purchase cost, referred to as a *load fee*, the management fee, and other operating expenses, however, often reduce the dividend and capital gains income to a rate below that achievable through a hypothetical investment into the popular averages. The choice between making a direct investment in common stocks or in shares of investment companies should depend upon (1) the amount of funds available for investing (small investors frequently prefer investment company shares), (2) the extent of diversification desired, (3) the amount of time the stockholder is willing to devote toward the management of his account, and (4) the ability of the owner to manage his own account.

Securities of locally owned and operated firms are often traded in the *over the counter market*, that is, not on an exchange, while common stocks of large nationally known companies are often traded on so-called *stock exchanges*, or organized auction markets. Becoming familiar with the functions of brokers, dealers, and security exchanges and with the ways they assist investors will enable the individual to make the most appropriate use of their services. This subject will be discussed in Chapters 7 and 8.

Securities may be classified on the basis of the type of industry of the issuer. One such classification consists of government, finance, transportation, industrial, and public utilities. Since each of these areas of investment offers some advantages and disadvantages, a study of these categories is important. The interest earned on bonds of local and state governments, called *municipals*, is exempt from federal income taxes, and these instruments may be used to advantage by individuals and financial institutions in high income tax brackets (see Chapters 2 and 4). Since the financial statements and expenses incurred by the transportation, industrial, and public utilities groups differ widely, a separate study of these major categories is useful and appears in Chapters 12–15. Operating performances and portfolio management of financial institutions are discussed in Chapter 24.

The investor is interested in a return on his investment in the form of interest, dividends, growth in capital, or a suitable combination of these. He is also concerned with the variability of the expected return and with the numerous other risks that may be associated with the investment.

Securities differ in their risk characteristics. Long-term marketable government bonds, for example, possess both interest rate risk and inflationary risk. These bonds are of the highest *credit quality*, that is, the chance of a default in the interest or principal repayment is remote, and the bonds are highly *liquid* because large amounts are traded in each transaction without unduly affecting prices. The bonds carry an assured interest return and a high probability of principal repayment at maturity, and thus have a low risk of financial failure.

Common stocks, conversely, have no guarantee of dividend payment and no maturity date with a guarantee of principal repayment. Moreover, many have limited liquidity, and their market value may oscillate widely. In addition, some companies suffer financial reverses and bankruptcy. However, the stock prices of numerous corporations generally rose from 1945 through 1965, so that stocks of selected firms provided protection against inflation. With all other risk characteristics, however, the degree of risk in a common stock investment is likely to be much greater than in U.S. government bonds.

Many investors attempt to locate securities that appear to be underpriced at their current market value. Depressed prices may be due to the fact that the stocks of companies within a given industry all reflect temporary unfavorable investor sentiment and trade at low *multiples of earnings*, that is, the ratio of the market value per share to the earnings per share, commonly referred to as the *price–earnings ratio*.

Other issues, however, may trade at higher than average earnings multiples because of a significant change in management, competitive position within the industry, product improvement, mineral discovery, and similar factors that are expected to enhance substantially the long-run earnings of the company. The investor may purchase the securities at current market prices or he may attempt to improve the timing of the purchase through the application of the *technical approach*, that is, the attempt to gauge the short-term movement of stock prices by using price and/or volume of trading information. If he correctly forecasts a downward price movement, the stock may be acquired on a later date at a lower market value. There is always the possibility, of course, that the market price will move up rather than down.

Many speculators attempt to use the technical approach in locating issues to be bought or sold. A stock that moves up on relatively heavy volume is ordinarily assumed to be in heavy demand by buyers, while an issue that declines on relatively heavy volume is assumed to be low in demand. Although some traders, those who buy for short-term capital gains, reap attractive returns on their investments, numerous investment writers suggest that the average stock trader is less successful than the average long-term investor.

A number of investment schemes may be followed by the investor, such as dollar averaging, formula investing, or buying undervalued issues. *Dollar averaging* is a plan for committing a definite fixed amount of money at stated intervals into the shares of one company or into investment company shares. *Formula investing* is a plan for determining the appropriate balance of a portfolio to be held in fixed-return securities, such as long-term government bonds, and in common stocks. *Undervalued issues* may be located by contrasting companies within a given industry for growth in earnings per share and for the price-earnings multiples, or ratios, at which they trade. The advantages and disadvantages of these and other methods are considered in Chapter 22.

Finally, the investor must have patience in awaiting his hoped-for results. Otherwise he may sell his security just before a rise in market value in order to buy either a stagnant or a declining issue.

chapter 2 | Security Types: Fixed Return

Introduction

The savings and investment habits of individuals and business firms vary widely. During World War II a large portion of disposable personal income was saved. After companies returned to peace-time production, heavy demand for consumer goods reduced current savings to a fraction of war-time levels. During the 1950s and early 1960s, however, individuals generally saved from 6 to 8 percent of their disposable personal income, investing some of the funds in various types of fixed- and variable-return securities. Since World War II business corporations have retained about one half of their after-tax profits for expanding plant and working capital.

This chapter describes types of savings media, government and corporate fixed-return issues, life insurance contracts, and other types of fixed-return securities. Each medium has peculiar characteristics that make it attractive to investors seeking certain attributes and having particular investment goals. The risks associated with each are analyzed in Chapter 4.

Savings Media

Six types of savings media are available for the individual investor. These include shares in savings and loan associations, time deposits with mutual savings banks, time or savings deposits with commercial banks, shares of credit unions, U.S. government savings bonds, and deposits in the postal savings system.

Shares of Savings and Loan Associations

Savings and loan associations are of two types—stock companies and mutual companies. While mutual companies outnumber stock companies by about 10 to 1, there is little difference between the operation of the two. In the stock savings and loan association, initial capital is raised through the sale of common shares, and the depositors are creditors. The shareholders then participate in the profits after payment of operating costs and interest expenses to depositors and elect the board of directors in the manner as in an ordinary business corporation.

7

In the mutual savings and loan corporation, the initial operating capital is frequently provided by businessmen who are interested in forming a savings association. Some of the initial contributors usually become the directors and officers of the concern. After the firm has been in operation for a period of time, the capital is composed primarily of retained profits. In the mutual savings and loan company, each stockholder has one vote in the election of the directors, and each shareholder, that is, each depositor, has a pro rata claim against the retained earnings account. Ownership in a savings and loan association is ordinarily represented by a passbook, which must be submitted with each deposit and withdrawal. These associations typically pay interest, sometimes referred to as dividends, semiannually, but some declare dividends quarterly. Any funds withdrawn prior to the dividend payment date will usually not receive any interest for that portion of the interest period prior to withdrawal.

Savings and loan associations may operate under state or federal charter, and at the end of 1965, about one third of the 6300 savings and loan associations in the United States were operating under federal charter. Federal associations are required to be, and state-chartered savings and loan associations may be, members of the Federal Savings and Loan Insurance Corporation (FSLIC). This corporation insures each shareholder's account up to a maximum of $15,000. At the end of 1965, almost 30 percent of all savings and loan associations were state, noninsured associations but these accounted for only 4 percent of total share deposits. In most states the associations have the power to require 30 to 60 days notification for share withdrawal, but the associations rarely impose the restrictions for small withdrawals. Others require a few days notification for large deposit withdrawals such as $10,000.

Savings and loan associations invest a large percentage of their funds in residential mortgages, with the balance distributed among commercial property mortgages, cash, government securities, and other assets.

Deposits with Mutual Savings Banks

Mutual savings banks, which numbered only about 520 in 1965, were located predominantly in the Atlantic seaboard states, with New York, Massachusetts, and Rhode Island accounting for more than one half of the number. These banks operate similarly to mutual savings and loan associations, permitting each shareholder one vote in the election of directors and increasing their capital through the retention of profits. The savings banks may elect to be insured by the Federal Deposit Insurance Corporation (FDIC) or the FSLIC. Their assets are primarily invested in mortgages and high-grade fixed-return securities.

Time and Savings Deposits at Commercial Banks

A majority of commercial banks offer two types of savings plans to individuals. *Savings accounts*, on which the individual earns interest, usually compounded semiannually, are offered by virtually all commercial banks.

Each demand deposit and savings account at a national, state-member, and state-insured nonmember bank is insured by the FDIC up to $15,000, while time certificates of deposits are insured by the FSLIC. Since profit-making institutions are not permitted to open savings accounts at such banks, commercial banks have developed for these investors *time certificates of deposits*, sometimes referred to as CD's. Individuals are also eligible to acquire CD's. While funds in savings accounts may be withdrawn on 30 days notice, as in a typical savings and loan association, time certificates of deposit are issued with definite maturities. A slightly lower rate is usually paid on shorter maturities than on those for six to twelve months, and the interest rates paid on CD's may be slightly higher than those paid on savings accounts. In 1965, the Board of Governors of the Federal Reserve System raised the maximum interest rate permitted to be paid on CD's from 4.5 to 5.5 percent. In its announcement the board said that the step was taken to permit commercial banks to pay higher rates and to attract more short-term investments from foreigners. However, it is doubtful that many commercial banks can afford to pay a rate as high as 5.5 percent. In early 1967, insured banks were limited to a 4 percent rate on savings accounts, 5.5 percent on CD's of greater than $100,000 and 30 or more days to maturity, and 5 percent on smaller CD accounts.

Credit Union Shares

Many individuals are eligible for membership in either a state or a federally chartered credit union. At the end of 1965, more than 22,000 credit unions with more than seven million members were in operation in the United States. This is a cooperative-type association, where each member must buy at least one share of interest, each share usually having a value of $5. Members are encouraged to save systematically by making weekly or monthly purchases of shares in the association. A majority of the associations pay dividends semiannually, and the assets acquired by the credit unions are reloaned to members for the purchase of consumer durable goods, for current living expenses, or for emergencies. The members are co-owners of the association, and each has one vote at the annual stockholders meeting to elect the board of directors. Notification of share withdrawals is ordinarily not required, and the credit union often provides debt-cancellation insurance to the borrowing members and share life insurance to the stockholders. The accounts of the shareholders were not insured in 1966, but some discussion of such a plan was being considered by the Credit Union National Association.

U.S. Savings Bonds

Although U.S. savings bonds were authorized in the 1930s, they did not gain in popularity until the 1940s, when vast sums were placed in U.S. savings bonds to help finance the war effort. Series E bonds in 1967 were yielding 4.15 percent when held to maturity of seven years and redeemed at

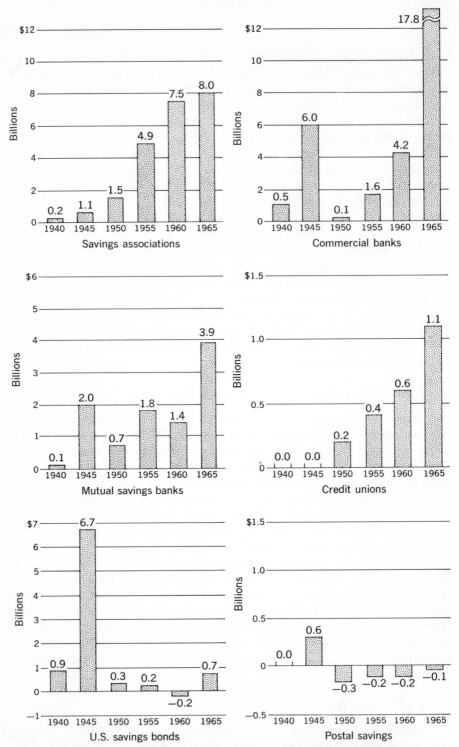

FIGURE 2-1 / Changes in flow of savings to selected media, 1940–1965.
From U.S. Savings and Loan League, *Fact Book,* Chicago,
1966, p. 11.

par. The bonds are sold on a discount basis at 75 percent of face value and are not negotiable. Series H bonds were carrying yields similar to Series E, were sold at par, matured in 10 years, and paid semiannual interest to the registered holder. The savings bonds (E and H) are issued by the U.S. Treasury Department through commercial banks and are redeemable at the banks upon demand at a fixed price schedule. They are not marketable other than by being resold to the Treasury through its bank agents, nor may they serve as collateral for a loan.

Postal Savings

The U.S. Postal Savings System was authorized in 1910. Under this type of savings, individuals are permitted to open a savings account witnessed by a passbook. The deposit of each individual is limited to $2500, and during the early 1960s the Treasury Department was phasing out this savings operation. Initially, some communities that did not have a bank possessed a post office, and this provided individuals within these locations with a savings medium. Although this type of savings medium accounted for about $3 billion in 1947, the figure had declined to less than $0.5 billion by 1966, influenced largely by the 2 percent annual rate being paid at that time.

Annual Flow of Savings to Savings Media

Figure 2–1 indicates the changes in savings in selected media from 1940 through 1965. The annual increase in savings for these six types of savings media in 1940 amounted to only $1.7 billion. More than one half of this amount was invested in U.S. savings bonds, while $0.5 billion flowed to savings deposits in commercial banks. During 1965, however, more than $28

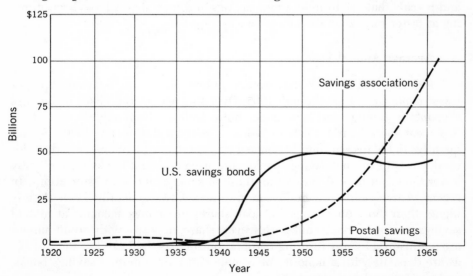

(See following page for continuation of figure and caption.)

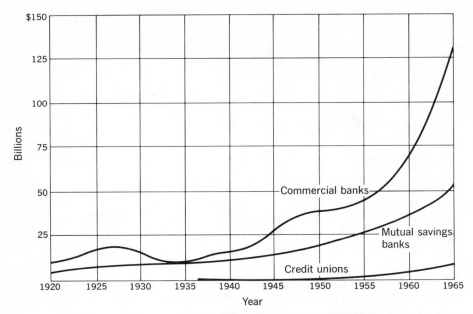

FIGURE 2-2 / Changes of savings in selected media, 1920–1965. From
U.S. Savings and Loan League, *Fact Book,* Chicago, 1966,
p. 12.

billion was invested in these types of savings media, with slightly more than
one third going to savings and loan associations and a similar share to commercial banks. The balance was divided among mutual savings banks, credit
unions, and U.S. savings bonds. From 1950 through 1965, amounts in postal
savings declined. Figure 2–2 compares the growth of savings for the six types
and reveals that credit unions and savings and loan shares have been growing at faster rates than the other security types.

Average Annual Yields

Figure 2–3 indicates the average annual yields on selected types of
investments from 1930 through 1965. Over this period, the yields on savings
accounts in savings and loan associations declined from slightly more than
5 percent in the early 1930s to below 3 percent during the 1940s. Subsequently, yields rose to slightly above 4 percent. Over this same period, yields
on deposits of mutual savings banks and of commercial banks were slightly
lower than, but moved parallel to, those of savings and loan associations. In
recent years, yields on credit union shares have generally been slightly
higher than those on savings and loan shares or savings accounts at mutual
savings or commercial banks. However, share deposits with credit unions
are not insured by any insuring corporation such as the FDIC or the FSLIC,
as are deposits with a majority of commercial banks, mutual savings banks,
and savings and loan associations.

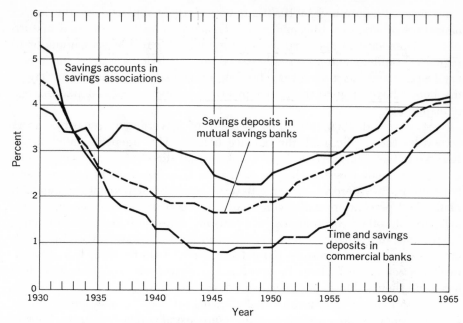

FIGURE 2-3 / Average annual yields on selected types of investments, 1930–1965. From U.S. Savings and Loan League, *Fact Book*, Chicago, 1966, p. 17.

Although not shown in Figure 2–3, yields on Series E and H bonds were 2.9 percent during World War II, but had risen in several steps to 4.15 percent in early 1966. Whereas there was a yield preference for savings bonds during World War II, that is, the yields compared favorably to those of other savings media, this was untrue during the latter 1950s and early 1960s, so that other types of savings media gained relative to the investment in Series E and H bonds. The interest paid on postal savings was only 2 percent per year in 1966.

Government Issues

U.S. Marketable Securities

The U.S. Treasury Department was using a number of different types of issues to finance the current federal debt of approximately $330 billion in 1966. The marketable issues consisted of Treasury bills, certificates, notes, Treasury bonds, and other bonds, while nonmarketable securities were U.S. savings bonds, Treasury savings notes, Treasury bonds–investment series, special issues, and others. *Treasury bills* were three-, six-, or twelve-month noninterest-bearing debt instruments that were sold at a discount adequate to provide the investor with the prevailing yield. For example, a six-month bill issued at 98 percent of par yielded slightly more than 4 percent. *Certifi-*

cates were discontinued in 1963 and were largely replaced by the longer maturities of Treasury bills and notes. *Treasury notes* have original maturities of from one to five years, carrying interest payable semiannually to registered holders, and are usually issued once or twice a year as the Treasury Department has a need for refunding other maturing obligations. Treasury bonds have original maturities in excess of five years and pay interest semiannually.

At year-end 1966, about 66 percent of government securities were owned by the public, with the balance held by U.S. agencies and Federal Reserve banks. The breakdown of ownership of direct and fully guaranteed U.S. government securities in late 1966 was: U.S. government agencies and trust funds, 20.9 percent; Federal Reserve banks, 13.4 percent; commercial banks, 17.3 percent; mutual savings banks, 1.4 percent; insurance companies, 2.9 percent; other corporations, 4.5 percent; state and local governments, 7.2 percent; individuals, 22.9 percent; foreign and internationals, 4.4 percent; other miscellaneous investors, 5.0 percent. From 1945 to 1966, U.S. government agencies, the Federal Reserve banks, individuals, and foreigners had increased their holdings of U.S. government securities.[1]

When monetary authorities are following an "easy" money policy, interest rates on U.S. government securities are usually relatively low. During periods of "tight" money, that is, in boom periods, interest rates on U.S.

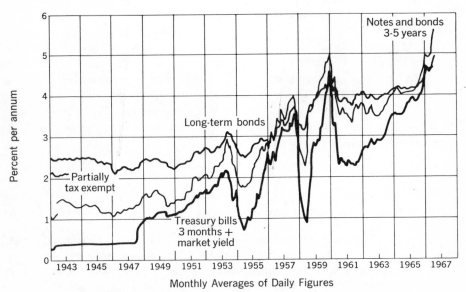

FIGURE 2-4 / Yields on U.S. government securities. From the Federal Reserve System, *Historical Chart Book,* Washington, D.C., U.S. Government Printing Office, 1966, p. 25.

[1] Volume outstanding and ownership is reported in the current issue of Board of Governors of the Federal Reserve System, *Federal Reserve Bulletin* (Washington, D.C.: U.S. Government Printing Office).

government securities are relatively high. Interest rates, or yields to maturity, on three-month Treasury bills normally oscillate much more than those on intermediate-term notes and long-term Treasury bonds. Figure 2–4 indicates that the yields on the intermediate notes usually vary somewhere between those on short-term Treasury bills and those on long-term government securities.

Federally Sponsored Agencies

Yields of U.S. government agency securities have averaged slightly higher than those on U.S. Treasury obligations. These agencies include federal home loan banks, the Federal National Mortgage Association, banks for cooperatives, federal intermediate credit banks, federal land banks, and the Tennessee Valley Authority. Each of these agencies typically finances a part of its assets through the sale of short- or intermediate-term notes or long-term bonds. Yields on these securities are typically 0.1 to 0.2 of 1 percent higher than those on similar maturities of government securities, because these securities are not guaranteed by the federal government as to principal and interest. The Treasury Department does have a lending agreement with a majority of its agencies, however, under which loans are to be made available to the agencies in times of need. The agency securities are considered to have an Aaa rating, only slightly lower than those of U.S. government securities.[2]

State and Municipal Securities

The annual amount of financing by state and local governments had increased from approximately $5.5 billion in 1956 to more than $10 billion in 1964. By mid-1965 there was an estimated $75 billion in municipal securities outstanding, which represented an increase of almost 400 percent during the past 20 years. A further doubling of the amount by 1975 was anticipated.

Issues of state and municipal securities are generally classified by types of taxing authority associated with the debt servicing. These include *general obligations*, which are backed by the full taxing authority of the issuer; limited tax bonds, or *special assessment bonds*; and *revenue bonds*. Servicing the interest and principal payment for the latter is limited to the revenues

[2] For a complete list of the securities outstanding that have been issued by federally sponsored agencies, the investor should refer to the current issue of the *Federal Reserve Bulletin*. Current yields for these securities may be obtained by checking a recent issue of *The Wall Street Journal*, *Barron's*, or *Commercial and Financial Chronicle*. Moody's Investors Service and Standard & Poor's Corporation rate municipal, agency, and corporate bond issues with one of nine bond ratings, ranging from Aaa, the highest, to C grade. The ratings are dependent upon the services' estimation of the debt-servicing ability of the issuer, taking into account such factors as earning stability, amount of debt, number of times interest is earned, and senior debt issues.

generated from the project for which the issue proceeds were used, such as the erection of a toll road or bridge. Frequently a revenue issue will also be backed by the full taxing authority of the municipality. During 1965, almost 64 percent of the municipal issues sold were general obligations, another 31 percent were revenue obligations, and the remaining 5 percent were Public Housing Administration (PHA) bonds and U.S. government loans. The interest earned on municipal and PHA bonds is exempt from federal income taxes, but capital gains are taxed.

The 1949 housing act authorized the creation of local public housing agencies that would cooperate with the PHA in an attempt to eliminate unsafe and unsanitary housing. Funds are provided by bonds that are issued by local housing agencies and directly guaranteed by the PHA. These bonds have an Aaa rating, are considered to be municipal bonds for federal income tax purposes, and the recipient is not taxed on the interest. Long-term capital gains, however, are taxable at the applicable rate.

Since the interest received on investments in state and local government securities is exempt from federal income tax, the securities trade at lower

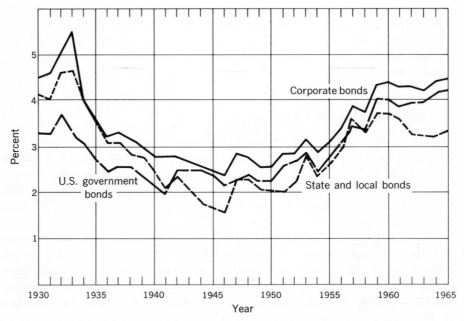

FIGURE 2-5 / Average annual yield on selected types of investments, 1930–1965. From U.S. Savings and Loan League, *Fact Book,* Chicago, 1966, p. 17.

yields to maturity than do the fully taxable issues. For example, Figure 2–5 compares the yields on state and local government securities to those on corporate issues and on long-term U.S. government securities from 1930 through 1966. Throughout this period the yields on state and local government issues were approximately one percentage point lower than those on long-term U.S. government securities.

However, during certain periods of time, such as in late 1957, the spread between the yields on municipal securities and Treasury issues became very narrow. Because of favorable tax treatment of interest, this type of issue is in demand by individuals who are in high income tax brackets and by certain financial institutions.

The larger of the municipal issues are rated by Moody's Investors Service, Standard & Poor's Corporation, and/or Fitch Bond Rating Service. Each of these bond-rating services assigns one of nine possible grades to a given bond. In interpreting the ratings, bonds with the highest grades have the greatest degree of servicing assurance, that is, assurance of payment of interest and principal, while bonds of Ba grade or lower are somewhat speculative in nature, and the degree of servicing assurance is substantially lower.

Corporate Debt Issues

Types of Corporate Securities

The one million corporations operating in the United States in 1966 were using many different types of fixed-return securities. Types of debt used by corporations include accounts payable to trade creditors, accrued wages, accrued taxes, other accruals, short-term notes to the general public, term loans to banks and other financial institutions, bond issues, mortgage loans, and subordinated loans to officers or stockholders. In addition to long-term debt, some corporations issue preferred stock.

American corporations make extensive use of debt. From 1950 to 1964, the long-term debt of American corporations increased from $72.2 billion to $227.4 billion, or by 214 percent. During the same 15-year period, short-term debt increased from $94.9 billion to $252.9 billion, or by 166 percent. Long-term debt is used as the major source of external funds by U.S. corporations because (1) the interest is a business expense, whereas dividends on stock are paid from after-tax income, and ordinarily costs less than equity capital; (2) the use of debt provides the corporation with leverage (generating a larger return than the cost of the funds increases the return to the common shareholders); and (3) large blocks of bonds may be readily sold to financial institutions or to the general public at low underwriting costs.

From 1955 through 1965, American corporations annually raised from $10 to $15.8 billion by the sale of new securities. Some 70 to 80 percent of the issues made in any one year are usually in the form of bonds or notes, while much of the balance consists of common stocks. Only 2 or 3 percent of the new issues in any one year has been in preferred stocks. About 50 to 60 percent of the bond issues are sold directly to financial institutions such as large life insurance companies, while the balance is sold to the general public through investment banking firms.[3] When compared to internally generated funds, for example, net income and noncash expenses such as depreciation, external financing is small, with the former annually averaging roughly $40 to $55 billion in the early 1960s.

Characteristics of Corporate Bonds

Although they vary considerably in amount and legal characteristics, bond instruments usually have a number of common features. Almost all have *definite maturities.* They are usually issued in denominations of $1000, although some may be of smaller size or in multiples of $1000. For the most part, interest is paid semiannually. Some are *bearer bonds,* that is, unregistered as to principal and interest, with coupons attached. To collect the interest payments the owner of the bond clips the appropriately dated coupon and mails it to the corporation or paying agency. Other bonds are *registered* as to principal and/or interest, so that the registered owner receives his semiannual interest payment automatically by mail.

Yields Versus Grade

There is a wide spread between the *yields to maturity* on corporate issues of different grades, because the high-grade issues carry little risk of nonpayment of principal and interest to the holders.[4] Others are much more speculative and are assigned low ratings by bond-rating agencies. The higher-rated bonds, all other things being equal, trade at lower yields to maturity than do the lower-rated bonds. High-grade bonds are usually issued by corporations with substantial financial strength and ability to service their debt. Although default is not completely ruled out, it is unlikely. One of the tests of bond quality is the number of times the firm earns the interest plus other fixed charges, such as sinking fund payments or leasing rentals. The ratio is usually significantly larger on high-grade bonds than on low-grade bonds.

A comprehensive study of American corporate bond financing from 1900 through 1942, conducted by the National Bureau of Economic Research, disclosed some interesting facts on corporate bond defaults. The default rate was slightly lower for public utilities, intermediate for industrial issues, and slightly higher for railroads. Although many corporations defaulted in the payment of either principal or interest, the amounts owing were usually ultimately paid, since the weak corporation often reorganized

---

[3] This topic is explained in greater detail in Chapter 10.
[4] The rate of return when held to maturity. See Chapter 4 for the method of computation.

or merged with another corporation. Where investor bought bonds at depressed prices upon default and held them until the debt was extinguished, handsome returns ranging from 10 to 40 percent per annum were realized.[5]

Debt Structure

A privately owned utility or railroad is typically a heavier user of debt than an industrial corporation. It is not uncommon to find an electric utility with 50 or 55 percent of its total capitalization, that is, long-term debt, preferred stock, and common equity, provided by long-term bonds. Typically the utility uses an *open-end first mortgage bond* issue, which permits the corporation to issue additional bonds of equal rank and secured by the same "real assets," for example, land and buildings. Railroads, while providing from 40 to 45 percent of their total capitalization with long-term debt instruments, typically have a much more complicated debt structure. Frequently it consists of a number of different bond issues secured by liens, or pledges of property as security for a debt, on the railroad's right of way, terminals, or rolling stock. Although many industrial corporations do not use long-term debt, it is not uncommon to find a company with from 20 to 30 percent of its total capital represented by long-term debt.

Bond Indenture

The terms under which bonds are issued are contained in the legal agreement between the issuing corporation and the bondholders (or bond trustee). This document is commonly called the *bond indenture* or *trust agreement.* The indenture ordinarily includes a description of the pledged property, the coupon rate, the maturity date, provisions for early retirement of the issue, provisions for modifying the characteristics of the bonds, limitation on other debt issues, and other items.[6]

Mortgage Bonds and Debentures

Bonds secured by a lien on the real property of the issuer are commonly referred to as *first mortgage bonds*; others may be secured by a lien on personal tangible property such as furniture, machinery, or, in the case of railroads, rolling stock. Still other issues, particularly those made by holding companies or financial institutions, may be secured by a pledge of stocks and/or bond instruments and are called *collateral trust bonds.*

[5] For a more complete analysis of corporate bond financing, see W. Braddock Hickman, *Statistical Measures of Corporate Bond Financing Since 1900,* a study by the National Bureau of Economic Research (Princeton, N.J.: Princeton University Press, 1960).

[6] The duties of a bond trustee are covered in Chapter 9.

Debentures, which are most commonly used by industrial corporations, are not secured by a pledge of a specific asset. For a given corporation, secured bonds usually rank higher in quality and trade at lower yields than do unsecured issues, but debentures of industrial firms may trade at lower yields to maturity than some of the secured railroad issues.

The financial strength of the issuer and its ability to service adequately its indebtedness is of greater importance in making a bond-purchase decision than the type and amount of security pledged behind the bond. Where the investor has the option of investing in two securities of approximately equal merit with the exception that one is secured and the other is unsecured, the secured bond would normally be preferred.

Income Bonds, Convertible Bonds, and Warrants

Other types of debt issues that are frequently issued by corporations are income bonds, bonds with warrants attached, and convertible debenture issues. The interest on *income bonds* is not required to be paid unless earned (it may be cumulative or noncumulative), and the bonds are usually issued in connection with a reorganization of a financially weak firm. Cumulative interest or dividends accumulate from year to year and must be paid prior to dividend payment on lower-ranking securities. Noncumulative interest or dividends are not carried forward when passed, and such securities offer a low assurance of income. Since interest is not assured and the bonds are usually unsecured, they normally carry low quality ratings and trade at relatively high yields.

In order to make a bond issue attractive, corporations frequently attach *warrants* to the bonds that permit the holders to buy shares of common stock in the corporation during a stipulated time period at a definite price. The warrants, which are usually detachable from the bonds, are often listed for trading on one of the major stock exchanges and may offer speculative investment opportunities to investors when the market price of the common shares is expected to rise.[7] The market value of the warrants usually oscillates more widely than that of common stocks, although the warrants receive no dividends. Warrants that are not exercised by the expiration date become worthless, and the exercise of a large number of warrants may dilute the earnings per share and market price of the common stock.

Corporations unable to sell bonds or companies reluctant to sell common stock at the prevailing market price may elect, however, to offer *convertible bonds.* The bonds are ordinarily convertible into common shares at premiums of 25 to 50 percent above the common share price on issuance

---

[7] Corporations with stock purchase warrants may be determined by consulting the capitilization structures of companies analyzed by standard investment services. Trading in outstanding warrants is reported in *The Wall Street Journal, Barron's,* and other security-transaction sources.

date, and the bonds frequently trade at low current yields because of the speculative value of the conversion feature. As the market value of the common stock rises above the conversion price, the bonds trade approximately at their conversion values. Although many of the issues are *callable,* that is, the bond indenture permits the corporation to retire the issue at a fixed price, usually slightly above par, prior to the stated maturity dates, the holders ordinarily have 30 or 60 days after the call to convert into stocks. The conversion of a large debenture issue may dilute the earnings per share and market value of the common stock.[8]

Preferred Stocks

Characteristics

Preferred stocks do not offer the tax advantage to the issuing corporation provided by long-term bond instruments. Whereas the interest on bonds is a deductible expense, dividends paid on preferred stock are paid out of after-tax income; therefore, corporate sale of preferred stock during the 1950s and early 1960s constituted only about 2 to 3 percent of the total annual issues.[9]

Most preferred issues are in denominations of $100 and most provide that preferred shareholders receive a set dividend before the common shareholders receive any. The typical preferred stock has a *cumulative* feature, which means that unpaid dividends accumulate from year to year and must be paid to preferred shareholders before cash dividends are paid to the common stockholders. Many preferred issues also carry, in case the corporation is dissolved, *liquidation preferences* over common stockholders. Liquidation privileges are usually limited to the par value of the stock, and unless otherwise stated, preferred shareholders may vote share for share with common stockholders. However, most preferred issues do not have voting rights unless the preferred stock has been in arrears on its dividends for a specified number of years. In such a case the preferred shareholders often have the right to elect a majority of the firm's board of directors.

Preferred shares have many disadvantages possessed by both corporate bonds and common stocks. The dividends paid to the shareholder are almost always limited to a specific amount, and the board of directors of the corporation is not required to declare dividends to preferred shareholders. However, corporations that wish to maintain good relations with their stockholders normally pay dividends on their preferred stock.

[8] For a current list of convertible bonds and preferred stocks, see *Moody's Bond Survey* and *Moody's Stock Survey.*
[9] U.S. Securities and Exchange Commission, *Statistical Bulletin* (Washington, D.C.: U.S. Government Printing Office), monthly issues.

Grades and Yields

Preferred stock is usually rated as high, intermediate, or low grade. Yields on high-grade preferred stock were considerably greater than those on high-grade bonds from 1940 to 1963, with the spread disappearing from 1963 to 1965. During the same periods, higher but parallel yields to maturity have prevailed on intermediate-grade corporate bonds and preferred stock (see Fig. 2–6). Since the individual may obtain substantially the same yield

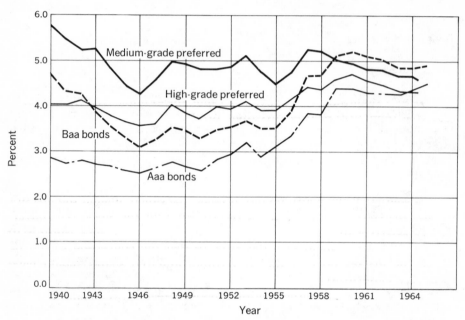

FIGURE 2-6 / Yields on selected grades of corporate bonds and preferred stocks. From *Moody's Industrial Manual,* New York, Moody's Investors Service, selected issues.

on corporate bonds as on corporate preferred stocks, which bear more risks than bonds, he has little incentive to purchase preferred stock other than the tax motive of dividend exclusion up to $100 per year per stockholder.

Participating and Convertible

Corporations may offer preferred stock issues that are either participating or convertible, or both. The *participating preferred* shareholders receive a set dividend rate and then "participate" with the common shareholders for extra dividends when dividends to common shareholders exceed a certain amount or rate. For example, at the end of 1965 Standard Fruit and Steamship Company had outstanding a 106,000 share issue of *cumulative participating preference stock* that was authorized to receive a $3 annual cumulative dividend and four times the current dividends paid on each common share. The stock, issued in 1933, had liquidation rights of $100 per share plus dividend arrearages, that is, dividends accumulated during past periods, and the owners were entitled to vote only if dividend arrearages on the preferred exceeded $9 per share, in which case a majority of the directors were to be elected by the preferred stockholders as a group. Other companies with outstanding participating issues in early 1966 included Arden-Mayfair, Inc.; Chicago, Milwaukee, St. Paul and Pacific Railroad; and Southern California Edison. The tendency in the 1950s and 1960s was for corporations to issue preferred stock convertible to common stock rather than to sell participating preferred stock.

Convertible preferred stocks are frequently convertible into the firm's common stock at a graduated scale over time, for example, each $100 preferred share into two and one half common shares through 1969, two common shares from 1970 through 1974, and so forth. The stocks are normally callable at a slight premium above par value, for example, 105 from 1965 to 1969, 104 from 1970 to 1974, 103 from 1975 to 1979, and at par thereafter. For a $100 par, $4 cumulative convertible callable preferred share with the above features, the market price is influenced by current dividend yields on straight preferred issues and the value of the common into which it is convertible. Assume that in 1967 when the market value of the common was $44 per share that the above preferred issue was called. Should the investor exercise his conversion privilege or receive $105 for the stock? To convert each preferred share to common provides the holder with stock worth $110 ($44 × 2½), or $5 more than the $105, so that the conversion should be made. The market price of the convertible preferred shares should have been very close to $110. A floor, or lower market price, of a convertible cumulative issue is established by the dividend feature. Assuming that the current yield on straight preferred stock of similar grade is 5 percent, the market price of each share should be $80 (.04 ÷ .05 × $100, or the dividend rate as a percentage of par divided by the current dividend yield times the par value of each share). Investors who desire some assurance of a preferred dividend but some opportunity for capital appreciation may choose convertible preferred stock.

Life Insurance

Importance of Life Insurance

Although the need for insurance coverage for a given family varies widely, each family should maintain some life insurance, particularly on the life of the head of household in order to provide income in the event of his death. During 1964, when disposable personal income per family was $7200, average life insurance coverage per family amounted to $13,300, and premiums as a percentage of disposable personal income amounted to 4 percent. Of the $800 billion insurance in force in 1964, 57 percent represented ordinary policies, 32 percent group policies, 5 percent industrial policies, and 6 percent credit life insurance. *Ordinary life insurance* policies are written on an individual, usually in an amount in excess of $1000, while *group insurance* is written on a group of individuals having some common bond, such as employees of the same business firm. *Industrial policies* are individual policies that are written in smaller amounts, such as $250 or $500, while *credit life insurance* is usually written on a group policy basis and covers debtors of a given financial institution.

Types of Policies

The important types of life insurance policies are group term, individual term, whole life, limited payment plans, endowment plans, and combination plans. *Group term insurance* is normally a blanket policy written on all employees of a given business firm. Individuals obtain coverage without a medical examination, and as long as the employee continues under the coverage, it is noncancellable. *Individual term insurance* is usually written for a limited period of time, called a term. Often it may be renewed for additional terms, at higher premiums, of course, at the option of the policyholder. *Whole life insurance* requires a periodic constant premium payment throughout the life of the policyholder. Under *limited payment plans*, the insured makes premium payments over a limited period of time, such as 20 years, at which time the policy is paid up for the remainder of the life of the individual. With *endowment plans*, premium payments are usually made for a limited period of time, and at the end of the endowment period, that is, the period, such as 20 years, during which premiums are paid, the insured usually has the option of taking paid-up insurance or cash equal to the face amount of the insurance policy. *Combination plans* are frequently a combination of whole life and level term or decreasing term insurance.

A majority of insurance agents consider whole life insurance to be the best buy when comparing investment costs to probable lifetime benefits. However, young people who wish to have a substantial amount of insurance when their dependent children are between the ages of 1 and 20 may seek additional coverage through term insurance. Some whole life insurance, however, should be obtained on the life of each head of household to provide some liquidity to the estate or some funds to the surviving spouse in the event of the untimely death of the insured.[10]

Other Investments

Foreign Securities

Although some speculative investors may wish to purchase foreign securities at yields slightly higher than those prevailing on domestic issues, he is confronted with some disadvantages. The rates of default of foreign

[10] The insurance afforded by the Social Security program is explained in Chapter 6 under "Retirement Needs."

securities are considerably higher than those of domestic issues, and many of the series that carry unusually high coupon rates have been in default for years. The high interest rates may have contributed to the inability of the issuer to service the bond indebtedness. At mid-1964, the United States imposed a so-called interest equalization tax, whereby purchasers of foreign securities from foreign owners were obliged to pay a tax on the transaction. This tax was equal to 15 percent of the purchase price on equity instruments and on bonds of more than 10 years to maturity. On securities with a shorter maturity, a graduated scale ranging from 2¾ percent up to 15 percent was assessed. Other disadvantages of owning foreign securities are lack of financial information about the issuer and/or the inability of the holder to bring suit for collection of the debt in the event of a default in payment. Frequently political upheavals render outstanding foreign securities value-less.

Mortgages

The yield that an investor may earn on a real estate mortgage is influenced significantly by the type of mortgage, the geographical location of the property on which the mortgage is held, and the risk associated with the loan. Although Veterans Administration (VA) and Federal Housing Administration (FHA) first mortgages had maximum interest rates of 5.75 percent in 1966, the notes were trading at slight *discounts*, that is lenders were paying the sellers less than face value for the mortgage notes, so that the yield to maturity to the investor was about 6 percent. Yields earned on conventional mortgages, that is, mortgages not guaranteed by the VA nor insured by the FHA, were in 1966 generally higher than on the latter types, depending primarily upon the geographical location of the mortgaged property. The mortgage debt for residential property is normally amortized over a period of years, usually 20 to 40. The investor in real estate mortgages, although he may realize slightly larger returns on his investments than bond investors, should be in a position to care for the property in the event of default by the mortgagor. The foreclosure rate, particularly for FHA residential mortgages, was relatively high during the mid-1960s. The cost of collecting the monthly rent, in addition to the risk involved in this type of financing, may more than offset the difference in yields obtainable on investments in mortgages and on other fixed-return securities.

Taxation of Investment Income

The income earned on most of the above securities is fully taxable for federal income tax purposes, but a few are only partially taxed while others are tax free. Interest earned on savings accounts, shares of savings and loan associations, credit union shares, savings bonds, U.S. Treasury securities, mortgages, and corporate bonds is fully taxable. Interest on municipal bonds is fully tax exempt, which makes these bonds of value to the high tax bracket individual and to tax-paying corporations such as banks. For federal income tax purposes, each stockholder is entitled to a $100 annual dividend exclusion, and a joint account owned by a husband and wife receives a $200 dividend exclusion. A corporation, however, may exclude 85 percent of the dividend income it receives from holding preferred or common stocks of other corporations.

Summary

During the early 1960s the annual savings of individuals was approximately $25 to $35 billion, while the cash flow of American corporations was about $50 billion. Whereas the latter is invested largely in expansion of plant and facilities, the savings of individuals are generally channeled through financial institutions into other types of investment media. An investor may select a savings account at a commercial bank or shares at a local savings and loan association or credit union, or he may wish to commit his funds to U.S. government or federal agency securities.

Some individuals prefer to make direct commitments into securities rather than investing indirectly through financial institutions. The individual has a variety of fixed-return investment media from which to choose, such as U.S. Treasury issues, federal agency securities, corporate bonds and stocks, and foreign issues. Individuals in high tax brackets should consider the advantages of investing in tax-free municipal securities. Although because of tax advantages some individuals commit a limited amount of funds into corporate bonds and preferred stocks, these securities are generally held by large institutional investors and/or other corporations. In order to insure against the failure of an adequate estate, many heads of households carry life insurance on themselves.

In selecting an investment, the individual should consider, among other things, the expected return, the taxes on the income that is expected to be earned, and the risks associated with the investment. This subject is covered in Chapter 4.

QUESTIONS FOR REVIEW /

1. Contrast the different types of savings media available to the individual with regard to safety and expected level of return.
2. Compare the relative amounts of the various components of the U.S. government debt outstanding during 1966. To whom is the government debt owed?
3. Enumerate advantages and disadvantages of investing in U.S. government agency securities rather than in direct U.S. government issues.
4. What investors are usually interested in municipal bonds? Why?
5. Contrast the usual characteristics of the corporate bond with those of a preferred stock.
6. How are security types graded? How do grades affect yields?

7. What should the head of the household consider in determining the amount of life insurance to carry on each member of his family?
8. The income of which types of investment media are fully taxable? Which types are exempt from federal income taxes?

PROBLEMS /

1. Contrast the flow of savings in various types of financial institutions during the last five years. How would you account for the differences in savings flow to these financial institutions? (Refer to the *Federal Reserve Bulletin, Finance Fact Yearbook,* or *Savings and Loan Fact Book.*)
2. Determine the rate of interest currently being paid by a local savings and loan association, a commercial bank, a federal credit union, and the rate paid on Series E bonds. Assume that you have $1000 that you wish to invest for a period of four years in some type of safe, liquid investment. Contrast the interest income that you would receive on this investment with that offered by each of the above types of media.
3. Prepare a list of six foreign bonds and six common stocks and contrast their current yields with those obtainable on domestic issues. How would you account for these differences?
4. Determine three cumulative, convertible, callable preferred issues that are trading at relatively low current yields. Would you recommend the stocks for immediate purchase? Defend your answer.
5. Assume that you own a $1000 bond in the Apex Corporation, which is convertible into 200 shares of common stock. The bond has a 6 percent coupon rate and the common stock pays no dividends and is trading at $7.50 per share. In two weeks the conversion ratio declines to 166⅔ shares per bond. Should you convert the bond, sell it in the open market, or continue to hold it? Support your answer with computations.
6. The General Utility Company is permitted to earn 7 percent before taxes on its total capitalization, which includes 50 percent debt, 15 percent preferred stock, and 35 percent common stock. The firm pays 5 percent bond interest, 5 percent preferred stock yield, and 75 percent of its earnings per share to common stockholders in dividends. Assuming a corporate tax rate of 50 percent, determine (a) the number of times bond interest and preferred dividends are earned and (b) the rate of earnings and dividends paid on the book value of common equity.
7. Contrast the annual after-tax return from an investment in $10,000 of 5 percent corporate bonds and 5 percent preferred stock for (a) a corporation in the 50 percent tax bracket and (b) an individual in the 30 percent tax bracket.

REFERENCES /

American Bankers Association, *The Commercial Banking Industry.* Englewood Cliffs, N.J.: Prentice-Hall, Inc., 1962.

Board of Governors of the Federal Reserve System, *Federal Reserve Bulletin.* Washington, D.C.: Federal Reserve System, October 1964.

———, *Historical Chart Book.* Washington, D.C.: Federal Reserve System, 1966.

Bogen, Jules I., *Financial Handbook,* 3d ed. New York: The Ronald Press Company, 1952.

Cohen, Jerome B., and Arthur W. Hanson, *Personal Finance,* 3d ed. Homewood, Ill.: Richard D. Irwin, Inc., 1964.

Commerce Clearing House, Inc., *Explanation of '64 Revenue Act.* New York: Commerce Clearing House, 1964.

Curvin, Winthrop, *A Manual on Municipal Bonds.* New York: Smith, Barney & Company, 1956.

Davis, E. H., *Of the People, By the People, For the People* (municipal bonds). New York: John Nuveen & Company, 1958.

Hickman, W. Braddock, *Corporate Bond Quality and Investor Experience.* Princeton, N.J.: Princeton University Press, 1958.

————, *Statistical Measures of Corporate Bond Financing Since 1900.* Princeton, N.J.: Princeton University Press, 1960.

Insurance Information Institute, *Insurance Facts, 1964, Property Liability, Inland, Marine, Surety.* New York: The Institute, 1964.

Investment Bankers Association of America, *Fundamentals of Municipal Bonds.* Washington, D.C.: The Association, 1959.

Life and Health Insurance Handbook. Ed. D. W. Gregg, 2d ed. Homewood, Ill.: Richard D. Irwin, Inc., 1956, 1964, 1965, and 1966.

Meiselman, David, *The Term Structure of Interest Rates.* Englewood Cliffs, N.J.: Prentice-Hall, Inc., 1962.

Moody's Government Manual. New York: Moody's Investors Service, Inc., selected issues.

Moody's Public Utility Manual. New York: Moody's Investors Service, Inc., selected issues.

Pilcher, James C., *Raising Capital with Convertible Securities,* Michigan Business Studies, Vol. 12 No. Z. Ann Arbor, Mich.: University of Michigan, 1955.

Prather, Charles L., *Money and Banking.* Homewood, Ill.: Richard D. Irwin, Inc., 1961.

Reed, Edward W., *Commercial Bank Management.* New York: Harper & Row, Publishers, Inc., 1963.

Robinson, Roland I., *The Management of Bank Funds.* New York: McGraw-Hill Book Company, Inc., 1962.

————, *Money and Capital Markets.* New York: McGraw-Hill Book Company, Inc., 1964.

U.S. Savings and Loan League, *Conference on Savings and Residential Financing* (proceedings). Chicago: The League, selected annual issues.

————, *Savings and Loan Fact Book, 1964.* Chicago: The League, 1965.

U.S. Securities and Exchange Commission, *Statistical Bulletin.* Washington, D.C.: U.S. Government Printing Office.

chapter 3 | Security Media: Variable Return

Introduction

The individual who is concerned with price appreciation may select from a number of different types of assets. He may make a direct investment in unincorporated business firms, for example, in the form of a proprietorship or partnership; he may acquire common stock of a corporation; he may purchase real estate; or he may hold precious metals, stones, paintings, or even other assets. The purpose of this chapter is to provide a brief description of the important types of variable-return securities, with emphasis on common stock and real estate investments.

Citizens of the United States are direct or indirect owners of many types of variable-return securities. In 1965, about 8 million individuals were single proprietors or partners in unincorporated firms; about 20 million were shareholders in U.S. corporations; and others were indirect equity owners by holding investment company shares, by being participants in uninsured pension fund plans or common trust funds, and by owning insurance policies of companies having substantial amounts of stock investments. Approximately 60 percent of the 57 million family units in the United States owned real estate in 1965.

When one studies the statistics reported on the rates of return on investments in common stocks listed on the New York Stock Exchange as reported in Table 3–1, he understands why common stock ownership gained in popularity from 1932 to 1960. This study embraced a 36-year period and included all issues trading on the New York Stock Exchange. Through the joint efforts of Professors Lorie and Fisher of the Graduate School of Business of the University of Chicago, the Ford Foundation, and Merrill Lynch, Pierce, Fenner & Smith, Inc., and the use of a large electronic data processing system, this report was made possible.

Table 3–1 presents rates of return on all New York Stock Exchange common stocks for selected time periods from 1926 to 1960. Under columns 2 and 3, the statistics assume that no federal income taxes are paid by the holders of the securities, for example, certain financial institutions, and that dividends are reinvested. Column 2 refers to portfolio-to-portfolio annual growth rate, while column 3 portrays the portfolio-to-cash annual rate of return for selected investment periods. The latter amounts are slightly

TABLE 3-1 / **Rates of Return on Investment in Common Stocks Listed on the New York Stock Exchange with Reinvestment of Dividends**

Period	Portfolio to Portfolio	Portfolio to Cash	Portfolio to Portfolio	Portfolio to Cash	Portfolio to Portfolio	Portfolio to Cash
	No Federal Income Taxes		$10,000 Average Annual Income		$50,000 Average Annual Income	
1926–60	9.03	9.01	8.44	8.20	7.42	6.84
1926–29	20.40	20.28	20.40	20.28	20.35	19.44
1926–32	−16.49	−16.76	−16.49	−16.76	−16.51	−13.37
1926–40	2.39	2.35	2.37	2.38	2.22	2.38
1926–50	6.80	6.77	6.32	6.15	5.53	5.14
1929–32	−48.36	−48.73	−48.36	−48.73	−48.19	−40.65
1929–40	− 2.98	− 3.04	− 3.00	− 2.85	− 3.00	− 2.28
1929–50	4.88	4.84	4.31	4.16	3.52	3.21
1929–60	7.74	7.71	7.05	6.81	5.97	5.39
1932–40	21.11	20.99	21.08	20.63	20.63	19.36
1932–50	18.61	18.56	17.83	17.43	16.48	15.47
1932–60	17.39	17.35	16.52	16.18	14.98	14.12
1950–52	12.50	11.97	11.09	10.00	8.99	7.12
1950–54	17.93	17.65	16.55	15.32	14.36	11.64
1950–56	16.98	16.79	15.78	14.80	13.72	11.43
1950–58	16.50	16.36	15.41	14.55	13.43	11.37
1950–60	14.84	14.72	13.85	13.09	12.01	10.30
1955–56	6.44	5.37	5.67	4.56	3.98	2.80
1955–57	− 3.66	− 4.19	− 4.38	− 3.98	− 5.99	− 4.22
1955–58	13.02	12.62	12.23	11.10	10.48	8.24
1955–59	14.00	13.70	13.26	12.16	11.58	9.23
1955–60	11.20	10.95	10.48	9.62	8.88	7.20

SOURCE: "Rates of Return on NYSE Common Stocks: 1926 to 1960," *The Commercial and Financial Chronicle*, December 12, 1963, p. 2887.

smaller than the former because of the selling costs involved in liquidating the portfolio. Figures in both columns include the initial brokerage fees. From 1926 through 1960, an annual rate of return slightly in excess of 9 percent was achieved. During more recent times, 1950 to 1960, conversely, an annual growth rate of 14.84 percent was realized from portfolio to portfolio compared to 14.72 percent from stock to cash. An investment in 1929 and a sale in 1932, conversely, produced an annual deterioration rate of almost 50 percent.

Columns 3 and 4 assume that (1) the investor had an average annual income of $10,000 per year, (2) he took the standard deduction, and (3) his income taxes were computed at the prevailing rates from 1926 through 1960. Because of the income tax burden, the annual rates of return were substantially lower for this individual than for the types of financial institutions that pay no federal income taxes.

The last two sets of columns in Table 3–1 were designed for the individual within the $50,000 average annual income tax bracket and utilized the capital gains tax rates that were in effect at the end of each of the respective time periods when securities were liquidated. All these portfolios assume a reinvestment of dividends and equal initial investment in stock of each company listed on the New York Stock Exchange.[1]

Common Stocks of Domestic Corporations

First Issue

Ownership in a business corporation is represented by common stock certificates designating the number of shares held by a given shareholder. Corporations may issue *par value*, that is face value as stated on the stock certificate, or *no par value* stock. The par value, which bears no relation to the market price of the firm's stock, is usually in the neighborhood of $1 to $5. While the par value of par stock and the *stated value* of no par stock serve an accounting purpose, these concepts have no investment significance in themselves. They merely reflect that portion of the issue price of new shares to be shown on the balance sheet as "capital stock," with the balance credited to a "paid-in-surplus" or "capital in excess of par" account.

Risk Bearer

The managers of the firm may be stockholders, but they are frequently management specialists hired to operate the business. The board of directors, which is elected by the stockholders, is responsible for the operation of the corporation. As the firm grows, the managers may elect to sell other types of securities, such as preferred stock, bonds, or short-term notes. Holders of these *senior issues* have a superior position to that of common stockholders with respect to payment of interest and preferred dividends. In most cases, holders of preferred stock have rights to passed up dividends and must, by law, be paid these cumulative dividends before cash dividends may be declared on common stock. Since other types of investors rank ahead of common stockholders in liquidation, the latter bear the brunt of the risks of fluctuating earnings and liquidation at less than *book value*.[2] The liabilities of the stockholders are limited to their investments, and they may not be assessed additional amounts.

---

[1] For an analysis of this study, see "Rate of Return on NYSE Common Stocks: 1926 to 1960," *The Commercial and Financial Chronicle*, December 12, 1963, pp. 2286–2287.

[2] Book value per share of common stock is computed by dividing the equity of common stockholders (capital stock, paid-in-surplus, and retained earnings) by the number of outstanding common shares.

Freely Transferable

The owner of stock has the right to transfer his interest to someone else. The buyer should ascertain that the issuing corporation has transferred the ownership on its books so that dividends, voting rights, and other privileges will accrue to the new owner. Although the individual has the right to sell his stock, there is little or no trading in the shares of many small corporations due to the lack of interested buyers. For this reason, common stocks of many small businesses are nonliquid and difficult to market.

Fluctuating Earnings

If a corporation increases its profits, the common stockholders benefit, since income remaining after payment of interest to creditors and dividends to preferred stockholders accrues to them. Usually only a portion of these earnings will be distributed as dividends, with the balance reinvested in fixed assets, for example, land, buildings, and fixtures, and in working capital, for example, current assets such as cash, accounts receivable, and inventories. Where there is active trading, the market price of common shares frequently moves somewhat in proportion to current earnings and dividends. However, the relationship varies among companies, and market price per share may either lead or lag the improvements or declines in profits.

Market Performance

Figure 3–1 reveals that from 1940 to 1962 Moody's average of 125 industrial stocks (the 125 industrial stocks utilized by Moody's in computing the average of industrial common stock prices) had risen about 500 percent. The rate of growth in the market value of the typical industrial common stock far outdistanced the increase in the consumer price index. In late 1965, average industrial stock prices were about 950 percent of their 1940 levels, a rise of 850 percent, while the consumer price index had risen by about 135 percent.

Moody's 25 railroads (the 25 railroads utilized by Moody's in computing the average of railroad common stock prices) did not perform nearly as well as did the industrial common stocks. Prices of rail stocks did not decline as much as industrial stocks during World War II. Immediately after World War II rail stock prices declined by approximately 25 percent. From the 1947–1949 lows, the recovery was slow, and the railroad stock price index did not reach its 1945 level until 1951. Some reasons for the decline in railroad profits and, hence, the poor market performance included the stiff competition provided by growing truck lines and air carriers and rising wages and interest costs. Many rail stocks, however, enjoyed substantial capital appreciation from 1962 through 1965.

In comparing the relative price performance of utility stocks to industrial issues over the 1940–1965 period, utilities declined more from 1940 to

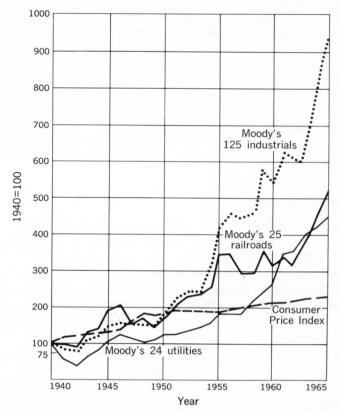

FIGURE 3-1 / Indexes to selected prices, 1940–1965. From U.S. Department of Commerce, *Survey of Current Business.*

1942, rose slightly faster from 1942 to 1946, declined less rapidly from 1947
to 1948, rose slightly less from 1949 to 1954, rose more rapidly from 1955 to
1962, and rose more slowly from 1963 to 1965. Individual utility companies
ordinarily have growing earnings and dividends, which contribute to relatively stable or rising common stock prices, while sales, earnings, and market
prices of industrial issues oscillate more widely. Since the sale of electricity
increased annually by about 6 percent from 1950 to 1965, the stocks of electric utility companies are believed to have some future growth potential.

Bank stocks declined in market value approximately 25 percent from
1940 to the low in 1942 and rose by more than 300 percent from the 1942
low to the 1962 average. During 1963 and 1964, bank stock prices appreciated tremendously, with the values of many of the issues increasing by 50
to 100 percent. Most bank stocks trade in the over the counter market.[3]

Large life insurance companies enjoyed a good growth trend in the

---

[3] For a detailed description of the operation of security markets, see Part II of this
text. The Securities Act Amendments of 1964 requires that the larger over the counter
companies provide the Securities and Exchange Commission and the general public with
substantially the same information that is required of the listed companies. Late in 1964,
one bank had applied for a New York Stock Exchange listing and a few others were
considering the move.

market value of their common stock from 1957 to 1961, but the issues generally declined from 1962 to 1965. These stocks offer long-term appreciation, since the increasing life expectancy of U.S. citizens since World War II, as a result of advances in medicine, has led to a decline in death benefits paid to policyholders without offsetting decreases in premium income to the insurance companies. Such companies are required by law to build up premium reserves in order to meet benefit claims. Therefore, in time, the assets are likely to exceed these claims, spelling rising profits to the stockholders over the long term. Thus, it is argued that shares of life insurance companies could prove to be profitable long-term investments.

Investment Companies

Numerous investors elect to purchase common stocks of investment companies. *Closed-end* investment companies have a fixed amount of resources available for investment, but they may enhance this by borrowing on a long-term basis or selling additional shares of stock. The market price of their own outstanding shares, like the stock of other business corporations, depends upon demand. About 22 such companies were listing their securities on the New York Stock Exchange in 1966, while about 80 others were traded in the over the counter market or on other exchanges.

In contrast to a closed-end company, an *open-end* investment company stands ready to buy and sell its outstanding shares continually. The price at which these shares will be sold or redeemed depends upon the market value of the securities held by the open-end investment company. For example, if the market value of its security holdings is $9.5 million and if the company has outstanding one million shares of its own stock, the price of each share is $9.5 million/1 million, or $9.50. A commission, called the *load*, is often assessed the purchaser. Typically this ranges from 6 to 10 percent of the price and covers the transaction of buying and redemption. In our example, assuming an 8 percent load, the company would sell new shares for $10.26 and offer to rebuy them at $9.50. There were approximately 250 open-end investment companies in the United States in 1965. Whereas the closed-end investment company may use debt financing, the open-end company is permitted to sell only common shares. It may, however, borrow from commercial banks in an amount up to one third of its assets.

Since open-end investment companies are not permitted to invest over 5 percent of their assets in any one corporation nor to purchase more than 10 percent of the outstanding issues of any one company, the portfolio of the investment company is quite diversified. Closed-end companies have less strenuous diversification requirements.

The two primary advantages afforded the investors of a mutual fund, or an open-end investment company, and closed-end fund are diversification and professional management. The investor may not have the time or the skill necessary to manage his portfolio; but by participating in an investment company, he is afforded some degree of professional management. Investment companies are administered, of course, by professional managers, whose fees amount to ½ of 1 percent per year on average assets.

One of the 22 closed-end investment companies listed for trading on the New York Stock Exchange at the end of 1965 was Lehman Corporation. The company was formed in 1929, and in 1965 it had a stated investment policy of "conservation and growth of capital, together with provisions for a reasonable rate of income." The company was concentrating its investments in a few industries.

The Investment Company of America, one of the larger open-end companies, was investing about 86 percent of its assets in a diversified list of common stocks in late 1965, with the balance held predominantly in cash and government agency securities. The fund was formed in 1933 to acquire the assets of a closed-end company, but was converted to open-end status in 1939. "Long-term growth of capital and income" is the primary investment objective of the fund, with current income a secondary consideration.

The management groups for both types of investment companies, with the approval of their respective boards of directors, operate their security portfolios to achieve broad investment objectives. For some funds the objective is capital growth through a diversified common stock fund; others stress current income, that is, dividends and interest; while still others strive for a balance between the two.[4] In order to achieve capital growth and limit the risk of losses, the fund managers determine a number of industries from which to select common stocks. Other assets, to meet working capital needs or "advantageous buying opportunities," are held in cash or invested in short-term securities. Fund managers seeking income, conversely, invest in a diversified list of bonds, preferred stocks, and common stocks with high current yields.

The broad policies under which the open-end fund is operated are set forth in the *prospectus*, or offering circular, and/or the annual report and cover such areas as (1) broad investment objectives; (2) types of share accumulation programs offered, for example, lump-sum or equal monthly payments; (3) alternate choices of each holder for receiving cash or investing in additional shares the net income and realized capital gains; (4) provisions for partial, systematic, or lump-sum resale of shares to the company; and (5) other important policies. The operating policies of the closed-end fund differ somewhat from the above, since these funds are not continually selling and redeeming their own shares.

Yields

The *earnings yield* refers to the annual earnings per share divided by the market value per share, while the *dividend yield* is the annual dividend per share divided by the market value per share. The market value used in each denominator may be the current share price, the average of the past year's high and low prices, or some other suitable measure. As suggested by

---

[4] Investment companies are further discussed in Chapter 23.

Figure 3–2, yields on common stocks vary over a wide range. In early 1966, for example, dividend yields on the common stocks of sales finance companies, railroads, and natural gas companies were about 4.5 to 5.5 percent, but on other stocks, such as growth companies in the airline, office machine, and electronics industries, dividend yields were frequently less than 1 percent. An individual seeking a generous dividend return should pay particular attention to the average dividend yield of selected types of common stocks, but such shares normally provide little capital appreciation.

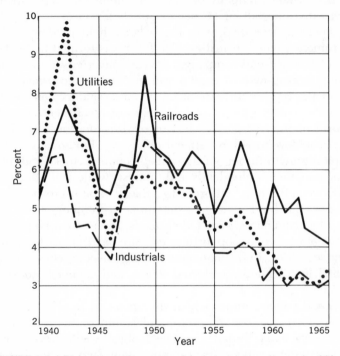

FIGURE 3-2 / Dividend yields on Moody's industrials, rails, and utilities, 1940–1965. From U.S. Department of Commerce, *Survey of Current Business.*

Investors normally demand a high earning and/or dividend yield for the more volatile issues, while the securities of high-grade companies that have enjoyed and are expected to continue a rapid growth in sales and earnings may trade at low yields. Growth stocks often trade at yields of 1 or 2 percent and at price–earnings multiplies, that is, the market price divided by annual earnings per share, of 30 or more. Market values of certain growth issues, however, may be increasing at an annual rate of 10 percent or more.

Ownership of Common Equities

The owners of common shares may be classified into four categories: U.S. citizens, financial institutions, including governments, business corporations, and foreign holders. Although current holdings by each of these categories of over the counter issues and listed securities [5] are not available, the New York Stock Exchange does provide some annual breakdown of its shareholders. In late 1965, New York Stock Exchange-listed securities were valued at about $550 billion, with financial institutions holding 21 percent of the securities, having increased their relative ownership from 13 percent in 1949. The *1965 Census of Shareowners—Shareownership USA*, conducted by the New York Stock Exchange in 1965, disclosed that there were 19,963,000 shareholders in the United States, with foreign ownership of U.S. corporate securities in 143 different countries.[6] Many of the larger corporations owned stocks of subsidiary corporations, that is, corporations controlled by virtue of stock ownership, or had substantial investment portfolios of listed securities.

The number of shareholders in the United States more than tripled from 1950 through 1965. Growing popularity of share ownership over that time was influenced by the rapid annual growth in stock prices, the rising level of family income, the predominantly inflationary trend in consumer prices (equities normally rise in market value as consumer prices rise), and an increasing understanding on the part of the "average" citizen of common stock ownership.

Tax Treatment of Dividend Income and Capital Gains

The investor in both preferred and common stocks has a slight tax advantage over the investor in many other types of savings media. Each shareholder may exclude the first $100 of dividend income for federal income tax purposes. Husband and wife may jointly own common stocks and exclude up to $200 in dividends on a joint tax return. If the dividend yields on the husband and wife's holdings amounted to 3 percent, and they were in the 25 percent income tax bracket, the after-tax income on the common stocks would equal the after-tax earnings on a 4 percent savings account, up to the exclusion.

The stated motive of most foreigners in buying securities is to acquire dividend income, while, in contrast, a majority of American investors report their primary purpose to be capital appreciation. The income tax law gives some benefit to holders of securities who have made a profit through capital appreciation. *Short-term capital gains*, or realized profits from the sale of a capital asset, such as securities, held for a period of six months or less, are fully taxed, while *long-term capital gains* on securities, that is, stocks and bonds, that are held for more than six months are taxed at one half the taxpayer's ordinary federal income tax rate or at 25 percent, whichever rate is lower. In arriving at the taxable income from capital gains transactions, the investor must offset long-term capital gains with long-term capital losses;

[5] These markets are explained in detail in Part II of this book.
[6] See, for example, U.S. *Statistical Abstract* (Washington, D.C.: U.S. Government Printing Office, 1965), p. 476. For a detailed breakdown of security holdings by financial institutions, see Chapter 24 of this text.

offset short-term capital gains with short-term capital losses; and then offset net long-term gains or losses with net short-term capital gains or losses. If the net long-term capital gain exceeds the net short-term loss, the capital gains treatment applies to the excess. When capital losses exceed capital gains, the individual may deduct up to $1000 a year against ordinary income and carry the balance forward to future years to offset capital gains or to deduct up to the $1000 annual limit from ordinary income.[7] For example, assume that Mr. Smith had $600 in capital gains on stocks held for more than six months, $200 in long-term capital losses, $150 in short-term capital gains, and $200 in short-term capital losses. He would compute his net taxable capital gain as follows:

Long-term capital gains	$600	
Less: Short-term capital losses	(200)	
Net long-term capital gains		$400
Short-term capital gains	$150	
Less: Short-term capital losses	(200)	
Net short-term capital losses		(50)
Taxable net long-term capital gain		$350

(Margin note: ERROR → LONG)

Assuming that Mr. Smith was in the 30 percent income tax bracket, he pays taxes on one half the $350, or an equivalent rate of 15 percent. Another stockholder, however, who was in a tax bracket above 50 percent would pay the maximum capital gains rate of 25 percent.

A stock split, that is, when a corporation increases its common shares outstanding proportionately among all shareholders, such as, say, two for one, or a stock dividend, that is, a stock split, except that the ratio between the shares held and the shares received is ordinarily less than 25 percent, is not taxable to the recipient, but the cost basis of the total shares held is then adjusted for these divisions.[8] Suppose, for example, that 100 shares of stock in the Boeing Company were purchased in 1964 at a cost per share of $40. After the stock split of two for one in 1966, the stock then had an adjusted cost basis of $20 per share. Dividends paid in stock of another corporation or in property dividends (such as merchandise samples) are ordinarily taxable at fair market value to the recipient.

The corporation, in computing its taxable income, excludes 85 percent of dividends received from its stock holdings of other firms and is afforded a slightly different capital gains treatment than the individual. The corporation cannot offset capital losses with ordinary income, but may carry them forward for five years to offset future capital gains. During years in which

[7] Federal income tax treatment of capital gains resulting from the sale of stock purchase rights (short-term options issued to stockholders that permit the purchase of additional shares at a stated price) and of profits made on the sale of stocks purchased under a restrictive stock option plan is explained in Chapter 17.

[8] See also Chapter 17, "Stock Splits and Stock Dividends."

the corporate federal tax rate was above 50 percent, the use of the maximum long-term capital gains tax of 25 percent was advantageous over paying the ordinary tax rate on one half the capital gain.

Security Options

Put and *call* dealers stand ready to buy and sell certain contracts to the investing public. These contracts are referred to as puts and calls, and spreads and straddles. For the payment of a stipulated premium, depending upon the contract, the owner has the right to buy and/or sell a stipulated number of shares of common stock of a given company within a certain time period at a specified price to the put and call dealer.

Put

A *put* is an option to sell a specified number of shares, usually 100, on or before a fixed date at a predetermined price. The predetermined price is usually the market value at the time the contract is consummated.

When the holder of a given stock with a sizable paper profit thinks that the market price of his security might move down substantially within the next few months, he may protect his profit by the use of a put contract. Suppose that a holder of American Telephone and Telegraph Company stock on March 14, 1966, believed the stock might decline to a lower level. Filer, Schmidt & Company, Inc., a large put and call dealer, on that date offered put contracts on 100 shares of AT&T at $58.75 per share, good through June 13, 1966, at a cost of $200. Suppose the shareholder buys this contract. Assume that on June 8, 1966, the market value of the stock declines to $53. If the investor then exercises his option, he would sell the 100 shares of AT&T to the dealer at the agreed price of $58.75 per share even though the current price is $53. He would thus minimize his losses.

A speculative individual who currently does not own the stock may nevertheless buy a put in hopes of later, during the contract period, acquiring 100 shares of AT&T at a price markedly below $58.75.

High tax bracket individuals sometimes use puts to extend the holding period of an issue from a short-term to a long-term capital gains period. For example, suppose that Mr. Brown bought 100 shares of Collins Radio on November 15, 1965, at $45 per share and wished to sell it in April 1966, when the price was about $80 per share. Since he was in the 50 percent federal income tax bracket, he desired to take a long-term capital gain. *The Wall Street Journal* (April 22, p. 23) quoted a special put option per 100 shares of Collins Radio at $80 per share for a cost of $300, good through June 22, 1966. Mr. Brown bought the contract, saving $602 in after-tax profits. Had he desired, the stock could have been repurchased in early May, 1966, for as low as $52 per share.

ALTERNATE 1: IMMEDIATE SALE

Sale of stock on April 22, 1966	
Proceeds net of brokerage and New York taxes	
($8000 − $52)	$7948
Cost	(4500)
Short-term gain	3448
Tax: 50 percent	(1724)
After-tax profits	$1724

ALTERNATE 2: PURCHASE OF PUT CONTRACT WITH ITS EXER-
CISE BETWEEN MAY 15 AND JUNE 22, 1966

Selling price to dealer		$8000
Less: Cost	$4500	
Two-way brokerage plus		
New York transfer taxes	99	
Option	300	
Total cost		(4899)
Long-term capital gain		3101
Taxes: 25 percent		775
After-tax profits		$2326

Call

A *call* is an option to buy a specified number of shares in a given stock, usually 100, on or before a fixed date at a predetermined price. If an individual believes that the price of an issue will rise substantially within the next few months, but does not have adequate funds for making the investment at that time, he may assure himself of being able to buy the stock at a stipulated price, plus the premium for the call contract, by using this device.

Suppose that Mr. Jones desired to buy 100 shares of Eastern Air Lines common stock on March 18, 1966, at 79¾ per share. Because of a temporary shortage of cash, he bought a *call option* on 100 shares of Eastern which cost $550 and was good through April 25, 1966. In early April 1966, when the price of Eastern was $110 per share, Mr. Jones exercised the option and bought the stock from the put and call dealer at the contract price 79¾ per share, simultaneously selling it "at the market" and earning a generous return on his investment. His actual profit was $2370, computed as follows:

Selling price ($110 × 100 shares)		$11,000
Less: Two-way brokerage plus New York		
transfer taxes ($50 + $50 + $5)	$ 105	
Contracted price	7975	
Cost of call	550	
Total cost		8630
Profit before taxes		$ 2370

Spread

A *spread* consists of both a put and a call contract. The option price at which the put or call is executed is specified in terms of a number of dollars away from the market price of the stock at the time the option is granted. The put may be exercised at a specified number of dollars below the market and the call at the corresponding number of dollars above the market. For example, assume that a spread is bought on XYZ common stock which permits the buyer to buy or sell 100 shares at $4 per share, or 4 points, above or below the current market price within the next 90 days at a premium cost of $250. If the market price of the stock fluctuates either upward or downward by substantially more than $7.50 per share including brokerage cost per share, the owner of this contract can make a profit. The $7.50 per share was computed as follows:

Approximate per share brokerage and New York taxes	$1.00
Cost of contract ÷ 100 shares	2.50
Spread from cost	4.00
Total	$7.50

If the fluctuation is less than this spread either on the upside or the downside, the investment is valueless and results in a complete loss to the purchaser.

Straddle

A *straddle* is similar to a spread except that the execution price of either the put or call option is at the market price of the stock at the time the straddle is granted. In essence, both the straddle and the spread accomplish the same thing.

Other Options

There are at least two other combinations of put and call contracts. A *strap* is a combination of two calls and one put contract, while a *strip* is a combination of one call and two put contracts.

Premiums

The cost of these contracts depends on the volatility of the market price of the issue involved, the number of shares, and the length of the contract period, such as 30 days, 60 days, 90 days, or six months. The cost of a put or a call for 100 shares on a typical stock averages about 8 percent of the market value for a 90-day contract, while the cost of a six-month contract is approximately 12 percent of the market price of the stock. Since the spread, straddle, strap, and strip are combination contracts, the cost increases above the basic rate on puts or calls.

Investment in Foreign Equities

Indirect Investment

Shareholders of many large U.S. corporations are investing indirectly in foreign operations. By mid-1964 more than 2100 U.S. corporations were operating in Europe. They were, at that time, active in 102 of the 112 United Nations countries, and private investment abroad increased $6 billion in 1964, reaching a total of about $73 billion.

Some of the larger U.S. companies derive substantial revenues from foreign sales; for example, in 1963, General Motors' revenue from foreign sales amounted to $2.3 billion, an increase of approximately 20 percent over the 1962 figure. Of course, U.S. corporations with foreign operations run the risk of nationalization of these properties, but because of the good growth potential, firms have taken this calculated risk. Not only were American goods being accepted by foreigners but in 1965 there was less competition in foreign countries than in the United States. It was estimated that the outlay for plant and equipment in foreign countries by U.S. corporations would approximate $4–5 billion each year in 1965 and thereafter.

Direct Investment

The American investor can acquire common stocks of foreign corporations. In fact, at the end of 1965, 25 foreign companies had listed their securities on the New York Stock Exchange, and 70 foreign issues were listed on the American Stock Exchange. Others were traded over the counter. For the most part, these issues were Canadian corporations, although some European stocks were included in the list.

In 1963, foreigners made net purchases of $150 million in stocks, while American citizens and institutions made net purchases of $6.1 billion in foreign bonds. The fact that foreign bond interest rates were one to two percentage points higher than those on U.S. issues probably accounted for the outflow of funds from this country into foreign bonds. At the same time, the dividend yields on foreign common equities were no higher than on U.S. securities, and U.S. issues were generally appreciating more in market price, resulting in a net inflow of equity investments.

In order to curb the outflow of funds from the United States, a law was passed in July 1964 that taxed foreign debt securities from 2.75 to 15 percent, depending on their maturity, increasing by one percentage point the interest cost to foreign borrowers. Common stocks were taxed at a flat rate of 15 percent. The tax was made retroactive to July 1963, so that in effect American purchasers of foreign securities from other than an American owner were required to pay the additional tax based on the market value of their issue. This interest equalization tax was intended to be temporary, to reduce the gold outflow from the United States; but just how long the tax will last is anyone's guess. If the U.S. citizen, wishing to avoid the payment of the interest equalization tax, is able to obtain a certificate of U.S. ownership of his securities, that is, show that the security was bought from a U.S. citizen, he is not required to pay the tax.

Real Estate Investments

For a number of reasons the investor should have some knowledge of the real estate and mortgage markets. During early married life, a majority of families must resolve the problem of whether to buy a home or continue to rent, and as the wage earner approaches middle age, he may have some savings which he wishes to invest in income-producing rental property.

Trends in Home Ownership

From 1945 to 1965, the population of the United States increased by about three million per year, and the number of housing starts in the United States is expected to accelerate in the latter 1960s as the large number of war babies reaches the home-buying age. This trend should place more pressure on the market for land and housing, and as the young people reach marriageable age, the demand for housing, particularly apartment units, is likely to be strong. As these individuals grow older, they have a greater tendency to buy homes rather than to rent.

Home Ownership Versus Renting

In weighing the advantages of owning a home over renting one, the individual should consider such things as the income tax advantage of owning; more space, privacy, and satisfaction; and the building of equity through monthly mortgage payments. Conversely, disadvantages of owning are also present, particularly in cases where the individual is uncertain about the length of time he plans to remain in a given location, since the cost of disposing of a home often approximates 10 percent of the home's appraised value. Therefore, if a family intends to remain in a given geographical location for a relatively short period of time, renting is more prudent than owning a home. The renter should also consider his low cost of occupancy, that is, he has few or no upkeep expenses, and the convenience of his present location before deciding to buy a home in some less desirable location.

Types of Financing

After one decides to invest in a home, he should consider the merits of financing the home with a loan guaranteed by the Veterans Administration (VA), a loan insured by the Federal Housing Administration (FHA), or a conventional mortgage, that is, a loan not insured or guaranteed. The no down payment VA mortgage was made available to World War II and Korean War veterans, and a low down payment VA loan program was passed for Cold War veterans in 1965. The VA mortgage requires little or no down payment, and the borrower receives up to 35 or 40 years to repay the mortgage note, which in 1966 carried an interest rate of 5¾ percent. The buyer of the FHA home was required to make a down payment on a graduated scale, depending on the price of the home. In 1966, the down payment for the FHA home was 3 percent of the first $15,000, 10 percent of the next $5000, and 25 percent of any additional amount, with a maximum loan of $25,000 on a single-unit dwelling. A slightly lower down payment is required of Cold War veterans. In addition to the 5¾ percent interest on the FHA mortgage, the borrower also had to pay ½ of 1 percent annually for FHA insurance. The FHA mortgages carried maximum 35-year maturities on new homes and 30-year maturities on older homes.

Many borrowers desire to finance conventionally, that is, other than through the VA or the FHA, by borrowing 75 to 80 percent of the market value of the home from a savings and loan association, a commercial bank, an insurance company, or some other real estate lender. For the conventional loan the maturity is normally shorter and the down payment is larger than for the insured and guaranteed type, although the purchaser's closing costs, such as loan origination costs, legal fees, recording fees, survey expenses, and prepaid insurance and taxes, are usually less on the conventional-type mortgage.

The closing costs to buy a home ordinarily run from 2 to 3 percent of the value of the property, while the seller of a refinanced home or one initially financed with a VA or FHA mortgage must suffer the discount below par at which fixed-rate, that is VA and FHA, mortgages trade. For example, when FHA rates were 5¼ percent in early 1966, some lending institutions were discounting the notes by more than 5 percent, which produced an effective return to the lender of about 6 percent. Selling commissions ordinarily cost the seller from 4 to 6 percent of the appraised value of the property.

Since transfer costs on refinancing are so expensive, it is wise financial policy for someone planning a near-term relocation to either rent or buy a small *equity*, that is, the owner's share of the real estate value not encumbered by a mortgage, in a used home. Reselling a used home with a small ownership is often easier than selling one with a substantial equity. The greatest danger of permitting someone to assume the loan is that the original mortgagor, or buyer, remains liable for the mortgage debt in the event that the new buyer defaults.

Rental Property

Individuals investing in rental property may acquire single-unit dwellings in the form of a prefabricated house or a low-priced older home in order to receive a substantial return on their investment; however, during recent years there has been a tendency toward the erection of multiunit dwellings, such as one- or two-story apartment buildings. In considering a rental real estate investment the individual should consider the initial cost and problems involved in maintaining the property, the vacancy rate within the surrounding geographical area, and the cost of disposing of the property should he wish to liquidate his investment.

Until 1964, gains on the disposition of rental property held for more than six months received the favorable long-term capital gains tax treatment, but beginning in 1964, owners who depreciate their property with an accelerated method [9] came under a different rule. Gains on such property held for less than 20 months are taxed as ordinary income; gains on property held for more than 120 months are classified as long-term capital gains; and gains realized between 20 and 120 months must be prorated to ordinary income and capital gains on a linear basis. Thus a $10,000 gain realized in 60 months is prorated 40 percent to capital gains (60 − 20) and 60 percent to ordinary income. The new tax law is likely to result in a lower turnover rate of apartment unit ownership, since the full amount of the gain is not subject to the capital gains rate unless the property is held for more than 10 years.

Real Estate Investment Trusts

In 1960, real estate investment trusts were afforded a tax treatment similar to that for investment companies. Real estate investment trusts are corporate-type ventures that invest in real estate, rent the property to commercial or residential tenants, and pay out 90 percent or more of the income to the shareholders without suffering the ordinary corporate income tax burden that applies to other types of companies. The law is very strict and its violation subjects the entire income to the ordinary corporate tax rate. Some individuals prefer to see their investments in tangible property such as real estate rather than in common stocks, and this medium offers a hedge against inflation, since the value of real estate generally rises in relation to rises in the consumer and wholesale price indexes.

Summary

An investor who wishes to commit his funds to a variable-return security may elect to invest in a single proprietorship or a partnership, in common stocks of corporations, or in real estate. It is normally easier for the small saver to invest in the shares of a corporation than in the other three types of media, because an equity in an unincorporated business firm usually demands a substantial cash outlay and continuous, time-consuming management by the proprietor or partners. Investments in real estate also require considerable sums of money and, for purposes of direct management, such investments require that the owner be located near his property. An invest-

---

[9] These depreciation methods are explained in Chapter 12.

ment in the shares of a corporation may be made in small or large amounts. Ownership of common stocks is freely transferable, and the holder's liability is limited to the amount of his investment. The common stockholder, however, bears more risk than does a bondholder in the same corporation, since (1) in the event of liquidation, he receives the residual assets, and (2) dividends on common stock are not contractual obligations, as is the interest on bonds.

From 1950 through 1965, the number of stockholders in U.S. corporations increased from approximately 6 million to more than 20 million. This increase is a reflection of the more affluent American society, with higher average family incomes, and was influenced by the desire for an investment that appreciates more rapidly than the cost of living index, and other factors. Over the 1940–1965 period, industrial stocks appreciated 800 percent, while the consumer price index rose about 135 percent. On the average, the prices of industrial and insurance stocks appreciated at a more rapid rate than did those of railroads, utilities, or bank issues. However, there was wide variation in the price movements of individual issues.

In addition to common stock, real estate—in the form of home ownership, rental property, or shares of a real estate investment trust—offers a hedge against inflation. In 1965, approximately 60 percent of the family units in the United States owned the homes in which they lived, and an estimated 8 to 10 percent of these families owned income-producing property.

QUESTIONS FOR REVIEW /

1. Contrast an investment in an unincorporated firm with an investment in a corporation.
2. Compare the risks assumed by the common stockholder to those assumed by the bondholder of an American corporation.
3. What is meant by a price-level hedge? What type of investment meets this objective? Why is this important in an economy such as that of the United States?
4. Contrast the market performance and capital appreciation of the various types of common stocks (for example, utilities) since the close of World War II.
5. How does the open-end investment company differ from the closed-end investment company?
6. Contrast the open-end investment company and the real estate investment trust.
7. Contrast the current income yields obtainable on variable-return securities, particularly common equities, with those available on fixed-return securities.
8. Why do American corporations elect to invest substantial sums of money abroad?
9. How may security options be used?
10. Is it more advantageous to rent or to own one's home? What factors should be considered before making this decision?
11. Contrast the methods available for financing home ownership.

PROBLEMS /

1. From an up-to-date source of financial data (for example, *Moody's Handbook of Common Stocks*) determine three common issues that are yielding above 5 percent; between 3 and 4 percent; and below 1.5 percent. How would you explain the differences? Assuming that you had placed $1000 in each of the nine issues exactly 10 years ago, contrast the present market value of the issues, assuming that you did not reinvest the dividends. Compare the dividend income. Which issues offered more income and appreciation?
2. By the use of *The Value Line Investment Survey, Moody's Stock Survey,* or the *Wall Street Journal* and Wiesenberger's *Investment Companies* compile a list of five closed-end investment company shares that are trading at depressed levels. Which of these issues would you recommend for purchase at the present time?
3. Morgan and Mary Dougall are considering the purchase of a new home. They have just been transferred to a medium-sized Midwest city, and the company has promised Morgan that he will not be transferred for at least four years. Morgan is earning $15,000 per year and Mary is the housewife for her husband and two small children. The Dougalls have been saving their money for the past six years until the day when they can own their own furniture and their own home, and they now have $8400 in a savings account. You have been asked to counsel the family.

REFERENCES /

Amling, Frederick, *Investments: An Introduction to Analysis and Management.* Englewood Cliffs, N.J.: Prentice-Hall, Inc., 1965.

Bogen, Jules I., *Financial Handbook,* 3d ed. New York: The Ronald Press Company, 1952.

Bryant, Willis R., *Mortgage Lending, Fundamentals and Practices,* 2d ed. New York: McGraw-Hill Book Company, Inc., 1962.

Clendenin, John C., *Introduction to Investments,* 4th ed. New York: McGraw-Hill Book Company, Inc., 1964.

Cohen, Jerome B., and Arthur W. Hanson, *Personal Finance,* 3d ed. Homewood, Ill.: Richard D. Irwin, Inc., 1964.

Commerce Clearing House, Inc., *Explanation of '64 Revenue Act.* New York: Commerce Clearing House, 1964.

Crane, Burton, and Sylvia Crane Eisenlohr, *The Sophisticated Investor.* New York: Simon and Schuster, Inc., 1964.

Graham, Benjamin, *The Intelligent Investor.* New York: Harper & Row, Publishers, Inc., 1959.

Graham, Benjamin, David L. Dodd, and Sidney Cottle, *Security Analysis, Principles and Techniques,* 4th ed. New York: McGraw-Hill Book Company, Inc., 1962.

Holmes, Lawrence G., and Carrie M. Jones, eds., *Real Estate Handbook,* Englewood Cliffs, N.J.: Prentice-Hall, Inc., 1948.

Husband, William H., and Frank Ray Anderson, *Real Estate.* Homewood, Ill.: Richard D. Irwin, Inc., 1960.

The International Reference Day Book. New York: Professional & Technical Programs, Inc., 1964.

Jordan, David F., and Herbert E. Dougall, *Investments,* 7th ed. Englewood Cliffs, N.J.: Prentice-Hall, Inc., 1960.

Kahn, S. A., F. E. Cose, and A. Schimmel, *Real Estate Appraisal and Investment.* New York: The Ronald Press Company, 1963.

Lerner, Eugene M., *Readings in Financial Analysis and Investment Management.* Homewood, Ill.: Richard D. Irwin, Inc., 1963.

Merrill, Lynch, Pierce, Fenner & Smith, Inc., *Security and Industry Survey.* New York: Merrill Lynch, Securities Research Division, selected issues.

Moody's Industrial Manual. New York: Moody's Investors Service, Inc., selected issues.

Moody's *Public Utility Manual.* New York: Moody's Investors Service, Inc., selected issues.

Moody's Transportation Manual. New York: Moody's Investors Service, selected issues.

New York Stock Exchange, *The Exchange.* New York: The Exchange, selected issues.

Pilcher, James C., *Raising Capital with Convertible Securities,* Michigan Business Studies, Vol. 12, No. Z. Ann Arbor, Mich.: University of Michigan, 1955.

Ratcliff, Richard U., *Real Estate Analysis.* New York: McGraw-Hill Book Company, Inc., 1961.

"Rates of Return on NYSE Common Stocks: 1926 to 1960," *The Commercial and Financial Chronicle.* New York: December 12, 1963.

Real Estate Handbook, ed. Lawrence G. Holmes and Carrie M. Jones. Englewood Cliffs, N.J.: Prentice-Hall, Inc., 1948.

Sauvain, Harry, *Investment Management,* 2d ed. Englewood Cliffs, N.J.: Prentice-Hall, Inc., 1959.

Standard & Poor's Corporation, *Standard & Poor's Stock Guide.* New York: Standard & Poor's, year end, 1963.

U.S. Securities and Exchange Commission, *Statistical Bulletin.* Washington, D.C.: U.S. Government Printing Office.

The Value Line Investment Survey. New York: Arnold Bernhard & Company, Inc.,

Welfling, Weldon, *Financing Business Enterprise.* New York: American Bankers Association, 1960.

Wu, H. K., and A. J. Zakon, *Elements of Investments: Selected Readings.* New York: Holt, Rinehart and Winston, Inc., 1965.

chapter 4 | Investment Risks

Introduction

An investment in any form of security possesses some risks, with no type being completely free from some danger. Investment media are subject to such hazards as the purchasing power risk, the credit or business risk, the interest rate risk, the market risk, the monetary value risk, and the political environment risk. The last two are more likely to be associated with foreign securities than with domestic issues.

This chapter considers how the above types of hazards relate to the security media described in Chapters 2 and 3 in periods of recession and inflation. A security that bears a substantial degree of purchasing power risk during a period of rising prices, for example, long-term government bonds, may offer a considerable hedge against loss in purchasing power during a depression. Conversely, other investments that increase in value during a period of inflation, as measured by changes in the consumer price index, usually decline in value during a recession or depression.

The investor should determine the dangers associated with each type of investment medium and decide which of these risks he is willing to assume and which he desires to avoid. His decision will largely depend upon his intermediate or long-term forecast for inflation or deflation in the level of consumer prices.

In addition, the investor must decide whether he wishes to commit his funds for the long term, disregarding short-run oscillation in security prices, or whether he wishes to be a speculator, that is, to buy and sell financial assets over a short time period in order to profit from the price changes.

Purchasing Power Risk

The *purchasing power risk* is the probability or chance of a deterioration in the value of a security medium relative to an index of consumer purchasing power, for example, the consumer price index. Security media that are relatively free from this risk are said to provide a hedge against inflation. These include certain common stocks, shares of many investment companies, real estate investments, and variable annuity insurance policies. Other securities, conversely, offer some hedge against deflation. These generally include, insured savings accounts with banks and savings and loan associations, U.S. government securities, high-grade municipal and corporate bonds, and others. High-grade preferred stocks, credit union shares, and mortgages offer this attribute to a limited degree, since their income is less assured.

Variable-Return Securities

During a period of rising consumer prices it is prudent financial policy to commit a portion of one's portfolio to variable-return securities, such as stocks, investment company shares, or real estate, since indexes of stock prices normally appreciate in value about equal to or in excess of the change in the level of consumer prices. For example, Figure 3–1 contrasts the consumer price index (1940 = 100) to the index of industrial, rail, and utility stocks; one finds that from 1940 through 1965, the consumer price index increased by 135 percent, industrial stocks increased by 830 percent, rail issues appreciated by 440 percent, and utility shares gained by 330 percent. In terms of purchasing power, a $1000 investment in the average of Moody's 125 industrials over the period would have increased to $9300 ÷ 2.35, or $3957, disregarding brokerage costs, dividend income, and income taxes on the profits. Over this same period the market performance of investment company shares has at times exceeded that of the popular averages and at times has fallen short.[1]

The rates of return on an investment in all common stocks listed on the New York Stock Exchange for various time periods between 1926 and 1960, assuming reinvestment of dividends, was compiled by Professors James H. Lorie and Lawrence Fisher of the University of Chicago.[2] The study revealed that the average New York Stock Exchange stock produced an annual return of 9.03 percent, disregarding income taxes, over the 24-year period. For the 1932–1960 period, an annual rate of return of 17.39 percent was achieved, whereas the yearly gain was 14.84 percent for the 1950–1960 period. Conversely, the stocks declined at an annual rate of 48.36 percent from 1929 to 1932, thus indicating that such securities contain a high degree of risk from price declines during major depressions.

The value of *real property*, for example, land and buildings, increased substantially from 1940 to 1965. The "Balance Sheet of Agriculture: 1940 to 1965" listed the value of farm real estate as $33.6 billion in 1940 and $158.5 billion in 1965, an increase of 372 percent.[3] Over this period farm acreage declined, but substantial amounts (unknown) were invested in drainage improvements, irrigation projects, and building construction. Construction

---

[1] See Chapter 23 for a discussion of the performance of investment companies.

[2] See, for example, "Rates of Return on NYSE Common Stocks: 1926 to 1960," *The Commercial and Financial Chronicle*, December 12, 1963, p. 2287, or Table 3-1 of this text.

[3] *U.S. Statistical Abstract* (Washington, D.C.: U.S. Government Printing Office, 1965), p. 631.

costs and the value of urban property also generally increased over the period. For example, the average construction cost of private nonfarm houses was $7850 in 1948 and $15,575 in 1964,[4] an increase of 98 percent, attributable to rising construction costs and to increasing size and luxury of homes. Over a similar time period, 1946–1964, the Department of Commerce construction cost index doubled.

Fixed-Return Securities

Fixed-return securities, such as long-term bonds, long-term mortgages, or insurance contracts, other than variable annuity plans, offer no hedge against inflation, but become very profitable investments during periods of declining consumer prices. For example, suppose that a $1000 Series E savings bond was acquired in 1950 at an initial cost of $750, redeemable at a face value of $1000 some 9⅔ years later, and issued to yield a 3 percent annual return if held to maturity. At the end of the holding period, the bond was worth 1.333 times its cost, disregarding federal income taxes owed on the $250 interest income, while the consumer price index had risen to 123 percent of its 1950 level. The interest income was barely adequate to pay the federal income taxes—assume a rate of 20 percent—and to offset the increase in consumer prices. Over the 1940–1960 period the consumer price index rose by 111 percent, which was greater than the increase in the value of Series E bond investments ($1.333 \times 1.333 - 1.00 = 78$ percent). Although one cannot be sure of the extent of future price-level changes in the United States, economists in 1966 were generally expecting a 1½ to 2 percent annual increase in the consumer price index for the intermediate-term future.

Fixed-amount insurance contracts also carry a substantial risk of erosion in purchasing power because of inflation. For example, suppose that Mr. Simon acquired a $20,000 insurance policy on his life in 1940, payable to his wife upon his death. Upon Mr. Simon's death in 1960 the $20,000 was worth only $9478 ($20,000 ÷ 2.11) in terms of 1940 purchasing power, having been eroded by more than 50 percent through inflation.

Over the 1940–1965 period other types of fixed-return securities, such as bank savings accounts, shares of savings and loan associations, or credit union shares, possessed a slightly lower degree of inflationary risk than did long-term contracts. As interest rates rose over the period, the investor in these savings media participated in the increases, whereas the level of return on long-term bonds or life insurance contracts is limited to a stated rate and does not increase with changes in current interest rates. Of course, an investment in high-grade bonds when interest rates are at historically high levels would prove to be a profitable investment should the following years be a deflationary period.

[4] See, for example, U.S. Savings and Loan League, *Savings and Loan Fact Book* (Chicago: The League, 1965), p. 44.

Credit Risks

The *credit risk*, sometimes referred to as the *business risk*, is the probability or chance of an obliger, either a business firm or a government, failing to meet interest and/or principal payment on its bonded indebtedness. This meaning may also be extended to embrace the payment of cumulative dividends on preferred stocks and the maintenance of a regular dividend policy on common stocks. Many business firms become insolvent, bankrupt, or develop financial difficulties each year. Large, well-established companies frequently operate in a depressed condition for a number of years before being rehabilitated. Examples of corporations that weathered financial storms and were restored to profitable operation during the early 1960s include American Motors, Chrysler Corporation, Eastern Air Lines, and KLM Royal Dutch Airlines.

Fixed-Return Securities

Fixed-return securities that carry substantial degrees of credit hazards include speculative-grade corporate bonds, low-grade municipal issues, preferred stocks of companies with significant amounts of senior capital, for example, bonded indebtedness, foreign government bonds, and corporate debt. A much lower credit risk is involved with the purchase of U.S. government obligations, issues of federal agencies, high-grade corporate bonds, and municipal issues. To an intermediate degree, mortgages and life insurance contracts carry this type of risk.

Table 4–1 relates the quadrennial default rates for outstanding corporate bond issues with high (AAA, AA, A, and BAA) and low (BA, B, CAA, CA, and C) agency ratings at the beginning of periods between 1912 and 1943. This comprehensive study was published by the National Bureau of Economic Research in 1958 and revealed that the default rate during each of the four-year periods between 1912 and 1939 was in excess of 18 percent for all low-grade issues but declined to 8.9 percent during World War II. The performance was generally best for public utilities, intermediate for industrials, and poorest for railroads. More than two thirds of the low-grade railroad issues were in default at some time between 1932 and 1935. The performance of the high-grade issues, conversely, was substantially better, with default rates in 1932–1935 amounting to 10.5 percent for the high-grade rail issues, 7.2 percent for the high-grade industrials, and 1.8 percent for the high-grade public utilities.[5] The study also revealed that investments in the defaulted issues offered substantial speculative appreciation since many of the corporations were ultimately restored to profitable operation, merged

[5] See, for example, W. Braddock Hickman, *Corporate Bond Quality and Investor Experience,* a study by the National Bureau of Economic Research (Princeton, N.J.: Princeton University Press, 1958), selected pages.

with other financially strong firms, or liquidated for funds adequate to retire the bonded indebtedness. In liquidation, assets left for preferred and common stockholders, being junior or subordinate to the credit issues, are normally less than the book value of the outstanding equity securities.

TABLE 4-1 / **Quadrennial Default Rates for Outstanding Corporate Bond Issues and Low Agency Ratings at Beginning of Periods, 1912–1943**

Period	Grade I–IV	Grade V–IX	Not Rated	Grade I–IV	Grade V–IX	Not Rated
	ALL ISSUES			RAILROADS		
1912–15	7.0%	49.3%	8.5%	7.1%	48.8%	13.5%
1916–19	3.4	21.6	9.2	1.7	12.3	24.2
1920–23	1.0	18.2	14.9	1.0	20.1	11.1
1924–27	1.1	23.5	13.8	0.6	29.5	13.1
1928–31	1.4	22.6	7.2	0.8	23.6	0.0
1932–35	6.2	48.9	49.2	10.5	68.8	0.0
1936–39	3.3	21.7	8.0	6.3	43.4	0.0
1940–43	0.4	8.9	6.8	0.6	7.7	23.3
	PUBLIC UTILITIES			INDUSTRIALS		
1912–15	0.0%[1]	100.0%[1]	6.7%	0.0%[1]		11.2%
1916–19	8.6	30.1	3.7	0.3	17.2%	4.4
1920–23	0.9	16.6	25.2	1.0	28.1	3.6
1924–27	0.7	16.6	13.1	3.1	29.4	14.1
1928–31	1.3	18.1	2.9	2.9	27.6	8.4
1932–32	1.8	41.9	45.6	7.2	38.2	51.9
1936–39	1.1	10.9	14.5	1.4	12.2	8.7
1940–43	0.4	9.7	8.8	0.0	11.9	2.2

[1] Based on fewer than five issues.

SOURCE: W. Braddock Hickman, *Corporate Bond Quality and Investor Experience,* a study by the National Bureau of Economic Research (Princeton, N.J.: Princeton University Press, 1958), selected pages.

In a given corporation debentures, that is, unsecured credit instruments, rank between secured creditors, if any, and the stockholders. Therefore, since junior issues possess a higher credit risk than senior securities, they normally carry a lower bond rating and trade at higher yields to maturity.[6] Clearly, a higher return, either from interest or a capital gain, on bonds can usually be secured only by sacrificing some assurance of a stable income and payment of principal upon maturity. In short, if more credit risk is assumed,

[6] The yield to maturity on a bond is the discount rate that equates the market value with the total of the expected future interest receipts and principal repayments. This concept is illustrated in the following section.

then the investor expects to receive additional compensation in the form of an increase in yield to maturity.

Ratings on corporate bonds are influenced largely by the number of times the company earns its *fixed charges*, for example, interest on contractual obligations, rent on leased facilities, and principal repayments. The average number of times that fixed charges have been earned during the past 7 to 10 years and the results during the poorest of these years should be considered. According to one outstanding security analyst, a safe coverage before rent, interest, and taxes, computed on average 7- to 10-year earnings, is four times on public utilities, five times on railroads, and seven times on industrials. During the poorest earnings years, the coverage should be three, four, or five times, for utilities, rails, and industrials, respectively.[7]

Since some of the lower-quality municipal issues also default in the payment of their interest or principal, an investor in this type of security should study the past debt-servicing record of the government, relate the government's present debt structure to its probable future ability to service such debt, and periodically check the bond rating on his issue to see whether or not some financial weakness has been recognized by the bond-rating services.[8]

Other types of fixed- or semifixed-return securities such as shares of credit unions or mortgages also possess the credit risk. Some credit unions are liquidated with less than 100 percent of the share balance being paid to the share depositors. Repossession of property by a mortgagee is sometimes necessary when the mortgagor defaults in his payments. Losses on the resale of such property frequently occur.

Variable-Return Securities

An investor in preferred or common stock who is seeking a high level of current income with a substantial degree of assurance of payment should study the dividend and long-term earnings record of the company. Whereas some corporations, such as American Telephone and Telegraph Company, have a lengthy record of uninterrupted dividend payments, many others pay irregular dividends. Some investment services, such as Standard & Poor's, provide, among other data, the number of years of continuous dividends. Similar information may be obtained by consulting other investment sources.[9]

Whereas the ranking of corporate bonds depends upon the degree of protection for interest and principal repayment, the ranking of preferred

---

[7] For a more complete study of this topic, see Benjamin Graham, David L. Dodd, and Sidney Cottle, *Security Analysis*, 4th ed. (New York: McGraw-Hill Book Company, Inc., 1962), pp. 324–363.

[8] See, for example, the most recent issue of *Moody's Government Manual* (New York: Moody's Investors Service, Inc.).

[9] See Chapter 11.

and common stocks is generally based on the relative stability and growth of corporate earnings and dividends. Standard & Poor's composite earnings and dividend ranking for stocks is one of seven groups: A+, A, A−, B+, B, B−, and C. Certain issues, for example, companies that sell predominately to the Defense Department, are not ranked because of their unstable earnings picture. The higher the ranking, generally, the greater is the assurance to the investor of increasing earnings and dividends per share for his company's preferred and common stock.

An owner of real estate is also faced with the credit risk in that his tenants may become delinquent in their rent payments, relocate to another area and remove some of the owner's furnishings, or damage the property without making restitution.

Interest Rate Risk

The *interest rate risk* refers to the probable fluctuation in the market prices of fixed-return securities, such as bonds, the values of which move in the opposite direction as yields to maturity.

The market price of long-term bonds fluctuates considerably over the business cycle. Even though the earnings of a company may be relatively stable and the fixed charges of the corporation appear to be adequately covered, the market price of its bonds may vary by 10 or 20 percent over its cyclically high and low trading range. During a boom, interest rates charged by banks and yields to maturity on bonds are relatively high. Monetary authorities may be taking a "tight" money stand, and the demand for funds is ordinarily in excess of the supply of loanable funds. Conversely, as a recession gains momentum, business firms reduce their inventory holdings, decelerate the rate of capital expansion, and repay some of their existing loans. In addition, consumers repay installment debt at a more rapid rate than they create it. As the pressure on funds decreases, interest rates tend to decline.

Since World War II interest rates have been unstable. From 1946 to 1959, long-term interest rates increased, while from 1960 to 1964, they declined slightly. During the last half of 1965 and early 1966, rates were again increasing. Intermediate-term yields were between 4¾ and 5 percent on U.S. government notes at the end of 1959, declined to approximately 3½ percent at the end of 1964, and rose to almost 5 percent in early 1966. The yields to maturity on the intermediate-term issues normally fluctuate more widely than those on long-term issues. (see Fig. 2–4).

Timely investments in high-grade bonds, that is, when prices are low and yields to maturity are high, will produce capital gains or generous interest returns for the investor, while untimely commitments often produce capital losses. For example, suppose that an investor in 1957 had bought a 10-year 4 percent bond to yield 3½ percent to maturity and sold it two years later at a price that provided the buyer with a yield to maturity of 5 percent. What gain or loss did the investor suffer on his bond commitment?

Table 4–2 provides a list of values for a 4 percent coupon bond with selected maturities ranging from 1 to 10 years and yields of from 1 to 6 percent. In determining the price for a 10-year 4 percent bond yielding 3.5 percent, the investor enters the table at a 3.5 percent yield and moves across to the appropriate number of years to maturity, 10. The figure, 104.19, represents the price of the bond as a percent of its par or maturity value. The price would thus be $1041.90 for a $1000 bond. After two years the bond was sold at a price to yield the new buyer 5 percent. The student should verify that this implies that the price of the bond had declined to $934.70 during the two-year period and that the original investor had suffered a capital loss of about $107. During the two-year period the bondholder did receive $80 interest, which was significantly less than the amount of his capital loss, however.

TABLE 4-2 /   Table of Values for a 4 Percent Coupon Bond with Selected Maturities

	Years to Maturity						
Yield	1	2	3	4	6	8	10
1.00	102.98	105.93	108.84	111.73	117.43	123.01	128.48
1.50	102.47	104.91	107.31	109.67	114.29	118.78	123.14
2.00	101.97	103.90	105.80	107.65	111.26	114.72	118.05
2.50	101.47	102.91	104.31	105.68	108.31	110.82	113.20
3.00	100.98	101.93	102.85	103.74	105.45	107.07	108.58
3.50	100.49	100.96	101.41	101.85	102.68	103.46	104.19
4.00	100.00	100.00	100.00	100.00	100.00	100.00	100.00
4.50	99.52	99.05	98.61	98.19	97.40	96.67	96.01
5.00	99.04	98.12	97.25	96.41	94.87	93.47	92.21
5.50	98.56	97.20	95.90	94.68	92.42	90.40	88.58
6.00	98.09	96.28	94.58	92.98	90.05	87.44	85.12

Bond tables are prepared from present-value tables. At any given point in time a bond is worth the sum of (1) the present value of the face of the bond discounted by the effective yield to maturity and (2) the present value of the interest to be received per period over the life of the bond discounted by the effective yield to maturity. Since most bond issues pay interest semiannually, and thus provide the investor with the equivalent of semiannual compounding of his return, the coupon rate is divided in half and the number of years to maturity is doubled to determine the number of periods.

Let us now determine the market value of a $1000 10-year 4 percent bond that yields 3.5 percent to maturity by using (1) a table of present values of $1 for 20 periods discounted by 1¾ percent per period, to determine the value of each dollar of the bond principal, and (2) a table of present values of $1 per period for 20 periods discounted by 1¾ percent per period, to determine the present value of the expected future flow of each dollar of interest income. The following are extracts from present-value tables:

PRESENT VALUE OF $1			PRESENT VALUE OF $1 PER PERIOD		
	Discount Rate			Discount Rate	
Periods			Periods		
	1¾%	2½%		1¾%	2½%
16	.7576163	.6736249	16	13.8504968	13.0550027
20	.7068246	.6102709	20	16.7528813	15.5891623

Value of 10-year bond ($1000 × .7068246)	= $ 706.82
Value of interest ($20 × 16.7528813)	= 335.06

Value of 10-year 4 percent bond sold to yield 3½ percent = $1041.88

The value of the bond as computed from present-value tables is identical to the figures within the bond table, except for rounding differences.

The student should now compute the value of the 8-year 4 percent bond sold to yield 5 percent to maturity by use of the above present-value tables and compare his results with those shown in the bond table (Table 4–2).

Of course, should yields on bonds decline, then this is equivalent to saying that the market value of bonds has risen. In this case the investor realizes a capital gain rather than a capital loss. From 1940 through 1966, however, the long-term trend of interest rates, that is, yields to maturity, was up, so that during this period bonds frequently had to be sold at capital losses. Although the trend has been up, there have been substantial short-term fluctuations in yields; hence, the investor is perhaps wise to commit funds to bonds when it appears that yields are at historically high levels or when he is reasonably sure that he can commit his funds until the bonds mature.

Because the operating performance of firms with top-graded bonds is almost always adequate, fluctuations in the market value of these bonds are influenced much more by yield structure, that is, the level of yields to maturity on similar-grade short-, intermediate-, and long-term maturity issues at any given point in time, than by operating performance. Companies that experience operational problems eventually get into financial difficulties or go into receivership or bankruptcy proceedings. For example, when a company is unable to generate adequate cash flows, it may have difficulty in meeting its interest payments to bondholders and in setting aside the required *sinking fund payments*.[10] When this situation leads to an actual default in servicing the issue, the market price of the securities often falls to

---

[10] The bond indenture frequently requires that a corporation set aside a certain percentage of the initial size of a bond issue in a so-called sinking fund, such as 4 percent per year, in cash, with a bond trustee to be used to retire a portion of the outstanding bonds or to invest in high-grade securities in order to build up funds for retiring the issue at maturity.

depressed levels. If an investor or speculator believes the insolvency to be a temporary condition, his purchase of the bond at a depressed price may produce a high capital gain. Since corporations with bond issues in default have, in many instances, made payment of accumulated interest and principal to the bondholders, many purchasers of such instruments at depressed prices have reaped large gains.

The cyclical behavior of interest rates suggests that long-term bonds, whether government or corporate, should be acquired at the peak of a boom when bond prices are extremely low, that is, during periods of high yields to maturity. During the following recession, market values will increase, thus providing the investor who wishes to sell the bond with some capital gain. Attempting to gauge the exact peak of bond yields to maturity, however, is very difficult.

Market Risk

Although the interest rate risk is associated with marketable fixed-return securities, such as certain U.S. Treasury bonds, U.S. agency securities, municipal bonds, corporate bonds, and preferred stocks, a similar risk, sometimes called the *market risk*, that is, the probability or chance of a decline in market price, is shouldered with the purchase of common stocks. From 1940 to 1957, average dividend yields on common stock ranged from one to one and a half percentage points above those on Aaa corporate bonds. From 1959 to 1965, however, the reverse was true. Market prices of many common stocks remained at such high levels that the average dividend yields of the stocks were considerably less than the average yields on Aaa corporate bonds. At that time prices on common stocks would have had to decline by some 25 to 35 percent in order to bring dividend yields into equality with yields on high-grade corporate bonds. The risk of a decline in market price is borne, of course, by the shareholder. Yields on Aaa corporate bonds are shown in Figure 2–6 and stock yields appear in Figure 4–1.

Market prices of common stocks, as measured by the popular Dow Jones Industrial Average (DJIA) index or the Standard & Poor's Average of 500 Stocks, have historically oscillated very widely. For example, the DJIA was about 375 in 1929 and declined to 50 by 1932 before beginning a five-year rally to 190 in 1937. It then declined by about 45 percent to 100 in 1939 and oscillated between 90 and 210 between 1939 and 1950 before rising to 1000 in early 1966. The long upward move, however, was not without major downward readjustments. A sharp four-month decline in 1957 dropped the DJIA about 20 percent. Prices fell about 22 percent in 1959 and 1960 before reaching new highs, declined roughly 25 percent in 1962, fell by about 10 percent in 1965, and were very volatile in early 1966. Even during a period of generally rising stock prices, sudden sharp declines frequently occur.

Numerous financial advisers and economists, because of the disparity between yields on corporate bonds and stocks, expect a major downward adjustment in common stock prices within the future. Some argue that it started in 1966 and may last for a few years until stock prices fall more in line with historical standards as measured by dividend yields or price–earnings multiples. Only time will tell whether this forecast is accurate.

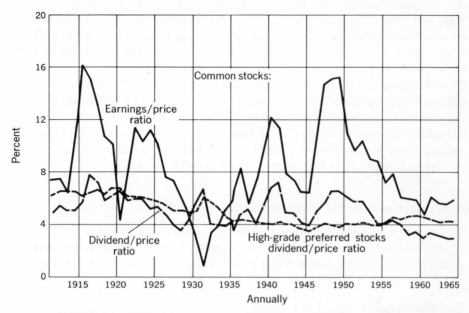

FIGURE 4-1 / Yields on common and preferred stocks, 1911–1965. From Board of Governors of the Federal Reserve System, *Historical Chart Book*, 1966, p. 37.

The DJIA is an index of the market price of 30 large industrial stocks. These giant companies have relatively stable sales, earnings, dividend payments, and common stock prices when compared to their smaller competitors. It is not uncommon when these issues decline 10 to 20 percent in market value to find that the market value of other more volatile stocks falls by two or three times this percentage. Because of the wide swings in the market prices of common stocks, an investor or speculator in such securities bears a considerable risk of loss in capital; on the other hand, one who is successful reaps generous returns on his investment.

Other Risks

Other types of risks, particularly those associated with investments in foreign securities, are the *monetary value risk* and the *political environment risk*. The interest and principal repayment of some foreign bond issues are payable in foreign currency rather than in U.S. dollars. Such an investment in the government or corporate bonds of a country that undergoes a shrinkage in the value of its currency relative to the American dollar, for example, Canada, where the Canadian dollar declined from 103.122 to 92.743 percent of the U.S. dollar between 1960 and 1965, deteriorates an investor's capital, since his return is in less valuable units than his commitment. Conversely, with countries whose rate of exchange relative to the U.S. dollar is favorable, the investor benefits, for example, Austria and the Netherlands between 1960 and 1965. Of course, the investor who buys foreign government bonds or securities of foreign corporations, often in an attempt to gain a slightly higher yield than obtainable on domestic issues, runs the calculated risk of (1) a change in the foreign government and repudiation of outstanding debt, (2) nationalization of business firms, that is, seizure by the government, or (3) the desire but inability of the foreign government or corporation to handle its indebtedness. The investor should weigh carefully the possibility of the additional risks associated with foreign investments against his expected return, either in the form of interest or dividends or capital gains, when investing in foreign securities rather than in domestic issues.

Risks Assumed by the Investor and the Speculator

The investor and the speculator differ in a number of respects, such as in (1) the characteristics desired in a security, (2) the approach to security selection, and (3) the amount and types of risks each is willing to assume.

The Investor

In the broadest sense an investor is a person, corporation, or government that commits funds to financial assets. Investing is, of course, merely the act of committing funds. For example, Mr. Jones may invest $10,000 in a partnership, XYZ Company may invest in a new delivery truck, or a state retirement fund may invest in U.S. government securities.

In security analysis, "investment" has a narrower connotation. One outstanding text defines investing as follows: "An investment operation is one which, upon thorough analysis, promises safety of principal and a satisfactory return." [11] The "analysis" deals with both qualitative, that is, desirable characteristics, and quantitative, that is, numerical evaluation, aspects. The "satisfactory return" may be either interest or dividend income or capital appreciation, while "safety of principal" refers to a high degree of both marketability and liquidity and to little fluctuation in market value. Securities that are actively traded and that can readily be turned into cash are said to be highly *liquid*. A security is *marketable*, if it can be traded in large blocks without substantially affecting its market price. U.S. government securities are highly marketable, since bond dealers stand ready to buy or sell large blocks of these securities, and security prices change very

[11] Graham, Dodd, and Cottle, p. 40.

little when such blocks are traded. Of the securities listed on the New York Stock Exchange, some 70 to 75 percent trade daily. For corporations such as General Motors, Chrysler, or Sperry Rand, an offer to sell 1000 or 10,000 shares has relatively little effect on the market value of the stock; but for a more thinly traded issue, for example, one in which average daily trading is below 2000 shares, an order to sell 1000 or more shares may cause a significant drop in the market price of the stock.

The investor buys a security—bonds, stock, or real estate—only after a thorough analysis of the quantitative and qualitative factors surrounding the asset. Before making a corporate bond investment, he wishes to assure himself that the issuer is financially sound and is reasonably expected to adequately service the debt. He places importance upon the debtor's historical debt-servicing record, the progressiveness of company management, the trend in sales and profits of the firm, and the adequacy of corporate income or cash flows to service the company's contractual obligations. When these factors appear unfavorable, the investor either requires collateral or seeks another bond issue offering the desired strengths. Since these factors are almost always favorable in bonds that are rated Aaa or Aa, such securities have sometimes been labeled as *investment grade,* with all others being called *speculative grade.*

Investment-grade stocks are stocks issued by financially strong companies operating in industries with promise of growth. Stocks rated as A+, A, or A— are generally considered to be investment-grade equities, while the lower grades are regarded as speculative in nature.[12] With investment-grade stocks, the owners expect a high stability of income and a liquid, marketable security. When choosing a stock, the investor prefers one with a long-term promise of growth in market value and disregards the short-run oscillation in the market price of the security. He may prefer a growth company selected from a growth industry, that is, an area that can reasonably be expected to grow more rapidly than the U.S. economy because of shifting population components and consumer preferences or aggressive research and development of new products. The investor, of course, analyzes his security holdings periodically—at least annually—to ascertain that they continue to be of investment quality.

The real estate investor seeks either land that is strategically located and offers long-term capital appreciation potential or structures—commercial, industrial, or consumer dwellings—that appear to offer a satisfactory return. With buildings, the quality of construction, location, and probable future rental demand are of prime importance.

The purchaser of investment-grade bonds, of course, assumes some risks. There is a slim probability of the credit risk, that is, the loss of capital through the unwillingness or inability of the firm to service its contractual obligations. The inflation risk, however, particularly on bonds, savings ac-

---

[12] See Chapter 3.

counts, and other fixed-return securities, is great when the probability of continued erosion of purchasing power is high. High-grade bonds, while oscillating somewhat less in market price over the business cycle than the lower-quality issues, do, nevertheless, carry a substantial interest rate risk. High-grade securities offer a higher degree of liquidity, marketability, and price stability than the more speculative issues.

Investment-grade stocks carry certain risks but offer some strengths. The continued payment of dividends is not assured, nor do stocks have definite maturities. The credit risk is, moreover, higher on investment-grade equities than on high-grade bonds. The market value of many common equities grows with the economy—usually as rapidly as the increase in the level of consumer prices—and, therefore, these securities are relatively free from the inflation risk. An investment in equities bears a substantial market risk. Sudden, sharp price drops occur with little warning, which can erase within a few months about one fourth or one half of the invested principal in common stocks.

Real estate investments bear some risks while they guard against others. The amount of well-situated land is fixed, and as demand increases, through population growth, prices are expected to rise. Hazards borne by owners of structures include not only such insurable ones as destruction by fires, hurricanes, tornadoes, or hail but also such uninsurable ones as high vacancy rates, relocation of highway arteries, and shifts in the business community. Real estate is also poor in marketability and liquidity and requires substantial maintenance and transfer costs.

The Speculator

Speculation is the act of committing funds to a speculative-grade security, that is, one of low quality and with wide price movements. The speculator seeks to take a capital gain in a relatively short period of time and almost wholly disregards the promise of income, either in the form of interest or dividends. The individual, of course, may "speculate" in a wide range of security media, such as marketable U.S. government securities when prices are severely depressed, corporate bonds, common stocks, security options, real estate, or commodities.[13]

The speculator in stocks is interested in capital gain and seeks a security that provides wide oscillation in market value. He disregards the higher-quality issues that have little price variation but seeks a security that is actively traded.

Some speculators disregard the fundamental strengths and weaknesses of the issue in which they trade, while others assign them some importance. Speculating in an issue with good fundamental strengths, for example, in-

[13] Because of the complexity of commodity markets and trading, this subject is not discussed in this text.

creasing sales and profits with adequate liquid assets to meet operating and contractual obligation needs, is far less risky than buying stock of a corporation that has been and is expected to continue to show losses. *Selling issues short,* that is, selling issues not owned, borrowing them to make immediate delivery to the purchaser, and buying replacement issues at a later date—hopefully at a lower cost, conversely, should be either in (1) "strong" issues that have had a very recent rapid rise and are expected to decline because of "profit-taking" selling, (2) low-quality issues that are excessively priced when related to current and future expected earnings, or (3) weak, declining (bear) markets.

The speculator is willing to take a substantial market risk or interest rate risk in hopes of obtaining a high return. Since he commits his funds for only a short time—a few days or months—his exposure to the inflation and credit risk is less than in a longer-term investment. Because of the low quality of the issues in which he trades, however, the credit risk may be substantial.

Some financial analysts advocate that few individuals make "good" speculators. Sauvain suggests that a "successful speculator," that is, one who consistently earns better than average returns,

> must have a burning desire to make money. He must be willing to work very hard as well as to neglect his wife or sweetheart in order to make the profit. In addition, he should have an instinct for determining favorable situations and for warning him against unfavorable developments.[14]

He must also have patience—a virtue often lacking in a speculator but present in an investor—and be willing to shift from a "long position," that is, owning securities, to a "cash position" or to a "short position," that is, owing securities, as the direction of the market dictates. He must buy when others are "panic selling" and sell when others are "recklessly buying," disregarding current security prices relative to earnings prospects.

Summary

Since no single investment medium is completely free from all risks, a commitment of funds into any type of security presents some danger. The purchasing power risk refers to the possible decline in the purchasing power of an investment, while the credit risk is the probable inability of the corporation or governmental agency to fulfill the obligations of the instrument, for example, payment of interest and redemption of bonds upon maturity. The interest rate risk refers to the fluctuation in the market value of a bond or preferred stock, while the market risk applies to the possible loss in market value of common stocks, security options, or real property.

[14] Harry Sauvain, *Investment Management* (Englewood Cliffs, N.J.: Prentice-Hall, Inc., 1959), p. 424. See also Chapter 16 of this text.

The purchasing power risk associated with securities is dependent upon the probable future direction of movement in consumer prices. During periods of inflation, many common stocks, investment company shares, variable annuity insurance policies, and real estate investments offer hedges against inflation. Fixed-return securities are high in this type of risk, since the principal and periodic income are eroded by the shrinkage in the value of the dollar. The opposite is true during a long period of declining consumer prices.

Fixed-return securities, particularly those with an assured income, for example, insured bank savings or savings and loan accounts, are low in credit risk. This risk is almost nil in U.S. government and agency securities, low in high-grade corporate and municipal bonds, and increases with an investment in low-quality municipal or corporate bonds.

The interest rate risk is high for debt instruments with fixed maturities and fixed-interest coupon rates, such as intermediate- or long-term government, municipal, or corporate bonds; corporate preferred stocks; and mortgages. The risk is absent, however, from savings media, for example, bank savings accounts, savings and loan shares, credit union shares, savings bonds, or postal savings.

All equity investments possess some degree of market risk, but the degree of danger is less with a high-grade, sometimes called investment-grade, common or preferred stock than with one of low quality. An investment-grade security is one that offers safety of principal and a high degree of marketability and liquidity along with a reasonable interest or dividend yield. An investment-grade security may also provide some year-to-year growth in capital appreciation.

The investor purchases a security that, based upon thorough analysis, offers safety of principal and a yield commensurate with the various types of risks assumed. The speculator, conversely, purchases a security that he believes will offer him a quick capital gain.

The primary difference between an investment and a speculation is the intent of the buyer. For example, an individual may buy International Business Machines (IBM) stock with the intention of holding the security for several years. This act is classified as an investment. The speculator buys IBM stock if he believes the market price of the issue will increase appreciably within the next few days. The speculator is willing to assume a greater market risk than the investor, but he also expects a higher return on his commitment of funds.

The security owner must (1) formulate his objectives, whether income or capital gains, (2) determine the risks he is willing to assume, and (3) select a portfolio that meets these objectives. If the investor desires some protection from each type of risk, for example, those of purchasing power, credit, interest rate, or market, he should follow the policy of investing in a mixed portfolio of high-grade bonds or other high-quality fixed-return investments and common stocks.

[handwritten: CORP BONDS / CDS / TREAS Bonds / MUNIC Bonds / MORTS / Pref Stks / Common Stocks]

QUESTIONS FOR REVIEW /

1. Consider the security media that were discussed in the previous chapters and rank these from high to low for (a) purchasing power risk, (b) credit risk, (c) market risk, and (d) interest rate risk.
2. What risks are associated with an investment in foreign securities in addition to those associated with an investment in domestic issues?
3. How may one select a low market risk security?
4. How would you choose a common stock that offers higher than average capital appreciation potential?
5. Which of the following investors need safety of principal and assurance of income: (a) the young widow with two children; (b) the retired; (c) the medical doctor; (4) the speech professor; (e) the industrial worker.
6. What investment policies should be followed by the person seeking safety of principal?
7. How does an investor differ from a speculator?
8. Describe briefly the difference between a speculation and an investment.

PROBLEMS /

1. With the use of *Security and Industry Survey* by Merrill Lynch, Pierce, Fenner & Smith, Inc., information distributed by E. F. Hutton & Company or other brokerage firms, *The Value Line Investment Survey, Moody's Stock Survey,* Standard & Poor's *Security Owner's Stock Guide,* or other up-to-date investment information, compile a list of six common stock issues that are currently suitable investments for the individual seeking stability of principal and assurance of income; then recommend six stocks for the speculator who is attempting to maximize his capital gains. Defend your recommendations.
2. Make a study of the market price fluctuation and yield changes from the peak of the last business cycle to the bottom of the subsequent trough and determine the change in the market value of Aaa- and Baa-grade industrial and public utility bonds. You may elect to work with industry averages or to select individual issues representative of the categories. You may refer to publications of Moody's Investors Service, Inc., for the desired information. How do the market values and yield variations of corporate bonds compare with those of U.S. government issues with similar maturities (10 years or more to maturity)? Evaluate their investment worthiness.

REFERENCES /

Board of Governors of the Federal Reserve System, *Historical Chart Book.* Washington, D.C.: Federal Reserve System, 1966.

Hickman, W. Braddock, *Corporate Bond Quality and Investor Experience.* Princeton, N.J.: Princeton University Press, 1958.

———, *Statistical Measures of Corporate Bond Financing Since 1900.* Princeton, N.J.: Princeton University Press, 1958.

Meiselman, David, *The Term Structure of Interest Rates*. Englewood Cliffs, N.J.: Prentice-Hall, Inc., 1962.

U.S. Department of Commerce, *Business Statistics*. Washington, D.C.: U.S. Government Printing Office, 1963.

Wu, H. K., and A. J. Zakon, *Elements of Investments: Selected Readings*. New York: Holt, Rinehart and Winston, Inc., 1965.

chapter 5 | Investment Priorities

Introduction

After becoming familiar with the different types of security media and the risks associated with each, the investor should formulate some goals or investment priorities. The order of priorities may differ for each household because of different family circumstances, but the following are suggested: (1) liquid funds, (2) insurance coverage, (3) home ownership, (4) education of dependent children, (5) supplemental income, (6) retirement income, and (7) estate planning.

For the total of all households in the United States in 1965, about 20 percent of family assets were held in cash or savings media; about 43.3 percent was invested in other current financial assets such as insurance reserves, corporate issues, and government securities; and of the balance, 37.5 percent, two thirds was represented in home ownership and one third in consumer durable goods, for example, automobiles, furniture, and clothing. Table 5–1 and Figure 5–1 reveal that mortgage debt, consumer debt, and consumer net worth were 9 percent, 3.9 percent, and 87.1 percent, respectively, of total assets. The above figures are the arithmetic averages for all families, and the asset holdings and outstanding debts of any one family varies widely from these averages. This chapter together with Chapter 6 will consider some of the goals or priorities that influence the choice in the modes of wealth held by an individual family.

Liquid Assets

Need for Liquid Assets

The three primary needs for liquid funds are to meet ordinary living expenses, emergencies, and to provide temporary investment media. Families should own some liquid assets, such as currency, demand deposits, time and savings deposits, savings shares, and U.S. savings bonds, for meeting ordinary living expenses. In order to minimize the loss of interest on uninvested funds, the head of the household should maintain an adequate but not excessive demand deposit balance. Inconvenience may arise if the account is too small. The size of the account should depend in part upon the frequency of income. For example, a family that receives weekly wages

TABLE 5-1 / The Consumer Balance Sheet, 1961–1965 (End of period in billions of dollars)

	1961		1965	
	$	%	$	%
Currency and bank deposits	189.7	11.2	269.1	12.2
Currency and demand deposits	80.0		105.4	
Time and savings deposits	109.7		163.7	
Savings shares	75.7	4.5	117.9	5.3
Insurance and pension reserves	201.3	11.9	270.5	12.3
Private	156.8		208.7	
Government	44.5		61.8	
Government securities	103.9	6.1	119.9	5.4
U.S. savings bonds	46.4		49.6	
Other U.S. government	26.7		32.3	
State and local government	30.8		38.0	
Corporate and other securities	489.3	28.8	619.2	28.1
Bonds and notes	20.9		23.3	
Investment company shares	32.6		46.3	
Other preferred and common shares	435.8		549.6	
Total current (financial) assets	1060.0	62.5	1396.5	63.3
Nonfarm family home ownership	420.0	24.8	535.0	24.3
Value of consumer-owned durable goods (depreciated 10% annually)	216.5	12.7	273.5	12.4
Fixed assets	636.5	37.5	808.5	36.7
Total assets	1696.5	100.0	2205.0	100.0
Mortgage debt	139.9	8.2	197.9	9.0
Short- and intermediate-term consumer credit	57.7	3.4	86.0	3.9
Total liabilities	197.6	11.6	283.9	12.9
Consumer net worth	1498.9	88.4	19.21.1	87.1

source: National Consumer Finance Association, *Finance Facts Yearbook* (Washington, D.C.: The Association, 1966), p. 39.

ordinarily has less need for a large liquid fund than one with a monthly salary. The demand deposit account should be adequate to meet ordinary recurring bills such as rent or house payment, food, utilities, installment debts, and other living expenses. In 1966, the ratio of consumer debt to disposable personal income was above 14 percent, and many families were paying either rent or a house payment ranging between roughly 15 and 25 percent of their disposable personal income.

There is some relation between the use of consumer debt and family income level. In early 1964, about half of all U.S. spending units owed on installment debt. About 60 percent of families with annual income of $5000 to $10,000 were making consumer installment payments, and approximately three fourths of this group had less than $500 in liquid assets. Some 39 per-

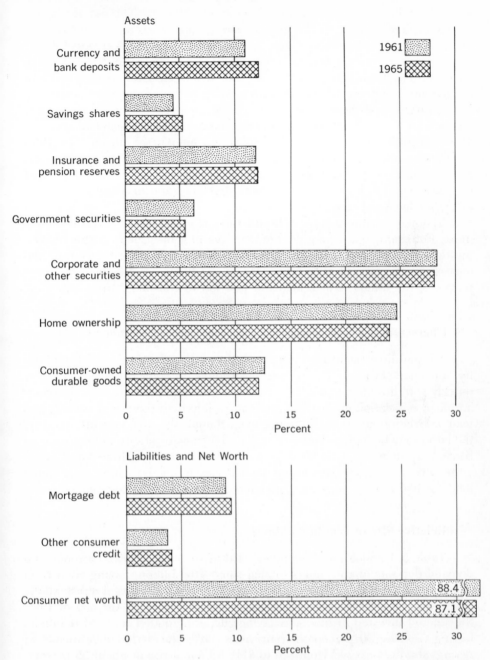

FIGURE 5-1 / The consumer balance sheet, 1961 and 1965. From Table 5-1.

cent of the total in the survey, or about 78 percent of those owing on installment debts, had installment liabilities in excess of $500.[1] The use of average
consumer debt declines as the level of family income rises.

Emergency funds should also be maintained in order to meet living
costs during an unexpected period of unemployment or sickness, although
health insurance and wage continuation insurance may reduce this need, or
to meet other expenses that arise with a death in the family, car breakdown,
home repairs, and the like. When unemployment occurs or an emergency
arises, a family with no liquid fund is very susceptible to financial reverses.
This susceptibility varies inversely with the amount of income. In 1963,
nearly 10 percent of families with income between $3000 and $6000 was
rated as being very vulnerable to financial reverses, and another 8 percent
was considered to be somewhat vulnerable.[2] The ratio declined for families
in higher income brackets.

Another possible use for a liquid fund is a temporary investment medium. For example, a young couple may live in a furnished apartment, saving their money until they have adequate funds to buy their furniture and
make a down payment on a home. When the funds are adequate for these
purposes, the family is in a financial position to consider home ownership.

Characteristics of Media That Qualify as Liquid Investments

A liquid investment medium should have three features—safety, liquidity, and marketability. The investment should be convertible to cash very
quickly with little loss in market value. For example, shares in a local savings
and loan association are usually more accessible than those in a savings and
loan association across the country, even though the dividend rate paid on
the latter may be higher. Since savings and loan associations and commercial
banks may demand 30 to 60 days notice of withdrawal, these types of investments are slightly less liquid than Series E bonds, which after being
held for two months may be liquidated on demand at a commercial bank.

Relative Size of Liquid Holdings

Table 5–1 and Figure 5–1 reveal that at the end of 1965, currency and
demand deposits of consumers totaled some $105 billion, having risen from
$80 billion in 1961. Certain types of savings media increased substantially
from year end 1961 to 1965, while others changed little. At the end of 1965,
the amount invested in time and savings deposits totaled some $164 billion,
having risen by 50 percent in four years. Over the period investments in
savings shares increased from $76 to $118 billion, a rise of about 55 percent.

---

[1] National Consumer Finance Association, *Finance Facts Yearbook* (Washington,
D.C.: The Association, 1965), pp. 45–47.
[2] National Consumer Finance Association, pp. 45–47.

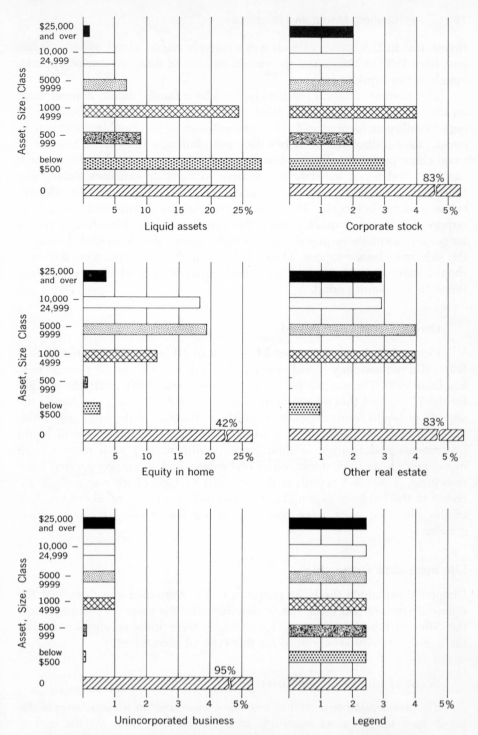

FIGURE 5-2 / Distribution of assets of spending units, by asset size class,
1963. From *U.S. Statistical Abstract*, 1965, p. 349.

Investment in U.S. savings bonds was relatively stable, about $47 to $50 billion, from 1950 to 1965, since the annual amount of new investment approximately offset liquidation.

The amount of liquid funds to be held by a family should depend more on the needs of the household than on its income level or total asset holdings. Stability of income and a large investment in marketable securities, of course, may reduce the need but does not eliminate it. A schoolteacher or some other professionally employed person with an assured stable income has less need for a "substantial," relative to monthly expenses, emergency fund than a salesman, industrial worker, or self-employed person who receives a variable income. The owner of marketable bonds and stocks may require funds more quickly than the assets will provide—four days or longer are normally required—or if security prices are depressed, timing of the sale may be very poor. Depending upon the circumstances, a family should strive to maintain a liquid fund equal to normal expenses over a three- to six-month period.

Ownership of Liquid Funds

Figure 5–2 shows that about 24 percent of all family units in the United States did not own any liquid assets at the end of 1963, and 53 percent held less than $500. The median for the entire group was $400, while the median for the 76 percent that owned liquid assets was $900. For a given family the amount of liquid funds depends primarily on the size of the total asset holdings. Families with small asset holdings tend to concentrate them in liquid investments and equities in their home, while families with more wealth invest more heavily in stocks, other real estate, and in unincorporated business firms. Table 5–1 reveals that from 1961 to 1965, there was a slight increase in the holdings of liquid assets. On balance, however, about one half of the spending units were poorly prepared for meeting financial emergencies.

Life Insurance Ownership

Chapter 2 explained the basic purposes of life insurance and described the different types of contracts. Let us now consider the scope of coverage, how the different types of insurance, for example, term, meet varying needs, and the average family expenditure for this type of investment.

Scope of Life Insurance Coverage

The average amount of life insurance coverage on a large sample depends to a major extent upon age and sex (see Fig. 5–3). At the end of 1960, approximately half the individuals under 18 were insured, while the ratio was 60 to 65 percent for the 18- to 64-year age brackets. The ratio

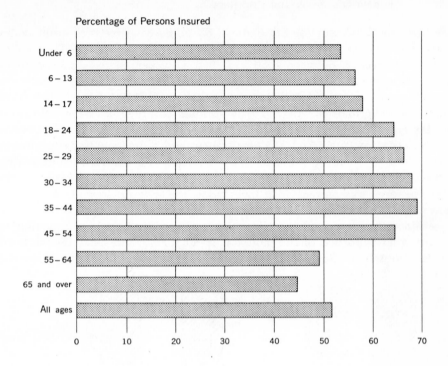

Percentage of Persons Insured

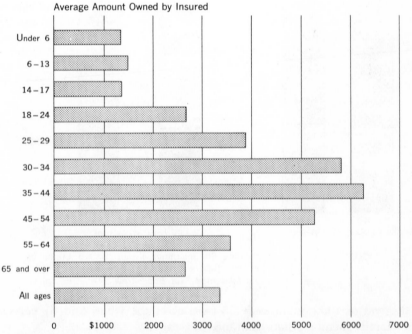

Average Amount Owned by Insured

FIGURE 5-3 / Characteristics of individual life insurance ownership in the United States in 1960. From Institute of Life Insurance, *Life Insurance Fact Book*, New York, 1965, pp. 13–14.

declined to 42 percent for those above 65. Some 65 percent of adult males were then insured, while only 54 percent of the females above 18 years of age were covered. Between 1956 and 1965, however, there was some trend toward more life insurance coverage at an older age, that is, among the retired group, and individuals in the 25-to-34 and 35-to-44 age brackets were also increasing their coverage. This additional coverage has been influenced by the growth in disposable personal income, inflationary trends that prevail in the economy, increased life expectancy, and more aggressive insurance salesmanship. Some 89 percent of the ordinary life insurance sold during 1963 was on males, but on a cumulative basis only 70 percent of such insurance in force was on males. In most cases, the wife or dependent children are named as beneficiaries of the insurance policies.

Since the income of most families is limited and there is rationing of assets, a large portion of the money is spent for life insurance on the head of the household. Some two thirds of heads of households were insured

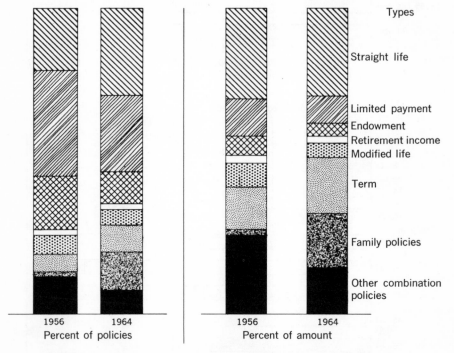

FIGURE 5-4 / Sales of ordinary life insurance in the United States by types of policies, 1956 and 1964. From Institute of Life Insurance, *Life Insurance Fact Book,* New York, 1965, p. 13.

at the end of 1960, while only 55 percent of the wives and 51 percent of other family members had insurance coverage.

In 1964, the largest number of insurance policies was sold to individuals with annual income of $3000 to $7500, which, of course, included a majority of U.S. families. Although the purchase of ordinary life insurance by individuals earning more than $10,000 annually accounted for only 12 to 14 percent of the number of policies, the amount purchased by these individuals totaled some 32 percent in 1956 and in 1964.

There has been a relative decline in the purchase of straight life, limited payment life, and the endowment policy. During the eight-year period 1956–1964, there was an increase in the sale of term insurance and family policies, the latter usually being a combination of permanent and term insurance (see Fig. 5–4). There was also a noted shift from the purchase of the smaller policies, with more emphasis on the sale of larger units at lower cost per unit, for example, term insurance. Many wage earners, for example, prefer a $5000 or $10,000 term or straight life insurance policy to a $1000 or $2500 endowment policy. In 1956, 22 percent of the policies were written in amounts of $10,000 or larger, and the percentage had increased to 36 by 1964.

Type Versus Need

The type of life insurance contract to purchase depends, of course, upon the needs of the insured and/or his beneficiaries. A reputable insurance agent should analyze a family's insurance program, but the following ideas may be helpful:

1. Some permanent-type insurance, for example, straight life, should be purchased, particularly on the head of the household. This type of policy builds a cash surrender value and offers protection after the insured reaches age 65 (beyond which age term insurance is ordinarily not written).

2. Additional term insurance may be added, providing maximum protection during the "term" of policy, such as 5, 10, or 20 years, in order to supplement Social Security benefits to the spouse and dependent children in the event of the wage earner's death.

3. Some families prefer a combination of straight life and term or decreasing term insurance, for example, $25,000 the first five years, $20,000 the next five years, and so on, to meet the above needs.

4. Educational endowment plans may be acquired to meet the cost of higher education.

5. Credit life insurance, or group term insurance, carried by lending institutions, and mortgage cancellation policies, decreasing term, or a combination of straight life and term, offer substantial protection for the cost and reduce the need for permanent insurance.

The amount of insurance to carry depends upon (1) the age of the head of household, his spouse, and other dependents; (2) the standard of living the head of household wishes to assure his surviving family; (3) his other assets and debts; (4) the income-earning ability of his spouse; (5) Social Security benefits (Chapter 6); and (6) other factors, for example, the health of the insured, supplemental retirement plans, and income available for premiums.

Let us analyze the insurance coverage of the Doak family. Mr. Doak, 36, and his wife, age 32, have three children, ages 8, 5, and 2. Present insurance ownership consists of (1) maximum Social Security coverage; (2) $5000 straight life on Mr. Doak; and (3) $20,000 10-year term on Mr. Doak, $5000 on his wife, and $1000 on each of the three children. Mr. Doak's annual before-tax income is $12,500; he owes $2000 on installment debts and $18,000 on a home mortgage; and his equity in assets amounts to $15,000, divided 10 percent to liquid funds, 20 percent to equity in home, and 70 percent to household items, automobile, and other durables.

After the death of Mr. Doak the insurance proceeds were found to be inadequate to provide the "accustomed standard of living" for the wife and children. The proceeds from the term policy could be applied to the automobile and mortgage debt or invested to provide income, leaving about $5000 to cover funeral costs, living expenses until Social Security payments begin, and other items. The $368 (maximum) monthly Social Security survivors benefits, payable only until the children reach the age of 22 if in school or 18 otherwise, are helpful, but far less than the $800 monthly family budget prior to Mr. Doak's death. Between the wife's age of 52, when the youngest child is 22, and age 60, Mrs. Doak is eligible for no Social Security benefits. Upon reaching age 60, she may claim survivor's retirement benefits of $120 per month. Obviously, Mrs. Doak must take a job, incurring child care expense, lower her standard of living, or seek remarriage. The Doaks are underinsured for the periods (1) of the children's dependency, (2) when Social Security benefits cease and before retirement benefits begin, and (3) in which the wife is expected to outlive the husband.

Share of Budget Spent for Life Insurance

The percentage of disposable personal income spent for life insurance fluctuated over the past. Some 4.7 percent was spent in 1934 compared to 5.1 percent in 1940, 3.5 percent in 1950, and 4 percent in 1964. Thus, in 1964, the "average" family with $10,000 annual disposable personal income spent about $400 for life insurance in addition to the payment for Social Security benefits (Chapter 6).

Home Ownership

Characteristics of Owners

The promotion of home ownership by various federal programs since the mid-1930s has increased the relative number of families who "own" their homes. Housing units occupied by owners increased from 43 percent in 1940 to 62 percent in 1963. Figure 5–2 indicates that some 58 percent of the families had equities in their homes in 1963 compared to 54 percent during 1960. In 1963, the *modal* group, that is, the most numerous category, had equity investments ranging from $5000 to $10,000, with 5 percent of the equity owners investing less than $1000.

During recent years there has been a trend for young married couples and retired individuals to move to apartment units. Multiunit dwelling starts increased from 8 percent of the total in 1955 to more than 34 percent in 1964, indicating a significant shift in the preference for apartment units over this period.

Size and Type of Mortgages

In 1958, approximately 40 percent of the housing units were being financed with some type of real estate credit compared to 47 percent in 1963. In the postwar period increases in the price of land and dwelling costs necessitated more mortgage financing per unit. From 1950 to 1964, for example, the average cost of a dwelling increased 80 percent, from $8675 to $15,575, while the average size of the mortgage increased from $5440 to $9478, maintaining an almost constant relationship between cost and mortgage debt.[3]

The three types of mortgages, VA, FHA, and conventional, have shifted somewhat in relative importance. The percentage of total homes financed with VA mortgages declined from 8 percent in 1958 to 4 percent in 1963 and 1964, while FHA mortgages were used to finance 13 to 14 percent of the housing starts in those years. The others were financed with conventional mortgages. Lack of eligibility for VA mortgage credit reduced its usage from 1958 to 1965, but reinstatement of the GI Bill of Rights in 1966 for Cold War veterans may repopularize the VA mortgage.

Size of Home To Purchase

The size of the home that a family should purchase depends primarily upon the size and income level of the family. Many families prefer to purchase a three- or four-bedroom house containing two or three baths rather than a smaller one because of the relative ease in selling a medium-sized structure and its better adaptability to a growing family. There are two good reasons for "slight overbuying." The transfer costs for a residence are approximately 10 percent of the appraised value of the home, including closing costs of purchase and sale, and an inflationary trend in the United States makes debt retirement easier on the individual as time progresses, since the payment of principal and interest remains constant and the amount of disposable personal income for the average family increases.

Many lending institutions recommend that the home mortgage be

[3] U.S. Savings and Loan League, *Savings and Loan Fact Book* (Chicago: The League, 1965), pp. 43 and 52.

limited to two and one half times annual family income. For example, a family with an annual income of $8000 should not borrow more than $20,000 for financing a home. If their down payment is inadequate to cover the difference, they should look for a smaller unit or postpone the purchase. When a family finances more than two and one half times their annual income, it may become difficult to meet monthly house payments and other necessities of life.

Outlook for Real Estate Values

The real estate market is shaped primarily by the age of the population seeking housing, the availability of mortgage credit at reasonable interest rates, and the general level of the U.S. economy. A large segment of the population will be entering college age from now until 1980 and will later be forming household units. This age group should provide strong demand for apartments, and multiunit dwellings should continue to account for a large percentage of the housing starts in the late 1960s and early 1970s. The relative demand for single-unit dwellings should increase after about 1970, when the demand for homes should accelerate.

Since the amount of vacant land in suitable locations is limited, the cost of building sites is likely to follow the upward trend. Clearance of low-value homes from convenient locations and their replacement with apartment units is likely to continue. Many of the new single-family dwellings will probably continue to be erected in residential subdivisions located outside the city limits of metropolitan areas. From 1955 to 1965, labor and material costs were rising about 1.8 percent annually, and this upward trend is likely to continue.

From 1946 to 1955, an individual could have purchased a home, lived in it, and then sold it for a profit; but during the early 1960s, the value of real estate did not appreciate so rapidly, and the obsolesence associated with home ownership approximately offset the inflationary trend. In the mid-1960s, however, three- to five-year-old homes were being sold, generally, at cost or slightly less, and investments in landscaping, fencing, carpets, draperies, and other extras were difficult to recapture in the sale of a home.

Education of Dependents

Income Differential

The lifetime income expectancy of an individual depends to a large extent upon the type of work for which he is trained. In 1965, for example, the salary of the average medical doctor was much higher than the salaries of most other types of jobholders. Doctors, dentists, lawyers, and scientists were within the top four brackets, followed by engineers, economists, and college professors, in that order. Not all individuals can enter these profes-

sions, of course, but the youth—and his parents—should consider the expected lifetime earning differential between a high school graduate and
a college graduate. U.S. Department of Labor estimates in 1963 indicated
that the expected lifetime earnings of a high school graduate are $247,000
compared to $417,000 for a college graduate. If the trend in inflation con-
tinues, the amount of lifetime income will no doubt reach still higher figures.
Each college-age person must decide for himself whether or not this 70 percent increase in expected income is a worthwhile reward for the expense
and work required to obtain a college education. The prestige and work
environment obtainable with different educational attainments should also
be considered. With the occupational need for more highly trained technicians, rather than semiskilled workers, it is becoming increasingly more
difficult for individuals with less than a college degree to qualify for a job
with promotional opportunities. Since most parents want their children to
have the opportunity of competing with other individuals for good jobs, they
encourage their offspring to attend a college or a university.

Cost of Education

The cost of a college education increased substantially from 1946 to
1964, and it is probable that the increase will continue. In 1964, approximately $2500 per year was required for a student to pay tuition, fees, room
and board, and miscellaneous costs for attending many of the private, prestige universities, while the basic cost associated with attending state-sup-
ported institutions ranged from about $1500 to $2000. This is approximately
twice the cost level at the end of World War II, and it is probable that the
expense will double again by 1980 or 1985.[4] In the early 1960s, a college
degree required some $8000 to $10,000 in out-of-pocket expenses, and the
student was foregoing some $4000 to $5000 annual income while pursuing
his degree. The cost of four years of college, then, was approximately
$10,000 in cash outlay, plus about $20,000 in lost income, or a total of about
$30,000.

Number of College Students Expected

In 1960, there were approximately 3.6 million students enrolled in U.S.
colleges and universities, and by 1965 the number had increased to approximately 5.4 million. Projections indicate that about 7 million students will be
enrolled by 1970 and about 8.3 million by 1975, with some two thirds of
these individuals being male. The median years of school completed is likely
to increase from about 10.6 in 1960 to approximately 12 by 1970, and perhaps to 12.3 by 1980.[5]

[4] Department of Labor estimates.
[5] Department of Labor estimates.

Since World War II there has been a greater emphasis placed on a college degree than in earlier decades. In 1940, for example, only 16 percent of high school graduates entered college. In the mid-1960s, however, over 40 percent of high school graduates were enrolling in a college or university, resulting in crowded classrooms, a shortage of qualified instructors, and a rising salary scale for professors. With the increasing need for more technically trained personnel, a college degree has generally become the expected norm in many fields.

Funds to Meet Educational Costs

The expenses associated with a college education may be financed in a number of ways, including dependence upon some type of scholarship, borrowing through a student loan program, working one's way through college, the savings of the parents, or a combination of the above methods.

Although many business firms and foundations grant scholarships to worthy students, only about 10 percent of the students in college in 1965 were receiving this type of aid—which was often limited to the payment of tuition and room and board. The student who attends college on a scholarship, then, must have some funds to meet other out-of-pocket costs. The usual criteria for granting scholarships are (1) economic need and (2) average or higher ability. Since this type of financing is often unavailable to the needy below-average student, parents should not depend upon this method but should seek other means for financing the college education of their children. Scholarships, if and when they are granted, should be considered windfall gains.

Another method for financing a college degree that grew in acceptance in the early 1960s is the student loans. Many universities, foundations, commercial banks, and savings and loan associations grant loans to needy students who are doing passing work. Financing under these programs is usually limited to students who have completed one or more years of acceptable college work, requires little or no interest during the remaining period of schooling, and requires a systematic repayment beginning about 6 to 12 months after the student takes his degree or after he drops out of school. Complete repayment is usually expected within five or six years after graduation or withdrawal from the college or university. Loan limits under these programs are usually adequate to cover only the real necessities, such as tuition, books, and room and board.

It has become increasingly difficult to work one's way through college because of the high cost of education and the low pay scale of part-time students. Some students alternate between being a full-time student and a full-time worker, for example, during the summer, although in some cases this postpones completion of the degree. Reinstatement of the GI educational benefits for those who entered military service after January 31, 1955, should be a real aid to students who qualify.

The most dependable method for financing a college education is through a savings program. A large number of families with children in college have an annual income of less than $6000, and since many families expect to have more than one child in college at the same time, it is imperative that some planning and systematic saving be done in order to finance these costs. The parent may select from a number of methods for building an educational fund, such as: (1) the purchase of 15- to 18-year endowments on the children soon after their birth, thus providing benefits during the critical college age; (2) borrowing against the cash surrender value of permanent insurance; (3) a long-range savings plan that involves investing in shares of a savings and loan association or Series E bonds; or (4) a systematic investment in common stocks or in the shares of an investment company.

Supplemental Income

Distinguishing among the last three priorities—supplemental income, retirement income, and building an estate—may be difficult. This is true because many of the types of investments that qualify for one of these purposes also meet the objectives of the others. Assets acquired for these priorities do not demand a high degree of liquidity and marketability, since the owner expects to hold them over an extended period of time. The investor may be willing to assume a higher than average credit risk or market risk in order to obtain high yields. He should, however, protect himself somewhat against the inflation risk and should not be tempted to use the funds for some other purposes, for example, for a vacation or a new automobile.

Numerous investments, such as rental property, common stock, and fixed-return securities, are capable of providing a supplemental income before retirement. Each of these has some advantages and disadvantages. Real estate investments, for example, usually offer a hedge against inflation, an adequate return to the investor, and a tangible asset to the holder. Some offsetting disadvantages include the high cost of transferring ownership, the time and effort required to manage the property, and the possible loss of mobility to the owner. The investor in rental property should reside near his rental units in order to manage them with a minimum of effort; otherwise, the property may be assigned to some realtor who will manage the assets for a stipulated percentage, commonly 4 to 6 percent, of rental income.

An investment in well-chosen common stocks offers some hedge against inflation. Although the rate of growth from 1967 to 1980 may not equal the 1950 to 1967 appreciation, some increase in market value is expected for a number of reasons. Many corporations in 1966 were retaining approximately one half of their earnings and reinvesting them in other fixed assets and working capital (equal to about 3 to 4 percent of the market value of common stock); general price levels were increasing by 1 or 2 percent per year; and the increase in productivity, about 3 percent annually during this century, should in the aggregate increase corporate profits. Should these trends continue, average annual increases in common stock prices from 1965 to 1985 of about 6 or 8 percent do not appear to be unreasonable estimates. Of course, stock prices do oscillate widely over time.

Figure 5–2 indicates that at the end of 1963, some 17 percent of the spending units in the United States owned real estate other than their homes, and, with some overlap, another 17 percent owned corporate stocks. From 1960 to 1963, common stock ownership increased from 14 to 17 percent of total spending units, whereas real estate investors remained constant at 17 percent. Approximately one half of the individuals who owned corporate stock and about one half of those owning other real estate had investments in excess of $10,000 on the latter date. Few low-income families owned stocks (Fig. 5–5).

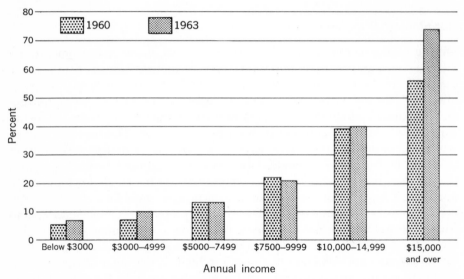

FIGURE 5-5 / Spending units owning shares of stocks, by levels of annual income, 1960 and 1963. From *U.S. Statistical Abstract*, 1965, p. 476.

High-grade bonds offer a more assured return of principal and interest than do real estate or equity investments, but during a period of inflation such an investment is less desirable than one in either real estate or common equities. Since one receives a fixed return of principal and interest on bonds, it is to his advantage for consumer prices to decline. The purchasing power of an investment in bonds, however, deteriorated during the inflationary period 1940–1965. Certain investors, such as high-income individuals, institutional buyers, and corporate investors, prefer to hold tax-free municipal securities rather than other fixed-return issues.

When the children are no longer dependent upon their parents for their livelihood, the wage earner can begin to plan for his retirement. Since Social Security payments alone are not adequate to provide the average family with its accustomed standard of living, many families attempt to provide additional retirement income. If the asset holdings of the family are substantial, proper estate planning may preserve a sizable part of family assets upon the death of the husband or wife. These priorities, retirement income and estate planning, are discussed in Chapter 6.

Summary

Although investment priorities differ among families because of the age of the husband and wife, the number and ages of dependents, the asset holdings of the family, and the educational and income levels of the husband and wife, it is generally recommended that the following financial priorities be met in the recommended order:

1. The family should maintain a liquid fund adequate to meet family expenses for three to six months in the event of temporary unemployment or sickness of some family member. These funds may be held in cash or invested in marketable, liquid securities such as Series E bonds, savings and loan shares, credit union shares, or the savings account of a commercial bank.

2. Some insurance coverage, particularly on the wage earner or head of the household, should then be obtained. This insurance coverage should supplement the Social Security benefits paid to dependent children and spouse upon the death of the wage earner. During recent years, there has been some shift from permanent-type to term insurance.

3. Home ownership gained in popularity from 1940 to 1964, when owner-occupied homes increased from 43 to 62 percent of U.S. households. Apartment dwelling is common during early married life, with home ownership more prevalent as the family increases in size. In order to finance the purchase of a home, many families borrow with a VA, FHA, or conventional mortgage an amount two or two and a half times the wage earner's annual income, amortizing the debt over 25 to 35 years.

4. Providing for the costs of higher education may be done in one or more of the following ways: working one's way through college; receiving a scholarship; borrowing under a student loan program; or through systematic savings. The latter method is recommended, and the funds should be invested in a medium not easily appropriated for another purpose, such as a vacation, a boat, or a new automobile. Educational insurance plans or investment company shares promote systematic savings and discourage misuse.

5. Supplemental income before retirement may be from real estate, fixed-return securities, or equities. Although high-grade bonds offer a safer return of principal and interest than does an investment in real estate or stocks, the inflationary trend during postwar years has been a prime disadvantage for bond investors. Ownership of common stocks increased in popularity from 1950 to 1963, with some 17 percent of all spending units owning common stocks on the latter date.

QUESTIONS FOR REVIEW /

1. What factors should influence the size and type of investment medium for liquid funds?
2. What factors should influence the amount of life insurance carried by the average head of household?
3. Discuss the shifts in popularity of various types of life insurance policies over the past 10 years.
4. What factors should be present before a family buys a home?
5. Evaluate the advantages and disadvantages of obtaining a college degree.
6. Discuss expected lifetime income in relation to the cost of higher education.
7. How should a college educational program for dependent children be financed? What percentage of the average budget is required?
8. How important is the fifth priority, supplemental income before retirement?
9. What investment media appear to be suited for meeting the fifth priority, supplemental income before retirement?
10. Discuss briefly the trends in stock ownership that have prevailed since 1950.

PROBLEMS /

1. You are requested to outline an appropriate investment plan, including specific recommendations as to investment purchases, for Mrs. Jones.

Mrs. Mary Jones, widow and mother of a five-year-old girl and a two-year-old boy, has just received $50,000 from a life insurance policy. Mortgage cancellation insurance paid off the home mortgage and note on the one-year-old Buick.

The husband's will left his share of the community property in trust with the wife for the benefit of the children. The family was receiving no income other than $240 a month from Social Security. Mary was 27 years old and had had two years of secretarial training, although she wished to remain at home until her children were in school.

Mrs. Jones's property and debts were as follows:

Assets

Cash in bank	$ 600	Clothing	$ 2000
Bank savings		Car	3000
account	1200	Cash surrender	
Life insurance		value of life	
proceeds	50,000	insurance	200
Home	22,000	Total	$85,500
Furniture	6000		

Liabilities and Equity

Furniture loan	$ 2400
Charge accounts	300
Equity	82,300
Total	$85,000

Her estimated monthly budget was as follows:

Income (Social Security)		$240
Expenses		
Insurance* ($15; $12; $8)	$ 35	
Food	120	
Household items (loan repayment)	50	
Clothing	60	
Contributions	20	
Recreation	15	
Utilities	45	
Taxes on house	15	
Car maintenance and expense	50	
New car fund	60	
Christmas fund	20	490
Funds needed		$250

* Auto, home, life.

2. Advise the Smiths on their financial planning.

Mr. and Mrs. Robert Smith have been anticipating his retirement for several years, and in another month the dream is to be realized. Although the Smiths have lived in furnished apartments all their married lives, they have often contemplated home ownership. Mr. Smith is 65 and Mrs. Smith is 62. Together they expect to receive about $205 per month in Social Security. Mr. Smith has been a salesman at Sears Roebuck & Company for 20 years, has some 800 shares of the stock in his account, and may elect to either keep the stock or receive its cash value upon retirement.

Their financial condition is as follows:

Cash	$ 200	Debts	
Series E bonds	800	None	0
Sears stock	?	Equity	?
Car	800		XX
Personal items	1500		
	XX		

Mr. Smith has a $10,000 paid-up policy on himself and $1000 policy on his wife. The Smiths need about $350 a month for meeting living expenses. In addition, they desire a $2000 vacation trip each year. How would you recommend that they handle their financial program?

3. Assume that a family with $25,000 in assets maintains the financial asset distribution in Figure 5–2. Allocate the total into the various components and comment on their adequacy to meet the first five investment priorities. Do the same for a family with $7500 in assets.

4. Attempt to estimate the annual expenditure for various types of insurance "needed" by a typical homeowner who earns $10,000 annually and who has a wife and two preschool age children.

5. Estimate the period of time over which a family earning $8000 annually which saves 10 percent per year must save in order to accumulate an educational fund for two children. Assume that educational costs amount to $1500 per year per student and that savings earn 5 percent annually.

REFERENCES /

Amling, Frederick, *Investments, An Introduction to Analysis and Management.* Englewood Cliffs, N.J.: Prentice-Hall, Inc., 1965.

Cohen, Jerome B., and Arthur W. Hanson, *Personal Finance,* 3d ed. Homewood, Ill.: Richard D. Irwin, Inc., 1964.

National Consumer Finance Association, *Finance Facts Yearbook.* Washington, D.C.: The Association, 1965 and 1966.

Post, Ray C., *Student Loan Fund Programs: A Response to the Problem of Financing Higher Education.* Unpublished thesis, Louisiana State University, 1964.

U.S. Department of Commerce, *Statistical Abstract of the United States,* 86th ed. Washington, D.C.: U.S. Government Printing Office, 1965.

chapter 6 | Investment Priorities— Continued

Introduction

Many wage earners are approximately 45 to 50 years of age before completing the first four priorities discussed in Chapter 5: liquid funds, insurance coverage, home ownership, and the education of dependent children. During middle age the individual begins to plan seriously for supplemental income before retirement and for retirement income and begins his estate planning. The evaluation of the adequacy of one's retirement plan should begin with an analysis of Social Security benefits, since more than 80 percent of adult workers are covered by the program. If the head of the household determines that the Social Security retirement income is inadequate to meet his retirement needs, he begins to consider other pension plans that will provide supplementary retirement benefits.

This chapter will review (1) the retirement needs of the elderly, (2) the income of the retired, (3) benefit provisions of numerous pension plans, and (4) estate planning. The latter subject is devoted primarily to an analysis and application of federal gift tax and estate tax laws for building and preserving an estate.

Retirement Needs

A Social Security administration estimate for a modest, though adequate, level of living in 1959 suggested that a range between $2640 and $3370 annually would be adequate for both man and wife just past 65. This estimate was based on reasonably good health for the couple and assumed that they would require no unusual medical or other service and would keep house by themselves in a two- or three-bedroom rented unit. For the debt-free homeowner the median was reduced to $2500, and the estimated cost of living for one person was $1800. An additional annual expense of $500 was estimated for families who maintained an automobile, and medical expenses were gauged to be about $315 per year for the couple, although with Medicare the latter figure should be reduced.

The median estimate for a modest, though adequate, level of living for a retired man and wife was $3000 in 1959, but from 1959 through 1965, the consumer price index rose by 9 percent, so that the approximate need at the end of 1965 would have been $3300. A large portion—27 percent—of the total family budget was allocated for food for the family, while smaller amounts were allocated for other necessities, such as medical, clothing, household operation, insurance, and miscellaneous expenses.

Income for the Retired

Retirement income for the elderly in the early 1960s was substantially less than the amount considered necessary for providing an adequate budget. The 1959 median income for 5.1 million aged married couples, that is, couples with one spouse 65 or older, was $2600. The median income was $2670 for the 3.7 million elderly families maintaining their own homes, compared to a median income of $2400 for those living with other relatives. Conversely, the 7.8 million nonmarried persons aged 65 and over had a median income of $790 ($1160 for males and $670 for females). Another survey made in 1962 indicated that when both husband and wife were receiving only Social Security, the median amount per year was $1400, compared to less than $900 for the nonmarried workers. The average couple received $365 per year from sources other than Old Age, Survivors and Disability Insurance (OASDI); nonmarried men, nonmarried women, and widowed women, respectively, drew $65, $45, and $35 per year from other sources.

BENEFITS BELOW SPECIFIED AMOUNTS

	Retired Men	Retired Women	Widow Beneficiary
$2000	81%	90%	92%
$1800	76	86	87
$1300	57	71	72

The Social Security Administration's estimate of the cost of living in 1962 for one person was $1800. The above schedule shows that 76 percent of the retired male workers, 86 percent of the retired female workers, and 87 percent of the widowed beneficiaries were receiving less than that amount annually. More than 70 percent of the retired female workers and beneficiaries were drawing less than $1300. It was estimated that about 3.1 million nonmarried beneficiaries were living at the poverty level of income, while another 4.1 million were without sufficient income for an adequate level of living. The need for additional retirement income, then, is greater for nonmarried individuals and surviving beneficiaries of the wage earners than for couples. Since the husband usually dies some 6 to 10 years before his spouse, he should provide for an adequate standard of living during that period. Although Social Security survivors' benefits are helpful, additional amounts should be generated from other sources.[1]

[1] See U.S. Department of Health, Education and Welfare, Social Security Administration, *Research and Statistics, Note No. 2: Retirement Income and Measure of Need* (Washington, D.C.: U.S. Government Printing Office, February 24, 1964).

Pension Plans

Social Security

Social Security retirement benefits, survivors' benefits, and disability benefits as of 1965 are shown in Table 6–1. In order to qualify for these retirement benefits the wage earner must (1) have paid Social Security taxes for a number of quarters (10 years, or less in some cases, provides permanent coverage); (2) receive annual income below $1500 from wages (partial benefits are received with annual wage income between $1500 and $2700) for persons below age 72 (there is no limit on wages for those above 72); and (3) have reached the specified age requirement (65 for full benefits or 62 for partial benefits for the wage earner or retiring spouse and age 62 for full survivors' benefit and 60 or 61 for partial benefits). Income from insurance, dividends, interest, rent, royalties, or capital gains are not considered in the income limitations. Disability income is available only to someone who is completely disabled from employment of any type, and the coverage and amount are computed in the same way as if the disabled were retiring at age 65. Should the person recover from his disability, he loses the right to disability benefits. In some instances, an individual may have a choice between retirement income at his present age, with reduced benefits, or full benefits under the disability program. For example, suppose that Mr. Adams has a heart attack at age 62 and is advised by his physician not to work. He may retire with three-fourths benefits at that age, or he may apply for full disability benefits. His spouse, of course, does not receive full benefits until she is 65, or she may elect to receive partial retirement benefits at age 62, 63, or 64.

Social Security benefits were extended to farmers, military service personnel, and other groups during the 1950s and early 1960s, so that in 1963 more than 114 million people had wage credits toward the Social Security program. The amount of benefits being paid under the program increased by more than 2000 percent from 1950 through 1963.

Other Public Plans

For each 16 persons entitled to OASDI benefits, one was covered under some other public retirement plan in 1963, with practically none receiving payments under both programs. At the end of 1963, some 800,000 persons connected with railroads were covered by the Railroad Retirement Act and the Railroad Unemployment Insurance Act. These special industry-wide laws provide retirement annuities for the aged, disability and survivors' protection, and unemployment and maternity benefits.

Railroad workers and their dependents are protected under the Social Security Act until the worker has 10 years of creditable service with a railroad, at which time he qualifies under the Railroad Retirement Act, which

TABLE 6-1 / Monthly Cash Benefit Payments under the Social Security Program[1]

Average yearly earnings after 1950	$800 or less	$1800	$3000	$3600	$4200	$4800	$5400	$6600
Disability benefits before 65	$44.00	$78.20	$101.70	$112.40	$124.20	$135.90	$146.00	$168.00
Retirement at 64	41.10	73.00	95.00	105.00	116.00	126.90	136.30	156.80
Retirement at 63	38.20	67.80	88.20	97.50	107.70	117.80	126.60	145.60
Retirement at 62	35.20	62.60	81.40	90.00	99.40	108.80	116.80	134.30
Wife's benefit at 65 or with child in her care	22.00	39.10	50.90	56.20	62.10	68.00	73.00	84.00
Wife's benefit at 64	20.20	35.90	46.70	51.60	57.00	62.40	67.00	77.00
Wife's benefit at 63	18.40	32.60	42.50	46.90	51.80	56.70	60.90	70.00
Wife's benefit at 62	16.50	29.40	38.20	42.20	46.60	51.00	54.80	63.00
One child of retired or disabled worker	22.00	39.10	50.90	56.20	62.10	68.00	73.00	84.00
Widow age 62 or over	44.00	64.60	84.00	92.80	102.50	112.20	120.50	138.60
Widow at 60, no child	38.20	56.00	72.80	80.50	88.90	97.30	104.50	120.20
Widow under 62 and 1 child	66.00	117.40	152.60	168.60	186.40	204.00	219.00	252.00
Widow under 62 and 2 children	66.00	120.00	202.40	240.00	279.60	306.00	328.00	368.00
One surviving child	44.00	58.70	76.30	84.30	93.20	102.00	109.50	126.00
Two surviving children	66.00	117.40	152.60	168.60	186.40	204.00	219.00	252.00
Maximum family payment	66.00	120.00	202.40	240.00	280.80	309.20	328.00	368.00

[1] Generally, in figuring average yearly earnings after 1950, five years of low earnings or no earnings can be excluded. The maximum earnings creditable for Social Security are $3600 for 1951–1954; $4200 for 1955–1958; $4800 for 1959–1965; and $6600 starting with 1966. Because of this, the benefits shown in the last two columns will not generally be payable for some years to come. When a person is entitled to more than one benefit, the amount actually payable is limited to the largest of the benefits.

SOURCE: U.S. Department of Health, Education and Welfare, Social Security Administration, *Social Security* (Washington, D.C.: U.S. Government Printing Office, 1965), p. 21.

provides higher benefits in most cases than does the Social Security program. An employee with 10 years or more of service may draw a lifetime annuity at age 65. Full lifetime disability annuities are payable to workers under this age if they are permanently disabled from any regular gainful employment. Monthly annuities are payable to the following survivors if the deceased was completely insured: the widow or dependent widower at age 60, payable for life unless she or he remarries; dependent unmarried children under age 18; and dependent parents at age 60, provided no qualified widow, widower, or child survives.

The 1965 monthly compensation for the retired railroad worker was based on the average of the employee's creditable railroad earnings for the months included in the years of service. He counted up to $300 per month prior to July 1954, up to $400 from then until October 1963, and up to $450 per month beginning in November 1963. The monthly disability or retirement annuity was derived by multiplying the employee's years of credit service by the sum of the following: 3.35 percent of the first $50 of average monthly coverage; 2.51 percent of the next $100; and 1.67 percent of the remainder up to $300.

For railroad retirement, survivors', and disability benefits, the total tax rate in 1965 was 14½ percent of the worker's earnings up to $450 per month divided equally between the employer and the employee. As Social Security rates are raised, the rates for railroad retirement benefits also rise, and total costs are scheduled to increase to 18¼ percent on January 1, 1968.

The expense of insurance premiums for unemployment and sickness benefits are incurred only by the employer. The cost is based on a sliding scale between 1.5 and 4 percent of the worker's earnings up to $400 per month during 1964, the rate depending upon the balance in the railroad's unemployment insurance account on September 30 of the preceding year.[2]

In 1964, there were 14 federal retirement systems and more than 2200 state and local government public employee retirement systems in the United States. Between 1935 and 1963, the number of federal employees with retirement coverage increased from 2.5 million to about 7.5 million. Federal civil service employees were contributing 6½ percent of their regular salaries with no ceiling, and the government was spending an estimated 8 percent of its payroll to make up the deficiency. In 1965, the employees could retire at age 62 after five years of service, or at age 60 with as much as 30 years of service. Retirement and disability pension benefits ranged from 40 to 80 percent of the highest five years' salary, depending upon the length of service and the age of retirement.

Retired military personnel generally qualify for one or more federal retirement plans. Twenty or more years of active duty provides immediate monthly retirement benefits of 2½ percent per year times the number of

---

[2] U.S. Department of Health, Education and Welfare, Social Security Administration, *Social Security Programs in the United States* (Washington, D.C.: U.S. Government Printing Office, 1964).

years service times monthly base pay. Thus, a retired officer with 26 years of active service and $600 monthly base pay (base pay excludes allowances for shelter, food, and clothing) should draw monthly retirement of (.025 × 26 × $600) = $390 for life. He also qualifies for Social Security benefits upon reaching the appropriate age, 62 or 65. Personnel with less than 20 years of service in active duty may accumulate additional retirement points by remaining in a military reserve unit. In the latter, points are accumulated about one fifth as rapidly as for full-time service, but retirement benefits begin at age 60. For example, suppose that after 10 years of military service Officer Jones transfers from active duty to reserve status for another 10 years. Assuming a base pay of $600 per month for his rank and years of service at retirement, he qualifies for monthly retirement benefits at age 60 equal to $180 = (.025 × 10 + ⅕(10) × $600).

Servicemen were also afforded disability and survivors' benefits. Benefits in 1965 for service-connected disabilities ranged from $20 to $250 per month, or up to $720 per month for a person house bound, and pensions for disabilities not connected with the service varied from $40 to $85 per month, with additional amounts for dependents. Monthly survivors' benefits were the smaller of $120 or 12 percent of monthly base pay, payable to the widow, plus $28 times the number of dependent children less one, not to exceed $128 monthly, reduced by Social Security and/or railroad retirement survivors' benefits.

Thus the surviving widow of a major with base pay of $600 with three dependent children should qualify for the following monthly benefits:

Widow's benefits ($600 × .12) =	$ 72
Children's benefits (3 − 1) × $28 =	56
Total	$128
Less: Social Security benefits (assume $4800 average Social Security base)	$309.20
Military survivors' benefits	–0–

Bringing servicemen under the Social Security program in 1957 practically eliminated survivors' benefits for deaths of servicemen after that date because of the relatively generous survivors' benefits under the OASDI program.

More than $3.4 billion in benefits were paid to 1.5 million retired federal, state, and local government employees and about 262,000 surviving families during 1962. Retired employees received about 74 percent of the benefits, disabled workers about 17 percent, and the surviving families the remainder. The 14 federal systems accounted for 55 percent of the beneficiaries and 58 percent of the benefits, while some 2200 state and local government employer systems accounted for the remainder. At the end of 1962, almost 98 percent of retired federal employees were divided about equally between federal civil service and armed forces employees.

Private Pension Plans

At the end of 1960, more than 20 million workers were covered by funded retirement plans, while unfunded retirement programs were providing old age pension coverage for 462,000 workers and additional long-term disability, death, and other benefits for another 904,000 laborers. Benefits paid by the *unfunded* schemes are paid out of the general assets of the employers, while benefits of *funded* plans are paid from special funds held by trustees or insurance companies. Most of these plans were established after World War II, and slightly less than half were covered by collective bargaining between management and labor unions. Some 60 percent of the coverage under nonfunded schedules was for manufacturing industries, which accounted for about 8 percent of the business firms, while the balance was for nonmanufacturing industries such as communications, utilities, railroad transportation, trade industries, and others.[3]

The Welfare and Pension Plans Disclosure Act of 1958 requires administrators to furnish certain financial information to the Secretary of Labor, who then makes it available to the public. Originally, all plans with more than 25 employees were required to submit specified information, but a 1962 amendment exempted plans having less than 100 participants. At the end of 1961, there were 120,500 plans with more than 25 covered employees; all except one of the 100 largest pension funds were pension or retirement plans. Of this group, 91 were administered by employers or employer groups, eight by joint management–labor boards, and one by an employee organization. Some 93 plans covered workers of a single employer, 6 covered employees of more than one employer, and 1 covered the members of an international union.

The assets of welfare and pension benefits plans amounted to $30 billion at the end of 1959, and this total was increasing at the rate of about $4 billion per year during the early 1960s, with the 100 largest plans holding well over half the total assets for all reporting programs. About 88 percent of the assets of these 100 plans was invested in corporate securities, with a slightly larger figure devoted to bonds than to common stocks. The smaller funds devoted a small percentage of their assets to common stocks, and roughly 15 percent of their assets was invested in government obligations.[4]

Based on a sample of almost 16,000 private pension plans that were studied by the Department of Labor for the 1961 calendar year, about 80 percent of the contributory schemes, that is, plans in which the employees share the cost provided for *vesting protection*, or permanent interest upon termination of employment, for the employee as against 55 percent for

[3] U.S. Department of Labor, *Prevalence and Characteristics of Unfunded Pension Plans* (Washington, D.C.: U.S. Government Printing Office, January 1963).
[4] U.S. Department of Labor, *Welfare and Pension Plan Statistics: The 100 Largest Plans, 1959–1961* (Washington, D.C.: U.S. Government Printing Office, 1963).

workers of noncontributory plans. Vesting was far more common in single-employer plans than in multiemployer plans, amounting to 70 percent for the former and only 33 percent for the latter. These vested rights may be in the form of immediate cash withdrawals or future retirement benefits. The vesting of interest is of particular importance to older workers who may stay with an employer for 15 to 20 years but may not remain with the firm until retirement age. Should these persons be dismissed from service or take jobs with other firms, the loss of retirement benefits would work hardships on them and their families.

From 1960 through 1963, the number of persons covered by private health and pension plans increased by roughly 20 percent. At the beginning of 1964, some 24 million workers, most of whom were also covered by Social Security, were covered by these plans, and about one half were under collective bargaining plans that had been negotiated between employers and unions. Some two million persons were receiving private pensions in 1964, in most cases supplementing OASDI benefits. Figure 6–1 indicates that a large segment of the working population was covered by surgical and medical, temporary disability, unemployment, and retirement benefits on July 1, 1963. The cost of these plans was primarily borne by the employers, although some were financed by a contribution of the employee. Almost 73 percent of the pension plans and 36 percent of the welfare plans were financed by the employer. Less than 1 percent of the pension plans was financed entirely by the participants, while 9.7 percent of the welfare plans was so financed. Almost half of the welfare plans or combination pension and welfare plans were financed jointly by the employer and the plan participants, and less than 1 percent of all plans provided for the payment of benefits out of general labor union funds.

Although the amount of retirement benefits from private pension plans was small in 1959, the amount of such benefits has been increasing since that date, so that retired workers in the future, say by 1980, should be receiving a significant portion of their total retirement benefits from private pension plans. The amount of the monthly benefit that an individual may expect to receive beginning at age 65, assuming that his employment began on January 1, 1962, at age 25, ranges from a low of 20 percent of his wages for OASDI primary benefits, which were increased about 7 percent in 1965,[5] to a high of 95 percent for retired workers of Grumman Aircraft (Table 6–2). An analysis of the benefits under 26 selected private pension plans as of January 1963 indicates that 10 of the plans provide for retirement benefits ranging from 30 to 40 percent of wages, while another 10 provide for retirement income in excess of 50 percent of wages if the employee has been with

---

[5] The Social Security base on which payments are made and benefits are determined was raised from $4800 to $6600 annually in early 1966. At that time the rate was also increased from 3⅝ to 4.2 percent. Thus a worker receiving a $500 monthly gross income pays $500 times 4.2 percent, or $21 monthly into his account, and his employer pays a similar amount.

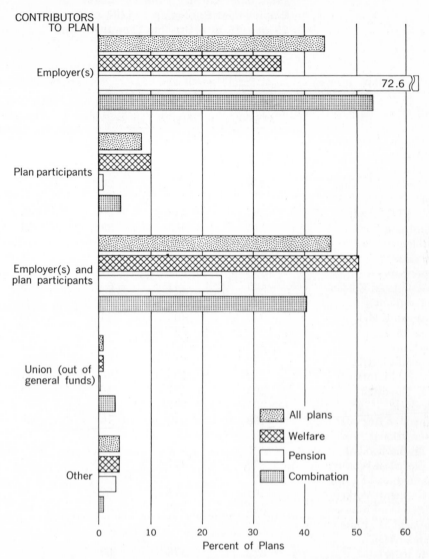

FIGURE 6-1 / Distribution of 162,000 welfare and pension benefit plans, July 1963. From U.S. Department of Labor.

the firm for 40 years or more. These projections were based on an assumed final monthly wage of $595 for individuals with 30 years of service and $645 in monthly wages for employees with 40 years of service.

Other Retirement Income

Many business corporations provide a profit-sharing pension fund for their employees in addition to or in lieu of a funded retirement plan. One very generous savings and profit-sharing pension plan is provided by Sears,

TABLE 6-2 / **Monthly Retirement Benefits at Age 65 (Including OASDI Primary Based on Employment Beginning 1/1/62 at Ages 25 and 35 at a Starting Monthly Wage of $450**

Plan	Total Benefit		Total Benefit as Percent of Wage	
	30 Years of Service	40 Years of Service	30 Years of Service[1]	40 Years of Service[2]
Aluminum company of America	$251	$321	42%	50%
Amalgamated Clothing Workers	176	177	30	27
American Telephone and Telegraph	239	318	40	49
Armstrong Cork	315	400	53	62
Bethlehem Steel	218	296	37	46
Chrysler	201	227	34	35
Cities Service	305	391	51	61
Consolidated Edison	408	441	69	68
E. I. duPont	315	401	53	62
Eastman Kodak	320	405	54	63
Firestone	201	227	34	35
Ford	210	239	35	37
General Electric	296	373	50	58
General Motors	210	239	35	37
B. F. Goodrich	201	227	34	35
Goodyear	201	227	34	35
Grumman Aircraft	452	610	76	95
International Brotherhood of Electrical Workers	176	177	30	27
International Ladies Garment Workers	191	192	32	30
Johnson and Johnson	310	386	52	60
National Maritime Union	251	252	42	39
Standard Oil of Indiana	373	478	63	74
United Mine Workers	201	202	34	31
U.S. Rubber	235	312	39	48
U.S. Steel	218	206	37	46
Westinghouse	216	247	36	38
U.S. Civil Service	329	484	55	75
OASDI Primary	126	127	21	20

[1] Based on a final monthly wage of $595.

[2] Based on a final monthly wage of $645.

SOURCE: U.S. Department of Health, Education and Welfare, Social Security Administration, Division of the Actuary, *Anaylsis of Benefits under 26 Selected Private Pension Plans* (Washington, D.C.: U.S. Government Printing Office, January 1963).

Roebuck and Company. About 200,000 employees of Sears were entitled to participate in the savings and profit-sharing fund at the end of 1965. From 5 to 10 percent of the net profits of the company, depending upon its level of net income, were set aside annually for the participants. An employee of Sears was permitted to deposit up to 5 percent of his annual compensation in the fund, not to exceed $500 per year, if he had been with the firm for more than one year. The trustees of the fund invest the monies in common stock of Sears, Roebuck (in 1965 the fund held 25 percent of the outstanding common shares) and in other assets.

The extent to which an individual benefits from the profit-sharing plan depends upon his length of service with the company. Employees with from 1 to 5 years of service receive one unit, those with 5 but less than 10 years receive two units, those with 10 to 15 years receive three units, and those with more than 15 years of service receive four units. Assuming that the profits of the company are adequate to contribute 80 cents for each one dollar unit contributed by the employee, the individual who has been with the company for more than 15 years receives credit for his $500 contribution plus $1600 from the company's portion ($500 × $.80 × 4).

Upon ceasing to be a member of the fund, a depositor who has completed five years of continuous service is entitled to withdraw the monies and securities in his account, but when a member dies, the credit in his account is paid to his surviving beneficiaries. A member who withdraws from the fund before the expiration of the five-year period because of a permanent disability receives the credit in his account, but anyone who ceases to be a member of the fund through termination of his employment before the expiration of the five-year membership period is entitled to receive only his contribution plus simple interest of 5 percent per year. It was not unusual in the early 1960s for a Sears, Roebuck employee to retire with a common stock fund of more than $50,000.

In order to provide for supplementary retirement benefits for entrepreneurs, that is, proprietors or partners, and for their employees, the Self-Employed Individual Tax Retirement Act of 1962 was passed. This law permits these employers a tax deferral equal to 50 percent of the amount set aside, up to an annual maximum amount of $2500, for investment into qualified retirement funds. A qualifying firm is required to maintain retirement plans for all full-time employees who have three or more years of service. Some seven million self-employed individuals in the United States were eligible to participate in 1965. The earnings on the funds and the tax-exempt portion are taxable when withdrawn, presumably at retirement, when the income tax rate is lower for the self-employed individual than during earlier years. In order to qualify, the plan must be nondiscriminatory and funded, and the owner–employer is required to contribute the same percentage of pay or provide benefits that constitute the same percentage of pay for his employees as he does for himself. Contributions on behalf of employees are deductible expenses, but they must be nonforfeitable at the time they are made. Cash contributions may be made to a trustee bank, which places them in a custodial account and invests them in open-end regulated investment company shares or in insurance policies.

In order to provide educators with a source of supplementary retirement benefits in addition to Social Security and teachers' retirement income, a special tax law provides for deferring up to 20 percent of their gross income until retirement, when the individual may elect to take annuity benefit payments over his expected remaining life. The income is taxed only when withdrawn, presumably at lower tax rates, and the assets are invested in insurance policies.

Estate Planning

Building an Estate

An estate may be built through the accumulation of wealth from inheritance, savings, investment, or insurance proceeds. From 1940 to 1966, federal income tax laws favored the building of an estate through investments in capital assets, for example, stocks, land, and structures, with gains realized on such assets held for more than six months being taxed at a lower tax rate than investment income, for example, dividends of interest.[6] A wise —and lucky—investor in common shares or real estate often builds a small fortune over a few years, but unless proper estate planning is followed, much of an estate reverts to the federal government rather than to beneficiaries upon the owner's death. In order to avoid or minimize estate taxes, a portion of the assets may be distributed to the beneficiaries prior to the owner's death, and familiarity with federal estate laws, or consultation with an attorney, may provide additional savings to the estate.

Federal Gift Taxes

The purpose of the federal gift tax law is to prevent an individual from giving away all of his property to his relatives before his death. The transfer is not forbidden, but a gift tax is imposed where the gift exceeds a certain amount. The first $3000 of a donation made to any person during a given year is exempted from the gift tax. Where both the husband and the wife own property, or where the nonowning spouse consents, they may make a joint gift of up to $6000 to any person in any year without the amount being subjected to the federal gift tax. Each person also has a $30,000 lifetime exemption for gifts exceeding the tax-free $3000 per year per person limit, but each donor, must file a gift tax return for each year in which a gift above the $3000 is made. If husband and wife give a joint gift, the $6000 limit applies; but if the gift exceeds this amount, each must file a gift tax return. Gift tax rates on donations above these amounts are shown in Table 6–3, and these federal gift taxes are not deductible in computing federal income taxes.

---

[6] The 1965 revision in the long-term capital gains law that applies to gains on real estate was explained in Chapter 4.

TABLE 6-3 /   Table of Federal Gift Tax Rates (Applicable to Gifts Made after December 31, 1941)

Taxable Gifts[1] From	To	Tax on Lower amount	Rate on Excess[2]
$ 0	$ 5000	$ 0.00	2¼ %
5000	10,000	112.50	5¼
10,000	20,000	375.00	8¼
20,000	30,000	1200.00	10½
30,000	40,000	2250.00	13½
40,000	50,000	3600.00	16½
50,000	60,000	5250.00	18¾
60,000	100,000	7125.00	21
100,000	250,000	15,525.00	22½
250,000	500,000	49,275.00	24
500,000	750,000	109,275,00	26¼
750,000	1,000,000	174,900.00	27¾
1,000,000	1,250,000	244,275.00	29¼
1,250,000	1,500,000	317,400.00	31½
1,500,000	2,000,000	396,150.00	33¾
2,000,000	2,500,000	564,900.00	36¾
2,500,000	3,000,000	748,650.00	39¾
3,000,000	3,500,000	947,400.00	42
3,500,000	4,000,000	1,157,400.00	44¼
4,000,000	5,000,000	1,378,650.00	47¼
5,000,000	6,000,000	1,851,150.00	50¼
6,000,000	7,000,000	2,353,650.00	52½
7,000,000	8,000,000	2,878,650.00	54¾
8,000,000	10,000,000	3,426,150.00	57
10,000,000	Balance	4,566,150.00	57¾

[1] After all deductions and exemptions.

[2] Effective January 1, 1942, for 1942 and subsequent calendar years.

For example, suppose that Mr. Brown and his wife give a farm worth $80,000 to their only son. The gift taxes, assuming joint ownership by husband and wife, that each owes are computed as follows:

Value of gift (one half for each)		$40,000
Less: Annual exclusion	$ 3000	
Lifetime additional gifts	30,000	33,000
Taxable gift		7000
Gift taxes (112.50 +.05¼ × $2000) =		$ 217.50

The Browns could have elected to conserve a portion of their allotted additional lifetime exemption for later use, thus paying a larger gift tax on this particular distribution. Perhaps a wiser method would have been to divide the land into numerous tracts, giving one each year to the son and benefiting more from the $6000 annual gift exclusion before using up the additional lifetime exemption.

Where a gift is made in contemplation of death, that is, within three years of death, the amount must be included in the gross estate of the decedent. A significant amount of the total assets may, however, be given to the children in the form of gifts prior to the death of either spouse, thus leaving a lower taxable estate with a smaller amount of federal estate taxes.

Federal Estate Taxes

Federal estate taxes are imposed upon an estate on the death of the owner, are paid by the executor of the estate, and are due within 15 months after the death of the property owner. The executor may elect the market value at the date of death of the decedent, one year later, or at an interim date when assets are disposed of, whichever benefits the parties concerned.

All the property, such as insurance proceeds, real estate, included at full market value, and domestic and foreign stocks and bonds, is included in the gross estate. Proceeds from insurance policies are ordinarily included in the estate where they are payable to the estate or to a beneficiary of the decedent. If the insured owned an *incident of ownership*, that is, if the insured had a right to borrow against the policy or to change the beneficiary where the value of such interest exceeds 5 percent of the face amount of the policy, immediately prior to his death, the proceeds must be included in the gross estate. One legal method for avoiding the taxation of insurance proceeds is to set up a nonrevocable insurance trust, leaving the income from the trust to be paid to the spouse for her remaining life, with the principal to be paid to the children upon the death of the spouse.

Every estate has a number of deductions: an automatic $60,000 exemption; funeral expenses, for example, cost of the casket, burial plot, tombstone, and funeral; and administrative expenses, for example, the executor's commission, the attorney's fees, and miscellaneous expenses of settling the estate. Administrative expenses may be limited by estate law to a certain percentage of the total estate and may average from 5 to 8 percent of the value of the property. Deductions may also be taken for the payment of unsecured debts, mortgages, and liens and for unpaid federal and state income taxes on income up to the date of the decedent's death. Miscellaneous losses incurred while the estate is being settled, such as losses from fire, flood, or theft, are also deductible.

When the decedent is survived by a spouse, up to one half of the amount of the adjusted estate may be taken as a marital deduction as long as the spouse has the complete right to the property. The estate gets a marital deduction for the property left to the spouse (1) by an outright bequest under a will; (2) by intestacy, that is, when no will is left, with the legal share going to the spouse; (3) under a trust created by the will whereby the wife receives the income for life and has the right to name the person or persons to receive the principal; (4) by insurance on the life of the decedent, which is included in the gross estate in cases where the proceeds are payable in a lump sum or in installments to the wife, or payable to an insurance trust in cases where the spouse has the right to income and principal; (5) by property that passes to the wife as a joint tenant or as a tenant by the entirety (that is, the wife was part or complete owner when the husband was alive); (6) by survivors' benefits under an annuity where there is no possibility of payment to anyone else; or (7) by a legal life estate where real property is left in trust and where the wife has the right to receive the income during her life and has the right to name the principal upon her death. Insurance proceeds do not qualify for the marital deduction in cases in which an insurance trust is set up with the spouse to receive the income only until her remarriage or in which the wife has lifetime rights to the income with no rights to the principal.

Charitable contributions are also deductions from the taxable estate, with no limit as to the amount of deduction. The contribution may be made to the United States or to a municipality for a public purpose, to a nonprofit organization such as a religious, charitable, scientific, literary, or educational institution, or to various types of veterans' organizations.

In certain cases, the executor of an estate may be able to claim tax credits against the federal estate tax liability. These are for federal gift taxes that were paid on property transferred in contemplation of death or for federal estate taxes that were paid on prior transfers. The amount of credit that may be claimed for the latter depends upon the amount of time that has passed between the death of the two spouses.

DEATH OF SECOND SPOUSE	PERCENT CREDIT
Within 2 years	100
2–4 years	80
4–6 years	60
6–8 years	40
8–10 years	20
Beyond 10 years	0

The executor, under the terms of the will, may pay the federal estate taxes as though they were a debt of the estate, or the taxes may be prorated against each person's share of the estate. If a portion of the tax must be paid by the spouse and/or by a charitable institution, then the marital and charitable deductions will be reduced by the amounts of the taxes prorated to them. Offsetting, or payment of, federal estate taxes dollar for dollar with marketable U.S. securities is permitted, and therefore executors buy low-priced issues in order to retire the debt at a discount.[7]

[7] For tax-saving ideas and a description of federal estate and gift taxes, see J. K. Lasser Tax Institute and Ralph Wallace, *How to Save Estate and Gift Taxes* (New York: American Research Council, 1961).

Table 6–4 illustrates proper tax planning for the John Smith family. Assume that Mr. Smith retires at age 65 and that his wife is 61 years old at the time of his retirement. At retirement his assets are valued at about $500,000, and he is able to draw Social Security and other retirement benefits. Although Mr. Smith does not know how many years he will continue to live, he wishes to reduce his federal estate tax burden to the very minimum, maximizing the estate he leaves to his wife and four children.

TABLE 6-4 / Illustration of Estate Planning for the John Smith Family

Value of assets at Mr. Smith's retirement (age 65)		$500,000
Prior usage of lump-sum gift by Smith and wife		None
Less: $6000 annual gifts by Smith and wife to each of four children for the next seven years		168,000
Lump-sum gifts by Smith and wife to the four children		60,000
Value of Smith's estate at age 72 (assuming income is consumed)		$272,000
Deductions (Smith dies at age 77; wife is living at age 73)		
Debts	$ 15,000	
Funeral expenses	5000	
Expenses of executor	12,000	32,000
Adjusted estate		$240,000
Marital deduction (one half of adjusted estate)	120,000	
Charitable deduction	14,000	
Exemption	60,000	194,000
Taxable estate		$ 46,000
Federal estate taxes [4800 + (.22)(6000)]		6120
Provisions of will		
Insurance trust with lifetime benefits to wife, with proceeds to be divided equally among children at her death		100,000
Expenses, including federal estate taxes		38,120
To charity		14,000
To wife		119,840
Total		$272,000

Mr. and Mrs. Smith discuss the situation and decide that they will each make a $3000 annual gift to each of the children for the next seven years and make an initial lump-sum gift of $60,000 to the four children. Their income is assumed to equal their living expenses. At the end of the seven-year period, the value of the Smith's estate has been reduced to $272,000. The gifts were discontinued when Mr. Smith reached the age of 72, and he died at the age of 77. The debts against the estate were $15,000, the funeral expenses were $5000, and the administrative expenses were $12,000. The adjusted estate, then, had a balance of $240,000. Mr. Smith's will left $14,000 to various charitable institutions, and his $100,000 paid-up life insurance had been placed in an insurance trust prior to his death, with his wife to receive lifetime benefits and the principal to be equally divided among the four children or their heirs on the death of his wife.[8] The balance of the estate was to go to the surviving spouse. Up to one half of the amount of the adjusted estate may be taken for the marital deduction, while an additional $60,000 may be taken as the exemption for the estate. Only $46,000 is left as the taxable estate, and Table 6–5 indicates that federal estate taxes on holdings of this size amount to $6120. The Smiths, through proper tax planning, reduced the taxes on a $500,000 estate to about $6000 without paying any federal gift tax.

TABLE 6-5 / Table for Computation of Estate Tax

(A)	(B)	For Total Tax	
Taxable Estate Equaling:	Taxable Estate Not Exceeding:	Tax on Amount in Column (A)	Rate of Tax on Excess over Amount in Column (A)
			(%)
—	$ 5000	—	3
$ 5000	10,000	$ 150	7
10,000	20,000	500	11
20,000	30,000	1,600	14
30,000	40,000	3,000	18
40,000	50,000	4,800	22
50,000	60,000	7,000	25
60,000	100,000	9,500	28
100,000	200,000	20,700	30
200,000	250,000	50,700	30
250,000	400,000	65,700	32
400,000	500,000	113,700	32
500,000	600,000	145,700	35
600,000	750,000	180,700	35
750,000	800,000	233,200	37
800,000	1,000,000	251,700	37
1,000,000	1,250,000	325,700	39
1,250,000	1,500,000	423,200	42
1,500,000	2,000,000	528,200	45
2,000,000	2,500,000	753,200	49
2,500,000	3,000,000	998,200	53
3,000,000	3,500,000	1,263,200	56
3,500,000	4,000,000	1,543,200	59
4,000,000	5,000,000	1,838,200	63
5,000,000	6,000,000	2,468,200	67
6,000,000	7,000,000	3,138,200	70
7,000,000	8,000,000	3,838,200	73
8,000,000	9,000,000	4,568,200	76
9,000,000	10,000,000	5,328,200	76
10,000,000	—	6,088,200	77

[8] When a person dies intestate, that is, leaves no will, state law determines the division of the estate assets among the relatives.

Mrs. Smith has received full rights to approximately $120,000 in property and lifetime benefits from the $100,000 insurance policy. Her Social Security survivors' payments and other retirement benefits should be sufficient to provide an adequate standard of living for the remainder of her life. Upon the death of Mrs. Smith, only the $120,000 plus any additional savings and minus any reduction in principal will remain in her estate, presumably to pass to her children. Assuming that she does not remarry, Mrs. Smith's estate will receive an exemption of $60,000, and if she wishes, she may further reduce her estate by making annual gifts to each of her children. Conversely, gifts made within three years of death are *assumed* to be made in contemplation of death and would not serve to reduce further the federal estate tax burden. Nevertheless, if Mrs. Smith leaves a taxable estate of $60,000, federal estate taxes will be only $9500. The total federal estate tax burden for both estates, therefore, would amount to only about $15,600, less any credit for federal estate taxes paid on the prior transfer if Mrs. Smith dies within 10 years of Mr. Smith.

Familiarity with federal estate and gift tax laws and proper tax planning will permit a husband and wife to eliminate or to reduce the over-all federal estate tax burden to a manageable fee. In the case of the Smiths, distribution of a part of the estate by gift and the use of the insurance trust reduced the total estate taxes by about $60,000 from the tax burden that would have been imposed had Mr. Smith left all of his assets to his wife outright. This difference should be verified by the student.

Taxable Basis of Assets Received by Gift or Bequest

It is important to the recipient of an asset by gift or bequest to maintain a proper federal income tax cost basis for the item so that a proper accounting of any loss or gain on the property may be recognized when the asset is liquidated. The proper cost basis may be different on an item received by gift as opposed to an asset received through a bequest. On assets received by gift, the donee's (receiver's) cost for the purpose of recognizing a gain is the donor's cost plus any gift tax paid by the donor, but the cost may not exceed the fair market value on the date of the gift. For purposes of recognizing a loss, the cost to the donee is the donor's cost, or the fair market value at the date of the gift, whichever is less. Gifts held to be in contemplation of death are subject to the inheritance tax unless the property has already been transferred by the donee.

For assets received by bequest, the fair market value at the time of death is used to determine any gain or loss on the disposition of the assets. As an alternate cost basis for determining gains or losses, the executor of the estate may elect the market value one year later or at an interim date if the estate is settled in less than a year.[9]

---

[9] Federal tax treatment of gains and losses on assets received by gift or bequest dates back to 1942 and 1943, but the individual should consult an up-to-date income tax service to determine the current ruling, since a change in this portion of the tax code has recently been considered.

Summary

Statistics released by the Bureau of the Census and the Department of Labor in 1964 indicated that a significant percentage of retired family units in the United States were receiving retirement income insufficient to provide an adequate level of living. The estimated need in 1960 was $3000 for a couple and $1800 for an unmarried person, with these amounts rising with inflation. The inadequacy was far greater for a single person than for a couple. Some 76 percent of the retired male workers and more than 85 percent of the retired female workers or female beneficiaries were receiving an amount smaller than necessary to provide an adequate standard of living.

The problem, inadequacy of retirement income, may be less severe in the future than in 1964. During the latter 1950s and early 1960s, many labor unions demanded higher retirement benefits. In addition to the 114 million people covered by Social Security in 1964, more than 20 million workers were covered by funded retirement plans, and an additional 8 million were covered either by the federal civil service employment act or by the railroad retirement system. These combined benefits of private and public pension plans should in the future provide a more reasonable living scale for the retired.

The family that owns a significant amount of assets should use proper tax planning in order to reduce the over-all federal estate tax burden imposed upon the death of one of the spouses. This may be done through the use of the annual and/or $30,000 lifetime gift deduction afforded to each donor and through knowledge of the federal estate and gift tax laws as well as through proper tax planning.

QUESTIONS FOR REVIEW /

1. Why is it important that an investor consider his plans for retirement while he is still in middle age?
2. How much retirement income is needed for a husband and wife upon reaching retirement age?
3. Contrast the retirement income of the single person with that of the married couple.
4. Assuming that your father and mother retire under the maximum Social Security retirement benefits, determine the adequacy of these benefits.
5. Contrast the retirement benefits provided under other retirement plans with those provided under Social Security.
6. How does the creation of private pension plans affect the future growth and stability of the economy?
7. Explain briefly the ways that may be used in building an estate.
8. Outline the procedure for computing federal estate taxes.
9. Outline the procedure for computing federal gift taxes.
10. Explain what is meant and illustrate with an example the term "tax planning" with regard to preserving an estate.
11. How important is a will?

PROBLEMS /

1. Assuming that you are 25 years old and are qualified to be hired as an employee of any of the companies analyzed in Table 6–2, determine the expected retirement benefits from five of the companies for which you have a possible occupational interest, plus the benefits that you would expect to receive from Social Security.

2. Assume that an individual retired from the military at age 40 at a monthly retirement income of $175 and took a job with Sears, Roebuck and Company at a salary of $500 per month. Also assume that the person will receive a built-in wage increase of about 5 percent a year. He elects to contribute the maximum amount permitted to the profit-sharing plan, and he desires to remain with the company until his retirement at age 65. His wife is three years younger, so that both will begin drawing Social Security upon his retirement from Sears. Compute his expected amount of retirement income, and on the basis of the past and expected future performance of the Sears Roebuck common stock, determine as nearly as you can the value of the individual's stock fund at the end of the 25-year period. Assume that the trustees for the fund invest 75 percent of the monies in Sears stock and the remaining 25 percent in securities that return an annual compounded rate of 4 percent. (This is a problem and is not intended to illustrate the exact management of the profit-sharing fund of Sears, Roebuck.)

3. A college professor who is 55 years of age (wife is 56) is receiving an annual salary of $15,000. He will be eligible for retirement in six more years, or he may continue to teach until he is 70. His teacher's retirement will be one third of his average five-year highest salary if he elects not to receive survivors' benefits or 25 percent with survivors' benefits. His standard of living will permit him to save $3000 annually, since his two children are married and self-supporting. He is in a financial position to elect the 20 percent of income, tax-sheltered annuity plan, which will offer him an annual compounded rate of return of 4 percent. His home is paid for, he carries $30,000 insurance on his life, he owns $15,000 in a diversified list of common stocks, and holds $5000 in a federal credit union. Advise him as to the decision concerning the income deferral plan, his probable retirement benefits, and the type of retirement plan (survivors or nonsurvivors benefits) to elect. Also compute his Social Security retirement benefits, assuming maximum coverage and current rates.

4. Assume the same facts about Mr. Smith (Table 6–4) except that the estate was $800,000 and one half was given equally to the four children over the same seven-year period. Compute the total federal gift and estate tax liabilities.

REFERENCES /

Buckley, Joseph C., *The Retirement Handbook*. New York: Harper & Row, Publishers, Inc., 1962.

Casey, William J., *Estate Planning Desk Book*. New York: Institute for Business Planning, 1961.

Fundamentals of Federal Income, Estate and Gift Taxes; with Emphasis on Life Insurance and Annuities, ed. Edwin H. White, 8th ed. Indianapolis, Ind.: The Research and Review Service of America, Inc., 1962.

Hall, Harold R., *Some Observations on Executive Retirement*. Boston, Mass.: Division of Research, Graduate School of Business Administration, Harvard University, 1953.

J. K. Lasser Tax Institute and Ralph Wallace, *How To Save Estate and Gift Taxes*. New York: American Research Council, 1961.

Metzger, R. L., *Profit Sharing in Perspective*. Chicago: Wallace Press, Inc., 1964.

Sears, Roebuck and Company, *The Savings and Profit Sharing Pension Fund of Sears, Roebuck and Company Employees*. Undated.

Soule, George, *Longer Life*. New York: The Viking Press, 1958.

U.S. Department of Health, Education and Welfare, Social Security Administration, *Analysis of Benefits under 26 Selected Private Pension Plans*. Washington, D.C.: U.S. Government Printing Office, 1963.

———, *Farm People and Old-Age Survivors, and Disability Insurance in the United States*. Washington, D.C.: U.S. Government Printing Office, 1964.

———, *Research and Statistics Note No. 2: Retirement Income and Measure of Need*. Washington, D.C.: U.S. Government Printing Office, February 24, 1964.

———, *Social Security*. Washington, D.C.: U.S. Government Printing Office, 1965.

———, *Social Security Handbook*, 2d ed. Washington, D.C.: U.S. Government Printing Office, 1963.

———, *Social Security Programs throughout the World*. Washington, D.C.: U.S. Government Printing Office, 1964.

———, *Social Security Programs in the United States*. Washington, D.C.: U.S. Government Printing Office, 1964.

U.S. Department of Labor, *Labor Mobility and Private Pension Plans*. Washington, D.C.: U.S. Government Printing Office, 1964.

———, *Prevalence and Characteristics of Unfunded Pension Plans*. Washington, D.C.: U.S. Government Printing Office, January 1963.

———, *Private Pension Plans and Manpower Policy*. Washington, D.C.: U.S. Government Printing Office, 1963.

———, *Research and Statistics Note No. 6: Benefits and Beneficiaries under Public Employee Retirement Systems, Calendar Year 1962*. Washington, D.C.: U.S. Government Printing Office, May 16, 1963.

———, *Welfare and Pension Plan Statistics: The 100 Largest Plans, 1959–1961*. Washington, D.C.: U.S. Government Printing Office, 1963.

U.S. Securities and Exchange Commission, *Statistical Bulletin*. Washington, D.C.: U.S. Government Printing Office, selected monthly issues.

part two | Security Market Operations

The complex of institutions through which the exchange of securities takes place is referred to as the security markets. One of these markets, the stock market, can be classified in two ways, on the basis of new or existing issues and on the basis of the degree of regulation imposed upon the markets. *Primary markets* handle original or new issues of securities, that is, instruments of finance issued to the public for the first time (frequently through financial intermediaries), while *secondary markets* cover the exchange of securities after they have been issued in the primary markets.

Secondary markets are further subdivided into regulated exchanges and over the counter trading. The regulated stock exchanges are said to be true auction markets, in that exchange members act as agents for their buying and selling customers. Over the counter dealers, conversely, buy and sell for their own account, attempting to take a profit on their activities.

Part II considers (1) the development of the security markets, (2) the mechanics of security trading, (3) the regulation of securities, (4) the marketing of securities, and (5) financial literature useful to the investor.

chapter 7 | History of Security Markets

Introduction

Markets for securities may be broadly divided into primary markets, the channels through which new securities are sold, and secondary markets, the registered exchanges and the over the counter markets through which trading in outstanding securities is facilitated. The purpose of this chapter is to give a brief history of the secondary markets, along with a short discussion of early security trading, the New York Stock Exchange, other registered exchanges, and the over the counter markets.

Exchanges are true auction markets. The exchange neither buys nor sells the securities but merely provides a trading place where exchange members act as agents for the buyers and sellers of stocks and bonds. In some instances, the exchange member may act as a dealer of securities rather than as an agent for the buyer or seller, but when he performs in this capacity he is required to advise his customer of this relationship.

Over the counter dealers do not act as agents for their customers but serve as merchants of securities, since they actually own the stocks they sell and take title to those they buy. Exchange members, serving as agents, charge a commission for their buying and selling services, while the profit of over the counter dealers is the difference between what they pay for the stock, the *bid price*, and what they receive for it, the *ask price*. The bid and ask quotations in financial newspapers merely refer to the price range within which the stocks have recently traded and do not commit the over the counter dealers to these prices on subsequent days. The bid price is usually a more reliable figure than is the ask price, since the latter may be inflated by as much as 5 or 10 percent. Since the over the counter dealer must sell his securities at a price higher than what he paid for them in order to cover his expenses, the spread between the bid and ask price is usually about 4 to 10 percent. The spread is usually much narrower on a stable, actively traded stock than on an irregularly traded issue.

Early Trading in Securities

The first recorded security trading in the United States took place on Wall Street, New York City, when the 1789–1790 Congress authorized an $80 million stock issue to finance the Revolutionary War. In scattered market

111

places, such as coffeehouses, auction rooms, and offices, trading was carried on in government stock and in shares of the banks and insurance companies being formed in the eighteenth century. Trading in the issues was very irregular because individuals were reluctant to commit their funds to unmarketable, nonliquid securities.

In May 1792, a group of merchants and businessmen decided to meet daily at regular hours in order to buy and sell securities. The market place was under an old tree located on Wall Street, a few blocks from the present site of the New York Stock Exchange. These men were the original members of the exchange and handled the buy and sell orders of government issues, insurance company stocks, and shares in the First United States Bank, the Bank of North America, and the Bank of New York. In the following year the brokers moved indoors to the Tontine Coffee House. New York state bonds, issued to pay for the Erie Canal, bank stocks, fire insurance company stocks, shares of the Delaware and Hudson Canal Company, of the Merchants Exchange, and of the New York Gas Light Company were traded on the exchange by 1827; and 10 years later eight railroads had listed their securities for trading.

The New York Stock Exchange

Early Development

The New York Stock Exchange, also called the Big Board, developed as increasing trading activity among merchants and businessmen created the need for a more formal organization than that provided for by the 1792 agreement. On March 8, 1817, the first constitution of the New York Stock and Exchange Board was adopted. The constitution provided for a president, who was to call out the names of the stocks at 11:30 A.M. each business day, fix commissions, and set fines for violations or nonattendance of roll call. As the name of the stock was called, the brokers made their bids and offers. The New York Stock and Exchange Board was located in about a dozen different offices between 1817 and 1827 before it settled at its present site on the corner of Broad and Wall streets. In 1863, its name was changed to the New York Stock Exchange.

Stock Ticker

The stock ticker, first installed in 1867, is a high-speed printing telegraph that prints and codes the transactions of round lots (generally 100 shares or multiples of 100 shares; less than a round lot is called an odd lot) that trade on the New York Stock Exchange. The moving tape is flashed on a screen so that any observer in a brokerage office may see the transactions that occur on the floor of the exchange a few minutes after the actual transactions take place. The old ticker system had a maximum speed of 285 characters per minute and often ran several hours behind during the frantic trading of the 1929 stock market crash. In 1930, a faster ticker system with a maximum speed of 500 characters per minute replaced the old ticker service; however, with very heavy trading, the tape still ran a few minutes late, and an even faster model was installed in 1964. Although the exchange now has complete control over the distribution of ticker services, the tickers are owned by both the New York Stock Exchange and Western Union. In early 1962, some 3800 tickers were in operation, with approximately one third owned by the New York Stock Exchange.[1]

```
   GE        X       C
      97 ¼      61     58 ⅛
```

The ticker tape appears approximately as shown in the diagram, with GE referring to General Electric, X symbolizing U.S. Steel, and C referring to Chrysler, each of which traded 100 shares at the respective prices shown. Where more than one round lot of 100 shares trades at a given price, the number of round lots followed by an "s" precedes the price. Units of trading equal to or in excess of 1000 shares are written in full. Where the issue is preferred stock, Pr immediately follows the ticker tape symbol.

```
   GE              C                X Pr
      2s  97 ⅜       1,000  58 ¼        98 ⅞
```
200 shares

Other Developments

There were a number of developments in the history of the New York Stock Exchange between 1871 and 1938. Membership in the exchange began to be sold in 1871, and a telephone was installed in the exchange in 1879. Other interesting milestones were when the daily volume of trading topped one million shares in 1886; trading in nonlisted securities was discontinued in 1910; quotations began to be reported in dollars and eighths of dollars instead of in percentages of par in 1915; the exchange required an independent audit of financial statements for listed companies in 1933, a requirement that later became a part of the Securities Exchange Act of 1934; and the exchange was reorganized in 1938, providing for the payment of a salary to the president, who previously had not received any compensation for his administrative duties.

Membership

Since the New York Stock Exchange is a cooperative-type organization, the expenses of the exchange, ranging from $7 to $10 million annually, must be met by its membership. A membership on the exchange is referred to as a *seat*, although "membership" is a more descriptive term. The original con-

---

[1] See George L. Leffler and Loring C. Farwell, *The Stock Market*, 3d ed. (New York: The Ronald Press Company, 1963) pp. 148–166.

stitution of the New York Stock Exchange provided for 1375 members, but by early 1966 the number had been reduced to 1366. The membership is classified as (1) commission brokers, who buy and sell for their customers; (2) floor brokers, who assist the commission brokers; (3) specialists, who maintain an "orderly market" in a few assigned issues; (4) traders, who ordinarily buy and sell for their own account and frequently double as floor brokers; (5) odd lot specialists, who buy and sell securities in less than round lots; and (6) bond brokers.

Roughly 70 percent of the members of the New York Stock Exchange are partners or officers of member investment firms. These members, commonly referred to as *commission brokers*, act as agents in buying and selling securities for their customers on the floor of the exchange. In payment for this service they receive a brokerage commission (see Chapter 8).

The *floor brokers* assist the commission brokers in the transaction of the market orders. For example, a large chain of brokerage houses may own only three or four seats on the exchange and, therefore, may maintain only this number of representatives, other than clerical workers, on the floor of the exchange. When business becomes rushed, the services of floor brokers are frequently engaged. At one time the floor broker received $2 for his services and was called the "two-dollar broker," but the fee has now advanced above this level.

Some 20 percent of the members are *specialists*, each concentrating in a few assigned issues in which they handle away from the market orders, that is, orders limited as to price and/or time. For example, suppose an individual places an order to buy 100 shares of General Motors at 96 (stocks are quoted in points, a point being a dollar, and eighths and dollar signs are omitted), "good until cancelled," when the current market price is 97½. The specialist receives the order from the individual broker and fills it when he receives an offer from another broker to sell 100 shares at 96. He thus matches buy and sell orders at specified prices, and for this service he charges each broker a small commission. Orders may also be limited as to time, such as one day, three days, one week, 30 days, or longer.

Away from the market orders are entered in a book by the specialist, who must fill the orders on the basis of first price and then time of receipt of the order. For example, if someone places a limited order to buy 100 shares of General Motors at 96 and someone else places an order to buy the stock at 95⅞, the first order ranks ahead of the second. Where the price limit is the same, the order that is received first is filled first. A divergence from this rule may be followed when some of the limited orders are for more than one round lot. If a person placed a limited order to buy 300 shares of General Motors at 96, he would be given preference for acquiring a 300-share offer at this price over persons placing orders to buy only 100 shares, but the price and time preferences usually prevail.

The specialist buys and sells for his own account, but he must subordinate his own position and interest to those of the public. He may not buy or fill an order from his own account if stocks are demanded or offered by the general public at the same price. He may, however, narrow the spread between bid and ask by bidding higher or asking less than the general public. The specialist receives a portion of the commission paid to the brokerage firm for executing away from the market orders.

Specialists may be either long or short in the securities they maintain markets in, and frequently a large specialist may be long in one issue and short in another. *Long* refers to the ownership of shares, and a *short* interest, or position, refers to the sale of securities that the individual borrows from a broker. A later purchase, for example, in order to replace the lender's shares, at a lower price will produce a profit to the short seller, but if he must pay a price higher than the selling price, he loses money. Normally, about 25 percent of the trading by a specialist is on the short side. As demand for an issue rises and owners are reluctant to sell the issue at the current market quotation, the specialist may "offer stock" from his own account and even go short in the issue. As demand subsides and the market value declines, the specialist rebuys enough shares to cover his short position and to rebuild his inventory. He has been a supplier of stock in a rising market and a buyer of shares in a falling market, thus reducing the upside–downside oscillation in the market price of the issue.

The *odd lot specialists*, sometimes called odd lot dealers, buy and sell odd lots, which are from 1 to 99 shares in most issues, while a few high-priced inactive issues, that is, stocks with little or no daily trading, trade in round lot units of 10 instead of the normal 100 shares. In reality the odd lot specialists are dealers who obtain as their commission one fourth of a point for stocks trading at or above $55 per share or one eighth of a point for stocks trading below $55 per share on the New York Stock Exchange (the breaking point is $40 for the American Stock Exchange). Two odd lot dealers account for about 99 percent of New York Stock Exchange dollar trading volume in odd lots, which averages about 10 to 12 percent of total dollar volume of trading in New York Stock Exchange common shares.[2]

The odd lot specialist is usually long some 100 to 500 shares for each New York Stock Exchange issue, the amount depending on the activity of trading in each of the issues. The odd lot dealer is obligated to buy all odd lots offered at the market, less his commission, and to fill all market orders to buy an odd lot at the market price plus the odd lot differential or commission. When an odd lot order is placed, the next round lot trade for the issue determines the price at which the odd lot order will be executed by the odd lot dealer, plus or minus the odd lot differential, of course. The customer must pay a regular commission to his broker in addition to the odd lot commission (see Chapter 8 for an example).

Other exchange members, called *traders*, buy and sell for their own account while other members act as *bond brokers* for the corporate bonds

[2] For a comprehensive analysis of odd lot dealers and the odd lot public, see Leffler and Farwell, pp. 254–272.

that trade on the Big Board. The traders act as floor brokers or brokers' brokers at times, but may not trade during the day for their own account in any stock in which they transact buy or sell orders as a floor broker. This would provide the trader with an unfair advantage over the general public, since he (1) may see immediately the rise and fall in security prices; (2) does not pay brokerage fees, although he does pay transfer taxes and helps to pay operating costs of the exchange; and (3) may profitably buy and sell securities on a very narrow profit margin. The purchase and sale of a security by a trader in the same day does not require any cash payment. For example, suppose that a trader buys 1000 shares of Bell and Howell in the morning at 43 and sells them in the afternoon at 43¾. His gross profit of $750 is reduced by transfer taxes of about $50, and he has made same-day settlement and therefore does not have to put up any cash. The trader's own buy and sell orders are, however, subordinate to those of the general public. That is, a customer's order to buy the above stock at 43 would be filled before the trader's order.

Operation

The Board of Governors of the New York Stock Exchange, which sets rules and regulations governing exchange members, consists of 33 board members, three of whom represent the general public and have no direct contact with the securities markets. Other board members, called allied members, are elected from the members. An *allied member* is a general partner or voting stockholder in a member organization but is not an exchange member. If a brokerage firm has six general partners and only two of these are members of the New York Stock Exchange, the other four are classified as allied members. The exchange has more than 1300 employees, about 500 of whom work on the trading floor. The floor of the exchange looks something like a football field, with 18 horseshoe-shaped trading booths, each handling about 85 to 100 security issues. Trading activities at booths 2 and 4 on the New York Stock Exchange is shown in Fig. 7–1.

Brokerage offices are located in each of the 50 states and in about 13 foreign countries.[3] More than 3400 offices are linked with the New York Stock Exchange by telephone and telegraph and receive almost instantaneous quotations of floor transactions on the stock ticker tape or by means of a gigantic computer that records transactions and relays them to brokerage offices on a *teleregister*, a machine that looks much like a desk calculator. With this device an individual may determine for each listed security the daily range and volume, the last bid and ask prices, the daily opening and closing prices, the time of the last trade in the security, the annual dividend rate, the price–earnings ratio, the date of the last stock split, and other information. This data can be obtained in two or three seconds by depressing

---

[3] See New York Stock Exchange, *Understanding the New York Stock Exchange* (New York: The Exchange, 1964).

FIGURE 7-1 / New York Stock Exchange (Courtesy New York Stock Exchange)

a ticker tape symbol and the appropriate buttons on the teleregister. The device has become very popular because of its speed in providing a wide range of information and to a large extent is replacing the ticker tape service. Within time the teleregister will be equipped with a small television screen on which the ticker tape will be projected. An account executive may have to watch the ticker tape for several minutes before he gets a current quotation on a given stock, but he may determine almost instantaneously with the teleregister the last transaction price and the time at which the trade took place.

The American Stock Exchange

The American Stock Exchange is also located in New York City. A firm may not list its securities on both the New York and the American exchanges, but it may list its securities on one of these exchanges as well as on exchanges located in different cities.[4] If trading for a given security were permitted in the same city on more than one exchange, a great number of investors would attempt to arbitrage their trading transactions, thus creating confusion. *Arbitrage* refers to the simultaneous purchase and sale of securities on different exchanges at different prices.

Development

The American Stock Exchange, once called the Curb Market, had a colorful outdoor era prior to 1921, but since that time it has been indoors. The exact birthdate of the American Stock Exchange is not known, but it probably followed the Gold Rush of 1849 when mining shares began to be actively traded. The exchange grew and developed with the Industrial Revolution that took place in the United States in the late nineteenth century.

With the growing need for capital by the economy and by businessmen who sought public support through the sale of common stocks, secondary trading in the new industrial issues found its way to the Curb Market. Although the brokers were operating on the curbstones of Wall and Hanover streets, they frequently overflowed into the street. In order to receive buy and sell orders promptly, the curb traders placed telephone clerks at upper-story windows overlooking the market on the sidewalks below. The clerks, seated at the windows, would relay their orders to their broker by a shout or a hand signal. So that the telephone operators could locate their brokers, the curb traders were dressed in colorful costumes and wore unusual hats and caps. After the clerk relayed an order to his broker, the latter raced to the hydrant, lamp post, or mail box where the stock was being traded, executed the order with another member, and raced back to signal the confirmation to the clerk, who relayed the information by telephone to the brokerage office, which then contacted the customer. The Curb Market changed its name to the New York Curb Exchange in 1929, and in 1953, the present name, the American Stock Exchange, was adopted.

Although security trading by the Curb Market provided a colorful scene for sightseers and visitors, it created congested pedestrian and traffic

[4] Listing requirements for the New York and the American exchanges are given in Chapter 9.

situations, to say nothing of the discomfort caused by the weather. Deciding that an indoor exchange would permit a speed-up in transactions and the use of a ticker service, in 1919 the members voted to move indoors. Property was selected and purchased through the sale of stock to the members, and the New York Curb Market was located in a building on its present site at 86 Trinity Place, New York City.

Operation

In 1965, there were 21 trading posts at strategic locations throughout the 152-foot long trading floor of the American Stock Exchange. One special bond post is located centrally at the southern end of the floor. The stock posts are open octagons that contain eight chest-high writing spaces for members, who work on the outside, and provide room for two or three clerks on the inside who are hired by the specialists to write confirmation of orders. The stock and bond posts are equipped with hundreds of tiny open compartments under the writing spaces and counters for filing the "good until cancelled" orders, limited orders, odd lot orders, and records of the specialists. Telephone booths, for use by the brokers, line the east and west sides of the trading floor. The ticker transmission station, located at the northern end of the trading floor, flashes reports of the exchange's transactions instantaneously to ticker units in about 200 U.S. and Canadian cities. A portion of the floor of the American Stock Exchange is shown in Figure 7-2.

Some 500 or more individuals circulate on the floor of the American Stock Exchange, about 340 of whom are regular members, and the remainder are pages, who dispatch the memos to the ticker station by pneumatic tube, or members' clerks, who are used to facilitate trading. Members, pages, and clerks dress differently so that an observer may distinguish them.

The constitution of the American Stock Exchange in 1964 provided for 499 regular members, but an increase was being considered. In 1964, 340 of the members were floor brokers (168 were specialists, 132 were commission brokers, and 40 were floor traders). Associate members have no direct trading privileges but are required to pay the same annual dues as regular members. Associate membership may be purchased on an auction basis according to the latest regular seat sale. Associates pay an initial cost based on a percentage of the last sale price of a regular membership. The associate's privilege is limited to trading through regular members at reduced commission rates.

The execution of a buy or sell order on the American Stock Exchange is similar to that on the New York exchange. The duties of the specialist are different, however, since on the American exchange he also serves as the odd lot dealer for the securities for which he is maintaining a market. The specialist receives an odd lot differential, equal to one fourth or one eighth of a point per share, for stocks trading at and above or below $40, respec-

FIGURE 7-2 / American Stock Exchange (Courtesy American Stock Exchange)

tively. He is obligated to buy all odd lots offered or to fill all odd lot purchase orders at the price determined by the next round lot transaction minus
(or plus) the odd lot differential. Although the odd lot specialist obtains the
odd lot differential, he may lose money on certain types of transactions. For
example, on April 1, 1964, a very favorable earnings report was made public
on Mohawk Airlines after the markets closed. A large number of buying
orders flooded the American Stock Exchange for this particular issue on the
following day. Although the stock had closed on Wednesday at 7⅛, it
opened on Thursday at 8. Assuming that a large number of odd lot purchase
orders had been placed at the market, the odd lot specialist handling this
issue of stock would have been obligated to fill these orders at the opening
market price plus the one eighth of a point differential. Since the market
price of the stock was rising so rapidly, the odd lot specialist could have
suffered a tremendous loss on the odd lot orders. In this particular issue,
trading was suspended in the late morning and was continued on the following day. The market price of the stock continued to rise on the following
day to 11½, but within about four months it had declined to almost $6 per
share. This decline was brought about primarily through the dilution in
earnings per share, which was created by the conversion of a large debenture issue into common stocks.

Not only does the American Stock Exchange assist the domestic economy through the provision of a secondary market for the trading of securities but it also facilitates the financing of foreign companies by a unique system of American depository receipts, or American certificates of deposit. These certificates are issued by an approved New York bank or trust company against the deposits of the original, or foreign, shares with a European branch of the New York institution. As foreign shares are deposited abroad, the equivalent American depository receipts are issued in New York upon cabled advice from the foreign depository of the deposit of such shares. As the transactions in these shares are made, the depository receipts change hands—not the stock certificates. Actual shipment of stock certificates back and forth between the United States and foreign countries is eliminated, immensely expediting arbitrage transactions and securities traded on foreign exchanges. Dividend notifications and payments to American holders of foreign securities are also facilitated.[5]

The American Stock Exchange is the nation's leading market for foreign securities. Some 18 to 20 percent of total trading in the exchange was in foreign securities during the early 1960s, but the amount declined after the imposition of the interest-equalization tax of 1964.

In 1965, a majority of American Stock Exchange common stock issues traded at prices below $15, and the average daily volume of trading was only about one third that on the New York exchange. The dollar volume of these transactions was some 10 percent as great as on the New York Stock Exchange, but the ratio varies widely over the stock cycle. American Stock Exchange listing requirements are much less restrictive than those of the New York Stock Exchange, and this exchange is oftentimes a proving ground for an intermediate or large company that later lists on the New York exchange.

Other Registered and Exempt Exchanges

The Securities and Exchange Commission (SEC), under the Securities Exchange Act of 1934, forbids transactions on an exchange that is not registered or specifically exempt from registration with the SEC. The exchanges must file registration statements and other supporting documents with the SEC, including the constitution and rules under which the exchange operates). These exchanges must also set forth disciplinary action to be taken in the event that exchange members, allied members, or employees violate such rules and regulations.

The *18th Annual Report of the SEC* states that there have been more than 100 stock exchanges in operation in the United States. The number operating in 1929 was 30 but had declined to 17 by 1966. Of these 17 stock exchanges, 3 were exempt from registration because of their insignificant size and total dollar volume of stocks listed and traded. The largest of these

[5] For a more complete description of the American Stock Exchange, see American Stock Exchange, *The American Stock Exchange* (New York: The Exchange, undated).

TABLE 7-1 / Market Value and Volume of Sales Effected on Registered and Exempted Securities Exchanges in 1965 (in Thousands)

REGISTERED EXCHANGES

	Total Market Value (Dollars)	Stocks[1]		Bonds[2]		Rights and Warrants	
		Market Value (Dollars)	Number of Shares	Market Value (Dollars)	Principal Amount (Dollars)	Market Value (Dollars)	Number of Units
All Registered Exchanges	93,313,298	89,213,821	2,586,856	3,794,216	3,288,676	305,260	81,690
American Stock Exchange	9,025,800	8,611,828	582,212	150,925	138,327	263,047	19,632
Boston Stock Exchange	381,825	381,824	7151	0	0	1,000	10,000
Chicago Board of Trade	0	0	0	0	0	0	0
Cincinnati Stock Exchange	72,481	72,074	1248	41	53	366	137
Detroit Stock Exchange	619,100	618,970	14,064	0	0	130	160
Midwest Stock Exchange	3,086,052	3,085,808	69,605	5	5	239	669
National Stock Exchange	290	290	238	0	0	0	0
New York Stock Exchange	76,877,502	73,199,997	1,809,351	3,643,109	3,150,159	34,396	57,872
Pacific Coast Stock Exchange	2,180,025	2,172,958	59,427	102	98	6966	3014
Philadelphia–Baltimore–Washington Stock Exchange	1,009,257	1,009,107	21,696	35	35	115	196
Pittsburgh Stock Exchange	48,407	48,407	1155	0	0	0	0
Salt Lake Stock Exchange	4742	4742	8984	0	0	0	0
San Francisco Mng. Exchange	1653	1653	5180	0	0	0	0
Spokane Stock Exchange	6164	6164	6546	0	0	0	0

EXEMPTED EXCHANGES

All Exempted Exchanges	18,683	18,545	1853	44	20	94	613
Colorado Springs Stock Exchange	163	163	1172	0	0	0	0
Honolulu Stock Exchange	15,072	14,944	598	44	20	94	613
Richmond Stock Exchange	3279	3279	73	0	0	0	0
Wheeling Stock Exchange[3]	159	159	9	0	0	0	0

NOTE: Data on the value and volume of securities sales are reported in connection with fees paid under Section 31 of the Securities Act of 1934. They include all securities sales effected on exchanges, except sales of bonds of the U.S. government, which are not subject to the fee. The data cover odd lot as well as round lot transactions. Reports of most exchanges for a given month cover transactions cleared during the calendar month; clearance occurs for the most part on the fourth day after that on which the trade actually was effected.

[1] Includes voting trust certificates, certificates of deposit for stocks, and American depository receipts for stocks, but excludes rights and warrants.

[2] Excludes U.S. government Bonds

[3] Includes figures through April 30, 1965, when the Wheeling Stock Exchange was dissolved.

SOURCE: U.S. Securities and Exchange Commission, *Statistical Bulletin* (Washington, D.C.: U.S. Government Printing Office, March 1966), p. 9.

registered exchanges, the New York and the American exchanges, were discussed above, and a list of the other registered and exempt exchanges appears in Table 7–1. The Midwest Stock Exchange is third in size, based on volume of security sales during recent years, followed by the Pacific Coast Stock Exchange and the Philadelphia–Baltimore–Washington Stock Exchange. In 1965, none of the other registered or exempt exchanges accounted for as much as one half of 1 percent of the total U.S. market value of share transactions.

The decline in the number of registered and exempt stock exchanges occurred because of mergers and withdrawals from operation. In general, the exchanges are similar in organizational structure and membership requirements to the New York Stock Exchange. Each exchange must file registration material and annual reports with the SEC unless it is specifically exempt from these requirements, and the trading procedures on the exchanges are similar to those on the New York and the American exchanges except that many do not have specialists. Some of the smaller exchanges have odd lot dealers similar to those on the New York Stock Exchange, while odd lot trading on others is handled by specialists. Some of the smaller exchanges permit trading in securities not listed on that exchange but listed on some other registered exchange. For example, unlisted trading privileges are extended to all New York and American stock exchange issues by a majority of the smaller exchanges. Brokerage commissions, on the issues traded with unlisted trading privileges, are usually those required by the New York or the American exchange.[6]

Market Value of Listed Securities

Table 7–2 compares the market value of securities traded on exchanges at the year end 1962 and 1964. Although there were approximately as many stock issues listed on the American Stock Exchange and exclusively on other exchanges as on the New York Stock Exchange, the market value of the shares listed on the Big Board amounted to more than 90 percent of the total market value of all listed stocks, while some 99 percent of the bonds listed on a registered or an exempt exchange were traded on the Big Board.

From 1962 to the end of 1964, the market value of stocks traded on the exchanges increased by approximately one third. An insignificant part of this rise was due to an increase in the number of listed issues, but a major portion was due to the capital appreciation of listed issues. The volume of bonds listed on registered or exempt exchanges increased about 15 percent over the two-year period.

While the New York Stock Exchange has been more important for the trading of domestic issues, Table 7–3 reveals that the American Stock Exchange lists more foreign issues with a larger market value than does the

[6] For a more comprehensive analysis of regional and local stock exchanges, see Leffler and Farwell, pp. 314–325.

New York Stock Exchange. Listing and trading in foreign securities on exchanges other than the New York or the American were relatively unimportant at the end of 1962 and 1964. Canadian issues accounted for roughly one half of the foreign issues listed on the New York Stock Exchange, but amounted to only 25 percent of the foreign issues listed on the American Stock Exchange.

TABLE 7-2 /   Market Value of Securities Traded on Exchanges on December 31, 1962, and December 31, 1964 (amounts in millions of dollars)

	December 31, 1962		December 31, 1964	
	Number of Issues	Market Value	Number of Issues	Market Value
Stocks				
New York Stock Exchange	1559	$345,846	1606	$474,322
American Stock Exchange	1018	24,365	1022	28,220
Exclusively on other exchanges	470	4016	445	4315
Total stocks	3047	$374,227	3073	$506,857[1]
Bonds				
New York Stock Exchange	1202	$111,094	1186	$127,725
American Stock Exchange	84	1170	91	1267
Exclusively on other exchanges	26	143	23	124
Total bonds	1312	$112,407	1300	$129,116
Total stocks and bonds	4359	$486,634	4373	$635,973

[1] About 22 percent of the issues and 2 percent of the values were for preferred issues.

SOURCE: U.S. Securities and Exchange Commission, *29th and 31st Annual Reports* (Washington, D.C., U.S. Government Printing Office, 1963, and 1965), pp. 41 and 45, respectively.

The total market value of annual security sales is influenced largely by the level of stock market prices. Share volume of trading turnover frequently increases substantially with sharp advances or declines in security prices. Dollar volume of trading is ordinarily significantly higher in a strong bull market than in a depressed market, however. For example, assume that the average price of a New York Stock Exchange share is $55 at the height of a bull market and only $44 at the bottom of a bear market. Dollar volume of trading has declined 20 percent on the same share turnover. Tables 7–1 and 7–2 indicate that roughly 15 percent of the listed shares changed hands in 1965, the turnover rate being slightly higher for securities listed on the American Stock Exchange than for those traded on the New York Stock Exchange.

Table 7–1 indicates that the trading in bonds through an exchange is dominated by Big Board transactions, while the American Stock Exchange

TABLE 7-3 /   Foreign Stocks on Exchanges (amounts in millions of dollars)

Exchange	Canadian		Other Foreign		Total	
	Issues	Values	Issues	Values	Issues	Values
DECEMBER 31, 1962						
New York	12	4210.1	13	1779.8	25	5989.8
American	91	6454.7	36	207.1	127	6660.8
Others only	1	0.5	2	10.7	3	11.2
Net Total	104	10,664.3	51	1997.5	155	12,661.8
DECEMBER 31, 1964						
New York	14	6374.7	12	2272.2	26	8646.9
American	66	7721.6	36	518.5	102	8300.1
Others only	2	25.8	3	18.4	5	44.3
Net Total	82	14,122.1	51	2869.1	133	16,991.3

SOURCE: U.S. Securities and Exchange Commission, *29th and 31st Annual Reports and Exchange Commission* (Washington, D.C.: U.S. Government Printing Office, 1963 and 1965), pp. 42 and 46, respectively.

is more important for warrants and rights. Only 7 of the 17 exchanges list bond issues, but 9 of the 17 exchanges traded in rights and warrants in 1965. The American Stock Exchange accounted for some 86 percent of the total market value of trading in rights and warrants during 1965, but for only 24 percent of the number of units traded. Trading of rights and warrants on the New York Stock Exchange amounted to some 11 percent of the total market value but for some 70 percent of the total number of units traded.

Over the Counter Market

Over the counter trading in securities refers to the sale of securities by individuals and/or dealers other than that which takes place through registered or exempt exchanges. During recent years, there has been an increasing amount of over the counter trading in listed securities. Such trading is done to a large extent by financial institutions, but some security dealers maintain a market in a selected list of securities and are willing to buy and sell the securities at a narrower spread than the round-trip brokerage commission charged by member brokerage firms. The *30th Annual Report of the SEC* indicated that about 4500 stocks with 300 or more holders representative of approximately 4200 domestic companies were quoted in only the over the counter market. These stocks had an aggregate market value of $100 million at the end of 1963, and approximately one third of this amount was for bank stocks, about one fourth for insurance stocks, and the remainder for industrials, utilities, and other miscellaneous issues. The over the counter stocks, in general, are associated with smaller, more closely held corporations than are listed securities. Only those companies with 300 or more holders must report regularly to the SEC, and many smaller companies may have actively traded stocks. At mid-January 1964, about 8200 stock issues were listed with approximately 35,000 dealers.[7]

In the latter 1950s, about 40,000 issues of securities were traded in the over the counter markets, whereas 80,000 or 90,000 different issues could probably have been traded if the shareholders had wanted to market their securities. Of the trading in outstanding securities, some 73 percent of the issues traded daily was in stocks, some 10 percent was in corporate bonds, and the remainder was in government issues.[8]

Frequently the securities that are traded in the over the counter market belong to local or regional companies in which there may be active local trading but very little national interest. Few bank stocks and insurance company stocks are listed on registered exchanges, but many are traded actively in the over the counter markets, and many have a national market. Generally, over the counter markets are representative of companies that have short histories or that are closely held. For this reason, the shares are less marketable, generally trade at lower multiples of earnings than do listed securities, and in many cases, the market price oscillates less violently than for listed stocks. However, "third market sales," of over the counter trading, in 1965 represented 2 percent of the total number and 2.9 percent of the total value of shares traded on national security exchanges. Some 97.6 percent of these third market sales were in New York Stock Exchange issues.[9]

The SEC estimated in 1964 that about 150 foreign stocks, or American shares representing foreign stocks, had active daily trading in the over the counter market. In addition, there were many other foreign stocks that were less actively quoted in the regional over the counter markets.

The over the counter markets are "made" by over the counter dealers. Section 15-A of the Securities and Exchange Act of 1934 encourages associations of security dealers to promote investor interest and self-regulation. To date, the National Association of Security Dealers (NASD), a nonprofit membership corporation, is the only such organization that has been formed, with some 4000 security dealers belonging to it. The NASD attempts to promote fair dealing between security dealers and their clients. It encourages its members to maintain a spread between bid and ask of no greater than 5 percent and restricts commission splitting to members of the NASD. When a security dealer violates the regulations and requirements of the NASD, he is subject to disciplinary action or loss of membership.[10]

[7] See Securities and Exchange Commission, *29th and 30th Annual Reports* (Washington, D.C.: U.S. Government Printing Office, 1963 and 1964).

[8] See Erwin Friend, and others, *Over-the-Counter Securities Markets* (New York: McGraw-Hill Book Company, Inc., 1958), or Leffler and Farwell, pp. 402–418.

[9] Securities and Exchange Commission, *Statistical Bulletin* (Washington, D.C.: U.S. Government Printing Office, March 1966), p. 10.

[10] For a more comprehensive analysis of the National Association of Security Dealers, see Jules I. Bogen, *Financial Handbook* (New York: The Ronald Press Company, 1952), pp. 118–120.

Summary

The 1966 secondary markets for the trading of equity securities consisted of the over the counter markets and 17 security exchanges, 3 of which were exempt from registering with the SEC. Unless specifically authorized by the SEC, an exchange must register with that commission. Over the counter trading refers to the trading in securities that take place other than through the exchanges. Since there are no complete records maintained on over the counter securities, the exact relative importance of this kind of trading as against that through exchanges is not known.

The New York Stock Exchange is the oldest of the registered exchanges, formed in the latter part of the eighteenth century to facilitate trading in stocks issued to finance the Revolutionary War and stocks issued by a few banks and insurance companies. Since that time, more than 100 exchanges have been in operation, but only 17 were in existence in 1966.

The dollar volume of trading in domestic issues of common stocks on the New York Stock Exchange accounts for 80 to 85 percent of the total dollar volume of trading in stocks of U.S. exchanges, while the American Stock Exchange normally accounts for 7 to 8 percent, with the remainder divided among the other 15 exchanges. The American Stock Exchange is relatively more important for trading in rights, warrants, and foreign issues than is the New York Stock Exchange.

QUESTIONS FOR REVIEW /

1. Explain how the first stock exchange in the United States evolved.
2. Explain what is meant by a seat on a stock exchange.
3. How are the expenses incurred by stock exchanges financed?
4. Differentiate among the following: (a) commission brokers, (b) floor brokers, (c) specialists, (d) floor traders.
5. What are the functions of odd lot dealers on the New York Stock Exchange? How does odd lot trading on the Big Board differ from that on the American Stock Exchange?
6. How does the American Stock Exchange differ from the New York Stock Exchange?
7. What is meant by unlisted trading privileges?
8. How does the over the counter market operate?
9. What reasons can you suggest for the greater importance of trading in warrants and rights on the American Stock Exchange as contrasted to the New York Stock Exchange?
10. Show how trading in foreign securities is facilitated on the American Stock Exchange.

PROBLEMS /

1. From a current issue of *Barron's* or *Commercial and Financial Chronicle* prepare a list of the warrants listed on (a) the American and (b) the New York stock exchanges. Save these lists for future use.

2. By a review of "Whose New on the Exchange," in *The Exchange* (published by the New York Stock Exchange), determine three recent listings on the Big Board. Contrast the listing requirements of the exchange with those that exist for the companies. What possible reasons account for the management's choice to list on the New York Stock Exchange?

3. For the past two years, contrast the share volume and dollar value of stock trading on the New York, the American, and other regional exchanges. Do you believe that there is a real need for the latter group? Explain.

REFERENCES /

American Stock Exchange, *The American Stock Exchange*. New York: undated.

Commerce Clearing House, Inc., *American Stock Exchange Guide*. Chicago: Commerce Clearing House, 1962.

Bogen, Jules I., *Financial Handbook*, 3d. ed. New York: The Ronald Press Company, 1952.

Cooke, Gilbert W., *The Stock Market*. New York: Simmons-Boardman Publishing Corporation, 1964.

Friend, Erwin, and others, *Over-the-Counter Securities Markets*. New York: McGraw-Hill Company, Inc., 1958.

Leffler, George L., and Loring C. Farwell, *The Stock Market*, 3d ed. New York: The Ronald Press Company, 1963.

New York Stock Exchange, *The Exchange*. New York: The Exchange, selected monthly issues.

———, *The New York Stock Exchange Factbook*. New York: The Exchange, 1964.

———, *Understanding the New York Stock Exchange*. New York: The Exchange, 1964.

U.S. Securities and Exchange Commission, *Annual Reports*. Washington, D.C.: U.S. Government Printing Office, selected issues.

chapter 8 | Mechanics of Security Trading

Introduction

Knowledge of how the securities markets operate is important to the buyer of common stocks. The individual investor, however, has only an indirect association with the major exchanges and must buy and sell his listed securities through an *agent*, commonly referred to as an account executive, of a brokerage firm that owns a membership on the security exchange.

Before attempting to trade in listed securities, the individual should discover (1) how to open an account with a security broker or dealer, (2) what it costs to buy and sell stocks, (3) the various types of orders that may be placed, (4) how these orders are executed, and (5) the differences between cash and margin trading. These and other topics are described in this chapter.

Opening an Account

After an individual decides that he can safely afford the risk associated with the ownership of common stocks, his next step is to visit a reputable brokerage firm, where he is assigned to an account executive who will ask him to provide certain types of financial information. Ordinarily, the office manager attempts to maintain the number of accounts in fairly equal balance among his account executives to insure adequate handling of each account. The account executive will first ascertain that the prospective customer has a good credit rating, that he will actually pay for the stock that he orders for purchase, and that he is in a financial position to invest in securities. The account executive will perhaps ask for a bank reference, two or three credit references, and the names of two or three other individuals who are acquainted with the applicant. He may also ask the prospective customer whether he is interested in stability of principal, a liberal dividend income, growth issues, or speculative issues with wider price movements. Knowledge of the types of securities the customer is seeking and the degree of market risk he is willing to assume will aid the account executive in meeting the needs of the individual customer.

The prospective investor may find his enthusiasm dampened after the account executive quizzes him about his financial condition, the types of securities he may already own, and his knowledge about the stock market; but account executives, most of whom are well trained in the area of security analysis and devote their lives to the study of security trading, must have all this information in order to render their full services to investors. The attitudes and services performed by an account executive vary widely, and his treatment of one customer may differ significantly from his attitude toward another. The account executive must be a psychologist and determine the types of services expected by each client. Some account executives act only as order takers, while others carry on active selling practices with their clients. The account executives, of course, attempt to aid their customers in making a profit on their stock transactions, but some customers dislike short-term trading and prefer to hold their stocks for several years. This attitude may be desirable, but it should depend on the position of the market, for example, whether the early stages of a rising market, the top of a mature market, or a market down turn. Most account executives have favorite issues that they are recommending for purchase at the time the customer asks for a suggestion. Account executives are not fortune tellers, however, and they do make bad guesses in timing and price recommendations. While this situation is irritating to the stockholder, he can always change to another account executive. Even though he should listen to the counsel of his account executive, he is the final judge in deciding when and what issues to buy and sell.

Cost of Buying and Selling Securities

An investor buys stock from an over the counter dealer at the ask price and sells it at the bid price, thus paying the dealer's profit only once. If a stock is bid 20, ask 21, the investor may buy the issue today at $21 and sell it back tomorrow at $20, assuming that the bid–ask spread does not change. However, when he buys or sells shares of common stock through a brokerage firm, he must pay a brokerage fee. If he is dealing in a sizable amount of money, say $3800, the fee is only 1 percent on each occasion, or substantially lower, in most cases, than the difference in the spread between bid and ask quoted by over the counter security dealers. In addition, the seller of stock traded through either the American or the New York Stock Exchange must pay New York state transfer taxes; federal transfer taxes were discontinued in 1965. As mentioned earlier, an odd lot differential of one eighth or one quarter of a dollar is charged for the purchase or sale of an odd lot of a stock trading below $55 or at $55 and above, respectively, on the New York Stock Exchange, with the break at $40 on the American Stock Exchange. In 1966, the round lot and odd lot brokerage commission and the New York State transfer tax schedules were as follows:

ROUND LOT (100 SHARES) BROKERAGE COMMISSION*

Amount Invested	Commission
Up to $100	As mutually agreed
$100–$400	$3 + 2%
$400–$2400	$7 + 1%
$2400–$5000	$19 + ½%
More than $5000	$39 + ⅒%

* An odd lot commission is $2 less than the round lot commission, but the investor must also pay the odd lot differential.

NEW YORK STATE TRANSFER TAX (PAID BY SELLER)

Market Value per Share	Tax per Share
$20 or more	$.05
$10–19⅞	.0375
$5–9⅞	.0250
Below $5	.0125

Assuming that a person bought 50 shares of Fluor Corporation in November 1965 at $50 per share and sold the stock in December of that year at $65 per share, the cash outlay, proceeds, and profits were as follows:

Cost of stock ($50 × 50)		$2500.00
Odd lot differential (50 shares × 25)*		12.50
Brokerage $17 + ½% × ($2500 + 12.50)		29.56
Total investment		$2542.06
Selling price of stock (50 shares × $65)		$3250.00
Less: Odd lot differential	$12.50	
New York State transfer tax	2.50	
Brokerage $17 + ½% × (3250.00 − 12.50)	33.19	48.19
Net Proceeds from sale		$3201.81

* The breaking point for a one eighth or one quarter point odd lot differential was changed from $40 to $55 at mid-1966 on the New York Stock Exchange.

In the above example, the investor made a net profit after all expenses of $659.75, a return of approximately 25 percent of his investment for the six-week holding period. Since the securities were held for less than six months, the investor was taxed on the entire amount of his capital gain.

The brokerage fee is computed on each round lot transaction and/or each odd lot transaction and is a smaller percentage of the dollar investment on higher-priced issues. For example, assume that an investor has a choice of buying 1000 shares of a $10 issue or 100 shares of a $100 issue, each of which he expects to rise by 10 percent. His profit is greater on the latter by 46 percent, computed as follows:

	$10 Stock	$100 Stock
Market price of 100 shares	$ 1000	$10,000
Brokerage ($7 + 1%); ($39 + ⅒%)	17	49
Total per round lot	1017	10,049
Number of lots	10	1
Investment	10,170	10,049
Gross selling price per lot	1100.00	11,000.00
Less: Brokerage ($7 + 1%);		
($39 + ⅒%)	18.00	50.00
New York State transfer taxes	3.75	5.00
Total selling costs	21.75	55.00
Net proceeds per lot	1078.25	10,945.00
Number of lots	10	1
Total net proceeds	10,782.50	10,945.00
Net profit	$ 612.50	$ 896.00

Of course, the lower-priced issues frequently oscillate somewhat more widely than the higher-priced stocks, but brokerage and transfer taxes are much more severe on the lower-priced issues.

Types of Orders

Size of Order

Orders for common stocks are classified as round lots, usually 100 shares or multiples of 100 shares, or odd lots, that is, less than 100 shares. In terms of total volume of trading, round lot transactions on the New York Stock Exchange are about seven or eight times as great as the dollar volume trading of odd lots. Odd lot transactions are conducted only through odd lot dealers on the New York Stock Exchange (specialists transact odd lot orders on the American Stock Exchange), with 99 percent of New York Stock Exchange odd lot business being done by the two largest dealers, who also fill odd lot limited orders, odd lot stop orders, and monthly investment plan orders. Limited and stop orders are discussed in the following paragraphs, while the monthly investment plan is presented in Chapter 22.

Orders may, of course, be submitted in multiples or fractions of round lots. Some investors buy 200, 500, or 1000 share units, while investment companies and pension funds frequently trade in blocks of 5000, 10,000 or larger. Such a large trade is frequently substantially above or below the previous trade price, and some security analysts place significance upon the large trades and whether they are at increased or decreased prices, using the figures as a gauge to what "smart investors" are doing. For example, a trade on the up side is gauged to mean accumulation, while a trade on the down side is assumed to indicate distribution. A majority of the New York Stock Exchange trades, however, are for 100 shares. The sale of 150 shares involves both a round lot and an odd lot transaction, where the round lot is 100 shares. The 100 shares are traded on the floor of the exchange, while the 50 shares are sold to an odd lot dealer at the next round lot transaction price less the odd lot differential. A few of the higher-priced issues, particularly preferred issues of utility companies, trade in round lot units of 10, and some Canadian exchanges have round lots in units of 10, 25, or 100, depending upon the issue.

Types of Transactions

When an investor buys securities, he is said to be long in the issue; if he sells securities, he eliminates this long position; and when he strongly believes that an issue is overpriced and will probably fall within the foreseeable future, he may request his broker to "sell the stock short." A *short sale* involves selling an issue that one does not own. The broker borrows the stock for his customer in order to make delivery, but expects the seller to "buy back in" at a later date in order to repay the borrowed stock certificate. Short selling is legal by certain types of investors but may be done only from a margin account that provides for borrowing a portion of the purchase price of stocks from the brokerage firm. Certain types of accounts, such as those of financial institutions and investment clubs, are not permitted to sell securities short or to buy on margin. Some individuals frequently take a short position in an issue, but short selling is actually undertaken more by specialists on the exchanges and by professional traders than by the general public.

Many investment advisers recommend that a short position not be taken in a listed security issue that has less than one million shares outstanding, while some suggest that it is dangerous in an issue with less than three million shares outstanding. Although the exact number is not important, the investor should give some consideration to the trading volume of the stock and to the floating supply, that is, the amount of stock in the hands of traders or investors willing to part with it at some price. For an issue that has a substantial amount of daily trading and for which the floating supply is fairly great, relative to the amount of the total shares, the investor may safely make a short sale and expect to cover it fairly close to the market price at the time when he requests his account executive to "cover."

From 1950 through 1965, the primary market trend for common stocks was upward, and many account executives were reluctant to advise their customers to make short sales, since for the average investor the short sale is more risky than the long purchase. For example, a stock trading at $8 has a tremendous potential capital gain, since the market price can rise 200 or 300 percent over a period of time. Conversely, a stock may not fall by more than 100 percent. The stock sold short at $8 will probably not decline to less than $2 or $3 per share, but suppose that the individual goes short in an issue at $8 and it rises to $20. Then his loss amounts to 150 percent of his investment, while the maximum loss on the long purchase cannot exceed 100 percent.

Limits as to Price

A majority of account executives encourage their customers to make *market orders* to insure that the transaction is executed at the best possible immediate price. When the buyer or seller of stocks feels that he can purchase or sell a stock at a slight advantage to himself within the next two or three days, he may place a *limited order* to sell at a specified price. For example, assume that XYZ common is trading for 25¼, and the prospective purchaser believes that the market price of the stock will decline to 24½ within the next few days. He places a limited order to purchase 100 shares of the stock at this price. The order form is completed, transmitted to the floor of the New York Stock Exchange, and transferred to the books of the specialist who handles the issue. When the market price of the stock drops to 24½, the order is filled. Assuming that more than one order for XYZ common appears on the books of the specialist at 24½, the order received first is filled first. Similarly, a shareholder may place a limited order to sell an issue if and when it reaches a designated price. However, all orders at a given price may not be filled because of inadequate supply of or demand for the stock.

Limits as to Time

Market orders and day orders, unless reactivated, are cancelled at the end of the trading day. For example, if an order is placed to buy 100 shares of Fluor late in the trading day and there is no more trading in the issue, the order is cancelled at the close of the day unless it is reactivated by the purchaser. Where there is inactive trading in a security, the buyer may instruct his account executive to enter a week order, which expires at the end of the calendar week, or a month order, which expires at the end of the last trading day of the month. While an individual may place an order for 7 days, 10 days, or 30 days, *open orders*, or orders that are good until cancelled, are easier for the stockholder to remember.

Investors are advised not to place market orders in stocks that are very irregularly traded, since the spread between bid and ask may be as much as fifty cents, one dollar, or sometimes more per share. An order at the market authorizes the floor broker to execute the order at the best offer price, meaning that the purchaser is paying a premium for the issue. Knowing that the bid–ask price for a stock is 49½, 50, the purchaser may place a limited order to buy the stock during the trading day at 49⅝ or 49¾, since some owners of the security may be willing to sell at this price. Frequently, in order to narrow the spread between bid and ask for a given issue, the specialist who maintains a market in the security buys or sells from his own account. For example, in the above illustration, the specialist may offer or buy the stock at 49¾. The customer who offers his stock at 50 may be willing to accept 49¾ per share for the issue, and another wishing to make the purchase may raise his bid to 49¾. In this way, the spread between bid and ask has been narrowed so that trading may be facilitated.

Stop Orders

Another type of order that may be used to limit the amount of losses or to protect the amount of capital gains is the *limited stop order*. Assume that in mid-October 1964 an investor bought 100 shares of Fluor common at 27 per share. After adjustments for the 5 percent stock dividend in January 1965, the stock had increased to 38 per share at the close of a trading day near the end of February 1965. The holder of the security did not know whether the market value would continue to rise or recede. In order to protect a part of his profits, he placed a stop order at 34⅞, so that if the market price of the stock declined to that level, the stop order would become a market order. Of course, the issue might be sold at a price lower than the 34⅞, because there are frequently gaps in the trading price (more than one eighth of a point difference in adjacent trades) when the market prices of securities are falling very rapidly. The investor could have placed a limited stop order at 34⅞ so that the order would not be executed unless (1) the price of the security fell to this point and (2) another buyer was willing to pay 34⅞ for these shares. The danger in this type of order, however, is that a buyer of the shares may not be available at this price and the order may not be transacted. The positions for setting stop orders are open to debate, but should probably be (1) about 10 to 15 percent below the market value of the issue when the stop is set (the usual fluctuation is important), (2) slightly below a dollar value (as 30⅞; 39¾; 79⅝, and so forth), and (3) slightly below a support level (an area of congested trading in the recent past that is below the current price). Where stops are set too close to the market price or above a support level, say 30⅛, a move to 30⅛ or 30 will frequently trigger the transaction just before a price rally.

Other Types of Orders

Some investors prefer a *discretionary account*, which provides the account executive with wide latitude in the selection of securities to be purchased and sold. The investor who feels that his knowledge of the stock market is limited and who wishes to place reliance upon his account executive may follow this plan. Should the performance of his account be less than he expects under this method, he may cancel the discretionary order privilege of the account executive.

Even after a limited order has been placed with an account executive and relayed to the member specialist, the investor is free to change his mind and submit a *cancel order*. He should not abuse this privilege by repeatedly using it, however, since cancellation of an order involves considerable paper work and communications expense. One danger in using a limited order, good until cancelled, is that an investor may later sell an issue at the market and forget his original order, which is later transacted. In order to fulfill the contract, he may have to buy another round lot at a price higher than the selling price. At best, the round-trip brokerage fee and transfer taxes will cost him at least 2 or 3 percent of his investment, or the firm may be willing to change the order to a short sale and permit him to replace the issue at a later date.

In order to limit the amount of actual losses on a short sale, the investor may use the *stop buy order*. For example, suppose that an individual believes that an issue will move down from its current price of 39 to roughly 32. He may short the issue at the market, intending to cover his short position at 32 or 33. However, instead of falling, the issue may continue to rise in price, and in order to limit his loss, the investor may place a stop buy order at a price above his selling price, say 41¼. In this way he has lost 2¼ per share plus his round-trip brokerage fee and transfer taxes, but with a steep upward price progression, the market price of an issue may move quickly and extensively. As the market price falls for a shorted issue, one may place a stop buy order two or three points above the current market price, thus providing some profit if the decline is not to the anticipated level.

A speculator who is interested in short-term capital appreciation and who finds one or more issues that oscillate regularly between two price limits may make use of the *double stop sell* or the *double stop buy* order. For example, suppose that an investor noticed that Eastern Air Lines common moved between 30 and 40 per share three or four times between 1963 and 1964. He may have decided to buy 100 shares of the stock each time it falls to 30 and to sell the stock each time it reaches 40. He may have been willing to take a short position in the stock at 40 and attempt to cover his short position at about 30 per share. He could have done this automatically by using the double stop sell and double stop buy limited orders. Assuming that he purchased the stock at 30 and that the price is approaching his imaginary upper limit of 40, he may place a double stop sell order at 40. His 100 shares are sold at 40 or above, and a similar number of shares are sold short at that price. He would continue to be short in the issue until his short interest is covered. Assume that the issue fell to 30 and that he had placed a double stop buy limited order. His 100 shares would have been covered at that point and he would have gone long in the issue for 100 shares. There is one danger in this type of transaction. Suppose that instead of leveling off at 40 the price had moved up to 80, 100, or 120, as occurred with Eastern Air Lines common in 1966. If the investor had remained short in the issue, he could have had a net loss of $80 per share. Conversely, if he had placed an order to purchase the security long when it reached 30 and the market price of the stock continued to drift lower, he may have had a book loss in the issue for a period of time, but could have held on for a hoped-for later recovery. Trading long and short in an issue is recommended only for the professional or the individual who is willing and able to assume a tremendous risk.

How Orders Are Executed

After the individual has opened an account, he may place an order with his account executive to buy or sell securities by almost any means of communication, including telephone, mail, telegram, or in person. When a telegram is used, the account executive may ask for a letter of verification within a few days.

The action that occurs between the placing of an order and the appearance of the trade on the ticker tape requires only a few minutes. When an order is placed for a security listed on the New York or on the American exchange, an employee of the brokerage office wires the order to the floor of the exchange, where an exchange member receives it and attempts to transact the order at the best possible price. For example, suppose that XYZ common is bid 25¼, ask 25½. The commission broker may ask, "XYZ common?" He does not disclose whether he is in the market to buy or sell the issue. The specialist for the stock gives him the bid–ask quotation, 25¼, 25½. The commission broker may say, "Bid 25⅜" or "Bid ⅜." Another broker who is waiting to sell an order at the market or at that price may shout, "Sold!" Simultaneously, a buy and a sell contract has been filled. The reporter writes the price and volume on a small slip of paper, noting the details of the trading, and gives it to a page, who calls out the information and places the report in a small plastic container which travels through a pneumatic tube to the ticker tape room. The slip of paper is extracted from the container, stamped as to time received, and placed on a moving belt. A clerk or typist punches out the sales data on a tape, the information is fed through the stock ticker, and almost instantaneously it is flashed to the offices of numerous brokerage firms. The ticker mechanism is geared to take care of about 10 million shares per day. When the volume of transactions is substantially higher or increases in tempo near the end of the trading session, the ticker may run a few minutes or hours late, as in May 1962, when the ticker fell behind more than four and one-half hours. Ordinarily, however, the ticker reports the transaction only two or three minutes after it takes place on the floor of the exchange.

After a buy or sell order is executed, the customer is notified by mail as to the price of the transaction and the brokerage fee and/or transfer taxes involved. With a purchase the investor is expected to make payment within four business days, and with a sale of stock he may instruct his account executive to credit his account or to mail him the check, which he expects to receive within four business days. When a security is sold, the seller must supply the account executive with his stock certificate as soon as possible, but in any event, earlier than the fourth business day. For safekeeping or with a margin account customers may leave their stock certificates with their brokerage firm in *street name,* that is, the brokerage firm being the registered holder rather than the original owner. In this case a monthly statement is mailed to the customer showing (1) the securities held by the brokerage firm for the customer, (2) the amount of dividends that have been credited to his account, (3) the interest charge for borrowing, in the case of a margin account, and/or dividends owed on shorted stock, and (4) the debt balance for the amount of margin due the broker.

The New York Stock Exchange requires that companies listing their securities on the exchange maintain a registrar and a transfer agent in New York City. The transfer agent must be sure that a person buying the stock becomes a stockholder of record, while the person selling the stock is removed from ownership. Ordinarily, the voided stock certificate is attached to the certificate stub and a new certificate is issued to the buyer. The registrar maintains a separate list of the stockholders of record of a company whose securities trade on the New York Stock Exchange. Ordinarily the duties of the registrar and the transfer agent are delegated to trust companies or trust departments of large commercial banks.

The buyer of a security deals directly with his account executive. When he purchases stock and requests his account executive to mail the stock certificate to him, he may ordinarily expect to receive it within two to eight weeks. However, one of the advantages of leaving stock certificates in street name is that the buyer may want to sell his shares before he receives the stock certificate, and if they are credited to his brokerage account he may proceed immediately with the sale. On the other hand, a certificate that has been mailed to the buyer may be in transit and require several days to reach the owner, thus making it difficult to redeliver it to his account executive within the required time period. Also, in the event that a stock dividend or a stock split has occurred, the owner of the security may sell his stock either on the old basis or on a "when issued" (adjusted) basis where the security is deposited to his account. Otherwise, he may be required to surrender the security to be voided so that other stock securities with different par values, in case of a split, can be issued to him. When this occurs, there may be a short period in which the owner will be unable to dispose of his securities. On the other hand, he may authorize his account executive to perform this clerical work for him and credit his account for the securities and/or proceeds from a sale.

Account executives of member brokerage firms will usually act as dealers in over the counter securities when requested to do so by the customer. For example, suppose that an individual desires to purchase 100 shares of Ethyl Corporation common, which in early 1965 was traded only in the over the counter market. Suppose that the price was bid 42, ask 43, and the account executive acquired the 100 shares of Ethyl for the customer and sold it to him at the ask price of 43. The member firm probably had to buy the security from an over the counter dealer. Ordinarily, the over the counter dealer and the member firm split the profit, but the brokerage firm sometimes charges the customer its cost plus a commission determined by the New York Stock Exchange brokerage schedule.

Margin

In opening a margin account, the New York Stock Exchange ordinarily requires that each customer *maintain a margin,* that is, own an equity, in his account of at least $1000. The amount that a customer may borrow to finance either a purchase or a short sale of a listed security is determined by the Board of Governors of the Federal Reserve System. In early 1966, the *initial margin* requirement for a listed stock was 70 percent, and if an individual wished to purchase 50 shares of a stock in a company that was trading for $100 a share, he would be required to put up $3500 of the price and could borrow the additional $1500 from his brokerage firm. The Board of Governors may set the margin between 30 and 100 percent, and from 1960 to 1965 it ranged from 50 to 70 percent. When stock prices are relatively depressed as they were in mid-1962, the margin requirement is usually lowered from 70 to 50 percent, but when stock prices are relatively high, it is sometimes increased to 100 percent. Between 1955 and 1965 70 percent was the usual margin ratio. By changing the margin requirement the Board of Governors of the Federal Reserve System can control the amount of credit used in security transactions.

One well-known brokerage firm, Merrill Lynch, Pierce, Fenner & Smith, requires that the customer maintain at least $2000 in cash and/or securities in his margin account. Some firms limit the use of margin to securities that are trading above a stipulated price, such as $10 per share.

The requirements for maintaining margin on stocks (ordinarily 25 to 30 percent) are less severe than those for initial margin. Suppose that an individual buys 50 shares of a stock at $100 per share including odd lot commission and brokerage fee and the price falls to $40 per share. Instead of being worth $5000, the stock is worth $2000 and the amount still owed on the margin account is $1500 plus the accumulated interest. The customer's margin has dropped below 25 percent, so that he is asked to deposit more margin or allow the security to be sold at the market price, with the proceeds being used to pay off the margin account and the balance being credited to his account. Some brokerage firms require that a margin of at least 30 percent be maintained, rather than the minimum 25 percent required by the New York Stock Exchange for its member firms.

The Board of Governors of the Federal Reserve System also sets the margin requirement on primary issues of securities. In 1966, the margin requirement for the purchase of primary securities was only 30 percent, as compared to the 70 percent required for the purchase of secondary issues. An example of the use of margin in the purchase of a primary issue is as follows: In mid-1964, American Telephone and Telegraph Company made a large rights issue of securities, permitting each stockholder to purchase one additional share of the stock at $100 with each 20 rights. The holder received one right for each share of the common stock of AT&T that he owned. Assuming that an individual held 100 shares of the stock, he received 100 rights, which permitted him to purchase five additional shares at $100 per share directly from the company and not through a brokerage firm. At the time the offer was made, the market price of the stock was between $138 and $142 per share, and before the rights had expired, the company announced that the stock was to be split two for one. A new sale of securities by the rights method frequently depresses the market value of the stock. Conversely, when a corporation raises the dividend rate, declares a stock dividend, or splits a stock into a lower price range, the market price of the security may respond favorably. Many of the recipients of the rights chose to sell them to other interested individuals and did not elect to purchase shares for their own account. The rights were trading for approximately 1¾ to 2¼ each. An individual could have bought 20 rights at about $2 each, paid an additional $100, and received one share of stock in American Telephone and Telegraph Company which was equivalent to the $140 market value on the stock at that time. Assuming that an individual was willing to invest $2000 in rights of AT&T at that time, he could have opened a margin account, bought the rights, and instructed his account executive to exercise them for him. The account executive would have purchased the 50 shares of stock, thus advancing the remaining $5000 in funds. After the stock split two for one, the investor owned 100 shares of AT&T, each worth approximately $68. Two years later, the market price per share had fallen to $52. Although the customer who borrowed the $5000 to purchase the shares was expected to repay the loan within a reasonable amount of time, no time limit was set. The stockholder was receiving the cash dividend of about 3 percent and paying an annual rate of interest on the margin account of from 5 to 6½ percent. Margin calls were made, of course, as the equity of the stockholder declined below 25 percent.

Interest expense is a deductible tax item, with the first $100 in dividends for each stockholder of record exempt from federal income tax. There could conceivably be a tax advantage in buying stock on margin, particularly if the issue is paying a generous dividend. Although some leverage may be generated in this manner, more capital gain can ordinarily be acquired from investing in other than high-dividend-yielding issues.

When a customer maintains a margin account, he is expected to leave the securities in street name or assign the securities to the brokerage firm. The member exchange may then use the securities as collateral for a bank loan that may be needed to finance the margin buying, or the brokerage firm may lend the securities for short-sale transactions.

Payment for a stock purchase is handled differently for a cash account and a margin account. For example, in a cash account a customer may buy a stock one day and sell the securities the next without being required to put up any cash, assuming that his selling price was adequate to cover his purchase price plus his round-trip commission and transfer fees. For a margin account, the transaction must be completed the same day; otherwise, cash, or securities, must be deposited equivalent to the margin required by the Board of Governors of the Federal Reserve System. An investor with a margin account with less than the required margin ratio loses a part of his margin buying power when he sells a security and does not reinvest on the same trading day. For example, assume that the equity in an account is only $7000, the margin is $5000, and an issue is sold for $2000. The customer may reinvest the $2000 in some other issue on the same day without losing his buying power, but if he waits until the following day to place an order for additional securities, a part of his buying power has been lost. He now has equity of $7000, margin of $3000, and no buying power. Many brokerage firms grant the margin buyer the privilege of taking a cash loan up to the amount of his unused buying power.

Summary

Opening a stock account with a member brokerage firm is similar to opening a charge account at a retail store. Certain types of credit information must be supplied, an account number is assigned, and orders for purchasing or selling stocks may be transmitted in person, by telephone, by mail, or by telegram. The account executive should be instructed whether the account is to be a margin or cash account and whether to hold or mail the stock certificates to the customer.

The cost of trading in securities depends upon the type of securities firm, that is, whether a dealer or a brokerage firm, the number of shares bought or sold, and the amount of money involved. Over the counter dealers take a profit equal to their spread between bid and ask prices, while member brokerage firms charge a fixed schedule of brokerage commissions on each purchase and sale. The commission declines in relative cost as the dollar size of the order increases. Purchasers of odd lots must pay a slight premium for their shares.

The security trader may use a wide range of orders in buying or selling stocks, for example, long purchase, short sale, at the market, limited as to time, limited as to price, stop buy orders, stop sell orders, double stop buy or stop sell orders, and numerous others.

Orders for buying or selling listed securities are given to the account executive, and relayed to the floor of the exchange, where the commission broker acts as agent for the customer in obtaining the best possible price for the issue, in keeping with the type of order. The completed transaction appears a few minutes later on the stock ticker. The customer is advised by mail of the price he received or paid for the issue, and cash settlement is made within about four business days.

A customer may use a cash account or a margin account. With the former, he must finance the entire purchase price of the stock, while he is free to borrow a portion of the purchase price in a margin account, at least when the margin requirement as set by the Board of Governors of the Federal Reserve System is below 100 percent. Short sales are permitted only from margin accounts.

QUESTIONS FOR REVIEW /

1. What information does a broker request in opening an account?
2. Why should a customer be willing to give information concerning his financial situation to his account executive?
3. How does the cost of trading in odd lots differ from that of dealing in round lots?
4. Assuming that an individual can invest $200 per month in a given security. Would you suggest that he invest $200 monthly or $600 quarterly? Explain.
5. How is an odd lot order executed?
6. How is a round lot order executed?
7. Explain briefly the significance of the ticker system.
8. What is meant by margin?
9. How is the amount of margin that an individual may use determined?
10. In the event that a security purchased on margin declines, when is a call for more margin ordinarily made?
11. Contrast the advantages and risks involved in the long purchase and the short sale of securities.
12. When would you recommend the use of double stop buy limited orders and double stop sell limited orders?
13. When should limited orders be used?
14. Explain how ordinary stop orders may be used with long purchases and short sales of securities.

PROBLEMS /

1. In May 1964 you opened an account with a brokerage firm and instructed your broker to buy 1000 stock purchase rights that permitted you to purchase 50 shares of American Telephone and Telegraph. Your cost basis for each of the warrants, or rights, was $2 each. You then borrowed the balance, $5000, from your brokerage firm and subscribed to 50 shares of the company. Subsequent to that date, the stock was split two for one, so that you now have 100 shares. Assume that your margin account was assessed at an interest rate of 6 percent per year, computed monthly, and that you repaid one fourth of the margin at the end of each quarter, including accrued interest. Assume that you sold the shares at the closing price in yesterday's market. Determine the total investment cost, including the interest paid, dividends, and the proceeds from the sale of the stock. What was your average return per year on the investment?
2. On January 2 you bought 100 shares of the Acme Company Common at $25 per share, excluding brokerage, and on July 5 you sold the stock at $31 per share. Compute your cost basis, your net selling price, and your profits.

3. Referring to problem 2, contrast the annual rate of return that you would have realized on your commitment of funds using 30 percent margin if you could have borrowed the funds at 6 percent per annum with the return on a cash account. Assume that $1000 minimum equity permits you to use a margin account and the stock paid no cash dividends during the period.

4. In your association with some New York financiers, you heard that the bottom was about to drop out of Xerox common in May 1965. You therefore sold 50 shares of the stock short at $135 per share, including the odd lot differential. You used the maximum amount of margin permitted at that time, 30 percent, and financed the other 70 percent from your savings. Since the broker does not really have to borrow funds for the financing of short sales, you were not required to pay any interest on the margin account. Your account was, however, penalized with the dividends that were declared from the above date to the present time. Assuming that you instruct the account executive to cover the short position, determine the gain or loss from the transaction. Consider any stock dividends or stock splits that may have occurred since 1965. You may find this information by referring to *Moody's Handbook of Common Stocks* or some other source of investment information.

REFERENCES /

Bogen, Jules I., *Financial Handbook*, 3d. ed. New York: The Ronald Press Company ,1952.

Cooke, Gilbert W., *The Stock Market*. New York: Simmons-Boardman Publishing Corporation, 1964.

Federal Tax Course. Prentice-Hall Editorial Staff. Englewood Cliffs, N.J.: Prentice-Hall, Inc., 1961.

Leffler, George L., and Loring C. Farwell, *The Stock Market*, 3d ed. New York: The Ronald Press Company, 1963.

New York Stock Exchange, *Understanding the New York Stock Exchange*. New York: The Exchange, 1964.

chapter 9 | Regulation of Security Trading

Introduction

Prior to the stock market crash of 1929, there were no federal laws requiring that American corporations provide financial and accounting information to their shareholders or to the general public. Although numerous state security laws existed, they were, in many cases, lax or ill defined. Manipulation in security trading and widespread misrepresentation in the financial statements that were distributed to the general public prevailed. These poor security laws and the speculative fever that pervaded the stock market before the 1929 crash resulted in the passage of federal laws to promote a stronger securities market.

The stock market crash of 1929 caused some distrust of the security exchanges and fear of common equities in general and led to a thorough investigation of the whole process of marketing security issues. This investigation led to the passage of six federal security acts and the creation of a new federal agency, the Securities and Exchange Commission (SEC).

On September 5, 1961, Congress ordered the SEC to set up a group of professionals to take a hard look at security markets and trading. The findings of this committee were reported in the *Special Study of Security Markets,* which made recommendations for changes that resulted in the Securities Act Amendments of 1964.

In order to comply with this act, numerous changes have been made in the listing requirements of registered companies, in over the counter security dealing, and in the by-laws of registered exchanges; other proposed changes are still under consideration.

The objectives of this chapter are to summarize the purposes of the federal security laws, indicating their implications for security traders and investors; to describe briefly the state security laws; to explain the by-laws and other requirements of some of the more important registered exchanges; and to outline the requirements and regulations imposed by the National Association of Security Dealers (NASD) upon the over the counter dealers who are members of this organization.[1]

---

[1] Due to the small amount of space that can be allocated to this topic, only brief comments may be devoted to each of these subjects. Where the reader wishes more details concerning the various security laws, the *Special Study,* or other topics dealing with security regulations, he should refer to the footnotes within this chapter or to the list of references at the end of the chapter.

Federal Security Laws

Creation and Purpose of the SEC

For 17 months following President Roosevelt's assumption of office in 1932 the administration conducted a Senate investigation into banking practices and security market operations which culminated in the Securities Act of 1933 and the Securities and Exchange Act of 1934. Although the enforcement of the Securities Act of 1933 was assigned to the Federal Trade Commission, in 1934 it came under the aegis of the SEC when this special governmental agency was created. The SEC is composed of five members, not more than three of whom may belong to the same political party, who are appointed by the President with the advice and consent of the Senate for five-year staggered terms. The chairman of the commission is designated by the President, and the commissioners may not have conflicting outside interests. The commission employs a staff of lawyers and accountants who carry on the activities of opinion writing, general counsel, regulation, and other functions. One of its major objectives has been to improve accounting and auditing standards for companies registering with the SEC and to assist in the establishment and maintenance of high standards of professional conduct by accountants who certify the statements. In addition, the SEC has been assigned the task of enforcing the requirements of the Securities Act of 1933, the Securities Exchange Act of 1934, the Public Utility Holding Company Act of 1935, the Trust Indenture Act of 1939, the Investment Company Act of 1940, and the Investment Advisory Act of 1940. It is authorized to serve in an advisory capacity under Chapter X of the Federal Bankruptcy Act, which provides for the reorganization of a registered industrial company.

Securities Act of 1933

The Securities Act of 1933, often referred to as the "truth in securities law," has two basic objectives, to provide investors with financial and other information concerning the securities offered for public sale and to prohibit misrepresentation, deceit, and other fraudulent acts and practices in the sale of securities. Before a new security offering may be made to the general public, a registration statement must be filed with the SEC. In general, the registration statement must include a description of the registrant's business and its development, a description of any unusual characteristics of the securities to be offered for sale and their relation to the registrant's other capital securities, information concerning the management of the registrant, and certified financial statements. Twenty days after this statement is filed, provided that it has not been amended or the commission does not issue a stop order, the securities may be offered to the general public. The law also requires that a *prospectus,* or an offering circular, setting forth pertinent financial and management information about the concern be furnished to prospective security buyers.

In 1965, the following types of issues were exempted from registration under the Securities Act: first-lien notes; securities of cooperative housing corporations; shares offered in connection with certain transactions, for example, rights issues, shares exchanged for property, or shares issued under a profit-sharing plan or with restrictive stock option plans; U.S. and Canadian government issues; and fractional undivided interest in oil or gas rights up to $100,000.[2] The SEC was also authorized to make a conditional exemption from registration under the Securities Act of 1933 the securities of small business investment companies that are licensed under the Small Business Investment Act of 1958 or that have received the preliminary approval of the Small Business Administration (SBA) to apply for such a license. As long as the small business investment companies comply with the requirements of the SBA, the SEC may exempt them from the provisions of the Securities Act.

In order for an issue to be classified as public and thus require compliance with the Securities Act of 1933, it must be offered to the general public through the mail or through interstate commerce. A private offering of securities or an offering of securities restricted to the residents of the state in which the issuing company is organized to do business is exempt from this registration. Securities of municipal, state, federal, and other governmental instrumentalities, charitable institutions, and certain other regulated industries are exempt from registration, but corporate stock issues made in excess of $300,000 to the general public must comply with this federal law.

The accounting requirement for companies registering under the Securities Act of 1933 and the other acts administered by the commission are set forth in Regulation S-X of the SEC. The principal changes in the Securities Act of 1933 that were made by the Securities Act Amendments of 1964 dealt with the nature of the information to be filed and the kinds of forms that were required to be submitted to the SEC, but the basic law was not changed.

Securities Exchange Act of 1934

The Securities Exchange Act of 1934 was designed to accomplish the following goals: to make available to the public reliable information regarding securities; to eliminate fraud, manipulation, and other abuses in security trading; to insure that just and equitable principles of trade are observed by exchange members and others; to regulate the use of credit for the purchase of securities (the margin requirement is set by the Board of Governors of the Federal Reserve System but is enforced by the SEC and by the NASD);

[2] For an analysis of the various types of exemptions, see Securities and Exchange Commission, *General Rules and Regulations under the Securities Act of 1933* (Washington, D.C.: U.S. Government Printing Office, April 1965), pp. 15–27.

and to regulate trading in securities by insiders in listed securities and the use of voting proxies by corporations whose shares are listed. Extensive changes in the Securities Exchange Act of 1934 were made by the Securities Act Amendments of 1964. Numerous additional changes will no doubt be made by the leading security exchanges and the NASD in order to comply with the provisions of the Securities Act Amendments and in order to eliminate the weaknesses that were revealed in the *Special Study of Security Markets*.

The act requires that exchanges that operate in interstate or foreign commerce and through the mail be registered with the SEC unless they are specifically exempted from such registration. The exchange must file a registration statement providing data on the organization, constitution, by-laws, rules of procedure, and membership. Registration is not granted unless the exchange has adequate rules for disciplining its members. Although the exchanges have wide latitude in their requirements, the rules of the exchanges may not be inconsistent with the act. The commission is permitted to exempt organized stock exchanges from regulations where, in the opinion of the commissioners, exemption would not be contrary to public opinion. In early 1966, 14 exchanges were registered and 3 were exempt from registration, with the latter accounting for less than one tenth of 1 percent of total trading in listed securities.

The *Special Study of Security Markets* pointed out certain dangers in the activities permitted traders and specialists on the New York and American stock Exchanges. The new requirements for these exchanges set a minimum capital standard for the trader, required at least 75 percent of trading to be against the tide, that is, counter to the direction of price movement for an issue, prohibited traders from trading for their own accounts and handling floor orders in the same issue on the same day, and required them to buy or sell in a subordinate position to the general public. These provisions restricted the operations of the trader to the extent that some 270 of the 300 traders did not apply for this type of activity under the new requirements imposed by the New York Stock Exchange.

Under the new rules adopted by the New York Stock Exchange, the specialist has an obligation to utilize his capital as a dealer in assisting in the maintenance of a fair and orderly market. Each exchange must establish minimum capital amounts for specialists and provide effective methods of surveying the activities of these individuals. The exchange must design and enforce rules that assure that the specialists' brokerage customers receive the best possible prices available and that the specialist does not give himself preferential treatment over his customers. The SEC has a right to review and disapprove new exchange rules relating to specialists when it believes them to be inadequate. It was also given the power to bring proceedings directly against the specialist when the exchange fails to do so or when the commissioners feel that the penalities imposed by the exchange are inadequate.

A corporation, except when it is dealing in exempt issues, must be registered with the SEC before its securities may be traded on a registered exchange. Annual reports on Form 10-K must be filed with the commission in order to keep the registration statements up to date, and semiannual and monthly reports are required under certain circumstances. The latter reports take the form of interim financial statements and statements showing transactions in the companies' securities by insiders or individuals holding more than 10 percent of their voting securities.

The Securities Exchange Act of 1934, as amended in 1964, was extended to cover over the counter companies having more than 750 shareholders in mid-1965, more than 500 shareholders beginning in mid-1966, and more than $1 million in assets. Many of the intermediate- and larger-sized corporations that had previously been trading their securities in the over the counter markets are now required to register under the Securities Exchange Act of 1934, and this may encourage some of the companies to apply for listing on one of the major exchanges. Numerous commercial banks have already begun to consider listing on the New York Stock Exchange or on one of the other registered exchanges. Insurance companies, which meet certain conditions, were exempted from this requirement.

The Securities Exchange Act of 1934 was amended in 1936 to provide for the registration of all brokers and dealers who do business in the over the counter markets. This registration consists of filing an application with the commission containing such information as is considered necessary by the SEC. The commission has the power to deny registration, to revoke registration, and to suspend or expel from membership in the NASD. Brokers and dealers who are registered with the SEC are required to file financial reports each calendar year. Criminal penalties, including fines up to $10,000 and/or imprisonment for up to 10 years for individuals and fines up to $500,-000 for exchanges, have been imposed.[3]

Public Utility Holding Company Act of 1935

The purpose of the Public Utility Act was to free electric and gas utility companies from the control of absentee and uneconomical holding companies and their abuses; to give the SEC the power to regulate the sale and issuance of securities, dividend payments, and other factors where the public interest was affected; to forbid parent companies from borrowing from subsidiaries or providing services at excessive costs; and to require reorganization of the companies by January 1, 1938, in order to simplify the corporate structures of public utility holding companies and to liquidate second-degree holding companies. The law provides that a holding company may not have a subsidiary whose subsidiary is in turn a holding company.

[3] The provisions of the Securities Exchange Act of 1934, as amended by the Securities Act Amendments of 1964, that apply to the NASD and its regulation over member brokers and dealers are in a later section of this chapter.

TABLE 9-1 / Registered Holding Company Systems in the United States on June 30, 1965

	Solely Registered Holding Companies	Registered Holding Operating Companies	Electric and/or Gas Utility Subsidiaries	Non-utility Subsidiaries	Inactive Companies	Total Companies	Aggregate System Assets, Less Valuation Reserves, at Dec. 31, 1964[a] (thousands)
1. Allegheny Power System, Inc.	1	1	12	7	1	22	$ 679,623
2. American Electric Power Co., Inc.	1	0	12	9	1	23	1,752,683
3. American Natural Gas Co.	1	0	2	4	—	7	1,003,389
4. Central and South West Corp.	1	1	4	1	1	8	835,215
5. Columbia Gas System, Inc.	1	0	10	9	—	20	1,497,786
6. Consolidated Natural Gas Co.	1	0	4	3	—	8	920,193
7. Delaware Power & Light Co.	0	1	2	—	—	3	246,796
8. Eastern Utilities Associates	1	0	4	—	2	7	108,745
9. General Public Utilities Corp.	1	0	6	3	—	10	1,177,305
10. Middle South Utilities, Inc.	1	0	5	1	3	10	939,702
11. National Fuel Gas Co.	1	0	4	3	—	8	258,146
12. New England Electric System	1	0	16	1	—	18	759,178
13. Ohio Edison Co.	0	1	4	—	—	5	764,204
14. Philadelphia Electric Power Co.	0	1	1	—	1	3	57,810
15. Southern Co.	1	0	5	2	—	8	1,799,000
16. Utah Power & Light Co.	0	1	1	—	—	2	323,488
Subtotals	12	6	92	43	9	162	13,123,263

							[a]
Less: Adjustment to eliminate duplication in count resulting from 3 companies being subsidiaries in 2 systems and 2 companies being subsidiaries in 3 systems[b]		—	—6	—1	0	—7	—
Add: Adjustment to include the assets of these 5 jointly owned subsidiaries and to remove the parent companies' investments therein which are included in the system assets above							293,073
Total companies and assets in active systems	12	6	86	42	9	155	13,416,336

[a] Represents the consolidated assets, less valuation reserves, of each system as reported to the commission on Form U5S for the year 1964.

[b] These five companies are Beachbottom Power Co., Inc., and Windsor Power House Coal Co., which are indirect subsidiaries of American Electric Power Co., Inc., and Allegheny Power System, Inc.; Ohio Valley Electric Corp. and its subsidiary, Indiana-Kentucky Electric Corp., which are owned 37.8 percent by American Electric Power Co., Inc., 16.5 percent by Ohio Edison Co., 12.5 percent by Allegheny Power System, Inc., and 33.2 percent by other companies; and The Arklahoma Corp., which is owned 32 percent by Central and South West Corp. system, 34 percent by Middle South Utilities, Inc., system and 34 percent by an electric utility company not associated with a registered system.

SOURCE: Securities and Exchange Commission, *Annual Report* (Washington, D.C.: U.S. Government Printing Office, 1965), p. 86.

It also stipulates that the operating subsidiaries of a holding company must be limited to an integrated area in one or more adjoining states.

On June 30, 1965, there were 23 holding companies registered under the act, but 5 were relatively small in size and were excluded from the active holding company systems. These included the American Gas Company, British–American Utilities Corporation, Kinzua Oil and Gas Corporation and its subholding company Northwestern Pennsylvania Gas Corporation, and Standard Gas and Electric Company (which was in the process of dissolution). Of the remaining 18, two were classified as subholding companies. On June 30, 1965, the 16 remaining public utility holding company systems were composed of 155 companies with total net assets of $13.4 billion. A list of these companies appears in Table 9-1.

Trust Indenture Act of 1939

The Trust Indenture Act was intended to protect holders of corporate bonds and required that the *indenture*, or the contract between the issuer and the bond trustee, contain standard protective provisions, that essential provisions of trust indentures be more fully disclosed to the holders, and that responsible, disinterested trustees be selected by the companies falling under the jurisdiction of the act. A corporation that makes a public sale of bonds in excess of $1 million must, in general, comply with this act, but where the issue is for an amount smaller than $1 million or where the issue is sold in private placement, it is exempt from registration under this law. Although the bond trustee is paid for his services by the corporation that makes the issue, he is an agent of the bondholders and must report to them within 90 days in cases where an interest payment, principal repayment, or sinking fund payment is omitted or where the corporation has committed an act of bankruptcy.

Investment Company Act of 1940

The Investment Company Act regulates investment companies not registered under the Securities Act of 1933 or the Securities Exchange Act of 1934. The act requires honest and unbiased management; greater participation in management by security holders—for example, two thirds of the directors must be elected by the shareholders; adequate and feasible capital structure, with limitations on the amount and the number of issues of bonds and preferred stock; transmission of financial reports to security holders containing prescribed information, at least semiannually; and compliance with certain selling practices. It limits the amount of load charge, or selling commission, that may be assessed and requires investment companies to furnish a prospectus to prospective customers which gives some financial information about the concern and a description of its management and operating policies.

Investment Advisory Act of 1940

All individuals or organizations that for compensation act as security advisers, either directly or in writing, must be registered with the SEC. Registration statements and semiannual reports must be submitted to the SEC. Certain types of individuals, such as bankers, attorneys, teachers, accountants, and others are exempt.

Adviser to a Reorganization Plan

In addition to being the enforcement agency for the above six security laws, the SEC is authorized under Chapter X of the Federal Bankruptcy Act, which is designed for reorganization of an industrial corporation that lists with a registered security exchange, to appear as a party to a reorganization proceeding, either on its own motion if approved by a federal judge or at the request of a judge. It is the function of the SEC to study the reorganization plan and to submit a report on whether the plan or plans submitted are feasible, fair, and equitable. In order to be feasible, the plan should eliminate the need for further reorganization on subsequent dates. In order to be fair and equitable, the plan should treat each class of securities or creditors and each security owner in each of these categories in accordance with their legal priority and on a parity with others. The judge may accept or reject the report of the SEC, since the commission serves only in an advisory capacity, with the final decision left to the federal judge.[4]

State Security Laws

All except two states have formulated security laws to combat fraud in the issuance of securities. These laws are commonly referred to as "blue-sky laws," since the laws of some states were once so lax as to permit a piece of sky to be sold to prospective security owners. The Securities Act of 1933 provides for state regulation of security issues even though a company may be required to register under the federal act. For companies that make an issue (1) too small to require registration under the Securities Act of 1933, (2) sold in intrastate commerce, or (3) exempted from registration under the federal act, only registration under the state act is required. Some states, such as New York, Illinois, and California, have adopted relatively rigid laws dealing with security regulations, while the laws of other states are considerably more lenient.

The registration of securities in most states usually takes one of three forms. Registration may be made by *qualification* and becomes effective by

---

[4] For an up-to-date listing of companies that have recently undergone reorganization and for which the SEC has served in an advisory capacity, see the current SEC *Annual Report*.

affirmative action taken by the state security official, or registration may be through *notification,* which merely requires an apprisal by the issuer filed with the state security commission advising it of the pending security offer. Where no positive opposition is taken by the state regulatory agency, the registration becomes effective within a stipulated time period. Some states provide for a third type of registration, *coordination,* which is available only for issues registered under the Securities Act of 1933.

In order to promote the uniformity of state security antifraud laws, the commissioners on uniform state laws developed a Uniform Securities Act in 1956, but by the end of 1961 only 14 states had adopted it. The state security laws that are enforced in a majority of states continue to be much more lenient, in most cases, than the federal laws. The weaknesses associated with state security laws are failure on the part of state administrative officials to formulate tools for the guidance of the security industry and to publicize adequately the administrative practices with regard to these security laws.[5]

Exchange Regulations

The New York Stock Exchange

The listing requirements of the New York Stock Exchange are much more severe than those of other exchanges, and the by-laws and regulations that control the operation of the members of the exchange are extensive. In order to list its securities on the New York Stock Exchange, a company must meet certain qualifications and must be willing to keep the investing public informed with regard to the state of its finances. The company must either be a going concern or a successor to a going concern (through acquisition, merger, or consolidation). In considering whether to accept or reject listing, the New York Stock Exchange gives attention to the degree of national interest in the company, the relative position of the company within an industry, the firm's growth potential or lack of it, and other factors. Although each case is decided on its own merits, the general requirements for initial listing by the exchange are as follows: a demonstrated earning power under competitive conditions of at least $2 million annually before taxes and $1.2 million after all charges and taxes; net tangible assets of at least $10 million, with emphasis being placed on the amount of the stock that is held publicly; and at least 600,000 common shares publicly held among not less than 1500 round lot shareholders.

Listing on an exchange does offer some advantages to a corporation in that millions of investors view the trading transactions daily for the outstanding securities. Frequently stocks trading on the Big Board sell at higher multiples of earnings than do those traded on other exchanges. About 80 to 87 percent of the dollar volume of trading in listed stocks on registered ex-

---

[5] See Richard W. Jennings and Harold Marsh, Jr., *Security Regulations* (Brooklyn, N.Y.: The Foundation Press, Inc., 1963), pp. 467–468.

changes takes place on the New York Stock Exchange. Although the company that lists its securities on any registered stock exchange must comply with certain security regulations, listing on the Big Board gives a company prestige. On the other hand, when the listed company gets into financial difficulty, the general public becomes aware of the situation almost immediately. The market prices of listed securities frequently fluctuate more widely than do those of unlisted securities, because more financial information is available on the former, which influences investor sentiment.

The exchange reserves the right at any time to suspend or delist a company when the board of governors of the exchange considers that continued dealing in the security is not in the public interest. In 1965, the exchange normally considered the suspension or removal of a company from its list if (1) the number of round lot holders fell below 600, (2) less than 250,000 shares were in the hands of the general public, (3) the market value of publicly held shares declined to below $2 million, (4) the aggregate market value of all outstanding common shares fell below $4 million, or (5) the earnings after taxes averaged less than $400,000 during the last three years.

Listed companies are required to provide, through timely disclosures to the general public, their earnings statements, dividend notices, and other information affecting security values and investment judgments. The exchange also requires that active operating companies agree to solicit proxies for all meetings of stockholders, to advise the shareholders on the items to be voted on at the meetings, and to show how management recommends the proxies to be voted. The exchange refuses to list nonvoting common stocks or voting common stock issues for a company that has a class of nonvoting common stock.[6]

The 1366 members of the New York Stock Exchange are regulated by the constitution and by-laws of the exchange, the rules of the stock clearing corporation and those of the board of governors of the New York Stock Exchange, and the Securities Exchange Act of 1934, as amended.[7] Before an individual may acquire membership on the exchange, he must make a personal statement concerning his business history, pass a physical examination, be sponsored by two or more individuals who have been members or allied members of the exchange for at least one year, pass an examination showing a knowledge of the securities industry, and present letters of recommendation from three or more persons. The applicant and his exchange-member sponsors must appear before the subcommittee for admissions—a committee of the board of governors of the exchange. Election to membership then requires a two-thirds affirmative vote by the 33 members of the board of governors of the exchange. The seat may be paid for in cash or

[6] See New York Stock Exchange, *The New York Stock Exchange Factbook* (New York: The Exchange, 1964), p. 7.

[7] These rules are much too detailed and complex to explain in the small amount of space allocated to this subject; however, they may be found in New York Stock Exchange, *The Guide* (New York: The Exchange, 1962).

amortized over three years.[8] Until 1953, membership on the New York Stock Exchange was limited to individuals or to partnerships, but since that date employees of corporations have also been admitted to membership. In 1965, an unincorporated member firm was required to maintain a capital account of at least $50,000, while the amount was $60,000 for a member corporation. The rules of the exchange require that each member firm that maintains accounts for its customers be audited annually by a certified public accountant.

Misconduct by members of the exchange, which may take the form of violation of the exchange constitution, rules, or capital requirements, fraudulent acts, fictitious transactions, material misstatements, or violation of the Securities Exchange Act of 1934, may result in disciplinary action being brought against the member. Such action may be in the form of a fine, suspension, expulsion, or a combination of these. The board of governors of the New York Stock Exchange may impose fines of up to $5000 per violation, and severe penalties may result in suspension of trading on the exchange for a limited period of time, such as one month, one year, or permanently. The SEC reserves the right under the Securities Act Amendments of 1964 to impose additional penalties upon members if in its opinion the member has not been subjected to adequate disciplinary action. In cases where the laws of the registered exchanges are judged adequate for chastising the members, the SEC leaves disciplinary action to the exchanges.

The American Stock Exchange

Numerous scandals were associated with the American Stock Exchange before its reorganization in 1962, and criticisms were leveled at the "free-wheeling attitude" and conduct of the members of the exchange. As a result of the 1960–1962 investigation of the American Stock Exchange, its president resigned and 14 of its members were either suspended or disciplined in some other way. Since 1962, however, the exchange has been reorganized and has pledged itself to the handling of better-quality stocks, to maintaining more stable markets, and to tightening its discipline of members. The American Stock Exchange also enacted a program of increasing its membership.

In order to be eligible for membership on the American Stock Exchange a person must meet certain requirements. An individual must be between 21 and 60 years of age when making application, be a citizen of the United States with a good character and reputation, have at least $10,000 in liquid assets above the cost of his membership, be trained under the supervision of a floor member before he is permitted to execute orders on the floor without

---

[8] For a detailed analysis of membership and organization of stock exchanges, see Gilbert W. Cooke, *The Stock Market* (New York: Simmons-Boardman Publishing Corporation, 1964), pp. 196–209.

supervision, and if he is a specialist candidate, pass an examination for specialists after a period of training. The applicant for membership makes a bid for a seat on the exchange, is required to take a physical examination by a qualified physician, and must deposit with the exchange an amount equal to at least 20 percent of the purchase price of the seat and sign a note for the balance. The applicant and/or his sponsors must appear for an interview before the admissions committee; in the case of out-of-town applicants a letter may be submitted instead of a coming in for a personal interview. The admissions committee then either recommends election of the candidate or decides not to recommend membership and presents its findings to the board of governors. A majority of the members of the board of governors present at the meeting (at least 10) must vote in the affirmative to accept the new applicant; otherwise the application is not approved. During the early 1960s, seats on the American Stock Exchange traded for from $50,000 to $60,000.

An individual may apply for associate membership on the exchange if he is at least 21 years of age and is actively engaged in the business of buying and selling securities as a broker or dealer, either as a partner of a firm or as an executive, director, or officer of a corporation.[9] In 1963, the cost of becoming an associate member of the exchange was $5000, and the associate member was required to pay a brokerage commission and clearing charges of 40 percent of the nonmember rate. This figure was raised from 35 to 40 percent in 1963 in an attempt to gain full membership from many of the associate members, and some 100 elected to become full members. Associate members are generally subject to the same restrictions as members regarding (1) business affiliations, (2) application procedures, and (3) obligations of membership.

Members and associate members of the American Stock Exchange who violate the constitution, by-laws, or requirements of the exchange or perform an act detrimental to the interest or welfare of the exchange are subject to a written charge, an appearance before the board (without counsel) to answer charges, and possible disciplinary action. Disciplinary action may take the form of a fine, suspension, expulsion, or a combination of these. Members or associate members are subject to suspension or expulsion for fraud, fictitious transactions, action leading to demoralization, for example, upsetting the market balance between supply and demand, misstatement of material fact in information given to the board of governors of the exchange or to one of the exchange officers, fraud prior to becoming a member of the exchange, dealing on another exchange, violating the constitution or rules of the exchange, or violating the Securities Exchange Act. Fines not to exceed $10,000 may be imposed on the member or associate member in lieu of suspension or expulsion.

[9] For a more complete analysis of the admission of members to the American Stock Exchange, see Commerce Clearing House, Inc., *The American Stock Exchange Guide* (Chicago: Commerce Clearing House, 1962), pp. 8495–8497.

The National Association of Security Dealers

The Securities Exchange Act of 1934, as amended by the Maloney Act in 1938, requires that associations of security dealers be registered with the SEC. The NASD is the only such association that had been registered by 1966. Membership in the NASD is made up of brokers and dealers across the nation, and its objectives are as follows:

> To adopt, administer, and enforce rules of fair practice and rules to prevent fraudulent and manipulative acts and practices, and in general to promote just and equitable principles of trade for the protection of investors;
>
> To promote self-discipline among members, and to investigate and adjust grievances between the public and the members and between members.
>
> To promote a medium through which its membership may be enabled to confer, consult, and coordinate with governmental and other agencies in solution of problems affecting investors, the public, and the investment banking and securities businesses;
>
> To promote through cooperative effort the investment banking and securities business, to standardize its principles and practices, to promote therein high standards of commercial honor, and to encourage and promote among members observance of Federal and state securities laws.[10]

Some 4000 broker–dealers are members of the NASD and must comply with its rules and regulations. Section 1 of the NASD Rules of Fair Practice states that "A member, in the conduct of his business, shall observe high standards of commercial honor and just and equitable principles of trade."[11] These rules, some 28 sections in number, cover such areas as recommendations of securities, charges for services performed, fair prices and commission, the use of information obtained in fiduciary capacity, disclosure requirements, fraudulent devices, selling concessions, and others. The Rules of Fair Practice established by the NASD recognize that the security dealers are in the business to make a profit, but require that the practices be fair. In general, the NASD encourages that the spread between bid and ask, or the profit margin made by the over the counter dealer, be 5 percent or less. This stated percentage does not apply to certain types of transactions, such as primary issues or the sale of investment company shares. The NASD recognizes that a larger markup is needed for a stock trading at a low price than for an issue trading at a high price. A proper markup should consider the type of security, the marketability of the issue, its price, the amount of the transaction, and the nature of the member's business.

There are a number of advantages in having a voluntary association of security broker–dealers such as the NASD. This association has generally

---

[10] National Association of Security Dealers, *The National Association of Security Dealers* (Washington, D.C.: Board of Governors of the Association, 1959), p. 2.

[11] See, for example, National Association of Security Dealers, *NASD Manual* (Washington, D.C.: The Association, March 1964), d-5.

promoted fair dealing in the security market, and members are authorized to split their fees in cases where several broker–dealers are involved in a transaction. Members are prohibited from splitting their fees with non-members.

Disciplinary action of the NASD is administered through a complaint process, with charges of violating one or more of the rules of the association forming the basis for a complaint. The NASD examines the charges in order to establish whether they are based on reasonable grounds, and if it finds that they are justified, a complaint is filed, which may be initiated by the general public or by one member of the association against another. The penalty may be in the form of a censure, fine, suspension, or expulsion from the association. If a delinquent member believes that the penalty imposed upon him is unjustly severe, he may register a complaint with the SEC. The SEC then reviews the findings of the NASD and may uphold the action, waive the penalty, or impose a more severe sentence.

A major function of the NASD is to continuously inspect the books and records of members to ascertain whether or not the rules have been or are being violated. Althought the NASD has been doing a difficult job, the SEC's *Special Study of Security Markets* of 1961 and 1962 pointed out some areas of weaknesses within the association. One of the major criticisms was that the association has too few qualified examiners. Although it is the stated intention of the NASD to examine one third of the main offices of its members each year, it has been falling far short of this goal. In one of the 13 districts of the NASD, for example, no member was examined between 1954 and 1957. The branch offices were examined on approximately 10-year cycles. Another problem is the inability of the association to examine new members within six months of their admission. Important areas of violations of NASD membership are the requirements of Regulation T, which concerns cash and margin accounts, and operation by NASD members while insolvent without disclosing that fact to the customer.

The *Special Study of Security Markets* also emphasized the weakness in the *wholesale quotation system* through which dealers advertise their buying and selling interest in securities traded over the counter. These *quotation sheets*, published in three different divisions of the United States and covering both equities and bonds, must indicate whether the bid–ask quotations are entered for the broker–dealer on behalf of himself or in conjunction with another broker–dealer. In cases where several broker–dealers are involved, this information must be indicated.

Summary

Inconsistent accounting practices, poor financial reporting, outright fraud by many corporate officials, and manipulation of the securities markets contributed to the overvaluation of security prices up to 1929 and to the stock market crash of 1929. An investigation into the causes of the crash resulted in the creation of the SEC and the passage of six federal security laws designed to promote a more healthy atmosphere in the security market in general and a greater public trust in investment in American business. These laws included the Securities Act of 1933, the Securities Exchange Act of 1934, the Public Utility Holding Company Act of 1935, the Trust Indenture Act of 1939, the Investment Company Act of 1940, and the Investment Advisory Act of 1940.

No major changes in the federal security laws were made between 1941 and 1964, but a thorough investigation of the operation of the securities markets and practices of members of registered exchanges and over the counter dealers resulted in the 1964 passage of the Securities Act Amendments. Although this legislation made numerous modifications in the original laws, two of these probably have particularly far-reaching effects on the operation of the securities markets. Under these amendments, the New York and the American stock exchanges were required to impose greater restrictions on the trading of specialists and floor traders. The positions of these members were required to be subordinate to that of the general public. In addition, corporations that traded their securities over the counter and that had more than $1 million in assets and more than 750 shareholders were required to register with the SEC during 1965, and those with more than 500 but less than 750 shareholders were required to register by mid-1966. Generally, life insurance companies were exempted from this registration provision in cases where certain requirements were met. However, numerous banks and other companies that had been trading their securities in the over the counter markets were required to comply. Many of these companies may well apply for listing on one of the major exchanges.

The Securities Act Amendments gave the SEC greater regulatory authority over the NASD and members of that voluntary association. Where NASD dealer–brokers violate the requirements of the SEC or the requirements of the NASD, the SEC may bring action directly against the individual where the penalties imposed by the NASD are deemed to be inadequate by the SEC.

QUESTIONS FOR REVIEW /

1. Do you believe there is a need for a federal agency such as the SEC? Explain.
2. How does the Securities Exchange Act differ from the Securities Act of 1933?
3. Explain briefly the other acts that have been assigned to the SEC for enforcement. Do you believe that these acts are necessary for the promotion of a healthy securities market?
4. What actions led to the 1961–1962 Senate investigation of the securities markets? What were the results of this investigation?
5. In general, how do the state security laws differ from the federal security laws? Must a company comply with both sets of these rules? Are these federal rules consistent with your state security laws?
6. Do you believe that all companies that are eligible for listing on the Big Board should seek such listing? Why or why not?

7. How may an associate membership on the American Stock Exchange be obtained? Would this be advantageous for an over the counter dealer? Explain.
8. What useful purpose(s) does the NASD fulfill?
9. How are over the counter dealers regulated?
10. What disciplinary action may be brought against NASD members by either the association or by the SEC for violation of NASD rules and regulations?
11. Do you believe that security markets should be regulated or unregulated? What additions or deletions in the federal regulations would you recommend.

PROBLEMS /

1. From the most recent issue of an *Annual Report* of the SEC, analyze the action taken by the SEC against some company for violation of the provisions of the Securities Act of 1933 or the Securities Exchange Act of 1934. Do you believe that the action taken by the SEC was justified or excessive?
2. Analyze the proceedings brought by the SEC against some member of a registered exchange and comment on the fairness of the penalties imposed.
3. Make a listing of the public utility holding systems that are required to register under the Public Utility Holding Company Act of 1935 and indicate the relative holdings of these companies compared to the total public utility industry. Has there been any recent action by the SEC against any of the companies required to register under this act? Explain.
4. By reference to the most recent *Annual Report* of the SEC, summarize the action and penalty imposed against a certified public accounting firm for failure to observe the accounting requirements of the SEC for registered companies as outlined in Regulation S-X. Do you believe these penalties were justified? What possible outcomes could severe penalties have upon the continued operation of accounting firms? Do you believe that accounting firms should attempt to practice under the SEC?

REFERENCES /

Commerce Clearing House, Inc., *The American Stock Exchange Guide.* Chicago: Commerce Clearing House, 1962.

Cooke, Gilbert W., *The Stock Market.* New York: Simmons-Boardman Publishing Corporation, 1964.

Bogen, Jules I., *Financial Handbook,* 3d. ed. New York: The Ronald Press Company, 1952.

Friend, Erwin, D. Wright Hoffman, and Willis I. Winn, *The Over-the-Counter Security Markets.* New York: McGraw-Hill Book Company, Inc., 1958.

Leffler, George L., and Loring C. Farwell, *The Stock Market,* 3d ed. New York: The Ronald Press Company, 1963.

National Association of Security Dealers, *The National Association of Security Dealers.* Washington, D.C.: Board of Governors of the Association, 1959.

———, *NASD Manual.* Wilmington, Del.: The Association, March 1964.

U.S. Securities and Exchange Commission, *Annual Reports.* Washington, D.C.: U.S. Government Printing Office, selected issues.

———, *General Rules and Regulations under the Securities Act of 1933.* Washington, D.C.: U.S. Government Printing Office, April 1965.

———, *Statistical Bulletin.* Washington D.C.: U.S. Government Printing Office, February 1965.

chapter 10 | Marketing Security Issues

Introduction

During the early 1960s, American corporations were investing about $40 to $50 billion annually in new plant and equipment in this country and an additional $3 to $5 billion in the same investment in foreign countries. With the liberalization of the depreciation method permitted by the Internal Revenue Service, and with the retention of approximately 50 percent of net income for reinvestment purposes, American corporations have found a need to float new corporate security issues each year, the total approximating some $10 to $16 billion annually.

The various types of new corporate securities, for example, bonds and preferred and common stock, sold for cash in the United States are listed in Figure 10-1, which indicates that from 1953 to 1965 debt issues accounted for some 80 to 90 percent of the total new corporate securities offered for cash in the United States. During 1962 and 1963, when the prices of common stocks were relatively low, debt issues increased in importance. Conversely, common stock offerings grew in relative importance during 1961 and 1964, when common stock prices were relatively high. Although this timing of a sale proves to be advantageous to a corporation in that it raises a larger supply of funds with fewer shares or bonds, the individual investor must be careful not to pay an excessive price for such issues, since there is a likelihood that their market price will fall during a subsequent bear market.

Of the total debt issues made in the United States from 1953 through 1965, public offerings were relatively more popular from 1953 through 1958, while private placements gained in relative importance from 1959 through 1965. Private placement of debt is primarily with large life insurance companies rather than with the general public through underwriters, but pension funds, trust funds, and other financial institutions also buy large blocks of bonds directly from the issuers.

In addition to the sale of new corporate securities in the primary markets, parent corporations, financial institutions, large estates, or corporate officers frequently find it desirable to make block distributions of shares in a given company, and a considerable amount of trading in outstanding securities is facilitated through registered exchanges and in the over the counter markets.

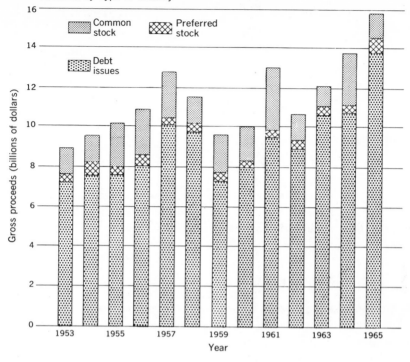

Classified by Type of Security

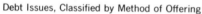

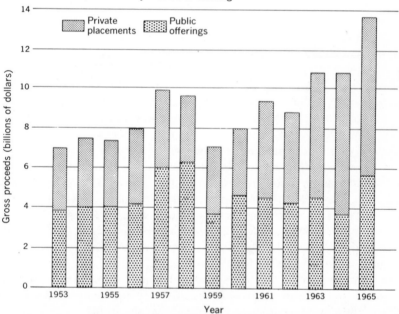

Debt Issues, Classified by Method of Offering

FIGURE 10-1 / New corporate securities offered for cash in the United States, 1953–1965. From Securities and Exchange Commission, *Statistical Bulletin,* Washington, D.C., U.S. Government Printing Office, February 1965, p. 15.

The purposes of this chapter are to discuss some of the advantages and disadvantages of various types of primary issues, for example, public sales, rights issues, and private placements; to describe the methods used for making block distributions; and to show the relative importance of trading in the outstanding securities by listed and nonlisted business corporations.

Primary Issues

Before the board of directors of a corporation decides to make a preemptive rights issue of stock, a public sale of stock, or a private placement of securities or to offer the securities for sale on a competitive bid basis, a number of factors are considered. First and most important, the board of directors considers the legality of the issue and whether or not the market will absorb it.

Preemptive Rights Issues

The corporation laws of some states require that a new issue of common stock or securities convertible to common stock first be made to the old shareholders on a prorated basis before being offered to the general public. Some states do not require privileged subscriptions unless specifically provided for in the charter or by-laws of the corporation, while others permit this privilege to be waived by a corporation's charter or by-laws. Before deciding to make a preemptive rights issue, the board of directors of the corporation determines the legality of the issue. If the shares must be offered to the old stockholders before being offered to the general public, authorization and a waiver of this privilege must be obtained from the shareholders before the securities can be offered to other individuals. This method is frequently used by a business corporation that makes shares of the company stock available to officers and employees under a restrictive or employee stock option plan (see Chapter 17).

In a preemptive issue, *rights*—sometimes referred to as *stock purchase warrants*—are issued to the holder of stock which authorize him to purchase additional shares at a lower price than the prevailing market value. For example, in May 1964 the American Telephone and Telegraph Company made a rights issue of common stock, which was being traded at approximately $142 per share (prior to a two for one stock split that occurred in September 1964). Each holder of AT&T stock received the number of rights equivalent to the shares of stock he held, and 20 rights plus $100 were required for the purchase of one additional share. In a situation such as this, the shares of stock trade *rights-on,* that is, with the rights, for a period of time and trade *ex-rights,* that is, separate from the rights, during the period in which the owners may exercise their rights. The ex-rights period lasts from about two weeks to one month, and during this period the recipients of the rights may either exercise them or sell them to someone else. For securities listed on a registered exchange, the shares go ex-rights four business days prior to the date of record, which is the date used to determine who receives the rights. On the ex-rights day, each share is expected to be reduced by the value of one right, and the theoretical value of one right may be computed as follows: $V = (M - S)/(N + 1)$, where V represents the value of each right, M represents the market value of one share of stock prior to going ex-rights, S represents the subscription price per share, and N denotes the number of rights required to purchase one additional share of stock. In our example, the theoretical value of one right was equal to $(142 - 100)/(N + 1)$, or 21, or $2 per right. The actual trading range for the rights of American Telephone and Telegraph Company was slightly above and slightly below this figure. The rights traded from approximately $1\frac{3}{4}$ to $2\frac{3}{16}$, and the value of the rights was influenced directly by the fluctuation in market value of the common stock. During the ex-rights period, the ratio for determining the theoretical market value of a right is similar to the above, except that the 1 is dropped from the denominator. The management of a corporation should consider the value of each right in setting the subscription price of the stock, since the key to a fully subscribed rights issue is the relative size of the issue compared to the number of shares already outstanding and the difference between the subscription price and the prevailing market value. Since the market value of common shares fluctuates widely, the period in which the rights trade on their own merits and within which they may be exercised is usually relatively short. Rights that expire are worthless.

An investor must decide whether (1) to exercise his rights, thus acquiring additional shares of stock in the corporation or (2) to sell the rights and let someone else exercise them; in any case he must make a proper accounting to the taxing authorities. He may consider the entire proceeds from the sale of rights as a capital gain, or he may elect to prorate his old cost basis for each share between each right and each share of stock on the basis of the market value of each on the day of the sale. The latter method is required if the value of one right is equal to more than 15 percent of the market value of the share of stock and may be elected irrespective of their values. The holding period for the shares of stock determines the long-term or short-term capital gain position. Where rights are exercised, the old cost basis per share is prorated between the old shares and the value of the rights.

Mr. Hadley, who had bought 500 shares in the Watley Corporation at $20 per share in 1965, received 500 rights that permitted him to subscribe to 100 new shares of common stock at $15 per share. The market value of the stock was $30, rights-on. The theoretical market value of each right was:

$$V = \frac{M - S}{N + 1} = \frac{\$30 - 15}{(5 + 1)} = \frac{\$15}{6} = \$2.50$$

Since the value of each right is less than 15 percent of the market value of one share, Mr. Hadley may elect either of the two methods for determining his capital gain on a sale of the rights. Under the former method, the entire $1250 selling price may be considered a long-term capital gain. As an alternative, his gain may be computed by allocating the cost of the old shares between the shares and rights on the basis of market value of each on the date of sale. Assume that the rights are worth $2.50 each and the stock worth $27.50 per share during the ex-rights period. The adjusted cost basis of each share is $27.50/($27.50 + $2.50) × $20 = $18.33, and the cost basis of each right is $2.50/($27.50 + $2.50) × $20 = $1.67. The long-term capital gain is computed as follows: (500 shares)($2.50 − $1.67) = $415. Assuming the same facts except that the rights are exercised, the cost basis on the old 500 shares is computed as above, $18.33 per share, and the cost basis of each new share is $15 + 1.67, or $16.67. The owner is required to use the first-in, first-out method of accounting in assigning a cost to shares actually disposed of unless he can specifically produce each stock and show the date he acquired the stock and its exact cost.

There are at least three reasons why the market value of shares sold on a rights basis is expected to decline. First, since the subscription price of the stock is lower than the prevailing market price, the market value of each share is expected to fall by the value of one right. Second, the floating supply of the issue has been increased, and the demand for the issue may have been overcome by the supply, thus resulting in some additional selling pressure and lower market prices of the shares. Third, when a corporation raises new amounts of capital, the funds may earn a lower return for several months after their acquisition than other corporate assets, leading to a dilution in the earnings per share of the stock and resulting in a decline in the market value of the stock. Of course, this reasoning also applies to the sale of an issue of common stock to the general public, but the discount on a rights issue is usually greater than the flotation costs, for example, underwriting and registration fees, of a public stock sale.

A study that appeared in the October 1958 issue of *The Magazine of Wall Street* indicated that rights issues are usually made during a bull market. In many cases the market value of the shares later falls below the subscription price, and the investor would have made money by selling his rights and buying additional shares at subsequent depressed prices. Theoretically, the market value of each share of stock should be diluted by the value of one right, so the investor has little to gain or to lose in making the new acquisition. He may, however, wish to protect his present holdings in the corporation and may have a feeling of responsibility to aid the corporation in financing an expansion program. The investor is not unduly concerned with upward and downward oscillation in his stock's market value, but the trader is reluctant to buy new shares in a corporation that is making a rights issue. One who elects to sell his rights and/or his shares of stock in the corporation may usually maximize the selling price of his rights and/or the purchase of additional stock by selling the rights at an early date. One who buys rights, conversely, usually should wait until near the end of the ex-rights period when the rights are somewhat depressed in value.

Usually some 5 to 25 rights offerings are made each year by companies that list their securities on the New York Stock Exchange. For example, when the market prices of securities were rising during the strong bull markets of 1955 and 1956, some 21 and 22 rights issues, respectively, were made by industrial companies that listed on the New York Stock Exchange. In 1957, when stock market prices had begun to decline, only 15 companies made rights issues: the number fell to 7 in 1958; and in 1963, only 3 industrial corporations, Burroughs Corporation, Celanese Corporation of America, and National Aviation Corporation, made common stock rights offerings. Five utility companies also elected this method, and 4 other New York Stock Exchange industrial companies chose to make convertible debenture offerings. One utility, Pacific Telephone and Telegraph Company, offered stock in Pacific Northwest Bell Telephone Company on a rights basis. In 1963, the general level of stock market prices was recovering from a 20 percent decline that occurred during the second quarter of 1962, as measured by the popular averages.[1]

If the board of directors of a corporation believes that the old stockholders or purchasers of the warrants will not exercise all their rights, a *stand-by underwriting agreement,* that is, an agreement to offer unsubscribed shares to the general public, may be made with an investment banking firm or an underwriting syndicate. When General Motors Corporation made a $325 million stock issue in 1955, it negotiated a stand-by underwriting agreement. Only 2 percent of the rights were not exercised, and therefore only $6 million of the stock had to be offered to the general public by the underwriting group, which consisted of more than 300 investment banking firms.

Instead of arranging for a stand-by public offering, which requires registration with the SEC and the payment of an underwriting fee, some corporate management groups prefer to extend an oversubscription privilege to their shareholders, which permits them to subscribe to more shares of stock than they have rights. The rights that have not been exercised are then redistributed to the oversubscribers on a prorated basis.

A similar method is for a corporation to attempt to raise a larger amount of funds than it actually needs, so that if only 80 or 90 percent of the rights are exercised the proceeds from the sale will meet the need for funds. Since corporations that make rights issues without the stand-by arrangement are not required to file with the SEC, it is difficult to find statistics on the number of rights that have been exercised and the number that have expired. If substantially all the rights have been exercised, the corporation may frequently advertise this fact; but if the issue is poorly subscribed, there is usually no public notice.

[1] For a list of rights offerings by New York Stock Exchange companies, see *The Exchange* or *The New York Stock Exchange Factbook.* The latter may be obtained free of charge by writing to the New York Stock Exchange and requesting the booklet.

Public Sales of Securities

Domestic corporations that sell shares of stock to the general public in excess of $300,000 or corporations that make public bond issues in excess of $1 million must register under the Securities Act of 1933 or the Trust Indenture Act of 1939, respectively. After effective registration with the SEC and after a 20-day waiting period, assuming that no amendment to the registration material has been filed and that the SEC has not issued a stop order, the corporation's underwriting group may proceed with the public sale of securities.

Table 10-1 indicates that of the $16 billion in new securities offered for cash in the United States during 1965, about 47 percent was represented by public issues, and of this amount, issues totaling $6.4 million were registered under the 1933 Securities Act. Additional issues totaling $999 million were unregistered, while railroad issues, which do not have to be registered with the SEC, accounted for some $262 million. Small issues, which are made under Regulation A, a simplified registration procedure, of the SEC amounted to $43 million during the year, and private placements totaled some $8.5 billion. Noncorporate issues, which include issues made by the federal government, agencies, and states, amounted to some $24 billion in 1965. Comparative statistics for 1962–1965 are shown in Table 10-1 and reveal that both private and nonprivate borrowers were raising more funds in 1965 than in 1962 and 1963.

The Securities Act and the Trust Indenture Act require that a prospectus be made available to the prospective purchasers of new securities. The prospectus makes public information concerning the history and operations of the company, presents audited financial statements and descriptions of other security types as well as the characteristics of the issue being made, and indicates how the proceeds are to be used, the underwriting costs, and the offering price of the issue. The latter is ordinarily not set until one or two days prior to the offering date in order to determine the market price of similar issues. To facilitate the sale of the issue, the selling group, or underwriters, sets up a trading account and "pegs the price of the issue" during the offering period. For example, suppose that World Wide Drug Corporation elects to sell one million shares of stock to the public when the market price of the stock is 20¼. The underwriting group decides to offer the stock to the general public at 20 per share (no brokerage commission is required with a primary issue), and limited buy orders are placed with the specialist for the issue at 19¾ to 20 per share, thus maintaining the market value at about 20. After the sale is completed—which may require only one to three days, or in a weak market, more than a month—the limited buy orders are cancelled, thus permitting supply and demand to set the market value. Assuming that the underwriting agreement called for the payment

TABLE 10-1 / Securities Offerings: Estimated Gross Proceeds from the New Securities Offered for Cash in the United States (in thousands of dollars)

	1962	1963	1964	1965
All Offerings	29,956,043	31,616,257	37,121,630	40,108,205
Corporate	10,704,562	12,236,646	13,956,774	15,992,343
Noncorporate	19,251,482	19,379,611	23,164,857	24,115,862

CORPORATE OFFERINGS, BY INDUSTRY

	1962	1963	1964	1965
Manufacturing	3,249,364	3,543,191	3,046,227	5,416,839
Extractive	208,927	214,132	420,946	342,074
Electric, gas, and water	2,825,367	2,668,319	2,759,885	2,936,022
Railroad	225,529	431,268	333,088	283,743
Other transportation	340,809	533,269	649,023	729,053
Communication	1,302,528	1,094,423	2,189,219	947,137
Financial and real estate (excluding investment companies)	1,892,608	3,119,757	3,856,407	4,275,779
Commercial and other	659,429	632,287	701,977	1,061,697
Memorandum: Foreign corporate issues included above	510,851	717,861	455,540	1,021,813

CORPORATE OFFERINGS, BY TYPE OF OFFERING

	1962	1963	1964	1965
Public	6,064,172	5,823,354	6,453,158	7,442,304
Registered under 1933 Act	5,543,601	5,070,060	5,808,714	6,442,854
Unregistered	520,571	753,294	644,443	999,450
Railroad	216,044	381,199	286,015	261,923
Issues $100,000–$300,000 in size	126,865	58,112	44,031	43,271
Other	177,662	313,983	314,397	694,256
Private	4,640,389	6,413,292	7,503,616	8,550,039

NONCORPORATE OFFERINGS, BY TYPE OF ISSUER

	1962	1963	1964	1965
United States government (including issues guaranteed)	8,590,216	7,213,142	10,655,918	9,347,765
Federal agency (issues not guaranteed)	1,187,788	1,168,325	1,205,286	2,731,237
State and municipal	8,558,201	10,106,663	10,544,126	11,148,138
Foreign government	553,427	771,978	480,294	460,304
International	180,339	0	153,433	200,723
Nonprofit institutions	181,513	119,502	125,800	227,695

SOURCE: Securities and Exchange Commission, *Statistical Bulletin* (Washington, D.C.: U.S. Government Printing Office, February 1965 and February 1966) pp. 13 and 13.

of $19 million to the corporation on the offering date, the selling group must peddle the stock to the general public in order to recapture its cost and earn a profit.

Private Placements

Under a private placement of securities the issuing corporation is not required to register with the SEC nor to issue a prospectus. For example, an issuing corporation may elect to make a sale of its bonds to large financial institutions, which are in a position to solicit financial information from the corporation adequate to permit them to make logical decisions concerning the worthiness of the investment. Since large life insurance companies and uninsured pension funds have come to dominate the purchase of corporate bonds, and since 80 to 90 percent of the new securities issued by corporations in the early 1960s were in the form of bonds, their sales to these two types of investors were important means for financing business expansion.

Competitive-Bid Basis

The Federal Power Commission (FPC) requires that electric utility companies that operate in interstate commerce and that come under its jurisdiction offer their securities for sale on a competitive-bid basis. Some 18 percent of the corporate· offerings made during 1965 were made by electric, gas, and water utility companies, although not all of the companies are regulated by the FPC. Investment banking firms and large financial institutions compete for these issues. Frequently large insurance companies are successful in obtaining a major portion of a bond issue, and since no underwriting or SEC registration fees are involved with a direct placement, the sale of the securities to financial institutions rather than to the general public through an investment banking syndicate will result in more proceeds to the issuing corporation. Although this method works to the advantage of both the issuing corporation and the buying financial institution, it reduces the revenues to investment banking firms engaged in the underwriting of securities. (In reality, the negotiated price is somewhere between the expected offering price in a public sale and the proceeds per share that the corporation could expect to receive.) Competitive bids are also used by the federal government and by the state governments in their sales of securities. Each commercial bank has the privilege of subscribing for $200,000 or less of each Treasury bill offering at the average market price for which the issue is sold, and this permits these institutions to maintain an adequate amount of secondary reserves, or liquid investments.

Block Distributions

Block distributions of outstanding stock in the secondary market may be through registered exchanges or in the over the counter market.

Through Registered Exchanges

Two types of plans are in effect that permit block distributions of securities to be handled through a national exchange when it has been determined that the regular market of the exchange cannot absorb the particular block of stock within a reasonable period of time without undue fluctuation of the security price. These plans are referred to as the *special offering plan* and the *exchange distribution plan*. The former is a plan under which a fixed-price offering is made based on the market price; under the latter distribution is made at the market price. With either plan orders are solicited off the floor but are executed on the floor. The special offering plan has been permitted on the American, Boston, Cincinnati, Detroit, Midwest, New York, Pacific Coast, and Philadelphia–Baltimore–Washington stock exchanges since 1942. In 1966, the exchange distribution plan was permitted on the American, Midwest, New York, and Pacific Coast stock exchanges.

Table 10-2 lists the block distributions that were made on the New York and American stock exchanges during the three-month period that ended December 31, 1965. No special offerings were made during the period. Fourteen exchange distributions were made on the New York Stock Exchange and three on the American Stock Exchange during that time. In most instances, the exchange distribution required only two or three trading days, but for a few of the issues a longer period was required. The largest issue was made by Colgate-Palmolive Company in the amount of 225,000 shares having a value in excess of $6 million. The last column in Table 10-2 lists the types of sellers of the security, with individuals and mutual funds occurring most frequently. One exchange distribution on the New York Stock Exchange was made by a brokerage firm.

Over the Counter Distributions

Block distributions of securities in the over the counter market often take the form of *secondary distributions*. This kind of distribution takes place when one financial institution sells a large block of securities to another such institution or when an investment company purchases a large block of stock from a single stockholder or when mutual funds exchange blocks of securities. The method of secondary distribution is used when it has been determined that it is not possible or is not in the best interests of the buyers and sellers of the securities to sell the shares on the exchange in the regular way or to make a special offering or an exchange distribution. Usually the secondary distribution is done after the close of the exchange, and the trading takes place at a price similar to the closing price of the security on the registered exchange. It is usual for the members to obtain the approval of the exchange before participating in the secondary distribution. In this type of distribution, the brokerage firms act as dealers of the securities rather than as agents.

TABLE 10-2 / Block Distributions of Stocks[1]: Three Months Ending December 31, 1965

	Distribution		Number of Shares		Offering Price per Share (Dollars)	Value of Shares Sold (Dollars)	Type of Vendor
	Began	Ended	In Original Offer	Sold			
Special Offerings	THERE	WERE	NO SPECIAL	OFFERINGS	DURING	THE FOURTH	QUARTER 1965
Exchange Distributions							
New York Stock Exchange							
Continental Oil Co.	10-7	10-12	37,200	25,000	77.19 av.	1,929,625	Invest. Co.
Emhart Corporation	10-18	10-18	89,000	89,000	31.50	2,803,500	Funds
Colgate-Palmolive Co.	10-28	10-29	225,000	225,000	28.75	6,468,750	Funds
Central Illinois Public Service	11-11	11-18	103,700	63,524	26.44 av.	1,679,747	Fund
General Telephone & Electronics Corp.	11-16	11-17	38,250	36,750	46.125	1,695,094	Invest. Co.
S. D. Warren Company	11-23	11-24	21,000	18,800	46.49 av.	874,025	Fund
National Can Corp.	11-24	11-26	90,000	78,500	26.18 av.	2,054,750	Fund
The Glidden Company	12-7	12-6	43,100	42,900	22.125	949,163	Fund
Ashland Oil & Refining Co.	12-9	12-9	9,500	9,500	55.75	529,625	Broker
Calgon Corp.	12-13	12-15	19,100	19,100	37.375	713,863	Fund
Sharon Steel Corp.	12-13	12-15	61,456	36,756	28.84 av.	1,059,930	Individuals
Socony Mobil Oil Corp.	12-17	12-20	27,000	16,400	90.00	1,476,000	Individual
Chesebrough Ponds	12-17	12-20	20,400	20,400	27.86 av.	568,350	Insurance Co.
Dana Corp.	12-29	12-29	12,910	12,910	47.50	613,225	Bank
American Stock Exchange							
Allied Paper Corp.	10-14	10-14	42,000	42,000	12.625	530,250	Fund
Riegel Textile Corp.	10-14	10-14	12,060	12,060	22.25	268,335	Directors & Officers
Community Public Service Co.	10-26	10-27	38,000	38,000	41.47 av.	1,575,750	Fund
Total Exchange Distributions			889,676	786,600		25,789,982	

Secondary Distributions
New York Stock Exchange

	10-1	10-4	37,000	39,632	38.75	1,535,740	Fund
Miles Laboratories, Inc.							
U.S. Borax & Chemical Corp.	10-4	10-4	73,800	80,600	30.75	2,478,450	Fund
American Enka Corp.	10-5	10-5	147,000	162,900	42.50	6,923,250	Funds
Colgate-Palmolive Co.	10-7	10-8	150,000	159,650	29.625	4,729,631	Invest. Co.
Max Factor & Co.	10-14	10-14	112,500	116,910	33.375	3,901,871	Fund
Liggett & Myers Tobacco Co.	10-14	10-14	87,500	94,400	84.125	7,941,400	Funds
Amerada Petroleum	10-14	10-15	74,700	77,225	75.625	5,840,141	Fund
Amerada Petroleum	10-18	10-18	62,900	62,900	75.75	4,764,675	Funds
Wickes Corp.	10-18	10-18	53,000	55,400	26.50	1,468,100	Fund
American Airlines, Inc.	10-19	10-20	285,714	288,500	61.75	17,814,875	Insurance Co.
National Airlines, Inc.	10-19	10-20	135,000	164,000	112.50	18,450,000	Funds
Kaiser Cement & Gypsum	10-21	10-22	120,000	126,300	15.50	1,957,650	Invest. Co.
Torrington Company	10-26	10-27	19,400	11,675	44.625	520,997	Insurance Co.
Parker-Hannifin Corp.	11-9	11-12	285,000	285,000	35.00	9,975,000	Estate
Ethyl Corporation	11-12	11-12	269,700	319,200	42.50	13,566,000	Fund
E. J. Korvette, Inc.	11-16	11-16	150,000	164,300	28.75	4,723,625	Individuals
Oklahoma Natural Gas Co.	11-16	11-16	43,700	43,700	37.00	1,616,900	Funds
Consolidated Foods Corp.	11-23	11-24	171,212	174,740	43.00	7,513,820	Individuals
Niagara Mohawk Power Corp.	11-23	11-24	210,000	212,675	26.75	5,689,056	Invest. Co.
Revere Copper & Brass	11-24	11-26	67,100	72,050	46.875	3,377,344	Fund
Ametek, Inc.	11-29	11-29	35,900	35,900	25.125	901,988	Fund
Alleghany Corp.	12-1	12-1	200,000	200,000	11.50	2,300,000	Company
Tektronix, Inc.	12-2	12-8	635,000	643,965	33.25	21,411,836	Individuals

[1] Common or capital stock unless otherwise indicated.

SOURCE: Securities and Exchange Commission, *Statistical Bulletin* (Washington, D.C.: U.S. Government Printing Office, February 1966), p. 11.

TABLE 10-2 (Continued)

	Distribution		Number of Shares		Offering Price per Share (Dollars)	Value of Shares Sold (Dollars)	Type of Vendor
	Began	Ended	In Original Offer	Sold			
Grand Union Co.	12-3	12-3	241,800	258,500	25.00	6,462,500	Fund
Rohr Corp.	12-7	12-7	111,400	111,400	38.50	4,288,900	Fund
North American Car Corp.	12-7	12-7	113,000	113,000	29.25	3,305,250	Fund
Boise Cascade	12-10	12-10	30,000	31,300	56.00	1,752,800	Fund
Northern Industrial Public Service Co.	12-16	12-17	20,000	20,100	64.00	1,286,400	Fund
Swingline, Inc.	12-16	12-20	250,000	263,020	62.00	16,307,240	Individual
Associates Investment	12-21	12-21	95,000	103,285	24.125	2,491,751	Fund
Atlantic City Electric Co.	12-21	12-22	73,800	78,365	32.75	2,566,454	Fund
American Stock Exchange							
Aerosol Techniques, Inc.	10-26	10-26	80,000	84,885	22.50	1,909,913	Officers & Directors
Selas Corp. of America	10-27	10-28	100,000	100,000	22.00	2,200,000	Officer
Revco D.S., Inc.	10-28	10-28	127,429	139,379	21.25	2,961,804	Individuals
Berkshire Frocks, Inc.	11-10	11-19	4,500	4,500	10.875	48,938	B/D & Individuals
Berkshire Frocks, Inc.	11-10	11-24	150,000	160,670	10.875	1,747,286	Officer/Director
National Video Corp.	11-15	11-16	389,100	389,100	63.125	24,561,938	Company & Indivs.
Total Secondary Distributions			5,211,655	5,449,126		221,293,523	
TOTAL BLOCK DISTRIBUTIONS			6,101,331	6,235,726		247,083,505	

During 1964 and 1965, numerous complaints were registered by the mutual funds and other large investors in common stocks concerning the relatively high brokerage commissions that must be paid for buying and selling listed securities. Financial institutions have begun to exchange large blocks of securities with one another, thus eliminating the cost of trading on registered exchanges. This "swapping" does not have a depressing or stimulating effect on the market, but it does reduce the business of member brokerage firms. Finding a buyer or seller of a large block of securities at the market may also prove difficult. Suppose that Fund A desires to sell 100,000 shares of Sperry Rand. Managers of other funds may be suspicious of the action and begin to sell from their own account, thus depressing the market price of the issue.

Numerous open-end investment companies have advertised for large blocks, valued at $10,000 or more, of domestic issues of common stock to be exchanged for shares of equal market value in the investment company. When this exchange agreement is reached, the investment companies often forgo the load charge or selling commission. For federal income tax purposes, the "trade" is a taxable exchange, but it does provide the individual with some diversification and frees him from the responsibility of managing his own account. This type of trade may be desirable for a retired individual who receives a large block of shares as a lump-sum retirement benefit payment. In such an exchange, the recipient is taxed on the difference between his cost basis and the fair market value of the assets received and uses the capital gains tax treatment for computing his federal income taxes.[2]

Trading on the New York Stock Exchange

Round lot transactions on the New York Stock Exchange may be conducted by (1) specialists; (2) odd lot dealers who are either building or selling inventory; (3) other members of the exchange, who initiate the transactions either on or off the floor; and (4) commission brokers for the accounts of nonmembers. The latter account for buying and selling for the general public and is the largest of the above categories. Although the odd lot dealers and specialists must fill all odd lot orders that they receive, these transactions appear only indirectly in the volume of trading reported by the exchanges. It is only as the odd lot dealer or specialist trades in round lots, reducing or building his inventory holdings, that his transactions appear on the ticker tape, in financial pages, and the like.

Round Lot Transactions

Round lot transactions on the New York Stock Exchange by months for the year 1964 are shown in Table 10-3. The table reveals that round lot trading was considerably smaller in February, June, August, and November

---

[2] For a detailed explanation of qualified profit-sharing plans, see the most current issue of *Federal Tax Course* (Englewood Cliffs, N.J.: Prentice-Hall, Inc). See also Chapters 5 and 12 of this text.

TABLE 10-3 / Round Lot Transactions on the New York Stock Exchange for the Year 1964, by months (shares in thousands)

Month	All Round Lot Sales		Transactions of Specialists Except for Odd Lot Accounts in Stocks in Which They Are Registered			Transactions for Odd Lot Accounts of Odd Lot Dealers and Specialists		
				Sales			Sales	
	Total	Short	Pur-chases	Total	Short	Pur-chases	Total	Short
January	119,367	6143	16,082	16,815	3582	3304	3149	0
February	89,821	4515	11,291	11,428	2572	2218	2491	0
March	119,459	5651	15,078	15,098	3301	2843	3082	0
April	127,260	6466	16,712	16,645	3145	3001	3163	0
May	100,803	6014	13,141	13,290	2873	2193	2708	0
June	97,750	5378	13,092	12,997	2561	2447	2681	0
July	104,379	4604	13,825	13,772	2733	2585	2814	0
August	83,778	4196	11,476	11,645	2597	1957	2211	0
September	111,294	5875	15,026	14,963	3351	2278	2796	0
October	108,602	5050	14,723	14,658	2921	2491	2629	0
November	95,415	5078	12,828	12,461	2910	2184	2346	0
December	106,221	4660	13,699	13,440	2196	2278	3057	0
Total for Year	1,264,151	63,632	166,973	167,213	34,742	29,779	33,127	0

Month	Other Member Transactions Initiated on the Floor			Other Member Transactions Initiated off the Floor			Transactions for Accounts of Nonmembers		
	Pur-chases	Sales Total	Short	Pur-chases	Sales Total	Short	Pur-chases	Sales Total	Short
January	2686	3077	529	6080	6233	778	74,191	73,248	1078
February	1938	2120	211	4489	4712	800	69,885	69,069	931
March	2316	2429	290	5882	6376	1012	93,341	92,474	1049
April	2762	2962	559	6662	6937	1133	98,123	97,553	1630
May	2582	2672	437	5631	5763	848	77,256	76,370	1855
June	2077	2244	335	5158	5857	1066	74,975	73,970	1416
July	1632	1684	133	5795	6102	970	80,541	80,008	769
August	576	588	113	5035	5145	664	64,734	64,189	822
September	766	867	204	7398	7598	1130	85,826	85,070	1190
October	741	821	110	7186	7339	987	83,461	83,155	1033
November	546	528	67	6032	6385	886	73,826	73,696	1215
December	789	764	90	7294	6327	912	82,161	82,633	1461
Total for Year	19,414	20,756	3077	72,643	74,773	11,186	958,319	951,434	14,451

SOURCE: Securities and Exchange Commission, *Statistical Bulletin* (Washington, D.C.: U.S. Government Printing Office, February 1965), p. 4.

than in the other months. Short sales amounted to some 5 percent of the total volume of transactions.

The specialist, who is charged with maintaining a market in the securities assigned him but who is permitted to trade for his own account, is expected to maintain an orderly market in the securities in which he is dealing. In cases where there is a spread between public bid and ask price for a given issue, the specialist may sell from or buy for his own account. He may buy an order only at a price higher than the one offered by the general public or sell at a price lower than the one offered by the general public. In maintaining this market, the specialist is frequently short a considerable number of shares. Short sales accounted for some 20 percent of total sales volume by specialists in 1964 (see Table 10-3). Since a short sale may be made only in a rising market, a majority of these short sales are made contrary to the trend in the market price. As the market price of an issue rises rapidly, the odd lot specialist tries to maintain a more orderly market in the issue. These short sales, to some extent, counter the buying pressure that is generated with rising volume. If the shares were not provided by the specialist through the short-selling technique, the market price of an issue would oscillate much more than it actually does. Conversely, the specialist must cover his short position, which is usually done during a falling market, so that buying to cover the previous short sales has a stimulating effect upon the market price of a stock.

It can be seen from Table 10-3 that some 2.5 million shares were sold monthly by the odd lot public through the New York Stock Exchange. Sales by the odd lot accounts, most of which were purchased by the odd lot public, were some 10 percent higher during 1964 than were sales of odd lots by the general public. No short sales were recorded by the odd lot accounts during 1964. Although these statistics appear to indicate that the odd lot public was accumulating stock during 1964, one must consider that odd lot buyers frequently accumulate an individual issue with several odd lots until they reach 100 shares and later sell the round lot.

"Other member transactions initiated on the floor" (for example, by floor traders) in Table 10-3 indicates that short sales accounted for approximately 15 percent of the total sales during 1964. Purchases were slightly less than sales during the year, even though common stock prices were generally rising.

The table also indicates that transactions for accounts of nonmembers, that is, the general public and financial institutions, amounted to some 75 percent of total round lot trading on the New York Stock Exchange in 1964. Sales were approximately 1 percent behind purchases, and short sales accounted for about 1.5 percent of total sales volume.[3]

---

[3] For a comparative listing of and volume of exchange trading by years since 1935, see the most current *Annual Report* of the SEC. A copy may be obtained through the documents library of most colleges and universities or from the U.S. Government Printing Office, Washington, D.C. Daily and monthly volume of transactions on the New York and American stock exchanges are reported in the SEC's monthly *Statistical Bulletin*.

Odd Lot Sales

Odd lot dealers and specialists must frequently buy and sell securities in round lots through the New York Stock Exchange in order to maintain their desired inventory position for all New York Stock Exchange securities. The odd lot transactions on the New York Stock Exchange, some 99 percent of which go to two of the largest odd lot dealers, are shown in Table 10-4. During 1964, the odd lot public sold more shares than it purchased but received 10 percent less for its sales than it paid for their acquisitions. Thus it was either "trading down" to lower-priced issues or losing money on its transactions. Short sales by odd lot customers aggregated about 1 percent of total odd lot sales in units and ½ percent of the market value. These statistics reveal that the size of the average purchase, using the arithmetic mean, was about $550, and the average sale by the odd lot customer was approximately $500. With a transaction of this size, the brokerage charge to buy and again to sell is approximately $10.

Comparative Trading Volume on Registered Exchanges

Between 1935 and 1963, sales on the New York Stock Exchange ranged from a low of 65 percent of the total on all exchanges in 1961 to a high of 78.23 percent of the total in 1939. Share volume for the first six months of 1964 amounted to almost 74 percent of total trading on registered exchanges. The dollar volume from 1935 through 1963 varied from approximately 82 percent to 89 percent. During the first six months of 1964, the dollar volume on the New York Stock Exchange amounted to some 82.75 percent of the total volume of trading on registered exchanges. The share and dollar volume of trading on the American exchange oscillates more widely than does that on the New York exchange. For example, less than 12 percent of the total trading on listed exchanges occurred on the American exchange in 1938, 1939, and 1942. However, in 1959 and again in 1961 trading on the American exchange amounted to about 25 percent of the total. For the first six months of 1964, conversely, trading in American Stock Exchange stocks amounted to some 18.07 percent of total stock trading. As measured by the dollar volume of transactions during recent years, the volume has been about 7 to 10 percent of total trading. Shares on the American Stock Exchange trade at considerably lower prices, on the average, than those on the New York exchange. The Midwest and the Pacific Coast stock exchanges each account for between 2 and 3 percent of the dollar and share volume of trading. The balance of the trading, which is fairly insignificant, occurs on the other regional exchanges.[4]

[4] See Securities and Exchange Commission, *Annual Report* (Washington, D.C.: U.S. Government Printing Office), selected issues.

TABLE 10-4 / Odd Lot Transactions of the New York Stock Exchange for the Year 1954, by months

Month	Purchase by Customers for Odd Lot Dealers and Specialists		Sales by Customers to Odd-Lot Dealers and Specialists		Short Sales by Customers	
	Number of Shares	Market Value (Dollars)	Number of Shares	Market Value (Dollars)	Number of Shares	Market Value (Dollars)
January	10,440,426	638,339,429	10,139,553	531,335,317	111,741	7,619,426
February	7,457,960	419,775,412	7,567,487	374,764,092	95,774	7,139,625
March	9,593,752	507,596,532	9,635,086	459,034,345	76,785	5,522,682
April	10,189,415	551,895,133	10,126,547	494,261,280	119,011	7,719,461
May	7,660,399	427,067,636	8,045,378	410,035,922	114,385	7,200,243
June	7,707,322	426,118,703	7,827,548	392,043,017	120,863	8,050,342
July	8,198,191	441,337,841	8,333,099	407,779,178	48,009	3,351,025
August	6,571,242	358,708,866	6,733,437	336,178,319	59,853	4,653,263
September	8,123,765	430,520,092	8,582,098	424,063,249	78,581	5,722,679
October	8,314,189	433,692,844	8,365,164	407,883,167	66,569	4,462,467
November	7,309,915	382,739,895	7,431,195	359,832,916	63,329	4,251,643
December	8,058,848	397,410,264	8,853,303	404,184,798	109,383	6,912,135
Total for Year	99,625,424	5,415,202,647	101,639,895	5,001,395,600	1,064,283	72,604,991

SOURCE: Securities and Exchange Commission, *Statistical Bulletin* (Washington, D.C.: U.S. Government Printing Office, February 1965), p. 6.

Summary

Security markets may be divided into primary and secondary markets. The primary market refers to the initial sale of stocks, bonds, or other negotiable securities by business corporations to the general public or to other types of investors. Trading in outstanding securities refers to block distributions, round lot orders, and odd lot transactions in the over the counter markets and through the registered exchanges.

A corporation may sell new, or primary, issues to the old shareholders on a preemptive rights basis, to the general public, either directly or through an underwriting group, or to financial institutions, either by private placement or on a competitive-bid basis. Public sale of stocks in interstate commerce for issues in excess of $300,000 and for bond issues in excess of $1 million requires registration with the SEC under the Securities Act of 1933 and the Trust Indenture Act of 1939, respectively.

A large estate, individual, or financial institution that holds a considerable block of a security may elect to make a block distribution. This may be made through a registered exchange in the form of a special offering plan or under an exchange distribution plan. Although the former was first made effective in 1942, it has been losing in popularity to the exchange distribution plan initiated in 1954. The primary difference between the two plans is that under the former the security is offered through the exchange at a fixed price, whereas the market price determines the offering price of the security under the latter plan. If it is felt that the market will not absorb these block distributions without the market price of the issue being adversely affected, a secondary distribution may be made after the closing of the exchange. Distributions of large blocks of stock may also be made in the over the counter market between financial institutions or between a wealthy individual and a financial institution.

In 1940–1964, trading through the New York Stock Exchange accounted for some 83 to 86 percent of the dollar volume of trading on registered exchanges; trading through the American Stock Exchange accounted for another 7 to 10 percent; and trading through the other registered and exempt exchanges totaled 6 to 8 percent. During the early 1960s, over the counter trading in corporate securities was increasing in importance as many over the counter dealers were becoming active traders of listed securities, and some mutual funds and other financial institutions had begun to exchange large blocks of securities rather than going through the registered exchanges.

QUESTIONS FOR REVIEW /

1. List and discuss briefly the advantages of a preemptive rights issue.
2. List and discuss briefly the advantages to the corporation and to the buying stockholders of a public sale of corporate stocks.
3. Why has the private placement of securities been more dominant in the bond market than in the stock market?

4. Describe briefly what is meant by a competitive-bid security offering and indicate the types of securities that are sold in this manner.
5. Differentiate between the special offering plan and the exchange distribution plan. How is each priced?
6. How are block distributions handled in the over the counter market?
7. How does a secondary distribution differ from the exchange distribution plan?
8. Why does the New York Stock Exchange specialist use the short sale so frequently?
9. How important is the short sale to New York Stock Exchange members and to the general public other than the specialist?
10. Evaluate the buying and selling by the odd lot public.

PROBLEMS /

1. With the use of the most recent edition of *The New York Stock Exchange Factbook,* determine the rights offerings that were made during the most recent year. How did the rights offerings affect the market prices of the securities under review?
2. Use *The Wall Street Journal, Barron's,* or *Moody's Stock Survey* to compile a list of five companies that made public sales of stocks during the last six to twelve months. Was there any noticeable change in the market values of the securities immediately before or after the public flotations?
3. From a recent copy of "Odd Lot Customer's Purchases and Sales on the New York Stock Exchange in 75 Selected Stocks," which is published in each monthly issue of the *Statistical Bulletin* of the SEC, determine three common issues for which there was very active purchasing and three for which there was very active selling by the odd lot public and evaluate the timing of these purchases and sales. Do you believe that the odd lot public has been acting wisely in its purchases and sales of individual issues? Explain.
4. By using the most recent February, May, August, or November edition of the *Statistical Bulletin* of the SEC, determine three issues of common stock that have been sold in large block distributions within the last three or four months. Have these block distributions had any dampening effect on the market prices of the issues?

REFERENCES /

Cooke, Gilbert W., *The Stock Market.* New York: Simmons-Boardman Publishing Corporation, 1964.

Bogen, J. I., ed., *Financial Handbook,* 3d. ed., New York: The Ronald Press Company, 1952.

Leffler, George L., and Loring C. Farwell, *The Stock Market,* 3d. ed. New York: The Ronald Press Company, 1963.

New York Stock Exchange, *The Exchange.* New York: The Exchange.

————, *The New York Stock Exchange Factbook.* New York: The Exchange, 1964.

U.S. Securities and Exchange Commission, *Annual Report.* Washington, D.C.: U.S. Government Printing Office, selected issues.

————, *Statistical Bulletin.* Washington, D.C.: U.S. Government Printing Office, February 1965.

chapter 11 | Sources of Investment Information

Introduction

It is important for the investor to be informed about world affairs, economic conditions within the nation, the general level and direction of stock market prices, and developments within individual companies. Such information is reported almost instantaneously by news tickers, in daily newspapers, in weekly financial magazines, in monthly publications and by investment services. In order to keep up to date on these topics, the investor should have access to and periodically review the sources of information discussed within this chapter. Since an attempt to buy and review all of the publications mentioned here would require a tremendous monetary expense and a full-time reading job, this list is only suggestive, and the investor should determine which of these sources are most helpful to him and of these, which are available through his university or public library. He is then in a position to supplement the available information with subscriptions.

Instantaneous News

News Ticker

Dow Jones and Company owns the only news ticker service in the United States. The printing telegraph operates continuously and is located in many of the larger brokerage offices. By means of the ticker, news items are instantaneously flashed over wires to the printing telegraph, which relays the news to the board room of brokerage firms. Many news flashes have an immediate effect on the general level of stock prices, for example, war news or legislative action, or on the market price of a particular company's stock, for example, an airline crash, strike, or a mineral discovery.

Stock Ticker

The *stock ticker*, commonly referred to as the *stock ticker tape service*, permits trading information to be flashed to member exchange offices almost as soon as a transaction takes place. Since the development of the stock ticker service in the 1920s, volume of trading on the listed exchanges has increased, and the need for a more rapid ticker service has often been felt. In the mad scramble to unload securities during the stock market crash of 1929, the ticker tape ran more than five hours late, and on occasions after that date it sometimes ran one to two hours late. In late 1964, the 900 Series ticker was installed, which automatically runs at 500, 600, 700, 800, or 900 characters per minute. When trading is relatively slow, the ticker moves at the lower rate of speed, changing automatically to a more rapid speed when trading becomes more active, and reverting to a slower pace when trading declines. Whole-number price digits are frequently deleted in order to accelerate the reporting. Under normal conditions, the improved ticker service for the New York Stock Exchange can handle trading volume up to 10 million shares a day without running late. Although many account executives within a brokerage firm and some traders or interested bystanders watch the board room ticker tape for long periods of time in order to see the trend of individual issues, this is a rather difficult method for gauging the intraday volume of trading and the price activity within a specific issue.

Teleregister

With the development of large electronic data processing systems and with the invention of the teleregister, the account executive or an investor who happens to be in a brokerage office may quickly obtain a large amount of trading information about any listed issue. By depressing the ticker tape symbol and the appropriate button, the operator may determine the most recent trading price, the present bid and ask, the amount of time since the last trade, the volume of trading for the day, the opening and closing price, the daily range, the last dividend payment date, and other financial information. This new method of obtaining instantaneous information has largely eliminated the need for posting prices from the ticker tape on a large blackboard at the front of the brokerage office. Since the advent of the teleregister many brokerage offices no longer post ticker tape reports, and some have discontinued the use of the ticker tape altogether.

Daily Newspapers

The Wall Street Journal

One of the largest news services in the United States is Dow Jones and Company. In 1965, the company was publishing eight issues of *The Wall Street Journal* in various geographic areas within the United States. Some 850,000 subscribers to this daily business and financial newspaper receive *The Wall Street Journal* either the same day it is published or on the following day. Although Dow Jones itself considers *The Wall Street Journal* to be a business rather than a financial newspaper, it does give complete daily financial information. The front page of the paper summarizes longer articles and financial news items that appear in detail within the paper. Some 50 to

60 percent of the publication is devoted to news items, while the balance is used for advertising space. The *National Observer* is its weekly counterpart.

The *New York Times* is another newspaper that contains a large amount of business, economic, and financial information. Other regional newspapers, too numerous to mention, also present unbiased business and financial news. Since delivery of the New York newspapers to some locations may require two or three days and the reader may prefer more up-to-date information, he may seek a regional newspaper that offers an unbiased presentation of the news.

Financial Magazines

Dozens of weekly, biweekly, or semimonthly financial magazines are available to the investor. In addition, some professional journals published either monthly or quarterly may also prove to be of value. Although the following list is not intended to be exhaustive, it indicates the extent of the types of information available. The items are generally arranged by frequency and type of publication, and the arrangement is not intended to denote the desirability or usefulness of the data presented within these periodicals.

Barron's National Business and Financial Weekly is devoted almost entirely to financial rather than business news. The publication presents articles on various industries, developments within numerous companies, some news articles on domestic and world-wide situations that are expected to have an impact upon the financial situation in the United States, and a complete enumeration of weekly transactions in the over the counter markets and on the registered exchanges. The periodical contains lists of the new annual highs and lows on the New York and American stock exchanges, annual and interim earnings reports, changes in various stock averages and other technical indicators, commodity news, and other information.

Commercial and Financial Chronicle is a biweekly financial magazine that presents information similar to that carried in *Barron's*. Although there are numerous differences in the format and types of data carried, both magazines present a wealth of financial information.

Other weekly journals that carry a substantial amount of economic, business, and financial data and that enjoy a wide circulation include *Business Week, Newsweek,* and *U.S. News and World Report*. Many newsstands carry these periodicals, or they may be acquired on a subscription basis.

If an individual wishes to read articles on specific industries and companies and obtain recommendations as to buy and sell action, he may refer to *Financial World, Forbes Magazine, Investment Dealers' Digest,* or *The Magazine of Wall Street*. Special industry studies, especially in the January 1 issue of *Forbes,* and individual company studies, particularly in *The Magazine of Wall Street,* appear from time to time, as well as surveys of the general economy, the level of the stock market, and the technical approach to security analysis.

Two of the more widely read professional journals in the area of finance are *The Journal of Finance,* published quarterly by the American Finance Association, and *The Financial Analyst Journal,* published six times a year by the Financial Analysts' Federation. The articles in these two publications are, for the most part, written by university professors and security analysts. The articles that appear in *The Journal of Finance* are primarily theoretical in nature, while those in *The Financial Analyst Journal* are usually empirical studies.

Newsletters

Kiplinger's, Whaley-Eaton, and dozens of other newsletters are published weekly. Some of these command a very large following, while others have smaller subscription lists. Numerous large commercial banks and all Federal Reserve banks prepare monthly business reviews that are available to interested subscribers. Many of these may be acquired free of charge, while others require a small subscription fee. An investor should not wholly rely on the "tips" within the newsletters, but interesting situations for further investigation are often presented.

Federal Publications

One of the most comprehensive publications dealing with money, banking, and credit is the *Federal Reserve Bulletin,* published monthly by the Board of Governors of the Federal Reserve System. Each issue includes two or three articles on current topics of interest and some 100 pages of statistical data dealing with Federal Reserve banks and member commercial banks, U.S. government securities, various types of credit, industrial production, employment, gold reserves, international transactions, and other topics. For an individual who prefers graphic rather than tabular data, chart books are published monthly and annually by the Board of Governors of the Federal Reserve System in series similar to those presented monthly in the *Federal Reserve Bulletin.*

Some series reported in the *Federal Reserve Bulletin* also appear in the *Survey of Current Business,* published monthly by the Department of Commerce, Bureau of Business Economics. A biannual supplement to the *Survey of Current Business* is *Business Statistics,* which presents historical tabular information covering the last 30 to 35 years. This publication gives general business indicators and indexes to stock prices and includes data on commodity prices, construction, domestic trade, employment, population, finance, foreign trade, transportation and communications, industry, and other segments of the economy.

The *Monthly Labor Review* is published by the Department of Labor and includes series dealing with employment, hours worked, pay levels, price indexes, and the like. Although these series are published by the Department of Labor as primary data, they are also recorded by the *Federal Reserve Bulletin* and the *Survey of Current Business* as secondary information. The materials are available almost simultaneously in the secondary and primary sources.

The SEC has two regular publications, the *Statistical Bulletin,* which is published monthly, and the *Annual Report.* In addition, the SEC publishes from time to time numerous brochures and information sheets on various topics. The *Statistical Bulletin* presents data on volume of trading on the security exchanges, primary security issues, expenditures on new plant and equipment, savings by individuals in the United States, portfolio holdings of private noninsured pension funds, and other topics. The *Annual Report* contains a description of the various acts administered by the SEC. Historical series of data dealing with security trading, new security offers, security listings, and action brought by the SEC against exchanges, exchange members, or over the counter dealers are included in the *Annual Report.* A majority of the better libraries, particularly those that maintain extensive public documents sections, receive these governmental publications. For the individual who wishes to have immediate access to these sources, subscriptions may be ordered directly from the U.S. Government Printing Office, Washington, D.C., at nominal charges.

The *Statistical Abstract of the United States* is published annually and includes reference material on many of the topics compiled as primary data by the other governmental agencies. Much of the data tabulated from periodic census information is maintained and updated with estimates within the *Statistical Abstract of the United States.*

Exchange Material

The New York Stock Exchange, the American Stock Exchange, the Midwest Stock Exchange, and numerous other registered exchanges maintain information on their own operations as well as on the companies listed on the respective exchanges. Much of this information may be acquired at little or no cost by writing to the exchange. For example, *The Exchange,* published monthly by the New York Stock Exchange, presents only factual data, but much of the material in this source may be used by the individual in reaching investment decisions regarding New York Stock Exchange issues. The periodical presents a monthly summary of how various industries have fared, and this type of information is frequently useful to the investor. Newly listed companies are discussed and special studies also appear in each issue.

Publications of Security Firms

Most large security exchange members or over the counter dealers publish and distribute information to their clients, and in most instances the information may be acquired free of charge from the respective exchange members or security dealers. Special studies on various industries or on specific companies are frequently made by security houses, and these exchange members often compile a list of recommended stocks. The list may be so extensive, however, that the individual still has a difficult job in determining which of the recommended issues are desirable commitments at their current market prices. It is recommended that the individual investor consider the "tips" given by others but investigate before he invests. Widely circulated recommendations do usually have a stimulating effect on market prices, with subsequent declines in price and very slow, disappointing recoveries. One frequently buys on such a tip (after a 15 to 25 percent price rise) only to have the issue decline to its previous level.

Reports of Corporations

One source of current information about a particular corporation is the annual or quarterly report that is prepared by many of the large corporations and distributed periodically to shareholders. Many annual reports are very elaborate, including comparative financial statements and descriptions of new and old products being marketed and plans for future expansion. Although the reports are frequently optimistic in nature and are intended to point out the strengths of a given company, the information reported may be very useful to a security analyst. The large corporations are eager to send annual reports to prospective stockholders and to mail them to their own shareholders. Corporations that list their securities on a registered exchange must, as one of their requirements, distribute annual reports to their shareholders, file a registration statement with the SEC, and update it annually with materials similar to those that appear in the annual report. The information is filed with the SEC either on Form F-1 or 10-K. In certain instances, listed corporations are also required to furnish quarterly or semiannual information to the SEC on Forms 8-K and 9-K, and listed companies are required to show the buying and selling activity within their stock by insiders of the corporation. The general public may view the buying and selling transactions by the directors and officers of a company and thereby gauge the desirability of buying or selling the issue. This type of information is published periodically in the *Statistical Bulletin,* but much of the information that is filed with the SEC is also distributed by various investment services and made available to the general public in secondary sources of information, for example, in *Value Line, Barron's,* and other publications. Prospectuses describing new security issues are also helpful.

Industry Surveys

Numerous cooperative organizations publish industry reports describing recent progress within their industries and their outlooks for the future. These surveys aid the investor in determining which industries are likely to be dynamic or stagnant within the future. Some of the better-known ones include the American Iron and Steel Institute, the American Petroleum Institute, the Cotton Textile Institute, the National Association of Wool Manufacturers, and others.[1]

Investment Services

Moody's Investors Service

Perhaps one of the more widely recognized investors' services is Moody's Investors Service, which is published in seven different volumes and includes statistical data on industrial companies, public utility companies, municipal governments, transportation companies, and financial institutions. Each of these areas is treated in a bound volume and is supplemented weekly with looseleaf sheets that present interim reports, dividend news, and the like. Moody's Investors Service also publishes a *Bond Survey* and a *Stock Survey*, which indicate expected primary security issues and provide recommendations as to buy, sell, and hold for various issues of common and preferred stocks, convertibles, and bonds. These weekly surveys also present economic and business indicators and attempt to forecast future developments within the economy and the stock market.

Standard & Poor's Corporation

Standard & Poor's Corporation, which resulted from a merger of the two companies (now a division of McGraw-Hill Publishing Company, Inc.) provides a number of services, one of which, *Corporate Records,* is similar in nature to that provided by Moody's Investors Service. Many college, university, and public libraries subscribe to one or both of these services. Standard & Poor's Corporation also publishes a monthly *Stock Digest,* which presents a condensation of financial information on some 4000 corporations. This source is useful to the account executive or investor desiring certain types of information, for example, industry data and ticker tape symbol, on a large number of companies. The publication makes recommendations as to convertibles, most favorably situated companies, defensive issues, and industry groups. Standard & Poor's *Industry Survey* is helpful in analyzing some 45 industries, while its *Stock Market Encyclopedia* presents two pages of key financial data and comments on each of about 2500 large corporations. The

---

[1] See, for example, George L. Leffler and Loring C. Farwell, *The Stock Market,* 3d ed. (New York: The Ronald Press Company, 1963), pp. 628–636. In addition to these trade journals, Merrill Lynch, Pierce, Fenner & Smith publishes a quarterly, *Security and Industry Survey,* that gives some insight into the expected outlook for about 30 different industries and a list of recommended stock issues that are representative of these industries. Another such publication is the January 1 issue of *Forbes Magazine,* which is devoted to an industry analysis, with emphasis upon expected developments in the foreseeable future.

service corporation rates corporate and government bonds on the basis of their safety of interest and principal repayment (one of nine grades) and preferred and common stocks on the basis of earnings and dividend stability (one of seven ratings).

Fitch Publishing Company

The Fitch Publishing Company publishes *Fitch Stock Record* and *Fitch Bond Rating*. The three companies, Moody's Investors Service, Standard & Poor's Corporation, and Fitch are the three leading bond-rating services within the United States, and national banks may buy only corporate bonds of the top four grades, as indicated by two of these leading bond-rating services.

The Value Line Investment Survey

The primary purpose of *The Value Line Investment Survey* is to report quarterly on some 1100 companies that are kept under constant surveillance by A. Bernhard & Company, Inc. The report is mailed weekly to subscribers and includes statistical financial information, an analysis of new products being designed and marketed, sales outlooks, and recommendations as to probable market strength within the next 12 months and within the next three to five years. The weekly survey provides information on about 90 companies and includes industry surveys, discussions of special situations, and reports on investment companies.

Investment Companies

The most complete annual study of closed- and open-end investment companies is made by Arthur Wiesenberger and Company and is entitled *Investment Companies*. A survey of about 300 of the leading open- and closed-end investment companies is made, covering investment objectives, evaluation of management, the portfolio holdings of the various funds, and a comparison of the performance of the funds with that of the general market. Information is also provided on the Investment Company Act and small business investment companies. For periodic information on investment companies, the reader may refer to the *Statistical Bulletin* of the SEC or to periodic reports published by *The Value Line Investment Survey, Barron's,* or other sources.

Chart Services

Dozens of chart services are available to the investor, but before subscribing to any of these publications he should determine which are available in his public or college library or in his brokerage office or subscribe to one or more of these on a trial basis. If he determines that a specific chart service meets his needs, and if he believes that the benefits afforded will be worth the cost to him, he may desire to become a subscriber.

Range charts may be obtained on a monthly, weekly, or daily basis. Monthly range charts on a large number of companies appear in *Moody's Handbook of Common Stocks,* Standard & Poor's *Stock Market Encyclopedia,* and *The Value Line Investment Survey.* Trendline Corporation publishes *Trendline's Current Market Perspectives,* which gives an industrial grouping (some 96) for 960 listed stocks, publishes charts on unlisted securities, and has a daily basis stock chart which provides the daily range and closing prices of about 600 issues. Other chart services include M. C. Horsey Company, Robert Mansfield and Company, F. W. Stephens Company, Securities Research Corporation, and others. The investor may refer to descriptions of these in advertisements that appear in *The Wall Street Journal, Barron's, Commercial and Financial Chronicle,* or other leading financial magazines.

Numerous point-and-figure chart services are available. These include Chartcraft, Inc., Morgan, Rogers and Roberts, Inc., W. R. F. M. Financial Service Corporation, and others.

Summary

A businessman or an investor should be informed about current business, economic, and stock market news, and he should have access to various types of financial data. Instantaneous news reported over the stock ticker service, the news ticker service, or the teleregister may be of particular value in attempting to make short-range predictions about the price movement of individual issues. The investor may also wish to subscribe to one or more leading financial newspapers and magazines.

Weekly newsletters or monthly news summaries are published by numerous publishing companies, commercial banks, and Federal Reserve banks, while other information that may be useful to the businessman or to the investor appears in various federal publications. The Board of Governors of the Federal Reserve System, the Department of Commerce, the Bureau of Labor Statistics, the Bureau of the Census, the SEC, and other governmental agencies publish monthly, annual, or semiannual reports.

Other sources include the major security exchanges, listed corporations, cooperative associations within industries, and investment services, which include Moody's Investors Service, Standard & Poor's Corporation, Fitch Publishing Company, and *The Value Line Investment Survey.*

As an aid to improving the timing of purchase and sale of securities, the investor may wish to devote some time to the study of chart services.

A variety of financial literature is available in college or public libraries or in brokerage houses, so that the investor may already have access to this information. For convenience or more timely reports, an investor may find it desirable to subscribe to a daily financial newspaper, to one or two weekly or monthly financial magazines, to one newsletter, and to one or more investors' services.

QUESTIONS FOR REVIEW /

1. Contrast the use of the stock ticker service and the teleregister in determining the daily price trend of an individual issue.
2. Of what value is the stock ticker?
3. What types of information appear in the leading daily business and financial newspapers?
4. Enumerate briefly the various types of weekly, semimonthly, monthly, and quarterly financial magazines. Evaluate their usefulness to you as an investor.
5. Compare and contrast the information that appears in the *Federal Reserve Bulletin* and the *Survey of Current Business*.
6. What periodicals are published by the SEC? How may these be used by the investor in reaching logical decisions concerning his investment program?
7. Describe briefly the various types of investment services that usually appear in public or college libraries.
8. What type of information appears in Arthur Wiesenberger's *Investment Companies?*

PROBLEMS /

1. Select three financial magazines discussed in this chapter and make a listing of 10 items that are periodically described or covered by each of these.
2. Contrast the various series of statistical data that appear in the monthly *Statistical Bulletin* with the information that appears in the *Annual Report* of the SEC. How may the information on security purchases and sales on the leading exchanges be used by the investor in making logical investment decisions? Explain and give examples.
3. Make a detailed study of two of the investment services described in this chapter and compile a list of 15 types of financial information that are provided by each of these services. How much overlap exists between the two services?
4. List the bar chart and point-and-figure chart services that are available in your college or local public library.

REFERENCES /

Cohen, A. W. *The Chartcraft Method.* Larchmont, N.Y.: Chartcraft, Inc., 1961.

Cooke, Gilbert W., *The Stock Market.* New York: Simmons-Boardman Publishing Corporation, 1964.

Bogen, Jules I., *Financial Handbook,* 3d. ed. New York: The Ronald Press Company, 1952.

Leffler, George L., and Loring C. Farwell. *The Stock Market,* 3d ed. New York: The Ronald Press Company, 1963.

Merrill Lynch, Pierce, Fenner & Smith, *Security and Industry Survey.* New York: Merrill Lynch, quarterly issues.

New York Stock Exchange, *The Exchange.* New York: The Exchange.

————, *The New York Stock Exchange Factbook.* New York: The Exchange, 1964.

U.S. Securities and Exchange Commission, *Annual Report.* Washington, D.C.: U.S. Government Printing Office, selected issues.

————, *Statistical Bulletin.* Washington, D.C.: U.S. Government Printing Office, February 1965.

part three

The Fundamental Approach to Security Analysis

Before studying the financial position of a business corporation, the analyst should be aware of the kind of financial information that is published concerning American corporations. Although the investor is primarily concerned with growth in sales, earnings, and dividends, he should also be familiar with the operating differences among industrial, public utility, and transportation firms.

Chapter 12 is a study of the typical financial statements published by business corporations and the important ratios that may indicate strengths and weaknesses in individual companies. Chapters 13, 14, and 15, respectively, are studies of industrial companies, public utilities, and transportation firms. Chapter 16 discusses the problem of evaluating the "real worth" of common equities, while the final chapter in the section is concerned with special situations, such as mergers, exchange listing, stock splits, dividend news, and research and development and indicates how these special events normally influence the market values of common equities.

chapter 12 | Analysis of Financial Statements

Introduction

The financial analysis presented in this and the following five chapters is geared primarily toward a study of the financial position of a business firm and its influence on the investment decision. While an analysis of the type suggested in this chapter is of value, the investor should also be able to interpret the financial data, key ratios, and key per share figures that are reported in numerous investment advisory services. With knowledge of the latter he can analyze the financial information of a large number of companies in the process of determining worthwhile investments. An analysis of a large number of issues should produce some stocks that are underpriced in the market relative to their earning ability. The financial statements for the New Jersey Zinc Company and subsidiaries, now a part of Gulf and Western Industries, were selected as examples for analyzing the kind of information that usually appears on the balance sheet and combined income statement and statement of retained earnings. The notes that are required by Regulation S-X of the SEC are described, and an interpretation of key financial statements is presented.

Balance Sheet Analysis

The balance sheet of a business corporation is a static picture of the assets, liabilities, and equity ownership of the business firm at a stated point in time. *Assets* refer to the properties actually possessed by the business firm. *Liabilities* are the amounts owed to creditors for such things as materials, wages, taxes, and other accruals. The *stockholder's equity* refers to the funds that have been obtained by the corporation either through the sale of common or preferred shares and/or past profits that have been retained in the business.

In discussing accounting treatments of assets, liabilities, and equity accounts, references are made to the 1963 and 1964 financial statements of the New Jersey Zinc Company and subsidiaries (see Table 12-1). Dollar amounts and percentages of total assets are shown for the accounts. By studying common size statements, that is, those expressed in percentages of the total rather than in dollar figures, the analyst may very easily compare relative changes in the financial statements over a period of time. Although the table includes financial statements for only two years, the financial analyst may wish to include data for a much longer period of time before he is willing to commit his funds to the securities of the firm. For the sake of brevity, however, the financial statements for only two years are considered here.[1]

TABLE 12-1 /   New Jersey Zinc Company and Subsidiaries Consolidated Balance Sheets on December 31, 1963 and 1964

	1964		1963	
	($)	(%)	($)	(%)
Assets				
Current assets				
Cash	3,588,135	2.5	3,987,586	3.1
Marketable securities, at cost (Note 1)	33,452,085	23.4	20,101,472	15.6
Accounts and notes receivable	9,314,184	6.5	7,895,956	6.1
Inventories (Note 2)	13,655,985	9.6	13,667,431	10.6
Prepaid insurance	132,692	0.1	143,552	0.1
Total current assets	60,143,081	42.1	45,795,997	35.6
Investments and advances at cost (Note 3)				
Quebec Iron and Titanium Corporation (33⅓% owned)	19,381,959	13.6	19,381,959	15.0
Radiation Research Corporation (20% owned)	2,152,829	1.5	—	—
Catalysts and Chemicals, Inc. (16% owned)	1,027,472	0.7	1,027,472	0.8
	22,562,260	15.8	20,409,431	15.8
Property, plant, and equipment, at cost (Note 4)	130,198,208	91.1	130,771,275	101.5
Less accumulated depreciation and depletion	(72,782,323)	(50.9)	(71,249,366)	(55.3)
	57,415,885	40.2	59,521,909	46.2
Deferred exploration and other assets	2,865,089	2.0	3,092,413	2.4
Total assets	142,986,315	100.0	128,819,750	100.0

SOURCE: *1964 Annual Report* of the New Jersey Zinc Company, pp. 16 and 17.

[1] The financial statements within this chapter are taken from the *1964 Annual Report* of the New Jersey Zinc Company and subsidiaries. The percentage breakdown of the figures has been added in order to facilitate interpreting the information.

TABLE 12-1 *(Continued)*

	1964		1963	
	($)	(%)	($)	(%)
Liabilities				
Current liabilities				
Accounts payable and accrued expenses	5,286,709	3.7	4,697,948	3.6
Notes payable within one year (Note 6)	1,250,000	0.9	1,250,000	1.0
Federal income taxes	6,218,368	4.3	1,609,077	1.2
Production payments sold, less federal and state taxes (Note 5)	5,517,500	3.9	—	—
Total current liabilities	18,272,577	12.8	7,557,025	5.9
Notes payable, noncurrent, (Note 6)	13,750,000	9.6	15,000,000	11.6
	32,022,577	22.4	22,557,025	17.5
Stockholders' Equity				
Capital Stock, $12.50 par value (Note 7)				
Authorized: 4,200,000 shares; issued: 1964, 3,985,190 shares; 1963, 3,928,980[1] shares	49,814,875	34.8	49,112,250	38.1
Capital surplus (Note 7)	694,575	0.5	688,750	0.5
Retained earnings (Note 6)	63,689,325	44.5	59,565,850	46.2
	114,198,775	79.9	109,366,850	84.9
Less, capital stock reacquired at cost: 1964, 212,280 shares; 1963, 206,480[1] shares	3,235,037	(2.3)	3,104,125	(2.4)
	110,963,738	77.6	106,262,725	82.5
Total liabilities	142,986,314	100.0	128,819,750	100.0

[1] Adjusted for a two for one stock split in 1964.

Assets

In general, the assets of a business firm may be divided into current assets, investments, fixed assets, intangible assets, and deferred charges. Some accountants also add a sixth classification, other assets, for items that are not reported in the above five sections.

Current assets refer to properties that are either in the form of cash or that are expected to become cash within one year. Most accountants consider cash, marketable securities, accounts and notes receivable, inventories, and prepaid items to be current assets. Generally, these assets are expected to be converted to inventories, to receivables, and to cash during the ordinary operation of the business.

Cash refers to currency and coin and demand deposits at United States banks, but near-cash items, such as Treasury bills and time certificates of deposits, should be shown as a temporary investment.

The marketable securities are frequently reported at cost, as has been done for New Jersey Zinc, but they may be carried at the lower of cost or market. Whereas this account usually refers to very liquid marketable issues, such as short-term investments in U.S. government securities, this company has elected to include under this account investments in U.S. government Treasury bills and bonds, municipal bonds, preferred stocks, and common stocks. The equities are representative of companies that are listed on major exchanges or for which there is active trading in the over the counter markets. The financial analyst should recognize, however, that the stocks are subject to a considerable risk in market fluctuation, and he should compare the market value of these equities with the actual cost when analyzing the financial statements.

A study of the December 31, 1963 and 1964 balance sheets for New Jersey Zinc Company and subsidiaries (Table 12-1) reveals that total assets increased by approximately $13 million over the period. A substantial part of this increase was in the marketable securities account, with about one half allocated to U.S. government Treasury bonds or bills and the other half to listed common shares. The company did a substantial amount of trading during the period and in 1964 realized $1 million in profit from the sale of marketable securities.

The *accounts and notes receivable* should be subdivided into trade accounts; notes; acceptances receivable; and receivables from officers, employees, affiliates, and others. In order for these accounts to be classified as current assets they should be collectible in the ordinary course of business within a year from the balance sheet date. The portion of installment or deferred accounts and notes receivable that is expected to be collectible within one year should also be classified as a current asset. The balance that is expected to be collectible beyond one year should be classified within the investments section as a noncurrent asset.[2]

Whereas retail concerns and wholesale firms carry only two types of inventories—merchandise and supplies—a manufacturing company generally has four types of inventories. These include raw materials, work in process, finished goods, and miscellaneous supplies. Numerous methods may be followed in the reporting of inventories. A corporation may adopt the principle of using the last-in, first-out method or the first-in, first-out method of accounting for the flow of costs from the raw materials inventory to the work in process. Some companies elect to use the cost basis for evaluating the inventories on the balance sheets, while others use the lower of cost or

---

[2] See, for example, American Institute of Certified Public Accountants, *Accounting Trends and Techniques,* 17th ed. (New York: The Institute, 1965), p. 45.

market. Although any of these rules is in keeping with generally accepted accounting principles, a company should be consistent in its method of accounting for its cost of goods sold and in its evaluation of inventories on the balance sheet. There are more than a dozen methods of determining the *flow of costs* for inventories, but a survey of 600 industrial and commercial corporations that were included in the 1965 *Accounting Trends and Techniques* indicated that 190 were using the last-in, first-out method, another 163 were using the average-cost method, 199 were using the first-in, first-out method, and the balance were using some other method. Some 70 percent, or 416 of the 600 companies, were using the lower of cost or market for reporting the cost of inventories on the balance sheet. About 11 percent of the companies were reporting the inventory at the lower of cost or market and at cost, while other companies reported the inventory at the lower of cost or market and one or more other bases.[3]

The prepaid items, consisting of, for example, prepaid insurance, rent, and interest, for most business firms amount to a relatively small figure when compared to the total assets of the business. For New Jersey Zinc Company in 1964 the account amounted to only 0.1 percent of total assets. Although these items are not expected to be converted to cash during the following year, if these assets were not owned by the corporation, a cash expenditure would be required for their acquisition.

Many large American corporations have investments in other U.S. corporations or in foreign affiliates. In the American Institute of Certified Public Accountants Study of the 600 companies during 1964, some 99 of the 261 that reported investments in unconsolidated subsidiaries used the cost basis. The next most frequently used method was the "equity in the net assets," which 47 companies elected. Some 27, 22, and 27 companies were using cost less reserve, cost or below cost, and cost plus accumulated earnings or equity in earnings, respectively.[4] The footnotes that accompany the financial statements frequently denote the costs, the market values, and the undistributed profits of the affiliated companies.

Fixed assets includes such items as land, plant, and equipment. It is generally preferred that these assets be recorded separately at their costs, since the buildings and equipment are subject to depreciation. Of the 600 companies covered in the previously mentioned 1965 study, 542 were using the cost basis of evaluation for the property account. In keeping with a full disclosure rule, the property, plant, and equipment accounts should be stated separately, with the accumulated depreciation shown as a reduction from the accounts to arrive at the net property account.

The Internal Revenue Service (IRS) has prepared guidelines for numerous classes and types of assets indicating the minimum lives that may be used for federal income tax purposes. The IRS permits the taxpayer to elect many types of depreciation methods, including straight line, sum-of-

[3] American Institute of Certified Public Accountants, p. 57.
[4] American Institute of Certified Public Accountants, p. 83.

the-years digits, declining balance, and many others. The more rapid amortization methods permit a postponement of income taxes to more distant years because of greater expenses claimed during earlier years, and many businessmen have elected either the sum-of-the-years digits or the declining-balance methods for tax purposes. Frequently a company elects one of these accelerated methods for tax purposes but recognizes depreciation expense by the straight-line method (in order to maximize reported profits). Where the latter system is followed, the taxpayer should set up a tax reserve, that is, a contingent liability, equal to the difference between the federal income tax burden incurred by following the straight-line method and one of the accelerated depreciation methods. This tax reserve is merely the postponement of income taxes to future periods, when, using one of the accelerated methods, the depreciation allowance will be smaller. With the tax reserve method, reported net income and earnings per share are more stable than they are if the method is not used.

When the business corporation uses the declining-balance method, at double the straight-line rate, or the sum-of-the-year-digits method for income tax and/or accounting purposes, the depreciation charges are large during the early life of the assets, the cost of goods sold is inflated, and both taxable and reported income are relatively small. Conversely, since both net earnings per share and noncash expenses (depreciation and depletion) increase the cash earnings per share, the cash flow is greater during early years of depreciating an asset by an accelerated depreciation method than by the straight-line method, thus providing more operating capital. The calculation of depreciation under the three methods is as follows: Suppose that the XYZ Corporation purchased a machine for $5500, which had an estimated useful life of 10 years with no scrap value. Under the straight-line method, 10 percent of the asset cost was charged as depreciation expense each year, resulting in an annual claim of $550. In using the sum-of-the-years digits method, the digits 1+2+3+4+5+6+7+8+9+10 equals 55 were inverted and 10/55 of the cost of the machine was amortized the first year, 9/55 the second year, and so forth, producing depreciation of $1000 the first year, $900 the second year, and $800 the third year. The maximum amount of depreciation allowance permitted in using the declining-balance method is found by doubling the straight-line rate and computing the depreciation charge on the decreasing book value. In our example, 20 percent of the initial cost of $5500, or $1100, was deducted the first year, and ($5500 − $1100).20, or $880, during the second year. The accountant follows this procedure for five years (one half the life of the asset), and then switches to the straight-line method so that the asset may be completely depreciated over its estimated useful life.

In addition to the depreciation charges listed above, an unincorporated business firm may take an additional 20 percent depreciation on the cost of an asset during the year of acquisition, but the additional deduction may not exceed $25,000 for a separate return or $50,000 for a joint return. This 1958 tax law has been beneficial to unincorporated business firms because more rapid amortization of assets permits the postponement of income taxes to later years.

In 1961, the federal income tax law authorized a 7 percent tax credit for the acquisition of certain types of assets, such as machinery and equipment, when the estimated useful life is greater than eight years. With a six- to eight-year asset life, two thirds of this rate was granted; only one third was authorized for assets with four- to six-year lives; and when the estimated useful life is four years or less, no credit at all is allowed. The depreciable cost basis was reduced by the amount of the tax credit. Thus only $9300 of a $10,000 machine with a 10-year life could be depreciated after taking the $700 investment credit. This tax credit does not apply to real estate, but only to machinery, equipment, and the like and is a direct reduction from the tax liability. Incorporated and unincorporated business firms and individuals were authorized this tax credit, but public utilities received only one third the rate afforded to industrial companies.

The income tax amendments of 1964 authorized the investment credit without reducing the depreciable base of the asset, but when the asset is disposed of prior to the expiration of the period used in computing the tax credit, additional tax may be owed the federal government. For example, assume that a corporation purchased machinery with a 10-year useful life valued at $70,000 during 1964 and claimed a tax credit of $4900. Should the assets be disposed of prior to a four-year holding period, the entire amount of the investment credit is owed to the federal government in additional income taxes. Should the assets be sold before the eight-year period used in determining the tax credit, a tax liability equal to a part of the previously claimed credit is owed. If the $70,000 machine is sold in its seventh year, one third of the tax credit of $4900 becomes a tax liability.

The term "depletion" may be encountered on the financial statements of certain types of business firms. A depletion allowance refers to a reduction in the cost basis or book value of a natural resource due to consumption of this asset. For example, a coal mine may have estimated coal resources of 100 million long tons. The cost to the coal mining company for the land under which the coal is located is estimated to be 15 cents per long ton. As the coal (or other natural resource) is removed from the land, the total value of the natural resource is depleted. The corporation may elect either the cost basis for matching the cost of the mined product and expenses incurred or the percentage method of depletion for tax purposes. Since the latter method normally produces higher income tax deductions than does the cost method, many corporations, especially petroleum companies, elect to use the former. For oil and gas wells, the allowance for depletion is 27½ percent of gross income from the property, which may not exceed 50 percent of the taxable income of the taxpayer figured without the allowance for the property depletion.[5] Smaller rates are granted to other extracting companies.

The term "amortization of intangible assets" refers to an allocation of the cost of certain intangible assets, such as (1) organizational costs, (2) capitalized research and development expense, (3) leaseholds, (4) leasehold improvements, (5) patents, and (6) copyrights. Many businessmen and accountants follow a conservative rule of amortizing the intangible assets as rapidly as taxing authorities permit, or for accounting purposes, perhaps more rapidly. This rapid amortization reduces the assets and the reported earnings and produces an understated asset section.

Any asset that is owned by the business firm and that has not been classified as (1) a current asset, (2) an investment, (3) a fixed asset, or (4) an intangible asset may be classified either as a deferred charge or as "other assets." *Deferred charges* are costs incurred for services or benefits that are expected to be realized over a long period of years and include bond-issuance costs and developmental and improvement costs. These long-term prepayments are recorded on the balance sheet under the heading "deferred costs" or "deferred charges" and are usually amortized over the expected useful life of the asset, or in some instances over a shorter period. The "other asset" designation includes such assets as miscellaneous deposits received from customers, deposits made with vendors to secure contracts, advances to officers, construction in process, and others.[6]

Liabilities and Capital

The credit side of the balance sheet is devoted to a presentation of the liabilities and capital accounts of the corporation. These accounts merely reflect the sources from which the assets were acquired. The liability section of the balance sheet for a corporation is usually divided into current liabilities, long-term liabilities, and deferred credit to income. The capital section may be divided into capital stock, capital in excess of par value, and retained earnings. Some balance sheets also include sections on minority interests and on reserves, the latter being merely an appropriation of retained earnings.

The *current liabilities* for a business concern are debts owed by the firm that are expected to be liquidated within one year from the balance sheet date during the ordinary course of operation. This section includes such items as accounts payable to trade creditors, notes payable within one year, federal income tax liabilities, accruals of withholding taxes, and miscellaneous accruals (such as wages, interest, and insurance premiums payable). After

---

[5] For an analysis of current federal tax laws that apply to depletion allowances, see the most recent issue of *Federal Tax Course* (Englewood Cliffs, N.J.: Prentice-Hall, Inc.) or some other current tax service.

[6] See, for example, Wilbert E. Karrenbrock and Harry Simons, *Intermediate Accounting*, 3d ed. (Cincinnati, Ohio: South-Western Publishing Company, 1958), pp. 12–13.

cash dividends have been declared by the board of directors, this amount also becomes a current liability to the corporation and should be shown as a debt.

Long-term debts are liabilities owed by a business firm that are expected to be paid at a time more distant than one year from the balance sheet date and include such items as bond issues, term loans, and mortgages payable. Annually, the portion of the debt that is expected to mature within one year should be transferred to a current liability account.

A deferred credit to income account does not appear on the balance sheets of most companies, but some firms, such as publishers that receive magazine subscriptions for more than a year, have an obligation to provide services to these customers and show these debts as deferred credit to income.

Corporations formed by a merger or consolidation of two or more companies may have a minority group of stockholders who refused to accept the stocks in the surviving corporation but continue to hold their old securities. This minority interest is shown between the long-term liability section and the capital stock section on the balance sheet, but few American corporations have such an account.

The capital stock section of a balance sheet consists of accounts for (1) the par value of the preferred stock, (2) the par value of the outstanding common stock, (3) paid-in surplus or capital in excess of par value of capital stock, and (4) retained earnings, that is, earned income of the corporation that has not been paid out in the form of dividends. Frequently a corporation may acquire its own stock, called *treasury stock,* in the market and may deduct its cost from the total of the capital stock section.

Many corporations offer restrictive stock option plans to key officers and employees of their firm in an attempt to permit them some ownership in the company and to reduce employee turnover. These restrictive stock options must comply with state corporation laws, the by-laws of the corporation, and federal income tax rulings. Options are usually granted to key employees at the current market value and may usually be exercised in whole or in part over a stipulated period of time, such as five years. In order for the difference between the cost price and the market price on date of purchase to benefit as a long-term capital gain upon sale of the stock, the individual must hold the stock for at least three years. For example, suppose that a restrictive stock option plan was granted to a young executive, permitting him to purchase 1000 shares of stock in his employer corporation at $19, that the option was granted when the stock was trading for $20 a share, that the option was exercisable in whole or in part at any time during a five-year period, and that the individual exercised the option in whole at the end of the third year, paying $19,000 for the 1000 shares at the time they were trading at $30. In order for the difference between his option price and the market value at the time the shares were acquired to be considered a long-term capital gain ($11,000) for tax purposes, the individual must hold the stock for at least three years. Some 500 of the shares were sold one year after their purchase at $35 per share. The ordinary income was $5500 ($500 × $11), and the difference between the market price per share at the time the shares were purchased and the market price per share at the time the shares were sold, or $5 per share ($35 − $30) times 500 shares, produced a long-term capital gain of $2500. Had the executive continued to hold the stock for three years or longer, the entire gain would have been a long-term capital gain and subject to a maximum tax rate of 25 percent, or one half the ordinary tax rate of the taxpaying individual. Although the tax laws are designed to permit corporations to offer attractive stock purchase plans to their key employees, they are intended to discourage the officers and directors from taking short-term capital gains in the corporation on the basis of their inside knowledge.

Where there are a large number of restrictive stock options outstanding that were granted at prices substantially below the current market value per share, exercise of such options may dilute earnings and market value per share of the securities. However, the owners will normally hold these stocks long enough to take the long-term capital gain, so that the additional number of shares outstanding usually does not increase the marketable supply of the issue.

Under the federal income tax laws prevailing in 1966, the officer or director of an American corporation could not sell short or take short-term capital gains on the stock of the company in which he is employed.

Income and Retained Earnings Statements

Some companies prepare individual statements showing the net income from operations and changes in retained earnings, while others combine these into one statement, as was done by New Jersey Zinc in Table 12-2. The sales, expenses, and earnings of the company show a significant improvement during 1964. The cost of goods sold declined from 85.1 percent of sales in 1963 to 78.2 percent in 1964. Few changes occurred in the relative importance of selling and general administrative expenses, but federal income taxes increased by about 250 percent, while net earnings increased by almost 200 percent. Net earnings rose from 4.1 percent of sales in 1963 to 9 percent in 1964. This improved profitability was influenced by increasing demand for zinc by industry, a world shortage of zinc at that time, and price increases for the basic metal. Favorable earnings reports, expectations of continued future expansion, and other factors caused a substantial rise in the price of the issue during 1965.

The lower section of Table 12-2 indicates that the retained earnings increased $1,592,000 in 1963 by special credits, that is, by income from the sale of securities and land. The balance in the account increased during 1964 even though dividends per share were raised from 50 cents to 90 cents.

TABLE 12-2 / New Jersey Zinc Company and Subsidiaries Consolidated Statements of Earnings and Retained Earnings

	1964		1963	
	$	%	$	%
Net sales	83,222,682	100.0	70,055,454	100.0
Cost of goods sold	65,114,329	78.2	59,640,104	85.1
	18,108,353	21.8	10,415,350	14.9
Gain on sales of marketable securities	1,054,738	1.3	10,873	—
Interest, dividends, and other income	1,007,094	1.2	969,257	1.4
	20,170,185	24.2	11,395,480	16.3
Selling, general, and administrative expenses	5,302,932	6.4	4,569,163	6.5
Exploration	852,087	1.0	676,654	1.0
Research	1,568,266	1.9	1,255,126	1.8
Interest	672,980	0.8	725,940	1.0
Federal income taxes (Note 8)	4,273,000	5.1	1,317,084	1.9
	12,669,265	15.2	8,543,967	12.2
Net earnings	7,500,920	9.0	2,851,513	4.1
Retained earnings, beginning of year (Note 8)	59,565,850		57,022,691	
Special credits, less $349,000 of applicable federal income taxes (Note 9)				
Income from Texas-Zinc Mineral Corporation investment	—		987,751	
Gain on sale of land	—		604,395	
	67,066,770		61,466,350	
Cash dividends: 1964, $.90 per share; 1963, $.50 per share[1]	3,377,445		1,900,500	
Retained earnings, end of year (Note 6)	63,689,325		59,565,850	

[1] Adjusted for a two for one stock split in 1964.
SOURCE: *1964 Annual Report* of the New Jersey Zinc Company, p. 15.

In comparing year-to-year earnings for a company the financial analyst should determine whether consistency has been followed in the preparation of financial statements and that the company's financial statements are prepared on a comparable basis. Since the adoption of certain types of inventory policies will either adversely or favorably affect the reported income for a corporation, for example, the cost of goods sold and profits are drastically changing over a short time period, the investor should consider the effects of such a change on the reported profits.[7] Depreciation policies, special tax treatments, the use of tax carry backs or tax credits and how these influence the earnings per share should also be considered. Extraordinary gains and losses, unless they are expected to occur with some degree of regularity, should be excluded from the earnings per share figure in trying to judge the "real" earning power of a share of common stock.

The profits of foreign subsidiaries should be considered to some extent in determining the profitability of the parent company. The investor should realize that the actions of foreign governments, for example, Mexico's restrictions of sulphur exports in early 1965, may hamper the operations of business firms in their countries. Many corporations do not recognize the income from their subsidiaries until it has been received in the form of cash dividends, while others recognize their portion of the subsidiaries' profits when it is earned rather than when it is distributed. When the latter occurs, the reported earnings of the parent corporation may be exaggerated, and some financial analysts suggest that only 25 to 50 percent of foreign earnings be recognized because of the substantial risks associated with foreign operations.

Notes to Financial Statements

Regulation S-X of the SEC requires that companies which register with the SEC must make certain disclosures regarding their financial condition. Some of this information, which may appear in the form of footnotes to financial statements, covers such areas as: (1) changes in accounting principles, (2) any material retroactive adjustments, (3) significant purchase commitments, (4) long-term lease agreements, (5) assets subject to lien, (6) preferred stock data—any callable, convertible, or preference features, (7) pension and retirement plans, (8) restrictions on the availability of retained earnings for cash dividend purposes, (9) contingent liabilities, (10) depreciation and depletion policies, and (11) stock option or stock purchase plans.

The nine financial notes of Table 12-3 present an interesting insight into various financial aspects of New Jersey Zinc Company during 1964. Note 1 indicates the amount of marketable securities held by the company at year end 1963 and 1964. The company had a book profit of $3 million in the stock investment on the latter date. Although there was not a significant change in the total inventory holdings between year end 1963 and 1964, the amount of raw materials and work in process increased substantially,

[7] During a period of rising prices, the use of the last-in, first-out method for costing inventories will result in (1) carrying the inventory at a fairly low figure, (2) reporting the cost of goods sold at a relatively high figure, and (3) a lower before-tax earnings and a lower income tax burden than the use of the first-in, first-out method. When using the latter method, the inventory, to a large extent, is made up of the more recent acquisitions, so that the cost of goods sold account is slightly understated and the gross profits are exaggerated. When price changes occur, such as in the basic selling price of a metal, wide swings in reported earnings may occur. For this reason, many companies use the lower of cost or market rule, thus eliminating some of the swings.

TABLE 12-3 / New Jersey Zinc Company and Subsidiaries Notes to Financial Statements

1. Marketable securities are summarized as follows:

	1964			1963	
	Par Value	Cost	Value Based on Market Quotations	Par Value	Cost
U.S. government Treasury bonds and bills	$14,043,000	$13,758,844	$13,732,851	$6,166,000	$ 6,084,206
Municipal bonds	75,000	76,458	75,937	145,000	147,840
	Shares			Shares	
Preferred stocks				420	27,590
Common stocks					
American Smelting and Refining Co.				21,600	1,658,335
The Continental Insurance Co.				10,000	583,580
Firestone Tire and Rubber Co.				15,300	526,154
Ford Motor Co.	75,000	3,841,896	4,078,125	20,000	1,014,230
General Electric Co.	105,000	8,817,435	9,791,250		
General Motors Corp.	30,000	2,351,250	2,936,250		
The Goodyear Tire and Rubber Co.				70,000	2,559,326
Hartford Fire Insurance Co.				20,000	1,380,896
Kennecott Copper Corp.	50,500	3,812,856	4,646,000	50,000	3,747,226
Northern Canada Mines, Ltd.	50,000	87,605	90,800	50,000	82,382
Time, Inc.				1,000	84,224
Union Carbide Corp.	20,000	705,741	850,000	20,000	2,205,483
Westinghouse Electric Corp.					
Total		$33,452,085	$36,201,213		$20,101,472

SOURCE: *1964 Annual Report* of the New Jersey Zinc Company, pp. 18–20.

2. Inventories are stated at the lower of average cost or market and comprise:

	1964	1963
Manufactured products	$ 3,681,338	$ 5,783,174
Raw materials and work in process	7,519,556	5,563,015
Fuel and supplies	2,445,091	2,321,242
Total	$13,655,985	$13,667,431

3. At December 31, 1964, based on unaudited financial statements, equity in the net assets of Quebec Iron and Titanium Corporation exceeded the Company's investment therein by approximately $6,293,000 (Canadian currency) and the Company's share of this affiliate's net income amounted to approximately $1,759,000 and $197,000 (Canadian currency) for 1964 and 1963, respectively. No dividends were declared by the affiliate in 1964 or 1963. Refer to pages 4, 13, and 14 for additional comments about investments in affiliates.

4. Property, plant, and equipment is summarized as follows:

	1964	1963
Mines and mineral rights	$ 20,352,516	$ 20,251,055
Other land	1,938,661	1,937,334
Mining plants and equipment	34,254,187	35,590,342
Manufacturing plants and equipment	65,137,644	67,141,226
Other property plant and equipment	6,786,192	6,681,735
Construction in progress	1,729,008	1,169,583
Total	130,198,208	130,771,275
Less: accumulated depreciation (1964, $60,240,859; 1963, $59,076,545) and depletion	72,782,323	71,249,366
	$ 57,415,885	$ 59,521,909

Provision for depreciation and depletion amounted to $5,335,238 in 1964 and $5,211,631 in 1963.

5. In December 1964 the Company sold a portion of the proceeds to be realized from future mineral production at three of its principal properties for $7,800,000. The sale together with related costs and expenses will be taken into income as the minerals sold are produced, which is expected to occur in 1965. Accordingly, the proceeds, less federal and state taxes payable currently thereon, have been deferred in the accompanying financial statements.

6. These notes bear interest at 4½ percent per annum and mature in annual installments of $1,250,000 through 1976. The loan agreement restricts the payment of dividends (other than stock dividends) on the Company's stock and the purchase, redemption, or retirement of its stock to the sum of (a) income subsequent to December 31, 1955, (b) net proceeds from sale of stock of the Company subsequent to September 1, 1956, and (c) $5,000,000. At December 31, 1964, approximately $8,600,000 of retained earnings was free of such restrictions.

7. The Incentive Stock Option Plan, as amended by the Board of Directors to conform to the requirements of the Revenue Act of 1964, provides for the issuance of qualified stock options to officers and other key employees at a price not less

than the fair market value on the dates the options are granted, but not less than par value. The options become exercisable two years after date of grant and the option terms are for a period of 5 to 10 years from date of grant. Unissued shares of Company stock under option at the beginning and end of 1964 and changes during 1964, adjusted for the two for one stock split, are summarized as follows:

Shares under option, December 31, 1963	121,000
Less:	
Options exercised during 1964 at $12.40 to	
$13.25 per share	56,210
Shares under option and exercisable at December 31, 1964,	
at prices ranging from $12.50 to $13.25 per share	64,790

At December 31, 1964, 76,500 shares of unissued stock were reserved for future options.

Capital surplus increased $5825 in 1964, representing the excess of the amount received for capital stock issued under the Plan over the par value thereof.

8. In financial statements included in annual reports to stockholders for 1963 and 1962, the investment credit was being amortized over the productive lives of the acquired properties. In 1964, the Company adopted the method of recognizing the credit as a reduction of federal income taxes of the year in which the credit arises. The provision for federal income taxes in 1963 and retained earnings, December 31, 1962, have been restated to give effect to this change resulting in an increase in net earnings of $372,916 for 1963 and an increase in retained earnings at December 31, 1962, at $121,038.

9. These special credits arose from the receipt of a dividend from Texas-Zinc Minerals Corporation, the sale of the capital stock in that corporation, and the sale of Lake Wawayanda, New Jersey timber tract.

while the manufactured products declined (Note 2). The company's investments in Quebec Iron and Titanium Corporation (reported on the balance sheet at cost) were approximately $6 million less than its equity in the net assets at the end of 1964, and the company's share of the affiliates' net income amounted to $1,759,000 in Canadian currency in 1964. No dividends were declared by the affiliate in 1964, and the parent's share of subsidiary income was not reflected on the earnings statement (Note 3). Although the financial statements of the company do not reflect the depreciation method, the company did charge off depreciation, depletion, and other noncash items in an amount totaling $5,352,000 during 1964. Its net income of $7,501,000 and other income of almost $900,000 produced earnings per share of $3.43 based on the average number of shares outstanding during the year (Note 4). Note 5 describes the sale for future delivery of mineral production at three of its principle properties. The proceeds from the sale, less federal and state taxes currently payable thereon, were deferred. Note 6 describes the interest rate, installment payments, and restrictions upon cash dividends under the loan agreement. Note 7 indicates that at the end of 1964, 64,790 shares were under option to key employees and officers of the firm at option prices ranging from $12.50 to $13.25 per share, and 76,500 shares of unissued stock were reserved for future options. Note 8 indicates a change in the accounting treatment for investment credit, which created an increase in net earnings of $372,916 for 1963 and an increase in retained earnings on December 31, 1962 of $121,038. In 1964, the company adopted the method of recognizing the credit as a reduction of federal income taxes for the year in which the credit arose, whereas before that time the investment credit had been amortized over the productive life of the acquired property.

Accountant's Report

An *accountant's report,* sometimes referred to as the *auditor's certificate,* sets forth the scope of the examination of the financial statements and the opinion of the auditors as to the fairness of the financial statements prepared in conformity with generally accepted accounting principles applied on a consistent basis. The accountant's report for New Jersey Zinc has been modified only slightly from the standard short form audit report to embody the change in accounting principles indicated in Note 8. This report is presented in Table 12-4.

TABLE 12-4 /   Accountant's Report

To the Board of Directors of The New Jersey Zinc Company:

We have examined the consolidated balance sheet of The New Jersey Zinc Company and Subsidiaries as of December 31, 1964, and the related statement of earnings and retained earnings for the year then ended. Our examination was made in accordance with generally accepted auditing standards, and accordingly included such tests of the accounting records and such other auditing procedures as we considered necessary in the circumstances. We previously examined and reported upon the consolidated financial statements of the Company for the year ended December 31, 1963, which have been restated to reflect the change in method of accounting for the investment credit adopted in 1964, in which we concur, as described in Note 8 to the financial statements.

In our opinion, the accompanying financial statements present fairly the consolidated financial position of The New Jersey Zinc Company and Subsidiaries at December 31, 1964 and 1963, and the results of their operations for the years then ended, in conformity with generally accepted accounting principles applied on a consistent basis.

Lybrand, Ross Bros. & Montgomery

SOURCE: *1964 Annual Report* of the New Jersey Zinc Company.

Key Ratios

It is helpful for the analyst to prepare key ratios from the financial statements of a corporation for more than one year in order to determine the trends and operating results of the firm. By comparing the ratios from one year to another, it may be possible to detect improvement or deterioration. The financial analyst may also wish to compare the operating ratios of different companies within the same industry or with industry totals.[8]

The short-term creditor is interested in the current debt-paying ability of the borrowing firm, but the long-term bondholder or the equity investor is concerned with the long-range earning ability of the corporation and is more interested in a profitability analysis of the business firm than in its current liquidity position. There is some overlap, however, in the ratios that are used by the short-term creditors and the long-term investors. Dun and Bradstreet reports annually 14 important ratios for 72 different industries in the September through November issues of *Dun's Review and Modern Industry,* covering manufacturing, wholesalers, and retail firms, respectively. These ratios are frequently used as industry bench marks; a list of these 14 important ratios are shown in Table 12-5 for nonferrous metal foundries and for retail grocery and meat stores.

Definition of Terms

Before the analyst attempts to compute important ratios for a business concern, he should become familiar with certain terms. The following definitions are those reported in *Dun's Review and Modern Industry* and correspond to those that are generally accepted by accountants and financial analysts.

> *Collection Period*—The number of days that the total of trade accounts and notes receivable (including assigned accounts and discounted notes, if any), less reserves for bad debts, represents when compared with the annual net credit sales divided by 365 days to obtain the average credit sales per day. Then divide the total of accounts and notes receivable (plus any discounted notes receivable) by the average credit sales per day to obtain the average collection period.
>
> *Current Assets*—Total of cash, accounts and notes receivable for the sales of merchandise in regular trade quarters, less any reserves for bad debts, advances on merchandise, inventory less any reserves, listed securities when not in excess of market, state and municipal bonds not in excess of market, and United States Government securities.
>
> *Current Debt*—Total of all liabilities due within one year from statement date including current payments on serial notes, mortgages, debentures, or other funded debts. This item also includes current reserves such as gross reserves for Federal income and excess profit taxes, reserves for contingencies set up for specific purposes but does not include reserves for depreciation.
>
> *Fixed Assets*—The sum of the cost value of land and the depreciated book values of buildings, leasehold improvements, fixtures, furniture, machinery, tools, and equipment.

[8] See, for example, the current issue of Internal Revenue Service, *Corporate Income* (Washington, D.C.: U.S. Government Printing Office).

Funded Debt—Mortgages, bonds, debentures, term notes, serial notes, or other obligations with maturity of more than one year from the statement date.

Inventory—The sum of raw material, material in process, and finished merchandise. It does not include supplies.

Net Profits—Profit after full depreciation on buildings, machinery, equipment, furniture, and other assets of a fixed nature; after reserves for Federal income and excess profit taxes; after reduction in the value of inventory to cost or market, whichever is lower; after charge-offs for bad debts; after miscellaneous reserves and adjustments; but before dividends or withdrawals.

Net Sales—The dollar volume of business transacted for 365 days net after deductions for returns, allowances, and discounts from gross sales.

Net Sales to Inventory—The quotient obtained by dividing the annual net sales by the statement inventory. This quotient does not represent the actual physical turnover, which would be determined by reducing the annual net sales to the cost of goods sold and then dividing the resulting figure by the statement inventory.

Net Working Capital—The excess of the current assets over the current debt.

Tangible Net Worth—The sum of all outstanding preferred or preference stocks (if any) and outstanding common stocks, surplus, and undivided profits, less any intangible items in the assets, such as good-will, trademarks, patents, copyrights, leaseholds, mailing list, treasury stock, organized expenses, and underwriting discounts and expenses.

Turnover of Tangible Net Worth—The quotient obtained by dividing annual net sales by tangible net worth.

Turnover of Net Working Capital—The quotient obtained by dividing annual net sales by net working capital.[9]

By using the above definitions of terms, it is possible to compute the 14 important ratios that appear in Table 12-5.

In computing the median and quartile data for the foundries: nonferrous companies, 45 firms were included in the survey. Of this number, one fourth, or approximately 10, had current assets to current debt ratios in excess of the upper quartile figure, 4.51. In ranking the 45 companies for this ratio, the center (or 23d) company in the array had a current asset to current debt ratio of 2.8 times. One fourth of the companies, or 10, had a smaller current asset to current debt ratio than the lower quartile figure of 2.02 times. This procedure was followed by Dun and Bradstreet, who prepared the 14 important ratios for these 45 companies, ranking each individual ratio into an array. From these 14 different arrays, the upper quartile, median, and lower quartile figures were then determined.

A comparison of the ratios for the two industries reveals some major differences. Current assets to current debt was determined by dividing the former figure by the latter and expressing the answer as 2.8 times. The net profits on net sales was considerably higher for the nonferrous foundries

[9] Reprinted by special permission from *Dun's Review and Modern Industry* (Chicago: Dun and Bradstreet Corporation, November 1964).

TABLE 12-5 / Fourteen Important Ratios for Selected Industries, 1963

Foundries: Nonferrous (45 Companies)

Ratio	Quartile 1	Median	Quartile 3
Current assets to current debt ($\times$)	4.51	2.80	2.02
Net profit on net sales (%)	5.54	3.23	1.59
Net profit on tangible net worth (%)	15.68	10.09	4.55
Net profit on net working capital (%)	29.11	17.21	8.08
Net sales to tangible net worth ($\times$)	4.96	2.71	1.96
Net sales to net working capital ($\times$)	9.08	5.41	3.97
Collection period (days)	26	33	46
Net sales to inventory ($\times$)	29.9	16.2	8.9
Fixed assets to tangible net worth (%)	31.2	45.4	71.8
Current debt to tangible net worth (%)	16.9	27.9	49.3
Total debt to tangible net worth (%)	49.0	68.8	100.1
Inventory to net working capital (%)	22.0	48.2	81.3
Current debt to inventory (%)	71.5	111.9	215.6
Funded debt to net working capital (%)	33.2	53.5	97.4

Retail: Groceries and Meats (154)

Ratio	Quartile 1	Median	Quartile 3
Current assets to current debt ($\times$)	2.67	1.83	1.22
Net profit on net sales (%)	1.94	1.16	0.54
Net profit on tangible net worth (%)	19.56	10.36	4.19
Net profit on net working capital (%)	58.88	28.65	9.23
Net sales to tangible net worth ($\times$)	13.41	8.65	6.18
Net sales to net working capital ($\times$)	43.51	20.31	12.03
Collection period (days)	°	°	°
Net sales to inventory ($\times$)	27.3	18.6	13.0
Fixed assets to tangible net worth (%)	35.9	59.1	93.4
Current debt to tangible net worth (%)	26.6	49.5	76.6
Total debt to tangible net worth (%)	57.2	85.3	118.2
Inventory to net working capital (%)	72.4	111.6	191.5
Current debt to inventory (%)	66.7	94.8	135.5
Funded debts to net working capital (%)	25.3	58.3	165.7

° Breakdown on cash and credit sales not available.

SOURCE: Reprinted by special permission from *Dun's Review and Modern Industry* (Chicago: Dun and Bradstreet Corporation, September and December 1964).

than for the retail groceries. Conversely, there was no significant difference between the net profit on tangible net worth for the two groups. The range of net profits on net working capital, stated as a percentage, was much wider for the retail grocery stores than for the nonferrous foundries. Conversely, there was no significant difference between the net profit on tangible net worth for the two groups. The range of net profits on net working capital, stated as a percentage, was much wider for the retail grocery stores than for the nonferrous foundries. Net sales to tangible net worth was about one third as large for the metals as for the groceries and meats. Since there is such a wide disparity between the profitability and capitalization mix ratios for companies within separate industries, it is very important that the financial analyst contrast representative industry or company ratios.

With the exception of the collection period, each of the 14 ratios is computed by dividing the first item by the second. Some of the ratios are expressed in number of times, while others are stated as a percentage. When a ratio exceeds 100 percent, it is usually expressed in number of times, but where it is below 100 percent, the answer is denoted as a percentage. The collection period is ordinarily expressed in number of days that the total of trade accounts and notes receivable (including assigned accounts and discounted notes, if any, less reserve for bad debts) represents when compared with the annual net credit sales. In obtaining this figure, the annual net credit sales is divided by 365 days to obtain the average credit sales per day. Then the total of the net receivables is divided by the average credit sales per day to obtain the average collection period.

In the 14 important ratios reported by Dun and Bradstreet, the ratio of net sales to inventory differs as a result of inventory turnover. In computing inventory turnover, one should use the cost of goods sold to inventory so that both are reported at cost prices. It is acceptable practice to use the net sales to inventory figure to approximate the turnover, if one keeps in mind that the former figure is inflated by the gross profit markup. The analyst should be consistent in computing this ratio for the company when comparing it to the bench mark.

Table 12-6 compares the 14 important ratios for the New Jersey Zinc Company at the end of 1963 and 1964 with the 14 important ratios as reported by *Dun's Review and Modern Industry* for foundries: nonferrous. The 1963 ratios for the company were then ranked by quarters, since they corresponded to the quartile and median figures as reported for the nonferrous companies. In preparing ratios of a company for more than one year and also in contrasting these ratios to those of the appropriate industry, some over-all comparisons may be made between a company and its competitors.

During 1964, the current assets to current debt ratio declined from 6.06 to 3.29 for New Jersey Zinc. This may at first appear alarming until one realizes that almost all of this change was accounted for by a heavier federal income tax burden on higher profits and by recognizing as a liability the production payments sold that would require future delivery. Some accountants classify "production payments sold less federal and state taxes," as a deferred credit to income rather than as a part of the current liabilities

**TABLE 12-6 /   Fourteen Important Ratios for the New
Jersey Zinc Company, 1963 and 1964**

	1963	1964	1963 Quartile[1]
Current assets to current debt (×) *very liquid*	6.06	3.29	U.Q.
Net profit on net sales (%) *Profits up*	4.07	9.01	U.M.
Net profit on tangible net worth (%)	2.68	6.76	L.Q.
Net profit on net working capital (%)	7.45	17.91	L.Q.
Net sales to tangible net worth (×)	.66	.75	L.Q.
Net sales to net working capital (×)	1.83	1.99	L.Q.
Collection period (days)	41	41	L.M.
Net sales to inventory (×)	5.12	6.09	L.Q.
Fixed assets to tangible net worth (%)	56.0	51.7	L.Q.
Current debt to tangible net worth (%)	43.1	54.2	L.Q.
Total debt to tangible net worth (%)	21.2	28.9	U.Q.
Inventory to net working capital (%)	35.7	32.6	U.M.
Current debt to inventory (%)	55.3	133.8	U.Q.
Funded debts to net working capital (%)	39.2	32.8	U.M.

[1] Upper quartile, U.Q., = top 25 percentile; upper median, U.M., = 50 to 75 percentile; lower median, L.M., = 25 to 50 percentile; lower quartile, L.Q., = lower 25 percentile.

SOURCE: Computed from the *1964 Annual Report* of the New Jersey Zinc Company.

account. The current ratio for 1963 ranked within the upper quartile of the industry.

The net profit ratios, which include net profits on net sales, net profits on tangible net worth, net profits on net working capital, and the net worth and net working capital turnover ratios, were generally very low for the New Jersey Zinc Company when compared to its industry. Much progress was made from 1963 to 1964, however.

When comparing the ratios for the company in 1963 to those of its industry, some general observations may be made. The company was much more liquid than its competitors and depended much more heavily on short-term than on long-term debt. The company's heavy use of equity may have resulted in a smaller than average profit on tangible net worth. Profitability was, however, greatly improved in 1964. Some acquisition of the company's own common stock, either on the open market or from large holders of the securities, could have improved earnings per share. Note 6 to the financial statements (Table 12-3) describes a loan agreement that restricts such acquisition to (1) income subsequent to December 31, 1955, (2) net proceeds from sale of stock of the company subsequent to September 1, 1956, and (3) $5 million above the amount declared in cash dividends subsequent to that date. At the end of December 1964, the company had approximately $8.6 million of retained earnings that were free from such restrictions and that could have been used to reacquire the corporation's own stock.[10]

Summary

Although the investor may not be trained as an accountant, he should be able to analyze the financial statements that are prepared and distributed by business corporations and be able to compare them to industry statements and to statements of similar companies.

The analyst should compare financial statements for more than one year so that financial improvement or deterioration can be determined. He may wish to prepare comparative financial statements reported as percentages of total assets and as percentages of total net sales rather than using dollar amounts, since common-size statements clearly reflect changes in the breakdown of assets, liabilities, capital accounts, revenues, and expenses.

The analyst should prepare important ratios from the financial statement of the company that he is analyzing and compare these to key ratios for the company's industry or to the ratios of a similar firm. He may select as bench marks (1) ratios computed from the composite financial statements reported by industries and published in the Internal Revenue's *Corporate Income* or (2) the 14 important ratios for 72 industry lines that are reported each year by *Dun's Review and Modern Industry*.

One should not be overly concerned when a few of the ratios appear out of line. One should, however, determine the reasons for significant differences. The analyst should gain an over-all impression from the ratios regarding the financial strengths and weaknesses of the company rather than placing excessive importance upon one or two ratios. The preparation and interpretation of ratios do, to a large extent, locate weaknesses and strengths in a business firm and indicate areas where a more extensive study should be conducted.

QUESTIONS FOR REVIEW /

1. How does the financial analysis made by a short-term creditor differ from that made by a long-term investor?
2. State in your own words the meaning of current assets and current liabilities.

[10] The company did acquire 200,000 shares of its securities from St. Joseph Lead Corporation for approximately $9 million in late April 1965. This acquisition reduced the outstanding shares by some 5 percent and was undertaken in order to increase the earnings per share. The book value per share of $27.25 at the end of December 1964 was similar to the acquisition price per share of approximately $30. This reduction in the total number of shares outstanding, and a tremendous increase in the earnings per share in 1964 over 1963, perhaps accounted for the substantial increase in the market value of the stock in 1965.

3. What items should appear in the current assets section of the balance sheet? in the current liabilities section?
4. Of what significance is the method used in accounting for inventories important to the stockholder?
5. What assets on the balance sheet are subject to depreciation? depletion? amortization?
6. Should a financial analyst be concerned about a substantial decline in the current ratio for a business?
7. How does a capital surplus (capital in excess of par value) account arise?
8. Why are notes to financial statements frequently used? What items should be covered in these?
9. How much reliance should be placed upon the accountant's report?
10. What important ratios would you as a short-term creditor be interested in computing for a prospective client?
11. As a prospective investor in the stocks of a corporation, which ratios do you consider important?
12. How would you rate the New Jersey Zinc Company at the end of 1964 with regard to (1) liquidity, (2) profitability, and (3) over-all operating performance?

PROBLEMS /

1. With the use of *Moody's Industrial Manual* or annual reports, obtain financial statements on two companies in the metals industry and compare their operating performance and important ratios with their industry.
2. Prepare comparative financial statements for two food companies, such as the Great Atlantic and Pacific Tea Company and Winn-Dixie, for a period of three or four years. Compute important ratios for the two companies and compare them to those for the industry. Which company appears to rank more favorably? Would you recommend either of these companies for a short-term and/or a long-term investment? Defend your position.
3. For one or two of the companies mentioned above, consult the important ratios that appear in *Moody's Industrial Manual* and compare them to the 14 important Dun and Bradstreet ratios. How may the use of these ratios facilitate the work of the financial analyst?

REFERENCES /

American Institute of Certified Public Accountants, *Accounting Trends and Techniques,* 17th ed. New York: The Institute, 1965.

Dun's Review and Modern Industry. Chicago: Dun and Bradstreet Corporation, November 1964.

Federal Tax Course. Englewood Cliffs, N.J.: Prentice-Hall, Inc., selected issues.

Bogen, Jules I., *Financial Handbook,* 3d. ed. New York: The Ronald Press Company, 1952.

Forbes Magazine. New York: Forbes, Inc., January 1, 1965 and selected issues.

Graham, Benjamin, *The Intelligent Investor.* New York: Harper & Row, Publishers, Inc., 1959.

————, David L. Dodd, and Sidney Cottle, *Security Analysis*, 4th ed. New York: McGraw-Hill Book Company, Inc., 1962.

Internal Revenue Service, *Corporate Income*. Washington, D.C.: U.S. Government Printing Office, selected issues.

Karrenbrock, Wilbert E., and Harry Simons, *Intermediate Accounting*, 3d ed. Cincinnati, Ohio: South-Western Publishing Company, 1958.

Moody's Handbook of Common Stocks. New York: Moody's Investors Service, Inc., selected issues.

Moody's Industrial Manual. New York: Moody's Investors Service, Inc., 1964–1966.

The New Jersey Zinc Company, *1964 Annual Report*. New York: The Company, 1965.

New York Stock Exchange, *The Exchange*. New York: The Exchange, December 1963.

U.S. Department of Commerce, *Statistical Abstract of the United States*. Washington, D.C.: U.S. Government Printing Office, 1965.

————, *Survey of Current Business*. Washington, D.C.: U.S. Government Printing Office.

The Value Line Investment Survey. New York: Arnold Bernhard & Company, Inc., selected issues.

chapter 13 | Industrial Issues

Introduction

An individual who wishes to commit his funds to a long-term investment in industrial stocks should place tremendous importance upon the future outlook within industries. He should select industries having excellent potential for growth in sales and profits. From these industries he should then select companies that are expected to outperform their competitors. When an investor selects a growth company, sales, and in particular, profits, for the company should be increasing. Their continued increase will favorably affect the market value of the common stock.

The investor will find industries classified in a number of ways, the total number ranging from a low of approximately 17 to a high of perhaps 100. Since there are so many industrial groupings, and the number of actively traded stocks is so numerous, selection of individual issues becomes difficult. The statement and ratio analysis presented in Chapter 12 throws some interesting light upon the advisability of buying, holding, or selling a particular stock issue, but this type of analysis is time consuming when undertaken for a large number of companies. A more rapid method should be sought for eliminating as possibilities a majority of the companies under consideration, and a more detailed analysis should be applied to those that meet preliminary objectives.

The purpose of this chapter is to show how an investor may proceed in selecting individual industries and representative companies that appear to be desirable investment media. A brief comparison is made between the performances of companies operating in the durable and consumer nondurable goods industries. The operating performances of two companies selected from the nonferrous metals industry and from the food industry are contrasted in order to suggest methods for analyzing and interpreting key financial information.

Aids for Industry Selection

Population Projections

A key consideration in determining the attractiveness of an industry frequently is the outlook for population growth and the projected population "mix" in terms of both age and sex. Table 13-1 presents the population

221

TABLE 13-1 /   Population, by Age and Sex: 1960 and Projections to 1985

Year, Sex, and Series	Total, All Ages	Under 5 Years	5 to 9 Years	10 to 14 Years	15 to 19 Years
1960	180,676	20,364	18,825	16,910	13,465
1965—A	195,129	21,242			
B	194,671	20,783	20,420	18,888	16,977
C	194,136	20,248			
D	194,127	20,239			
1970—A	211,430	23,991	21,277		
B	208,996	22,013	20,821	20,469	18,941
C	206,110	19,660	20,289		
D	205,886	19,444	20,280		
1975—A	230,415	27,312	24,017	21,325	
B	225,870	25,192	22,047	20,870	20,516
C	220,133	22,330	19,703	20,339	
D	218,855	21,276	19,488	20,330	
1980—A	252,056	30,557	27,327	24,060	21,369
B	245,313	28,345	25,215	22,094	20,915
C	236,474	25,225	22,364	19,755	20,386
D	233,140	23,164	21,314	19,540	20,377
1985—A	275,622	33,048	30,561	27,363	24,096
B	266,322	30,469	28,358	25,255	22,136
C	254,016	26,974	25,250	22,410	19,804
D	247,953	24,235	23,197	21,363	19,591

projection of the Bureau of the Census from 1960 to 1985 based on four different fertility rates of adult women. By 1980, if the fertility rate, as measured by the average number of children per 1000 women at the end of child-bearing age is at the highest projected level, the population of the United States should approximate 252 million; but if the fertility rate is at the lowest projected figure, the population should be only 233 million. Although the population projection from 1965 through 1985 indicates an expected increase in all age groups, the number of persons between the ages of 25 through 44 was not significantly larger in 1965 than in 1960. From 1965 to 1970, the population within the 20- to 24-year age bracket should increase by one fourth, while the population within the 25- to 34-year age group should rise by only 12 percent. By 1970 and 1975, the projection of individuals between the ages of 35 and 44 shows a decline, while an increase in population is projected for the group between the ages of 20 and 34.

Since consumer preferences shift with sex and age differences, some importance should be placed upon these forecasts by the businessman, for example, in planning expansion, and by the investor, for example, in considering stock purchases. Increases in the number of infants, for example, accelerate sales of baby foods, infant wear, baby equipment, and the like,

TABLE 13-1 *(Continued)*

Year, Sex, and Series	20 to 24 Years	25 to 34 Years	35 to 44 Years	45 to 54 Years	55 to 64 Years	65 and Over
1960	11,112	22,909	24,223	20,581	15,628	16,659
1965—A B C D	13,623	22,374	24,462	22,067	16,973	18,102
1970—A B C D	17,104	25,220	22,997	23,360	18,501	19,571
1975—A B C D	19,057	31,139	22,458	23,574	19,846	21,171
1980—A B C D	20,624	36,517	25,267	22,194	21,056	23,087
1985—A B C D	21,472 21,021 20,494 20,485	40,004	31,089	21,718	21,266	25,006

SOURCE: U.S. Department of Commerce, *Statistical Abstract of the United States* (Washington, D.C.: U.S. Government Printing Office, 1964), p. 7.

and expansion of the school-age group produces greater demands for clothing, toys, shool supplies, books, and the like. College-age young people are prime customers for school supplies and books, automobiles, clothing, recreation, and vending machine products. Young adults (ages 20–35) who form new family units need housing, furniture and appliances, automobiles, life and nonlife insurance, and other necessities of life. Middle-aged adults (35–54) have more demand for single-unit dwellings, second automobiles, boats, summer homes, investments in stocks, travel, recreation, and so forth. The retired, conversely, normally spend their limited budget on necessities of life, largely food, housing, and medicines. By 1975, the number of persons between the ages of 15 and 24 will be some 33 percent greater than in 1965. Conversely, the number of adults from 25 through 54 will rise by only 10 percent. Sales of consumer goods, which are usually sold to individuals between the ages of 14 and 24, then, should be increasing from 1965 to 1975, while sales of goods to individuals between the ages of 25 to 54 should increase only slightly during the period.

Industry Groupings

The number of industry breakdowns varies widely, depending upon the source. The U.S. Department of Commerce, in each issue of its *Survey of Current Business* or in its biannual supplement, *Business Statistics,* lists 17 industrial classifications, which are further subdivided into 76 classifications. An individual who desires sales data, inventory levels, and other financial series on these 76 subclassifications may refer to these primary sources of information. Standard & Poor's Corporation lists group stock movements for 60 industries, while Trendline's *Current Market Perspectives* has 90 industry groups, and the quarterly, *Security and Industry Survey* published by Merrill Lynch, Pierce, Fenner & Smith, Inc., uses 33 industry classifications. The wide range between the number of industrial classifications is influenced by the differences in the combinations of these items. For example, the Department of Commerce includes air carriers, express operations, local transit lines, motor carriers, railroads, waterways, traffic, and travel in the transportation classification. An individual may subclassify the various industries into subindustries if he chooses or he may elect to work with a smaller number of breakdowns.

Before selecting an industry in which to invest, the prospective stockholder should consider such things as probable government expenditures during the next two or three years and how this factor is likely to affect sales and profits for companies in the aerospace, electronics, munitions, communications, and other industries; probable automobile sales during the next year or two and how this factor is likely to influence profits of automobile, automotive parts, and tire companies; probable future expenditures for recreation, for example, for air travel and motel or hotel accommodations; the government's agricultural program and how it may shape the future sales and profits of companies that produce agricultural equipment, fertilizer, insecticides, and basic commodities; the probable level of industrial production and how it will influence sales of heavy equipment, basic metals, chemicals, and the like. During the latter 1960s, Congress's emphasis on Medicare, automobile safety, food for freedom, a guaranteed standard of living in the United States; the conflict between the Communist and the Free World; labor's struggle to gain a larger share of corporate income; the rising population of young adults, with their job, consumer, and credit needs; the apparent shortage of investment funds; and the attempts to combat inflationary trends without stifling growth in industrial production should produce mixtures of pessimism and optimism for fixed- and variable-return securities.

Cyclical Patterns

Companies representative of a number of industries, such as beverages, drugs and cosmetics, foods, merchandising, and tobacco, vary relatively little in sales, profits, and market value fluctuations over the business cycle. Conversely, sales of other industries, for example, building materials, chemicals, steel, and transportation, vary widely from boom to recession.

If an individual believes that industrial production in the United States will continue to be strong during the next two or three years and that a shortage in basic metals will prevail within the foreseeable future, he may wish to commit his funds in these types of securities. On the other hand, if he expects a downturn in the growth rate, believes that the average price–earnings ratios are excessive, and feels that stock prices may run into weakness in the next few months, he may prefer to invest in more defensive issues, such as foods, certain types of beverages, and tobaccos. The investor should consider industry sales, profits, and market value fluctuations over the business cycle, attempt to analyze the probable growth in the gross national product and the index of industrial production, and gear his investment decisions to the outlook for a continued boom or recession period.

Published Recommendations

The investor may continuously obtain predictions of economists and security analysts for various industry groups in a number of sources. Various articles that appear in *Forbes Magazine, Barron's, Financial World,* and *The Magazine of Wall Street* as well as the publications of investment services contain analyses of individual industries and recommendations for purchasing, holding, or selling representative stock issues. The January 1 issue of *Forbes* is devoted each year to an annual report on American industry and presents outlooks for 18 classifications for the next 12 months and for the long range. Although the individual may not concur with these forecasts, it does stimulate thinking about the area, and the information is usually helpful in reaching a logical decision with regard to his security investments. Each monthly issue of *Security Owners' Stock Guide,* published by Standard & Poor's Corporation, contains breakdowns by industry, with recommendations of favorably situated companies. Industrial analyses also appear in *Moody's Stock Survey, Standard & Poor's Industry Surveys, The Value Line Investment Survey, The Security and Industry Survey, The Exchange,* and numerous other financial journals.

When an individual is interested in commiting his funds to an intermediate- or long-range investment, he should study the industry's prospects as reported by numerous periodicals or advisory services. If many of these services are concurrently recommending stocks representative of a given industry, buying pressure and rising stock prices may be generated for a time, but unless the industry actually does have some future growth prospects, the market rallies will probably be short-lived. Therefore, the investor should study the underlying strengths or weaknesses within a given industry and try to determine what effects population growth, population shifts in age groups, and the general level of economic activity within the nation will have upon the operation and profitability of an industry and of individual companies within the industry.

The Metals Industry

The metals industry includes companies that produce copper, aluminum, nickel, lead, and zinc. In the following section financial and operating data for two companies within the metals industry, New Jersey Zinc and St. Joseph Lead, are analyzed. Important ratios for the two companies are then compared with each other and with the industry average. Common-size income statements are then contrasted.

An investor should not attempt to analyze a company, such as a basic metal producer, and exclude an industry analysis, but he should determine whether or not there are reasonable expectations for future gains in sales and earnings for the company and the industry. The basic metal producers fared much better in 1964 than in 1963. This was not unexpected, however, since in 1964 lead prices rose 28 percent over 1963 prices. Aluminum prices increased by about 6 percent, copper prices edged up by almost 10 percent, and zinc prices rose by about 25 percent. As the selling price of a basic metal increases, a large percentage of the additional revenues is converted directly to the before-tax profits of the corporation. Phelps Dodge, which is a large copper producer, had relatively stable profits from 1959 through 1963, when earnings per share ranged between $3.41 and $3.94. Generally, however, earnings per share fluctuate very widely over the business cycle for producers of basic metals. Widely fluctuating earnings normally produce oscillating stock prices, with the price movements of the stock leading actual changes in profitability.

In the early 1960s, there was a shortage in world-wide production of lead; consumption had increased, and production capacity increased only moderately. Lead prices on the London Metal Exchange in early 1965 were some 31 percent above U.S. prices, when normally the English price level is about 5 percent lower than American. Although lead producers were reluctant to raise prices because of the fear of losing sales to competing metals, possible continued lead shortages were forecasted for a period of time.[1]

During 1964, zinc prices rose from $.115 to $.145 per pound, reflecting the supply–demand situation. The U.S. government released 75,000 tons of this metal from its stockpile during 1965, and despite the fact that the world supply rose by about 320,000 tons, the demand continued to be greater than the supply during early 1965. *Value Line* forecasted that the supply and demand for zinc could be approximately in balance during 1965 and that the supply could more than catch up with the demand during subsequent years. With stable or reduced prices of a basic metal, the market value of the equities usually declines.

The following sections will analyze important financial data of two of

---

[1] See *The Value Line Investment Survey* (New York: Arnold Bernhard & Company, Inc., March 12, 1965), p. 852.

the largest zinc producers, the New Jersey Zinc Company and St. Joseph Lead Company, in order to contrast their operating performances (1) over time, (2) with one another, and (3) with companies in a less cyclical industry, for example, foods.

The New Jersey Zinc Company

Table 13-2 presents a mass of financial information on the New Jersey Zinc Company from 1949 through 1964 which was extracted from *The Value Line Investment Survey*. The company was the largest U.S. producer of zinc products in 1965, accounting for about 15 percent of total U.S. output. Sales for the company increased each year from 1961 through 1964, and for each of the four years the profit margin improved over the preceding year. The net plant, in millions of dollars, was relatively stable from 1958 to 1964, but the depreciation rate had been increasing somewhat over that period of time. The percentage earned on total capital was relatively high from 1950 to 1952, lower in 1953 and 1954, recovered somewhat in 1955, and was at a relatively low level from 1956 to 1963. During 1964, conversely, net income to net worth rose to 6.8 percent. The book value per share at the end of 1964, although not revealed in Table 13-2, was only slightly larger than the market value on that date.

From 1949 to 1964, the average annual price–earnings ratio was 22 times. The market price of the stock, relative to earnings, appeared to be depressed during 1964, and if one multiplies the average annual price–earnings ratio of 22 by the forecasted earnings of $2.80 per share during 1965, a projected market value of $61 is obtained. Between the release date of the statement, March 12, 1965, and the end of April, the market price of the issue rose from $26 to $40 per share. *The Value Line Investment Survey* had suggested in early 1965 that the 12-month performance of the issue would be within the top rating, but did not believe this issue to be a desirable three- to five-year holding, and therefore rated it in the lowest of five groupings. In early 1965, the company was paying dividends at an annual rate of $1.25 per share. When the market price of a metal declines, the earnings and dividends per share are usually lowered, thus adversely affecting the market value of the issue. The investment service makes a study of the past seven years' actual growth rate in cash earnings per share and forecasts the probable growth rate during the next seven years. *Value Line* estimated the annual growth rate for New Jersey Zinc for 1965 to 1972 to be 5.5 percent, a figure higher than the historical growth rate of a −0.7 percent. The investment service, however, predicted that the 1967 to 1969 price of the issue would not be much greater than the March 12, 1965, price. Although *Value Line* estimated 1965 earnings per share to be $2.80, the service expected the 1967 to 1969 reported earnings per share to be only one half that figure (due to increasing world-wide production of zinc).

Individuals who have a limited amount of time to spend in computing

TABLE 13-2 / Financial Data on New Jersey Zinc Company, 1949–1965

841 NEW JERSEY ZINC NYSE- **NJZ**

Value Line Survey — Arnold Bernhard & Co., Inc. — MARCH 12, 1965

Recent Price **26** | Yield est'd next 12 mos. **4.8%** | Next div'd meeting about 4/16 if goes ex about 4/28

GROWTH RATE (Cash Earnings) — Past 7 years, Actual −.7% | Next 7 years, Value Line Est. 5.5%

Normal average price 1967-69, if our estimate of earnings is on target. **30**

9.0 × Cash Earnings (5 yr. Moving Avg., Centered)

2-for-1 split

HOW SUITABLE FOR YOU / YOUR Weights (4, 3, 2 or 1—use each weight only once)

Quality (C+)	4 ×	
12 mos. (I)	10 ×	
3-5 Years (V)	8 ×	
Yield (4.8%)	8 ×	
Sum (100 perfect, 60 average) =		

Percentage of outstanding shares traded monthly: 4.0%, 3.0%, 2.0%, 1.0%

Italicized numbers are estimates

Statistical array

	1949	1950	1951	1952	1953	1954	1955	1956	1957	1958	1959	1960	1961	1962	1963	1964	1965	1966	1967-69
Sales ($ mill) ①	NA	NA	NA	NA	NA	NA	NA	NA	NA	NA	NA	NA	61.9	63.2	70.1	83.2	88		72
Profit Margin ②	NA	NA	NA	NA	NA	NA	NA	NA	NA	NA	NA	NA	14.0%	14.2%	17.2%	26%	27%		18%
Working Cap'l ($ mill) ④		29.4	31.5	33.2	33.2	34.7	36.7	52.4	57.2	60.1	59.7	61.2	60.8	59.0	59.0				
Bonds & Pfd. ($ mill)								14.8	20.0	20.0	20.0	18.8	17.5	16.3	15.0				
Net Plant ($ mill)	NA	23.4	26.3	29.6	29.6	26.1	22.0	26.5	24.0	32.5	36.0	32.9	33.2	34.9	38.2				
Depreci'n rate ②		1.8%	2.0%	2.1%	2.1%	2.1%	2.2%	2.2%	2.5%	2.4%	2.8%	2.4%	3.2%	3.6%	4.0%				
% Earned Total Cap'l	NA	10.3%	9.7%	11.2%	2.6%	3.0%	4.5%	2.7%	1.7%	1.3%	3.4%	2.0%	2.2%	1.9%	2.7%				
% Earned Common Eq'ty	NA	10.3%	9.7%	11.2%	2.0%	3.0%	4.5%	2.4%	1.2%	0.8%	3.3%	1.6%	1.8%	1.5%	2.3%				
Book Value per sh.	NA	24.88	26.20	26.62	26.62	26.47	27.06	26.93	26.53	26.35	27.48	26.92	27.10	27.20	26.93				
Cash Earn'gs per sh.	NA	2.97	3.01	3.36	1.23	1.27	1.70	1.26	1.05	1.45	1.76	1.46	1.62	1.58	1.96	2.40	3.80		3.30
Capital Spending per sh.	NA	1.26	1.54	1.30	1.02	.92	1.04	4.59	1.73	1.65	.85	1.29	.95	.74	1.31	1.79			1.35
Reported Earn'gs sh.	1.25	2.56	2.53	3.08	.69	.79	1.23	.66	.32	.21	.89	.44	.49	.41	.66	1.79	2.80		
Div'ds Declared sh.	1.38	1.50	1.50	1.50	1.38	.63	.63	.75	.69	.15	.25	.50	.50	.31	.50	.90	1.25		.90
Div'd Payout Ratio	NA	51%	50%	42%	112%	49%	37%	60%	66%	16%	14%	34%	19%	20%	25%	25%	33%		27%
Avg Annual P/E Ratio	23.5	11.5	14.4	14.8	78.1	25.8	17.4	36.5	52.4	56.8	15.4	26.7	27.4	36.6	24.4	12.6			22.0
Avg Annual Div'l Yield	4.7%	5.1%	4.1%	4.6%	5.5%	3.1%	2.9%	3.1%	4.2%	1.3%	1.8%	4.3%	2.3%	3.1%	4.0%	4.0%			3.0%

Price to Earnings Ratio	Dividend Yield	Estimated 12 months to 3/31/66	
Current 9.3 ③	Current 4.8%	Cash Earnings $3.80	Div'd Declarations $1.25
13 yr. Median 26.7 ⑤	13 Jr. Median 3.1%	Reported Earnings $2.80	

Quality	12 Mos. Perform'ce	Desirability as 3-5 Yr. Holding	
C+	I (highest)	V (lowest) ‡	

Characteristic Growth Index	40	(Range 100 to 5)
Characteristic Stability Index	1.5	(Range 100 to 5)

SOURCE: *The Value Line Investment Survey* (New York: Arnold Bernhard & Company, Inc., March 12, 1965), p. 841.

important financial and operating ratios for a corporation may refer to the appropriate manual of Moody's Investors Service, for example, industrials, utilities, and so on. Table 13-3 reports a number of important financial and operating ratios that are regularly published by Moody's on the companies analyzed therein. Since these ratios were constructed in the previous chapter from the financial statements, no additional comments will be made on them at this time. Having access to the already constructed ratios, however, can conserve time for the financial analyst.

TABLE 13-3 /   Important Ratios for Two Lead and Zinc Companies, 1962–1964

Ratios	St. Joseph Lead, Year Ended Dec. 31		New Jersey Zinc Company, Year Ended Dec. 31[1]	
	1962	1963	1963	1964
Financial and Operating Ratios				
Current assets and current liabilities	5.35	4.00	6.06	3.29
Cash and securities to current assets (%)	55.62	55.27	61.59	52.60
Inventory to current assets (%)	29.99	24.91	53.19	29.84
Net current assets to net worth (%)	45.01	37.11	38.63	35.99
Property depreciated (%)	65.05	65.62	55.90	54.48
Annual depreciation to gross properties (%)	2.63	2.81	—	—
Capitalization Ratios				
Common stock and surplus (%)	79.51	84.30	84.9	79.9
Sales divided by inventory	4.82	6.68	5.12	6.09
Sales divided by receivables	10.46	10.67	8.94	8.87
Sales to net property (%)	142.67	158.71	144.95	117.70
Sales to total assets (%)	57.39	61.16	58.20	54.38
Net income to total assets (%)	2.36	8.01	5.25	2.21
Net income to net worth (%)	3.30	10.79	6.76	2.68
Analysis of Operations	(%)	(%)	(%)	(%)
Sales	100.00	100.00	100.00	100.00
Cost of merchandise sold	85.75	76.63	85.1	78.2
Operating and administrative expenses	15.41	13.01	10.3	9.3
Operating profits	(1.16)	10.36	5.6	12.5
Other income (net of expenses)	6.03	4.84	0.4	1.6
Total income	4.87	15.20	6.0	14.1
U.S. and Canadian income taxes	.75	2.10	1.9	5.1
Net income	4.12	13.10	4.1	9.0

[1] Computed from annual reports.

SOURCE: *Moody's Industrial Manual* (New York, Moody's Investors Service, Inc., 1964), pp. 407, 1189, and 2174.

St. Joseph Lead Company

In 1965, the St. Joseph Lead Company was the nation's largest producer of lead and one of the major miners of zinc. Lead was expected to be in a strong demand position through 1967, but after that time *Value Line* forecasted that supply would probably match demand, thus setting the stage for future declines in the price of lead. The profit margin of the company has historically been very susceptible to the business cycle. For example, according to Table 13-4 the profit margin declined from 11.3 percent in 1957 to 5.8 percent in 1958, while it declined from 11.4 percent in 1961 to 4.1 percent in 1962. From 1962 through 1965, however, the profit margin increased. While the percentage earned on total capital was 10 percent or greater from 1949 through 1957, the annual return from 1958 through 1962 averaged only about 5 percent. The percentage earned on total capital increased to 10 percent in 1963 and to more than 20 percent during 1964 and 1965. Although the book value per share had been increasing somewhat from year to year, the company had also been paying a generous dividend. The 13-year median price–earnings ratio of 13 times the estimated reported earnings per share of 1967 through 1969 would produce an expected market value of about $65 per share during that time interval, according to *Value Line* estimates.

An investor should consider the sales trend of a company, the demand for its product, and the future expected earnings per share by the company within the foreseeable future. All these factors, plus the fact that the stock in St. Joseph Lead Company was trading at a dividend yield of 4.8 percent when the average New York Stock Exchange stock was trading at about 3.2 percent, made the stock appear to be underpriced in the market. In early 1965, *The Value Line Investment Survey* rated the stock in the highest grouping for the next 12 months' performance, but in the fourth grouping for the three- to five-year holding period.[2]

A small rating schedule appears in the upper right corner of the *Value Line* chart (Tables 13-2 and 13-4) which permits the investor to weight the stocks for quality, 12-month expectations, three- to five-year expectations, and yield. If the investor places prime importance upon quality (price stability), he weighs this factor with 4; and if he places the 12-month expected performance as being next in importance, this item is weighted with 3. If values of 2 and 1, respectively, are used for the other two categories, the stock has an over-all rating evaluation of 62, which compares closely with an average rating of 60.

The financial and operating ratios on the St. Joseph Lead Company, which appear in Table 13-3, are similar to those on the New Jersey Zinc Company. During the early 1960s, the St. Joseph Lead Company increased

[2] In early 1965, The *Value Line* groupings were changed from quintiles of 220 stocks each to a more normal distribution; that is, I, 100 stocks; II, 250 stocks; III, 400 stocks; IV, 250 stocks; and V, 100 stocks.

TABLE 13-4 / Financial Data on St. Joseph Lead Company, 1949-1965

844 ST. JOSEPH LEAD NYSE-SJO

Value Line Survey
© Arnold Bernhard & Co., Inc.
MARCH 12, 1965

Recent Price **48** | Yield est'd **4.8%** next 12 mos. | Next div'd meeting about 5/18 goes ex about 5/25

GROWTH RATE (Cash Earnings)
Past 7 years, Actual : 3.2%
Next 7 years, Value Line Est. 12.5%

9.0 × Cash Earnings (5 yr. Moving Avg., Centered)

3-for-2 split · 10% div'd

Normal average price 1967-69, if our estimate of earnings is on target,

HOW SUITABLE FOR YOU?	YOUR Weights (4, 3, 2 or 1—use each weight only once)
Quality (C+)	___ 4 × ___ = ___
12 mos. (I)	___ 10 × ___ = ___
3-5 years (IV)	___ 4 × ___ = ___
Yield (4.8%)	___ 8 × ___ = ___
Sum (100 perfect, 60 average) = ___	

Percentage of outstanding shares traded monthly — 4.0%, 3.0%, 2.0%, 1.0%

Italicized numbers are estimates

	1949	1950	1951	1952	1953	1954	1955	1956	1957	1958	1959	1960	1961	1962	1963	1964P	1965	1966	1967-69
Sales ($ mill.) ①	82.7	103.9	110.8	105.2	88.0	95.0	121.5	119.9	106.9	75.6	86.2	79.6	70.7	67.7	75.7	109.5	115	125	125
Profit Margin	14.8%	19.4%	26.2%	14.5%	12.5%	14.5%	16.8%	14.1%	11.3%	5.8%	10.3%	9.3%	11.4%	4.1%	15.4%	23.8%	26%	28%	28%
Working Cap'l ($ mill.)	23.7	30.0	34.1	31.8	25.4	29.5	33.6	38.2	33.6	40.0	42.6	37.7	47.9	38.1	34.1				
Bonds & Pfd. ($ mill.)									8.5	23.5	27.7	26.8	23.1	21.8	17.1				
Net Plant ($ mill.) ② ⑥	11.9	12.0	14.1	18.0	21.0	19.6	19.1	19.7	31.7	40.4	45.6	47.5	46.7	47.1	47.6	47.9			
Deprecia'n rate	2.4%	2.6%	2.0%	2.1%	2.2%	2.9%	3.0%	3.0%	3.2%	2.4%	2.7%	2.9%	2.4%	2.6%	2.8%				
% Earned Total Cap'l	17.3%	21.6%	21.8%	15.1%	10.1%	11.6%	18.3%	14.4%	10.1%	5.0%	7.0%	3.9%	5.5%	2.6%	10.0%				
% Earned Common Eq'ty	17.3%	21.6%	21.8%	15.1%	10.1%	11.6%	18.3%	14.4%	10.8%	5.3%	7.9%	3.7%	5.9%	3.3%	10.8%				
Book Value per sh.	11.05	12.62	13.87	14.27	14.01	14.48	15.51	15.99	16.56	16.85	17.64	17.69	18.50	18.86	20.21				
Cash Earn'gs per sh.	2.28	3.14	3.36	2.51	1.81	2.23	3.43	2.89	2.45	1.50	2.14	1.50	1.79	1.75	3.03	4.93	5.60		6.65
Capital Spending per sh. ④	.24	.45	.85	1.26	1.09	.25	.50	.79	3.33	2.57	1.96	1.30	.54	.70	.95				5.00
Reported Earn'gs sh.	1.91	2.72	3.03	2.15	1.41	1.68	2.83	2.30	1.79	.89	1.39	.66	1.09	.62 ⑧	2.18	3.93	4.50		5.00
Div'ds Declared sh.	1.43	1.43	1.79	1.73	1.67	1.21	1.82	2.83	1.21	.61	.61	.61	.61	.67 ⑧	.84	1.67	2.20		2.60
Div'd Payout Ratio	63%	46%	53%	68%	91%	49%	52%	61%	50%	40%	28%	40%	34%	35%	27%	34%	39%		39%
Avg Annual P/E Ratio	9.6	6.9	6.9	12.3	15.4	13.6	13.0	11.9	11.3	19.0	14.1	26.0	18.3	27.8	11.0	10.9			13.0
Avg Annual Div'd Yield	7.8%	7.6%	6.9%	6.9%	7.7%	5.3%	6.3%	6.7%	6.0%	3.6%	3.1%	3.5%	3.1%	3.5%	3.5%	3.9%			4.0%

Price to Earnings Ratio		Dividend Yield		Estimated 12 months to 3/31/66	Div'd Declarations	Reported Earnings
13 yr. Median	13.6	13 yr. Median ⑤	3.9%	Cash Earnings (per share)	$2.30	$4.50
Current ⑦	10.7	Current ⑧	4.8%	$5.60		

Quality	12 Mos. Perform'ce	Desirability as 3-5 Yr. Holding
C+	I (Highest)	IV (Below Average)†

Characteristic Growth Index 10 (Range 100 to 5)
Characteristic Stability Index 20 (Range 100 to 5)

SOURCE: *The Value Line Investment Survey* (New York: Arnold Bernhard & Company, March 12, 1965), p. 844.

its earning ability more rapidly than the New Jersey Zinc Company and appeared to be in a slightly more advantageous earning position for the next two or three years. Both companies were expected to continue to increase their earnings during 1965 and 1966. After that time, their profitability is likely to hinge primarily upon the supply of and demand for their products, which will depend largely upon the levels of economic activity in the United States and other industrial nations. Since these types of equity issues fluctuate so widely over the business cycle, the investor should appraise them periodically and should not consider them to be safe from market deterioration during stock market breaks or during recession periods.

The Food Industry

The monthly price index of grocery store shares declined almost 40 percent from late 1961 through mid-1962. By the end of 1964, the prices of common stocks in the industry had recovered to approximately the mid-1961 levels. In April 1965, *Value Line* estimated that sales for the industry should increase approximately 5 percent during the subsequent year, contrasted to only a 2 percent gain for all industries, and that the net industry income should rise by some 10 percent compared to a zero expected gain for all other industries. Should these developments occur, the grocery store stocks could become more favorable investment media for the general public.[3]

Some food chains do much better in increasing their growth in sales and profits than do others, since the industry has become one of severe competition, as evidenced by the erection of a large number of new stores and use of trading stamps, weekend specials, contests, and the like. Depressed profits produced by a slight overexpansion in the industry in 1965 should benefit greatly from growing family units in the latter 1960s.

Since the sales profit trends for the food industry are relatively stable over the business cycle because consumers continue to purchase almost the same amount of these goods during boom or recession periods, during boom periods the market performances of these issues is usually poor relative to the market average. Food stocks sometimes perform much better than other stocks during recession periods, although these issues were hard hit by the 1962 stock market decline. For these reasons, the prices of common stocks of food, tobacco, confectionary, and some beverage companies are sometimes at a higher level during a recession period than the general level of stock market prices. These issues are sometimes referred to as defensive issues, in that they offer some hedges against declining market prices.

In this section, two grocery store chains are analyzed. The Great Atlantic and Pacific Tea Company, the largest grocery chain, which in 1965 had 4500 stores located in 39 states, is contrasted with Winn-Dixie Stores, Inc., which during the same year operated about 630 retail units throughout the southeastern portion of the country.

[3] *The Value Line Investment Survey* (April 2, 1965), p. 1121.

TABLE 13-5 /   Financial Data on Great Atlantic and Pacific Tea Company, Inc.

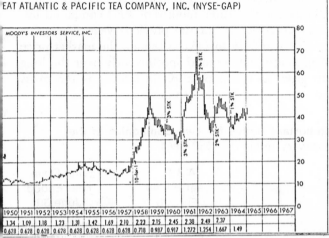

GREAT ATLANTIC & PACIFIC TEA COMPANY, INC. (NYSE-GAP)

MOODY'S INVESTORS SERVICE, INC.

CAPITALIZATION:	(2/29/64) (000)	(%)
Defer.inc.tax	$ 6,653	1.2
Com. & Surp.	559,144	98.8
Total	$565,797	100.0%

Shs. ($1) - (11/28/64) - 24,287,554

LATEST EARNINGS:	1964	1963
Period 39 wks.	11/28	11/23
Gross ($ Mill.)	3,780.2	3,782.6
Net ($ 000)	37,212	c38,369
Per Share	1.53	c1.58

INTERIM EARNINGS:

Qu.	5/31	8/31	11/30	2/28
61	0.56	0.58	0.60	0.64
62	0.56	0.54	0.62	0.77
63	0.52	0.47	c0.59	0.79
64	0.48	0.53	0.52	

DIVIDENDS:	Record	Payable
0.30Y	1/22/64	2/21/64
1% Stk.	1/22	2/21
0.30Q	5/4	6/1
0.30Q	8/5	9/1
0.30Q	11/5	12/1

PRICE RANGE: (1964) 44² - 34⁴

GREAT ATLANTIC & PACIFIC TEA COMPANY, INC. (MD.)

Operating results of this largest retailer reflect efforts to maintain its strong competitive position. The stock is high
de.

GROSS REVS. ($ MILL.)	OPER. PROFIT MARGIN %	NET INCOME ($ 000)	WORK CAP. ($ MILL.)	SENIOR CAPITAL ($ MILL.)	NO. SHS. OUT. (000)	CASH FLOW PER SH. $	EARN. PER SH. $	DIV. PER SH. $	DIV. PAY. %	PRICE RANGE	PRICE X EARN.	AVG YIELD %
3,989.1	1.7	30,396	185.5	25.9	23,252	1.65	1.23	0.628	51	15⁴ – 13	11.6	4.4
4,140.0	1.7	32,233	194.5	25.9	23,252	1.76	1.31	0.628	48	19⁵ – 14⁷	13.2	3.6
4,305.0	1.8	35,375	205.2	25.9	23,252	2.29	1.42	0.628	44	20 – 16	12.7	3.5
4,481.9	2.0	41,876	217.9	25.9	23,252	2.70	1.69	0.628	37	17 – 14	9.2	4.1
4,769.2	2.3	50,667	227.7	25.9	23,252	3.21	2.10	0.628	30	22 – 13⁴	8.5	3.5
5,094.7	2.3	53,905	245.7	Nil	24,120	3.42	2.23	0.718	32	52⁷ – 21⁴	16.7	1.9
5,048.6	2.1	51,996	257.4	Nil	24,120	3.47	2.15	0.987	46	49⁵ – 32	19.0	2.4
4,246.6	2.3	59,012	269.6	Nil	24,129	3.92	2.45	0.917	37	37 – 27⁷	13.2	2.8
5,240.3	2.3	57,464	279.9	Nil	24,174	4.00	'2.38	1.272	53	67¹ – 33¹	21.1	2.5
5,310.5	2.4	60,206	278.0	Nil	24,211	4.47	2.49	1.254	50	58⁷ – 33	18.4	2.7
5,189.2	2.0	57,489	289.2	Nil	24,251	4.22	c2.37	1.667	70	49³ – 37⁴	18.3	3.8

te: Adj. for 10-for-1 split 12/58; also stk. divs.: 1960-61, 3%; 1962-63, 2%; 1964, 1%. a-Year ends 2/28 of following year.
ncl. 15c a sh. spec. credit for prior yrs. deprec. adj.

KGROUND: Largest grocery chain with about 4,519 stores ated in 39 states, Washington, D.C., and in 3 Canadian vinces. Sales by regions were as follows: Middle-antic States, 40%; East-Central, 26%; Southeastern, %; New England, 8%; Canadian provinces, 4%. Items nufactured by subsidiaries and sold under company-ned brand names account for about 11% of total sales.

Company accounts for about 10% of food store sales in the U.S. The Hartford Foundation and members of the family own 74% of the common stock. Quarterly dividends have been paid since incorporation...Plaid trading stamps are offered in about 60% of the company's stores.   Dividends paid annually since 1905.

URCE: *Moody's Handbook of Common Stocks* (New York: Moody's Investors Service, Inc.,
ring 1965), p. 254.

The Great Atlantic and Pacific Tea Company, Inc.

Financial information appears in Table 13-5 on The Great Atlantic and Pacific Tea Company (A & P). The per share market price approximately tripled from 1953 through 1964, net income approximately doubled, and sales increased by about 25 percent. Market prices move irregularly, even though sales and profits may grow at relatively stable rates. The market value of the stock increased only slightly from 1950 through 1957, but rose by some 200 percent from early 1958 through early 1959. The market price of the stock fell from $50 to $30 during the 1959–1960 boom period, but rose from $30 to $68 during the 1960–1961 recession. During the subsequent boom period, the market value of the stock declined to approximately $35 per share. Earnings per share of $1.53 for the first three months of 1964 compared unfavorably with $1.58 for the same quarter of the previous year. The price range for the issue during 1964 was 34½ to 44¼. Although the market price of the common stock will probably not respond spectacularly over the long run, it should continue to grow as the population increases, as the gross national product rises, and as more families are formed.

TABLE 13-6 / Important Ratios for Two Companies in the Grocery Industry, 1962–1964

	A & P, Year Ended Feb. 28		Winn-Dixie, Year Ended June 30	
Ratios	1963	1964	1962	1963
Financial and Operating Ratios				
Current assets and current liabilities	2.25	2.34	3.35	3.77
Cash and securities to current assets (%)	31.27	31.72	38.14	30.23
Inventory to current assets (%)	65.39	65.67	57.71	65.08
Net current assets to net worth (%)	42.48	51.72	77.66	73.82
Property depreciated (%)	33.28	34.61	—	—
Annual depreciation to gross properties (%)	11.76	10.63	—	—
Capitalization Ratios				
Common stock and surplus (%)	100.00	100.00	86.98	88.36
Sales divided by inventory	14.28	15.63	14.59	14.19
Sales divided by receivables	318.83	392.75	608.64	522.22
Sales to net property (%)	2,139.20	1,975.28	2,659.65	2,790.74
Sales to total assets (%)	661.29	659.76	626.74	661.39
Net income to total assets (%)	7.84	7.31	14.19	14.93
Net income to net worth (%)	11.22	10.28	21.10	20.94
Analysis of Operations	(%)	(%)	(%)	(%)
Sales	100.00	100.00	100.00	100.00
Cost of merchandise sold	82.26	81.87	81.01	80.83
Operating and administrative expenses	15.38	16.14	15.07	15.40
Operating profits	2.36	1.99	3.92	3.77
Other income (net of expenses)	.02	.11	.74	.77
Total income	2.38	2.10	4.66	4.54
U.S. and Canadian income taxes	1.25	.99	2.40	2.28
Net income	1.13	1.11	2.26	2.26

SOURCE: *Moody's Industrial Manual* (New York: Moody's Investors Service, Inc., 1964), pp. 407, 1189, and 2174.

Table 13-6 reports important financial and operating ratios for the A & P and indicates that almost two thirds of 1963 current assets was in inventories. Annual sales volume during 1963 and 1964 amounted to more than six and one-half times the company's total assets, but net income to total assets was significantly lower than for other food chains. The net income to net worth for A & P was 11.22 percent and 10.28 percent, respectively, for the years ended February 28, 1963 and 1964. Net income to sales for the company amounted to 1.13 and 1.11 percent, respectively, for the two years.

Winn-Dixie Stores, Inc.

In 1965, Winn-Dixie was one of the smaller retail grocery chains listed on the New York Stock Exchange. The company had been following the acquisition route and had added some 296 stores between 1955 and 1958. Company management owned about 34 percent of the shares outstanding, and the firm planned to add 54 more stores during the 1965 fiscal year (see Table 13-7).

Table 13-6 presents some interesting financial information about Winn-Dixie. With the exception of 1951, the company reported an increase in earnings per share every year from 1950 through 1964. Dividends per share also increased each year over the 15-year period. Unlike its larger competitor, A & P, Winn-Dixie Stores was using some long-term debt. At the end of June 1964, about 9 percent of the total capitalization was composed of long-term debt, with the balance in common stock and retained earnings. Winn-Dixie sales increased by almost 300 percent from 1954 through 1964, while net income increased by almost 500 percent. A strong working capital position, a good dividend payment record—dividends having been increased for 21 consecutive years—and a generous dividend payout of approximately 70 percent made this a particularly attractive issue for the income investor in early 1965.

A study of the financial and operating ratios for Winn-Dixie (Table 13-6) indicates a 1963 current ratio of 3.77 to 1. The current assets held in the form of cash and securities declined from 38 to 30 percent from year end 1962 to 1963, while inventory as a percentage of current assets increased. This shift was not particularly alarming, since it may have been created by a temporary investment of idle funds until additional purchases of retail outlets or erection of new retail stores could be accomplished. A majority of the 1963 and 1964 ratios for Winn-Dixie and A & P were similar. The inventory turnover of Winn-Dixie was slightly greater than for the larger company in 1962, but slightly smaller during 1963. Conversely, the percentage of net income to total assets and return on net worth was almost twice as great for Winn-Dixie as for A & P. The higher profit potential has been possible because of a slightly lower operating ratio for Winn-Dixie. The cost of merchandise sold was only 80.83 percent of sales for Winn-Dixie as compared to

TABLE 13-7 / Financial Data on Winn-Dixie Stores, Inc.

WINN-DIXIE STORES, INC. (NYSE-WIN)

MOODY'S INVESTORS SERVICE, INC.

| EARN. | 0.34 | 0.31 | 0.36 | 0.39 | 0.46 | 0.55 | 0.73 | 0.86 | 0.98 | 1.10 | 1.25 | 1.34 | 1.38 | 1.45 | 1.62 | | |
| DIV. | 0.12 | 0.15 | 0.183 | 0.21 | 0.26 | 0.33 | 0.39 | 0.45 | 0.51 | 0.57 | 0.65 | 0.78 | 0.90 | 1.02 | 1.14 | | |

CAPITALIZATION:	(6/27/64)	
	(000)	(%)
Debt	$ 9,600	9.1
Defer.inc.tax	265	0.2
Com. & Surp.	95,978	90.7
Total	$105,843	100.0%

Shs. ($1)-(9/19/64)-12,622,308

LATEST EARNINGS:	1964	1963
Period 12 mos.	9/19	9/21
Gross ($ Mill.)	202.0	192.2
Net ($ 000)	4,334	3,976
Per Share	0.34	0.32

INTERIM EARNINGS: 6/30

Wks.	12	16	12	12
62	0.29	0.37	0.35	0.37
63	0.30	0.40	0.36	0.39
64	0.32	0.46	0.43	0.41
65	0.34			

DIVIDENDS:	Record	Payable
0.10M	11/16/64	11/20/64
0.10M	12/14	12/28
0.10M	1/15/65	1/30/65
0.10M	2/11	2/27
0.10M	3/15	3/31

PRICE RANGE: (1964)   40⁴ - 28⁴

WINN-DIXIE STORES, INC. (FLA.)

This is a medium grade stock which is backed by a faster than average expansion of the company in the grocery chain field.

YEAR 6/30	GROSS REVS. ($ MILL.)	OPER. PROFIT MARGIN %	NET INCOME ($ 000)	WORK CAP. ($ MILL.)	SENIOR CAPITAL ($ MILL.)	NO. SHS. OUT. (000)	CASH FLOW PER SH. $	EARN. PER SH. $	DIV. PER SH. $	DIV. PAY. %	PRICE RANGE	PRICE X EARN.	AVG. YIELD %
54	228.0	3.4	3,582	17.7	9.6	8,436	0.69	0.46	0.26	57	$10^2 - 5^2$	17.0	3.4
c55	358.6	3.1	6,820	24.4	9.2	12,402	0.81	0.55	0.33	59	$13^6 - 9$	20.4	2.9
56	421.3	3.5	h9,126	38.8	17.6	12,414	1.01	h0.73	0.39	46	$12^7 - 10$	13.6	3.4
57	513.5	3.4	10,626	40.5	17.6	12,454	1.19	0.86	0.45	53	$14^4 - 9^4$	14.0	3.8
58	588.6	3.4	12,270	44.3	16.8	12,562	1.34	0.98	0.51	52	$24^5 - 13^1$	19.4	2.7
59	666.4	3.4	14,012	48.2	16.0	12,626	1.58	1.10	0.57	52	$23^1 - 20$	19.6	2.6
60	721.5	3.8	15,800	54.9	15.2	12,631	1.80	1.25	0.65	52	$29^2 - 21$	20.2	2.6
61	767.0	3.8	17,051	60.2	14.8	12,710	1.94	1.34	0.78	58	$41 - 26$	25.0	2.3
62	772.3	3.9	17,483	64.4	12.4	12,654	2.04	1.38	0.90	69	$39 - 22$	22.1	3.0
63	831.3	3.8	18,279	66.2	11.8	12,641	2.21	1.45	1.02	70	$32^4 - 26^7$	20.5	3.4
64	871.8	3.9	20,414	72.2	9.6	12,631	2.37	1.62	1.14	70	$40^4 - 28^4$	21.3	3.3

c-Incl. acquisitions during 1955. h-Excl. $1.3 mill. (11c a sh.) special credit.

BACKGROUND: Company and its wholly-owned subsidiaries operate a chain of 631 retail units throughout the southeastern portion of the country (especially Fla. and the Carolinas) and in Southern Indiana. Also, 8 wholesale units, bakeries, ice cream plants and plants manufacturing salad dressing, jam, mayonnaise and peanut butter, and a trucking-fleet and warehouses which service most of its stores

...Acquisitions have contributed importantly to growth, adding 296 stores in 1955-58, including Dixie Home Stores in 1955 with its 115 outlets largely in South Carolina. Also 36 Hill Stores located in Birmingham, Ala. acquired 7/62. Management owns 34% of shares outstanding...Dividends have been increased for 21 consecutive years...Plans call for 54 new stores in fiscal 1965.

SOURCE: *Moody's Handbook of Common Stocks* (New York: Moody's Investors Service, Inc., Spring, 1965), p. 597.

about 82 percent for A & P. Operating and administrative expenses were also slightly lower for the smaller chain than for its largest competitor. Since the stores in this industry operate on such a small net profit ratio, a small savings of one half of 1 percent of sales is very significant in the over-all profitability of the firm. All in all, a large company such as A & P may have a greater stability of sales and profits, but a smaller concern such as Winn-Dixie has a greater potential for growth in sales and profits. This growth may be accomplished through mergers, consolidations, or internal retention of profits. A growing company, particularly one that absorbs outside units, frequently encounters management problems. This occurred for Winn-Dixie during the early 1960s, but despite such problems, the company was able to increase its sales and profits each year from 1954 to 1964. Should this rate of growth in sales, profits, and dividends continue, the market value of the stock should respond favorably over the long run.

Summary

Before an investor makes a long-term commitment of funds into the common stocks of a corporation, he should make some study of the industry and the companies operating therein. In attempting to determine one or a few industries within which to invest, the individual may be influenced by population projections that indicate growing demand for a product and by cyclical movements of industries. In addition, the investor may select stocks on the basis of recommendations by economists or security analysts. Periodicals such as *Forbes Magazine,* Standard & Poor's *Stock Guide,* Moody's *Stock Survey, The Value Line Investment Survey, Security and Industry Survey, The Magazine of Wall Street,* and others, recommend industries that are expected to outperform the general economy. An investor may wish to diversify into more than one industry, such as the basic metals and food industries. The former has widely swinging sales, profits, and market prices over the business cycle, while the food stocks offer somewhat more stability. Both industries should benefit from a growing population and increasing personal income.

In order to reduce the amount of time required for reviewing financial statements, the analyst may refer to the financial information presented by some of the leading financial services, including important ratios. By so doing he may review a larger number of concerns over a greater period of time than when he attempts to work out the ratios and to study comparative statements. Periodically, he should reanalyze the companies within which he holds stocks.

QUESTIONS FOR REVIEW /

1. In seeking to make a long-term commitment of funds, why is it important to seek a growth industry?
2. What techniques should be used in attempting to select four or five industries that will probably outperform the economy?
3. How would the procedure recommended for a "bull" be changed if a "bear" were seeking to find issues that are expected to deteriorate in market value?
4. How do population forecasts and trends in population components by ages and sex influence the decisions of prospective stock market investors?
5. List sources of investment information that provide breakdowns of various in-industries as well as of companies representative of these industrial divisions.

6. In general, how do sales, profits, and market values of common shares of durable and consumer goods companies react to the business cycle and/or stock market swings?
7. Why is it important to make a study of the industry as well as to consider price structures and supply and demand factors when selecting an issue in the basic metals industry? What other factors are important?
8. What financial information do you consider to be important to the individual who is seeking to commit some funds to common stock issues representative of the retail grocery industry?
9. In planning an investment portfolio, how much industry diversification is desirable?

PROBLEMS /

1. With the use of the January 1 issue of *Forbes, The Magazine of Wall Street*, or the *Security and Industry Survey*, determine three industries that are recommended as attractive investments for the next one or two years. Do you agree with the recommendations? If not, wherein do you differ?
2. From one of the industries chosen in problem 1, select two intermediate-sized corporations that are listed on one of the registered exchanges and make a financial analysis of these companies. Which of these competitors appears to be the more strategically situated at the present time for short- and long-term benefits? Would you recommend the purchase of the common stocks of either of these companies at prevailing market prices? Retain your analysis for future use.
3. Assume that you have been engaged as a financial consultant by a wealthy individual who wishes to place $100,000 in an investment portfolio of common stocks. Since he is in the 60 percent income tax bracket, he is seeking long-term capital gains. His other investments are limited to savings accounts, life insurance, and real estate. Indicate the industries and companies that you recommend for his investment and the amount of funds to be allocated to each.

REFERENCES /

Annual Report of The New Jersey Zinc Company. New York: New Jersey Zinc Company, 1964.

Dun's Review and Modern Industry. Chicago: Dun and Bradstreet Corporation, November 1964.

Federal Tax Course. Englewood Cliffs, N.J.: Prentice-Hall, Inc., selected issues.

Forbes Magazine. New York: Forbes, Inc., January 1, 1965 and selected issues.

Glover, John G., and Rudolph L. Lagai, *The Development of American Industries.* New York: Simmons-Boardman Publishing Corporation, 1957.

Graham, Benjamin, David L. Dodd, and Sidney Cottle, *Security Analysis,* 4th ed. New York: McGraw-Hill Book Company, Inc., 1962.

"Improvements in *The Value Line Survey*," *The Value Line Investment Survey.* New York: Arnold Bernhard & Company, Inc., April 23, 1965.

Internal Revenue Service, *Corporate Income.* Washington, D.C.: U.S. Government Printing Office.

Karrenbrock, Wilbert E., and Harry Simons, *Intermediate Accounting*, 3d ed. Cincinnati, Ohio: South-Western Publishing Company, 1958.

Merrill Lynch, Pierce, Fenner & Smith, Inc., *Security and Industry Survey*. New York: Merrill Lynch, Spring 1965.

Moody's Handbook of Common Stocks. New York: Moody's Investors Service, Inc., selected issues.

Moody's Industrial Manual. New York: Moody's Investors Service, Inc., 1964–1966.

U.S. Department of Commerce, Bureau of the Census, *Population Estimates*, Series P-25, No. 301. Washington, D.C.: U.S. Government Printing Office, February 26, 1965.

————, *Statistical Abstract of the United States*. Washington, D.C.: U.S. Government Printing Office, 1965.

————, *Survey of Current Business*. Washington, D.C.: U.S. Government Printing Office.

The Value Line Investment Survey. New York: Arnold Bernhard & Company, Inc., selected issues.

chapter 14 | Public Utility Issues

Introduction

Types of companies considered as utilities include electric companies, gas companies, gas pipeline companies, waterworks, and telephone companies. These firms are highly regulated and enjoy natural monopolies.

The privately owned sector of the electric utility industry was dominated by 214 companies in 1964 that accounted for about 98 percent of the total assets and revenues of all privately owned firms. Some 487 publicly owned utility companies were in operation at the end of 1962. Of these 433 were municipal ventures and 54 were federal projects. However, in 1964, the privately owned electrical utilities were producing about 77 percent of the total number of kilowatt hours of electricity being generated.

Many electric companies maintain natural gas divisions, and some of the larger natural gas companies have constructed pipelines for transporting natural gas from producing areas within the United States to more distant locations. Many water companies are municipally owned, while almost 90 percent of the telephones in service within the United States are furnished by the American Telephone and Telegraph Company and its wholly owned subsidiaries.

The public utility companies, especially the electrical companies, use a much larger amount of debt relative to total assets than do industrial companies. This is made possible because of stability in the sales of electricity, natural gas, and telephone services and the very stable earnings of the companies.

This chapter is devoted primarily to an analysis of the electric utility industry, but natural gas companies, natural gas pipeline companies, and the coal industry are also considered. In the strictest sense, coal mining companies are not utilities, since prices are set by competition rather than by rate regulation, but the outlook for the coal industry is closely allied to that of the electric utility industry.

Electric Utility Companies

History and Purpose

The first dynamo was put into operation in England in 1831. The dynamo, which converts mechanical power to electrical energy, led to the use of the arc light as a means of illumination. Up to that time flickering gas jets had been used to produce light. One of the first uses of electrical energy in the United States was for lighting the campus at Cornell University. Although the arc lamp could be used for outside illumination, it was too large and inefficient for interior lighting. The next development was the invention of the incandescent lamp by Thomas Edison in 1879. Edison, through his interest in the generation and transmission of electrical energy, was placed in charge of the first central station for large-scale commercial generating and distribution of electricity in New York City in 1882. Although the first electricity in this country was used for street lighting, about 500 houses were wired for electricity by 1884. Also in 1882, a hydroelectric station was placed in operation in Wisconsin.[1]

Electrical current is created when a certain type of wire is passed through a magnetic field. Dynamos may be turned in one of two ways. In the first case the hydroelectric generator is turned by the force of water falling on a wheel or on blades that have been designed to catch the force of the falling water. Steam-turned generators, however, are more widely used. With the use of the latter, some fuel such as oil, coal, or natural gas is burned to produce steam. The steam heats the water vapor, causing it to expand, thus releasing the force that turns the generator.

Electricity has become the dominant type of energy used in the United States because of the long distances over which it may be transmitted and the low cost of distributing it. In the early 1960s, about 98 percent of U.S. homes were wired for electricity. Commercial and industrial operations were also using vast amounts of electrical energy.

Since its beginning the growth rate of the industry has been about 6 percent per year, and from 1950 through 1965 the growth rate surpassed this annual rate. Total plant capacity approximately doubled from 1955 through 1965, and this rate of increase is likely to continue into the 1980s. The growth rate of generated electricity from 1962 to 1964 was 7.5 percent. There are a number of reasons why the sale of electricity has continued to increase at such a tremendous pace. First, the population and the number of family-owned dwelling units has been increasing. Second, utility companies have been emphasizing the ownership of major appliances. Third, the heavy industrialization of business firms and the growing usage of electronic data processing equipment also account for a continually growing consumption of electrical energy. In addition, more and more homes and business firms are beginning to use electrical energy for heating purposes.

The prerequisite for renewing the franchises of electric utility companies is the provision of adequate service at a fair price. In order to have an abundant supply of generating equipment on hand, electric utility plants maintain stand-by generating equipment. Many of the larger companies have an exchange agreement with other near-by utility companies, so that

---

[1] For an analysis of the electric utility industry, see John G. Glover and Rudolph L. Lagai, *The Development of American Industries* (New York: Simmons-Boardman Publishing Corporation, 1958), Chapter 8.

in the event of current failures a company is able to obtain electricity from another company while its own generating equipment and lines are being restored.

In general, the electric utility companies that operate in the southern states where air conditioning equipment is used during the summer months have a peak load factor during that period, but for companies located in colder climates, the peak load factor usually occurs during the winter months. In the early 1960s, southern utility companies arranged an exchange agreement with the Tennessee Valley Authority, since the two groups have opposing peak load factors, for the exchange of some three million kilowatt hours of electricity. Such an exchange program reduces the amount of stand-by generating equipment required by the utility companies and reduces the need for expansion through the construction of additional generating units.

The Importance of Population

A number of factors are important to the continued growth of the electric utility companies. These include growth in population, industrialization of the area being served by the utility, the climate of the area, and the availability of heating fuels.

Some classes of electricity users pay a lower price per kilowatt than do others. In 1963, of the 178 billion kilowatt hours of electricity sold by Class A and Class B electric utility companies in the United States, some 24.2 percent of the sales went to residential users, 18.7 percent to commercial users, and 39.3 percent to industrial users. The balance was accounted for by public lighting, other public authorities, railways, and interdepartmental use. As a percentage of the total revenue collected by the privately owned Class A and Class B electric utility companies, some 37.1 percent was paid by residential users, 26.6 percent by commercial users, 24.9 percent by industrial users, and the balance by miscellaneous classifications. Residential users were paying slightly higher rates than commercial users, but the large industrial users were paying only about 40 percent of the average rate per kilowatt hour as compared to the other two classifications. Some 14.2 percent of the total kilowatt hours and 6.4 percent of the revenues were from sales of electricity for resale to other privately owned companies, publicly owned municipals, and to Rural Electrification Administration co-operatives (REA's).

Although the degree of industrialization is important to an expanding community, increasing industrialization and population growth usually go together, and commercial businesses grow as the population grows. A study of the projections of population increases by states within the United States from 1964 to 1985 may be of value in attempting to project the growth rates of individual electric utility companies. Electricity sales for a firm operating in an area that is expected to continue to grow in population are likely to increase at a more rapid rate than for a firm located in an area where little growth or a decline in population is anticipated.

Table 14-1 is a projection of population increases by states within the United States from mid-1964 to mid-1985. These statistics are based on the population estimates of the Bureau of the Census and assume a slightly reduced fertility rate, an equal distribution of the 300,000 annual immigrants,

TABLE 14-1 /   Projections of Population Increases by States, 1964 to 1985

Division and State	Percentage Increase	Division and State	Percentage Increase
New England		South Atlantic (*cont.*)	
Maine	23	West Virginia	00
New Hampshire	41	North Carolina	32
Vermont	27	South Carolina	34
Massachusetts	28	Georgia	37
Rhode Island	24	Florida	93
Connecticut	44	East South Central	
Middle Atlantic		Kentucky	20
New York	25	Tennessee	27
New Jersey	46	Alabama	33
Pennsylvania	16	Mississippi	30
East North Central		West South Central	
Ohio	36	Arkansas	7
Indiana	32	Louisiana	45
Illinois	33	Oklahoma	21
Michigan	29	Texas	42
Wisconsin	33	Mountain	
West North Central		Montana	20
Minnesota	34	Idaho	35
Iowa	14	Wyoming	37
Missouri	24	Colorado	54
North Dakota	15	New Mexico	75
South Dakota	16	Arizona	88
Nebraska	17	Utah	55
Kansas	18	Nevada	37
South Atlantic		Pacific	
Delaware	58	Washington	41
Maryland	55	Oregon	31
District of Columbia	44	California	79
Virginia	45	Alaska	71
		Hawaii	36

SOURCE: Compiled from U.S. Department of Commerce, Bureau of the Census, *Population Estimates*, Series P-25, No. 301 (Washington, D.C.: U.S. Government Printing Office), p. 4.

the most recent mortality rates, and the same net migration between states as that which prevailed from 1955 through 1960.[2]

A number of states, for example, Florida, Arizona, New Mexico, and California, are expected to have population increases over the next 20 years in excess of 75 percent, but some states, for example, West Virginia, Arkansas, Pennsylvania, Iowa, North Dakota, and others, are expected to have very small increases in population. An individual utility company will not grow at exactly the same rate as the population within the state, since there may be numerous utility companies operating within the state, and some may deteriorate while others may expand. When the rate structure of an electric utility company is conducive to profitable operation and when the utility's area of operation is expected to increase in population and industrialization, the firm's future revenue and profit outlook should be optimistic.

Balance Sheet Analysis

Table 14-2 presents composite balance sheets for the privately owned Class A and Class B electric utilities in the United States as of the end of 1963 and 1964. The Class A utilities are those having annual operating revenues of $2.5 million, while Class B utilities are those having annual operating revenues of $1 million or more but less than $2.5 million. In 1964, Class A and Class B electric utility companies accounted for more than 98 percent of the privately owned electric light and power industry.[3] Table 14-2 indicates that on December 31, 1964, privately owned Class A and Class B utilities had 81.4 percent of their assets invested in net electric utility plant, an additional 9.1 percent in net other utility plant, 2.2 percent in other property and investments, and 6.8 percent of total assets in current and accrued assets. The total current and accrued liabilities amounted to 7 percent, or slightly more than the current assets. The debt and capital components were short-term debt, 7 percent; long-term debt, 45.7 percent; preferred stock, 8 percent; common stock and other paid-in capital, 25.1 percent; and earned surplus (retained income), 9.5 percent. Long-term debt amounted to some 40 percent of gross utility plant, and this ratio had declined slightly from about 43 percent in 1958. From 1957 to 1964, long-term debt had declined from approximately 52 percent to 50.5 percent of net utility plant. From 1955 through 1964, accumulated depreciation ranged from 19 to 22 percent of total utility plant.

Asset turnover varies widely for commercial, industrial, and utility companies. Some commercial businesses are able to generate $15 or $20 of sales for each dollar invested in business assets when a large amount of the fixed assets are acquired through renting or leasing. Industrial corporations

[2] For population estimates based on various fertility ratios, see U.S. Department of Commerce, Bureau of the Census, *Population Estimates,* Series P-25, No. 301 (Washington, D.C.: U.S. Government Printing Office, February 26, 1965), pp. 1–6.

[3] See Federal Power Commission, *Statistics of Electric Utilities in the United States Privately Owned* (Washington, D.C.: U.S. Government Printing Office, 1964), p. v.

TABLE 14-2 / Composite Balance Sheet of Privately Owned Class A and Class B Electric Utilities in the United States, December 31, 1963–1964

Item	1963		1964	
	Amount	Percent of Total	Amount	Percent of Total
Electric utility plant	$53,474,463,500		$56,326,587,506	
Accumulated provisions for depreciation and amortization	11,510,654,715		12,574,518,567	
Net electric utility plant	41,963,808,785	81.7	43,752,068,939	81.4
Other utility plant	5,813,384,708		6,189,423,702	
Accumulated provisions for depreciation and amortization	1,210,882,612		1,297,627,762	
Net other utility plant	4,602,502,096	9.0	4,891,795,940	9.1
Total utility plant	59,287,848,208		62,516,011,208	
Accumulated provisions for depreciation and amortization	12,721,537,327		13,872,146,329	
Net total utility plant	46,566,310,881	90.7	48,643,864,879	90.5
Utility plant adjustments			10,202	
Nonutility property less accumulated provisions for depreciation and amortization	110,661,341	0.2	117,740,358	0.2
Investment in associated companies	899,324,139	1.8	917,593,338	1.7
Other investments	119,361,885	0.2	154,850,953	0.3
Special funds	19,101,880	0.0	20,746,976	0.0
Total other property and investments	1,148,449,245	2.2	1,210,931,625	2.2
Cash	575,364,744	1.1	554,857,115	1.0
Special deposits	99,767,132	0.2	96,412,715	0.2
Working funds	16,735,142	0.0	16,751,890	0.0
Temporary cash investments	463,044,095	0.9	564,384,012	1.1
Notes and accounts receivable less accumulated provision for uncollectable accounts	1,116,965,650	2.2	1,221,046,351	2.3

SOURCE: Federal Power Commission, *Statistics of Electric Utilities in the United States Privately Owned* (Washington, D.C.: U.S. Government Printing Office, 1965), p. xv.

TABLE 14-2 *(Continued)*

Item	1963		1964	
	Amount	Percent of Total	Amount	Percent of Total
Receivables from associated companies	58,641,444	0.1	62,246,472	0.1
Materials and supplies	855,767,341	1.7	904,785,900	1.7
Prepayments	155,967,794	0.3	151,941,651	0.3
Other current and accrued assets	68,686,945	0.1	61,650,523	0.1
Total current and accrued assets	3,410,940,287	6.6	3,634,076,629	6.8
Unamortized debt discount and expense	72,816,437	0.1	71,664,579	0.1
Extraordinary property losses	18,359,486	0.0	15,215,508	0.0
Preliminary survey and investigation charges	11,734,912	0.0	11,774,599	0.0
Clearing accounts	8,567,720	0.0	9,790,988	0.0
Other deferred debits	151,706,767	0.3	156,058,478	0.3
Total deferred debits	263,185,322	0.5	264,504,152	0.5
Total assets and other debits	51,388,885,735	100.0	53,753,387,497	100.0
Common stock issued	10,560,310,737	20.5	11,063,584,110	20.6
Preferred stock issued	4,513,901,531	8.8	4,557,329,956	8.4
Premium on capital stock	1,802,605,865	3.5	1,920,984,045	3.6
Other capital stock items	5,179,697	0.1	4,173,126	0.1
Other paid-in capital	270,235,398	0.5	306,213,019	0.5
Capital stock discount and expense	(83,270,815)	(0.2)	(76,003,332)	(0.1)
Earned surplus	4,640,145,034	9.0	5,142,117,791	9.5
Reacquired capital stock	(5,097,262)	(0.0)	(7,700,972)	(0.0)
Total proprietary capital	21,704,010,185	42.2	22,910,697,743	42.6
Bonds (less bonds reacquired)	23,219,593,115	45.2	24,211,235,000	45.0
Advances from associated companies	122,476,529	0.2	108,665,229	0.2
Other long-term debt	289,761,864	0.6	269,064,477	0.5
Total long-term debt	23,631,831,508	46.0	24,588,964,706	45.7

Notes payable	467,382,499	0.9	518,981,741	1.0
Accounts payable	582,793,649	1.1	583,553,294	1.1
Payables to associated companies	71,283,971	0.2	87,206,093	0.1
Customer deposits	193,739,257	0.4	206,999,753	0.4
Taxes accrued	1,611,150,388	3.1	1,658,176,413	3.1
Interest accrued	222,473,340	0.4	233,924,303	0.4
Dividends declared	173,445,414	0.3	190,497,421	0.4
Tax collections payable	57,698,882	0.1	57,493,307	0.1
Other current and accrued liabilities	238,645,488	0.5	199,401,724	0.4
Total current and accrued liabilities	3,618,612,888	7.0	3,736,234,049	7.0
Unamortized premium on debt	66,553,212	0.1	64,327,793	0.1
Customer advances for construction	50,520,395	0.1	51,670,725	0.1
Accumulated deferred investment tax credits	—		147,111,332	0.3
Other deferred credits	205,388,119	0.4	71,078,058	0.1
Total deferred credits	322,461,726	0.6	334,187,908	0.6
Property insurance reserve	26,228,600	0.0	26,052,235	0.0
Injuries and damages reserve	34,162,672	0.1	36,328,230	0.1
Pensions and benefits reserve	28,912,013	0.1	29,300,875	0.1
Other operating reserves	48,942,851	0.1	49,786,835	0.1
Total operating reserves	138,246,136	0.3	141,468,175	0.3
Contributions in aid of construction	236,440,682	0.5	262,163,768	0.5
Accelerated amortization	1,098,642,342	2.1	1,067,585,838	2.0
Liberalized depreciation	637,532,337	1.2	711,424,338	1.3
Other	1,107,931	0.1	660,972	0.0
Total accumulated deferred income taxes	1,737,282,610	3.4	1,779,671,148	3.3
Total liabilities and other credits	51,388,885,735	100.0	53,753,387,497	100.0

normally have sales equal to about one to one and one-half times their total investment in assets, but the electrical utility company usually invests between $4 and $5 in plant for each annual dollar of revenue.

Public utility companies frequently use short-term bank debt, first mortgage bonds, debenture bonds, preferred stocks, common stocks, and the retention of a portion of internally generated funds in order to finance their assets. The bond issues are usually limited in amount and open-end in nature, so that each of the series ranks equally with the outstanding bond issues. For example, Gulf States Utilities Company, which serves a portion of southern Louisiana and east central Texas, was authorized in 1965 to issue up to $1 billion in first mortgage bonds. At the end of 1964, the company had outstanding $204 million in the bonds that had been issued in 14 series from 1946 through 1962. The corporation was authorized to issue up to $30 million in principle amount of debentures and in 1964 had outstanding $22.2 million of these securities. In order to provide the company with some flexibility in financing and to eliminate the sale of very small issues of bonds that are expensive to underwrite, the company had a $20 million line of credit with two large money market banks. The construction of a generating unit could be paid for chiefly with internally generated funds and through temporary bank borrowing, and the short-term debt could then be refinanced with a long-term bond issue. In this way, a bond issue in the amount of $10 to $20 million could be made by the company every year or every other year. The company was authorized to issue up to one million shares of $100 par cumulative preferred stock, and 625,000 shares were outstanding at the end of 1964. Eight preferred stock issues, carrying various dividend rates and call provisions, were outstanding at the end of 1964. The company was authorized to issue 20 million common shares, and 10,373,344 were outstanding on that date.

Since the average utility company was expanding its generating facilities by about 6 to 7.5 percent per year during the early 1960s, a majority of the companies floated new issues of securities. It is easier and cheaper to sell security issues in amounts of $10 or $20 million than in smaller units. Therefore, a bond issue every two or three years and a common stock issue every three or four years may provide the degree of financial flexibility needed by a large utility. The board of directors of a utility company should attempt to minimize the cost of financing over the long run and should issue bonds when interest rates are relatively low and sell common stock when the market values of the equities are at relatively high levels. The retention of profits contributes a substantial portion of the increase in the common stock equity of utility companies, although many companies pay 65 to 70 percent of net income as cash dividends.

Interpreting the Income Account

The composite income accounts for the years ended December 31, 1963 and 1964 for privately owned Class A and Class B electric utilities in the United States are shown in Table 14-3. Operating revenues are shown as

100 percent and other items are shown as percentages of that figure. In 1964, operating expenses amounted to 37.5 percent; maintenance was 6.4 percent; depreciation and amortization, 11.3 percent; taxes other than income taxes, 10 percent; income taxes, 11.1 percent; provision for deferred income taxes, 0.8 percent; and income taxes deferred in prior years, 0.3 percent. The cost of operating other utility facilities is considerably larger than for the electric utility operation. For example, operating expenses for other utilities (natural gas) amounted to 63.4 percent in 1964; maintenance expenses totaled 4.4 percent; depreciation amounted to 6.3 percent; taxes other than income taxes amounted to 7.6 percent; and other items, including income taxes, totaled 6.3 percent. Total income as a percentage of total utility operating revenues amounted to 21.8 percent. Some 6.1 percent was used in the payment of interest on long-term debt, and net income amounted to 16 percent of total utility operating income. Of this amount 1.4 percent was applied to the payment of cash dividends on preferred stock and 9.8 percent on common stock. The balance, 4.8 percent of total operating revenue, was maintained in the business for expansion purposes.

The cost of operation and maintenance as a percentage of electric operating revenues declined from about 50 percent in 1953 to 44 percent in 1964. During the same period depreciation increased from 9.1 percent to 11.3 percent, primarily because of the use of accelerated depreciation methods. A decline in federal income taxes from 12.5 percent to 10.7 percent of revenues was offset by the increase from 8.5 percent to 10 percent in other taxes paid. The interest on long-term debt as a percentage of operating revenue increased from 5 percent in 1953 to 6.2 percent in 1961 and 6 percent in 1964. Although Class A and Class B privately owned electric utility companies earned fixed charges, for example, interest costs and principal repayments, almost four times annually from 1953 to 1957, the amount declined to 3.4 percent from 1958 to 1961 and increased to 3.6 percent in 1963. Over the 1953–1963 period, dividend payments on common stock as a percentage of average common equity ranged from 7.4 percent to 8.2 percent. The average was approximately 7.9 percent.[4] Yields on market values, however, were significantly lower (3–3.5 percent), indicating that the shares were trading at about twice their book value during the period.

Evaluating Individual Companies

In evaluating the investment worthiness of a utility company, the investor should (1) make some estimate of future growth in the company's revenues, (2) attempt to determine how this growth will influence earnings per share, (3) forecast the expected price–earnings ratios of utility companies in general and of the individual company selected, and (4) attempt to determine the direction of the market prices of individual issues. If the individual finds one or more undervalued issues, he may wish to commit a portion of his funds to this investment.

[4] Federal Power Commission, *Statistics of Electric Utilities*, 1963, p. xxv.

TABLE 14-3 / Composite Income Account for Privately Owned Class A and Class B Electric Utilities in the United States, Years Ended December 31, 1963 and 1964

Item	1963 Amount	1963 Percent of Revenues	1964 Amount	1964 Percent of Revenues
Electric utility operating income				
Operating revenues	$12,018,473,940	100.0	$12,673,095,545	100.0
Operating expenses				
Operation expense	4,485,597,089	37.3	4,746,822,526	37.5
Maintenance expense	763,319,374	6.4	826,028,672	6.5
Depreciation and amortization expense	1,351,526,583	11.3	1,429,627,381	11.3
Taxes other than income taxes	1,191,107,981	9.9	1,267,805,504	10.0
Income taxes				
Federal	1,300,919,724	10.8	1,358,471,554	10.7
Other	52,775,287	0.4	57,265,403	0.4
Provision for deferred income taxes	143,254,850	1.2	103,117,213	0.8
Income taxes deferred in prior years—credit	39,385,749	0.3	46,324,528	0.3
Investment tax credit adjustments—(net)			53,654,984	0.4
Total operating expenses	9,249,115,139	77.0	9,796,468,709	77.3
Net operating revenues	2,769,358,801	23.0	2,876,626,836	22.7
Income from electric plant leased to others	2,147,954	0.0	2,772,188	0.0
Total electric utility operating income	2,771,506,755	23.0	2,879,399,024	22.7
Other utility operating income				
Operating revenues	2,161,493,808	100.0	2,317,762,234	100.0
Operating expenses				
Operation expense	1,383,633,485	64.0	1,470,105,840	63.4
Maintenance expense	103,648,744	4.8	103,642,370	4.4
Depreciation and amortization expense	137,647,719	6.4	145,243,630	6.3
Taxes other than income taxes	162,889,896	7.5	175,100,060	7.6

	Amount	%	Amount	%
Income taxes				
Federal	111,139,582	5.1	127,438,439	5.4
Other	3,630,450	0.2	3,994,408	0.2
Provision for deferred income taxes	9,495,607	0.4	9,506,828	0.4
Income taxes deferred in prior years—credit	1,652,274	0.0	1,458,080	0.0
Investment tax credit adjustments—(net)			7,115,920	0.3
Total operating expenses	1,910,433,209	88.4	2,040,689,415	88.0
Net operating revenues	251,060,599	11.6	277,072,819	12.0
Income from utility plant leased to others				
Total other utility operating income	251,060,599	11.6	277,072,819	12.0
Total utility operating income				
Operating revenues	14,179,967,748	100.0	14,990,857,779	100.0
Operating expenses				
Operation expense	5,869,230,575	41.4	6,216,928,366	41.5
Maintenance expense	866,968,117	6.1	929,671,042	6.2
Depreciation and amortization expense	1,489,174,302	10.5	1,574,871,011	10.5
Taxes other than income taxes	1,353,997,877	9.5	1,442,905,564	9.6
Income taxes				
Federal	1,412,059,306	10.0	1,485,909,993	9.9
Other	56,405,737	0.4	61,259,811	0.4
Provision for deferred income taxes	152,750,457	1.1	112,624,041	0.8
Income taxes deferred in prior year—credit	41,038,023	0.3	47,782,608	0.3
Investment tax credit adjustments—(net)			60,770,904	0.4
Total operating expenses	11,159,548,348	78.7	11,837,158,124	79.0
Net operating revenues	3,020,419,400	21.3	3,153,699,655	21.0
Income from utility plant leased to others	2,147,954	0.0	2,772,188	0.0
Total utility operating income	3,022,567,354	21.3	3,156,471,843	21.0
Other income				
Income from merchandising, jobbing and contract work	(1,170,769)		(976,163)	
Income from nonutility operations	2,005,071		1,985,748	

source: Federal Power Commission, *Statistics of Electric Utilities in the United States Privately Owned* (Washington, D.C.: U.S. Government Printing Office, 1965), p. xvi.

TABLE 14-3 (Continued)

Item	1963		1964	
	Amount	Percent of Revenues	Amount	Percent of Revenues
Nonoperating rental income	(203,845)		(368,759)	
Interest and dividend income	76,660,658		85,473,002	
Miscellaneous nonoperating income	7,725,717		34,576,565	
Total other income	85,016,832	0.6	120,690,393	0.8
Total income	3,107,584,186	21.9	3,277,162,236	21.8
Miscellaneous income deductions				
Miscellaneous amortization	2,648,370	0.0	7,530,621	0.0
Other income deductions	106,798,115		23,167,110	
Total miscellaneous income deductions	109,446,485	0.8	30,697,732	0.2
Income before interest charges	2,998,137,701	21.1	3,246,464,505	21.6
Interest charges				
Interest on long-term debt	859,795,598	6.0	898,929,818	6.0
Amortization of debt discount and expense	10,233,927		6,346,179	
Amortization of premium on debt-credit	5,371,904		5,505,024	
Interest on debt to associated companies	5,185,132		4,425,738	
Other interest expense	28,822,833		33,993,555	
Interest charged to construction-credit	78,881,231		85,142,140	
Total interest charges	819,784,355	5.7	853,048,126	5.6
Net income	2,178,353,346	15.4	2,393,416,379	16.0
Dividends declared—preferred stock	207,456,151	1.5	208,797,702	1.4
Dividends declared—common stock	1,360,012,221	9.6	1,472,904,119	9.8

Financial information on a large number of utility companies may be obtained from numerous sources. These include information filed by the electric utility companies with the Federal Power Commission and published in each annual volume of *Statistics of Electric Utilities in the United States.* The data are arranged by states, and thus the analyst can compare companies operating under similar circumstances as well as make use of projected population increases by states in forecasting revenues of specific utility companies. Public utilities that list their securities with a registered exchange or that make public issues or that belong to a public utility holding company group must file registration materials and annual reports with the SEC. This material is reported in each annual volume of *Moody's Public Utility Manual,* and certain interim reports are also published weekly in Moody's looseleaf volumes. *The Value Line Investment Survey* reports quarterly on about 90 companies in the electric utility industry. Standard & Poor's *Stock Market Encyclopedia* and *Security and Industry Survey* also include information on utility companies. Other studies on the electric utility industry appear in *Forbes Magazine, The Magazine of Wall Street, Business Week,* and many other leading financial magazines. The investor may obtain an annual report or a prospectus from a given company and thus receive more current information about the corporation.

In attempting to predict the future market value of the common stock of a utility company, the individual should consider the following: (1) the excess generating capacity of the utility, (2) the expected need for expansion over the next 5 or 10 years, (3) the estimated cost of the generating units, (4) the method of financing the expansion, (5) the expected trends in the sale of electricity and in the revenues generated by the company, (6) the projected income of the corporation, (7) expected earnings per share of the corporation, and (8) the projected price–earnings ratios of public utility companies in general and of the company in particular.[5]

Table 14-4 presents selected statistical data on 16 electric utility companies in the United States. Eight of these companies were selected from states that are expected to have unusually high rates of population growth during the next 20 years, while the other eight were chosen from states expected to have low rates of population growth over this period. The five-year moving average historical growth rate of the companies and the estimated growth rates for the next five to seven years as compiled by *The Value Line Investment Survey* are reflected in columns 1 and 2 of the table. The 15-year average price–earnings ratios of the companies are shown in column 3, while column 4 reflects the 1964 price–earnings ratios of the company. Some interesting results are revealed by comparing the rate of return on net plant and working capital for the companies from 1961 through 1963. The highest growth rate was experienced by the three Florida companies, and the 1964

---

[5] For another detailed method of evaluating public utility common stocks, see Benjamin Graham, David L. Dodd, and Sidney Cottle, *Security Analysis,* 4th ed. (New York: McGraw-Hill Book Company, Inc., 1962), pp. 570–600.

TABLE 14-4 / Statistical Data on Selected Electric Utility Companies

| | Projected Population Growth 1964–1985 (%) | 5-Year Moving Average[1] | | 15-Year Average Price–Earnings Ratios[1] | 1964 Price–Earnings Ratios[1] | Rate of Return[2] on Net Plant and Working Capital (%) | | |
		Historic Growth Rate (%)	Estimated Growth Rate (%)			1961	1962	1963
Florida	93							
Florida Power		9.0	8.5	20.0×	27.2×	7.54	8.08	7.87
Florida Power and Light		11.1	6.5	20.0×	27.5×	7.74	8.32	8.31
Tampa Electric		11.0	9.0	20.0×	33.2×	7.76	8.33	8.92
Arizona	88							
Arizona Public Services		7.0	10.5	17.0×	23.4×	6.65	6.63	6.23
California	79							
Pacific Gas and Electric		5.6	6.0	16.0×	17.7×	6.21	6.47	6.43
San Diego Gas and Electric		7.2	7.0	15.0×	15.4×	6.29	6.30	6.31
Southern California Edison		7.6	6.5	15.0×	17.9×	6.71	6.61	6.64
New Mexico	75							
Public Service Company of New Mexico		9.6	11.5	15.5×	25.0×	7.95	8.09	8.11
Kansas	18							
Kansas City Power and Light		5.5	7.0	15.0×	19.9×	6.69	7.00	7.31
Kansas Gas and Electric		6.2	7.0	14.0×	20.2×	6.74	7.02	7.50
Kansas Power and Light		5.0	6.0	13.5×	18.8×	7.80	8.03	8.12
Pennsylvania	16							
Duquesne Light		4.7	3.2	15.0×	18.2×	7.42	7.51	7.67
Pennsylvania Power and Light		2.8	4.6	15.0×	19.0×	6.51	6.47	6.63
Philadelphia Electric		4.0	3.5	15.0×	19.2×	6.27	6.44	6.55
North Dakota	15							
Montana–Dakota Utilities		5.8	6.5	16.0×	18.0×	5.34	5.42	6.42
Otter Tail Power Company		2.2	5.1	13.0×	14.9×	5.93	6.14	6.77

SOURCES: Compiled from [1] *The Value Line Investment Survey* (New York: Arnold Bernhard & Company, Inc., May 21, 1965) and [2] *Federal Power Commission, Statistics of Electric Utilities in the United States Privately Owned* (Washington, D.C.: U.S. Government Printing Office, 1963), pp. 651–652 and Table 14-1.

price–earnings ratios of these three utilities were also higher than those of any of the other 13 companies. Although the rates of return on net plant and working capital for the three companies from 1961 through 1963 were fairly generous, many of the other companies with lower price–earnings ratios had much higher rates of return. These included the Citizens Utilities Company, the Houston Lighting and Power Company, Kentucky Power Company, New Orleans Public Services, Inc., Texas Electric Service Company, Texas Power and Light Company, and West Texas Utilities Company.

If one assumes the estimated growth rates to be reasonably accurate, the information in Table 14-4 shows that in 1965 common shares of the Arizona Public Services Company and of some of the California issues were better investment prospects in 1965 than the issues of the other companies. It is interesting to note that the equities of the companies serving the states with lower rates of population growth have been penalized by trading at lower than average price–earnings ratios, and many of these companies were also handicapped by a low rate of return on net plant and working capital.

Figure 14-1 presents price–earnings ratios of selected companies in 1964

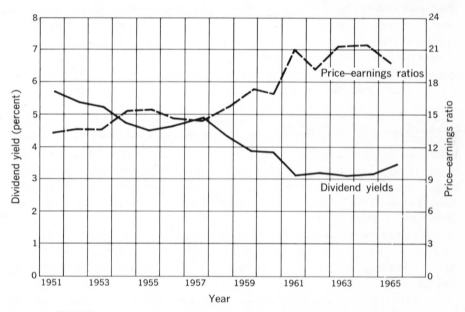

FIGURE 14-1 / Dividend yield and price–earnings ratios for Moody's 24 utility common stocks. From U.S. Department of Commerce, *Survey of Current Business,* selected issues.

as well as the dividend yield on Moody's 24 utility common stocks for the same time period. As measured by this index, price–earnings ratios increased from 11.92 times to 23.46 times from 1950 to 1964. The price, relative to earnings, rose from about 12 times earnings in 1950 to about 21 times earnings in 1963 and 1964. Although dividend yields in excess of 5 percent could be obtained on investments in utility stocks from 1950 through 1953, the relationship between current dividends and market price of each common share fell to almost 3 percent from 1961 through 1965. If utility stocks continue to trade at 20 or 21 times earnings and the companies continue to produce an annual increase in earnings per share of 5 to 6 percent, the average return on utility stocks should amount to about 3 percent from dividends, plus an average annual appreciation of 5 or 6 percent, resulting in an annual return on the investment of about 8 or 9 percent. Dividend yields and market values of utility company stocks do, however, oscillate over the stock cycle.

Industry Regulation

The primary function of a regulatory agency, particularly as it applies to the electric utilities industry, is to see that consumers are provided with the best possible service at the lowest possible cost but at a rate that is high enough to provide the security holders of the company with a reasonable return on their investment. Electric utility companies are regulated by both state and federal agencies. The state utility commissions of the states in which the electric utility operates regulate the rates that may be charged the various classes of customers—residential, commercial, and industrial. When electricity is sold at the wholesale level in interstate commerce, the FPC regulates the rates. Companies that sell electricity at the wholesale level and thus fall under the authority of the FPC must also seek permission from that regulatory agency before making a new security issue. In general, the agency attempts to maintain a fair balance between the debt and equity of the issuing corporation. The FPC has encouraged the utilities to use a considerable amount of debt, though not to exceed 60 percent of the total capitalization structure, and insists that common stocks of the companies and retained earnings accounts equal at least 25 percent of total capitalization. Preferred stock issues usually account for the balance of 10 to 15 percent of the total capitalization.

A summary of the indicated rates of return of electric utility companies on their electrical operations for the last three years appears in each annual issue of *Statistics of Electric Utilities in the United States Privately Owned,* published by the Federal Power Commission. In this publication, statistics are reported for the 188 companies having annual electric operating revenues in excess of $2.5 million. The rates of return on 16 of these 188 companies are reported in Table 14-4. The table indicates that only about 2 percent of the companies were earning less than a 4 percent return on their net plant and working capital while 9 companies were earning in excess of 9 percent. A majority of the companies were earning returns of between 5 and 7 percent.

Natural Gas and Pipeline Companies

The growth in population, the increase in the number of housing units, and the increasing use of natural gas for air conditioning, refrigeration, and home clothes driers should stimulate the sale of natural gas in the foreseeable future. Many electric companies have natural gas distribution facilities, but most of the larger natural gas companies operate only in the natural gas industry. The growth of the natural gas industry is perhaps not quite as assured nor as dynamic as that of the electric utility industry. However, the increasing usage of the commodity and the slightly more generous yields of these issues as compared to electric utility stocks sometimes make these securities attractive purchases.

Generally, when the natural gas company is regulated only by a state utility commission, adequate rates are set so that the stockholders and other security owners of the corporation receive a fair return on their investment. During recent years, however, natural gas pipeline companies that transport gas in interstate commerce and that must register with the FPC have come under severe rate-reduction pressures. Many rate cases have been brought by the pipeline companies against the FPC when the latter has ruled that rates for the wholesale of natural gas in interstate commerce should be at reduced prices. The most important of these cases had been resolved by the end of 1965, usually resulting in reduced rates, but some remain, and the decisions of the FPC and the courts may have an important influence on the operations of individual companies. Although the long-term outlook for the purchase of securities in the natural gas pipeline companies may be good, the short-range prospects are not as bright as for stocks of electric utility companies and of the natural gas companies that do not fall under the authority of the FPC.

Generally, natural gas and natural gas pipeline companies do not use as much leverage as do electric utility companies. A few corporations, however, such as Texas Eastern and Transcontinental Pipeline, use a high degree of leverage, providing some 70 to 75 percent of their total capitalization through the use of debt. Although these heavily leveraged companies are of low quality because of the risk of fluctuating earnings, an ability to operate profitably over the long run may produce handsome capitalization for the shareholders of these corporations.[6]

The Coal Industry

The coal industry is not classified as a public utility, but its destiny is closely allied to that of the natural gas and electric utility industries and to the level of industrial production. Coal is used primarily as a heating fuel by individuals, electric utility companies, and large steel mills. It has been estimated that the total resources of coal in the United States will be adequate to last about 2000 years at the current rate of consumption.[7]

In 1964, the consumption of coal was approximately 5 percent above the 1963 level. Electric utility companies were consuming some 54 percent of the product, steel mills were using an additional 19 percent, and the balance

[6] For an up-to-date analysis of the natural gas and natural gas pipeline industry, see the most current issue of Merrill Lynch, Pierce, Fenner & Smith, Inc., *Security and Industry Survey* (New York: Merrill Lynch).

[7] Glover and Lagai, pp. 175–212.

was purchased by other users. Many coal-producing companies have long-range contracts, ranging from 5 to 25 years, with electric utility companies. These long-range contracts add a considerable amount of stability to the operating revenues and expected profits of the industry. Recent wage increases have primarily been offset by rising coal prices, so that the producer should not be adversely affected by the trend in labor costs.[8]

The average price of steam-grade coal, which is obtained from the mouth of the mine, was $5.08 a ton in 1957 but had fallen to $4.40 a ton by 1964. In many cases the cost of transporting the coal from the mine to the consumer was a similar figure per ton. Because of heavy freight costs, a number of coal pipelines have been built as a cheaper alternative to rail transportation. Numerous large coal mining companies have erected generating units near the coal mines, converted the coal to electrical energy, and transmitted it over high frequency power lines to distant cities.[9]

Summary

During the twentieth century the sale of electric energy in the United States has approximately doubled during each 10-year period. This trend is expected to continue for the next 20 or 30 years. Although the growth rate of revenues and profits of the average utility company is in the vicinity of 5 to 7 percent a year, some electric utility companies are expected to perform better than the industry average.

In selecting a common stock of an electric utility company, the individual should consider the generating capacity of the company, the expected expansion to be undertaken within the near future, the trends in revenue and income, and the policy of the state utility commission in controlling the rates of the company. An individual should also select a utility company from an area that is expected to increase in population. As residential population increases, new family units are formed and new housing units are erected requiring additional electric energy for lighting, heating, and air conditioning and for the operation of major appliances. As population increases, commercial businesses usually also grow. Shifts in population are frequently correlated with industrialization, since industries normally do not expand in areas where there is not an abundant labor supply, nor do large masses of individuals move to areas where jobs are not available.

Electric utility companies are able to finance a significantly higher percentage of their total assets with debt than the average industrial company. This is possible because of the stability in revenues and earnings of the companies and the high percentage of revenue left as net income. The average utility company has some 15 or 16 cents of each revenue dollar left

---

[8] See Merrill Lynch, Pierce, Fenner and Smith, Inc., *Security and Industry Survey* (Spring 1965), pp. 14–15.

[9] See *The Value Line Investment Survey* (New York: Arnold Bernhard & Company, Inc., May 7, 1965), p. 352.

for the payment of dividends or the retention of earnings in the corporation. Although this may appear to be a large figure, revenues for an electric utility company amount to only some 20 to 25 percent of the total asset base; therefore, a high net return on sales is necessary to provide an adequate return to the security owners.

The stock market has generally placed a premium on the shares of the electric utility industry. Although the issues of many companies were trading in 1965 at price–earnings ratios of about 18 or 20 times, some of the utilities located in fast-growing areas were trading at from 25 to 35 times annual earnings per share. Natural gas, pipeline, and coal industry issues are expected to benefit in the long run from the growth in population and the growth in revenues, although these companies are not expected to grow as rapidly as the electric utility industry. In 1965, the shares were not traded at such high price–earnings ratios as the electric utility stocks, but dividend yields were higher.

QUESTIONS FOR REVIEW /

1. How does the capitalization of an electric utility company differ from that of an industrial corporation?
2. Enumerate the major sources of revenues and expenses of the electric utility company.
3. What possible advantages do the publicly owned electric utility companies have over the privately owned companies?
4. Differentiate between the Class A and Class B electric utility company as defined by the FPC. How important are these companies when compared to other producers of electricity?
5. Evaluate the growth potential of electric utility companies serving in nearby states.
6. Why do current assets appear so small for utility companies? Why are current liabilities frequently in excess of total current assets?
7. How would you forecast the expected earnings per share for a utility company for the next five years? Is it possible to forecast the price–earnings ratio of a utility issue? Why or why not?
8. How are electric utility companies regulated?
9. Contrast the future outlook of the natural gas industry with that of the electric utility industry. Wherein do these companies compete?
10. How would you rate the future prospects of the coal industry?

PROBLEMS /

1. Select a current annual report of an electric utility company and compute its growth rate in revenues and net profits for the last 10 or 12 years. By extrapolation, project these estimates for the next 5 or 10 years. Assuming that the electric utility company continues to maintain a similar capitalization mix and that the price–earnings ratio, dividend yield, and interest yield remain relatively

stable during this period, attempt to predict the market value of the stock 5 or 10 years in the future. How much reliance do you place on this estimate?

2. Through a study of population estimates and the listing of electric utility companies in *Statistics of Electric Utilities in the United States Privately Owned*, published annually by the FPC, compile a list of six utility companies that appear to have unusually high potential revenue and net profit increases. Contrast the average prices at which shares within the two groups are traded.

3. By reference to *Statistics of Electric Utilities in the United States Privately Owned*, determine three states that appear to be generous in setting the rates of return permitted on net plant and working capital, and select three other states that appear to be restrictive in setting these rates. Do the rates of return appear to have influenced average price–earnings ratios of the companies analyzed? Do you visualize any changes in the rigidity or laxity of the state utility commissions with regard to rate regulations within the states where the rates of return appear to be unusually low and unusually high? If so, how should this affect the market values of the common shares of these companies?

4. With the help of the most current *Annual Report* of the FPC, determine companies against which rate-reduction action has been recently brought by the FPC. Do you believe that these rate reductions were justified? What effects do you believe that this action has upon the market standing of the securities?

REFERENCES /

Annual Report of Gulf States Utilities Company. Beaumont, Texas: Gulf States Utilities Company, 1963 and 1964.

Glover, John G., and Rudolph L. Lagai, *The Development of American Industries.* New York: Simmons-Boardman Publishing Corporation, 1957.

Graham, Benjamin, David L. Dodd, and Sidney Cottle, *Security Analysis,* 4th ed. New York: McGraw-Hill Book Company, Inc., 1962.

Merrill Lynch, Pierce, Fenner & Smith, Inc., *The Electric Utilities* (*The Sixty Largest U.S. Companies with Revenues above $50,000,000 a year*). New York: Merrill Lynch, 1963.

———, *Security and Industry Survey.* New York: Merrill Lynch, Spring 1965.

Moody's Handbook of Common Stocks. New York: Moody's Investors Service, Inc., selected issues.

Moody's Public Utilities. New York: Moody's Investors Service, Inc., selected issues.

U.S. Department of Commerce, Bureau of the Census, *Population Estimates,* Series P-25, No. 301. Washington, D.C.: U.S. Government Printing Office, February 26, 1965.

———, *Statistical Abstract of the United States.* Washington, D.C.: U.S. Government Printing Office, 1965.

U.S. Federal Power Commission, *Annual Report.* Washington, D.C.: U.S. Government Printing Office, 1965.

———, *Statistics of Electric Utilities in the United States Privately Owned.* Washington, D.C.: U.S. Government Printing Office, 1963 and 1964.

The Value Line Investment Survey. New York: Arnold Bernhard & Company, Inc., selected issues.

chapter 15 | Transportation Issues

Introduction

Under Section XX of the Interstate Commerce Act of 1887, the federal government attempted to compel certain types of corporations to disclose financial and operating results to the general public. At that time, some railroads were expensing capital expenditures, that is, charging the entire cost as an expense during the year of purchase, while others were capitalizing and amortizing them over their estimated useful life. Today, the uniform system of accounting prescribed for common carriers by the Interstate Commerce Commission (ICC) is similar to that employed by industrial corporations and is extended to include many different types of carriers (see Table 15-1).

The ICC has a number of powers over the companies it regulates. One function of the ICC is to require certain accounting practices to be followed in preparing profit and loss statements and balance sheets. Another is to regulate the return on investments and rate schedules assigned to companies that come under the authority of the ICC. Companies that operate in interstate commerce must also have the approval of this governing body before opening new routes or disbanding old ones. In order that the ICC may be assured that the general public is being serviced adequately, operating schedules of such companies must be approved by that agency.

Table 15-1 lists the carriers subject to uniform systems of accounting as well as those that are required to file annual and periodic reports with the ICC. The former includes railroads, motor carriers, oil pipelines, water carriers, electric railways, express companies, stockyard companies, rail holding companies, and others. Carriers and other organizations that are required to file annual reports with the ICC but that are not subject to the prescribed uniform system of accounts include companies that furnish railroad cars, certain classes of motor carriers of passengers and property, small water carriers, small freight forwarders, motor holding companies, street electric lines, and rating bureaus and organizations. Local firms that operate intrastate, that is, within the state of organization and incorporation, do not fall under the jurisdiction of the ICC, but transportation companies that operate in interstate commerce must comply with ICC regulations.

At mid-1965, some 5160 companies were subject to the uniform system

TABLE 15-1 /   Carriers Subject to Jurisdiction of the Interstate Commerce Commission on June 30, 1965

Carriers subject to uniform system of accounts and required to file annual and periodic reports as of June 30, 1965

Railroads, class I	77
Railroads, class II	307
Railroad switching and terminal companies, class I	26
Railroad switching and terminal companies, class II	167
Railroad lessor companies	142
Motor carriers, class I passengers	248[1]
Motor carriers, class I property	1250
Motor carriers, class II property	2615
Oil pipelines	89
Water carriers	93
Maritime carriers	19
Electric railways	15
Freight forwarders	60
Protective service companies	7
Express companies	2
Sleeping car companies	1
Stockyard companies	37[2]
Holding companies (rail)	5
Total	5160

Number of carriers and organizations filing annual reports but not subject to prescribed uniform system of accounts as of June 30, 1965

Car lines (companies that furnish cars for use on lines of railroads)	155
Class II and III motor carriers of passengers	892
Class III motor carriers of property	11,700
Water carriers (less than $100,000 gross revenue)	104[3]
Freight forwarders (less than $100,000 gross revenue)	22
Holding companies (motor)	26
Street electric lines	4
Rating bureaus and organizations	105
Total	13,008
Grand total	18,168

[1] Includes combination property and passenger (9 carriers).

[2] Includes stockyard company lessors (12 carriers).

[3] Includes maritime carriers filing on water carrier Form K-C (2 carriers).

SOURCE: U.S. Interstate Commerce Commission, *Annual Report* (Washington, D.C.: U.S. Government Printing Office, 1965), p. 138.

of accounts and were required to file annual and periodic reports with the ICC. An additional 13,008 companies were required to file annual reports with the ICC but were not subject to its prescribed uniform system of accounts. In general, the system of accounting required by the ICC does not differ significantly from generally accepted accounting principles recommended for industrial companies. Revenue and expense classifications, however, are slightly different because of the nature of the businesses.

Companies Operating within the Transportation Industry

The operating revenues for ICC-regulated transport agencies from 1947 through 1964 are given in Figure 15-1. In 1947, the companies had operating revenues slightly in excess of $13 billion, and by the end of 1964, the amount had increased to $25 billion. The amount of operating revenues for railroads, including switching and terminal companies, increased slightly during the 17-year period. The operating revenues of motor carriers of property, conversely, increased from approximately $2 billion to about $9 billion. The rate of increase for airlines was much greater than for the other carriers, while little or no increase was reported for motor carriers of passengers, railway express companies, electric railways, and Pullman Company.

The 1947 to 1964 growth rates of the transport agencies are shown in Figure 15-2. Over this 17-year period, revenues increased 770 percent for airlines, 320 percent for motor carriers of property, and 170 percent for oil pipelines, compared to a gain of 155 percent in national income. The bottom portion of Figure 15-2 indicates that the revenues of railroads, motor carriers of passengers, and water lines increased slightly over the 17-year period, but their rates of gain were less than the growth in national income. There was a deterioration in the actual amount of operating income for railway express companies, electric railways, and Pullman Company.

For almost 200 years the railroad system in the United States has been the backbone of this nation's transportation system, and its strong position within the industry continued through World War II. Since then, however, competition with other segments of the transportation industry has become severe, so that the railroads have been hard pressed to maintain their previous revenue levels. It has been very difficult for the railroads, on the average, to increase revenues and profits. Since the railroad industry is such a tremendous one, and since there are vast amounts of railroad securities in the hands of the general public, the railroad industry will be treated in detail here. Airlines, because of their tremendous growth within the last 17 years and their potential future expansion possibilities, are also emphasized. Companies operating in other segments of the transport industries are not discussed at length, but the footnotes and references list sources of information on companies operating in these associated industries.

Although not covered in detail in this chapter, the railroad equipment industry may be of interest to the reader. From a low point in earnings for the industry in 1961, sales and earnings began to increase rapidly with 1966 railroad car production, reaching about three times the 1961 rate of output. Railroad cars remained in short supply in 1966, and backlogs of orders were at high levels. The duration of this sales boom will, of course, be influenced

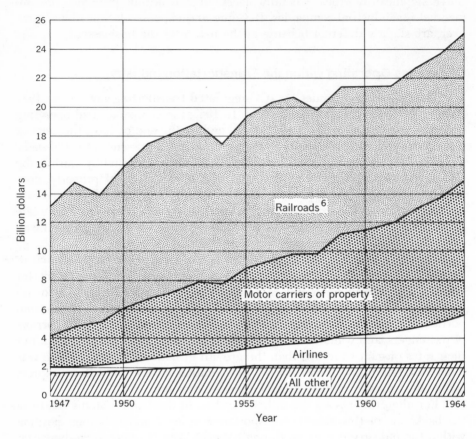

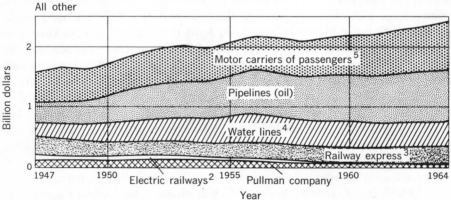

FIGURE 15-1 / Indexes of Operating Revenues[1] for selected transport agencies, 1947–1964. From U.S. Interstate Commerce Commission, *79th Annual Report,* Washington, D.C., U.S. Government Printing Office, 1965, p. 145.

(*See notes on following page.*)

by the level of industrial production; and when business declines, railroad revenues fall, buyers frequently cancel their orders for new railroad cars, and railroad equipment suppliers suffer from sales and profit declines. The following companies operate primarily within this industry: ACF Industries, Inc.; American Brake Shoe; Amsted Industries; General American Transportation Corporation; General Signal Company; General Steel Industries, Inc.; New York Air Brakes Company; North American Car Corporation; Pittsburgh Forgings Company; Poor & Company; Pullman, Inc.; Stanray Corporation; Union Tank Car Company; Westinghouse Air Brake Company; Youngstown Steel Door Company; and others.[1]

The future of the ocean shippers and shipbuilders depends upon a number of factors, for example, the volume of foreign trade, the speed-up that can be expected in loading and unloading, more specialized carriers, the cost of labor, and Cold War engagements. In the event that the world economy continues to grow and that the United States continues its pursuit of the Food for Freedom program, ocean shipping should have a healthy future. The market values of the equities do, of course, oscillate widely, and some of the issues, for example, American Export Isbrandtsen Company, were trading at extremely low multiples of earnings in 1966. Shipping and ship builders include the following companies: American Commercial Lines, Inc.; American Export Isbrandtsen Company, Inc.; Bath Iron Works Corporation; Lykes Brothers Steamship Company, Inc.; McLean Industries, Inc.; Merrit-Chapman & Scott Corporation; The Mississippi Valley Barge Line; Moore and McCormick Company, Inc.; Newport News Ship Building & Dry Docks Company; United States Lines Company; and others.

Figure 15-2 indicates that the revenues of motor carriers of property increased over 300 percent from 1947 to 1964, or at a growth rate that was twice that of national income during the same period, while motor carriers of passengers had revenue increases of only 50 percent. Truck lines do, of course, have some competitive operating advantages over railroads on short hauls. For example, a large segment of the young adult population annually moves from one geographical area to another in search of better-paying jobs, thus creating the need for moving vans. At the same time, bus lines gained

---

[1] For a review of operating statistics on these and other companies, see *Moody's Transportation Manual, Moody's Handbook of Common Stocks, The Value Line Investment Survey, Trendline's Current Market Perspectives, Standard & Poor's Corporate Records,* and other current investment services.

---

[1] Partly estimated.

[2] Shifts of carriers from electric to line-haul railroad and other classification, and partial and complete abandonments have affected the decline by an indeterminate amount.

[3] After deducting payments to others for express privileges.

[4] Includes only revenues from domestic traffic of carriers subject to the jurisdiction of the Interstate Commerce Commission.

[5] Does not include motor carrier revenues of electric railways, included under electric railways.

[6] Includes switching and terminal companies.

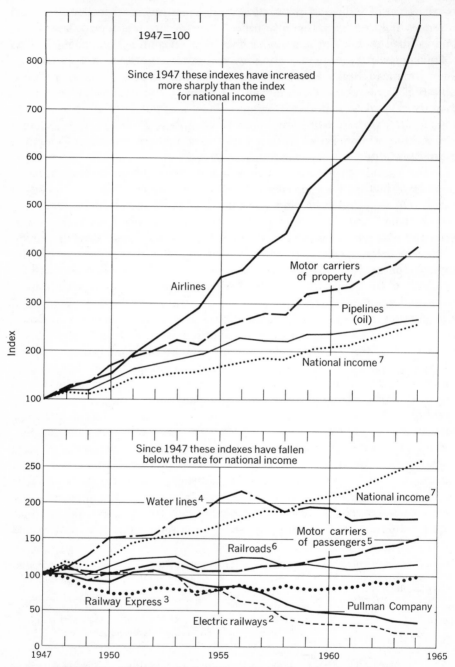

FIGURE 15-2 / Indexes of operating revenues[1] for selected transport agencies, 1947–1964. From U.S. Interstate Commerce Commission, *79th Annual Report*, Washington, D.C., U.S. Government Printing Office, 1965, p. 144.

(*See notes on following page.*)

some railroad passenger traffic but lost ground to the airlines and to private automobiles over the 1947–1964 period. Truck and bus line companies within which there is a large amount of public ownership of securities include Consolidated Freightways, Inc.; Cooper-Jerritt, Inc.; Greyhound Corporation; Interstate Motor Freight System; McLean Trucking Company; Merchants East Motor Lines; National City Lines, Inc.; Pacific Intermountain Express Company; Roadway Express, Inc.; Ryder's System, Inc.; Spector Freight System, Inc.; and U.S. Freight Company. Many of these corporations are holding companies for the common stocks of numerous operating subsidiaries.

Due to the large number of companies operating in these areas, a listing of railroads and airlines is not given.

The Railroad Industry

History

The railroad industry had its beginning in the United States in the early 1800s. The strap rail cars that were drawn on wooden rails by horse power were used in some cities until about 1830. The first steam locomotive in the United States was built in 1825, and the first trial run was made in 1830. From this beginning the railroad network began to expand in the United States and by 1918 had reached its maximum number of line miles.

As early as 1869 railroads within the United States began to consolidate in an attempt to operate more economically while providing customers with better and cheaper service. In order to facilitate westward expansion by providing settlers with transportation, agricultural implements, and staple foods, a federal land-grant program was inaugurated. This program, however, was much less important than is commonly realized. Companies that built only 8 percent of the railroad milage received land grants, while other companies received none. For these land grants, the railroads agreed to contribute their services to the federal government for the transport of goods and troops during national emergencies at 50 percent of the normal rate. In order to compete with these prices and receive federal government contracts,

---

[1] Partly estimated.

[2] Shifts of carriers from electric to line-haul railroad and other classification, and partial and complete abandonments have affected the decline by an indeterminate amount.

[3] After deducting payments to others for express privileges.

[4] Includes only revenues from domestic traffic of carriers subject to the jurisdiction of the Interstate Commerce Commission.

[5] Does not include motor carrier revenues of electric railways, included under electric railways.

[6] Includes switching and terminal companies.

[7] Revised national income.

other railroads that had not received land grants also provided these reduced rates. However, these rate reductions were discontinued in 1940.

The ICC is empowered to set railroad rates so that the carriers may obtain rates of return on their net investment ranging between 5½ and 6½ percent, although the actual rates of return have fallen far below these figures. Excluding the unprofitable depression years, the general range of returns was from 3.5 to 4.75 percent during the 1920–1964 period, well below the goal of the ICC. During World War I the railroad industry was controlled and operated by the federal government, which subsidized railroad income by about $1.6 billion over the four-year period. During World War II, however, when the railroads were operating with about 25 percent fewer box cars, passenger cars, and employees, the railroad industry was permitted to manage its own affairs. Not only was the need for subsidy eliminated during World War II, but the railroads paid almost $4 billion in federal income taxes.

All in all, the railroad industry has shown poor operating results since the 1920s. In the case of many of the companies the financial structures are unwieldy, being composed of large numbers of separate bond issues, vast amounts of noncallable preferred stock, and large amounts of fixed charges. Their heavy bonded indebtedness makes it difficult for the railroads to reduce their expenses during periods of declining revenues. The inability of the railroads as a result of restrictions imposed by the ICC to discontinue unprofitable operations, the growing severity of competition within the transportation industry, the expansion in private ownership of automobiles, the heavy ad valorem taxes imposed upon railroads, the strong position of labor unions within the industry, heavy retirement benefit costs, and numerous other factors all combined to hold the railroads at low profit margins during the latter 1940s and during the 1950s.[2]

Many railroads paid generous dividends during the 1920s, and shareholders believed that the railroad industry would have a strong future. However, the depressed state of the economy during the 1930s and the declining need for transportation facilities resulted in reduced revenues and cumulative losses for many companies. The overuse of debt and the inability to reduce fixed charges led to the reorganization of numerous railroads. With the vast need for transportation during World War II, however, the financial position of the companies improved and they were able to eliminate some bonded indebtedness and began to finance their operations more heavily with common stock and retained earnings. During and subsequent to World War II, railroads retained about one half of their after-tax net income for expansion purposes and/or for the repayment of funded debt. The reduction in fixed charges should produce more stable operating profits in the future.

Table 15-2 contains selected balance sheet items for 1954 through 1963

[2] For a comprehensive analysis of the railroad industry, see John G. Glover and Rudolph L. Lagai, *The Development of American Industries*, 4th ed. (New York: Simmons-Boardman Publishing Corporation, 1957), pp. 613–641.

TABLE 15-2 / Selected Balance Sheet Items, 1954–1963: Class I Line-Haul Railroads and Their Lesser Subsidiaries (in thousands of dollars)

Year Ended Dec. 31	Current Assets	Net Investment in Transportation Property	All Other Assets	Current Liabilities[1]	Long-term Debt	All Other Liabilities	Shareholders Equity
1954	3,346,911	24,702,048	3,278,552	1,805,377	10,744,715	1,193,348	17,584,071
1955	3,790,710	24,883,508	3,289,814	2,151,157	10,741,077	1,192,206	17,879,592
1956	3,575,204	25,285,612	3,262,526	2,130,785	10,801,320	1,111,210	18,080,027
1957	3,221,842	25,928,467	3,182,141	1,928,844	10,977,187	1,120,275	18,306,144
1958	3,147,256	26,012,615	3,015,483	2,129,840	10,614,720	1,061,404	18,369,390
1959	3,154,043	25,967,635	3,110,464	2,260,406	10,386,430	1,080,772	18,504,534
1960	2,939,773	26,098,028	3,089,336	2,259,987	10,244,727	1,095,178	18,527,245
1961	3,004,927	25,878,373	2,965,344	2,396,721	10,072,311	916,665	18,462,947
1962	3,055,840	24,595,106	4,376,231	2,371,290	9,927,493	956,654	18,751,740
1963	3,340,787	24,567,847	4,530,866	2,538,680	9,880,445	979,298	19,041,077

[1] Includes long-term debt due within one year in 1958–1963. This item was included in long-term debt in prior years.

SOURCE: U.S. Interstate Commerce Commission, *Annual Report* (Washington, D.C.: U.S. Government Printing Office, 1964), p. 141.

for Class I line-haul railroads and their lesser subsidiaries. Over this 10-year period, the current assets, net investment in transportation property, net investment in all other assets, and current liabilities remained relatively constant. The railroads did reduce their long-term debt by some 10 percent and their other liabilities by 15 percent while increasing the shareholders' equity by approximately 10 percent.

Table 15-3 lists the operating revenues, operating expenses, and net income for Class I line-haul railroads for the 1954–1964 period. Freight revenues increased from 1954 through 1956, generally declined from 1957 through 1961, and increased from 1962 through 1964. Passenger revenues, conversely, declined by approximately 25 percent over the 10-year period, and total operating revenues remained almost constant. The operating ratios, that is, the relationship between revenue and expenses, for the companies varied from a low in 1955 of 75.66 percent to a high of 79.52 percent in 1960. Although net income rose considerably from 1954 to 1955, it then began to decline until 1961 and by the latter year was about 40 percent of the 1955 level. Net income increased somewhat from 1961 through 1964.

Chapter 3 revealed that railroad stocks performed poorer as a group from 1940 to 1965 than did industrials, utilities, and financial institutions. In addition, the market price of many railroad issues oscillates widely over the stock market cycle. During boom periods, when railroads increase their net income, investor sentiment frequently shifts toward rail issues, resulting in increasing price–earnings ratios. During periods of falling net income and earnings per share, however, common stocks of railroads become more depressed in price, and not only do the earnings per share fall but the average price–earnings ratio also declines, thus producing wide fluctuations in the market value of railroad issues. Other railroads, particularly those in the East, have strong seasonal price movements, with generally rising market prices in the fall and winter and declining prices in the spring and summer (see Chapter 22).

Performance of Selected Companies

Table 15-4 gives selected statistics on six railroads operating within the United States. The companies included within this study are (1) Atchison, Topeka & Santa Fe; (2) Chicago, Milwaukee, St. Paul and Pacific; (3) New York Central; (4) Pennsylvania Railroad; (5) Southern Pacific; and (6) Union Pacific. As measured by the number of miles of railroad right of way, these companies are among the larger railroad systems operating within the United States.

In early 1966, the Atchison, Topeka & Santa Fe Railroad, which extends from Chicago to Los Angeles and San Francisco, had more than 24 million common shares outstanding, which were held by 128,000 stockholders. Almost 80 percent of the total capitalization of the company was made up of common equity, and the stock was trading at 40 percent below book value

TABLE 15-3 / Operating Revenues, Operating Expenses, and Net Income, Class I Line-Haul Railroads, 1954–1964

Year Ended Dec. 31	Freight Revenues (thousands)	Passenger Revenues (thousands)	Total Operating Revenues (thousands)	Total Transportation Expenses (thousands)	Total Operating Expenses (thousands)	Operating Ratio (percent)	Net Railway Operating Income (thousands)	Net Income (thousands)
1954	$7,797,885	$767,283	$ 9,370,826	$3,622,535	$7,384,499	78.80	$ 874,018	$681,690
1955	8,538,286	742,945	10,106,330	3,769,856	7,646,418	75.66	1,127,997	927,122
1956	8,951,423	756,582	10,550,943	4,043,452	8,108,353	76.85	1,068,246	876,333
1957	8,928,511	735,339	10,491,390	4,094,780	8,227,522	78.42	922,334	737,431
1958	8,070,826	675,296	9,564,568	3,834,340	7,543,842	78.87	762,296	601,737
1959	8,312,181	651,168	9,825,060	3,887,710	7,704,815	78.42	747,677	577,719
1960	8,025,423	640,268	9,514,294	3,832,882	7,565,336	79.52	584,016	444,640
1961	7,739,044	624,688	9,189,138	3,710,832	7,274,260	79.16	537,771	382,444
1962	7,991,146	619,056	9,439,895	3,755,092	7,418,562	78.59	725,679	571,017
1963	8,146,131	588,104	9,559,522	3,771,254	7,451,648	77.95	805,658	651,637
Jan.–June 1963	4,031,160	292,319	4,714,888	1,868,697	3,683,993	78.14	359,754	270,307
Jan.–June 1964	4,167,583	281,016	4,843,804	1,895,576	3,762,794	77.68	415,463	340,649

SOURCE: U.S. Interstate Commerce Commission, *Annual Report* (Washington, D.C.: U.S. Government Printing Office, 1964), p. 141.

TABLE 15-4 / Selected Statistics on Six Large U.S. Railroads, 1960–1965

Year	Revenue (Millions)	Operating Ratio	Percent Earned on Total Capital	Earnings per Share	Annual Price Range*	Average Price–Earnings Ratio
			ATCHISON, TOPEKA & SANTA FE			
1960	$614.0	78.5%	4.0%	$1.87[1]	21–20	12.5×
1961	604.5	77.2	4.2	2.00[1]	29–22	13.0
1962	612.3	79.2	5.2	2.65[1]	28–20	9.1
1963	616.1	80.6	4.9	2.52[1]	30–25	11.3
1964	659.8	80.3	5.2	3.04	37–28	10.5
1965	677.4	78.4	5.4	3.28	35–30	10.0
			CHICAGO, MILWAUKEE, ST. PAUL & PACIFIC			
1960	230.6	81.6	0.6	(.60)[1]	26–13	—
1961	221.8	79.3	2.8	1.29[1]	19–13	12.9
1962	227.7	79.5	2.4	.03[1]	18–7	—
1963	223.1	79.4	2.8	1.32[1]	17–9	10.2
1964	228.2	81.0	2.8	1.27[1]	37–14	20.2
1865	241.4	79.4	3.4	2.16	49–26	11.2
			NEW YORK CENTRAL			
1960	674.5	84.2	2.5	.16	32–15	—
1961	612.0	85.5	1.6	(1.92)	22–15	—
1962	622.6	83.9	2.1	(1.59)	21–11	—
1963	623.3	83.0	2.7	1.08	25–15	18.8
1964	641.5	81.7	3.8	4.06	53–25	10.1
1965	661.4	79.5	4.8	6.06	81–41	9.5
			PENNSYLVANIA RAILROAD			
1960	843.7	82.8	0.8	(.59)	17–11	—
1961	820.1	81.9	2.2	.27	18–11	54.1
1962	850.7	81.4	1.9	(.24)	19–10	—
1963	840.1	80.6	2.5	.68	26–13	27.4
1964	873.2	79.8	3.5	2.12	43–25	16.6
1965	892.6	78.4	3.8	2.45	65–35	19.3

* Rounded to nearest dollar.

[1] Including tax deferrals for accelerated depreciation.

SOURCES: *The Value Line Investment Survey, Moody's Handbook of Common Stocks,* and *Barron's,* selected issues.

TABLE 15-4 *(Continued)*

Year	Revenue (Millions)	Operating Ratio	Percent Earned on Total Capital	Earnings per Share	Annual Price Range*	Average Price– Earnings Ratio
		SOUTHERN	PACIFIC			
1960	760	77.4	4.3	2.41[1]	24–18	8.3
1961	771.0	75.6	4.4	2.58[1]	30–20	9.7
1962	805.9	76.2	4.8	3.02[1]	30–22	8.7
1963	809.9	76.7	5.0	3.25[1]	28–28	10.1
1964	838.6	78.0	5.1	3.50	46–31	11.9
1965	896.7	76.3	5.4	3.60	47–33	11.1
		UNION	PACIFIC			
1960	494.2	72.8	5.0	2.73[1]	31–25	10.0
1961	499.3	72.3	5.0	2.84[1]	27–27	11.9
1962	512.1	72.3	5.7	3.50[1]	35–27	9.0
1963	519.1	71.7	5.5	3.58[1]	42–32	10.9
1964	529.1	74.7	5.6	3.64[1]	49–39	12.0
1965	549.2	73.5	5.1	4.03	45–37	10.2

per share. From 1960 to 1965, common shares traded between 20½ and 37 per share, and the price–earnings ratio remained relatively constant. Although revenues from 1960 to 1965 increased by only 10 percent, earnings per share rose by about 75 percent.

The Chicago, Milwaukee, St. Paul and Pacific Railroad extends from Chicago to Seattle, Washington. Some two million of its common shares were held by 7400 shareholders in 1966. Although revenues for the company from 1960 to 1965 remained relatively constant, earnings per share oscillated widely. Each year between 1961 and 1965 the market value of the common stock increased from 50 percent to almost 200 percent from its low to its high market value. One reason for the fluctuation in earnings and market value was the high amount of leverage being used. In early 1966, the common shares had a market price considerably below the $145 book value per share.

In early 1966, approximately 6.8 million shares of the New York Central Railroad common stock were held by about 27,000 shareholders, and company officials were contemplating a merger with the Pennsylvania Railroad. In 1961 and 1962, the company reported large losses, while during 1963, 1964, and 1965 substantial improvements were made in the earnings per share on the common, thus causing the market price of the stock to respond favorably. The rate earned on total capital of the company averaged about 2.5 percent per year during the five-year period, and wide oscillation in the market value per share prevailed each year from 1961 to 1965.

In early 1966, almost 14 million shares of Pennsylvania Railroad common were held by about 137,000 stockholders. Although the revenues of the company were fairly stable over the six-year period, the company reported earnings deficits in 1960 and 1962. Profits increased significantly in 1963, 1964, and 1965 over each of the preceding years. The market value of the common stock oscillated by roughly 60 to 80 percent per year when comparing the low price to the high price each calendar year, and the average price–earnings ratio was also very volatile.

More than 27 million common shares of Southern Pacific Railroad stock were held by 82,000 stockholders during 1966. From 1960 through 1965 revenues increased by roughly 18 percent, while over the same period earnings per share indicated a stable rise from $2.41 to $3.60. In addition, the market price of the issue fluctuated within a narrower range than did some of the other railroad stock. Approximately one third of the company's total capitalization was financed with long-term debt (the company had no preferred stock), and the stock was trading at about a 50 percent discount from its book value per share. The rate earned on total capital during the period was very stable, ranging from 4.3 percent in 1960 to 5.4 percent in 1965, improving each year over this period. These operating statistics indicate that the company was efficiently operated, and since its area of operation extends from Portland, Oregon, to Los Angeles and across the Southwest to New Orleans, it is not as affected by severe weather as some of the northern railroads.

The Union Pacific Railroad extends from the Middle West to the West Coast, but some 40 percent of the net income of the company is derived from oil royalties and investments. In early 1966, more than 22 million common shares were held by almost 100,000 stockholders. Common stock provided some 85 percent of total capitalization, and in 1966 the stock was trading at a 25 percent discount from its book value per share. From 1960 through 1965, revenues increased by roughly 11 percent, while earnings per share rose by 48 percent. The percentage earned on total capital increased from 5 percent in 1960 to 5.6 percent in 1964. The market value of the stock and the average price–earnings ratio remained relatively stable over the six-year period.

In general, the security prices of southern railroads oscillate less widely during the year than do those of northern railroads. This seasonal movement is no doubt influenced by the effects of weather upon revenues and profits, but the timing of the purchases and sales of securities that oscillate widely then becomes very important to an investor who wishes to maximize his investment income and/or capital gains. Since the shares move widely over the business cycle, their purchase during a recovery phase of a boom period and their sale near the height of the economic expansion—if these can be determined—have in the past offered profitable opportunities for intermediate-term investments of, say, two to three years.

The Airlines Industry

History

The use of airplanes in the United States dates back to 1903 when the Wright Brothers sent an airplane into free flight. Although aircraft were not used extensively during World War I, they became commonplace during the 1930s and were much improved in the early 1940s. Propeller-driven planes continued to dominate the industry, but the aerospace companies had begun to experiment on jet aircraft for military use during the latter stages of World War II. Propeller-driven transport planes began to lose ground to jet aircraft during the 1950s, and by the early 1960s a company was not considered modern unless it had a large fleet of the latest design in jet aircraft.

During the 1950s, the airlines were faced with tremendous financing problems as they expanded their fleets, replaced propeller-driven planes with jet aircraft, and paid for costly maintenance. From the early 1950s through mid-1962, their low levels of profitability were reflected in the depressed market prices of stocks in the industry. The general public lacked confidence in the earning ability of airlines since investors for many years had been aware of their heavy fixed costs, reequipping costs, the federal mail subsidy, and other problems. Once these expansion costs had been met, however, and the heavy initial depreciation charges had been written off, the reported earnings per shares began to increase rapidly. From the latter part of 1962 to 1965 the common shares of many airlines increased by about 1000 percent. Some of the airlines were leaders in the 1962 and 1963 price movement, for example, Delta and Northwest, while others, such as Braniff and Eastern, were laggards and turned in a much better price performance in 1964 and 1965 than the industry average.

Figure 15-2 indicates that air transport companies increased their revenues by 650 percent from 1947 to 1964. Their future, of course, will be influenced by the strength of the over-all economy; the usage of air travel; and labor, operating, and financing costs. The price–earnings multiples and market prices at which the shares trade do vary widely over the years, however.

Operating Statistics on Selected Airlines

The six companies selected for this special study on airlines are the largest international air carrier and the five largest United States domestic airlines, arranged in the order of their size (see Table 15-5).

Pan American World Airways had a healthy growth rate in revenues and earnings over the 1960–1966 period because of increased foreign travel, more air freight shipments, and the situation in Vietnam. In early 1966, Pan

TABLE 15-5 / Selected Statistics on Six Large United States Airlines, 1960–1965

Year	Revenue (Millions)	Operating Margin[1]	Load Factor	Earnings per Share	Annual Price Range*	Average Price– Earnings Ratio
PAN AMERICAN WORLD AIRWAYS						
1960	$413.1	18.3%	62.5%	$ .54	12–8	17.1×
1961	460.4	18.5	59.3	.67	12–8	14.5
1962	503.9	20.5	58.1	1.12	12–8	99.0
1963	560.9	24.1	57.2	2.59	27–11	7.5
1964	604.7	19.8	58.1	2.64	42–26	12.5
1965	669.0	21.9	57.9	3.20	56–25	10.4
UNITED AIR LINES						
1960	379.1	16.3	65.2	1.11	16–10	11.4
1961	502.2	15.1	58.1	.29	22–14	62.8
1962	594.3	15.8	53.6	.61	18–9	22.7
1963	622.9	16.3	53.7	1.07	23–15	17.1
1964	669.4	17.1	53.9	2.02	33–22	13.5
1965	792.8	18.7	55.3	3.27	59–29	12.2
AMERICAN AIRLINES						
1960	428.5	14.1	65.1	1.50	26–17	14.1
1961	421.4	13.4	61.2	.85	27–19	26.7
1962	463.0	15.5	57.0	.83	24–15	22.7
1963	488.1	18.7	58.6	2.04	36–18	12.6
1964	544.0	21.8	59.6	3.93	51–34	11.3
1965	612.4	22.0	58.9	4.41	70–44	12.5
TRANS WORLD AIRLINES						
1960	378.4	14.1	63.4	.97	19–11	13.8
1961	362.5	12.7	55.1	(2.21)	20–11	—
1962	403.0	15.9	51.0	(.85)	14–8	—
1963	476.5	19.0	51.8	2.96	32–10	6.5
1964	575.0	23.3	56.6	5.47	52–31	7.8
1965	672.8	23.2	54.6	5.74	72–40	9.4

* Rounded to the nearest dollar.

[1] Before interest, depreciation, or federal income taxes.

SOURCE: *The Value Line Investment Survey, Moody's Handbook of Common Stocks,* and *Barron's.*

TABLE 15-5 (Continued)

Year	Revenue (Millions)	Operating Margin[1]	Load Factor	Earnings per Share	Annual Price Range*	Average Price– Earnings Ratio
		EASTERN	AIR	LINES		
1960	293.8	10.6	53.9	(1.74)	33–22	—
1961	295.4	6.1	52.2	(4.63)	32–21	—
1962	288.1	9.5	49.5	(4.61)	28–16	—
1963	355.0	8.8	50.5	(6.08)	30–19	—
1964	414.3	10.5	55.5	(1.80)	46–26	—
1965	507.5	17.6	57.3	7.04	98–41	9.3
		DELTA	AIR	LINES		
1960	120.2	15.4	58.0	.51	6–4	10.3
1961	146.1	18.4	60.0	.83	12–5	8.5
1962	169.8	19.3	58.1	1.10	16–8	8.7
1963	201.1	24.9	60.6	2.17	28–14	6.8
1964	224.7	24.4	60.1	2.46	42–27	11.4
1965	257.5	25.8	56.7	3.61	79–30	9.4

American had more than 15 million common shares owned by 51,000 share-holders. Operating revenue for the company had increased by approximately 60 percent from 1960 to 1965, while the load factor, that is, the percentage of seating space utilized, declined from 62.5 percent to 57.9 percent. Earnings per share for the company increased from 54 cents in 1960 to $3.20 in 1965. The market value of the stock oscillated rather broadly each year, but increased from 7⅞ per share in 1962 to 55⅝ per share in 1965.

Vacationers and businessmen are dependent upon United Air Lines, which serves cities from Boston and New York over northern transcontinental routes to the West Coast and Hawaii. In 1966, the company had about 15 million common shares outstanding, which were held by about 28,000 stockholders. Revenues of the company increased more than 100 percent from 1960 to 1965, but a part of this increase was a result of the merger with Capital Airlines in 1961. The operating margin increased from 15.1 percent in 1961 to 18.7 percent in 1965, which was favorable, but the load factor declined from 65.2 percent in 1960 to 53.6 percent in 1962 before rising slightly. Although earnings per share declined substantially from 1960 to 1961, a very good earnings trend was established from 1961 to 1965, with earnings per share increasing by about 60 percent per year in each of the four years. The relative range of market prices was roughly 50 percent of the lower price in each of the four years, and because of the fluctuating earnings pattern, the stock's price–earnings ratio over the period was also highly volatile.

Trans World Airlines in 1966 was the second largest domestic carrier in the United States, and in addition to its operation in the eastern region of the country, the company also had flights to Europe, the Near East, and the Far East. Revenues of the company increased by approximately 78 percent from 1960 to 1965, but earnings per share were very volatile. The company reported deficits of $2.21 and 85 cents per share in 1961 and 1962, respectively. Conversely, earnings per share increased to $2.93 in 1963 and to $5.74 in 1965. The market price of the stock was also very volatile with a low of 7½ in 1962 to a high of 71⅝ in 1965. The average price–earnings ratio during the 1963 to 1965 period was from 6.5 to 9.4 times.

American Airlines basically has an east–west route system with terminal points in Toronto and Mexico City. In early 1965 about nine million of its common shares were held by 43,000 shareholders. During the 1960 to 1965 period, revenues increased by roughly 43 percent, while the operating margin increased from 14.1 to 22 percent. This increase led to a tremendous improvement in earnings per share, from 85 cents in 1961 to $4.41 in 1965, and during this six-year period the market value of the stock moved from a low of 15⅜ in 1962 to a high of 69¾ in 1965.

Eastern Air Lines, the fourth largest domestic air transport system in the United States, has routes mainly from north to south, east of the Mississippi River. Although revenues of the company increased by approximately 35 percent from 1960 through 1964, a very low operating margin of 10.6 percent or less during the period, coupled with a load factor of about 50 to 55 percent, resulted in deficits per share over the 1960 to 1965 period of almost $19. Despite these losses, the market price of the common stock did not decline below 15⅞ in 1962, and by 1964 it had risen to 46. Failure of the company to keep up with its competitors in equipping and reequipping as well as inefficient cost controls produced tremendous losses. By 1965, however, substantial improvements had been made in the operating ability of the company and jet aircraft were put into service; revenues increased by 22 percent from 1964 to 1965. The operating profit margin rose to 17.6 percent of revenues, the load factor increased, tax-free earnings of $7.04 per share were reported, and the price of the stock more than doubled. The 1966 tax-loss carry forward was expected to be offset against net profits for a year or two.

In 1966, Delta Air Lines had a north–south system that linked Chicago, Detroit, and New York with southern cities, a transcontinental service from Florida and Georgia to the West Coast, and some Caribbean flights. Revenues for the company increased each year from 1960 through 1965, amounting to 120 percent over the six-year period. The operating profit margin also improved each year from 1960 to 1963, but stabilized at about 25 percent in 1964 and 1965. The load factor for Delta averaged almost 60 percent during the six-year period, and earnings increased each of the six years over the preceding year. Although the revenue record and earnings per share for the company were very stable, the average price–earnings ratio at which the stock traded was relatively low, ranging from 6.8 × in 1963 to 11.4 × in 1964. The book value per share of Delta Air Lines was about one seventh its market price in early 1966.

Delta, Western, Northwest Orient and a few of the other smaller airlines had a higher operating profit margin in 1965 than was generally permitted by the Civil Aeronautics Board. However, since many of the other airlines were earning a submarginal return on the investment of the shareholders, it was not believed that the CAB would take any prompt action in requiring the companies to reduce their rates. Should these companies reduce their charges for passenger service, their less fortunate competitors serving the same territories would be adversely affected.

Although not covered here, a study of the operating statistics of Braniff International Airways, Continental Airlines, KLM Royal Dutch Airlines, Northwest Orient Airlines, and Western Air Lines should prove of interest to the reader. Many of these smaller companies have grown more, relative to their revenue base, earnings per share, and appreciation in market value of common shares than have their larger competitors. In 1965, Continental was said to be a leader in efficiency.

Although one cannot know what the future sentiment of investors will be with regard to the attractiveness of airline stocks, projections suggest a bright future for the industry if the economy remains strong. This outlook could, however, be dimmed by heavy reequipping costs, rising labor costs, and/or rate reductions. Market prices of airline stocks oscillate widely from year to year. When purchased and held for the long run, however, the future outlook for airline stocks appeared to be favorable in early 1966.

Stock Movements within Industries

Figure 15-3 presents industry group charts for aerospace companies, including aircraft manufacturers, air transport companies, railroad equipment companies, and railroads. In comparing the market performance of the industry totals, aerospace companies declined from an index reading of 60 in early 1962 to approximately 44 by mid-1962. The market values of aerospace stocks continued to be very low until the second quarter of 1964, when price increases raised shares of the industry group back to the high reached in 1962. The common shares of air transport companies, conversely, were depressed in market value from the early 1950s to 1962. During 1963 and the first quarter of 1964, the market values of air transport stocks increased on average more than 200 percent. For the last three quarters of 1964, the market values of these stocks oscillated downward to some degree before beginning a rapid upward movement.

Railroad equipment shares declined by roughly 25 percent during the second quarter of 1962, but recovered their previous position by mid-1963.

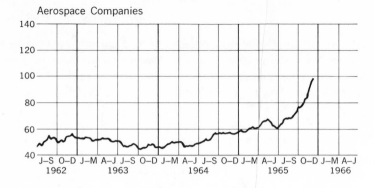

Aerospace Companies

Air Transport Companies

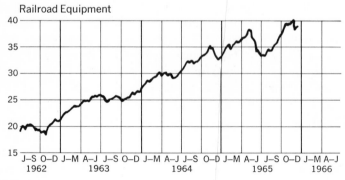

Railroad Equipment

Railroads

FIGURE 15-3 / Charts on selected industries. From *Trendline's Current Market Perspectives,* New York, Trendline Corporation, December 1965.

From mid-1963 through the end of 1965, these shares increased in market value by approximately one third. The market value of railroad shares, conversely, fell during the first part of 1962, rose in 1963 and 1964, declined in early 1965, and then rallied in late 1965.

Summary

The transportation industry is composed primarily of railroads, motor carriers of property and passengers, water carriers, oil pipelines, and domestic airlines. Statistics reported in this chapter indicate that the railroads have had difficulty in competing with other types of common carriers. Airlines increased their revenues by about 650 percent between 1947 and 1964, while motor carriers of property increased their revenues by about 300 percent. Motor carriers of passengers, water lines, railway express companies, electric railways, and the Pullman Company, conversely, fared poorer than the increase in national income.

Before an investor commits his funds into the common shares of a railroad issue, he should consider the outlook within the industry, determine whether or not he believes the railroads will be able to effectively control their expenses (including labor costs and retirement benefits), and attempt to determine what investors' sentiment will be toward these issues. In the railroad industry revenues, profits, and common stock prices fluctuate widely. Railroad bonds, while once thought to be of the gilt edge variety, had by the 1960s lost in favor to public utility and industrial bonds.

Future prospects for growth in railroad profits appear dim compared with the air transport industry. The investor, however, should not overlook the large amounts of convertible debentures that are outstanding for many of the latter issues. He should compute the effect that conversion of these convertibles may have upon earnings per share of the common stock. Conversion may also dilute the market price of the common stock. Many of these companies will outperform their competitors for a time, but then decline in profitability. This occurred with Eastern Air Lines and will no doubt occur with other companies from time to time. Although railroad common shares were generally trading at only 30 to 50 percent of their per share book values in 1966, many airline stocks were trading at three to seven times their per share book values. Future rate reductions, rising labor costs, and reequipping expenses may lead to decreases in earnings per share and market prices of airline issues.

QUESTIONS FOR REVIEW /

1. Explain the primary functions of the ICC.
2. What types of companies come under the jurisdiction of the ICC?
3. Contrast the growth in operating revenue among the various segments of the transportation industry.

4. What reasons can you suggest for the inability of the railroads to increase their revenues and earnings over the 1947–1963 period?
5. What steps should be taken by the railroads to improve operating results?
6. Contrast the market performance of air transport and railroad stocks.
7. Why have the market prices of aircraft and railroad equipment stocks fluctuated less than those of public carriers?
8. How would you account for the variation in market prices of the six railroads covered in this chapter?
9. Explain briefly what is meant by operating margin and by load factor when applied to domestic airline statistics.
10. Why have the price–earnings ratios of some airline stocks fluctuated more widely than others?
11. Why did Eastern Air Lines produce such tremendous deficits for a number of years? Do you believe that the company will regain its prior competitive position? Explain.

PROBLEMS /

1. For five of the smaller domestic airlines, compile important statistics for the past five years and try to determine which of the stocks of these companies are overpriced and underpriced from a strictly fundamental standpoint.
2. Determine from a recent *Annual Report* of the ICC a group of railroads that are considering merger or consolidation. Evaluate the operating statistics on each of the companies involved in the proposal and determine an equitable exchange ratio among the common shareholders of the involved companies should the merger or consolidation be consummated. Evaluate the earnings efficiencies that will result from the combined operation of the companies.
3. Make a statistical analysis of three (a) motor transports of passengers and (b) motor transports of property similar to the studies on railroads and airlines that appear in this chapter. Which companies are likely to show the best performance? After considering the market price at which each company's stock is trading, which issues, if any, would you recommend for immediate purchase?

REFERENCES /

Glover, John G., and Rudolph L. Lagai, *The Development of American Industries.* New York: Simmons-Boardman Publishing Corporation, 1957.

Graham, Benjamin, David L. Dodd, and Sidney Cottle, *Security Analysis,* 4th ed. New York: McGraw-Hill Book Company, Inc., 1962.

Merrill Lynch, Pierce, Fenner & Smith, Inc., *Security and Industry Survey.* New York: Merrill Lynch, Spring 1965.

Moody's Handbook of Common Stocks. New York: Moody's Investors Service Inc., selected issues.

Moody's Transportation Manual. New York: Moody's Investors Service, Inc., selected issues.

U.S. Department of Commerce, Bureau of the Census, *Population Estimates,* Series

P-25, No. 301. Washington, D.C.: U.S. Government Printing Office, February 26, 1965.

————, *Statistical Abstract of the United States*. Washington, D.C.: U.S. Government Printing Office, 1965.

U.S. Interstate Commerce Commission, *79th Annual Report*. Washington, D.C.: U.S. Government Printing Office, 1965.

The Value Line Investment Survey. New York, Arnold Bernhard & Company, Inc., selected issues.

chapter 16 | Market Prices and Intrinsic Values

Introduction

The market price of an actively traded stock can be obtained by simply phoning one's broker. In contrast, the *intrinsic value* of the stock, that is, its basic, or underlying, value, however, must be computed, usually by a rather involved process. Since the market prices of common equities do oscillate, an investor in a given stock must attempt to determine whether the stock is underpriced or overpriced relative to its future values. He may then be in a position to buy low and sell high.

In determining the intrinsic value of an individual issue, the investor cannot divorce his stock from the prospects for its industry nor from the over-all level of stock prices. Hence, he may begin his evaluation by viewing the general level of stock prices relative to corporate earnings. When the whole market appears to be depressed, he may be willing to invest a significant portion of his funds in common stocks; conversely, if the general market appears overvalued, he may reduce his commitment of funds in common stocks. He should then analyze individual issues for expected changes in earnings, dividends, and market value per share.

The Use of Historical Standards as a Guide

If one had used historical standards of price–earnings ratios as a guide, he would have concluded that stocks were grossly overvalued in 1965. For example, the price–earnings ratios of the Dow Jones Industrial Average (DJIA) group increased from about 7 times in 1949 to almost 19 times at the end of 1964. The data in Table 16-1 indicate that there was a gradual increase in the ratio from 1953 through 1956, that the ratio fell considerably during 1957, reached a high plateau at about 19 times in the last half of 1958, and remained at that level throughout 1960 before rising to an all-time high of more than 24 times in 1961. During 1962, the price–earnings ratio of the DJIA group declined to 16.2 times, but from 1963 to 1965 was around 18 or 19 times.

Numerous financial analysts use a price–earnings ratio of 12 times as a standard measure. The probable reason for the selection of this figure is that the average price–earnings ratio at which stocks have traded in the United

TABLE 16-1 /   Dow Jones Industrial Average

		Price (a)	Earnings (by quarter) (b)	Earnings of preceding 12 months (c)	Price–Earnings Ratio (col. a ÷ col. c)	Dividends
1964	Dec. 31	$874.13	$13.38[1]	$46.51[1]	$18.8[1]	$10.46
	Sept. 30	875.37	10.86	45.88	19.1	5.79
	June 30	831.50	12.06	44.46	18.7	7.16
	Mar. 31	813.29	10.21	42.60	19.1	7.83
			46.51[1]			31.24
1963	Dec. 31	762.95	12.75	41.21	18.5	7.39
	Sept. 30	732.79	9.44	40.18	18.2	5.35
	June 28	706.68	10.20	38.71	18.3	5.52
	Mar. 29	682.52	8.82	37.35	18.3	5.15
			41.21			23.41
1962	Dec. 31	652.10	11.72	36.43	17.9	7.65
	Sept. 28	578.98	7.97	35.52	16.3	5.25
	June 29	561.28	8.84	34.74	16.2	5.23
	Mar. 30	706.95	7.90	34.11	20.7	5.15
			36.43			23.30
1961	Dec. 29	731.13	10.81	31.91	22.9	7.57
	Sept. 29	701.21	7.19	29.03	24.2	5.09
	June 30	683.96	8.21	29.29	23.4	5.05
	Mar. 30	676.63	5.70	29.53	22.9	5.00
			31.91			22.71
1960	Dec. 31	615.89	7.93	32.21	19.1	6.55
	Sept. 30	580.14	7.45	31.64	18.3	4.85
	June 30	640.62	8.45	31.26	20.5	4.83
	Mar. 31	610.59	8.38	33.82	18.2	5.12
			32.21			21.35
1959	Dec. 31	679.36	7.36	34.31	19.8	6.73
	Sept. 30	631.68	7.07	35.70	17.7	4.53
	June 30	643.60	11.01	35.71	18.0	4.59
	Mar. 31	601.71	8.87	31.04	19.4	4.89
			34.31			20.74
1958	Dec. 31	583.65	8.75	27.94	20.9	5.83
	Sept. 30	532.09	7.08	27.97	19.0	4.59
	June 30	478.18	6.34	29.41	16.3	4.62
	Mar. 31	446.76	5.78	32.56	13.7	4.96
			27.95			20.00

[1] Estimated.

SOURCE: *Barron's* (New York: Dow Jones & Company, Inc.), selected issues.

TABLE 16-1 *(Continued)*

		Price (a)	Earnings (by quarter) (b)	Earnings of preceding 12 months (c)	Price– Earnings Ratio col. a ÷ col. c	Dividends
1957	Dec. 31	435.69	8.78	36.08	12.1	6.91
	Sept. 30	456.30	8.51	36.70	12.4	4.91
	June 28	503.29	9.49	34.82	14.2	4.79
	Mar. 29	474.81	9.30	34.30	13.8	5.00
			36.08			21.61
1956	Dec. 31	499.47	9.40	33.34	15.0	8.17
	Sept. 28	475.25	6.63	33.65	14.1	4.83
	June 29	492.78	8.97	35.51	13.9	4.98
	Mar. 29	511.79	8.34	36.02	14.2	5.01
			33.34			22.99
1955	Dec. 30	488.40	9.71	35.78	13.7	8.13
	Sept. 30	466.62	8.49	34.41	13.6	4.25
	June 30	451.38	9.48	32.11	14.1	4.24
	Mar. 31	409.70	8.10	29.65	13.8	4.96
			35.78			21.58
1954	Dec. 31	404.39	8.34	28.18	14.4	5.76
	Sept. 30	360.46	6.19	26.99	13.4	3.75
	June 30	333.53	7.02	27.52	12.1	3.92
	Mar. 31	303.51	6.63	27.20	11.2	4.04
			28.18			17.47
1953	Dec. 31	289.90	7.15	27.23	10.3	4.86
	Sept. 30	264.04	6.72	27.63	9.6	3.53
	June 30	268.26	6.70	26.93	10.0	3.95
	Mar. 31	279.87	6.66	25.78	10.9	3.77
			27.23			16.11

States during this century has approximated 12 times, being slightly higher for the DJIA group and slightly lower for Standard & Poor's 500 stocks. The ratios, however, were very low during and immediately following World War II and rose to extremely high levels during the latter 1950s and early 1960s. One may make one of three assumptions concerning future price–earnings relationships. He may (1) be very pessimistic and assume that these ratios will decline to or below their average levels of 12 or 13 times; (2) assume that the market price of stocks, relative to earnings, will approximately stabilize and reach a plateau, so that the average price–earnings ratios at which large, blue-chip stocks trade will approximate 18 or 20 times; or (3) conclude that the upward trend in price–earnings ratios will continue from 1965 through 1980 at approximately the same growth rate that prevailed during the previous 15 years. The latter supposition suggests that an investor should be willing to pay between 36 and 40 times earnings per share for the issues by 1980, a figure that appears to be excessive.

The demand and supply situation is likewise important to the investment decision. The demand on the part of financial institutions for securities was strong during the 1950s and early 1960s. Pension funds were investing a substantial part of their cash equities, open-end investment companies were increasing sales of mutual fund shares to individuals, and insurance companies were increasing their holdings of common stocks. Individuals, on balance, were liquidating stocks in the early 1960s, but the increasing level of family income, supply of money, and savings of individuals could stimulate the flow of personal funds into additional equities. The liquidity of business corporations in 1963 and early 1964 made it possible for these firms to become heavier investors in equities, and many corporations, such as New Jersey Zinc Company, accumulated a substantial investment in common equities. Demand for funds for expansion of plant and facilities in 1965 and 1966, however, caused corporations to be borrowers rather than investors. Deficit spending by the federal government, the cut in corporate and individual federal tax rates, and reductions in excise taxes during 1963–1964 resulted in a more liquid economy, with more funds available for investing. On the supply side, over this same time period, cash flows generated by corporations, that is, retained earnings plus noncash expenditures such as depreciation and depletion, resulted in smaller relative needs for outside financing during the early 1960s than in former years. From 1960 to 1965, from 75 to 80 percent of external financing undertaken by business corporations was in the form of bonds and notes rather than through equities,[1] and the supply of stocks was increasing more slowly than the demand for them, thus pushing stock prices to historical levels.

By early 1966, the complexion of the economy was changing. Corporations were rapidly expanding plant and equipment, savings as a percentage of disposable personal income had declined from earlier levels, the economy was operating close to full capacity, labor unions were pushing for higher income levels for workers, and inflation appeared to be a predominant force. Strong monetary policy, high interest rates, excessive demand for funds relative to supply, the uncertainties of the Vietnam situation, tax increases, and the possibility of a squeeze on corporate profits combined to produce weaknesses in stock prices. Interest rates on government issues reached historic levels by August 1966, and the level of stock prices had declined by 23 percent over the period February–August 1966. Future levels of stock prices will, of course, be largely influenced by the return obtainable on alternate types of investment media, the growth rate in corporate earnings, probabilities for changing price levels, and other factors.

Although it is well to be aware of the historical standards at which stocks usually trade relative to earnings, one should not overlook the fact

[1] See Chapter 10.

that the country does have a dynamic economy and that most U.S. Presidents promote an expanding gross national product (GNP). In the middle 1960s, the confidence of individuals appeared to be at a high level, and if the sentiment of investors remains strong, market values of stocks may continue to trade at high multiples of earnings. One must constantly remember, however, that stock market prices have fallen from 10 to 30 percent within three to six months on numerous occasions in the past, and these future short-range corrections will probably continue to occur about every three or four years. Attempting to forecast a general market downturn is difficult, but over the long run, an investment in common shares of well-chosen corporations should prove to be worthwhile.

How high should the DJIA have been in early 1965? This was a highly debated question, but two financial analysts determined a range of values by use of a discount method. If one had assumed a future growth rate for the DJIA of 5 percent per year for the next 75 years, and that investors require annual dividends and capital gains totaling 7.5 percent, then a multiple of current dividends of 36.7 and a DJIA of 1047 was indicated. If one had assumed an expected future growth rate of only 4 percent projected through the year 2040, and had required an annual yield of 7.5 percent, he should have paid 28.17 times annual dividends, or 803 on the DJIA. In effect, these two ranges were almost equidistant on either side of the 1965 DJIA. Of course, these statistics do not assure the present level of stock prices relative to earnings, because the assumptions on which the projections are based may prove to be incorrect. In addition, changing attitudes on the part of investors toward stock market commitments may shift and produce different multiples of earnings at which stocks trade.[2]

Determining an Intrinsic Value

Security Analysis

Graham, Dodd, and Cottle recognize that issues within various industries trade at different multiples of earnings and that these levels are influenced by a number of factors, such as a company's growth rate, its stability of sales and earnings, investor sentiment with regard to the industry, and other factors.[3] They also believe that the dividend payout has a substantial effect on the value at which a stock trades. The *present-value concept,* which

[2] See, for example, J. Fred Weston and David K. Eiteman, "Economic Trends in Security Values—A Bleak or Bountiful Future for Investors?" *Financial Analysts Journal,* March–April 1965, pp. 21–32.

[3] Benjamin Graham, David L. Dodd, and Sidney Cottle, *Security Analysis,* 4th ed. (New York: McGraw-Hill Book Company, Inc., 1962).

is illustrated in the following section, places a greater importance upon current cash inflows than distant cash inflows, because a dollar is worth more today than the expectation of receiving a dollar next year or five years in the future. These authors indicate that many companies that are retaining a large percentage of their earnings, reportedly for expansion purposes and in order to pay dividends during future years when earnings may be low, usually reduce their dividend rates or curtail them altogether when operating at losses.

Graham, Dodd, and Cottle believe that the intrinsic value of a stock equals $M(D + \frac{1}{3}E)$, where M is the multiple—or multiplier—at which similar issues trade, D is dividends per share, and E is earnings per share of the stock. In using this relationship, if the expected dividend payout is 66⅔ percent (that is, a company that earns $3 per share pays a cash dividend of $2 per share) and if similar stocks are trading at a multiple of 15, then the intrinsic value of the stock should be approximately 15 $[\$2 + (\frac{1}{3} \times \$3)] = \$45$ per share. The authors also suggest that for stocks trading at less than one half or more than twice their book value per share some upward or downward readjustment should be made to compensate for this wide divergency from the asset value underlying each share of stock. The authors note that the book value per share has frequently been weighted with 25 percent, while the earnings and dividend factors have been weighted with the other 75 percent.[4] Using the above illustration, one finds that if the book value per share were only $20, then the intrinsic value of each share of stock should be reduced by one fourth of the difference between the intrinsic value determined by using only the multiplier times $(D + \frac{1}{3}E)$ and the book value per share, or $[\$45 - (\$25 \times \frac{1}{4})] = \$38.75$. If the book value per share were equal to $100, then the intrinsic value should be increased by one fourth of $100 − $45, or almost $14 per share.

A number of methods have been recommended for defining the range of multiples that may be appropriate for use in attempting to determine the intrinsic value of common stock. Graham, Dodd, and Cottle suggest $E(8.5 + 2G)$, where E equals the average estimated earnings per share for the next seven years and G refers to the annual forecasted growth rate.[5] They apparently assume that an investor is willing to buy shares of stock in a company with a zero growth rate if the earnings yield is 11½ to 12 percent. Since the company is not growing and has little interest in expanding, a generous payout of 60 to 75 percent of earnings should produce a dividend yield of 7 to 9 percent. A range of multiples at which stocks should trade with varying growth in earnings rates is given in the following schedule:

[4] For a complete analysis of this approach see Graham, Dodd, and Cottle, pp. 518 and 557.

[5] Graham, Dodd, and Cottle, p. 538.

EXPECTED GROWTH RATE FOR NEXT SEVEN YEARS	ESTIMATED SEVEN-YEAR AVERAGE $E/S \times (8.5 + 2G)$
3%	14½ times
4	16½ times
5	18½ times
6	20½ times
8	24½ times
10	28½ times
12	32½ times
20	48½ times

Although these relationships may be reasonable for the lower expected growth rates, to extend these rates into the future at such a high return as 15 to 20 percent and to be willing to pay 38 to 48 times the current earnings per share of an issue may result in a substantial loss in the market value of the stock should the growth rate suddenly decline. For example, suppose that an issue that is currently earning $2 per share has had an average growth rate of 20 percent per year during the last five or seven years, compounded annually, and that this rate is projected into the future. Should the growth rate decline from 20 to 10 percent per year at the time earnings per share are only $2.40, the market value of the stock would decline by almost one third. For this reason a growth issue should probably not demand a multiple of much greater than 1½ to 2 times the ratio for an average stock (one with earnings growth of 4 to 6 percent).

Methods for Computing Historical Growth Rates

Numerous methods may be used by the financial analyst in computing the historical growth rate of a company. The growth rate may be based on the changes in earnings per share, cash flow per share, or some other factor. The investor may use a simple average method, the sum-of-the-years digits method, the annual compounded rate, or the three- or five-year moving average compounded rate. Other methods could no doubt be devised by the statistician or enterprising investor, but these indicate how the problem may be approached.

The earnings per share for Charles Pfizer Company are indicated in column 1 of Table 16-2. The increase in earnings per share from one year to the next was recorded in column 2 and then totaled. The average of this 10-year total produces the simple average growth rate of 8.9 percent per annum.

Some financial analysts argue that more recent growth is of greater relative importance than more distant growth rates. Hence, the individual may wish to place greater significance upon more recent growth trends. One easy way of doing this is to use a method similar to the sum-of-the-years digits depreciation method. Weighting the 10th year with 1, the 9th year

TABLE 16-2 / Selected Methods for Computing Historical Growth Rates of Earnings per Share: Charles Pfizer Company, 1954–1964

	(1)	(2)	(3)	(4)	(5) Annual Compounded Rate		(6)	(7)
Year	E/S¹	Increase over Past Year	Digits	Column 2 × Column 3	Year	E/S as Percent of Prior Year	Log of Percent	G Applied (trend of E/S)
1954	$ .98							$ .98
1955	.98	.000	1	0	1955	$100	2.0000	1.0653
1956	1.12	.142	2	.284	1956	114.2	2.0577	1.1580
1957	1.41	.259	3	.777	1957	125.9	2.1000	1.2587
1958	1.48	.050	4	.200	1958	105.0	2.0212	1.3682
1959	1.51	.020	5	.100	1959	102.0	2.0086	1.4882
1960	1.58	.046	6	.276	1960	104.6	2.0194	1.6166
1961	1.74	.101	7	.707	1961	110.1	2.0418	1.7572
1962	1.93	.109	8	.872	1962	110.9	2.0449	1.9101
1963	2.07	.073	9	.657	1963	107.3	2.0306	2.0763
1964	2.26	.092	10	.920	1964	109.2	2.0382	2.2569
Totals		.892	55	4.793			20.3624	
Average		.089		.087		Average (log G)		2.0362
		Simple Average		Sum of Digits		Antilog		1.087
						Growth rate		+.087

¹ From *Moody's Handbook of Common Stocks* (New York: Moody's Investors Service, Inc.), selected issues.

with 2, the 8th year with 3, and so forth up, to the most recent year, which is weighted with 10, produces total weights of 55. The increases in earnings per share (column 2 of Table 16-2) may then be multiplied by the weights assigned to determine the total. The total should then be divided by 55 to obtain the annual growth rate derived by the sum-of-the-years digits method. Over the 1955–1964 period, an annual increase of 8.7 percent was computed for Pfizer.

The annual compounded method requires the use of logarithms, and the earnings of one year are recorded as a percentage of the previous year's earnings (see column 5 of Table 16-2). The logarithms for the percentages are then determined from a table of logarithms and totaled, and the total is then divided by the number of items, in our case 10, to determine the average log. The antilog is then determined from a table of logarithms and is equal to 1 plus our growth rate. The antilog, in our case 1.087, was then applied to the 1954 earnings per share to determine what should have been the 1955 earnings per share if this growth rate (our annual growth rate was $1.087 - 1.0$, or 8.7 percent) had prevailed at a constant annual rate. The factor 1.087 was then multiplied by each of the items that appear in column 7 and noted for the following year. This procedure was followed for the 10 years, and the expected earnings per share during 1964 was exactly equal to the actual earnings per share. Of course, some of the actual earnings during the intermediate years were somewhat different from the expected earnings per share because of an irregular growth rate.

Should an individual wish to eliminate the effects of the business cycle upon the earnings per share he may prefer to compute a centered three- or five-year moving-average earnings per share. He may then apply this annual compounded rate method to the moving-average earnings per share, but his results will not be significantly different from those obtained with the log method.

Methods for Estimating Future Growth Rates

An investor may obtain some estimate of future sales, net profits, and earnings per share for a given company by referring to (1) estimates made public by the corporation, for example, in annual reports or financial journals; (2) forecasts made by investment services, for example, *Value Line*, Standard & Poor's, Moody's, and the like; or (3) projections made from past sales and profit data. The latter may be only rough approximations but they offer a bench mark against which actual quarterly performance can be gauged. Such forecasts for 1966 and 1967 net income and earnings per share of Continental Air Lines are shown in Figure 16-1 and Table 16-3.

Figure 16-1 is constructed much like a break-even chart, with dollar values appearing on both the *x* and *y* axis. The revenue is plotted on the diagonal line (drawn at a 45-degree angle) for the past two or three years and projected into the future for one or two years. Total expenses are then plotted immediately below the sales, joined by a straight line, and projected for a year or two. This method assumes that fixed costs will remain relatively constant over the next year or two and that variable costs will continue at the same percentage of revenues. Three or four factors could occur that would make these profit projections inaccurate, even with reasonably accurate estimates of revenues. These include changing load factors, improving operating efficiency, higher labor costs, and acquisition of more planes (higher fixed costs). Assuming that these factors will largely be offsetting, the projection for 1966 estimated earnings is $5.30 per share and for 1967, $7.50. It should be noted that these projections assume a 20 percent increase in annual revenues, which was the average for the 1963 to 1965 period.

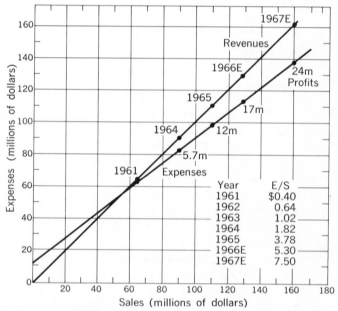

FIGURE 16-1 / Linear sales and profit projections for Continental Air Lines, 1966–1967. From Table 16-3.

Another estimate of 1966 and 1967 earnings per share for Continental Air Lines is shown in Table 16-3. Revenues projected for 1966 and 1967 are shown in column 2; before-tax profit margins are then extrapolated, the tax rate is applied, and earnings per share are determined. For Continental Air Lines, it was assumed that after-tax profits in 1966 would be 54 percent of before-tax profits—the same as for 1965—and that the rate could be reduced to as low as 50 percent in 1967 because of possible increases in corporate tax rates or discontinuance of investment credit. These projections produce slightly lower earnings estimates than those derived by the graphic method illustrated in Figure 16-1.

TABLE 16-3 /   Estimated Earnings per Share for Continental Air Lines, 1966–1967

Year	Gross Revenue (millions)	Increase	Before-Tax Operating Profit Margin	Net Increase (millions)	
1961	$ 63.0		7.8	$ 1.12	$ .40
1962	66.2	5%	7.5	1.78	.64
1963	78.3	20	9.5	3.01	1.02
1964	88.0	13	14.8	5.69	1.82
1965	116.7	33	19.4	12.10	3.78
1966E	140	20	22.0 × .54	16.60	5.20
1967E	170	20	24.0 × .50	20.40	6.40

SOURCE: *Moody's Handbook of Common Stocks*, 2d ed. (New York: Moody's Investors Service, Inc., 1966), p. 246.

Cash Flow Projections

The *Value Line Investment Survey* uses the five-year average, centered cash flow growth rate for the last 12 years. The service projects the expected cash flows into the future for two additional years. *Value Line's* computation of growth rate is in keeping with its philosophy that the average value of a stock is more closely allied to its cash flows per share than to the earnings per share. This may be true because of the variations in depreciation methods used by different companies, which distort the reported earnings per share. The average growth rate computed by *Value Line* for Charles Pfizer Company over approximately the same time period but using the earnings plus reserve for depreciation on a centered five-year–average basis indicated a slightly higher growth rate—10.5 percent—than that—8.7 percent—obtained by using the annual compounded rate illustrated in Table 16-2. Much of this difference can be attributed to the accelerated depreciation allowances permitted by taxing authorities, which have been applied by many companies during recent years.

Selecting a Method

Although the investor may use whatever method he wishes in determining the growth rate of the company he is studying, the compounded-rate method produces more valid and justifiable results than a simple method, since the former can be used with present-value techniques. The results obtained with the two methods may differ significantly. Although exactly the same figure was obtained for Pfizer by using the sum-of-the-years digits method and the annual compounded-rate method, this was a coincidence rather than an expected occurrence. When one wishes to find the historic growth rate in order to predict future growth rates by extrapolation, he should apply the same method to companies within the same industry; otherwise his comparisons will not be relevant.

The Importance of Dividends

After one has forecasted the expected earnings per share for a few years in the future, he should make some estimate as to the probable amount of dividends that will be declared by the company. This may be determined by analyzing the company's dividend payout ratio, which merely shows the relationship between earnings per share and cash dividends per share. The investor is then in a position to apply the present-value concept to the evaluation of common stocks.

Discounted Cash Flow Method

Some security analysts suggest that the value of a share of common stock is equal to future expected cash inflows, discounted by the appropriate rate of return. Since investors buy common stocks for both dividend income and capital appreciation, the sum of these two items should be considered. In 1965, it was possible to obtain a yield to maturity of 4 to 4½ percent on long-term government bonds. Therefore, an investment in common stocks—which, of course, carry more business risk than government securities—should have produced an annual return of 7 to 8 percent. If an investor is satisfied with a 7 percent return on his common stock investment, he should be willing to buy an issue paying a 3 percent dividend yield if the stock is expected to appreciate 4 percent per annum. In determining the present value of the earnings and the price at which one should dispose of the stock, the following formula may be used:

$$P_0 = \frac{D_1}{(1+r)} + \frac{D_2}{(1+r)^2} + \cdots + \frac{D_n}{(1+r)^n} + \frac{P_n}{(1+r)^n}$$

where P_0 is the value of the stock in period zero, or at the present time; D_1 is the expected cash dividend per share in year 1; D_2 is the dividend in year 2, and so fourth; r is the annual rate of return desired by the investors; and P_n is the expected selling price of the stock in the nth year.

The last term of this formula requires an estimate of the market price of the stock in the nth year. However, one dollar discounted by either 6 or 8 percent for 50 or 100 years is a minute figure. Therefore, if the stock is to be held for an extremely long time, the last term may be dropped without seriously invalidating the results. Instead of using compound interest tables to determine dividend multiples at which the stock should be trading, one may refer to tables that have been prepared for this particular purpose. Such tables were published in the March–April 1965 issue of *Financial Analysts Journal*. Separate tables were reported in the study of growth rates ranging from 1 to 20 percent, based on expected annual returns of 6, 7, 8, and 9 percent per annum.[6]

The computation of the discounted present value of future cash inflows is given in Table 16-4 for a hypothetical company. In our example, we will assume that the earnings per share in year one is $1, that the company's future annual growth in earnings per share is estimated to be 10 percent, that 50 percent of annual earnings will be distributed as dividends, and that the investor demands a 7 or 8 percent annual return consisting of dividends and capital gains. It is easy to determine the present value of the expected dividends for future years, but we must estimate the future market price of

TABLE 16-4 /   Present Value of a Share of Stock with a 10 Percent Growth Rate and a 50 Percent Payout Ratio Discounted by 7 and 8 Percent Annual Yields

Year	Earnings per share	Dividends per Share (50% Pay-out)	7% Rate P.V. Factor	7% Rate Amount	8% Rate P.V. Factor	8% Rate Amount
1	$1.00	$ .50	.9346	$ .467	.9259	$ .463
2	1.10	.55	.8734	.480	.8573	.471
3	1.21	.61	.8163	.498	.7938	.484
4	1.33	.67	.7629	.511	.7350	.492
5	1.44	.72	.7130	.513	.6806	.490
6	1.58	.79	.6663	.526	.6302	.498
7	1.74	.87	.6227	.542	.5835	.508
8	1.91	.96	.5820	.558	.5403	.519
9	2.10	1.05	.5439	.571	.5002	.525
10	2.31	1.16	.5083	.589	.4632	.537
11	2.54	1.27	.4751	.603	.4289	.545
12	2.79	1.40	.4440	.621	.3971	.556
13	3.07	1.54	.4150	.639	.3677	.566
14	3.38	1.69	.3878	.655	.3405	.575
15	3.72	1.86	.3624	.674	.3152	.586
16	4.09	2.05	.3387	.694	.2919	.598
17	4.50	2.24	.3166	.712	.2703	.608
18	4.95	2.48	.2959	.734	.2502	.621
19	5.45	2.73	.2765	.755	.2317	.633
20	6.00	3.00[1]	.2584	.775	.2145	.646
20		$142.50	.2584	36.825	.2145	30.573
Total (P)				$48.946		$41.493

[1] Assumed market price at end of 20 years $= M(D + \frac{1}{3}E)$, or $[8\frac{1}{2} + 2(10)] \times [3 + \frac{1}{3}(\$6)] = 28\frac{1}{2} \times \$5 = \$142.50$.

[6] See, for example, Nicholas Moldovsky, Katherine May, and Sherman Chottinger, "Common Stock Valuation (Principles, Tables, and Applications)," *Financial Analysts Journal*, March–April 1965, pp. 104–123.

the stock on the date of sale, say at the end of 20 years. By using the Graham, Dodd, and Cottle formulas given earlier to forecast the intrinsic value per share at the end of year 20, and by assuming that such an intrinsic value will equal the average market value at that time, we assume that $M = (8\frac{1}{2} + 2G)$ and $V = M(D + \frac{1}{3}E)$, or $[8\frac{1}{2} + 2(10)] \times [3 + \frac{1}{3}(6)] = 28\frac{1}{2} \times \$5 = \$142.50$ where M equals the multiplier at which stocks should trade, V equals the intrinsic value per shares, G represents the annual compounded growth rate in earnings per share, D represents annual dividends per share, and E equals annual earnings per share. We determine from Table 16-4 that an investor who demands a 7 percent annual return should pay \$48.95 per share for the stock, while one who requires an 8 percent annual rate should pay \$41.49. To assume that a 10 percent annual growth rate will continue uninterrupted for 20 years or longer is often no more than false hope, as the following section so vividly illustrates, and a tendency toward conservatism in the evaluation of a stock—by using a generous discount rate—is often prudent.

The Growth-Stock Concept

Just what constitutes a growth stock may be open to debate, but Standard & Poor's Corporation a few years ago began to publish a list of 200 rapid-growth stocks. The list was selected from about 6000 issues through the use of electronic data-processing equipment. In order for an issue to qualify as a growth stock, the following criteria had to be met:

(1) If growth in share earnings over the past five years has been steady, it must have amounted to at least 7 percent per annum, compounded;

(2) If growth has been interrupted in only one year and the decline has been less than 5 percent, annual growth must have been at least 10 percent;

(3) If growth has been interrupted in more than one year, or if in one year the decline was more than 5 percent, the annual growth rate must have been at least 12 percent.[7]

A review of the list indicates that of the original 200 issues that were selected as meeting these criteria, only 86 remained on the list three years later. Some 114 stocks had been dropped, 80 because of declines in the level of earnings below the previous year, 24 because of a slower growth rate than required by the standard set, and 10 because of mergers, bankruptcy, or other reasons. Of the issues dropped from the December 1962 list, about 28 percent had increased in market value by December 1964. For the replacement issues over the same two-year period, 60 percent had increased in market value, while 40 percent had either dropped in market value or were no longer trading in the market.

Suppose that you as an investor find an issue that has been increasing

---

[7] For a complete analysis of this study, see Stanley S. C. Huang, "Study of the Performance of Rapid Growth Stocks," *Financial Analysts Journal*, January–February 1965, p. 58–59.

its earnings per share by an annual rate of 15 percent for the last 10 years, and you wish to determine how much to pay for the issue. Using the method suggested above, where the multiplier is equal to 8.5 plus two times the growth rate, one has a multiple of 38.5 times the estimate of the average earnings per share for the next seven years (denoted as E).

Some issues, such as Xerox, or Syntex, sold at even higher levels of earnings in the mid-1960s, but this is projecting the expected future growth many years into the future. What happens to the market value if after two years the growth rate declines from 15 percent to 9 percent? Suppose for illustration purposes that we assume the earnings per share in zero year to be $1. They should be $1.15 for the first year, $1.32 for the second year, $1.52 for the third year, $1.75 for the fourth year, and so on. The individual should have been willing to pay 38.5 times $1.75, or about $67 per share for the stock, at a price–earnings ratio of 67 times current earnings. If after two years the growth rate diminishes to 9 percent and the investor uses the same 8.5 plus $2G$ relationship (revised $E = \$1.86$), he should be willing to pay 26.5 times $1.86, or $49 per share for the stock. Although the company would still be classified as a growth company, in that earnings per share are now increasing by 9 percent per year rather than the initial 15 percent, the indicated price of the stock has fallen from $67 to $49, a decline of about 30 percent, or almost 10 years of earnings per share. This inherent danger is assumed when one buys a so-called "growth stock" that is trading at 30, 50, or more times current earnings per share. Benjamin Graham offered empirical data which indicated that the average return made on average stocks over a period of years was better than the return made on growth stocks.[8] Growth issues were not nearly as popular in 1963 and 1964 as in the early 1960s because the market value of many of these issues decreased by 25 or 50 percent or more during the stock market decline in 1962. Some issues did, however, appear to be heading for lofty heights in 1965.

A Suggested Approach to Investing

One who has made a careful study of the price fluctuations of common stocks often concludes that the issues that are rising in market value may often show little improvement in earnings. Conversely, other issues that have been reporting substantial profit gains may be increasing little or declining in market value. Stocks are traded on the basis of future expected earnings rather than on historical profits, and at certain points in the stock cycle, issues representative of selected industries appear to be in popular demand while others are unpopular. An investor should realize that stock prices in relation to earnings swing widely over time. While earnings growth and increasing dividends are important to the investor, he should give some consideration to issues that are gaining in investor interest.

[8] See Benjamin Graham, *The Intelligent Investor* (New York: Harper & Row, Publishers, Inc., 1959), pp. 105–122.

One approach to security selection is the *undervaluation approach*. In applying this technique, the investor attempts to discover a number of industries that have tremendous potential for increasing profits. At the same time, the investor seeks to purchase issues that are trading at reasonable multiples of earnings. As profits improve, the average price–earnings ratios often also rise appreciably, so that one may realize a substantial amount of capital appreciation as well as increasing dividends on his commitment of funds. As the issues reach high price–earnings ratios, and if little additional improvement in earnings can reasonably be expected, the investor may wisely sell all or a portion of his stocks and look for other undervalued issues. Examples of issues that were low in investor esteem during the latter 1950s and early 1960s were airlines, aircraft, office equipment, radio and TV, and broadcasting issues. From 1962 through 1965, the earnings of many of these stocks increased substantially, and the average price–earnings ratios frequently doubled or tripled, resulting in capital appreciation of from 500 to 1000 percent.

Many electronics stocks, which had traded at price–earnings multiples of 30 to 40 in the early 1960s, declined to about 7 to 10 times earnings in 1962, but began to show improved profit margins in 1965 and regained investor interest. At any point in time certain industries appear to be gaining in popularity. In 1965, for example, such industries as ocean shippers; textile, railroad, and agricultural equipment manufacturers; radio and television; and metal specialty companies had bright prospects for future earnings. All industries gain in popularity for a time and then decline. The investor should not invest blindly on tips or rumors, but he should investigate as thoroughly as possible any leads that may develop. Although the investor is not concerned with day-to-day market oscillation, he should be concerned with the direction of movement of the market as a whole and with the trend in profits and price–earnings of the company in which he commits his funds as well as of similar companies.

Summary

Many analysts argue that the average price at which stocks trade relative to earnings should not be more than about 12 times. Others, for example, Benjamin Graham, suggest that an average price–earnings ratio of 12 times is probably too low and that a ratio of 14 or 15 times may be an expected level at which the market value of stocks may continue to trade within the future. In 1965, however, still other investors believed that it was possible for stocks to remain at price–earnings levels of 18 or 20 times for an indefinite time period. They reasoned that the supply of stocks relative to demand in 1965 was fairly low, that financial institutions had been net purchasers of stocks during the previous 15 years, and that the relative supply of common shares in the hands of individuals was smaller than in earlier years.

In attempting to determine the intrinsic value of an individual issue, the investor should give some attention to the historical growth rate in earnings per share and/or cash flow per share for the individual company, the expected growth rate within the future, the duration of this expected growth, and the level at which he believes securities in general will be trading in future years. Since a share of common stock is worth, according to some concepts, no more than the expected flow of dividends plus the future market price of the share discounted by an appropriate investment return factor, the individual should place some importance upon the present and expected future dividend policies of the company.

It is dangerous to assume that the growth rate of a company will prevail for an extended period of time. Therefore, the individual may wish to limit his cost of a stock to 30 or 40 times current earnings per share. Otherwise, the growth rate of the issue and the multiple at which it trades in the market may decline. Handsome profits can often be realized by buying issues that are trading at low price–earnings multiples but that are in potentially profitable situations.

QUESTIONS FOR REVIEW /

1. At what P–E levels have securities traded in the past?
2. Do you believe that future price–earnings ratios of common stocks will remain similar to their 1963–1965 levels, decline, or continue to increase? Support your answer.
3. Indicate how the security analyst may determine the intrinsic value of an individual issue.
4. Explain and illustrate the methods that may be used for calculating the historical rate of growth of a stock. Which method is preferable?
5. Explain briefly the discounted cash flow method for determining the current earnings multiple at which a stock should trade.
6. How much should be paid for a growth issue?
7. Explain the undervaluation approach. Determine two industries and four companies that should show substantial future appreciation. Defend your position.

PROBLEMS /

1. Through a study of the movement of DJIA for the past 12 or 15 years, determine whether or not there is any seasonal pattern to the upward and downward movement of the 30 industrial stocks.
2. For three companies, one that had a substantial increase in earnings per share from year to year, one that showed little change in earnings per share from year to year, and one that experienced a deterioration in earnings per share from year to year for the past 10 years, determine by either of the methods outlined in Table 16–2 the average annual growth rate.
3. Compare the growth rates of the companies that you used in problem 2 with those shown by *The Value Line Investment Survey* based on increases in cash flow per share. How do the results differ?

4. For each of the above companies project past growth trends in earnings per share and determine the P_0 to pay for a share, assuming the average of the last five year's pay-out ratio and that you desire an 8 percent annual return. You plan to hold the stock for 10 years and then sell it.

REFERENCES /

Barron's. New York: Dow Jones & Company, Inc., selected issues.

Graham, Benjamin, *The Intelligent Investor.* New York: Harper & Row, Publishers, Inc., 1959.

Graham, Benjamin, David L. Dodd, and Sidney Cottle, *Security Analysis,* 4th ed. New York: McGraw-Hill Book Company, Inc., 1962.

Molodovsky, Nicholas, Katherine May, and Sherman Chottiner, "Common Stock Valuation (Principles, Tables, and Application)," *Financial Analysts Journal.* Boston, Mass.: The Financial Analyst Federation, March–April 1965.

The Wall Street Journal. New York: Dow Jones & Company, Inc., selected issues.

Weston, J. Fred, and David K. Eiteman, "Economic Trends in Security Values— A Bleak or Bountiful Future for Investors?" *Financial Analysts Journal.* Boston, Mass.: The Financial Analyst Federation, March–April 1965.

chapter 17 | Special Situations

Introduction

Although one should consider the level of the stock market relative to corporate profits, the expected direction of movement of stock prices, and the fundamentals behind individual issues, special situations may arise that produce marked price changes in an issue. These special situations include listing of the security on a major exchange, the issuance of additional shares on a rights basis, a public issuance of stock, the granting or exercising of stock options, the conversion of a large debenture or preferred stock issue into common shares, a proposed secondary issue, or the discovery of a new product or process. This chapter is a discussion of the influences that these situations usually exert on the market value of common stock.

Big Board Listing

Chapter 9 discussed the 1964 revision of the Securities Exchange Act, which now requires a company with more than 500 shareholders to register with the SEC. No doubt many companies that are now required to register with the SEC will also elect to list on either the New York Stock Exchange, if they qualify, or on the American Stock Exchange. Big Board listing may offer some advantages, such as increased marketability of the stock, a broader share distribution, a higher price–earnings ratio, and more prestige. The name of the company is placed before the general public so that the company may derive some goodwill from the appearance of its name on the registered exchange.[1]

Although there is a charge for listing on the New York Stock Exchange, the fee is not a significant factor to most medium- or large-sized corporations that qualify for listing. For example, the initial listing cost in 1965 was only one cent a share for the first one million shares, one-half cent for the next million, and one-fourth cent for shares in excess of two million. Thus, the cost of listing for a corporation with four million shares outstanding was $15,000. An annual listing charge of one tenth of one cent per share was

---

[1] For an analysis of the advantages and disadvantages of listing on the Big Board, see "To List—Or Not To List?" *Financial World*, October 28, 1964, pp. 11–12.

being assessed on the first two million shares, with one twentieth of one cent per share on the remaining shares for the first 15 years of listing. Thereafter the latter charge is discontinued.

An investor may profit from observing the usual price action of the stock of a company that elects to list on the Big Board. The general tendency is for the market price to rise when listing news first becomes known, but to decline after listing takes place. An inspection of the price reactions of the stocks of corporations that listed on the Big Board during 1962 and 1963 reveals some interesting facts.

During 1962, 47 companies listed on the New York Stock Exchange. This was a year in which security prices suffered a tremendous drop from April through June. During this three-month period, stock prices declined by about 25 percent, as measured by Standard & Poor's Average of 500 stocks. By the end of 1962, this index had increased from its 1962 low of 52½ in the latter part of June to approximately 63 (1941–1943 = 10). The over-all decline from January through December, however, was roughly 15 percent. A comparison of the opening and closing 1962 prices of the 47 stocks reveals that 15 increased in market values, while 32 declined. It should be remembered, however, that 1962 was a period when prices were generally falling. None of the 20 issues listed between January 1 and May 31, 1962 had a market price as high at the end of the year as its initial listing price. Conversely, of the issues listed during the last seven months of the year, when market prices were depressed and subsequently rising, 15 of the issues rose in market value, while only 11 declined.

Table 17-1 is a compilation of the 1963 original stock listings on the New York Stock Exchange when 58 companies listed their securities on the Big Board. The 49 companies that listed from January through November 13, 1963, are shown, together with the opening market prices on listing date and the closing market prices on November 13, 1963, the cut-off date for the table. During this 11-month period, Standard & Poor's Average of 500 stocks increased by approximately 15 percent; however, 33 of these initial listings declined in market value, and only 16 increased. Thirty-seven of these 49 issues had been trading in the over the counter market prior to listing on the Big Board. Of these, 24 declined and 13 increased in market value. The performance of the over the counter stocks, when listed on the Big Board, was not significantly different from that of stocks that had been trading on the American or regional stock exchanges prior to Big Board listing.

Figure 17-1 illustrates the relative price changes from three months before to three months after listing date for the 58 companies that listed on the Big Board during 1963. The market value of 9 of the issues appreciated 25 percent or more from 90 days before until listing date; 12 increased between 15 and 24.9 percent; 14 increased from 5 to 14.9 percent; 12 increased by less than 5 percent or declined by less than 5 percent; and 8 declined from 5 to 25 percent. Three of the issues were not being traded 90

TABLE 17-1 / Original New York Stock Exchange Stock Listings: 1963

Company	Date Listed	Opened on Listing Date	Closed 11/13/63	Percent Change	Exchange Dealt on Previously	No. of Shares Listed on Date of Listing
The Papercraft Corp.	1/14	$ 8⅞	$ 7¼	− 18.3	OTC	2,332,724
The Welch Scientific Co.	1/21	19¼	15¼	− 20.8	OTC	1,812,000
American Cement Corp.	1/22	11¼	9⅞	− 12.2	OTC	4,589,577
Warner Brothers Co.	2/4	20¾	33⅛	+ 59.6	OTC	1,137,280
Loral Electronics Corp.	2/18	16¼	11½	− 29.2	American	2,317,365
Coastal States Gas Producing Co.	2/20	29	35	+ 20.7	OTC	6,222,923
Wesco Financial Corp.	2/25	40¼	38⅞	− 3.4	OTC	1,389,150
The Echlin Manufacturing Co.	3/4	14½	11⅞	− 18.1	American	1,807,400
Control Data Corp.	3/6	41¼	101⅜	+145.8	OTC	3,902,454
Uris Buildings Corp.	3/11	18¾	19¾	+ 5.3	OTC	3,471,540
Helmerich & Payne, Inc.	3/20	12½	10	− 20.0	American	1,919,779
Pacific Intermountain Express Co.	3/25	16½	14	− 15.2	OTC	1,755,763
Illinois Central Industries, Inc.	3/28	45¾	53	+ 15.8	—	2,909,634
Purolator Products, Inc.	4/3	21⅝[1]	24⅝	+ 13.9	OTC	659,149
Colonial Corporation of America	4/4	19⅞	22	+ 10.7	American	2,672,912
United Utilities, Inc.	4/10	37	39⅞	+ 7.8	OTC	5,247,146
Berman Leasing Co.	4/11	18½[1]	22⅝	+ 22.3	OTC	1,113,466
High Voltage Engineering Corp.	4/17	25½	43⅜	+ 70.1	OTC	2,362,832
Pacific Petroleums, Ltd.	4/22	13¾	11	− 20.0	American, Boston, & Pacific Coast	18,175,012
Hawaiian Telephone Co.	4/25	24¼	22½	− 7.2	Honolulu & OTC	4,909,037
The Fafnir Bearing Co.	5/1	47¾	42¾[2]	− 10.5	OTC	2,256,457
Petrolane Gas Service, Inc.	5/2	28¾	24	− 16.5	OTC	1,718,715
Emhart Manufacturing Co.	5/14	57½	44¾	− 22.2	OTC	1,036,142
Talon, Inc.	5/15	47¾	43⅜	− 9.2	American	1,171,062
Puerto Rican Cement Co.	5/24	21⅞	19¼	− 12.0	OTC	1,300,000

Norton Co.	6/10	40⅜	42¼	+ 4.6	OTC	5,752,930
Interstate Motor Freight System	6/18	27¼	22¼	− 18.3	OTC	831,000
Staley (A. E.) Manufacturing Co.	5/29	43	36½	− 15.1	OTC	2,273,163
Automatic Retailers of America, Inc.	6/7	38	35⅛	− 7.6	OTC	3,003,664
The Technical Materiel Corp.	6/24	27¼	20¼	− 25.7	American	2,414,962
Overnite Transportation Co.	6/27	22½	21¾	− 3.3	OTC	1,010,353
Electronic Specialty Co.	7/1	30½	35⅛	+ 15.2	American	1,443,505
Pennzoil Co.	7/8	40⅜	49⅝	+ 22.9	American	2,086,888
Atlas Credit Corp.	8/7	13	10¾	− 17.3	OTC	2,092,559
Arlan's Dept. Stores, Inc.	8/5	24	31½	+ 31.3	OTC	1,000,000
Servomation Corp.	7/29	22[1]	19⅜	− 11.9	OTC	3,466,355
Mattel, Inc.	8/12	48½	51¾	+ 6.7	OTC	1,911,396
Del E. Webb Corp.	8/19	12¼	10¼	− 16.3	OTC	6,522,593
William H. Rorer, Inc.	9/3	42	34¾	− 17.3	OTC	3,370,428
Indian Head Mills, Inc.	9/5	17¼	16	− 7.2	OTC	2,070,409
Warner & Swasey Co.	9/9	76½	68⅝	− 10.3	OTC	1,048,254
Dobbs Houses, Inc.	9/16	20	18⅞	− 5.6	OTC	3,081,568
Kirkeby-Natus Corp.	9/17	23	22½	− 2.2	American	2,236,865
Becton, Dickinson and Co.	9/25	43½	44¾	+ 2.9	OTC	2,321,636
Holiday Inns of America, Inc.	9/30	24½	19	− 22.4	OTC	3,497,446
Associated Spring Corp.	10/14	20⅝	19⅝	− 4.8	OTC	1,143,025
McLouth Steel Corp.	10/11	54⅞	49⅝	− 9.6	OTC	3,525,259
Nutone, Inc.	10/16	26⅝	23¾	− 10.8	OTC	1,571,456
Heli-Coil Corp.	10/21	29¾	25¾	− 13.4	American	703,500
National Propane Corp.	11/15[3]				OTC	1,017,868
The Permian Corp.	11/18[3]				American	3,083,579
The Japan, Inc.	11/19[3]				OTC	1,875,000
Weyerhaeuser Co.	11/25[3]				OTC	31,000,000
Santa Fe Drilling Co.	12/2[3]				OTC	1,500,964
The B.V.D. Co.	12/9[3]				American	2,937,299
Dymo Industries, Inc.	12/17[3]				OTC	1,812,827
Russ Togs, Inc.	12/17[3]				American	842,820
Yale Express System, Inc.	12/12[3]				American	1,134,062

[1] Adjusted for stock dividends and splits. [2] Bid price, no sale. [3] Scheduled.

SOURCE: New York Stock Exchange, *The Exchange* (New York: The Exchange, December 1963), p. 18.

days prior to listing. The market value 90 days after listing for 9 of the stocks was 15 percent or more above the initial listing price; 6 of the issues were trading between 5 and 15 percent above the listing price, 16 were trading within 5 percentage points of the listing price, and 27 had fallen in market price by more than 5 percent.

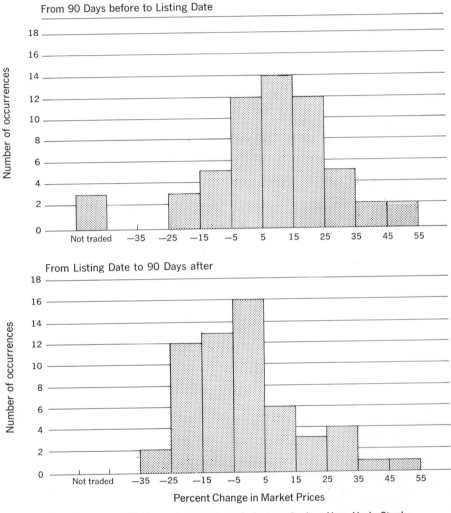

FIGURE 17-1 / Market price changes before and after New York Stock Exchange listing during 1963. Compiled from stock transactions as reported in *The Wall Street Journal*, selected issues.

The above statistics indicate that the market price of securities usually increases prior to listing, but normally declines by substantial margins subsequent to listing. The initial decision of a company to list on the Big Board attracts some speculative interest. Speculators who buy the stock expect the market value to rise between the date on which listing becomes public knowledge and the actual date of listing. They then sell the listed shares and look for other short-term–profit candidates. It is prudent financial policy for an investor to recognize this trend in market value with regard to listing and to wait 30 to 90 days after listing to buy an issue.[2]

Preemptive Rights Issues

Some financial managers and investors argue that the use of rights for the sale of new issues offers some advantages to the stockholders, since this system permits the holders to retain their proportionate share of equity ownership, claims on dividends, and voting interest. However, the method also has disadvantages. Some investment advisers believe that the use of rights for issuing additional shares of stock is a bull market phenomenon and that it is unprofitable for the recipient to exercise these rights. Frequently, in fact more often than not, the market value of the shares subsequently declines to a lower level than the subscription price of the stock even though the shares are offered to the old holders at prices substantially below market value.[3]

During the early 1960s, the use of right offerings by New York Stock Exchange companies declined in importance. From 1959 through 1963, the numbers of Big Board rights issues were 45, 21, 37, 8, and 13, respectively. Few public issues of stocks, including rights issues, are made during bear markets, since the management of a corporation is reluctant to create ill will through the sale of securities to the general public at a price below which subsequent prices will fall. In addition, investment bankers are reluctant to underwrite issues during bear markets. For these reasons, public and rights issues of equity securities are usually made during periods of vigorous stock market activity, when prices of common stocks are rising. In bear markets, conversely, numerous public utility companies have successfully used this method of financing for numerous reasons. First, the market values of such stocks are considerably more stable than those of industrial issues, so that the risk of downside price movement is low; second, financial institutions are large buyers of utility issues; and third, utility companies were increasing their fixed assets at a considerable rate each year in the early 1960s. Complete financing of expansion through the use of internally generated funds or through the sale of long-term debt was not possible for utility companies, and thus some equity financing was undertaken. Other reasons include low flotation costs, the absence of the requirement to register with the SEC, and compliance with state corporate law. During 1962, seven

[2] For names of companies that have recently listed on the Big Board, see *The Exchange, The Magazine of Wall Street*, or *Financial World*.

[3] See, for example, *The Magazine of Wall Street*, October 3, 1958, in which an article presents the rights issues that were made for Big Board industrial companies from 1955 to 1958 and indicates that a majority of these companies declined in market value subsequent to the rights offerings to prices lower than their subscription prices.

of the eight rights offerings on the New York Stock Exchange were made by public utility companies. National Cash Register was the only industrial company that marketed a rights issue, and although the subscription price of the stock in March 1962 was $100 per share, the market price of the stock had declined to $70 by early 1963. All seven of the public utility issues were sold at subscription prices that permitted price rises within the following year. Of course, public utility issues were gaining in popularity during that period.[4]

Public Stock Issues

Although liberal depreciation allowances, increased earnings, and retention of a substantial part of these earnings by American corporations lessened

TABLE 17-2 / Former "High Fliers" in the New Issues Market

| | | Offering | Bid | |
Issue	Date	Price	High[1]	Recent
Allied Maintenance	10–60	15¼	57½	21
American Bowling Enterprises	5–60	7½	12	1¼
American Heritage Publishers	10–61	14½	24½	8
American International Bowling	11–58	3	34½	1
Arlan's Department Stores	9–61	18	38¾	23
Carlon Products	4–59	9	41	4⅞
Charles of the Ritz	5–61	25	40¼	18
Clifton Precision	7–59	16½	56	15
Creative Playthings	10–61	10	17	5¼
Detroiter Mobile Homes	10–60	15	19¾	6
Dynatronics, Inc.	4–61	7½	22	2⅝
First Financial Corporation	11–59	10	24¼	7
Foods Plus	12–61	12	21	5¼
Gem International	6–60	7½	26⅜	8
Girltown 'A'	12–61	13	16½	5
Heath (D.C.)	5–61	38½	43¾	18
Industrial Timer	9–60	11½	20	5½
Kelly Girl Service	12–61	12½	27¾	12
King's Department Stores	8–61	13	33	11
Lowe's Companies	10–61	12¼	18¼	10
Mary Carter Paints	11–60	9¼	18	7
Melpar, Inc	9–60	14	28	9
Microdot, Inc.	4–60	14¼	33	9
Mother's Cookie	3–61	15	25	8
National Cleaning Contractors	10–61	16	28½	14

[1] Since offered.

SOURCE: "A Backward Glance," *Financial World*, January 9, 1963, p. 13.

[4] See "Stock Rights," *Forbes Magazine*, April 15, 1963, p. 33.

TABLE 17-2 *(Continued)*

Issue	Date	Offering Price	Bid High[1]	Bid Recent
New Hampshire Ball Bearing	5–59	18	43½	10
Ore-Ida Foods	8–61	13½	22½	5⅝
Playskool Manufacturing	10–61	12	34	13
Pneumo Dynamics	1–61	9	26¾	10
Pocket Books	1–61	25	41	6
Potter Instrument	5–61	10	26	6
Radio Shack	10–60	12⅝	30	2
Rotron Manufacturing	11–60	17	44	19
Standard Beryllium	8–59	1½	24½	4
Standard & Poor's	1–62	27½	44	23
Systron-Donner	4–60	13⅞	51½	13
Tastee Freez	9–61	13	30⅝	15
Technical Measurement	9–60	5	25	9
Trans-Sonics	7–59	12½	18¼	2⅝
United Servomation	12–61	18	33	17
Vacuum-Electronics	1–61	15	33	15
Vector Manufacturing	6–60	13¼	27	8
Vitamix Pharmaceuticals	5–61	10	20¼	7
Vitramon, Inc.	9–60	10	20⅜	7
Waldbaum, Inc.	9–61	14	30¼	10
Walter (Jim)	6–59	34	60¾	13
Welch Scientific	5–61	38	55	17
Western Publishing	8–60	42	83½	21
Work Wear	5–61	15	31¼	13
Wyle Laboratories	3–61	19½	43	8

the need for outside equity financing in the early 1960s, numerous companies did seek outside funds in the capital markets. Weekly offerings may be noted in *Barron's* or in *Moody's Stock Survey*. The investor should, however, avoid investing in small, unproved companies. During 1960 and 1961, many small companies made public sales of securities, some of which represented such "high-flying" industries as electronics, metals, the entertainment industry—bowling, particularly—publishing, and others. Although the market prices of many of these issues were higher in 1963 than the offering prices, for others they were much lower.

During 1960 and 1961, there appeared to be a buying fever for new security issues. Small corporations with unproved earnings records marketed public issues of securities that often doubled or tripled in value within a few weeks after the issue date. Table 17-2 presents a list of former "high fliers" in the new issue market that substantially increased in market value above the offering price, but that subsequently fell to a much lower level. Some of these issues—predominantly over the counter stocks—increased in market value by more than 1000 percent before declining by about 95 percent from their high levels. American International Bowling Company, for example, had a public offering in 1958 at $3 per share, increased in market value to $34.50, and then declined to $1 per share in early 1963. Standard Beryllium increased from $1.50 to $24.50 per share before declining to $4. Although some of these stocks ultimately recovered in price, investors were shocked during the 1962 stock market break, which all but wiped out their investments in these issues. One can imagine what happened to accounts that were financed on margin.

During early 1965, when stock prices were rising, numerous small companies again began to make public issues of securities. Intelligent investors should study the earnings records of the companies, critically analyze the prospects for future sales and earnings, and commit their funds to these investments only after serious consideration of the inherent risks involved and the potential future losses of investment principal.[5]

Stock Splits and Stock Dividends

Each year, about 5 to 10 percent of the Big Board companies either split their common stock or declare stock dividends of 20 percent or more. Some 103 New York Stock Exchange companies either split their stock or declared large stock dividends in 1962, while the number fell to 83 during 1963 and increased to 135 during 1964.[6] A stock split takes place as follows: If the board of directors of a corporation meets and splits the common shares two for one, then a stockholder who owns 100 shares receives 200 shares in exchange. The mechanics of distribution depend on whether the stock is a nonpar issue or whether it has a par value. When the stock is a nonpar series, the corporation must issue an additional number of shares to the stockholders of record equivalent to those presently owned. If, on the other hand, the old shares have a par value, they must be called in, retired, and replaced by other shares bearing only one half the par value. An alternate to the latter method is an endorsement to the old certificates showing the new par value and the issuance of new certificates for the additional 100 shares.

When a corporation declares a stock dividend, it merely pays dividends in shares of its own stock to the old stockholders of record. An amount equivalent to the market value of the newly issued shares should be transferred from the retained earnings account to the capital stock and paid-in surplus accounts.

With a stock split or a large stock dividend, the number of outstanding

[5] For an analysis of former "high fliers" in the new issues market, see "A Backward Glance," *Financial World*, January 9, 1963, pp. 13 and 26.

[6] For a complete listing of New York Stock Exchange companies that split their stock or issued stock dividends in excess of 20 percent during recent years, see late January issue of *Financial World*.

shares is increased, a situation that may create an additional floating supply of the stock. An individual who owns 100 shares that are split three for one may decide to sell 100 or 200 shares and diversify into other issues. This selling pressure may depress the market price of the stock for a time.

When the board of directors of the issuing corporation increases the cash dividend simultaneously with a stock split or a stock dividend, the market price of the stock frequently remains stable or rises. Ordinarily, however, a stock split or a large stock dividend has an adverse effect upon the market value of an issue slightly in excess of the expected dilution.

Figure 17-2 illustrates four companies in the office machine industry that had stock splits between 1962 and 1964. Dymo Industries common declined from $36 per share (adjusted for the three for one stock split) in April 1962 to $16 per share in June 1962. This substantial decline was during a period in which the general level of stock prices fell 25 percent. The market price of this particular issue then began a steady increase from mid-1962 through the end of 1964, appreciating from $44 to $60 per share subsequent to New York Stock Exchange listing. It then declined to approximately $20 per share late in 1964. Fluctuations in the market price of the issue were in the face of favorable earnings reports in 1962, 1963, and 1964, respectively, relative to the preceding years, since sales for the company increased by approximately 70 percent during each of the three years.

The common stock of International Business Machines has been split many times in past years. In the second quarter of 1964, the stock was split five for four, which gave each common share an adjusted market price of $490. By the end of 1964, the market value of the stock had declined to approximately $410. During the early 1960s, the company had an annual growth rate in earnings per share of 20 percent per year, and in 1964 and 1965 it traded at approximately 35 times earnings per share.

The market price of Control Data declined only slightly after its listing on the Big Board, and later it rose from $25 to about $75 per share (adjusted for a subsequent three for two stock split). After the stock split in October 1964, the market value of the issue declined from $62 per share (adjusted) to $45 per share. The market value of the issue was quite volatile during 1963 and 1964, despite increases in sales and earnings per share.

The market value of Xerox Corporation common stock declined only slightly after a five for one stock split in early 1964, and the stock then began to oscillate rather widely. The future market value of the stock will, of course, depend on trends in sales and profits, the development of new products, and encroachments into the copying field by competitors.

Generally, the market value of the common stock of a company appreciates prior to a stock split or the payment of a large stock dividend, but the market price of the issue ordinarily declines following the adjustment. A substantial increase in cash dividends along with a stock split or an unexpected stock split or stock dividend, conversely, may bring about a stimulating effect upon the market value. A speculator can frequently make a profit by buying

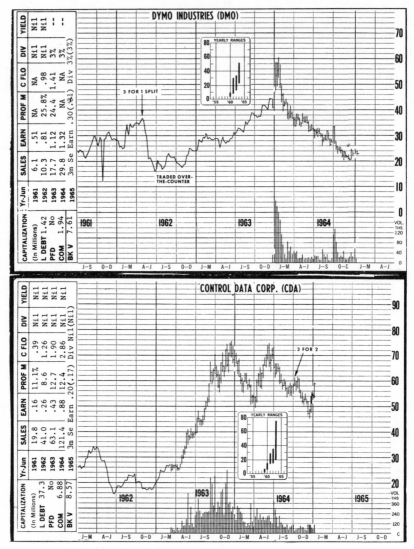

FIGURE 17-2 / The effect of stock splits on market values. From *Trend-line's Current Market Perspectives*, New York, Trendline Corporation, January 1965, p. 163.

an issue as soon as a proposed stock split becomes public knowledge and selling it on the day of or on the day preceding the meeting of the board of directors at which final action is to be taken. Should a proposed stock split or stock dividend be passed up, the market price of the issue becomes depressed. Perhaps the reason for the frequent declines in market value following positive action is that little new is anticipated and speculators liquidate their holdings and seek other upside movers.

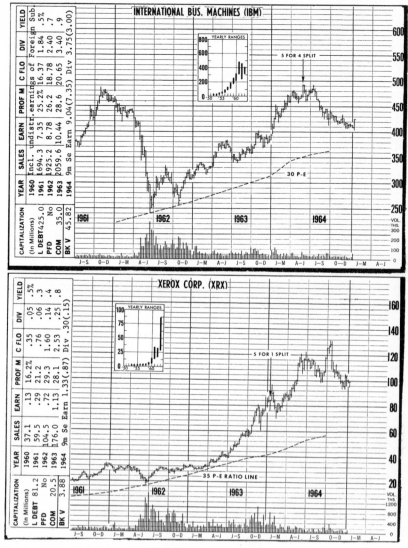

FIGURE 17-2 (Continued)

Stock Purchases by Corporate Officials

Frequently the news that the directors and/or officers of a corporation are accumulating their corporation's common stock encourages other investors and speculators to begin acquiring the issue. When the number of buy orders exceeds the number of sell orders, the issue rises in market value. In many cases, the officers of the corporation are merely exercising stock options that permit them to acquire shares; and although these acquisitions may produce a slight dilution in the earnings per share, little buying pressure normally occurs. The directors and officers of a firm are in a position to judge the future operating prospects of the company, and many investors believe that they possess more knowledge than the general public. Action taken by insiders is frequently copied by the general public, resulting in increased demand for and rising prices of an issue.

In order for corporate officers to obtain long-term capital gains equal to the difference between their purchase and selling price of stocks acquired under stock options, they must hold the shares longer than three years. Where the holding period is shorter, any gain is considered to be ordinary income rather than a long-term capital gain. For this reason the exercise of stock options should not substantially increase the supply of stock offered for resale within three years. Of course, the officers may sell other shares of stock that have been owned longer than the required holding period or that were acquired in the open market, in which case the stocks owned for more than six months qualify for long-term capital gains or losses. The first-in, first-out method of costing is required by the IRS for figuring the cost basis in determining the short- or long-term capital gains tax treatment for an issue unless shares can be identified.

In rare instances corporate directors or officers make use of their knowledge of the company without disclosing such information to the general public. When this occurs, the SEC may bring action against the corporate officials; or stockholders who suffered losses because of the sale of their shares—or in the case of adverse information because of holding shares—may bring suit directly against the guilty individuals and/or corporation. Under the provisions of the Securities Exchange Act of 1934, corporate officials are not permitted to gain personally from inside knowledge at the expense of the stockholders of the company. When short-term capital gains are taken, or when the inside information is used to the disadvantage of the general public, the corporation may bring suit against these individuals, forcing them to pay their profits to the company. Such funds then become a part of the paid-in surplus of the firm and benefit all the shareholders.[7] Insiders sometime have prior knowledge about the prospects of their corporation, but their stock accumulations ordinarily merely indicate their faith in the long-range earning ability and outlook of the company.[8]

Conversion of Debentures

The call of a convertible preferred stock or debenture issue frequently depresses the market value of the common stock. The conversion price of the issue may stimulate almost all of the bondholders or preferred stockholders

[7] In May 1965 such a suit was brought against Texas Gulf Sulphur, and the market price of the stock was adversely affected when the information of the suit became news. Despite the suit, the restrictive export action taken by the Mexican government against the two sulphur companies located in that country brought about such a critical world shortage of sulphur that the market price of Texas Gulf Sulphur common stock began immediately to recover.

[8] For a current listing of insider trading in common stocks, the reader may refer to the *Statistical Bulletin* of the SEC, *The Value Line Investment Survey*, or *Forbes Magazine*.

to convert into common shares rather than to receive a premium for the surrender of the issue, and such conversion may produce a substantial dilution in the earnings per share.

American Telephone and Telegraph Company, numerous airlines, some financial institutions, and other companies have successfully used convertible debentures as a method for raising equity capital. After the debentures have been outstanding for a period of years, the market price of the common issues may have risen adequately to force conversion by calling the issue. Since it is usually to the advantage of the preferred stockholder or debenture holder to convert rather than to receive the call price of the issue, a majority of the securities are converted. The terms of the conversion ordinarily grant the holders about 30 days to exchange their securities for common shares after the call is made. The increased number of common shares may dilute the earnings per share of the common stock and thus depress its market price.

A step-down conversion ratio frequently stimulates many of the convertible holders to exchange their issues for common stock. For example, Mohawk Airlines had a large convertible debenture issue outstanding in early 1964, with each $1000 bond convertible into 200 common shares, or a conversion price of $5 per share. On or after November 1, 1964, the conversion ratio increased to $6, or each $1000 debenture was exchangeable for only 166⅔ shares. Although each share of common earned about $1.25 for the year ended in March 1964, many holders of the debentures converted by October 1964, and earnings per share fell by almost one half during the following year.

The stockholder should consider the possible dilution effect of a call for issues that have large volumes of convertible debentures and preferred stock outstanding; and when the market price of the common stock reaches a point where exchange of the convertibles is advantageous, the holders may wish to (1) sell the issue and invest in another, or (2) watch the issue for sudden price weakness. In order to know which corporations have large convertible debenture issues outstanding, the individual should refer to *Moody's Stock Survey* and *Moody's Bond Survey* or other current sources of financial information. Periodically *Financial World* lists a number of companies for which the market price of the common stock is approaching the conversion relationship.

Mergers and Consolidations

Numerous "marriages" between large corporations occurred during the post-World War II years, and although many of the candidates had disappeared in some industries by 1966, there were numerous prospects remaining in other fields, for example, automobile parts, foods, insurance, and electronics.[9] Frequently a merger rumor remains just that—a rumor—but when the management of two companies begin to consider seriously the possibility of

[9] See, for example, *Financial World*, Novembr 4, 1964, pp. 4 and 22.

a merger, the market value of both issues frequently increases. Although it appears logical that the market value of one stock would decline while the other would rise, depending upon the bargaining position of each company, this is usually not the case. This is true because of the different price–earnings ratios at which the stocks trade. The stock of the company that is actively seeking the merger ordinarily trades at a generous multiple of earnings relative to the other merger candidate. Let us assume that Corporation A, with (1) two million common shares, (2) earnings per share of $2, and (3) a market value per share of $40 (a price–earnings ratio of 20 times), seeks to merge with Corporation B, which has (1) one million common shares, (2) earnings per share of $2.50 and (3) a market value of $30 (a price–earnings ratio of 12 times). The directors of Corporation A recommend that one share of A common be exchanged for each share of B common, and the directors of Corporation B, who will remain in active management of their division of Company A, vote to accept the proposal. Upon recommendation by their respective boards of directors, a majority of the shareholders accept the merger terms. Debts are assumed by the surviving corporation and shares of stock in A are exchanged for stock in B. What is likely to have happened to the market value of the stock of the two companies? The new earnings per share of the combined company is

$$\frac{\$2(2 \text{ million}) + \$2.50 \ (1 \text{ million})}{3 \text{ million}} = \$2.17$$

Capitalized at 20 times, this produces a market price of about $43. The common stock of both Corporation A and Corporation B should rise to about this level in anticipation of the merger. Some temporary decline in market price after the stockholders vote to accept or reject the merger is normal. Upon rejection, market prices may fall to or below their previous levels; but upon acceptance, there is little left to stimulate further price rallies and some profit taking reduces the market value.

The merger of two or more firms into a single unit may result in some savings for the companies concerned, but it frequently creates many problems. Proxy battles by large minority interest groups, court battles by some of the stockholders, or a negative decision on the part of the management of one or more of the companies may result in the abandonment of the merger idea, and these factors almost always lead to a reduction in the market price of both issues. In addition, antitrust suits are frequently initiated by the Federal Trade Commission.

Merger candidates are usually companies whose stock is trading at a substantial discount below book value, which may occur because of the lack of investor confidence in the company's management, poor recent earnings records, or lack of interest on the part of investors in the industry. A tax-loss carry forward, while of little value to a company that is unable to operate profitably, may be of tremendous value to an acquiring corporation, which may offset the tax loss against its taxable income. Frequently a small tax-loss company will be acquired by a larger, more profitable company.

Although the purchase of shares in one or more companies that are proposing a merger may result in some capital gain, this type of investment is hazardous for the individual and should be undertaken only by someone who is willing to assume the risk of possible loss in capital value on his investment because of a change in merger news or a reevaluation of the situation by the general public.

New Products

A company that is spending a significant amount of its funds for research and development may discover a new process or develop a product that is superior to that being sold by its competitors. Where the company can economically produce and sell the item to the general public at a profit-making level, a benefit ensues to the shareholders. Many corporations in the chemical, pharmaceutical, electronics, food processing, office equipment, and other industries spend a significant part of each sales dollar on research and development. These expenditures should ultimately result in rising sales and profits and higher market values of the securities of the corporation.

It is difficult to locate corporations that are preparing to market new, potentially profitable items. References to articles that appear in various newsletters, *The Wall Street Journal,* and other financial publications may provide clues. By the time the information is made public through a newspaper or periodical, however, much or all of the rise in the market price of the stock may have already occurred. The product may be so superior to that being manufactured by competitors, however—for example, the Xerox duplicator—that actual sales and profits far outshadow expectations, and the stock may continue to appreciate for years.

Shifts in Stockholder Attitudes

From the early 1950s through 1962, airline stocks were trading at very low multiples of earnings. From 1962 through mid-1966, however, these issues began to rise relative to earnings. Whereas airline stocks were trading at six to eight times earnings during 1962, many were trading at about 20 times current earnings in early 1966. After a period of popularity, when price–earnings ratios reach above-average levels, most issues lose their appeal and decline in market value. For example, electronics common stocks were trading at 30 or 40 times earnings per share in 1961, but after the stock market decline in 1962, many of the issues declined in popularity. The growth in sales and earnings of these companies was not as great as had been expected, and the market prices of electronics issues were very low in 1964 and 1965 relative to earnings. In 1965, many of these stocks were trading at 7 to 10 times earnings per share, but were gaining in investor interest.

The price–earnings multiples of numerous other industries oscillate upward and downward, depending upon the degree of pessimism or optimism of the general public toward a given industry. For example, during a boom period, tobacco stocks or utility stocks may be somewhat depressed in market price relative to earnings, but during a recession period, when sales and profits remain relatively stable, the issues may be in higher demand and thus sell at larger premiums relative to earnings.

Other Factors

Other factors that stimulate issues to rise in price relative to earnings include a shortage in a basic metal or mineral such as zinc, lead, sulphur, silver, or copper; the favorable working of leverage, such as in the airline industry during the early 1960s; an expanding consumer market, such as in the automobile industry; and a favorable tax change, such as may benefit companies selling goods that are subject to the federal excise tax. Of course, certain of these factors may be adverse to a company rather than beneficial. For example, when demand for a basic metal declines, the price at which the commodity trades may be reduced, thus lowering the profits and consequently the market price of the shares of the company. Although leverage works to the advantage of a company when sales and profits are rising, it creates an unfavorable profit situation when sales are declining. All tax laws are not favorable to corporations; in addition, certain companies may be adversely affected by shifts in consumer preference, the age composition of the population, and other factors.

Summary

A number of situations that occur infrequently for the average corporation may nevertheless have a tremendous impact upon the market value of the common stock of the company. For example, a corporation that is trading its securities on the American Stock Exchange, another exchange, or in the over the counter markets may decide to list its securities on the New York Stock Exchange. This action may bring about an immediate price stimulation, but the market price may subsequently decline after listing is accomplished.

A preemptive rights issue, a new public issue of common shares, and the conversion of securities to common stock, all of which bring about a dilution in the earnings per share of a corporation, normally produce short-range depressing effects upon the market value of the common shares. Of course, after the funds raised by the new sale of shares have been invested, some additional return on the new investments should produce a stimulating effect upon earnings per share and lead to a recovery in market price.

Other factors that frequently produce a decline in the market value of common shares include stock splits, stock dividends, a decrease in cash dividend payments, and a large secondary distribution of shares by corporate officials or by financial institutions. When cash earnings per share are increased at the time of a stock split or a stock dividend, however, the market value of the stock may respond favorably. Frequently the market value will accelerate until the actual split or stock dividend occurs and then decline.

Other factors that may affect the market value of common stock include the expectation of a merger or consolidation of two or more companies, the development of new products, or the expectation of rising or falling profits. Although the effect that such factors have upon the market value of the shares depends upon the circumstances surrounding each of the companies, before investing in such issues the individual should consider the usual effect of these special situations upon the market value of its securities.

QUESTIONS FOR REVIEW /

1. How does the listing of a security on the New York Stock Exchange usually affect the market value of the shares prior to listing? immediately following listing? for several years after listing?
2. Do you visualize an increase or a decrease in the number of issues listed on registered exchanges within the future? Explain.
3. Compute the cost of listing on the New York Stock Exchange for a firm that has 20 million authorized shares.
4. Enumerate the advantages and disadvantages to the corporation and to the shareholder associated with a rights issue versus a public sale of common stock.
5. Do you consider the use of the preemptive rights method for marketing common shares to be a bull market phenomenon? Explain.
6. How important is the use of rights when compared to public sales of common stock issues?
7. How does a new sale of stock to the general public affect the market value of the common shares? What factors account for these fluctuations?
8. How does the market value per share of a common stock usually respond to a large stock dividend? How can the market price be influenced by the cash dividend policy being followed by the board of directors of the corporation?
9. How important is insider trading in common stocks?
10. Under what circumstances are convertible preferred and debenture issues threats toward diluting the market values of common shares?
11. With regard to a proposed merger of two companies, how would you account for the favorable response in the market value of the stock of both firms?
12. What other factors usually have an effect upon the market value of the common shares of widely held corporations?

PROBLEMS /

1. Either (a) survey current financial periodicals and make a list of companies that have registered with the New York Stock Exchange during the past year and determine how the market value of the securities responded subsequent to the listing date; or (b) by referring to *The Exchange*, compile a list of 10 companies that have listed with the New York Stock Exchange and determine the market values of the issues 30 days prior to listing, the opening price on listing day, and the closing price 30 days after listing. How many of these issues responded

favorably to listing prior to the listing date but declined in market value from listing date to 30 days afterwards?

2. Compile a list of New York Stock Exchange companies that made preemptive rights issues during the most recent calendar year. This information may be obtained by referring to *The Exchange, The Magazine of Wall Street, Financial World, Forbes Magazine,* or other periodicals. Determine whether or not the market value of the issues responded favorably or unfavorably toward the rights issues subsequent to the issuance dates.

3. Locate three companies that made public issues of common stocks from three to six months ago and determine how the market values of the common shares responded prior to and following the public sale of securities. What does this indicate about the desirability of making an acquisition of a primary issue of securities compared to an acquisition through a registered exchange? Does the position within the stock cycle, that is, a bull or bear market, have any bearing upon this decision?

4. By reference to one of the leading chart services, such as *Trendline's Daily Basis Stock Charts, The Value Line Investment Survey,* or some other service, determine six companies that have either split their stock or paid stock dividends in excess of 20 percent during the past year. How did the market prices respond to the stock splits or stock dividends?

REFERENCES /

Financial World. New York: Guenther Publishing Corporation, January 9, 1963 ("A Backward Glance"); October 28, 1964 ("To List—Or Not To List?"); and November 4, 1964.

Forbes Magazine. New York: Forbes, Inc., April 15, 1963 ("Stock Rights"); January 1, 1965; and selected issues.

Graham, Benjamin, *The Intelligent Investor.* New York: Harper & Row, Publishers, Inc., 1959.

————, David L. Dodd, and Sidney Cottle, *Security Analysis,* 4th ed. New York: McGraw-Hill Book Company, Inc., 1962.

Huang, Stanley S. C., "Study of the Performance of Rapid Growth Stocks," *Financial Analysts Journal.* Boston, Mass.: The Financial Analysts Federation, January–February, 1965.

"Improvements in *The Value Line* Survey," *The Value Line Investment Survey.* New York: Arnold Bernhard & Company, Inc., April 23, 1965.

The Magazine of Wall Street. New York: Ticker Publishing Company, selected issues.

New York Stock Exchange, *The Exchange.* New York: The Exchange, December 1963.

Trendline's Current Market Perspectives. New York: Trendline Corporation, 1965.

The Wall Street Journal. New York: Dow Jones & Company, Inc.

part four

The Technical Approach to Timing Security Transactions

The technical approach, sometimes referred to as the price–volume analysis method, has been utilized by traders or speculators since the 1920s in an attempt to locate fast-moving issues. The users of the technique were blamed for contributing to the frenzied trading activities that preceded the 1929 stock market crash, and the method received little public attention for many years. However, the use of charts showing price and/or volume data gained in popularity in the early 1960s.

Many advisers recommend that technical patterns alone be used and that fundamental information with regard to securities be disregarded. The author, however, has had good trading—and investing—results from applying fundamental data with the technical approach. The location of a number of companies that have had substantial increases in sales, earnings per share, and backlogs of orders should be the first step. The technical strength of the issues should then be checked by an astute technician to determine an advantageous buying price and the proper timing of the acquisition. Both the fundamental and technical strengths of the issue should be checked periodically.

While some investors believe that the market values of securities oscillate in a haphazard method, a study of a large number of vertical bar and point-and-figure charts indicates that stocks quite frequently move within clearly defined upper and lower channels and that numerous formations are generally trustworthy in forecasting extensive upward and downward moves. Movements in stock prices and volume merely record the changing demand and supply of a stock at a given price and are influenced largely by expectations, earnings reports, dividend news, the ex-dividend date, and the degree of appeal of a group of stocks in a given industry.

Part Four summarizes the theories of the technical approach applicable to vertical bar charts (Chapter 18) and point-and-figure charts (Chapter 19). Market indicators are considered (Chapter 20), and some methods for locating bullish and bearish issues are analyzed (Chapter 21). Empirical data are presented in the Appendix and in Chapters 18 and 19, which evaluate the trustworthiness of the most frequently occurring chart patterns.

chapter 18 | Vertical Bar Charts

Introduction

The technical approach to security selection consists of the use of charts by an investor or speculator in an attempt to improve his timing in the purchase or sale of specific issues. Basically, there are two types of charts, the vertical bar chart, which is discussed in this chapter, and the point-and-figure method, which is described in Chapter 19. Vertical bar charts may be prepared with each bar representing the trading range within a day, week, or month. The volume of trading is ordinarily shown below the price range. The charts appearing in this chapter are adapted from *Trendline Daily Basis Stock Charts* and *Trendline's Current Market Perspectives* (weekly range charts).

Vertical bar charts compiled by months appear in *Moody's Handbook of Common Stocks*, Standard & Poor's *Stock Market Encyclopedia*, *The Value Line Investment Survey*, and numerous other publications. Usually the trading range and volume are shown for a number of years by months. Although some technicians prefer that the charts cover a long period of time, such as is possible with weekly or monthly range charts, buy and sell signals appear more quickly on daily rather than on weekly or monthly charts. Some technicians believe that patterns are easier to detect on weekly bar charts than on daily or monthly range charts.

Construction of Vertical Bar Charts

Purpose of Charting

The primary purpose of charting is to give the analyst a picture of the movement in market price and volume of an individual issue. By measuring the rises and declines in the market price of a stock along with the volume pattern of the issue, one attempts to determine whether the sentiment of investors is bullish—optimistic—or bearish—pessimistic. After studying thousands of chart formations, technicians have determined that certain bar chart patterns are usually bullish, that others are not reliable, and that still others are bearish. The more important of these formations are described and illustrated in the following sections.

Chart Base

Figure 18-1 illustrates how the daily-basis stock chart is constructed. Time is shown on the base of the chart, while either the number of shares traded or stock prices are recorded on the vertical axis. The volume is ordinarily recorded in hundreds of shares (or in thousands on the weekly or monthly range charts), and each square on the graph paper represents convenient units of round lot transactions. It is preferable to use a scale that is divided into eighths, since the market price of common stocks is quoted in dollars and eighths of dollars. Some technicians prefer to use semilog paper rather than arithmetic graph paper, so that equidistances represent similar rates of changes.[1]

Price Range

For each day's transactions a small vertical bar is recorded to represent the trading range of the stock on a given day, and the small horizontal tick represents the closing price of the stock. An issue that closes at the high range for the day often continues a price rise on the following day. This pattern does not always occur, however, because news may be reported during the night or over the weekend that alters the opinions of buyers and sellers of the issue.

Significance of Volume

The volume of trading is recorded on the vertical bar chart between the base and the daily price range. When a stock rises on high volume, it is said to be bullish. A stock that has been rising on heavy volume and has a mild decline on light volume is also said to be bullish. Conversely, a rise on relatively light volume is bearish.

Bullish Patterns

The types of bullish formations that occur most frequently on vertical bar charts are the inverted head and shoulders, saucer, up trend, gaps, and flags. These formations are illustrated in the upper section of Figure 18-1.

Inverted Head and Shoulders

The *inverted head and shoulders* has a right shoulder, the bottom of which does not penetrate as deeply as the head. The right shoulder penetrates slightly less than the head and its formation is similar to that of the

[1] See for example, Harry Lankford, *Quote American* (Wichita, Kan.: Harry Lankford). This is a weekly bar chart service of all American Stock Exchange issues.

Selected Bullish Formations

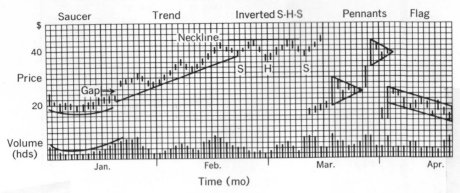

Time (mo)

Uncertainty Formations

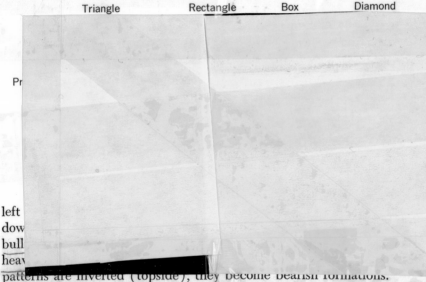

left
dow
bull
hea

patterns are inverted (topside), they become bearish formations.

The neckline is a straight line joining the high points that form the shoulders, or the extreme points on either side of the head. One suggested method for determining the approximate move, or the minimum move for the issue, is to measure the distance from the bottom of the head to the neckline. Some technicians argue that the market price of a stock should rise by a similar distance above the neckline before a major reversal in direction occurs. The neckline should be broken by at least 3 percent in order for the signal to be valid.

Radio Corporation of America (RCA) and Revlon display inverted head and shoulders in Figure 18-2. In September 1965, the neckline on RCA was broken by approximately 3 percent and the market price pulled back near the vicinity of the neckline and then rose by approximately 25 percent. The volume on the break out was very strong, and this heavy volume was the

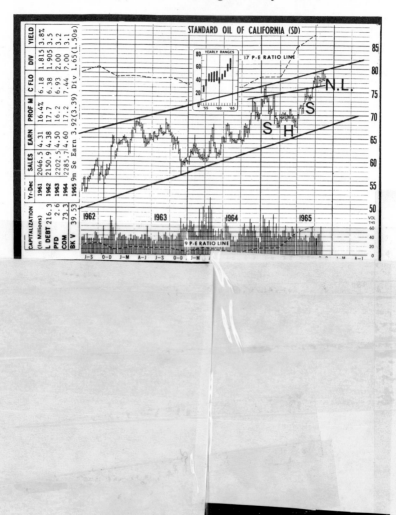

FIGURE 18-2 / Selected bullish patterns. From *Trendline's Current Market Perspectives,* New York, Trendline Corporation, Mid-March 1965, selected pages.

key to the reliability of the chart formation. Another inverted head and shoulders was formed for Revlon from mid-1963 through early 1965, and extremely heavy volume occurred with the break through the neckline.

Saucers

The *saucer* formation is concave, and the volume pattern closely resembles the pattern formed by the daily range. This formation is typical of stocks trading below $50 and usually signals a major up trend. Quite frequently a handle, that is, a slight decline on light volume, is built on the

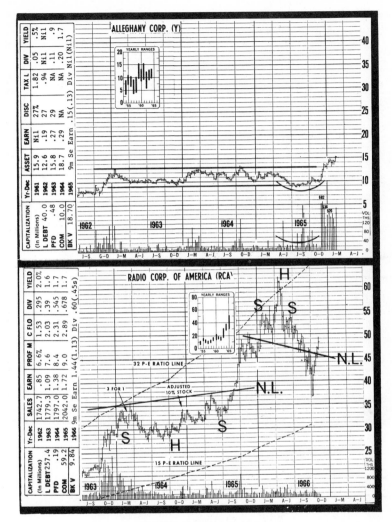

FIGURE 18-2 *(Continued)*

saucer, or cup-shaped formation, for a period of one to three weeks preceding the steep up trend in price. A saucer pattern is usually not dependable unless the volume is shaped similarly to the saucer and breaks the neckline by at least 3 percent. During December 1964, a small saucer appeared on the chart for RCA, and another small saucer formation appeared on Revlon from mid-October through November (Fig. 18-3). A small half-circle can be drawn inside the volume and below the lower trading range for Revlon during this period of time.

Figure 18-2 shows that a large saucer was formed for Standard Oil of California from mid-July through October 1964. During late July, when the market price of the issue declined, volume also declined. Near the bottom

FIGURE 18-3 / Bottomside reversals. From *Trendline Daily Basis Stock Charts*, New York, Trendline Corporation, January 8, 1965.

of the saucer volume remained fairly low, while it increased as the market price of the stock rose. The market price of the stock pulled back and built a handle for the saucer before ascending. The market price of a stock usually accelerates rather rapidly from such a deep saucer formation.

Gaps and Up Trends

Once an up trend has been initiated, the market price of the stock frequently oscillates between two imaginary trend lines, which are illustrated in Figure 18-1. The technician may join the low points with a straight line and find that the market price of the stock oscillates from this point upward and back to this line. Quite frequently the upward move is made in two or three similar stages.

These upward movements are sometimes sprinkled with gaps on the upside. No trading takes place at those prices, since the stock opens higher than the previous session's closing price and the issue does not pull back to fill the gap. These gaps are classified as *break-away gaps,* which occur at the

FIGURE 18-3 (*Continued*)

beginning of a bullish pattern, *measuring gaps,* which occur about two-fifths to one-half the distance up an entire move, and *exhaustion gaps,* which mark the termination of a move. These gaps occur more often on the daily-basis chart than on the weekly or monthly range chart.

When the gap is larger than the usual unit of trading, which is one eighth of a point, it is said to have significance. When the gap appears on the upside on very strong volume, the market price of the stock will probably continue to rise for a period of time. When gaps appear on the downside, accompanied by very strong volume, the market price of the stock usually declines for a time. Some common stock issues have a tendency to gap very frequently, while the market prices of others rise and fall in a more orderly fashion. An individual issue has some tendency to repeat its patterns, and when a stock issue usually fills its gaps—that is, when market price on subsequent days pulls back to close the gap or rallies to fill a gap that was left on the downside—it can be depended upon to do so. Some issues have a tendency to leave gaps, while others fill the gaps within a few trading days.

The market prices of many common issues appear to move up and back to an imaginary line similar to the one drawn in the chart for Unexcelled

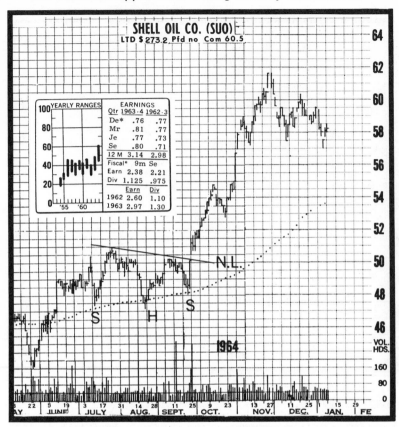

FIGURE 18-4 / Bullish formations. From *Trendline Daily Basis Stock Charts,* New York, Trendline Corporation, January 8, 1965.

Chemical Corporation (Fig. 18-4). When a person anticipates a purchase of this issue, he should wait until the market price declines to the trend-line area. When the market price of the stock remains above this trend line and the volume is strong on rising prices and weak on declines, the issue is said to be bullish. Once a market price breaks through the major trend line, however, this oftentimes signals a reversal in direction. Usually, but not necessarily, there will be a recovery to the trend line. Both Shell Oil Company and Unexcelled Chemical Corporation (Fig. 18-4) were forming up trends during the last half of 1964. The inverted head and shoulders followed by a gap through the neckline in late September 1964 signaled a major price increase for Shell Oil Company.

Pennants and Flags

Frequently small *pennants* and *flags* are formed by an issue as it moves upward or downward in market price. A pennant or flag has a staff that is rising, while a down flag and a down pennant have falling staffs. The latter

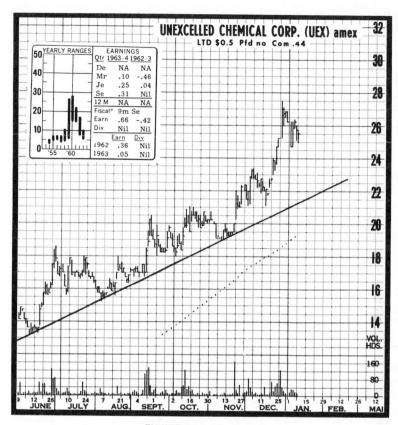

UNEXCELLED CHEMICAL CORP. (UEX) amex
LTD $0.5 Pfd no Com .44

YEARLY RANGES	EARNINGS		
	Qtr	1963-4	1962-3
	De	NA	NA
	Mr	.10	-.46
	Je	.25	.04
	Se	.31	Nil
	12 M	NA	NA
	Fiscal° 9m Se		
	Earn	.66	-.42
	Div	Nil	Nil
		Earn	Div
	1962	.36	Nil
	1963	.05	Nil

FIGURE 18-4 (*Continued*)

are bearish formations. In Figure 18-4 on Shell Oil Company, two small flags were formed during October and November 1964, which divided the entire move into thirds. Exhaustion gaps appeared near the top of the move. The small single-day island reversal, which formed in early January, may in reality be an uncompleted inverted head and shoulders. Until some additional price and volume information is available, however, it is impossible to predict accurately whether this formation will be a descending triangle, the first half of an inverted head and shoulders, or some other pattern. The volume appears to support a continued price rise for the stock.

Uncertainty Patterns

Uncertainty patterns usually take the form of triangles, wedges, rectangles, boxes, diamonds, and similar configurations, and these patterns have been named after the geometric shapes that they resemble. Many of these patterns are illustrated in Figure 18-1. They are called uncertainty patterns because one cannot forecast with a high degree of accuracy the direction of a break out from the formations.

FIGURE 18-5 / Uncertainty patterns. From *Trendline Daily Basis Stock Charts,* New York, Trendline Corporation, January 8, 1965.

Triangles and Wedges

Triangles are similar to *wedges* except that the latter are formed with two rising legs (a rising wedge) or two descending legs (a descending wedge). Triangles are a combination of one rising and one falling leg (a symmetrical triangle), one horizontal leg and a declining diagonal (a descending triangle), and one horizontal leg and a rising diagonal (a rising triangle). The configurations are frequently formed in reverse and are referred to as broadening, or inverted, patterns.

Triangle formations appear in Figure 18-5 on Texas Utilities Company and in Figure 18-2 on RCA. From July through October 1964, Texas Utilities common formed a triple top, which was enclosed in an ascending triangle. The ascending triangle is sometimes bullish; but the formation is not always reliable and should, therefore, be classified as an uncertainty pattern. In reality the market price of the stock broke from the bottom and began to form an inverted descending triangle. The descending triangle is usually, although not always, bearish.

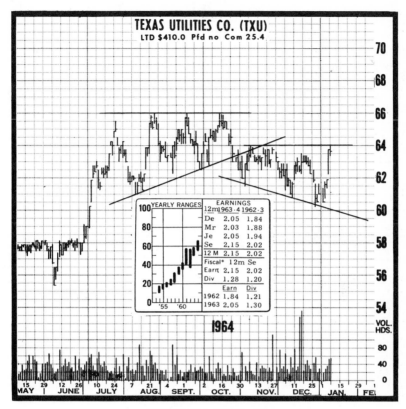

FIGURE 18-5 (Continued)

The pattern formed by Sinclair Oil Corporation (Fig. 18-5) common was more like a descending wedge than a descending triangle. The descending wedge, sometimes referred to as a coil, is more often a bullish than a bearish pattern, while the ascending wedge is more often a bearish pattern.

Rectangles and Boxes

Rectangles and *boxes* are similar in that the price of an issue moves up and back between two horizontal lines. The rectangle is simply an extended box with the base longer than the side. Prior to a break out from a box or rectangle, a small saucer or inverted saucer may form and give a clue to the probable direction of eruption. After breaking upward from a rectangle, the top of the pattern frequently serves as the bottom of another rectangle or triangle.

In Figure 18-6, Lear-Siegler common moved between $12 and $15 a share from July through December 1964. Since the decline in December was not to the bottom trend line at $12, the market price of the stock was ex-

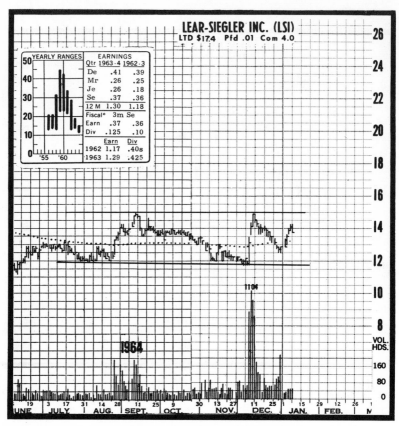

FIGURE 18-6 / Uncertainty. From *Trendline Daily Basis Stock Charts,* New York, Trendline Corporation, January 8, 1965.

pected to break through the $15 level, probably pull back to it on light volume, and then move upward. Very heavy volume, which occurred near the middle of December, sent the market price of the stock from $12 to $15 in only three trading days, which signifies accumulation of the issue by investors. If additional buying pressure is generated, the market price of the stock should continue to rise. Some technicians suggest that the extent of a move is approximately equal to the base of the rectangle; and if this is true, the market price of the stock should accelerate substantially. (In reality, the stock rose into the mid-30's within a year.)

A symmetrical triangle and a rectangle appear for Seeburg Corporation in Figure 18-6. These formations are uncertainty patterns in that the technician cannot tell in which direction the price will move until it has broken out of the formation. Since the market price declined through the bottom of the symmetrical triangle, it was expected to fall by approximately the base of the triangle, or about $4. The stock moved up and down from about 22¼ to 26 for about five months. During November and December,

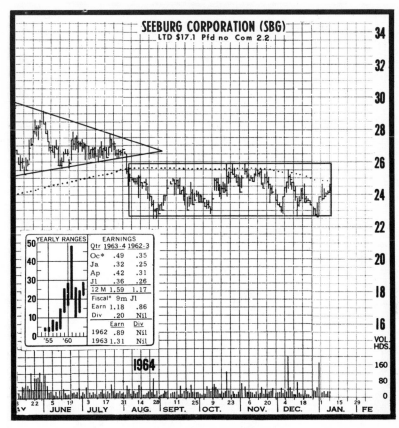

SEEBURG CORPORATION (SBG)
LTD $17.1 Pfd no Com 2.2

YEARLY RANGES	EARNINGS		
	Qtr	1963·4	1962·3
	Oc*	.49	.35
	Ja	.32	.25
	Ap	.42	.31
	Jl	.36	.26
	12 M	1.59	1.17
	Fiscal° 9m Jl		
	Earn	1.18	.86
	Div	.20	Nil
		Earn	Div
	1962	.89	Nil
	1963	1.31	Nil

FIGURE 18-6 *(Continued)*

the market price of the stock had difficulty in reaching the 26 level and was, therefore, expected to break from the bottom of the rectangle and continue its downward progression. The pattern resembled a head and shoulders top within the rectangle, which is a bearish pattern.

Bearish Formations

After the market price of a stock has been rising for a period of time, it frequently forms a topside reversal pattern, which may take the form of a head and shoulders, a compound head and shoulders—that is, multiple shoulders on either side of the head—an inverted saucer, a rounded top, a single-V top, a double top, a triple top, or single-day island reversal.

Head and Shoulders

Perhaps the easiest chart formation to recognize and the most reliable is the *head and shoulders*. The left shoulder is represented by an upward movement and a decline. The head is formed by a movement somewhat

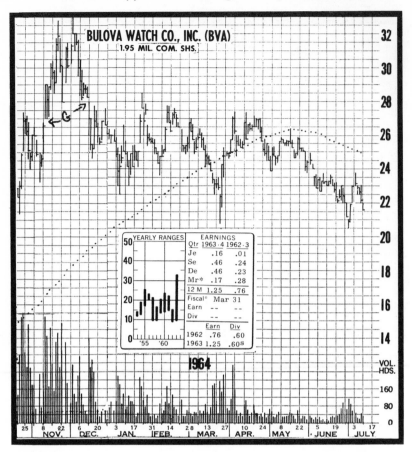

FIGURE 18-7 / Topside reversals. From *Trendline Daily Basis Stock Charts,* New York, Trendline Corporation, January 8, 1965.

higher than the preceding upward movement, with a decline similar to the preceding decline. The right shoulder is formed by an additional upward, wavelike motion and a decline that cuts the neckline by 3 percent or more. Two head and shoulders formations appear in the rounded top of Spiegel in Figure 18-7. The first head and shoulders was not completed, since the neckline was not broken by more than 3 percent. A compound head and shoulders was then formed which did break the neckline by more than 3 percent.

Double Top

The price rise of Bulova Watch (Fig. 18-7) common was capped by a *double top* set off by a gap on the upside that appeared in November and a down gap that appeared in December 1963. The reversal in trend could perhaps have been anticipated, since the price increases near the double top were on very light volume and the declines were on heavy volume, thus

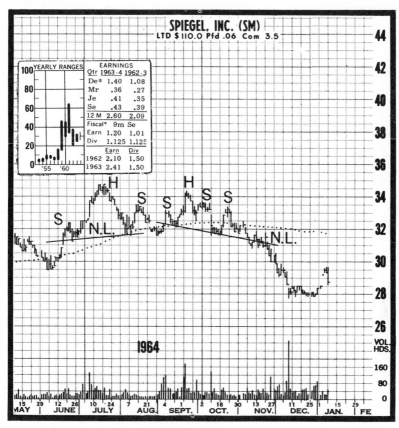

FIGURE 18-7 (Continued)

signifying weakness in the issue. The gap on December 16 was on unusually heavy volume and signified a major reversal in the up trend of the stock. Instead of selling the issue on December 17 or 18, 1963 at a relatively low price, the holder of the security should have waited for a rally. In mid-January 1964, the gap that had been formed on about December 16 was filled, and the market price of the stock continued to drift downward during the first half of 1964. The entire pattern for Bulova from mid-October to late December 1963 was a large head and shoulders formation.

Single-Day Island Reversal

An issue sometimes attracts widespread interest from speculators and traders, and when this occurs, the market value of the stock may rise rapidly. In late 1963 this occurred with Syntex Corporation (Fig. 18-8), one of the first companies to perfect birth control pills, and tremendous speculative interest was associated with the issue. From late November 1963 until mid-January 1964, the market price of the stock rose from about $65 to $190.

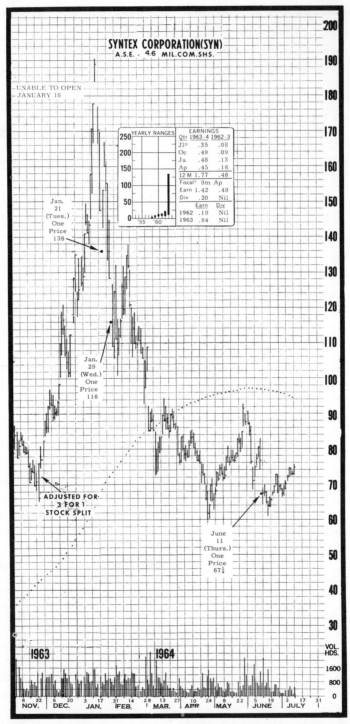

FIGURE 18-8 / Topside reversals. From *Trendline Daily Basis Stock Charts,* New York, Trendline Corporation, July 10, 1964.

On its upward movement, pennants, flags, and gaps were formed, which represent continuation patterns. A single-day island reversal was formed in early January 1964 by a gap on the upside and a gap on the downside. The upside gap was $6 in breadth and the downside gap was $7 in breadth, indicating that the market price of the stock was exhausted and would probably decline in a fashion similar to its preceding up trend. The stock rallied in February 1964, but was unable to break its preceding high. By the end of April 1964, the market price of the stock had fallen to $60. Some individuals who bought the stock in November and December 1963 and liquidated prior to the decline made handsome profits, but others who bought the stock at $160 to $190 a share may have to hold the issue several years before the market value of the stock again reaches this high plateau. Investing in a fast-moving, "high-flying" issue is extremely risky.

Other Topside Reversal Signals

Other topside reversal signals include the *triple top*, which is very similar to the double top; the *inverted saucer*, which is similar to the head and shoulders (except that the volume pattern for the inverted saucer is concave upward); and the *rounded top*. These formations will not be illustrated with charts, but the reader may detect these highly reliable reversal signals by consulting a large number of charts and looking for the formations.

The single-V top is almost impossible to detect because the stock changes direction without warning, but a one-, two-, or three-day island reversal may be a valid signal, or the volume may give a clue. Where the volume is very light on the upside but very heavy on the downside, a reversal in trend may be signified. The technician must be very alert and observe daily a particular issue in order to detect a price reversal before it has moved a significant distance.

The Down Trend

After a topside reversal signal has been completed, the market price of the stock usually moves downward, following a definite trend as illustrated in Figure 18-9. The market price of the stock frequently moves up to the major down-trend line, falls below it, and then approaches it again. This trend often continues for 6 to 24 months before the rate of decline drops or a reversal in trend is indicated.

Addressograph-Multigraph (Fig. 18-9) declined in price from 1961 through 1963, and during May and June of 1964, the issue appeared to be forming a rounded bottom (saucer) or an inverted head and shoulders. Either of these formations is bullish and indicates that a major reversal in the downward trend has taken place. The market price of the stock did move toward a more reasonable price–earnings relationship, and the earnings report for the quarter ended April 1964 was somewhat better than that for the same quarter of 1963.

FIGURE 18-9 / Bearish formations. From *Trendline Daily Basis Stock Charts,* New York, Trendline Corporation, July 10, 1964.

Estimating the Move

The distance a common stock is expected to move may be estimated with the use of gaps, flags, halfway consolidations, the base of a triangle or a rectangle, the distance from the head to the neckline of an inverted head and shoulders, or the radius of a saucer.

Gaps

In general, the three types of gaps recognized by technicians are the break-away, measuring, and exhaustion gaps. The *break-away gap* frequently occurs near the neckline of an inverted head and shoulders or just above the consolidation pattern in a break-out move from a saucer, rectangle, or triangle and is usually created by extremely heavy volume. *Measuring*

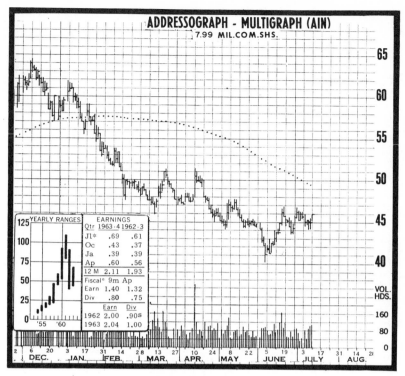

FIGURE 18-9 (*Continued*)

gaps frequently occur approximately 40 to 50 percent of the distance up the entire move. An *exhaustion gap* sometimes appears near the top of a completed move. A break-away gap and two measuring gaps appear in the chart on Stevens & Company (Fig. 18-10), but no exhaustion gap occurred. The highest measuring gap is almost equidistant between the break-away gap and the extent of the move, which was to $50. Another indication that Stevens common had approximately completed its move was indicated by the low volume in the final stage of the upward move. As the market price of the stock turned down, volume increased. Although the measuring gap may not indicate the exact amount of the move, it is indicative that the move is probably about half completed and is a signal to the technician to watch volume and price movements in order to determine a reversal in the trend.

Legs and Consolidations

Frequently an upward trend is completed in three similar legs with intermediate consolidations. The market value moves up for a distance, pulls back some one third to one half of this leg, moves up again, pulls back, and moves up in the final stage. Figure 18-10 on Stevens indicates a flag in September 1964 and a pennant in October 1964. Each of these legs is approxi-

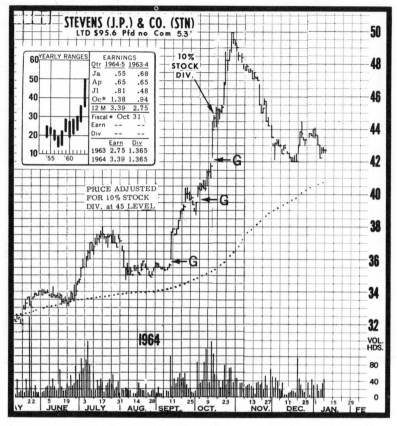

FIGURE 18-10 / Estimating the move. From *Trendline Daily Basis Stock Charts,* New York, Trendline Corporation, January 8, 1965.

mately one third of the total distance. Sometimes stocks move downward in two legs with a slight rally between them, as illustrated in the chart on Southern Pacific (Fig. 18-10). This issue formed a head and shoulders, broke the neckline, and went into a horizontal consolidation for about two months. The second downward leg was similar to the first one. During November and December 1964, the issue appeared to be forming a symmetrical triangle.

Consolidations may take the form of pennants or flags, symmetrical triangles, descending triangles, ascending triangles, descending wedges, or inverted head and shoulders. These figures are usually continuation patterns, although a reversal in trend sometimes occurs from these formations. Once the consolidation is spotted, the investor may wish to add to his holding of the issue, or he may wish to make a new acquisition of an issue that appears to have an additional substantial move in front of it. As long as the price continues to rise on heavy volume and to fall on light volume, the consolidation movement is normally a digestion period for the market. After a period of time, the stock usually continues its upward trend.

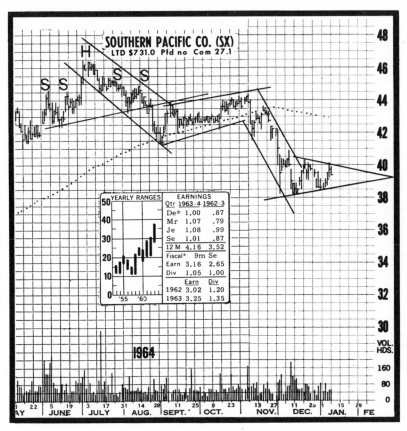

FIGURE 18-10 (*Continued*)

Part-way consolidations also appear approximately half way down a bearish movement. These often take the form of a down flag or a down pennant, but they may be in the form of a triangle, an inverted saucer, or a head and shoulders.

Bases of Triangles and Rectangles

When the price breaks from a triangle or a rectangle, the exent of the move is expected to be the distance of the base of the triangle or rectangle. After this distance has been reached, another continuation pattern or reversal pattern is usually formed.

Depth of Head and Shoulders and Saucers

When an issue breaks out of an inverted head and shoulders, technicians feel that it is expected to continue its move at least the depth of the head to the neckline above the neckline. When a greater move occurs, it is frequently marked with flags, pennants, or other consolidation movements, and if gaps occur in upward moves on especially strong volume, the issue is expected to rise for some additional distance.

Stocks that break from a saucer base are expected to move at least the distance of the radius of the saucer. Frequently the market value of the stock advances about this distance, forms another saucer, and moves upward again. Some issues form numerous saucers within a major trend channel.

Tools of the Technician

The primary tools of the technician are his supply of charts and his ability to interpret them. In order to locate 6 to 12 reliable formations, the technician should maintain charts on 75 to 200 different stock issues and should diversify his charts so that he includes some on issues in various industries. In this way, he may catch a movement in a certain industry and add other charts on companies within this industry. For example, if airlines become very strong, the technician may add charts on airlines so that he may detect some laggards in the industry and thus be able to take profits on some slow or late movers.

Support and Resistance Levels

A *resistance level* is a congested trading range above the current price level. In the Standard Oil of California chart (Fig. 18-2), there was a resistance level around $68 in 1964, and the issue had difficulty in rising above this price, but once it did break through on the topside, the resistance level became a support level. When the market price of the stock declined in December 1964, it did not break through this support level, but continued upward for a time. A resistance level in Unexcelled Chemical Corporation (Fig. 18-4) was formed in July at $17 per share. After the stock price moved above this figure, it had difficulty penetrating below $17 per share. As it increased above $18 per share, this figure became a *support level*, or a congested trading range below the current price, so that the stock had difficulty breaking below this price.

There is often a tendency for support and resistance levels to be on even dollars, and if the investor stops to think about the reasoning behind this pattern, it may become more obvious. The stock of Unexcelled Chemical hit $18 twice in June, twice in July, and once in August. When it rose to $20 per share, many individuals noted the rise and resolved to buy the stock if it dropped back to $18 per share. Limited orders to buy the issue at that price would have added some price support. As the market price of the shares increased, limited orders to buy the stock were given at the previous support levels. Texas Utilities common (Fig. 18-5) made three assaults on its resistance level at $66. The issue was unable to break this barrier, but it did establish a significant amount of trading at $64. When the issue finally broke from the bottom of the ascending triangle, the $64 then became a resistance level and the market price of the stock had difficulty in breaking the new, lower resistance level.

Stop Orders

Suppose that an individual had bought Shell Oil common at $45 (Fig. 18-4) and was holding the stock in early January 1965, when the market price was about $58. Assuming that he wished to protect a part of his book profits, where should he place his stop order? A congested trading area appears between 54 and 55, and if the market price of the stock is able to break through this area on the downside, it may fall to about 51. Therefore, approximately 53¾ appears to be a strategic position for a stop order. In reality, 57 appears to be a support level, but stop orders probably should not be set closer than 10 or 15 percent below the prevailing market value, or a momentary decline may activate the stop order prior to another upward movement.

For the individual who uses daily-basis stock charts as a tool in finding short-sale candidates, the use of a stop buy order is recommended. The stop buy should protect the short seller from a runaway, upward move in the stock, and the price should be set just above the resistance level. If the issue breaks through the resistance level, it will probably continue upward for a significant move. In general, the short sale is more dangerous than the long purchase because a stock sold short may move upward by 200 or 300 percent, while a stock may not decline by more than 100 percent. Rarely does an issue fall more than 25 or 50 percent over a short time period, but some unusual news, such as a proposed merger or a rich mineral discovery, may send a stock upward by 50 or 100 percent or more in a few weeks.

Limited Orders

Since most issues move up and back in a well-defined pattern, the patient investor or speculator may make use of these expected moves in setting his purchase price. Suppose that a stock is trading at 36 and the support level appears to be at 34. He may place an order to buy 100 shares at 34⅛ with a good chance that the order will be filled. There may be a large number of limited orders ahead of the purchaser at the even dollar; therefore, an order to purchase the stock at 34⅛ will have a greater chance of being filled than an order at exactly 34. Trying to squeeze the last eighth or quarter of a point may mean that the order is not executed.

Other Tools

The technician should use the measuring gap, the measuring consolidations, and other indicators of the distance of the probable move in determining when an issue should be sold. Perhaps most important, he should watch the volume pattern. When volume becomes relatively light on increased prices and when the price declines on heavy volume, the issue is probably preparing for a major reversal in direction.

An Evaluation of Bar Chart Patterns

In an attempt to evaluate the usefulness of the most frequently occurring vertical bar chart patterns as buying and selling signals, the 960 weekly range charts regularly carried in *Trendline's Current Market Perspectives* were analyzed for the period July 1961 through December 1964. The maximum actual moves above the break-out points were compared to the expected moves within 90 days and within 12 months of the break out.

The three bottomside reversal patterns analyzed were the (1) inverted head and shoulders, (2) saucer, and (3) rectangle base, while the three topside reversal patterns tabulated included the (1) head and shoulders, (2) inverted saucer, and (3) rectangle top. The relative moves were then classified for low-priced stocks (below $20), medium-priced stocks ($20 to $50), and high-priced stocks (above $50) at the break-out point. The time period, mid-1961 through 1964, was chosen because it (1) included the stock market break of early 1962, (2) covered the bull market of 1963–1964, and (3) permitted the pattern predictions in late 1964 to be checked against the results of the next 12 months. The formations were not tabulated as a pattern unless the break-out point was actually reached.

The frequency of occurrence and reliability of selected uncertainty patterns were also tested for the same period from the 960 charts. These patterns included: the broadening coil upward (the inverted ascending wedge); the broadening coil downward (the inverted descending wedge); the narrowing coil upward (the ascending wedge); the narrowing coil downward (the descending wedge); the symmetrical triangle; and the inverted symmetrical triangle.

The saucer pattern occurred almost twice as frequently as the inverted head and shoulders, while the number of occurrences of the rectangle was very small (see Table A-1 in the Appendix). The bearish head and shoulders pattern, conversely, occurred about one and a half times as often as the inverted saucer. A majority of the bearish patterns occurred at the top of the stock market cycle in early 1962, while a majority of the bullish patterns occurred late in 1962 and during 1963 and 1964.

Vertical bar chart users suggest that the expected move above the break-out point—the neckline of an inverted head and shoulders and the saucer or the top of a rectangle—is about equal to the depth of the pattern below the configuration. Some writers suggest that the move from a pattern is related to the time over which the pattern is formed, but the study described above produced little evidence to support this belief. There did, however, appear to be a high degree of correlation between the depth of a move below and above the pivotal point (the break-out line). The average move, expressed as a percentage of the expected move, that occurred within 90 days of the break out varied somewhat for the low-, high-, and medium-priced issues and for the types of formations analyzed. On the average, the maximum relative move that occurred within 12 months of the break out was about two to two and a quarter times that which occurred within 90 days, a finding that supports the strategy of trading frequently if one disregards the cost of stock transfer and income tax differences.

The average of the actual moves expressed as percentages of the expected moves for the patterns are shown in Figure 18-11. The data suggest that the bull has a slight advantage in taking profits when buying on a topside break out from the rectangle in low-priced stocks and from the saucer in medium-priced issues. The long-term investor should seek long rectangular consolidation patterns or very deep saucer patterns in order to obtain the highest profit potential with extended price rises for a year or longer.

The bear, conversely, should concentrate in the higher-priced issues that have formed inverted saucers or head and shoulders. Contrary to general belief, the low-priced issues did not prove to be as profitable in short selling as did the "high fliers" of 1962. The bear gained little by sticking with his short sale for more than 90 days, while the investor who bought at a pattern break out earned about two and a quarter times the move in a year that ordinarily occurred in a quarter. This difference was no doubt influenced strongly by the 25 percent decline in Standard & Poor's Average of 500 stocks during less than six months of 1962 and the more gradual recovery of 1963 and 1964 where a majority of the bullish formations were occurring.

Frequency distributions and histograms for six types of formations in which the actual moves are contrasted to the expected moves within 90 and 365 days are reported in the Appendix. The data should be studied carefully in order to evaluate the usefulness of these selected types of chart patterns. Similar studies should also be made of the daily-basis stock charts and the latter updated periodically. Chart patterns that occur during one type of market may be somewhat different from those that appear during another time period.

The frequency of occurrence and the reliability of selected uncertainty patterns that appeared on the 960 weekly range charts from mid-1961 through 1964 are shown in Table 18-1. The broadening coil and the inverted symmetrical triangle occurred only 15 times, approximately divided between topside and bottomside break outs. Warning signals—almost always in the form of a saucer or inverted saucer—occurred in all instances of the broadening coil upward and the broadening coil downward.

In the narrowing coil upward, topside and bottomside break outs were approximately equal in number, while 80 percent of the narrowing coils downward had topside break outs. Of these 30 formations, 2 gave no signal of a break out and 4 gave false signals. False signals occurred in about 20

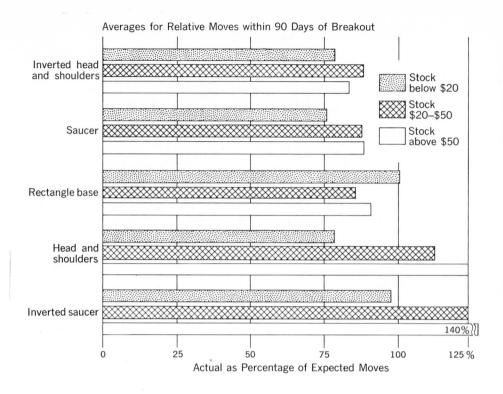

Averages for Relative Moves within 90 Days of Breakout

Inverted head
and shoulders

Stock
below $20

Stock
$20–$50

Stock
above $50

Saucer

Rectangle base

Head and
shoulders

Inverted saucer

140%

0   25   50   75   100   125 %

Actual as Percentage of Expected Moves

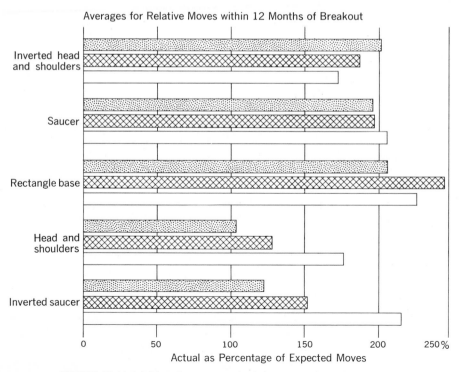

Averages for Relative Moves within 12 Months of Breakout

Inverted head
and shoulders

Saucer

Rectangle base

Head and
shoulders

Inverted saucer

0   50   100   150   200   250%

Actual as Percentage of Expected Moves

FIGURE 18-11 / Arithmetic average of relative moves for selected patterns
occurring on 960 vertical bar charts, 1961–1964.

TABLE 18-1 / Frequency of Occurrence and Reliability of Selected Uncertainty Patterns on 960 Weekly Range Charts from 1960–1965

Pattern	Topside Break Out			Bottomside Break Out		
	Number of Occurrences	Warning Signals	False Signals	Number of Occurrences	Warning Signals	False Signals
Broadening coil upward	7	100%	—	5	100%	—
Broadening coil downward[1]	1	100%	—	0	0	—
Narrowing coil upward	53	98%	2%	52	48%	38%
Narrowing coil downward	24	92%	—	6	33%	67%
Symmetrical triangle	32	97%	3%	9	67%	33%
Inverted symmetrical triangle[1]	1	1	—	1	—	100%

[1] Too few to be reliable.

SOURCE: Study of the 960 *Trendline's Current Market Perspectives* weekly range charts covering mid-1961 through 1965.

percent of the narrowing coils upward. The narrowing coil downward was much more reliable than the narrowing coil upward in forecasting a change in price direction.

Summary

The use of the vertical bar chart may aid the investor in improving the timing of his security transactions, and it is often an important tool for the speculator. Many technicians are able to recognize and profit from reliable chart formations which take the form of bullish, bearish, and uncertainty patterns.

Chart formations that are believed to be bullish in nature are the saucer, when accompanied by a similar volume saucer-shaped formation; the inverted head and shoulders, when trading volume is heavy on the upside and light on the downside; the up trend, when the volume is strong on the upside and light on the downside; the upside gap on heavy volume; and the flag and pennant.

When a saucer formation is reversed with a rounded top, and where the volume has a concave upward shape, the pattern is usually bearish. A downward trend is also bearish when the price decline occurs on heavy volume and the price rallies on light volume. Head and shoulders, down pennants, down flags, and gaps on the downside, if on extremely heavy volume, are bearish.

Some formations are not trustworthy because the technician cannot determine which direction the price of the stock will move prior to a break out from the formation. These include the symmetrical triangle, wedge, rectangle, box, and diamond. The ascending triangle is usually, although not always, bullish, while the descending wedge is also usually bullish. The descending triangle and ascending wedge are untrustworthy as forecasting devices.

The extent of a move may be predicted by noticing the location of the break-away, measuring, and exhaustion gaps or by counting the number of legs in the move from the depth of its formation. Some technicians also use the depth of a pattern in forecasting an expected move.

The technical approach to security analysis is an art and not a science. Therefore, the individual should not expect perfection from the use of this method. After using this tool for a period of time, however, one should become more proficient with the method.

QUESTIONS FOR REVIEW /

1. Describe briefly the base and the scale of the vertical bar chart.
2. Of what significance is volume on the vertical bar chart?
3. Contrast charts prepared with monthly, weekly, and daily price ranges.
4. Describe briefly the bullish formations that are discussed in this section.

5. Differentiate between the inverted head and shoulders and the saucer.
6. Enumerate the uncertainty patterns. How may the technician determine when a break out from an uncertainty pattern is expected?
7. How may the technician estimate the distance of an over-all upward or downward move?
8. Illustrate how stop orders and stop buy orders may be used by the technician.
9. How may resistance and support levels be used by the technican in setting his limited orders?
10. Describe briefly the numerous types of measuring consolidations.

PROBLEMS /

1. Using your library facilities, obtain charts on five issues that appear to be forming bottomside reversals. Does the technical strength appear to be preceding or following the upturn in earnings?
2. By use of the daily trading range, given in *The Wall Street Journal* or some other daily newspaper, or the weekly trading range, given in *Barron's, Commercial and Financial Chronicle,* or some other weekly newspaper, prepare charts for a period of six or eight months on five issues and identify the formations that appear thereon.

REFERENCES /

Edwards, Robert D., and John McGee. *Technical Analysis of Stock Trends.* Springfield, Mass.: John McGee, 1964.

Jiler, William, *How Charts Can Help You in the Stock Market.* New York: Commodity Research Publications Corporation, 1962.

Lankford, Harry, *Quote American.* Wichita, Kan.: Harry Lankford.

Moody's Handbook of Common Stocks. New York: Moody's Investors Service, Inc.

Standard & Poor's Corporation, *Stock Market Encyclopedia.* New York: Standard & Poor's.

Trendline Corporation, *Trendline's Current Market Perspectives.* New York: Trendline.

————, *Trendline's Daily Basis Stock Charts.* New York: Trendline.

The Value Line Investment Survey. New York: A. Bernhard & Company, Inc.

chapter 19 | The Point-and-Figure Chart Method

Introduction

The purposes of this chapter are to (1) present a brief description of the point-and-figure chart method, (2) indicate the usual types of bullish and bearish formations that appear on these charts, (3) show how up trends and down trends may be determined by the use of point-and-figure charts, (4) illustrate how the probable move of an issue can be estimated from the size and shape of the formations, and (5) evaluate the usefulness of the method.

Many of the formations that develop on the vertical bar chart (Chapter 18) also appear on the point-and-figure chart in approximately the same pattern. In some instances, however, the configurations are different, but one should be able to mentally transpose a pattern from one type of chart to the other.

There are some advantages as well as some disadvantages in using the point-and-figure chart rather than the daily or weekly vertical bar chart. Since on a bar chart the price range and volume of an issue are recorded for each day on a separate line, patterns may run over numerous pages. With the point-and-figure chart, however, price movements for six or eight years may be placed across a single page, since prices are recorded in the same column as long as they move in the same direction, and thus upward and downward trends are easily discernible. Patterns often repeat on a given stock, so that historical charts provide valuable information for estimating probable future price moves and in determining support and resistance levels. Another minor advantage of the point-and-figure chart is that small insignificant moves are disregarded and only the wider, more important moves are recorded (a move of less than three squares is ordinarily disregarded). Accumulation and distribution of the stock are also easily detected on the point-and-figure chart.

Construction of Point-and-Figure Charts

The point-and-figure chart is constructed on arithmetic graph paper, with the vertical axis representing the price of the issue and the horizontal axis showing the flexible time scale. One may select whatever scale is convenient, but it is recommended that a square represent 50 cents for stocks selling below $20 a share, $1 for stocks trading between $20 and $100, and $3 for stocks trading above $100. For stocks trading below $5 a share, some technicians choose to have a square represent 25 cents. The smaller the scale the smaller the moves that can be indicated, but the changes are more in line with the price at which the stock is trading. For example, with a $5 stock, a move of 25 cents represents 5 percent, which is as significant as a $2 move on a $40 stock. Only full square moves are recorded, and fractional squares are disregarded.

A daily-basis vertical bar chart covering at least six to eight months is usually needed before patterns are clearly discernible. The investor who wishes to use the point-and-figure chart, however, should have one that covers at least three or four years. For this reason, and because it is difficult and time consuming to prepare these charts by hand, it is more expedient to obtain prepared charts. Periodically, say at least once a year, the investor may wish to obtain a trial subscription to one of the leading point-and-figure chart services and maintain up-to-date charts on certain issues by posting from his financial newspaper. The costs of such services range from $3 to $25 an issue.

While some point-and-figure chart services use the single-square reversal method, others employ the three-square method.[1] Beginning at the starting point with Armour & Company in Figure 19-2, X's were placed in the first column as the price increased. No recording of a price reversal was made until the stock fell by at least three full squares, and then the squares were filled in with 0's. The small numbers that appear within the chart (1–12) represent the months of the year and indicate the period of time over which a given move took place. Some services, such as Chartcraft, Inc., prefer to use X's to denote rising prices and 0's to denote falling prices, but others use X's for both advances and declines. The former method is recommended, since the technician can more easily determine whether the price is rising or falling at any point in time, and it also facilitates chart posting. One should not attempt to maintain more charts than his time will permit, for once one falls a few weeks behind in posting, it is difficult to bring the charts up to date. Posting from the weekly trading range of *Barron's, Commercial and Financial Chronicle,* or some other newspaper will catch a majority of the three-point reversal moves, although small intraday and intraweek moves may be missed. Daily recording may be undertaken, but the amount of time required for posting is approximately equivalent to that required for noting weekly changes.

Alexander H. Wheelan, an associate of Morgan, Rogers, and Roberts, Inc., of New York City, a supplier of point-and-figure charts, uses the one-

---

[1] Chartcraft, Inc., of Larchmont, New York, has various types of chart services to which the individual may subscribe. See advertisements in *The Wall Street Journal* or in *Barron's* for this and other chart services.

square reversal method. This company provides charts showing intraday reversals for both stocks and commodities.[2]

Chart Patterns

The basic patterns that appear on the point-and-figure chart are presented in Figure 19-1. The patterns that are indicated at the bottom, or base, of a formation are almost identical to those that appear at the top except that the patterns are just flipped topside down. Point-and-figure chart analysts recognize about 13 basic chart patterns, with combinations and variation of these.

The *bullish signal formation* is illustrated in Figure 19-1,a. A downward move of several squares is followed by an upward move of five or six squares, which is then followed by another downward move repeated by an upward move that breaks the previous high and gives a buy signal. The *bearish signal formation* is the opposite of the bullish pattern. When a previous low is broken, a sell signal is indicated. Frequently the formation will be only four columns wide, but it may be substantially wider. If so, it is classified as a combination bullish signal and triple top (see Fig. 19-1,f).

Instead of regular ascending or descending triangles as are produced by bullish and bearish signals, variations of these formations may be less regularly shaped and therefore more difficult to recognize, although they are just as valid as the regular formations. In these irregular formations, the bottoms of the bullish patterns or tops of the bearish figures do not follow the diagonal trend line exactly but drop below it or fail to pull back to it.

In the formation of a *triple top* (Fig. 19-1,c), three assaults were made on the top of the formation before the break out appeared. Once the previous high was broken, a buy signal was indicated. Variations of the triple top and triple bottom patterns also appear in Figure 19-1,c.

The *bullish triangle* and the *bearish triangle* are actually formed identically. However, the move from the former is upward, whereas the break out from the latter is downward. This pattern is very similar to the symmetrical triangle that appears on vertical bar charts and is classified as an uncertainty pattern in that the analyst cannot tell the direction of the move until the break out occurs. A false signal frequently is given on this type of formation, with a break out in one direction immediately followed by a change in direction which carries to the other side of the pattern. Wheelan refers to this move as a swing.[3] The extent of the move from a swing is approximately

---

[2] Morgan, Rogers, and Roberts, Inc., offers point-and-figure chart services on New York Stock Exchange issues, American Stock Exchange issues, commodities, and numerous stock averages. A price list for these services may be obtained from the company, or from advertisements that appear in leading financial newspapers. Point-and-figure charts are also produced by W. R. S. M. Financial Service Corporation of New York, and other investors' services.

[3] See A. H. Wheelan, *Study Helps in Point and Figure Technique* (New York: Morgan, Rogers, and Roberts, Inc., 1954), p. 23.

Bottoms   Tops

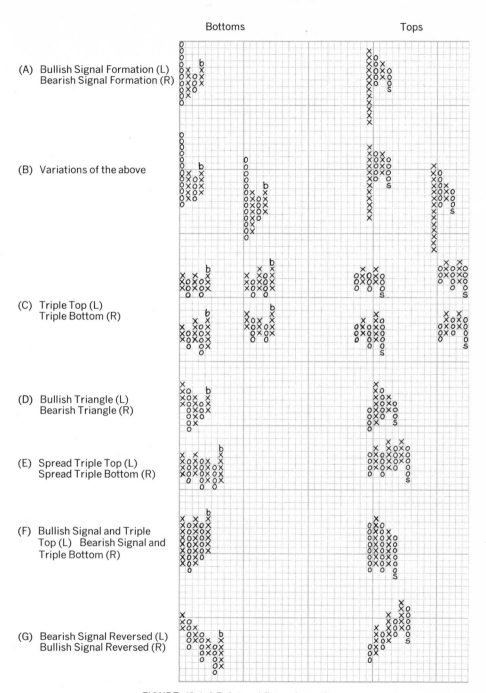

(A) Bullish Signal Formation (L)
    Bearish Signal Formation (R)

(B) Variations of the above

(C) Triple Top (L)
    Triple Bottom (R)

(D) Bullish Triangle (L)
    Bearish Triangle (R)

(E) Spread Triple Top (L)
    Spread Triple Bottom (R)

(F) Bullish Signal and Triple
    Top (L)   Bearish Signal and
    Triple Bottom (R)

(G) Bearish Signal Reversed (L)
    Bullish Signal Reversed (R)

FIGURE 19-1 / Point-and-figure formations.

equal above and below the center of the triangle. If a price breaks above the triangle by six squares and then immediately falls downward, it is presumed to fall about six squares below the triangle before resuming its formation of a new pattern.

The *spread triple top* is similar to the triple top formation, except that one or two assaults are made on the top of the formation in an attempt to break the resistance level, although some of the moves do not carry completely to the top.

The *bullish triple top* formation shown in Figure 19-1,f is a combination of the ascending triangle on the bottom of the formation, with the triple top appearing on the top. A break out above a previous high denotes a buy signal, while the inverse of this formation is a *bearish triple bottom* formation.

The *bearish signal reversal* appears to be somewhat like a series of bearish triangles, with the bullish signal formation completing the pattern. The *bullish signal reversal* (Fig. 19-1,g) indicates a reversal in an upward movement, and when a previous low has been broken, a sell signal is given. These formations appear on a vertical bar chart as the left shoulder and head of a head and shoulders or an inverted head and shoulders for the bullish and bearish signal reversal patterns, respectively. In fact, Wheelan refers to these formations by the same name.[4]

A large number of interesting formations appear on the point-and-figure chart for Armour & Company (Fig. 19-2). The configuration that formed from 1950 through 1952 appeared to be a gigantic bullish signal formation. The pattern was never completed by a break out, however, and a smaller bullish signal pattern formed from 1952 through 1955. When the stock rose to $11.50 in December 1955, the spread double top formation was completed. The issue broke from the bottomside of what appeared to be the beginning of a bullish signal pattern, but enough buying pressure was generated so that the swing was reversed, and the issue actually did move approximately the distance above as below the formation, or three squares. After moving to 22 per share in May 1956, the issue fell back to 14½. A slight rally in November 1956 completed a head and shoulders, when the price of the issue declined to 14. A large inverted head and shoulders formation appeared from January 1957 to June 1958. From 1958 to 1959, the issue formed a triple-top, and four assaults were made before a breakthrough actually appeared at 18½ in November 1958. Bullish triangles occurred on the ascent of the stock from 1959 through a part of 1960, when the issue fell from a bullish signal reversal pattern and then formed a bearish signal reversal pattern with a double base. A bullish signal formation was completed in 1961, and the sell signal was given in August when the price fell to 43. Almost immediately, the stock formed a bullish signal formation and moved upward to 51, at which point another bearish signal formation took

[4] Wheelan, pp. 16 and 25.

shape. The bearish triangle, or halfway consolidation, was formed in 1962, when a bearish signal reversal pattern was formed. A bullish signal reversal pattern was also formed in late 1962 and early 1963 prior to the formation of another bearish signal reversal pattern in 1963. In 1964 a broad-based bearish reversal signal appeared to be forming. Buy signals were given when the price of the stock hit 48 and 49. Almost all the formations that appeared on this point-and-figure chart became valid buy or sell signals, although they may have come so late as to wipe out a part of the profit the investor could have made.

Trend Lines

Trend lines appear somewhat differently on the single-square and the three-square reversal charts. With the latter method, a chart is squeezed together, and the trend line is drawn at a 45-degree angle, which is done by joining the opposite diagonals of each square. The price decline from 1957 through 1961 for Armour (Fig. 19-2) closely approached the trend line which appeared to support the market price of the stock. Once a stock has broken through a major up-trend line, point and figure technicians contend that a down trend has been established. In April 1962, when Armour stock fell to $46 per share, a bearish signal was given, the stock fell to the up-trend line, where a symmetrical triangle broke from the bottom, forming a bearish triangle, and another sell signal was given at $39 per share. The up trend was not signaled until a bearish signal reversal was formed in late 1962.

The use of the single full square reversal method by Morgan, Rogers, and Roberts, Inc., produces a chart pattern that is spread out and that shows intraday moves of more than one full square. One such chart is illustrated in Figure 19-3 for Class A stock of Columbia Broadcasting System. The trend line is drawn by joining the major rallies on the down trend, or the major declines on the up trend. An up trend was signaled when the stock broke above the down-trend line at $30 per share in October 1951. The charts are marked in a slightly different manner from those prepared by Chartcraft. For example, X's denote both falling and rising prices; the small letters are initials of the months, and $10 trading units are indicated by a 0 and $5 trading units by a 5. Dividend declarations are recorded with a circle, and dividend amounts are shown on the base of the chart immediately below the ex-dividend date. An up-trend line may be drawn on the chart from the $27 entry in November to the 40 in August 1952. In 1952 and 1953, the issue generally followed the up trend and appeared to be forming an inverted head and shoulders from December 1950 through August 1951. The extent of the upward move was not nearly as great as had been expected for the issue; frequently when a bullish signal is given below a major down-trend line, the signal is not reliable. A bearish signal given above a major up-trend line may also be misleading. Analysts maintain that bullish signals given above major up-trend lines as well as bearish signals given below major down-trend lines

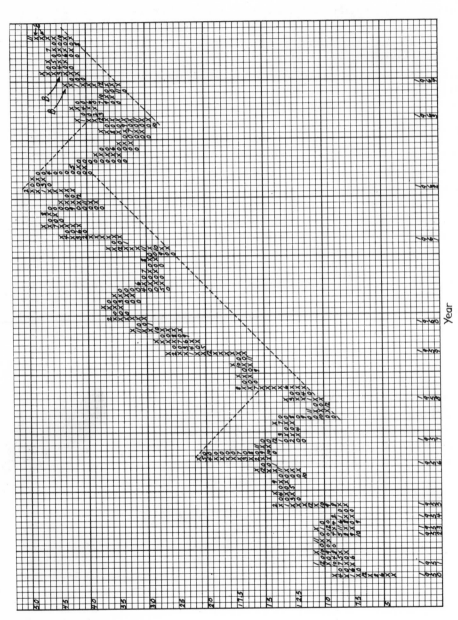

FIGURE 19-2 / Point-and-figure chart on Armour & Company, 1950–1964. From *Chartcraft Long Term P & F Chart Book*, Larchmont, N.Y., Chartcraft, Inc., 1965, p. 42.

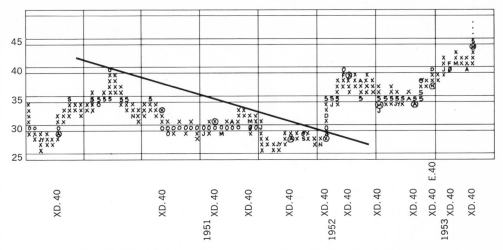

FIGURE 19-3 / Point-and-figure chart on Columbia Broadcasting System,
A. From A. H. Wheelan, *Study Helps in Point and Figure
Technique,* New York, Morgan, Rogers, and Roberts, Inc.,
1964, p. 35.

are usually reliable. The formation from June through July 1951 would be
referred to by Wheelan as a single fulcrum, and the width of this formation,
12 squares, approximates the expected extent of the move. Actually, the stock
moved 13 squares instead of 12, which provided a close approximation to
the extent of that move. The congested trading area that occurred during the
first half of 1952 gave a sell signal at $35 in April. Subsequent to that time,
the stock rallied to $39 per share before falling the expected six or seven
squares. After falling to the $34–35 support level, the market price of the
issue rallied to begin its upward move.

Support and Resistance Levels

Support and resistance levels are described in Chapter 19. However, some
slight differences which do not appear on the vertical bar chart are evident
on the point and figure chart with regard to them. The principle of the
levels is the same, but the analyst with a chart that covers 8 or 10 years is in
a better position to determine a resistance or support level than someone who
is using a chart with a range of only 6 or 12 months. When a stock has broken
into a new high, there is no overhanging supply, or resistance level, to depress the market price, and for this reason, an issue that breaks into a new
high may have a tendency to spring upward for an extensive move. Conversely, if an issue has declined in price and attempts a recovery, much of the
stock that is in weak hands (that is, owned by easily panicked holders) must
be traded before the issue can break through the congested trading areas.

Figure 19-4 for Occidental Petroleum Corporation contains a number
of support and resistance levels. In January 1962, the issue rose to $26 per

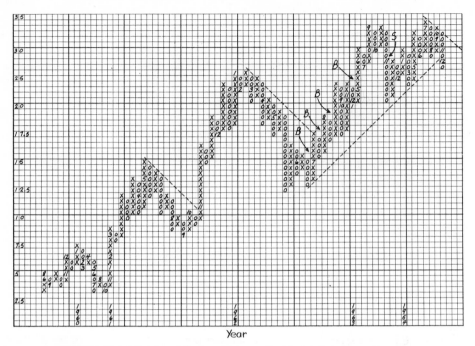

Year

FIGURE 19-4 / Point-and-figure chart on Occidental Petroleum Corporation, 1959–1965. From *Chartcraft Long Term P & F Chart
Book,* Larchmont, N.Y., Chartcraft, Inc., 1965, p. 301.

share and formed a bullish signal reversal, establishing the major down-
trend line. After falling to 12½, a decline of 50 percent in less than six
months, the market price of the stock began to rally upward. The issue
formed a symmetrical triangle from May through June 1962, broke out on
the bottomside, immediately formed a swing, and rallied to 17½. The stock
met some selling pressure at that point, declined to 15½, where it encountered support, rallied, and ran into selling pressure at 18½. A large number
of shares changed hands during the congested trading area from July through
August 1962, and the stock attempted to break into an all-time high. Selling
pressure, presumably by individuals who had bought the stock between 21
and 24 in early 1962 and some profit takers, drove the price down, and it was
only after many of these earlier purchasers had liquidated that the stock was
able to break above its all-time high and into a new trading range. The extent
of the move carried the stock to 34. The congested trading area at about 21
to 24 offered a resistance level when the price fell below this level, but after
the issue had broken above this point, it became a support level. It is
theorized that investors who had not purchased the stock at about 21 decided to do so if the price fell back to that position. Other investors—
perhaps those who had liquidated earlier at similar or higher prices—wanted
to buy the stock at around 25 or 26, so that a support level was formed at that

price. The stock formed a bearish signal reversal in the last half of 1964 and gave a sell signal at 28 in December, when a previous low was broken. After breaking through the major up-trend line, the downward extent of the move was expected to be significant. The 21–23 price range did, however, appear to offer some support on the decline.

Estimating the Extent of the Move

The analyst should make an estimate of a move from the number of rows that signify a reversal. If he uses a single-square reversal in changing columns for ascending X's and descending 0's, the extent of the move is expected to be approximately the width of the formation. On the other hand, if he uses a three-square reversal in direction before changing columns, the extent of the move is expected to be about three times the width of the rows. These are merely estimates, and the point-and-figure chart does not indicate the amount of time that will be required for the price to attain the expected level. The only way to obtain a clue with regard to the time element is to study past formations to determine whether the issue has usually moved quickly or slowly. For this reason, marking the years and months on a chart is an aid in gauging the probable time that will be required for a given move to be completed.

Close estimates of price moves appear on the 1960–1964 chart for Occidental Petroleum. The bearish signal reversal that was indicated in late 1961 is 8 squares wide. Multiplying 8 by 3, one obtains an estimated move of 24 squares. If the analyst measures the extent of an upward move from the lowest price row that includes the largest number of X's and 0's across the formation, 9½ or 10, and counts the squares from this point, he finds that the price objective is approximately 23. In reality, the price rose to 26. In estimating the distance of the move downward in early 1962, a bullish signal reversal of 6 squares wide times 3 represents 18 squares, so that the price was expected to fall from 25 to approximately 13 (it actually fell to 12½). The bearish triangle formed in mid-1962 produced a swing that was expected to carry some 5 points above the center of the triangle, and this level was attained exactly before another bullish triangle appeared (or in the opinion of some analysts, a bullish signal formation) of about 5 squares in width. The extent of the move was expected to be about 15 squares, but was actually 19. The sell signal that was indicated in October 1963 was expected to drop the stock approximately 12 squares, from a price of 33 to about 21, and in reality, the move was to 21.

In the charts illustrated in Figures 19-3 and 19-4, the formations were clearly discernible, and the estimated moves occurred with a high degree of accuracy. The value of a method, however, lies in its ability to outperform other methods. In order to evaluate the point-and-figure chart technique in terms of long-term investment results, the 30 Dow Jones Industrials were used as a sample for the five-year period, 1961 to 1965. Although the number of issues studied is too small to produce a fair evaluation of the method, it does indicate the type of analysis that should be undertaken on a broad scale. This study will be described in the following section.

Investing in the Dow Jones Industrials

Leading point-and-figure chart services suggest that greater profits may result if one invests in an issue which is "on the move." They note that a

TABLE 19-1 / Variation in Performance of International Harvester under Five Investment Schemes Using Three-Square Reversal Point-and-Figure Charts, 1961 to 1965

Date	Transaction	Shares	Net per Share	Amount
(1)				
1–61	Buy	396.04	25.25	$10,000
5–62	Sell	396.04	22.72	8998
2–63	Buy	329.96	27.27	8998
6–65	Sell	329.96	35.57	11,737
12–65	Buy	270.25	43.43	11,737
12–65	Sell	270.25	46.44	12,550
Net Gain of $2550, or 25.50%				
(2)				
1– 2–61	Buy	396.04	25.25	$10,000
12–31–65	Sell	396.04	46.44	18,392
Net Gain of $8392, or 83.92%				
(3)				
1–61	Buy	396.04	25.25	10,000
5–62	Sell	396.04	22.72	8998
5–62	Sell Short	396.04	22.72	8998
2–63	Cover	396.04	27.27	10,800
2–63	Buy	263.88	27.27	7196
6–65	Sell	263.88	35.57	9386
6–65	Sell Short	263.88	35.57	9386
12–65	Cover	263.88	43.43	11,460
12–65	Buy	168.36	43.43	7312
12–65	Sell	168.36	46.44	7819
Net Loss of $2181, or 21.81%				

(1) Buy on buy signal, sell on sell signal.
(2) Bought on 1/2/61, sold on 12/31/65.
(3) Buy on buy, sell on sell signal, short on sell, cover on buy, repeat.

SOURCE: Compiled from *Chartcraft Long Term P & F Chart Book*, 1966 ed. (Larchmont, N.Y.: Chartcraft, Inc., 1966).

TABLE 19-1 (Continued)

Date	Transaction	Shares	Net per Share	Amount
(4)				
1–61	Buy	396.04	25.25	10,000
2–61	Sell	396.04	27.66	10,954
2–62	Buy	387.34	28.28	10,954
5–63	Sell	387.34	30.63	11,864
2–64	Buy	367.08	32.32	11,864
5–64	Sell	367.08	35.57	13,057
12–65	Buy	300.64	43.43	13,057
12–31–65	Sell	300.64	46.44	13,962
		Net Gain of $3962, or 39.62%		
(5)				
1–61	Buy	380.81	26.26	10,000
6–62	Sell	380.81	25.69	9783
		Net Loss of $217 or 2.17%		

(4) Buy on buy, sell with 10% gross profit, repeat.
(5) After buy signal, wait for decline within two squares of the previous low and buy. After sell signal, wait for rally within two squares of previous top. Repeat.

stock that has broken a previous intermediate high is likely to continue in an upward direction for a time. Conversely, they suggest that if an issue falls below a previous intermediate low, it is likely to decline further. Chart services generally recommend that one of the following strategies be followed in using their charts: (1) buy on a buy signal (the breaking of a previous high), and sell on a sell signal (the breaking of a previous low); (2) buy on a buy signal, take a reasonable profit, such as 10 to 15 percent, sell, and wait for another buy signal to repeat the operation; or (3) after a buy signal is given, buy on a decline and hold the issue until a sell signal is given and then sell on a recovery into the bearish formation. The services do not stipulate the amount of the decline or recovery, but in the study of the 30 Dow Jones Industrials declines within two squares of the previous low and rallies within two squares of the previous high were used as guides. Since the services state that the bear signals are also reliable, a trader should profit by going long with a buy signal, selling on a sell signal, shorting the issue on a sell signal, covering on the subsequent buy signal, and repeating the cycle.

The results obtained by employing the above point-and-figure trading strategies with the 30 Dow Jones Industrials from January 1, 1961, through December 31, 1965, were contrasted to those obtained with a straight five-year investment in the issues. The various approaches are illustrated with a $10,000 initial investment in International Harvester common stock. Transfer costs were assumed to be 1 percent on buy orders and 1.2 percent on sell orders to facilitate computations, and the number of shares and net cost or

TABLE 19-2 / **A Comparison of the Rankings of Returns Obtainable on Investments in the 30 Dow Jones Industrials Using Point-and-Figure Charts, 1961 to 1965, with Five Trading Strategies**

	Type of Plan				
Stock	1	2	3	4	5
Allied Chemical	4	3	5	1	2
Aluminum Company of America	4	2	5	1	3
American Can	4	1	5	3	2
American Telephone & Telegraph	3	1	4	2	5
American Tobacco	2	4	1	5	3
Anaconda Company	1	2	3	4	5
Bethlehem Steel	4	5	2	3	1
Chrysler Corporation	2	1	5	3	4
du Pont de Nemours	3	1	5	2	4
Eastman Kodak	2	1	4	3	5
General Electric	4	2	5	1	3
General Foods	3	2	5	1	4
General Motors	3	1	5	2	4
Goodyear Tire	3	2	5	1	4
International Harvester	3	1	5	2	4
International Nickel	4	1	5	2	3
International Paper	5	1	3	2	4
Johns-Manville	3	2	5	4	1
Owens-Illinois Glass	3	1	5	2	4
Proctor and Gamble	2	3	1	4	5
Sears, Roebuck	3	4	2	5	1
Standard Oil of California	3	2	5	4	1
Standard Oil (N.J.)	2	1	4	5	3
Swift and Company	4	2	3	1	5
Texaco	3	1	4	2	5
Union Carbide	3	2	4	1	5
United Aircraft	3	1	4	5	2
U.S. Steel	1	3.5	2	5	3.5
Westinghouse Electric	4	1	5	2	3
Woolworth	4	2	5	3	1
Optimum selections	2	14	2	7	5
Average ranking	3.0	1.9	4.0	2.8	3.3

(1) Buy on buy signal, sell on sell signal.
(2) Bought on 1/2/61, sold on 12/31/65.
(3) Buy on buy, sell on sell signal, short on sell, cover on buy, repeat.
(4) Buy on buy, sell with 10% gross profit, repeat.
(5) After buy signal, wait for decline within two squares of the previous low and buy. After sell signal, wait for rally within two squares of previous top. Repeat.

sources Compiled from *Chartcraft Long Term P & F Chart Book,* 1966 ed. (Larchmont, N.Y.: Chartcraft, Inc., 1966).

proceeds per share were carried to two decimal points in order to reduce rounding errors. For International Harvester, the (1) buy on buy and sell on sell signal strategy produced a net gain of 26 percent over the period (disregarding cash dividends); (2) buy–hold strategy produced an 84 percent profit; (3) long and short strategy yielded a 22 percent loss; (4) taking a 10 percent gross gain after each purchase yielded a 40 percent, five-year gain; and (5) the decline and recovery method produced a 2 percent loss.

The results obtained with the Dow Jones Industrials, assuming an initial investment on or after January 1, 1961, and a final liquidation on December 31, 1965, and disregarding dividends, are reported in Table 19-2. Of the five strategies employed, (1) the buy on buy and sell on sell signal was optimum with two of the issues; (2) the strategy of buying and holding worked best with 14 of the 30 issues; (3) the long and short strategy was best for two of the companies; (4) the strategy of taking a 10 percent gross profit was most profitable with seven of the issues; and (5) the decline and recovery method yielded optimum results in five cases. The average ranking was best for buying and holding and poorest for going both long and short.

It should be noted that the Dow Jones Industrials are more stable stocks than secondary-grade securities, and point-and-figure trading strategies may produce more impressive results with wider-swinging stocks. Chart services, however, should test the success of the methods they recommend in order to produce optimum results for their subscribers. This small study strongly suggests that a long-term investment strategy may be superior to a trading strategy when one uses a set of rigid trading rules. The test, however, was somewhat biased against strategies (1), (3), and (5), since the funds were often idle in the accounts for lengthy time periods, while a trader would have sought other opportunities for short-term profits rather than keep funds idle.

The frequency of occurrence of the 13 chart patterns described in this chapter (six bullish, six bearish, and the swing pattern) and the actual as percentages of expected moves were tested for the 30 Dow Jones Industrials from January 1, 1961, through December 31, 1965; the results are reported in Table 19-3. The relative moves, as percentages of expected moves were classified into frequency distributions, with class intervals as follows:

Below 40%
40– 59.9%
60– 79.9%
80–119.9%
120–139.9%
140% and above

The relative frequencies within ±20 percent of the expected results were above one third for the swing, bullish signal, bearish triangle, bearish reversal, and bullish reversal patterns, but the estimates of the expected moves were less accurate for the other patterns in this study.

TABLE 19-3 / Actual as Percentage of Expected Moves for Selected Three-Square Reversal Point-and-Figure Chart Patterns Appearing for the Dow Jones Industrials, 1961 to 1965

Frequency of Occurrence Selected Bullish Patterns

Frequency Interval	Swing	Bullish Signal	Triple Top	Bullish Triangle	Spread Triple Top	Bullish Signal and Triple Top	Bearish Reversal
Below 40%	0	1	5	2	1	0	3
40–59.9%	3	8	10	12	2	1	4
60–79.9%	5	5	10	18	1	1	8
80–119.9%	17	9	9	26	2	1	16
120–139.9%	2	0	0	3	0	1	0
140% or above	7	1	0	10	0	0	4
Total	34	24	34	71	6	4	35
Average move[1]	114%	77%	67%	91%	62%	86%	91%
Within ±20%	50%	39%	26%	37%	33%	25%	46%

Frequency of Occurrence of Selected Bearish Patterns

Frequency Interval	Bearish Signal	Triangle Bottom	Bearish Triangle	Spread Triple Bottom	Bearish Signal and Triangle Bottom	Bullish Reversal
Below 40%	2	1	2	—	1	0
40–59.9%	12	3	9	—	1	7
60–79.9%	9	11	10	—	0	4
80–119.9%	7	3	11	—	1	4
120–139.9%	1	2	3	—	1	1
140% or over	0	0	4	—	0	1
Total	31	19	39	0	4	20
Average move[1]	66%	77%	88%	—	79%	75%
Within ±20%	23%	16%	28%	—	29%	35%

[1] Computed from raw data.

A Word of Caution

Every investor or trader should be suspicious of any method that is suggested as a "sure fire, get rich quick" gimmick. He should either ask for quantitative evidence in support of the claims made by the investment services or he should make independent tests of the method.

Numerous seasoned traders claim to have benefited from the use of point-and-figure charts, but most investors scoff at their usage. The charts are, in reality, no more than an orderly recording of past price data on individual issues. Whether or not a user can profitably employ the chart patterns will continue to be a moot question. The charts do provide a reasonable gauge to forecasting the extent of a move, and the support and resistant levels which are shown on the charts provides worthwhile information to the trader. While some individuals may profit from trading on the basis of charts, others have better operating results from a long-term commitment of funds into well-chosen, aggressive companies.

Summary

Some individuals prefer point-and-figure charts over vertical bar charts. The price movement may be shown for a period of 5 or 10 years on a point-and-figure chart, but the volume pattern is not shown, a factor which is oftentimes an early clue to the reversal in direction of an issue. Buy and sell signals are more clearly defined on the point-and-figure chart, but the timing of the purchase and sale of a stock is difficult.

The bullish formations that appear on the point-and-figure chart include the bullish signal formation, the triple top, the spread triple top, the bullish signal and triple top, the bullish triangle, and the bearish signal reversal pattern. When these formations are inverted they become bearish signals.

Bullish signals that are given above a major up-trend line and bearish signals that are given below a major down-trend line are described by chart analysts as being more reliable than bull signals below a down-trend line or sell signals above an up-trend line. The bullish and bearish triangles, which may be thought of as symmetrical triangles or as uncertainty patterns, may result in a swing without warning.

Point-and-figure chart services suggest numerous schemes for trading in issues, for example, (1) buying on a buy signal and selling on a sell signal; (2) taking a 10 to 15 percent profit after a buy signal and waiting for another buy signal before reinvesting; or (3) buying on a decline after a sell signal and selling on a recovery after a sell signal. The effectiveness of these strategies was contrasted to results obtained on a straight investment in the Dow Jones Industrials from 1961 to 1965. The straight five-year investment produced greater profits than the trading strategies.

Some technicians claim that charts are effective tools in estimating probable moves. A study of the formations appearing on the Dow Jones Industrials from 1961 to 1965 did indicate that some of the formations were reliable in forecasting the extent of the expected move while others were less effective. Support and resistant levels, as well as past chart patterns, are regarded as valuable trading information by numerous chart analysts.

Whether long-term investing or trading on the basis of chart patterns produces better results depends largely on the knowledge and skill of the individual. One must search for a method that one is able to employ profitably and utilize the method as long as it produces satisfactory results.

QUESTIONS FOR REVIEW /

1. Explain briefly how the point-and-figure chart is constructed.
2. What are the major differences between the single-point and the three-point reversal methods? How do the pattern formations differ?
3. What economic justifications can you advance for the formations of the various bullish signals? the various bearish signals?
4. How may support and resistance levels be used in making profits when one trades on the basis of chart patterns?
5. Do you prefer the 10 percent profit rule or the rule of buying on a buy signal and selling on a sell signal? Explain the advantages and disadvantages of each strategy.
6. Explain how one estimates the move of an issue that breaks out of a bullish formation? a bearish formation?
7. Point out some of the major differences between the various point-and-figure chart services that are available on a subscription basis.
8. What is meant by the swing rule?
9. What financial and personal attributes should an individual possess before applying the chart method?
10. Contrast the formations that appear on the daily-basis vertical bar chart with those on the point-and-figure chart.
11. What advantages and disadvantages accrue to the users of vertical bar and point-and-figure charts? How do these charts complement one another?

PROBLEMS /

1. Study the point-and-figure charts shown in Figure 19–5, indicate the types of formations, and compare the expected to actual moves. Would the 15 percent profit rule or the strategy of buying from purchase to sell signal produce more profits for the above stocks?
2. Analyze available up-to-date point-and-figure charts and determine six with buying and six with selling formations. Forecast the expected extent and duration of the move.

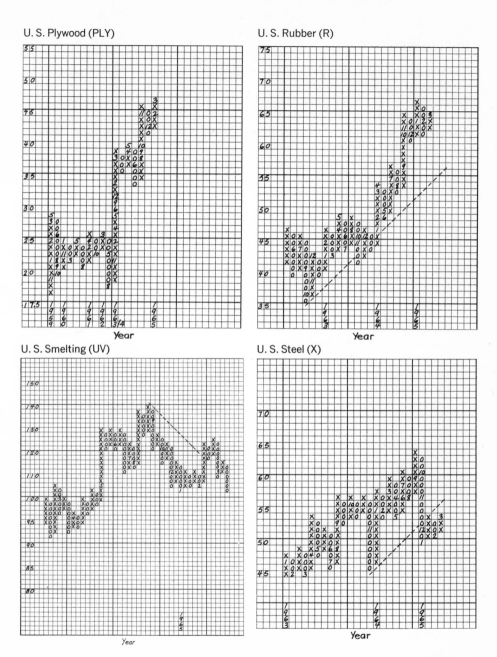

FIGURE 19-5

REFERENCES /

Chartcraft, Inc., *Chartcraft Long Term P & F Chart Book*. Larchmont, N.Y.: Chartcraft, 1965.

Cohen, A. W., *The Chartcraft Method of Point and Figure Trading*. New York: Chartcraft, Inc., 1961.

Wheelan, A. H., *Study Helps in Point and Figure Technique*. New York: Morgan, Rogers, and Roberts, Inc., 1954.

chapter 20 | Technical Indicators of the Stock Market Level

Introduction

Although many technicians believe that the patterns of the individual stock and the direction of its trend line are more important than the market as a whole, it is easier to pick a stock that follows the market trend rather than one that counters the tide. Since false chart signals more frequently appear near the top of an up trend or near the bottom of a down trend, an individual who depends on his charts for specific issues without considering the over-all direction of the market may make wrong decisions more often than correct ones.[1]

This chapter discusses numerous technical indicators that describe the general level of the stock market and that can be used to predict a change in direction. These include stock averages, price–earnings ratios, odd lot indexes, short interest ratios, the advance–decline line, and *Barron's* Confidence Index. Some of these indicators are illustrated graphically in order to show how they may be used to forecast a change in the over-all market direction. In many instances, the indicators point to a major reversal in the stock market weeks or months in advance of the actual change. Such information is important to the investor or speculator, since it provides him with an opportunity to readjust his investment position, to sell his long issues, or to go short.

Stock Averages

There are two conventional theories as to why stock prices fluctuate. The first is based upon the anticipation of a change in corporate earnings. If one multiplies this factor with regard to an individual company by the large number of firms that represent the popular averages, one may have a means of forecasting the wide fluctuations in general stock market prices. The second theory considers that the most important element influencing the movement of stock prices is rising and falling confidence on the part of

---

[1] See, for example, A. W. Cohen, *The Chartcraft Method of Point and Figure Trading* (New York: Chartcraft, Inc., 1961), p. 31.

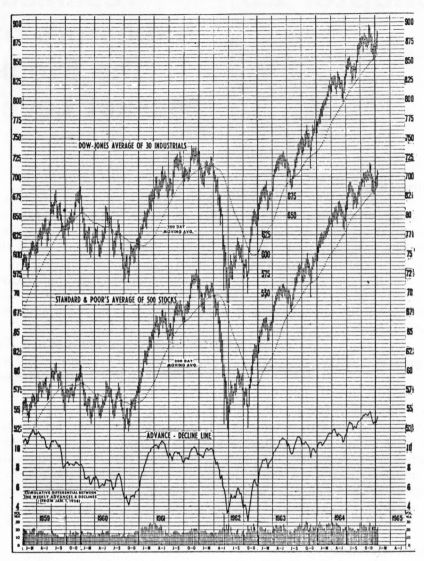

FIGURE 20-1 / Popular market indexes. From *Trendline's Current Market Perspectives,* New York, Trendline Corporation, Nov. 1966.

traders and investors in the future of stock prices, stock dividends, and earnings.[2]

There are numerous stock market averages that are used to indicate the general direction of the market, but only the more popular ones, the Dow Jones averages, Standard & Poor's Average of 500 Stocks, and Moody's Industrial Average, will be discussed in this chapter.[3]

[2] George L. Leffler and Loring C. Farwell, *The Stock Market,* 3d ed. (New York: The Ronald Press Company, 1963), p. 493.

[3] For a comprehensive analysis of stock price averages and indexes, see Leffler and Farwell, pp. 479–491.

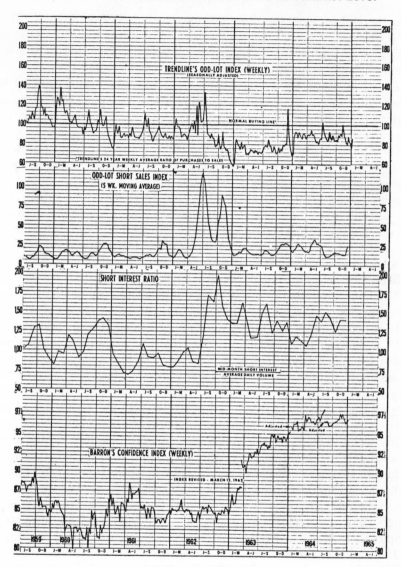

FIGURE 20-1 *(Continued)*

Dow Jones Averages

Charles Dow, founder of Dow Jones Company, which publishes *The Wall Street Journal, Barron's,* and *The National Observer,* developed the theory of the stock market average. His first index consisted of 11 stocks, composed almost entirely of railroads. The original Dow Jones Industrial Average, which used 12 stocks, dates back to 1897. Since that time, the company has devised four averages, the Industrial Average, the Rail Average, the Utility Average, and the Composite Index. Frequent changes have been made in the number of companies that are used in computing the averages, and at the end of 1966, the three averages included 30 industrials, 20 rails, and 15 utilities. These 65 companies are used to determine the Composite Index. For an up-to-date listing of the companies included in the index, the reader should refer to a current issue of *Barron's*.

The Dow Jones Industrial Average (DJIA) has been criticized for a number of reasons. One criticism stems from the fact that it includes American Telephone and Telegraph Company, the largest public utility company. Other criticisms are that the 30 stocks may be too small a number on which to base an index and that the list is comprised almost entirely of large, stable companies with blue chip stocks; that the index frequently drops one issue and replaces it with another; and that the higher-priced stocks included in the index carry more weight in the average than do the lower-priced issues. The index is not weighted by the number of shares of stock outstanding for the companies that comprise the index, a fact that has been another focus of criticism. Although the DJIA does have its weaknesses, as do all indexes, movements in the Dow Jones average of 30 stocks parallel almost exactly those of Standard & Poor's 500 stocks (see Fig. 20-1).

The Dow Jones theory is based on the belief that the averages discount everything that is known or expected about the issues. It recognizes three trends, called primary, secondary, and minor trends. The well-known stock market technician John McGee suggests that the *primary trend* determines whether the market is a bull or a bear market. This type of trend usually lasts for more than a year. The *secondary trend*, which may last for a few weeks or months, represents the reactions that interrupt the progress of prices in the primary direction. Secondary trends are composed of *minor trends*, or day-to-day fluctuations, and are unimportant to the investor. The primary trend in stock market prices was generally upward during the first 65 years of the twentieth century. The DJIA from 1920 to 1965 is illustrated graphically in Figure 20-1. The figure indicates that stock prices rose very rapidly during the 1920s but declined very rapidly from 1929 through 1932, recovered slightly from 1934 to 1937, and declined until 1942. From 1942 through 1965, the market generally rose, with downward adjustments. For example, there was a sharp drop in the average of stock prices during 1957 and 1958, another during 1960, and a substantial decline during 1962. From mid-1962 through the end of 1965, the DJIA showed a substantial rise, advancing from 550 to 940.

The Dow Jones theory is based on the premise that when a previous secondary low has been broken, a bear market signal has been given. This signal should be confirmed by both the Dow Jones Industrial and Rail averages in order to be completely valid, according to the Dow theory. Conversely, when a previous secondary high has been broken, a bull market signal has been given if this is confirmed by both the Industrial and Rail averages.[4]

---

[4] Robert D. Edwards and John McGee, *Technical Analysis of Stock Trends* (Springfield, Mass.: John McGee, 1964), pp. 15–18.

A. W. Cohen suggests that the direction and extent of movement in the DJIA may be forecasted by the point-and-figure chart method with a high degree of accuracy. Figure 20-2 is a point-and-figure chart for the DJIA from 1957 through early 1965. The author's interpretations of the formations that appear in Figure 20-2 are described below. Another technician would perhaps disagree with some of these interpretations and with the estimates of the projected moves. The patterns indicated are those that were described in Chapter 19, and the count from a bullish pattern was begun at the broadest point of the formation. The count from a triangle was started at the center of the triangle, while the count from a bearish pattern began at the broadest point within the formation. These estimates gave surprisingly accurate results.

1. A bullish signal formation (8 squares wide) was formed during 1957 and 1958 and indicated a move of 24 squares, each representing 5 points on the Dow Jones. The actual move was 25 squares.

2. A series of three bullish triangles was formed in 1959, indicating moves of 9, 9, and 15 squares, respectively, and the actual moves were 9, 9, and 10 squares.

3. During the last part of 1959, a bearish signal formation was given, which indicated a move of 12 squares, although the actual move was only 8 squares. A swing pattern occurred during the latter part of 1959, and the expected up swing, to follow the down swing, was exactly the projected move—7 squares.

4. During 1960, a bearish triangle was formed, indicating a downward projection of 9 squares, but the actual move was only 5 squares.

5. A bullish signal pattern was then formed, which indicated a probable move of 12 squares, and the actual move was 10 squares.

6. Later in 1960, a bearish signal formation indicated a probable downward move of 12 squares, while the actual move was 13 squares.

7. Late in 1960, a bullish signal formation indicated a potential upward move of 12 squares, but the actual move was 7 squares.

8. Two bullish triangles were formed during 1960 and 1961, which suggested over-all moves of 18 squares. The combined move was 22 squares.

9. A bearish triangle was formed in 1961, but developed into a swing, which may be considered a false signal. The indicated move was 9 squares, but the actual move was only 4 squares.

10. A bullish reversal signal was formed from September 1961 through February 1962. The astute chart analyst would have disposed of his stock in March 1962 before the 20 percent decline in stock market prices. The expected downward move was at least 24 squares, but the actual move downward was 40 squares.

11. In May 1962, a bearish triangle was formed, which suggested a downward move of 9 squares, but the actual move was 7 squares. A similar triangle was formed in the same month with a small attempt at recovery.

FIGURE 20-2 / Dow-Jones industrial average (5 x 15 chart based on prices at 11, 12, 1, 2, and close). From Chartcraft, Inc., Larchmont, N.Y.

12. From May to December 1962, a gigantic inverted head and shoulders pattern was formed. The width of this formation was 12 squares, which indicated a probable upward move of 36 squares. The actual move, before a bullish triangle was formed, was 23 squares.

13. A series of three bullish triangles was formed, with a swing from the third triangle during 1962–1963.

14. The DJIA continued to rise during 1964 until May, and then began to form bullish triangles.

To the technician who believes that a stock, or an average, moves up in three cycles, the first upward leg on Figure 20-2 (1957–1959) and the 1960 consolidations may represent the first cycle, the upward move and the 1962 consolidations may represent the second leg, and the final rise may appear somewhat later. This rise may be expected to carry the DJIA above the 900 mark before the onset of the next adjustment in stock prices.

Standard & Poor's Average of 500 Stocks

Standard & Poor's Corporation computes an average of 500 stocks, representing 425 industrials, 25 rails, and 50 utilities. The stocks in the average are weighted according to their importance (that is, the number of shares outstanding are multiplied by the market price per share) and represent the market values of about 90 percent of the New York Stock Exchange issues. This index, which is computed hourly by a high-speed computer, assumes a base period of 1941 through 1943 averages that has been assigned a value of 10.[5]

Other Averages

Moody's Investors Service prepares stock indexes on 125 industrials, 25 public utilities, 25 rails, 15 banks, and 10 insurance issues. The issues are weighted in importance by market value per share and number of shares outstanding. Other stock market averages are the New York *Times* average, the NYSE composite index, AMEX price level index, the Associated Press average, the Securities and Exchange Commission index, and the Merrill Lynch index.

Yields and Price-Earnings Ratios

The term *"yield"* has a number of meanings. *Yield to maturity* refers to the return on a commitment of funds into bonds or preferred stocks and is computed in a different way for stocks and bonds. A majority of bond issues have definite maturity lengths, and present-value tables and/or bond tables should be used to determine their yield to maturity (see Chapter 2). The yield to maturity on a preferred stock, however, may be found by dividing the annual dividend by the market value. For example, if a $100 par preferred

---

[5] For reports on the hourly and daily levels of Standard & Poor's index, see Standard & Poor's Corporation, *Security Owners' Stock Guide* (New York: Standard & Poor's). The publication, which is brought up to date monthly, also includes statistical data on some 4000 companies.

issue is paying a $6 cumulative annual dividend and is trading for $120 per share, the yield is computed by dividing $6 by $120, indicating a return of 5 percent.

Two types of yields relate to the return on common stock. The *dividend yield,* which is more widely used, refers to the annual amount of the dividend divided by the market value per share. The *earnings yield* may be computed by dividing the annual earnings per share by the average market value of the stock. The reciprocal of the earnings yield is the *price–earnings ratio,* which tells how many years a stock must be held in order for its current earnings to equal its market price, is a gauge to the over-all level of stock prices.

Two price–earnings ratio lines appear on Figure 20-3 for the DJIA. The reader may note that the Dow Jones average traded relatively close to the price–earnings ratio line of 9 during the latter 1940s and early 1950s. The ratio rose to 23 prior to the stock market decline of 1962. From 1962 through 1964, the earnings of the Dow Jones companies increased at a rate approximately equal to the increase in the DJIA. The average was trading at about 19 to 20 times annual earnings in early 1965, but had declined to about 15 by mid-1966.

The bottom left panel of Figure 20-3 illustrates the yields of Standard & Poor's 425 industrial stocks and of Standard & Poor's high-grade bonds. From 1920 to 1965 there were three periods when bond yields were higher than stock yields: from 1928 to 1929, in the middle 1930s, and from 1958 through 1965. This unusual stock versus bond relationship was extremely alarming to many investment counselors, who believed that the stock market was grossly overpriced in 1965 and that there would ultimately be a correction to bring the yields of common stocks substantially above those of corporate bonds.

Short-Sale Indicators

The short sale was described in Chapter 8 as the sale of stock that is not actually owned. The seller anticipates that the market price will fall, so that he may replace the issue on a later date at a lower price. Only listed securities may be sold short, and numerous types of investors may not use this method. An individual who maintains a margin account may ordinarily sell an issue short. Traders and exchange specialists also sell securities short, but corporate insiders who have significant stock holdings must register with the SEC and are not permitted to sell short stock in their own corporation. Financial institutions and investment clubs are not permitted to maintain margin accounts or to sell short.

Two short-sale indexes are given in Figure 20-1. Whereas the stock averages are frequently interpreted as an index of optimism, the *short interest ratio* may be regarded as an index of pessimism. This ratio is computed by dividing the midmonth short interest on the New York Stock Exchange by the average daily volume for the past 30 days.

Although it may appear confusing to the investor, it is bullish to have a large number of bears around. When there is a sharp rise in the short interest ratio without an offsetting decline in the general level of stock prices, substantial technical strength is imported to the over-all market. The sale of stock by the bears has already had its depressing effect upon the market. Covering the short sales (or buying back in) results in some buying pressures upon the market, thus stimulating stock prices. Therefore, a rise in the ratio is considered bullish, while a decline in the ratio is believed to be bearish. Generally, most analysts suggest that the ratio is bullish when the short interest is more than 1.5 times the daily trading volume and that the ratio is bearish when the short interest falls below one half of the average daily trading volume.[6]

Another odd lot index is the *odd lot short sale index* (see Fig. 20-1). A study of the chart reveals that short sales by odd lotters were low during the boom period of 1959 and early 1960, but rose somewhat in the final quarter of 1960 during the stock market decline. Odd lot short selling became almost frantic during June and July of 1962, but unfortunately the odd lotters were too late to take advantage of the greatest part of the decline, which occurred during April and May 1962. The indicators used by the odd lotters to go long or short in the market, in reality, appear too late to be applied profitably. From June through November 1962 many of the odd lot short sellers had to cover at losses during subsequent months. After odd lotters take losses in the stock market, they become disillusioned and decide to place their money in a safer type of investment. In going short in a market decline, or in going long during a boom period, the odd lotters frequently wait too long and then trade at a frantic pace, when the market is bottoming out or forming a rounded top. The investor should not be led into this trap.

The midmonth short interest for individual New York Stock and American stock exchange companies is reported from three to five days after the middle of each month in *Barron's, The Wall Street Journal, Value Line, Trendline's Daily Basis Stock Charts,* and other sources of financial data.

The Odd Lot Index

Only the buying and selling of round lots is reported on the financial page of a newspaper or on the ticker tape. In order to fill odd lots, the odd lot specialist must frequently replenish his inventory through the purchase of round lots. The purchase and/or sale of round lots by the odd lot specialist is then reflected in the daily volume. Odd lot volume on the New York Stock Exchange amounts to approximately 12 to 15 percent of the total trading volume on that exchange. Odd lot buying is relatively low when stock prices are depressed and less than normal during bull markets. Odd lot trading becomes heavier as the bull market approaches a climax, and buying becomes almost frantic in the beginning of a bear market and during the

---

[6] See, for example, William L. Jiler, *How Charts Can Help You in the Stock Market* (New York: Commodity Research Publications Corporation, 1962), pp. 169–173.

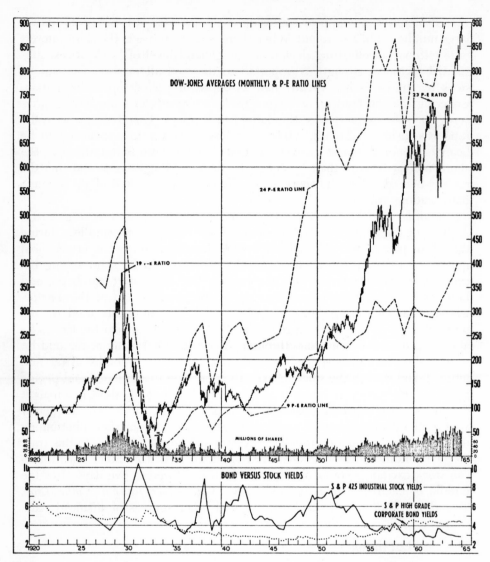

FIGURE 20-3 / Common stock averages. From *Trendline's Current Market Perspectives*, Trendline Corporation, New York, Nov. 1966.

following decline. Odd lotters usually time their transactions poorly and frequently suffer losses. Although some odd lotters make profits in the stock market, it is generally believed that on balance they lose money.

Figure 20-1 presents Trendline's Odd Lot Weekly Index, which is seasonally adjusted. The normal buying line of 100 percent is Trendline's 24-year weekly average ratio of purchases to sales. This index reveals that purchases were significantly higher than sales during 1959 and 1960, while the DJIA was declining, but in the latter part of 1960, during almost all of 1961, and

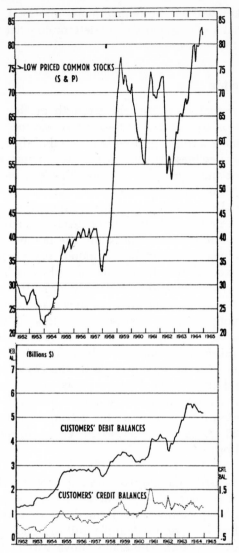

FIGURE 20-3 (Continued)

for the first five months of 1962, odd lot purchases were below odd lot sales. This was during a sustained bull market period. During the third and fourth quarters of 1962, when purchases became heavy relative to sales, the DJIA was declining by some 20 percent. During 1963 and 1964, there were only brief periods in which odd lot purchases exceeded odd lot sales. By the end of 1964, the confidence of the odd lot public had not been restored enough for purchases to exceed sales. During the final stages of most bull markets, the odd lotters become more frantic in their purchases of securities.

These past trends should discourage an individual from attempting to trade in the market without becoming more informed. Many investment advisers suggest that a wise trader should determine what the odd lotters are doing and do just the opposite.

The Advance-Decline Line

A market indicator that illustrates the strength of the market in general rather than of 30 or so selected issues is the advance–decline line. The *advance–decline line* is a running, cumulative total of the differences between daily advances and declines in stock prices on a major stock exchange. In constructing a point-and-figure chart to show this line one may begin at any point in time, and one may start with any number he chooses, such as 10,000. He should then mark off his scale arithmetically, since each block represents a definite number of advances or declines, such as 500. The differences between the number of advances and the number of declines on one of the leading exchanges should be computed daily and a running total should be maintained. In order for the advance–decline line to be contained on a single page, the scale should be relatively large. It is necessary to maintain a table that shows the cumulative advances and declines for each day from a starting point. One may then post from this table to the point-and-figure chart in the same manner as for an individual issue. The complete three-square reversal method should also be followed.

In combination with the signals given by the Dow Jones Industrial and Rail averages, Standard & Poor's Average of 500 stocks, and other technical indicators, the advance–decline line is sometimes helpful in judging over-all market strength. Figure 20-4 presents the advance–decline line from 1951 through early 1965. A careful analysis of figure formations reveals the following information:

1. In 1951, a bearish triangle was formed, which indicated a probable downward move of 9 squares, but the actual move was 10 squares.

2. In 1952, three patterns were formed: an uncertainty triangle appeared, from which a swing resulted, and a bullish signal formation indicated an upward move of 9 squares. The actual move was 11 squares.

3. During 1953, a bullish signal reversal pattern was formed, which indicated a probable move of 12 squares. The actual move was also 12 squares.

4. Late in 1953, a triple top formation indicated an upward move of 18 squares, but the actual move was only 15 squares. A swing, which is in reality a false signal, also appeared during the year.

5. During 1954, a bullish triangle indicated an upward move of 9 squares, although the actual move was almost twice this, or 16 squares. Later in 1954, a triple top was formed, which indicated an upward move of 15 squares, while the actual move was 17 squares.

6. During 1955, a spread triple top and a bullish signal formation indicated a significant rise. During the latter part of 1955 and the early part of

1956, however, a head and shoulders was formed, which indicated that a substantial decline was to follow.

7. In the latter part of 1956 and the first half of 1957, a gigantic bearish triangle was formed, which indicated a probable decline of 24 squares; the actual decline was 25 squares.

8. In 1957, a bearish signal reversal suggested that an upward move of 12 squares was in the making, but the actual movement was 11 squares.

9. In 1958, a bullish triangle indicated an upward move of 9 squares, but in using the three-square reversal, however, no consolidation pattern appeared until the upward movement had been 36 squares.

10. In 1959, a bearish signal reversal was formed, which indicated a decline of 12 squares; the actual decline was exactly 12 squares.

11. In 1959, a bearish triangle was formed. The indicated move was 9 squares, but the actual move was 14 squares.

12. In 1960, a spread triple top indicated an upward move of 24 squares, and in reality the move was exactly 24 squares from the point within the formation where the least number of unoccupied squares appeared.

13. In 1961, a triple bottom—a bullish pattern—indicated a probable decline of 24 squares, while the actual decline was 32 squares.

14. In 1962, a bearish signal reversal indicated a probable up trend of 12 squares, although the actual movement was a rise of 19 squares.

15. In 1962, a bullish triangle indicated an upward move of 9 squares, but the actual rise was 8 squares.

16. The pattern that was forming on Figure 20-4 during 1963 and 1964 appeared to be a large bearish signal reversal, which is called an inverted head and shoulders by some technicians, and suggested an advance of 33 squares. An advance of this magnitude would require an addition to the top of the chart and could come about in two or three stages, with the formation of consolidation triangles on the upward move.

From 1951 through 1958, the long-range trend of the advance–decline line was upward. From 1958 through 1963, however, the trend line was downward. With a reversal in direction of the trend for the advance–decline line during 1963, the secondary issues should remain relatively strong for an unknown period of time. One may gain a considerable amount of insight into the expected direction of movement of the market in general through a study of this and other technical indicators. Although a pattern may not provide an entirely accurate forecast of the expected move, only two false signals out of more than 20 were indicated on this chart, and thus this method appears to be highly reliable for predicting the probable direction of stock prices.

Barron's Confidence Index

Whereas the short interest ratio was described as an index that measures the degree of pessimism on the part of the investor, *Barron's Confidence Index* measures the degree of confidence that bondholders have in the economy of

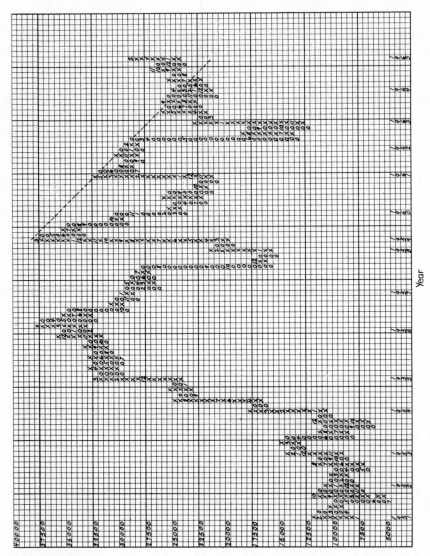

FIGURE 20-4 / Daily cumulative advance–decline line (three-square reversal). From Chartcraft, Inc., Larchmont, N.Y.

the nation and their faith in the ability of the issuing corporations to service their bonds. *Barron's* makes a daily comparison of the yields to maturity on high- and low-grade bonds. As investors grow more confident in the economy and the ability of business firms to handle their bonded indebtedness, they shift from high- to low-grade bonds in order to gain a higher yield. The difference between the yields of high- and low-grade bonds then narrows. Conversely, when confidence is lacking, there is a shift from low- to high-grade bonds. Bondholders are primarily large insurance companies and institutional investors, and the knowledge of the managers of these funds is assumed to be superior to that of the general bondholder or stockholder. Since these investors channel large sums of money into the bond and stock markets, their transactions are frequently adequate to depress or stimulate market prices. The confidence index usually leads the stock averages by some two to four months on a reversal in trend. Therefore, if the technician who is watching the index detects a downturn, he thus has from two to four months to reverse his position in the stock market. That is, he may wish to liquidate his long position and obtain a short position.[7]

Figure 20-5 illustrates *Barron's* Confidence Index from 1955 through 1964. Numerous chart formations appeared that indicated a change in the confidence of bondholders in the strength of the economy, the probable movement in bond yields and prices, and the ability of business corporations to adequately service corporate bond issues of various grades. The reader should determine the bullish and bearish patterns that appear on this chart and attempt to predict the direction and duration of the expected moves.

Industry Indicators

Although it is well to know the over-all direction of the stock market and the degree of pessimism and optimism being expressed by investors, the stocks in one industry may be moving up while those in another may be declining. If one can detect this trend, he may be able to concentrate his holdings within the industries that are moving up and to liquidate those in the industries that have declined in market favor. Locating bullish and bearish industries may be done in a number of ways. The investor may determine whether the price–earnings ratios within a given industry are moving upward or downward, comparing them to those of previous years and to those of the over-all market.

Industry studies are prepared by dozens of investment and chart services, and the following are merely suggestive. Again, the reader should not infer that this list is complete, but he should research whatever financial informa-

---

[7] For a more complete analysis of *Barron's* Confidence Index and how it may be used, see Jiler, pp. 168–169. *Barron's* Confidence Index is regularly reported by the leading investors' services, chart services, and financial newspapers. For the original data that will enable one to maintain his own charts, see "Study of Price Movements—Market Laboratory" in the most current issue of *Barron's*.

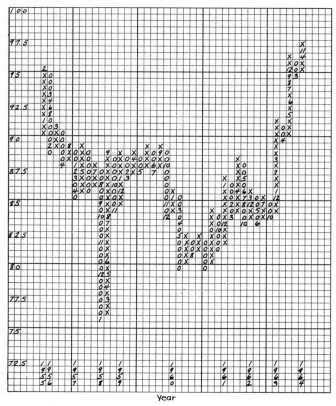

FIGURE 20-5 / Barron's confidence index. From Chartcraft, Inc., Larchmont, N.Y.

tion is available to him to find alternate sources. Where the information is sought on a weekly basis, the reader may refer to *Barron's* Group Stock Averages, which appears near the inside back cover of each issue. The information is presented in tabular form, so that one may construct charts on the trends in various industries. Similar information may be detected from a thorough analysis of the charts that appear in the midmonth issue of *Trendline's Current Market Perspective*, which provides weekly range charts on 960 listed stocks for a period of three to four years. The price–earnings ratios are indicated on a majority of the charts, as well as price and volume data and other statistical information. Since the charts are arranged by industry, the reader may study the chart patterns and determine industry leaders and laggards. For example, an industry that is 75 to 80 percent bullish is ordinarily more desirable than one that is only 40 to 50 percent bullish. Industry charts are also published in Chartcraft's point-and-figure charts, in *Trendline's Current Market Perspectives*, and in other investment services.

Information in text form is given in the quarterly *Security and Industry Survey*, published by Merrill Lynch, Pierce, Fenner & Smith. Similar information may be obtained from numerous other investment advisory services, chart services, or weekly newsletters.

Summary

While the analyst will probably find that the primary value of charts on industrial issues is to aid him in making market decisions, he may also find that charts help him to predict a probable reversal in the over-all direction of the stock market. In making such forecasts one may use a number of technical indicators, for example, the popular stock averages, short-sale indicators, trend line indexes, the advance–decline line, and *Barron's* Confidence Index.

The investor or trader may improve his profits by studying the price movement within industries. Often the stocks of certain industries are generally moving up while those in other industries are moving down. It is valuable for the investor to know which industries are currently in favor and which are losing in popularity.

Statistics indicate that odd lotters lose money on the average because they buy too late in a bull market and sell short after a bear market has already reversed its trend. A close study of the market indicators will frequently reveal a change in direction of security prices and permit the informed investor to make more timely buying and selling decisions.

QUESTIONS FOR REVIEW /

1. Why is it important that the technician devote some attention to the study of general market indicators as well as to the charts on individual issues?
2. Would you prefer to use a point-and-figure chart or a vertical bar chart in forecasting the direction and extent of the probable move of the DJIA? Explain.
3. How accurate were the buy, sell, and extent of move signals given on the point-and-figure chart for the DJIA (Fig. 20–2)?
4. How do the other popular stock averages differ from the Dow Jones averages? Contrast the advantages and disadvantages of using each of these.
5. How may odd lot indexes be used to gauge the probable trend in the market?
6. What can be learned from a study of the short interest ratio, and what strategy does this recommend for the odd lot public?
7. How may the advance–decline line be used by the technician?
8. What is the *Barron's* Confidence Index and what does it attempt to measure?
9. Explain the significance of dividend and earnings yields of common stocks.
10. How should an investor make use of the price–earnings ratio for an individual company? for a popular average?

PROBLEMS /

1. Determine the current earnings and dividend yields for some popular average, such as the Dow Jones Industrial and Rail averages.
2. Contrast the price–earnings ratios of various industries, for example, automobiles, airlines, electronics, chemicals, and petroleums.
3. Attempt to measure the probable future direction of stock prices in general by

using available financial material. Attempt to determine three industries that will probably decline in favor in the near future and three that are likely to gain in popularity within the next three months.

4. Study carefully the information that appears in "Study of Price Movements— Market Laboratory" in *Barron's* and explain how this information is helpful to the technician.

REFERENCES /

Barron's. New York: Dow Jones & Company, Inc.

Leffler, George L., and Loring C. Farwell, *The Stock Market*, 3d ed. New York: The Ronald Press Company, 1963.

Standard & Poor's Corporation, *Stock Market Encyclopedia*. New York: Standard & Poor's.

Trendline Corporation, *Trendline's Current Market Perspectives*. New York: Trendline.

————, *Trendline's Daily Basis Stock Charts*. New York: Trendline.

The Value Line Investment Survey. New York: A. Bernhard & Company, Inc.

The Wall Street Journal. New York: Dow Jones & Company, Inc.

chapter 21 | Methods for Locating Bullish and Bearish Issues

Introduction

There are countless methods for discovering issues that may prove to be profitable investments over a period of time. While the executive may have faith in a recently developed product which his company, his suppliers, or his customers are currently marketing, the general public must rely on current financial literature to discover worthy common stock investments. The most commonly recognized sources of financial information were described in Chapter 11, but some specific techniques for locating desirable issues are described in this chapter. These include the use of chart services, other investment services, the financial section of newspapers, the on-balance-volume method, the random-walk method, and the combined fundamental, undervaluation, and technical approaches to selecting securities.

The Use of Chart Services

Contrasting Chart Types

Stock charting is an art rather than a science, and a skilled user will often "sense" imminent price rises for a few issues from a large group of up-to-date charts. After a person has mastered the basic theories of vertical bar and point-and-figure charts, he should apply his new skill with paper investments before committing his funds to the market. Once he has developed his ability to interpret chart patterns and he has faith in the accuracy of forecasting by such means, he is ready to commit a limited amount of funds to actual investments. His commitment, because of the high risk in the market fluctuation of common stocks, should bear a reasonable relationship to his assets and income level.

Each type of chart offers some advantages and disadvantages over others, and some individuals prefer the bar chart while others like the point-and-figure method. The technician should utilize the tool with which he is most familiar and employ the type of chart that produces the most successful results. For the past few years the author has experimented with (1) the three-square reversal point-and-figure chart, (2) the daily-basis stock chart, (3) the weekly range chart, and (4) the monthly bar chart in an attempt to gauge the effectiveness of each of these methods. While the author's experience has undoubtedly differed significantly from that of other investors and traders, the information he gained may be of some benefit to new users of the techniques.

The true technician suggests that fundamental information be disregarded in making trading decisions, but the application of both fundamental and technical data should produce more impressive gains than the use of only one of these methods. This is true because one may have to keep his investment in a fundamentally strong issue for a long time before the market responds favorably. Bullish technical patterns, conversely, are frequently misleading or short-lived when unaccompanied by improved earnings.

The author found the chart patterns that appear on daily-basis stock charts to be less effective tools for discovering substantial moves (15 to 25 percent) than weekly range charts. Monthly range charts, however, do not reflect many of the patterns that appear on the daily or weekly range charts. Errors have frequently been made in attempting to gauge the top of a move from a daily-basis stock chart because of the limited time span for which the chart is constructed. Better results are possible if the chart analyst has a supply of charts covering a period of at least three years, and preferably longer.

Break outs from consolidations or sudden changes in direction in an issue, however, can be detected more quickly from the daily-basis chart than from weekly or monthly range charts or from point-and-figure charts. Gaps appear on the daily-basis charts that are hidden on the other charts in most cases, and these are important indications of strength (upside gaps) or weaknesses (downside gaps).

Point-and-figure charts offer some advantages and some disadvantages. The formations on these charts are more easily recognizable than on the range chart, the patterns offer a fair gauge to the expected move from a formation, the support and resistant levels are more clearly seen, and the charts are easy to maintain. The important ingredient of volume of trading is absent, however, and the point-and-figure chart is weak in its ability to forecast the time over which a move is expected to occur. It is believed that range charts and point-and-figure charts may be used to supplement one another, with the weekly bar chart being superior in detecting timely investments, the point-and-figure chart being more useful in forecasting a probable move, and the daily-basis stock chart being maintained daily to detect any sudden weakness in an issue.

Constructing Your Own Charts

For the individual who has sufficient time and who does not elect to spend much money for investment services, the construction of 50 or 100 charts may prove useful. The chart analyst may follow approximately the construction and format illustrated in Chapters 18 and 19. Although the charts described earlier were drawn on graph paper, some technicians prefer to use semilogarithmic paper. This type of paper may be acquired in many bookstores, and the use of it is described in a number of sources.[1]

The daily transaction page from *The Wall Street Journal* or from some other financial or local newspaper may be used as a source for constructing the daily basis vertical bar charts and volume patterns. The individual will find that some two hours is required daily to maintain 100 charts. If he has less time to devote to daily posting, the number of charts that he maintains should be reduced accordingly. Once one falls more than a week or two behind in his posting, he may as well discard the charts. If maintaining daily bar charts seems too time consuming, one may prefer to use weekly bar charts. No more time is required to post the weekly range, close, and volume than to post the daily transactions, and some 100 of these charts may be maintained in approximately two hours per week. *Barron's, Commercial and Financial Chronicle,* and other financial newspapers carry weekly summaries of price ranges and volume.

Recommendations by Investors' Services

The Value Line Investment Survey

Value Line regularly reports on about 1100 companies, and an especially recommended situation is given each week. A list of these recommendations appears in Table 21-1 for the period March 6, 1964, through February 26, 1965. One may observe the average performance of the 52 *Value Line* stocks when compared to the average performance of the *Value Line* 1100. The performance of the *Value Line* 1100, because of its broad coverage, is very similar to that of Standard & Poor's 500.

It may be noted that many of these issues did very well indeed, while others showed a small increase or a small decline. More impressive results have been noted for the *Value Line* rankings, however, since the service modified its ranking system to include 100 companies in the top group, 250 in group II, 400 in group III, 250 in group IV, and 100 in group V. In using the April 23, 1965, groupings for expected price performance within 12 months and comparing the prices on that date to the prices one year later, one finds that the following results were achieved:

Group I	+41.8%
Group II	+24.0%
Group III	+11.0%
Group IV	− 2.2%
Group V	− 2.4%[2]

---

[1] See, for example, Robert D. Edwards and John McGee, *Technical Analysis of Stock Trends* (Springfield, Mass.: John McGee, 1964), pp. 8–9.

[2] See "Selection and Opinion," *The Value Line Investment Survey* (New York: A. Bernhard & Company, Inc., April 22, 1966), p. 933.

TABLE 21-1 / *Value Line* Especially Recommended Stocks

Record of Recommendations

The up-to-date performance record of the Especially Recommended stocks selected during the past 52 weeks may be of particular interest to subscribers.

Thirty-six (36) of the fifty-two (52) recommendations (about 7 out of 10) have done better than the Value Line 1,100 Stock Average over comparable time periods.

| Stock | Recommended | | 3/3/65 Recent Price | Performance % Change Since Recommended | |
	Date	Price		Stock	VL 1100
Schlumberger	3/ 6/64	63	76	+20.6%	+16.3%
Lukens Steel	3/13/64	46	67	+45.7%	+15.2%
Edison Bros. Stores	3/20/64	29ᵃ	34	+17.2%	+15.0%
Hercules Powder	3/27/64	42	49	+16.7%	+14.0%
Hartford Fire	4/ 3/64	70	74	+ 5.7%	+12.7%
Hewlett-Packard	4/10/64	20	27	+35.0%	+12.0%
Kerr-McGee	4/17/64	36	52	+44.4%	+11.8%
Morgan Guaranty	4/24/64	123	114	− 7.3%	+13.4%
Catalin Corp.	5/ 1/64	4½	6¼	+38.9%	+13.6%
Mesta Machine	5/ 8/64	40	53	+32.5%	+12.5%
Ark.-La. Gas	5/15/64	34	44	+29.4%	+12.7%
Ayrshire Collieries	5/22/64	53	51	− 3.8%	+12.9%
Heinz	5/28/64	38	46	+21.1%	+13.2%
Universal Oil Prod.	6/ 5/64	33	47	+42.4%	+15.1%
Colorado Fuel	6/12/64	12	12	0	+14.7%
U.S. Shoe	6/19/64	30	35	+16.7%	+12.9%
ABC Consol.	6/26/64	14	20	+42.9%	+12.1%
Talcott, James	7/ 3/64	22	23	+ 4.5%	+10.9%
Amer. Express	7/10/64	38	61	+60.5%	+ 9.7%
Reichhold Chem.	7/17/64	13ᵃ	13	0	+ 8.9%
Wachovia Bk. & Tr.	7/24/64	33	37	+12.1%	+ 9.0%
Douglas Aircraft	7/31/64	28ᵃ	39	+39.3%	+ 9.4%
Lone Star Steel	8/ 7/64	12	14	+16.7%	+11.1%
Pitts. Coke & Chem.	8/14/64	18	21	+16.7%	+10.0%
Lear Siegler	8/21/64	13	16	+23.1%	+10.4%
Brown Co.	8/28/64	13	14	+ 7.7%	+10.6%
Rheem Mfg.	9/ 4/64	18	22	+22.2%	+ 9.4%
Kaiser Steel	9/11/64	26	22	−15.4%	+ 8.8%
Seaboard Finance	9/18/64	24	28	+16.7%	+ 8.7%

(a) Adjusted for stock splits and/or stock dividends.

The listed stocks, including those which did not appreciate or which declined, show an average appreciation since date of selection that is almost double the comparable advance in the Value Line 1,100 Stock Average.

SOURCE: *The Value Line Investment Survey* (New York: Arnold Bernhard & Company, Inc., March 12, 1965).

TABLE 21-1 *(Continued)*

Stock	Recommended Date	Price	3/3/65 Recent Price	Performance % Change Since Recommended Stock	VL 1100
First Nat'l Chicago	9/25/64	60	59	− 1.7%	+ 7.7%
Vanadium Corp.	10/ 2/64	18	21	+16.7%	+ 7.5%
General Dynamics	10/ 9/64	39	38	− 2.6%	+ 6.6%
Cont'l Assurance	10/16/64	136	129	− 5.1%	+ 6.7%
U.S. Vitamin	10/23/64	25	26	+ 4.0%	+ 5.9%
Ryder System	10/30/64	13	16	+23.1%	+ 6.3%
Raytheon	11/ 6/64	24	24	0	+ 6.3%
Air Products	11/13/64	51[a]	59	+15.7%	+ 5.8%
Stanray	11/20/64	15	15	0	+ 5.1%
Amer. Cement	11/27/64	11	13	+18.2%	+ 6.0%
Grumman	12/ 4/64	51	55	+ 7.8%	+ 7.1%
Lucky Stores	12/11/64	32	35	+ 9.4%	+ 8.6%
Colt Industries	12/18/64	11	17	+54.5%	+ 7.9%
Elec. Bond & Share	12/23/64	35	39	+11.4%	+ 8.2%
Cont'l Insurance	12/30/64	60	64	+ 6.7%	+ 8.2%
Twentieth Cen.-Fox	1/ 8/65	24	28	+16.7%	+ 6.1%
Ampex Corp.	1/15/65	17	19	+11.8%	+ 4.4%
Ling-Temco-Vought	1/22/65	18	25	+38.9%	+ 3.6%
Rex Chainbelt	1/29/65	56	59	+ 5.4%	+ 2.3%
Morrell (John)	2/ 5/65	30	30	0	+ 1.8%
U.S. Industries	2/12/65	11	13	+18.2%	+ 2.6%
Mont.-Dakota Util.	2/19/65	41	42	+ 2.4%	+ 1.6%
Castle & Cooke	2/26/65	37	39	+ 5.4%	+ 0.4%
52 Stocks				+16.5%	+ 9.1%

Whether or not the service will continue to achieve such gratifying results is not known.

Moody's Stock Survey

Moody's Stock Survey analyzes the international situation, the domestic economy, the leading business indicators, and specific industries that are in a unique situation and makes recommendations for purchase and sale of individual issues. *Moody's Bond Survey,* a sister publication, reports on outstanding and expected future bond issues, both domestically and internationally, and periodically reviews convertible bonds.

Other Services

Other services that make specific investment recommendations are the *Security Owner's Stock Guide,* which is published by Standard & Poor's Corporation, *Commercial and Financial Chronicle,* and *Fitch Stock Record.*

In addition, numerous leading financial magazines, for example, *Barron's, Business Week, Forbes, The Magazine of Wall Street, Financial World*, and *Investment Dealer's Digest*, present news articles on various companies that appear to be especially attractive. Some of these periodicals also make specific recommendations.

There are many newsletters that recommend individual stocks, and although a part of such information may be worthwhile, the prudent investor should not act strictly on tips but should investigate the situation thoroughly. In doing this, he may wish to use the technical, undervaluation, and fundamental approaches.

The Use of Daily High's, Low's, and Volume Data

Some technicians make considerable use of the daily high's, low's, and volume data that appear in his financial newspaper. On the inside back page of *The Wall Street Journal*, daily high's and low's are recorded for companies listed on the New York and the American stock exchanges. A stock that attains a new high on heavy volume is usually bullish, and when an individual issue makes a series of high's and then retreats, it may be in a strategic buying position prior to the next assault on the previous high. The maintenance of a table showing a complete listing of the New York and/or American stock exchange companies, with small squares for checking new high's and low's (a red pencil may be used to denote the low, while black indicates an increase), should provide the technician with the names of companies that will prove beneficial for charting. For the investor who subscribes to one or more chart services, the daily high's and low's may call his attention to some of the issues that he would otherwise overlook.

For those who cannot spend time checking out daily high's and low's, a weekly list is reported in *Barron's*. The purchase of a stock that has just broken into an all-time high is not necessarily recommended, but this signal does suggest that one should investigate the issue further. When a new high is reached, the investor—overnight if possible—should obtain a chart showing the historical price movement of the issue, or he should endeavor to chart the issue for the last four or five months. In this way, one may discover a valid buy signal, but if one waits too long, he may miss a major part of the upward move.

The daily low's should also be checked to see whether a stock may be forming a base from which a bearish reversal will occur, or whether the issue is likely to continue to decline. Attempting to forecast the exact bottom of a movement is very difficult, and it is recommended that long positions be taken in stocks only after a dependable buy signal has appeared on a chart.

The outstanding technician Joseph E. Granville believes that the volume pattern gives a clue to a break out before it becomes evident on the price chart. He also believes that more valid support and resistant levels exist for the volume of trading than for the price of an issue,[3] and he speaks of upward moves in stocks on heavy volume as being "energy." Granville suggests that a table be maintained on an issue recording the (1) date, (2) price, (3) volume, and (4) cumulative on-balance volume. Such a table is illustrated by Table 21-2 for Colt Industries for the period November 8, 1965, through December 23, 1965. On the first entry in the table the closing price of 18¼ was lower than the close of the previous day, so that the cumulative on-balance volume was assigned a −38, the volume turnover on that day. A decline occurred on November 9 and was assigned a negative value equal to the daily volume of trading; the November 10th closing price was unchanged from the previous day and received a zero weight. Subsequent price rises were rated with pluses equal to the daily volume. This process is continued day by day, and the tabular data for closing prices and on-balance volume may be recorded on a chart in much the same way as on a daily-basis stock chart except that points are recorded and joined by a broken line.

Granville maintains that when a stock is accumulating "energy" and has a higher on-balance volume at a given price than at the previous similar price, the issue is growing stronger and should advance in price. Conversely, when the on-balance volume is declining, the issue is gauged to be weaker. Of four such comparisons, aa, bb, cc, and dd, only the bb observation was a correct signal. One weakness of the method appears to be the assignment of a plus, zero, or negative rating to the entire day's volume based on the closing price even though the issue may have risen on heavy volume during an early part of the trading section but declined on light volume to ⅛ or ¼ point below the previous close. During its upward move, however, the stock did have a very regular upward move of four or five days followed by a downward adjustment of one or two days, and such information is useful to the short-term trader. The method appears to have merit but lacks refinement.

Charting Securities Other Than Common Stocks

Convertible Debentures

The point-and-figure method of charting, described earlier, may also be applied to convertible bonds. It is recommended that each square on the chart represent not more than 1 percent in par value of the bond. Of course, the use of one-half point squares will produce a chart that is more sensitive to small changes. The technician may use the one-square, two-square, or three-square reversal, whichever he desires. In determining which convertible bonds to chart, one should study "Moody's Convertible Bonds," which appears periodically in *Moody's Bond Survey*.

---

[3] See, for example, Joseph E. Granville, *Granville's New Key to Stock Market Profits* (Englewood Cliffs, N.J.: Prentice-Hall, Inc., 1963), pp. 56–59.

TABLE 21-2 /   On-Balance-Volume Method on Colt Industries, November 8 to December 23, 1965

	Date	Closing Price	Volume of Trading (00)	On-Balance Volume (00)
(a)	11/8/1965	18¼	38	− 38
	9	17⅞	63	−101
	10	17⅞	36	−101
(a)	11	18¼	51	− 50
	12	18⅞	58	8
	15	19¼	68	76
	16	20⅛	141	217
	17	20	261	− 44
	18	20⅜	136	92
(b)	19	20⅝	147	239
	22	21⅛	266	505
	23	21¼	213	718
	24	20⅞	62	656
(b)	—	20⅝	65	591
	26	20⅞	77	668
	29	21½	102	770
(c)	30	22⅞	405	1175
	12/1/1965	23	202	1377
	2	22¾	112	1265
	3	22⅜	307	958
	6	22½	83	1041
(c)	7	22⅞	104	1145
(d)	8	23⅞	168	1313
	9	24½	164	1477
	10	Holiday	Holiday	Holiday
	13	25	156	1633
	14	24¾	125	1509
	15	23⅞	94	1415
(d)	16	23⅞	74	1415
	17	23⅝	38	1377
	20	23	77	1300
	21	23⅛	120	1420
	22	23⅜	110	1530
	23	23¼	73	1457

SOURCE: Compiled from daily price and volume data.

Bonds that are trading close to the conversion value may prove to be profitable investments, because as common stocks rise, the market values of the bonds rises in direct proportion. When bonds are trading at a reasonable yield to maturity, these issues offer attractive investment possibilities to the investor who desires some chance for capital appreciation but who wishes to have some assured level of income. Although almost all of these issues are callable, the holder has 30 to 60 days, in most cases, after the call is exercised in which to convert to common shares.

Charts on convertible bond issues form approximately the same patterns as do common stock issues. Some technicians claim that a reversal signal may be indicated more clearly and at an earlier date on a chart for convertible bonds than on a chart for common stocks. For this reason, an individual may elect to maintain charts on both common stock and convertible bond issues for companies in which he has an interest and for which both are outstanding.

Another reason for investing in convertible bonds is that the margin requirement imposed by the Federal Reserve System does not apply to a purchase of convertible bonds. When the common stock of a company appears to be headed upward within the near future, the investor may be able to finance the purchase of convertible bonds with banks or brokerage firms at a lower margin than he can the purchase of stock.

Convertible Preferred Stock

The location of attractive convertible preferred stock issues may be undertaken in about the same way as the procedure outlined for convertible bonds. The investor should keep in mind, however, that where the call feature is present, the corporation may call the issue for retirement if it is to its advantage. For this reason, one should limit his purchase of convertible preferred stocks and convertible bonds to those issues that are not trading above their conversion values and to those that have a potential price rise in the near future.

Warrants

Stock purchase warrants are frequently issued by corporations as a means of marketing subordinated debenture issues and to facilitate a merger or acquisition of a second company. The stockholders in the absorbed company may be given debentures plus a certain number of stock purchase warrants in exchange for their old common shares. These stock purchase warrants may offer attractive investment opportunities to the risk investor.

Many New York Stock Exchange companies list their warrants for trading on the American Stock Exchange, and although a majority of the stock purchase warrants represent industrial companies, a few represent financial institutions and transportation companies. The market prices of warrants oscillate much more widely than the market prices of the common stocks. For example, an investment in 100 warrants of Trans World Airlines at the low price between January 2, 1964 and March 14, 1965 of 15⅛ would have increased by 160 percent to its high value during that time period, while the market value of the stock increased by almost 100 percent. The warrants for Universal American traded as low as ⅛ and as high as 2 during this period, representing an increase of 1500 percent from the low to the high price. Conversely, the market value of the common stock increased by only some 55 percent.

The technician may wish to compose a list of companies with warrants by consulting one of the standard investment services or the newspaper transaction page of the American Stock Exchange and maintain charts on stock purchase warrants. At least he should stay informed on the companies that have stock purchase warrants outstanding. If he maintains charts on the common stocks of these companies, he may find that larger returns will result from an investment in the warrants than from one in the stocks. He should also consider the expiration date of the warrant, since this factor influences the premium at which the warrant trades. The premium is the difference between the stock subscription price plus the cost of one warrant and the market value of a common share. Thus, a warrant that trades for $4 and can be used to purchase a share of stock at $15 which has a current market price of $13 is trading at a $6 premium: $[(\$4 + \$15) - (\$13)] = \$6$. As a warrant approaches the expiration date, the premium approaches zero, since warrants become worthless if not exercised.

Commodities

Many technicians suggest that the point-and-figure chart or the vertical bar chart may be used as effectively with commodities as with common stocks. The market prices of commodities swing so widely and frequently move so quickly, however, that the investor should maintain these charts daily, or perhaps even hourly, in order to catch the shifts. Since some commodity futures may be purchased with only 5 to 10 percent margin, a high degree of leverage may be obtained with this type of investment. A small reduction in market value will completely erase the capital of an investor in commodities who uses the maximum requirement, and a reduction in the market value by 1 or 2 percent may necessitate the call for additional margin. The rewards obtainable through an investment in commodity futures may be tremendous, but the risks are very great. Only someone who can afford to lose a major part or all of his capital commitment should trade in commodities. Technical writers suggest that one who trades in commodities should expect to take losses, but if he can keep his losses small and earn capital gains on other transactions, his over-all profits may be attractive.

Options

Puts, calls, and other types of option contracts were described in Chapter 2. Some technical writers suggest that the use of the technical approach may be an effective tool in selecting specific issues for dealing in put and call contracts.[4] A. W. Cohen, president of Chartcraft, Inc., suggests that only about 20 percent of these contracts are profitable to the buyers. The other 80 percent are profitable or at the break-even point for the put and call dealers. The buyer should keep in mind that the put and call dealer may be selling both types of contracts to different individuals. Whereas the put and call dealer is able to "hedge his position," this is not feasible or desirable for the individual investor.

The buyer of options should limit his purchase of this type of contract to one of either three months' or six months' duration and not a shorter time period and should buy only those that have a good chance of making a substantial price rise during the contract period. Since the holder of puts sells the issue at a stipulated price, he wishes to select an issue that will decline substantially within the contract period. He should, therefore, elect issues that have formed bearish consolidation patterns from which they are about to emerge. Because of the high risk associated with this endeavor, it is not recommended for the average investor.

Why Charts Work

Vertical bar charts and point-and-figure charts merely reflect the actions of the general public in buying and selling securities. The charts reflect the demand and supply of securities at a given price. When the price of a stock moves up on heavy volume, buyers are anxious to accumulate the issue, even at high prices, and these higher prices stimulate some additional supply of the stock. When the market price of an issue approaches a congested trading area the issue may find difficulty in breaking through this price level because many investors have held the issue for months or years and are anxious to sell without taking losses. Many of these investors will offer the stock for sale at their historic purchase price, and this additional selling pressure may cause the market price of the stock to decline for a time. After the buyers who are accumulating the issue absorb the supply being offered, the stock will usually resume its up trend. The opposite effect occurs for a falling stock. Investors who did not purchase the issue at its low point are anxious to do so if it ever again falls to that low level. Charts, then, merely reflect the economics of supply and demand, but signals that appear on the charts are no better than the technician who is using them. Some investors may find charts to be highly effective tools for gauging the timing of purchase and sales of securities while others may scoff at their usage. The results are what counts, however, and the direction of movement of individual stocks may be forecasted—sometimes—with uncanny accuracy. In weak stock markets, however, the tools are quite ineffective. Selling signals appear to be more

---

[4] The speculator who is interested in puts, calls, or other special option contracts should consult his brokerage firm or may note advertisements that appear in leading financial newspapers, such as *The Wall Street Journal, Barron's* or the *Commercial and Financial Chronicle.*

reliable in weak markets, while buying signals appear to be more accurate in rising markets.

The use of charts works because the method is unknown to many people; if all investors should become chart users, the usefulness of the technique would decline. As more individuals begin to use the method, chart formations should develop in a shorter time, the moves should be more rapid, and the extent of the moves should be less than generally expected.

An investor who has confidence in his charts and in his own ability to discern the bullish and bearish formations may be able to use the chart method very effectively. An individual who sees his stock decline two or three days in a row, without paying very much attention to the low volume of trading, may not be able to control his impulse to sell an issue before "the bottom falls out of it." Once the stock reaches the major up-trend line or a support level, however, it usually rebounds. If investors were able to discern (1) the probable direction of movement of a majority of issues and (2) the expected move, they would buy the issues that are expected to rise and sell them by placing limited orders slightly below the expected price potential. This series of limited sales would then drive the stock back, so that the relative extent of the oscillation would be reduced. If every investor had a perfect forecasting ability, the market prices of stocks would oscillate much less widely than they do. Wide oscillation is caused primarily by shifting investor sentiment and the irrationality of stockholders who base their decisions on impulse and unjustified feelings of bullishness or bearishness. However, if enough investors believe that the market is going to fall and place orders to sell their stocks, the market will assuredly fall, since the supply of stock offered is in excess of the demand.

During the 20 years from 1946 through 1965, financial institutions increasingly added support to the level of stock prices. When individual investors offer their stock for sale, prices may fall somewhat, but purchase orders placed primarily by financial institutions lend stability to the market. In the 20-year period financial institutions increased their holdings from slightly less than 13 percent to more than 20 percent of the market value of all issues on the New York Stock Exchange. However, a rising velocity of turnover by financial institutions, as evidenced in 1965 and 1966 (see Chapter 24), may lead to larger swings in the prices of common stocks in the future.

Weaknesses of Forecasting Methods

The technical, undervaluation, fundamental, and many other approaches to selecting securities have their weaknesses. Advocates of the random-walk theory argue that a random selection of securities of "equal risk" will provide the investor with results that are as good as those obtained with the use of the more sophisticated technical and fundamental methods. Numerous empirical studies have been made contrasting the performance of randomly selected portfolios with those of investment companies, and the performances differ little over time.[5] Eugene Fama has challenged both technicians and fundamental analysts to offer empirical evidence and operating results confirming the belief that their methods are superior to random selections.[6]

The relative attractiveness of the technical, undervaluation, fundamental, random-walk, and other approaches will long continue to be a moot question. Some analysts have a "feel" for their own tested method and prefer it to other, less-understood techniques. It is doubtful if a perfect method will ever be found for forecasting stock prices. However, the investor, or analyst, can search for methods that appear to work best for *him*. The confirmed fundamentalist will continue to believe his methods to be superior, while the devout technician will have faith in his charts. Other investors, no doubt, will benefit as well by using a random approach. The student of investments is urged to learn as much as possible about the numerous approaches to security selection. Actual investment experience, however, is imperative before one gains a "feel" for isolating potentially profitable or risky commitments. One who can shoulder the risk of being a stockholder should make use of whatever tools are available to him and pursue the investment strategy that he understands best and that provides him with the most successful results over time. Combinations of these methods may be utilized by an individual in order to improve his investment return, while other investors may continue to apply only one of these techniques. The author's personal preference is to combine the undervaluation, fundamental, and technical approaches to security selection, but other investors prefer to use a single approach, a different combination of these approaches, or the random-walk technique.

Summary

An investor may locate bullish or bearish issues in a number of ways. He may survey a large number of point-and-figure or vertical bar charts periodically and maintain those that have developed interesting patterns. If he does not have access to up-to-date charts, he may construct charts for the stocks that have been making new high's and low's. New high's frequently indicate that an issue has substantial strength, but it may be profitable for one to wait for a decline before committing one's funds. The 10 or 15 most active stocks that are reported daily are also interesting prospects, especially if the heavy volume was made on price rises. Other methods are to read financial magazines, journals, and business newspapers in order to locate interesting situations. One should make a further study of the technical position and fundamental strengths of an issue before making an investment. Investment services and newsletters are other possible sources.

[5] Irwin Friend and Douglas Vickers, "Portfolio Selections and Investment Performance," *The Journal of Finance,* September 1965, pp. 391–415.

[6] Eugene F. Fama, "Random Walks in Stock Market Prices," *Financial Analysts Journal,* September–October 1965, pp. 55–59.

The methods for locating bullish and bearish issues are countless. The individual should make use of whatever sources of financial data are available to him, and he should make sure that before he spends hundreds of dollars for materials he will devote a substantial amount of time to the study of the data.

Some writers argue, and support with substantial amounts of quantitative evidence, that a random selection will produce results equal to or superior to those obtained with the technical or fundamental approach. This is an interesting hypothesis and should produce numerous challenges from analysts who favor other methods.

QUESTIONS FOR REVIEW /

1. How should one construct and maintain the point-and-figure chart? How many charts should be maintained by the speculator–investor?
2. Contrast the types of charts that appear in *Trendline's Daily Basis Stock Charts* with *Trendline's Current Market Perspective*.
3. Explain briefly the advantages and disadvantages of the monthly range vertical bar charts over the weekly or daily range vertical bar charts.
4. Discuss the pros and cons of constructing one's own charts as opposed to subscribing to a chart service.
5. How may *Moody's Stock Survey* and *Moody's Bond Survey* be effectively used by the technician?
6. What possible uses could the investor make of *The Wall Street Journal*, *Barron's*, or the *Commercial and Financial Chronicle* in selecting bullish issues?
7. Describe briefly the financial and investment periodicals with which you are familiar and indicate the type of information included therein which is useful to the investor and to the speculator.
8. How may the daily or weekly high's and low's be used by the technician in locating probable bullish or bearish issues?
9. Can someone effectively use the list of most actively traded stocks in locating bullish or bearish issues? Support your answer with statistics.
10. Show how the technical approach may be applied to securities other than common stocks.
11. Select and defend either the technical approach to security selection or the random-walk approach.

PROBLEMS /

1. Using *The Wall Street Journal* or some other daily financial newspaper, determine from the list of the 10 or 15 most active stocks those that are forming bullish or bearish patterns.
2. By use of the daily or weekly high's and low's, reported in many leading financial newspapers, and through the use of some chart service, compile a list of (a) six companies that are showing bullish formation patterns, (b) four companies that are forming bearish formation patterns, and (c) three companies that are forming uncertainty patterns.

3. With the use of *Barron's* or some other financial newspaper, determine the warrants that are currently being traded on the American Stock Exchange. Of these issues, determine which ones appear to have a greater buying advantage at the present time than a similar investment in common stocks. Explain your choices.
4. Through the use of "Moody's Convertible Bonds," which appears periodically in *Moody's Bond Survey*, determine five issues that appear to be particularly attractive for the speculator's account. Defend your choices.
5. Read some of the recent articles on the random-walk method for selecting stocks and comment on the usefulness of the technique for the investor.

REFERENCES /

Fama, Eugene F., "Random Walks in Stock Market Prices," *Financial Analysts Journal*. Boston, Mass.: The Financial Analysts Federation, September–October 1965, pp. 55–59.

Friend, Irwin, and Douglas Vickers, "Portfolio Selection and Investment Performance," *The Journal of Finance,* September 1965, pp. 391–415.

Granville, Joseph E., *Granville's New Key to Stock Market Profits.* Englewood Cliffs, N.J.: Prentice-Hall, Inc., 1963.

Standard & Poor's Corporation, *Security Owners' Stock Guide.* New York: Standard & Poor's.

The Value Line Investment Survey. New York: A. Bernhard & Company, Inc.

The Wall Street Journal. New York: Dow Jones & Company, Inc.

part five | Portfolio Management

Parts One to Four of this book considered (1) the general characteristics and the risks associated with the major security types, (2) the operations of security markets, (3) the kind of financial information that is helpful in reaching an investment decision, and (4) the technical indicators that are sometimes an aid in gauging the direction of movement in security prices. It is important that the investor be familiar with the above areas if he is to do a good job in managing a security portfolio.

The following chapters will consider methods that are helpful to the individual in managing his investment account as well as the operating policies and performances of investment companies and other financial institutions. Both the individual investor and the manager of a large fund of securities must give some attention to (1) the frequency of stock trading, (2) the amount of industry or geographic diversification that is desirable, (3) whether to buy for the long term or to attempt to gauge advantageous buying and selling opportunities, (4) whether to invest completely in stocks or to balance the portfolio between fixed- and variable-return securities, and (5) whether to follow a defensive or an aggressive investment policy.

chapter 22 | Investment Management for the Individual

Introduction

Some stockholders prefer to use a mechanical device for making an investment in order to avoid the need for deciding when to buy or sell and how much to pay for individual issues. One such method is the dollar cost averaging plan, sometimes referred to as the monthly or quarterly investment plan. Another is a device for investing in certain stocks, such as the issues comprising the Dow Jones Industrial Average, that are trading at low multiples of earnings. Some analysts prefer to use a formula plan for determining the balance of funds to be committed to stocks and to fixed-return securities. Since many issues oscillate widely over the year or stock cycle, an attempt may be made to locate issues that are depressed in price and to sell them once they have gained in value. One who has successfully employed the technical approach may wish to combine it with some of the strictly mechanical devices. These and other investment plans are discussed in this chapter.

Since an investment in common stocks is only a part of an individual's over-all financial program, he should not overlook the importance of other investment priorities. Initially he should classify himself as a defensive investor, or one who desires to safeguard his principal, or an aggressive investor, or one who wishes to increase his principal by assuming greater risk, and pursue a program that is geared to accomplish these ends.

Investing in the Dow Jones Industrials

An investment in large, blue chip issues, such as those that compose the DJIA, offers a number of advantages. First, since a large amount of trading takes place in these securities each day, the individual has no difficulty in filling his buy or sell orders. Second, over a number of years, the performance of the DJIA has been approximately equal to that of the aggregate shares listed on the New York Stock Exchange. Although the Dow Jones Industrials do not fluctuate as broadly over the stock cycle as do lower-grade issues, they are in strong demand by many individuals and financial institutions, and thus they often trade at high multiples of earnings when compared to more speculative issues.

TABLE 22-1 / Average Price–Earnings Ratios of the 30 Dow Jones Industrial Average Stocks, 1954 to 1964

	1954	1955	1956	1957	1958	1959	1960	1961	1962	1963	1964
Allied Chemical	18.7	18.9	22.3	19.1	24.6	22.3	20.4	25.1	20.8	18.1	17.4
Aluminum Company of America	12.8	15.6	25.4	22.8	40.0	38.3	48.1	36.2	22.5	26.8	26.0
American Can Company	17.0	14.4	15.1	16.3	16.8	18.9	18.1	15.3*	15.2	17.2	16.7
American Tel. & Tel.	14.7	14.6	14.7	13.2	14.6	15.7	17.3	22.3	20.5	21.2	22.1
American Tobacco	10.0	9.7	10.2*	8.9*	10.1*	10.8*	12.6*	17.5	15.5	11.9*	11.8*
Anaconda	13.3	8.6*	5.9*	13.3	16.4	12.1*	12.8*	13.9*	9.7*	11.4*	9.4*
Bethlehem Steel	6.1*	7.5*	10.9*	10.2	15.7	22.2	18.8	17.4	19.7	15.0	12.0*
Chrysler	30.3	7.3*	32.0	4.9*	—	—	15.2	38.3	7.9*	7.8*	9.3*
duPont deNemours	18.7	22.0	25.1	21.6	26.6	27.0	27.5	24.8	21.8	23.9	27.0
Eastman Kodak	15.0	16.4	17.2	19.3	23.9	27.9	34.9	32.1	27.7	30.3	27.9
General Electric	16.6	22.7	24.0	22.0	24.5	27.1	37.6	26.0	22.4	25.4	25.2
General Foods	12.1	12.9	13.0	13.0	11.3*	14.4	18.3	23.2	30.4	24.5	25.2
General Motors	8.7*	9.8	14.7	13.5	19.3	17.0	14.3	15.8	10.8*	13.4*	14.9
Goodyear Tire & Rubber	8.1*	9.9	11.8	13.3	15.8	19.4	18.8	18.5	17.1	16.2	15.7
International Harvester	17.4	10.6	11.8	11.1	13.2*	8.7*	13.1*	16.2	13.1*	13.2*	10.7*
International Nickel	10.9	11.8	14.6	15.4	30.6	16.9	19.4	24.0	21.6	17.3	17.1
International Paper	11.4	13.3	17.4	15.5	18.6	20.0	20.8	19.6	19.1	20.7	18.5
Johns-Manville	14.6	11.9	14.2	17.4	15.4	14.2	17.2	23.3	17.5	14.4	14.7
Owens-Illinois Glass	23.5	23.8	43.1	38.0	31.1	30.0	45.1	41.9	31.3	31.7	24.1
Proctor and Gamble	15.4	16.8	16.5	14.9	18.8	20.7	23.4	32.9	28.6	27.5	27.6
Sears, Roebuck	11.7	15.0	14.6	12.4	14.6	17.0	20.2	25.5	24.0	25.6	29.1
Standard Oil of Calif.	9.1	11.2	12.0	11.3	12.9*	13.5	10.8*	11.5*	12.6*	14.0	14.2
Standard Oil (N.J.)	10.3	12.0	13.6	14.7	20.5	18.0	13.9	13.3*	13.5	14.2	17.2
Swift	14.5	12.6	18.7	15.1	20.0	12.9	14.7	22.0	14.9	14.6	12.3
Texaco	8.8*	10.7	11.1*	10.8*	13.6	13.4	11.7*	14.5*	14.1	15.6	18.1
Union Carbide	25.8	20.2	24.3	24.1	25.3	23.8	24.3	27.5	20.0	21.5	19.8
United Aircraft	8.1*	9.6*	11.2	7.4*	9.6*	12.0*	20.8	34.6	17.9	15.1	12.8
U.S. Steel	8.8	7.4*	10.4*	8.3*	14.5	23.2	16.7	27.3	22.8	15.3	14.7
Westinghouse Electric	12.9	27.8	—	15.3	17.0	20.4	24.8	35.6	20.6	28.7	18.5
Woolworth	17.1	14.0	13.1	11.7	13.5	12.1*	13.9	16.8	14.7	13.8	13.9

SOURCE: *Moody's Handbook of Common Stocks* (New York: Moody's Investors Service), selected issues.

* Within bottom five.

Certain of the Dow Jones Industrials trade at substantially lower price–earnings ratios than do others. An inspection of the average price–earnings ratios of the 30 DJIA stocks from 1954 through 1964 (Table 22-1) indicates that some issues were trading at relatively low price–earnings ratios during some years and at substantially higher price–earnings ratios in other years.

A study was made [to determine whether an initial investment, with annual substitutions, into the five Dow Jones Industrials issues that were trading at the lowest price–earnings ratios would have produced a higher rate of return in the 1955 through 1965 period than an equal investment in the over-all market average.] For this study (Table 22-2) it was assumed that a $20,000 investment fund was allocated to the purchase of the five DJIA issues that were trading at the lowest multiple of earnings. Approximately equal distribution into the five issues was made, except that fractional shares were not acquired. A 1 percent brokerage charge was paid for the purchase of securities, and the selling fee plus federal and state transfer taxes were assumed to be 1.2 percent of the value of the securities sold. Cash dividends received on the issues were reinvested during the following year in newly acquired shares.

Table 22-1 indicates the average price–earnings ratios of the 30 DJIA stocks from 1954 through 1964. Company earnings are usually reported by mid-March of each year, and the price–earnings ratios may then be computed for the preceding year. In 1954, the five companies whose common issues traded at the lowest multiples of earnings (denoted with an asterisk) were Bethlehem Steel, General Motors, Goodyear Tire and Rubber, Texaco, and United Aircraft. Approximately equal amounts of the $20,000 initial fund were placed in each of these issues. By early 1956, the stocks of General Motors, Goodyear Tire and Rubber, and Texaco were no longer among the lowest five with respect to multiples of earnings. Therefore, these issues were sold and the sales proceeds and dividends from the previous year were committed approximately equally to Anaconda Company, Chrysler Corporation, and U.S. Steel Company, which had declined to low price–earnings positions. The fund continued to hold Bethlehem Steel and United Aircraft. The above procedure was followed for the lowest price–earnings ratio companies of the DJIA for the 10-year period through March 1965, when the holdings were converted to cash. In this study all purchases and sales were assumed to have been made at the average March price for each calendar year. Prices and dividends were based on figures adjusted for stock splits and stock dividends. (See Table 22-2 for details of the transactions.)

At the end of the 10-year period the portfolio had a liquidated value of $99,957, which produced an annual compounded rate of return of 17.5 percent. Although some of the issues were sold at substantial losses, for example, United Aircraft, and Standard Oil of California, other issues showed tremendous gains, for example, U.S. Steel, General Foods, Woolworth, American Tobacco, Chrysler, and General Motors. This mechanical device of investing in the low-prestige Dow Jones Industrials and replacing them

TABLE 22-2 / An Illustration of Trading in the Lowest Five DJIA Price–Earnings Stocks, 1955 to 1965

Issue and Year	No. of Common Shares	Market Value per Share	Amount Invested (−) or Proceeds (+)	Dividends per Share	Cash Carry-over ( ) and Dividends
1955			$20,000		$ (+28)
Bethlehem Steel (bought)	124	$32	−4008	$1.81	224
General Motors	124	32	−4008	2.17	269
Goodyear Tire and Rubber	233	17	−4001	.59	137
Texaco	200	20	−4040	.952	190
United Aircraft	90	43½	−3915	2.29	206
					1054
1956					
General Motors (sold)	124	45	5513		
Goodyear Tire and Rubber	233	20½	4719		
Texaco	200	30	5928		(51)
Anaconda (bought)	68	83	−5700	5.00	340
Chrysler	300	18½	−5605	.721	216
U.S. Steel	100	58	−5858	2.60	260
Bethlehem Steel (held)	124	—		2.13	264
United Aircraft	90	—		2.50	225
					1356
1957					
Chrysler (sold)	300	18	5335		
United Aircraft	90	64	5691		(19)
American Tobacco (bought)	323	19	−6198	1.25	404
Texaco	218	28	−6165	1.057	230
Anaconda (held)	68	—		3.75	255
Bethlehem Steel	124	—		2.40	298
U.S. Steel	100	—		3.00	300
					1506

source: Table 22-1 and Mead', Her Book' (C...

1958

Security	Shares	Price	Amount	Per Share	Income
Anaconda (sold)	68	43½	2923		(11)
Bethlehem Steel	124	40	4900		
Chrysler (bought)	374	12½	−4722	.361	135
United Aircraft	80	57	−4606	3.00	240
American Tobacco (held)	323	—		1.25	404
Texaco	218	—		1.076	235
U.S. Steel	100	—		3.00	300
					1315

1959

Security	Shares	Price	Amount	Per Share	Income
Chrysler (sold)	374	14	5173	—	(+59)
Texaco	218	36	7754		
U.S. Steel	100	93	9188		
General Foods (bought)	200	40	−8080	1.28	256
International Harvester	350	22	−7777	1.00	350
Standard Oil of Calif.	155	48	−7514	1.727	268
American Tobacco (held)	323	—		1.25	404
United Aircraft	80	—		2.50	200
					1537

1960

Security	Shares	Price	Amount	Per Share	Income
General Foods (sold)	200	52	10,275		(+30)
Standard Oil of Calif.	155	37	5666		
Anaconda (bought)	160	53½	−8646	2.50	400
Woolworth	415	21	−8802	.833	346
American Tobacco (held)	323	—		1.36	439
International Harvester	350	—		1.20	420
United Aircraft	80	—		2.00	160
					1795

411

TABLE 22-2 *(Continued)*

Issue and Year	No. of Common Shares	Market Value per Share	Amount Invested (−) or Proceeds (×)	Dividends per Share	Cash Carry-over ( ) and Dividends
1961					
United Aircraft (sold)	80	42	3320	—	(+19)
Woolworth	415	24	9840	—	
Standard Oil of Calif.	172	43	−7470	1.727	297
Texaco	154	48	−7466	1.476	227
American Tobacco (held)	323	—		1.36	439
Anaconda	160	—		2.50	400
International Harvester	350	—		1.20	420
					1802
1962					
American Tobacco (sold)	323	46	14,680	—	(+55)
International Harvester	350	28	9692	—	
American Can (bought)	280	46	−13,009	2.00	560
Standard Oil (N.J.)	236	55	13,110	2.50	590
Anaconda (held)	160	—		2.50	400
Standard Oil of Calif.	172	—		1.813	312
Texaco	154	—		1.762	271
					2189
1963					
American Can (sold)	280	47	13,002	—	(+13)
Standard Oil (N.J.)	236	62½	14,573	—	253
Texaco	154	61	9281	—	852
Chrysler (bought)	600	22	−13,332	.421	588
General Motors	213	62	−13,338	4.00	400
International Harvester	490	27	−13,362	1.20	327
Anaconda (held)	160	—		2.50	2433
Standard Oil of Calif.	172	—		1.905	

1964					
Standard Oil of Calif. (sold)	172	58½	10,040	—	(421)
American Tobacco (bought)	310	32	−10,019	1.60	496
Anaconda (held)	160	—		2.50	400
Chrysler	600	—		.96	576
General Motors	213	—		4.45	948
International Harvester	490	—		1.35	661
					3102
1965					
American Tobacco (sold)	310	37	11,332		(+3,102)
Anaconda	160	63	1959		11,332
Chrysler	600	56	33,197		9,959
General Motors	213	107	22,518		33,197
International Harvester	490	41	19,849		22,518
					19,849
Value at end of 10-year period					99,957
Annual Compounded rate of return					17.5%

once each year with other issues that had fallen from grace produced a substantially larger rate of return on the investment per year than was achievable through a commitment of funds into the market average.[1]

Dollar Cost Averaging

Another strictly mechanical device for committing one's funds into securities is to select an issue that the investor believes has a good long-range outlook, to determine the amount of funds he is willing and able to commit to the issue at regular time periods, and to invest his funds systematically, regardless of the price at which the stock is trading. The individual may decide to

TABLE 22-3 /   1964 MIP Favorites on the New York
Stock Exchange

Stock	No. of Plans	Stock	No. of Plans
American Tel. & Tel.	8905	Lehman Corp.	922
General Motors	7519	Monsanto	836
General Tel. & Electronics	5076	Sperry Rand	806
Int'l Business Machines	4299	Litton Industries	738
Tri-Continental Corp.	3023	Union Carbide	729
Radio Corp. of America	2950	Ford	721
Sears, Roebuck	2913	American Bakeries	715
General Electric	2865	Merck	706
Minnesota Mining & Mfg.	2706	Westinghouse	667
Standard Oil (N.J.)	2685	American Machine & Fdry.	665
Dow Chemical	2019	Corn Products	655
International Harvester	1904	American Cyanamid	636
City Products	1677	Int'l Tel. & Tel.	632
Standard Oil of Calif.	1597	Long Island Lighting	625
Pacific Gas & Electric	1585	Florida Power	596
Eastman Kodak	1361	Columbia Gas	577
Pfizer (Chas.)	1346	Worthington Corp.	531
Scott Paper	1225	Madison Fund	503
Gulf Oil	1177	General Foods	497
Johnson & Johnson	1162	Rexall Drug & Chemical	491
Safeway Stores	1155	Great Northern Railway	489
duPont deNemours	1019	U.S. Steel	478
Phillips Petroleum Co.	1002	Lone Star Gas	467
Xerox	985	Lucky Stores	466
Texaco	971	El Paso Natural Gas	458

SOURCE: New York Stock Exchange, *The Exchange* (New York: The Exchange), January 1965.

[1] Although the idea was not illustrated with an example, such an investment plan was suggested by Benjamin Graham in *The Intelligent Investor* (New York: Harper & Row, Publishers, Inc., 1959).

invest $40 or $100 monthly, $300 quarterly, $1000 annually, or some other amount.

The monthly investment plan (MIP) has been sponsored by the New York Stock Exchange for a number of years, and from January through September 1964, 43,628 new monthly investment plan accounts were opened. At the end of September 1964, there were 115,195 of these plans in operation.[2] During recent years some of the most popular stocks with monthly investment plan purchasers have been American Telephone and Telegraph, General Motors, General Telephone and Electronics, International Business Machines, and Tri-Continental Corporation. MIP favorites are listed in Table 22-3.

If an individual has $100 each month to commit to the market, he must decide whether to invest monthly or at less frequent intervals. The 1965 brokerage cost schedule for an odd lot trading on the New York Stock Exchange is shown in Table 22-4. In the event that a monthly commitment of $100 is made, the brokerage commission is 6 percent, but if the investment is made on a quarterly basis, the brokerage commission is only 2.3 percent. Committing $300 quarterly rather than $100 monthly results in an annual rate of savings of about 6 percent on the amount of funds committed, since the investor saves $40.48 in brokerage fees on an average investment of about $665 ($\frac{1}{2} \times 12 \times 94.34). If the issue is rising at an average rate of less than 6 percent per year, it is more advantageous for the investor to commit $300 quarterly rather than $100 monthly. These rates change slightly as the amount of the monthly commitment changes.

TABLE 22-4 /   The Cost of Odd Lots in 1965 on the New York Stock Exchange

Payment	Amount Invested at Odd Lot Prices	Commission[1] Amount	Percent
$ 40	$ 37.74	$ 2.26	6.0
75	70.75	4.25	6.0
100	94.34	5.66	6.0
200	194.00	6.00	3.1
300	293.14	6.86	2.3
500	490.10	9.90	2.0
1000	985.15	14.85	1.5

[1] The commission may be less on high-priced stocks, but in all cases, the 6% minimum below $100 and the $6 charge above $100 applies.

SOURCE: Merrill Lynch, Pierce, Fenner & Smith, Inc., *Monthly Investment Plan* (New York: Merrill Lynch), p. 8.

[2] See M. S. Forbes, "Still Burned, Still Burning," *Forbes Magazine*, October 15, 1964, p. 11.

A dollar cost averaging plan for American Telephone and Telegraph common stock from 1955 to 1965 is illustrated in Table 22-5. In this case it was assumed that $300 per quarter was committed to AT & T common stock at the average January, April, July, and October market prices for the 10-year period January 1955 through October 1964. The value of the fund was computed at mid-January 1965, based on the prevailing market value per share and the number of shares held in the account at that time. This illustration assumes that (1) odd lot brokerage fees were paid each quarter, (2) cash dividends received during one quarter were reinvested the following period, and (3) no odd lot differential was assessed.

In January 1955, the investor placed $300 with his account executive to open a quarterly investment plan. The number of shares that his payment would buy was computed as follows: Since his brokerage fee was $1 plus 2 percent of the funds committed, we divide 1.02 into $299 to determine the amount to be invested. The odd lot dealer handling the account then credited the purchaser with 9.9369 shares of stock in AT & T (adjusted for subsequent splits). He received dividends per share during that quarter equivalent to $.375, and this operation was continued for 40 three-month time periods. At the end of the 10-year period, January 15, 1965, the investor owned 352.7172 shares of common stock, with a market value of $24,514, including the cash dividends which had accrued during the preceding quarter. This was a quarterly compounded rate of return of 3.34 percent, or an annual rate of return of about 13.4 percent.

Over the 10-year period, the market value of AT & T common increased at an annual compounded rate of slightly less than 9 percent, disregarding reinvestment of dividends. A dollar cost average investment in a stock that increased at a more rapid rate would have produced larger returns. In using this plan, the investor pays no attention to daily, weekly, or annual fluctuations in the price of his issue but commits his funds irrespective of the market price per share. He should look upon low prices as an opportunity to acquire more shares rather than being afraid to invest because stock prices have declined slightly from a previous high position.

Some individuals elect to use dollar cost averaging for building up their own permanent investment portfolio, for providing an educational fund for their dependent children, or for meeting retirement needs. Although it is not absolutely necessary that an issue be relatively stable in market value for this type of investment to be beneficial, it is imperative that the issue be one with a substantial long-range growth potential. For a widely swinging issue, more shares are bought when prices are depressed and fewer when prices are relatively high.

Formula Investment Plan

Formula investment plans have been designed so that an investor may determine the appropriate proportion of his total portfolio to commit to equity securities and to defensive-type issues (such as government bonds, high-grade corporate bonds, or shares of insured savings and loan associa-

TABLE 22-5 / An Illustration of Dollar Cost Averaging with a $300 Quarterly Investment in AT & T, 1955 to 1965

Mid-month Date	Cost per Share[1]	Cash to Invest	Shares Bought	Shares Held	Dividends per Share[1]	Cash Dividends Received
Jan. '55	29½	$300	9.9369	9.9369	$.375	$ 3.72
April	30½	303.72	9.9252	19.8621	.375	7.44
July	31	307.44	9.6912	29.5533	.375	11.08
Oct.	30	311.08	10.1333	39.8866	.375	14.95
Jan. '56	30½	314.95	10.0916	49.9782	.375	18.74
April	30½	317.74	10.2134	60.1916	.375	22.57
July	30	322.57	10.7190	70.9106	.375	26.59
Oct.	29½	326.59	11.0369	81.9475	.375	30.81
Jan. '57	29	330.81	11.3727	93.3203	.375	35.00
April	30	335.00	10.9150	104.2352	.375	39.09
July	29½	339.09	11.4606	115.6958	.375	43.38
Oct.	29	343.38	11.8062	127.5020	.375	47.81
Jan. '58	29½	347.81	11.9589	139.4609	.375	52.30
April	29½	352.30	11.6749	151.1358	.375	56.67
July	30	356.67	11.6232	162.7590	.375	61.03
Oct.	32	361.03	11.0303	173.7893	.375	65.17
Jan. '59	39	365.17	9.3377	183.1270	.375	68.67
April	42	368.67	8.5823	191.7093	.375	71.89
July	40¾	371.89	8.9231	200.6324	.4125	82.76
Oct.	40	382.76	9,3568	209.9892	.4125	86.62
Jan. '60	41	386.62	9.2209	219.2101	.4125	90.42
April	46	390.42	8.2995	227.5096	.4125	93.85
July	45	393.85	8.5588	236.0684	.4125	97.37
Oct.	47	397.37	8.2680	244.3364	.4125	100.78
Jan. '61	55	400.78	7.1262	251.4626	.4125	103.72
April	63	403.72	6.2670	257.7296	.4125	106.31
July	60½	406.31	6.5679	264.2975	.45	118.93
Oct.	60½	418.93	6.7724	271.0699	.45	121.98
Jan. '62	66	421.98	6.2534	277.3233	.45	124.79
April	63½	424.79	6.5429	283.8662	.45	127.74
July	53	427.74	7.8938	291.7600	.45	131.29
Oct.	54½	431.29	7.7404	299.5004	.45	134.77
Jan. '63	59	434.77	7.2078	306.7082	.45	138.02
April	61	438.02	7.0237	313.7319	.45	141.18
July	61	441.18	7.0745	320.8064	.45	144.36
Oct.	66	444.36	6.5858	327.3922	.45	147.32
Jan. '64	72	447.32	6.0773	333.4695	.45	150.06
April	70½	450.06	6.2447	339.7142	.50	169.85
July	73	469.85	6.2966	346.0108	.50	173.00
Oct.	69	473.00	6.7064	352.7172	.50	176.35
Jan. '65	69					

[1] Adjusted for splits.

SOURCE: Compiled from Table 22-4 and *Moody's Handbook of Common Stocks* (New York: Moody's Investors Service), Second Quarterly Edition, 1965.

tions). These plans are based on the premise that the general level of stock market prices fluctuates above and below a given norm. The commitment of a substantial portion of the total funds into equities when the general level of stock prices is low is advantageous, whereas a commitment of a larger percentage of the funds into defensive-type securities when the level of stock prices is high will result in smaller losses should stock market declines occur. The investor must arbitrarily determine the amount of funds he wishes to invest in stocks and what portion he wishes to commit to defensive-type investments at various levels of the stock market.[3]

Dince's article points out the similarity in movement of the DJIA and gross national product (GNP). The regression equation for the 1929 through 1962 period, using quarterly data taken as annual totals, resulted in a central value for the DJIA equal to 22.33 + 1.001 GNP. In applying the regression line that was established by using the DJIA and the GNP for the 1929 through 1962 period, one determines that the DJIA should be at 723.07 when the GNP is $700 billion, at 823 when the GNP is $800 billion, and so on. Assuming that the GNP is $700 billion at a point in time when the DJIA is at 900, how much above the expected norm is the DJIA? By dividing 900 by 723, one determines that the DJIA is approximately 24 percent above its base line. One then needs to determine what percentage of his funds to commit to stocks and what percentage to commit to defensive securities at this relative price level for stocks.

Table 22-6 divides the investment relationship between stocks and defensive investments into seven categories, as follows: 20–80; 30–70; 40–60;

TABLE 22-6 / Relationship of Percentage Difference Between Actual Dow Jones Industrial Average and Formula Value as Related to Zones Determining Variable Ratios of Stocks and Defensive Investments

Dow Jones as a Percentage of Formula Value	Zones	Stocks (%)	Defensive Investments (%)
141 or more	I	20	80
126–140	II	30	70
111–125	III	40	60
90–110	IV	50	50
75–89	V	60	40
50–74	VI	70	30
49 or less	VII	80	20

SOURCE: Marshall Ketchum, "Investment Management through Formula Timing Plans," *Journal of Business,* July 1947, p. 159; and Robert R. Dince, "Another View of Formula Planning," *Journal of Finance* 1964, p. 685.

[3] For an analysis of formula planning, see Robert R. Dince, "Another View of Formula Planning," *Journal of Finance,* December 1964, pp. 678–688.

50–50; 60–40; 70–30; and 80–20. Marshall Ketchum suggests that (1) the first zone prevail when the DJIA as a percentage of the formula value exceeds 141, (2) zone two should be followed when the DJIA as a percentage of the formula value ranges from 126 to 140, and so on, to the point where the DJIA is 49 percent or less of the expected norm.[4] In our example, 40 percent of the total funds should be devoted to stocks and 60 percent to defensive investments. An investor may use these suggested zones for determining a balance between stocks and defensive investments, or he may arbitrarily determine other zone allocations.

The results of such a formula investment plan in DJIA issues and in savings and loan shares at the average going rates of return from 1929 to 1962 are shown in Table 22-7. A hypothetical investment of $100,000 at the end of 1929 had grown to $431,249 at the end of 1962. As the DJIA fell from 1929 through 1932, defensive investments were liquidated and the proceeds were invested in stocks at the prevailing prices of the DJIA. Conversely, when switching from stocks to defensive investments, the equities were sold at the prevailing DJIA prices and the funds were transferred to shares of a savings and loan association. In this illustration, no provision was made for brokerage commissions, and interest and dividends were not reinvested. Switches were made from stocks to bonds or from bonds to stocks at the end of any quarter regardless of market fluctuations provided that the switch demanded by the formula involved more than $2000.[5]

The results of this study are not strictly comparable to the rates of return on investments in New York Stock Exchange stocks over a similar time period, 1929 through 1960,[6] because brokerage fees were disregarded and because in the investment illustration interest and dividends were not reinvested. The results obtained with the formula investment plan are not, however, impressive, since the growth in the fund amounted to only 3.75 percent compounded annually over the 33-year period, which is substantially less than a return obtainable over the same time period with a commitment of funds into common equities.

Because of the time required and the complexity associated with managing these plans—for example, determining the relative amount of holdings to commit to stocks and to defensive type equities, the periodic trading needed to maintain the predetermined relationship, and the need for making a decision about specific securities to purchase or hold—these types of plans are low in favor. In general, stock prices were moving up between 1940 and 1965 at such a rapid rate that it was disadvantageous for the investor to commit a large percentage of his funds to bonds. The investor would have committed less than half of his total holdings to stocks from 1955 through 1965, when the market prices of common shares were rising at a very rapid pace. At the same time, his investment in defensive-type issues

---

[4] Marshall Ketchum, "Investment Management through Formula Timing Plans," *Journal of Business*, July 1947, p. 159.

[5] Dince, p. 684.

[6] See the introduction to Chapter 3.

TABLE 22-7 / Year-end Portfolio Value and Yields, Using a Linear Equation

Year End	Total Value	Stock Value[1]	No. of Shares	DJIA	Income	Yield (%)[2]	Ratio (S/D)[3]
1929	$100,000	$ 20,000	80.500	286.10	$ 5,085	5.26	20/80
1930	93,339	14,358	113.427	164.58	4,727	5.54	20/80
1931	77,338	34,523	595.669	77.90	4,542	5.70	60/40
1932	81,935	45,620	957.027	59.93	4,580	4.54	70/30
1933	119,814	49,434	359.803	99.90	4,201	3.46	30/70
1934	122,691	63,837	471.709	104.04	4,795	3.62	40/60
1935	141,555	45,144	196.427	144.13	5,035	3.48	20/80
1936	147,916	32,541	166.291	177.90	5,254	3.72	20/80
1937	134,610	33,784	556.928	120.85	5,633	3.94	50/50
1938	151,434	48,340	195.702	154.76	5,377	3.31	20/80
1939	155,471	46,147	413.926	150.24	6,010	3.94	40/60
1940	149,395	59,348	569.645	131.13	6,695	4.69	50/50
1941	136,255	78,315	859.577	110.96	6,924	4.91	70/30
1942	145,958	119,994	977.944	119.40	6,876	4.46	80/20
1943	162,182	113,357	834.185	135.89	6,842	4.05	70/30
1944	175,809	124,029	814.266	152.32	6,791	3.55	70/30
1945	206,702	126,970	642.896	192.91	6,632	3.26	60/40
1946	199,929	121,266	789.787	177.20	8,653	4.29	70/30
1947	203,294	143,315	789.787	181.46	10,325	5.12	70/30
1948	200,180	139,889	903.237	177.30	11,493	5.52	80/20
1949	216,329	134,532	648.565	200.03	12,504	5.67	60/40
1950	238,741	145,482	608.491	235.41	12,472	5.01	60/40
1951	259,098	155,014	575.769	269.23	11,855	4.46	60/40
1952	272,151	168,067	559.405	291.90	12,414	4.60	60/40
1953	267,351	189,707	666.236	280.90	13,435	4.48	70/30
1954	332,782	175,948	411.462	404.39	13,470	3.87	50/50
1955	363,535	149,412	297.736	488.40	13,500	3.68	40/60
1956	368,969	189,069	369.361	499.47	13,755	3.85	50/50
1957	345,370	168,695	475.618	435.69	14,555	3.91	60/40
1958	398,287	168,232	272.963	583.65	14,585	3.57	40/60
1959	418,500	130,353	184.806	679.36	14,632	3.54	30/70
1960	407,438	168,656	264.618	615.89	15,817	3.76	40/60
1961	433,607	133,918	237.226	731.13	16,162	3.74	40/60
1962	431,249	229,406	330.662	652.10			50/50

[1] Before adjustment.   [2] On average portfolio.   [3] Ratio of stocks to defensive.

SOURCE: Robert R. Dince, "Another View of Formula Planning," *The Journal of Finance*, December 1964, p. 681.

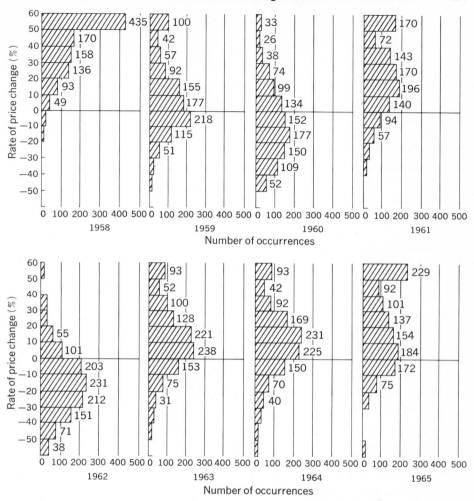

FIGURE 22-1 / Annual New York Stock Exchange common stock price changes, 1958–1965. From New York Stock Exchange, *The Exchange*, New York, selected issues.

would have been eroded by inflation. While the formula investment plan may work well in theory, it is difficult to apply, and it has resulted in less than spectacular results during the stock market booms of the 1940s, 1950s, and early 1960s. Such a plan, may, however, work to the advantage of the investor should a long bear market and deflationary period ensue. Formula investing may be classified more as a defensive-type investment "gimmick" than as an aggressive investment tool.

Annual Fluctuations in Common Stock Prices

The market prices of almost all common stocks fluctuate. Figure 22-1 illustrates the annual price changes of common stocks, from 1958 through 1965 for New York Stock Exchange issues. In each of the eight years, less than

2 percent of the issues were reported unchanged in market price from the previous year's close. The percentages of New York Stock Exchange issues that rose in price from 1958 through 1964 were 98, 60, 40, 85, 20, 75, and 75 percent, respectively. An analysis of the percentage changes in prices from one year end to the next, as reported in Figure 22-1, reveals that there was less oscillation near the end of the eight-year period. The narrowing oscillation may be attributed to the mildness of the business recession that occurred in 1960–1961 and the sustained boom period that prevailed from 1961 through 1965. Should business recessions and boom periods become more pronounced, greater fluctuation in common stock prices is to be expected.

Some security analysts contend that one reason why market prices oscillated less widely in 1965 than some seven or eight years before was that the floating supply of stock had been reduced. The acquisition of stock by financial institutions, including mutual funds, had reduced the number of shares in the hands of the general public. One writer, however, pointed out that a reduction in the floating supply of stock results in thinner issues, and that more thinly traded issues usually gyrate more widely than do issues with more market breadth.[7] Should mutual funds increase their volume of trading, stock prices could conceivably begin to oscillate more widely.

Some enterprising investors have investigated the seasonal patterns of market prices for certain groups of issues. Such a study was conducted by Merrill Lynch, Pierce, Fenner & Smith, (see Table 22-8). Although it would appear reasonable to assume that the common stock of department stores and soft drink companies would have wide seasonal swings, the actual oscillation was not adequate to be of much value to the investor. However, seasonal investing and selling in certain areas did prove to be advantageous, for example, in meat packing, eastern railroads, air conditioning, agricultural machinery, machine tools, aerospace, and fire and casualty insurance stocks. September and October were the preferred buying months for a seasonal strategy and January, February, March, or April were the optimum selling months. Whether one invested for a 5-year holding period, a 10-year holding period, or bought and sold seasonally, the latter produced substantially better results than a long-term commitment of funds. The mechanics of this study ignored the effects of capital gains taxes and selling commissions.

Between 1954 and 1964, the seasonal strategy of buying and selling common stock of Morrell between September and January produced profits of 706 percent, but the buy–hold strategy earned only 134 percent. During the 1960 to 1964 period, the buy–hold investor in Morrell common would have suffered a substantial loss.[8] Other industries may show seasonal swings in the future, while the expectations of seasonal swings in areas listed above may eliminate much of the annual oscillation in the prices of these issues.

---

[7] See, for example, E. D. Zinbarg, "Supply and Demand Factors in the Stock Market," *Financial Analysts Journal*, July 1964, pp. 84–88.

[8] "Personal Investing," *Fortune*, March 1965, p. 62, based on a report prepared by Merrill Lynch, Pierce, Fenner & Smith, Inc.

TABLE 22-8 /   How to Buy Stocks by the Calendar

Industry	Seasonal Strategy		5-Year Profits		10-Year Profits	
	Buy	Sell	Buy–Hold	Seasonal	Buy–Hold	Seasonal
Meat packing	Sept.	Feb.	15.9%	181.9%	81.9%	313.8%
Eastern railroads	Oct.	Feb.	33.7	164.8	49.3	165.4
Air conditioning	Oct.	March	46.0	129.8	63.4	347.2
Agricultural machinery	Oct.	Feb.	17.6	82.2	72.5	145.0
Machine tools	Sept.	April	30.7	78.0	82.5	235.8
Aerospace	Sept.	Jan.	2.6	46.6	36.8	215.7
Fire and casualty insurance	Oct.	Feb.	62.8	79.0	104.6	222.5

SOURCE: "Personal Investing," *Fortune*, March 1965, p. 62, based on a report prepared by Merrill Lynch, Pierce, Fenner & Smith, Inc.

Other Investment Plans

The use of the technical approach in timing security transactions was discussed in Part Four of this book. This method will not be considered here, although numerous technicians who have been writing in the area suggest a possibility of earning annual returns of more than 20 percent. Whether or not an individual is willing to spend an adequate amount of time in reviewing and/or maintaining his charts and whether he can become proficient in using them will influence to a large extent his ability to profit from the chart device.

It is generally recommended that the investor trade with the tide. For example, during 1963, 245 of the Big Board common issues closed at prices more than 30 percent above their previous year's closing price. Only 26 of the issues had declined by 30 percent or more. During 1964, 227 New York Stock Exchange issues increased by 30 percent or more, while only 37 declined by this amount. Conversely, during the 1962 stock market decline, only 25 Big Board issues closed at more than 30 percent above the 1961 year-end price, and 260 of the issues closed at prices greater than 30 percent below earlier levels.

It is possible for the investor to make profits both on a long purchase or on a short sale. Although no statistics are available to indicate the profitability of dividing an account between long purchases and short sales, some mixing may be desirable. When stock prices are extremely high and when all factors point toward a probable price decline, it is advisable to commit only a portion of one's funds, say 60 or 70 percent, to long purchases and to use the balance for short sales or cash reserves for buying "bargain issues" in market slumps. The investor may use his funds to purchase long securities and use the buying power generated through margin (assuming that the margin requirement is less than 100 percent) for covering his short positions. For example, assuming that the margin requirement is 70 percent and that an individual has $14,000 to commit to a stock fund, he may use additional buying power of $6000 created through margin borrowing. If he wishes, he may commit the $14,000 to long purchases of stocks and use the balance of his buying power to cover his short sale requirements. Although he must pay any dividends that are declared on the issues in which he is short, he is not required to pay interest to the brokerage firm. In many cases, the dividend yields on the securities sold are substantially less than the interest rate charged by brokerage firms for customer margin. Before an investor adopts this practice, however, he should become proficient in detecting the probable direction of prices of selected issues. Since short selling is more dangerous than long purchases in that a loss of more than 100 percent may occur, the bear should protect his position by the use of stop buy orders. Long purchasers may wish to use stop sell orders and thus limit their losses when stock market prices are declining. The enterprising investor may profit from investigating some of the issues that seasonally oscillate in order to locate long purchase candidates as well as issues to be sold short during appropriate periods.

Other Considerations

The Importance of Priorities

The student of investments should not overlook the importance of setting priorities in his investment program (see Chapters 5 and 6). He should review these priorities carefully before he commits a large percentage of his total net worth to equity investments, and he should recall that a logical investment program calls for the following seven priorities:

1. A cash reserve should be held in the form of demand deposit accounts, savings accounts, Series E bonds, or shares of an insured savings and loan association equal to one's expenses for three to six months. This liquid fund offers some protection in the event of sickness, inability to work, death in the family, or other emergencies. Otherwise, the loss of an automobile, household goods, or an equity investment in a home may result from an inability to meet monthly obligations.

2. Life insurance coverage adequate to provide the wage earner's dependent children with a suitable standard of living in the event of the untimely death of the wage earner is also important. Although the wage earner should consider the possible Social Security survivors' benefits that accrue to his dependent children, these are discontinued once the children reach the age of 18, or for full-time students, 22. Social Security benefits are insufficient to provide an adequate standard of living and should be supplemented with some private insurance.

3. It is also recommended that a substantial equity in a home be obtained prior to committing funds into the stock market. Home ownership,

particularly with a mortgage debt on the home, offers some tax relief if one elects to take deductions in computing federal income taxes. During inflationary periods, home ownership represents equity in a fixed asset and provides a hedge against inflation.

4. Some provision should be made for meeting the costs of higher education for dependent children. For the average student, the cost of a college degree in 1965 was about $10,000. Funds to meet this goal may be provided by an insurance plan, a systematic savings plan, a monthly investment in shares of a growing mutual fund, or through the dollar cost averaging method of investing in a common stock of a growing business firm.

5. Some individuals prefer to save during certain years so that they may have a supplemental income prior to their retirement. This provides more income during the years in which the children are in high school or college. Supplemental income may be provided through equity investments, investments in real estate, or other media.

6. In order to provide an adequate standard of living during retirement years, the wage earner should accumulate some savings or have other sources of income in addition to Social Security benefits. This may be in the form of additional insurance, an annuity plan, a private retirement plan, common stock or real estate investments, and others.

7. Before reaching retirement age the individual should give some thought to preserving his estate. He should consult the prevailing federal gift and tax laws to determine the advisability of transferring a portion of his estate to his beneficiaries prior to his death.

Although a major part of this book has been devoted to the study of common stocks, the individual should place this type of investment in its appropriate perspective. Common stock commitments may be used for priorities (4), (5), or (6) above, but the investor should not neglect the importance of the first three priorities.

Aggressive versus Defensive Policies

Before deciding on an investment route, the individual should classify himself as an aggressive or as a defensive investor. An aggressive investor is one who is willing to spend a considerable amount of time and some money for the purchase and study of financial services and to seek out capital gains situations. He is willing to take some losses, but attempts to maximize his gains through capital appreciation. The defensive investor, conversely, wishes to protect his investment from erosion, inflation, and capital losses due to declines in market value. Therefore, he may maintain a mixed fund of some bonds and some stocks. It may be prudent financial policy for both types of investors to commit a portion of their funds to fixed-return securities and the balance to equity investments. The amount committed to each depends upon the philosophy of the individual; the amount of time he can devote to managing the account; and the relative position of stock market prices, dividend yields, and bond yields.[9]

Both the investor and the speculator can make money in the stock market. The speculator, however, must maintain constant vigilance or a substantial percentage of his capital may be wiped out with falling prices. The investor, on the other hand, has confidence in the economy of the country and pays little attention to the fluctuating market values of his blue chip issues. His defensive position with some bonds and some stocks offers hedges against market risks and inflation. Although short-term speculation may offer substantial rewards to those who are able to obtain them, the risks are very great. A sound program of investment should be developed by the investor.

Summary

When an investor wishes to use some mechanical means for investing in a given stock or stocks, he may elect to invest in issues of the DJIA that have low price–earnings ratios. A commitment of funds into five of these low-priced issues, with annual trading and a reinvestment of dividends, resulted in an annual growth rate of more than 17 percent per year from 1955 through 1965. Another mechanical device for investing in a security is dollar cost averaging, which may be applied to a monthly or quarterly investment plan. Such a plan followed with the common stock of American Telephone and Telegraph Company on a quarterly basis from January 1955 through January 1965 resulted in an annual capital gain of 13.4 percent, including reinvestment of dividends.

Although some individuals suggest the use of a formula investment plan for determining the allocation of funds between common stocks and defensive investments, the investor is still faced with the problem of determining which issues to purchase and to sell.

The speculator who wishes to buy and sell securities and to attempt to make a greater return on his average investment than is possible through a buy–hold investment may consider the stocks that fluctuate rather broadly over the year, or he may wish to use the technical approach to security analysis. Regardless of the methods employed in attempting to make a profit, one should not overlook the importance of his investment objectives and priorities.

QUESTIONS FOR REVIEW /

1. During what time periods from 1929 through 1965 would it have been beneficial for the individual to have held bonds? to have held stocks?
2. How would you determine the price–earnings ratio at which a stock is trading?

[9] See Graham, *The Intelligent Investor.*

3. Explain how a trading account in the DJIA low price–earnings ratio stocks may be administered.
4. Explain the significance of the monthly investment plan. Should commitments of funds be made monthly or quarterly? Explain.
5. Contrast the results of a dollar cost averaging plan for the common stocks of American Telephone and Telegraph with a commitment into the low price–earnings ratio issues of the DJIA for the 10-year period 1955 through 1965.
6. What relationship exists between gross national product and the DJIA?
7. How would you determine the relationship between equity and defensive investments in a formula investment plan?
8. Contrast the results of a formula investment plan with those obtained by investing in the DJIA from 1929 through 1960 and from 1950 to 1960.
9. Do you believe that stock prices were fluctuating less violently during the early 1960s than during the latter 1950s? How would you explain this difference?
10. Certain industries suggest seasonal strategies for the purchase and sale of securities. Enumerate these. Do you believe that the knowledge of this fact by the general public will broaden or reduce the cyclical swing in the market values of these issues?
11. Should an individual maintain both a long and a short position in the stock market? Why or why not?
12. What place does an investment in common stock have in an individual's overall investment program?

PROBLEMS /

1. Assume that the general level of stock prices will decline within the near future. You propose to make short sales of certain Dow Jones Industrials that have been trading at high price–earnings ratios and to cover the short sales one year later. On that date you sell other issues short that are then among the top five with respect to price–earnings ratios. Would this plan produce significantly greater capital gains than buying low-priced DJIA issues long? Prepare such a study for the past five years, assuming that you commit $20,000 to a short interest in the five DJIA issues that are trading at the highest price–earnings ratios. You must pay the lender of the stock the amount of dividends declared on each of these issues. Include the amount of buying and selling costs involved in each of these transactions. What annual rate of return or deterioration in your account has come about during the five-year period?
2. For a DJIA issue for the last five years, assume that you make a quarterly investment of $300 at the opening market price on the first trading day of January, April, July, and October. These prices may be found in *The Wall Street Journal, Barron's, The Security Owner's Stock Guide, Commercial and Financial Chronicle,* and other sources. Compute the amount of brokerage fees and odd lot commissions that will be charged to your account, reinvest your dividends, and determine the number of shares of the issue that you will own at the end of the five-year period. Compare the market value of the stock at the end of the five years with the total amount of funds that you committed. What annual rate of return did you earn on this investment? Compare your results with those obtained by other members of the class with other issues to see which common stocks would have provided the best over-all results during the last five years.

3. By use of the formula investment plan outlined in this chapter and assuming a portfolio of $100,000, determine the amount of funds that you currently should have committed to stocks and the amount that should be invested in bonds (or other defensive issues). Suggest investment media for the portion of the funds that is to be committed to stocks.

4. Select one of the seasonal industries listed in Table 22–8 and compile a list of the companies within this industry whose common stocks usually fluctuate broadly over the year. If the current calendar date is near the strategic buying position, determine which of the issues should be acquired for the greatest possible gain. If the position is near or just past the strategic selling position, determine whether or not these issues would make good short-sale candidates. The use of point-and-figure charts or vertical bar charts may facilitate your study. How would you recommend that your funds be invested during the periods when they are not committed to these seasonal issues?

REFERENCES /

Dince, Robert R., "Another View of Formula Planning," *The Journal of Finance.* New York: American Finance Association, December 1964.

Forbes, M. S., "Still Burned, Still Burning," *Forbes Magazine.* New York: Forbes, Inc., October 15, 1964.

Graham, Benjamin, *The Intelligent Investor.* New York: Harper & Row, Publishers, Inc., 1959.

Ketchum, Marshall, "Investment Management through Formula Timing Plans," *Journal of Business,* July 1947.

Moody's Handbook of Common Stock. New York: Moody's Investors Service, Inc.

"Personal Investing," *Fortune,* March 1965.

"Rates of Return on NYSE Common Stocks: 1926–1960," *The Commercial and Financial Chronicle,* December 12, 1963.

Zinbarg, E. D., "Supply and Demand Factors in the Stock Market," *Financial Analysts Journal.* Boston, Mass.: The Financial Analysts Federation, July 1964.

chapter 23 | Investment Company Portfolios

Introduction

Investment companies are corporations organized for the primary purpose of holding common and/or preferred stock issues, corporate bonds, government issues, or a combination of these as investment media. In order to provide themselves with flexibility, investment companies generally maintain from 5 to 15 percent of their total assets in cash and/or short-term government securities, the amount of such holdings depending upon how investment company managers foresee the probable movement in stock prices versus bond yields. Individuals who do not choose to manage their own portfolio or who wish to obtain a higher degree of diversification than is possible through a small commitment of funds directly into common shares may elect to invest in investment company shares.

Investment companies may be divided into *open-end* and *closed-end* companies. The *open-end* investment company, or mutual fund, stands ready to sell additional shares of its own stock to the general public at the market value of each outstanding share plus a load factor of about 6 to 10 percent (a few funds charge no load fee) and is willing to redeem the shares at market value. For example, a mutual fund with $20 million in assets, 1 million common shares outstanding, and a load charge of 8 percent would offer to sell (ask price) additional shares at $21.60 and offer to redeem outstanding shares (bid price) at $20 each. Thus a short-term trader would forfeit his load charge, which is used to defray marketing costs. Conversely, the *closed-end* investment company does not continuously issue new shares of its own stock. Trading takes place in the outstanding shares of such companies, and the investor must acquire his shares on the open market. Although the closed-end investment company has a relatively fixed amount of capital, it may sell preferred stocks, debentures, debentures with warrants attached, or make new sales of common stocks in much the same manner as an ordinary business corporation (as illustrated later for Tri-Continental Corporation).

In 1966, about 300 open-end and 50 closed-end investment companies were operating in the United States, with 22 of the latter being listed on the New York Stock Exchange and the balance being traded through the American Stock Exchange, regional exchanges, or the over the counter markets.

This chapter will trace the development and growth of investment companies in this country and will consider the various objectives for which investment companies are formed, the relative sizes of some of the larger investment companies, the operating performance of open- and closed-end investment companies, the cost of owning investment company shares, the special tax provisions applicable to investment companies and to their shareholders, and how the buying and selling of securities in the open market by investment companies may affect the market price of individual issues.

Origin and Growth

Origin

The modern-day investment company originated in Europe in the early nineteenth century but did not spread to the United States until 1894. This type of corporation was not significant until the early 1920s, but during that decade the closed-end investment company became very important. Several hundred closed-end investment companies were in operation in 1929, owning approximately $7 billion in corporate securities. Their high degree of leverage left them very susceptible to the 85 percent decline in stock prices from 1929 to 1932, and the equities of many were entirely erased.

Open-end investment companies had not gained in popularity by 1930, but since they operated with little leverage, their shares were less adversely affected than were those of closed-end companies. Before 1930, there were about 20 mutual funds in operation, which held about $200 million in assets.

Because of the poor operating performance of investment companies during the stock market decline of the early 1930s, this type of security was very unpopular during that decade. The net amount of assets for investment companies continued to decline until the early years of World War II. From that date forward, and with the passage of the Investment Company Act of 1940, some confidence was restored in the operating ability of investment companies, and individuals began to buy their securities. Because of the inherent risk involved in using a substantial amount of leverage, closed-end investment companies have never regained the stature they had in the 1920s.

Growth

Table 23-1 traces the growth of mutual funds in the United States from 1940 through 1965. At the end of 1940, some 68 open-end investment companies were members of the Investment Company Institute. This did not include all of the operating investment companies, but it did account for substantially all of the assets held by mutual funds. The mutual funds grew between 1944 and 1965, with annual gross share sales during the early

TABLE 23-1 /   Growth of Mutual Funds, 1940 to 1965

Millions

Year	Total Net Assets	Gross Sales	Redemp- tions	Net Sales	Rate of Redemp- tions	Share- holder Accounts	Number of Funds
1965	$35,222	$4358	$1962	$2396	6.1%	6,709,000	170
1964	29,116	3403	1874	1529	6.9	6,301,908	159
1963	25,214	2459	1505	954	6.5	6,151,935	165
1962	21,271	2699	1123	1576	5.1	5,910,455	169
1961	22,789	2951	1160	1791	5.8	5,319,201	170
1960	17,026	2097	842	1255	5.1	4,897,600	161
1959	15,818	2280	786	1494	5.4	4,276,077	155
1958	13,242	1620	511	1109	4.7	3,630,096	151
1957	8714	1391	407	984	4.6	3,110,392	143
1956	9046	1347	433	914	5.1	2,518,049	135
1955	7838	1207	443	765	6.4	2,085,325	125
1954	6109	863	400	463	7.8	1,703,846	115
1953	4146	672	239	433	5.9	1,537,250	110
1952	3931	783	196	587	5.6	1,359,000	110
1951	3130	675	322	353	11.4	1,110,432	103
1950	2531	519	281	238	12.5	938,651	98
1949	1974	386	108	278	6.2	842,198	91
1948	1506	274	127	147	8.7	722,118	87
1947	1409	267	89	178	6.5	672,543	80
1946	1311	370	144	227	11.1	580,221	74
1945	1284	292	110	182	10.2	497,875	73
1944	822	169	71	98	9.2	421,675	68
1943	654	116	51	65	8.9	341,435	68
1942	487	73	25	48	5.6	312,609	68
1941	402	53	45	8	10.6	293,251	68
1940	448	°	°	°	°	296,056	68

° Not available.

SOURCE: *Investment Companies* (New York: Arthur Wiesenberger & Company, 1966), p. 20.

1960s amounting to about $2 to $4 billion. Over that period, however, from 30 to 60 percent of the number of shares sold were also redeemed. Nevertheless, annual growth in net share sales of $1 to $2 billion was attained in the early 1960s. At the same time, the number of shareholders increased from about 300,000 in 1940 to more than 6,700,000 in 1965. The number of mutual funds that were members of the Investment Company Institute increased from 68 to 170 over that time period, and it was estimated that about 300 open-end investment companies were in operation by the end of 1965. Many of these were not members of the Investment Company Institute and were very small in size. By the end of 1965, these funds held more than $35 billion in net assets.

Objectives and Relative Size of the Companies

Types and Objectives

Both open- and closed-end investment companies are classified by type of fund, with some investment companies maintaining only one type while others operate a large number, for example, Keystone. The generally recognized types of investment company funds are (1) diversified common stock, (2) industry-specialized, (3) balanced, (4) income, (5) tax-free exchange, (6) Canadian and/or international, and (7) bond and preferred stock.

In a diversified common stock fund, the assets are broadly diversified by industry and company. Some funds maintain investments in only 10 to 15 industries and perhaps 30 or 40 companies, but others are much more diversified and hold 100 to 150 different issues representative of more than 30 different industries. Diversified common stock funds have been the most important of the seven types for many years when measured in dollar amount of assets, and they place primary importance upon capital gains.

In an industry-specialized fund the assets are invested in one or a few different industries, such as the aerospace and airline industry or the petrochemical industry. Common stock is the predominant type of security held. Investors who believe that a particular industry has unusual growth potential may seek this type of investment.

The balanced fund consists of some balance among investments in common stocks, diversified as to industry and as to company; preferred stocks, bonds of corporations, and government securities. The balanced fund offers some protection against deterioration in common stock prices by maintaining a portion of its assets in fixed-return securities.

The income fund places primary importance upon obtaining a high return on investment either in the form of dividends or interest. During the latter 1950s and early 1960s, when dividend yields on common stocks were substantially lower than yields on preferred stocks and corporate bonds, income funds invested heavily in fixed-return securities. Because of the rapid capital appreciation in common stock prices during this period, the income funds did not produce the growth rates obtained by the common stock funds.

Tax-free exchange funds are invested predominantly in municipal securities on which the interest is exempted from federal income taxes, and this tax-free status is passed on to the shareholders. Investors who are in high federal income tax brackets are sometimes interested in the shares of tax-free exchange funds. Capital gains, of course, are taxable to the shareholders.

Canadian and international funds are organized for the purpose of buying only Canadian and/or international securities. Canadian shares grew in market value and were in demand for a time until the early 1960s but declined in popularity during 1963 and 1964. Rapid growth of the U.S. economy and a high level of stock prices, weak foreign security markets, and the interest equalization tax law of 1964 combined to produce lower returns on these types of funds than on those investing heavily in domestic common stock issues.

Bond and preferred stock funds are committed to investments in corporate bonds and preferred stocks. Although such securities pay a higher dividend or interest rate than most common stocks, they do not offer the growth potential of the latter. During periods in which common stock prices are increasing substantially, bond and preferred stock funds do not grow in market value nearly as rapidly as do the common stock funds. Conversely, there is some capital appreciation in the shares of bond and preferred stock funds during periods of recession, because as interest rates fall, the market values of these securities increase. Therefore, the capital gains realized in a bond and preferred stock fund are usually generated during recessions, when common stock prices are declining, interest yields are falling, and high-grade bond and preferred stock prices are rising.

Some investment companies operate more than one type of mutual fund and will permit an investor to switch all or a portion of his investment from one to another. It is sometimes wise to switch a portion of the investment from a diversified common stock fund to a bond and preferred stock fund when common stock prices are at unusually high levels, and the reverse is desirable, if permissible, when common stock prices are depressed. Some companies permit such switching without the payment of a load charge, while others require transfer fees.

Table 23-2 indicates that at the end of 1965 diversified common stock funds comprised almost two thirds of the total assets of all open-end investment companies. The balanced funds represented an additional 21 percent, while industry-specialized funds comprised 5 percent. The other funds combined held about 8 percent of the total assets of mutual funds. The ratios changed little between 1963 and 1965.

TABLE 23-2 /   Mutual Fund Assets by Types on December 31, 1963 and 1965 (dollars in millions)

Type of Fund	1963		1965	
Diversified common stock	$13,484	60%	$24,029	66%
Industry-specialized	2347	9	1815	5
Balanced	6277	24	7646	21
Income	906	3	1415	4
Tax-free exchange	565	2	801	2
Canadian and international	295	1	231	1
Bond and preferred stock	197	1	252	1

SOURCE: *Investment Companies* (New York: Arthur Wiesenberger & Company, 1964 and 1966), pp. 61 and 44, respectively.

Relative Size

Table 23-3 lists the 50 largest mutual funds that were operating in the United States as of December 31, 1965. The largest of the funds, Investors Mutual, had assets in excess of $2.9 billion, owned by 361,000 shareholders. Other open-end investment companies that had more than $1 billion in assets included Massachusetts Investors Trust, the Wellington Fund, the Dreyfus Fund, the Affiliated Fund, the United Accumulative Fund, and Fundamental Investors. Many of these mutual funds had in excess of 200,000 shareholders as of that date.

TABLE 23-3 / The 50 Largest Mutual Funds as of December 31, 1965

	Net Assets (millions)	Number of Shareholders (thousands)
Investors Mutual	$2977	435
Massachusetts Investors Trust	2252	217
Wellington Fund	2048	363
Investors Stock Fund	1801	346
Insurance Securities Trust Fund	1347	191
Dreyfus Fund	1339	324
Affiliated Fund	1294	202
United Accumulative Fund	1237	279
Fundamental Investors	1151	186
Massachusetts Investors Growth Stock Fund	898	145
United Income Fund	685	96
Fidelity Fund	636	75
Fidelity Trend Fund	636	98
National Investors Corp.	545	161
Investment Company of America	505	78
Hamilton Funds, Series H-DA	494	272
Television-Electronics Fund	487	111
Investors Variable Payment Fund	469	128
Puritan Fund	462	53
Chemical Fund	434	60
George Putnam Fund of Boston	404	52
Dividend Shares	386	87
Boston Fund	383	36
Broad Street Investing Corp.	364	36
Putnam Growth Fund	362	98
Fidelity Capital Fund	343	73
Financial Industrial Fund	342	96

TABLE 23-3 *(Continued)*

	Net Assets (millions)	Number of Shareholders (thousands)
State Street Investment Corp.	342	19
National Securities, Stock Series	337	62
American Mutual Fund	331	49
Keystone Lower-Priced Common Stock Fund (S-4)	310	127
United Science Fund	297	94
Delaware Fund	275	42
Group Securities, Common Stock Fund	275	45
Incorporated Investors	273	56
Axe Houghton Fund B	265	70
Eaton & Howard Stock Fund	253	32
One William Street Fund	247	60
Eaton & Howard Balanced Fund	225	25
T. Rowe Price Growth Stock Fund	197	42
Colonial Fund	196	19
Keystone Growth Fund (K-2)	194	43
Commonwealth Investment Co.	191	33
Founders Mutual Fund	187	85
Selected American Shares	185	26
Channing Growth Fund	181	67
Incorporated Income Fund	178	34
National Securities, Growth Stocks Series	174	64
Washington Mutual Investors	170	28
Diversified Investment Fund	163	27

SOURCE: Standard and Poor's Corporation, "Standard & Poor's Investment Companies," *Industry Surveys* (New York: Standard & Poor's, September 15, 1966), p. I-37.

Operating Performance

A graphic comparison of the market performances of investment companies and Standard & Poor's Average of 500 Stocks is shown in Figure 23-1. Using 1941 through 1943 as the base, one finds that the nine investment companies used in the investment company share index, computed from the bid price of selected open- and closed-end investment company shares, rated more favorably from 1929 through 1936 but slightly poorer from 1937 through 1942 than Standard & Poor's average. From 1942 through 1955, conversely, the investment companies performed slightly better than did the market average, but from 1960 through 1966, Standard & Poor's average outperformed the investment company shares included in this index.

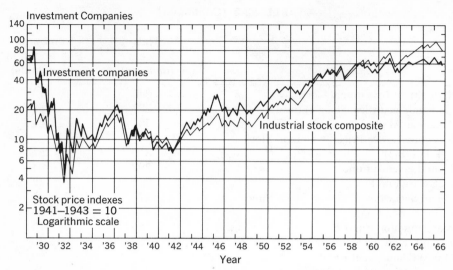

FIGURE 23-1 / A comparison between the stock indexes of investment company shares and Standard & Poor's 500. The investment company common stocks used in Standard & Poor's price index are: Adams Express, Dominick Fund, General American Investors, General Public Service, Lehman Corporation, Madison Fund, Niagara Share, Tri-Continental, and U.S. & Foreign Securities. From Standard & Poor's Corporation, "Standard & Poor's Investment Companies," *Industry Surveys,* New York, Standard & Poor's, September 15, 1966, p. 1–44.

Open-End Investment Companies

The market performance of the various types of open-end investment funds, which include (1) diversified common stock, (2) Canadian and/or international, (3) growth with income, (4) income with growth, (5) growth-income-stability, and (6) income, were compared with the performance of the Dow Jones Industrial Average by years from 1957 through 1964, and the results appear in Figure 23-2. For a majority of the years, the performance of the total of diversified common stock funds and those with objectives (3), (4), and (5) followed closely that of the DJIA. Income and Canadian and/or international funds, on the average, performed less well than the DJIA. The movement in the Dow Jones, however, is gross, while the change in the net asset value per share for the funds is net of brokerage and management costs. Before investing in the share of a mutual fund, the investor should study the objectives of numerous funds and the historical performance relative to the general stock market.[1]

---

[1] This type of study may be made from the annual reports or prospectuses published by a large number of the funds or by reference to a recent issue of *Investment Companies* (New York: Arthur Wiesenberger & Company).

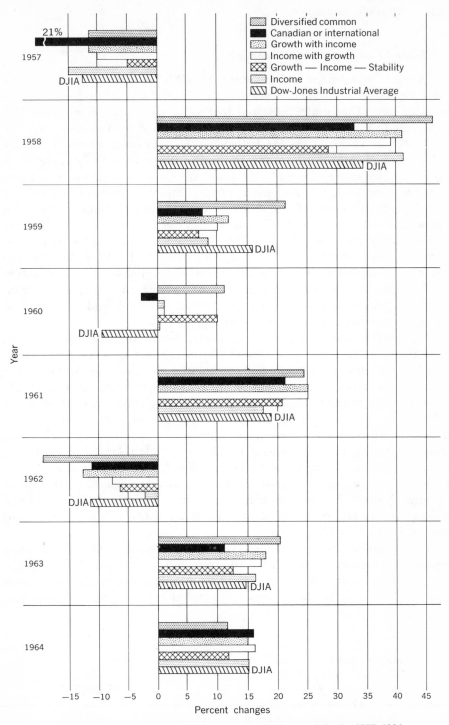

FIGURE 23-2 / Performance of selected types of mutual funds, 1957–1964.
From *Investment Companies,* New York, A. Wiesenberger
& Company, 1965, pp. 119–123.

Closed-End Investment Companies

A study was reported in *Financial World* (Table 23-4) on New York Stock Exchange closed-end mutual funds for the six-month period ended June 30, 1964. The results indicated that 21 of the 22 listed securities had appreciated in capital value. The Eurofund declined by 4 percent over the six-month period. All of the funds that had been in operation from January 1, 1954 through June 30, 1964 appreciated in value. Growth rates for 18 of the 22 companies for the past 10½ years are shown in column 3 of Table 23-4. The four funds that had capital appreciation in excess of 300 percent over this period included Central Securities, 399 percent; National Aviation, 358 percent; Niagara Share, 307 percent; and Carriers and General, 304 percent. Over the same period, the DJIA increased by 196 percent. Before investing in these or other funds the investor should (1) determine that the objectives of the fund are in line with his needs, (2) determine the operating results during recent market advances and declines, (3) analyze the probable performance of the portfolio holdings of the fund, and (4) evaluate the ability and honesty of the fund's management.

The market price of the shares is affected less by the asset value of each share than by the earnings ability of the investment company, and many closed-end shares were trading at substantial discounts in August 1964. For example, Tri-Continental, not withstanding capital appreciation of 244 percent during the previous 10½ years, was trading at a 25 percent discount below book value. The shares of other companies that were earning a more generous return on their investment during the first half of 1964 were generally trading at lower discounts. These included American European Securities, Lehman Corporation, Madison Fund, Central Securities, Petroleum Corporation, and Standard Shares. The market value of a majority of the funds had either remained relatively constant from the end of 1963 until August 1964 or had declined slightly, while for a few of the funds it had increased from $2 to $3 per share.

Mutual funds are permitted only one type of capital, common shares, but closed-end investment companies are frequently leveraged. For example, Tri-Continental Corporation, the largest diversified closed-end investment company, had the following types of capital outstanding on December 31, 1965:

Type	Number of Shares
Cumulative preferred stock ($2.50 dividend, $50 par, callable at $55)	752,740
Common stock ($.50 par)	15,266,592
Perpetual warrants (each entitles holder to buy 2.54 shares of common stock at $8.88 per share)	547,474

The corporation had called for redemption in 1965 a $20 million, 3⅞ percent debenture issue. The 1965 month-end discounts below book value per share

TABLE 23-4 / Market Performance of New York Stock Exchange Closed-End Mutual Fund Shares for Selected Years

	Performance*			Discount†		
	6 Months 1964	5½ Years	10½ Years	12/31/63	8/19/64	Stock Price 12/31/63 to 8/19/64
Diversified Companies						
Abacus Fund	+ 9%	+66%	—	11%	16%	42⅛–42½
Adams Express	+ 9	+45	+230%	9	15	26½–26⅞
American European Sec.	+10	+42	+172	8	9	29½–29
Amer. International	+10	+46	+228	6	15	16–15¾
Carriers & General	+10	+64	+303	8	13	32½–33⅜
Dominick Fund	+ 9	+52	+237	9	16	22–21
General Amer. Invest.	+18	+45	+215	3	11	31⅛–31¾
General Public Service	+ 8	+66	+289	15	19	5⅝–5¾
International Holdings	+ 8	+58	+224	19	14	34⅞–37
Lehman Corp.	+10	+56	+235	P1	10	30⅛–29⅛
Madison Fund	+12	+65	+272	P13	5	22⅛–19⅝
Niagara Share	+12	+77	+307	6	7	24–26
Tri-Continental	+ 8	+54	+244	21	25	46⅛–47½
U.S. & Foreign	+12	+45	+214	24	24	28⅝–31⅜
Nondiversified and Specialized Companies						
Amer. Research & Dev.	+ 2	+52	+217	P6	13	24–19¾
Amer.–S. African	+ 4	+59	—	34	30	30⅛–33
Central Securities	+ 8	+120	+399	P5	3	18¾–19⅛
Eurofund	– 4	—	—	24	30	13⅜–12
National Aviation	+13	+85	+358	2	12	28⅞–27½
Petroleum Corp.	+11	+45	+235	6	7	17⅛–18⅝
Standard Shares	+ 8	+83	—	8	8	31⅞–34
United Corp.	+ 6	+48	+176	12	12	8¼–8½

* Approximate change in net assets per share with capital gains (reinvested) plus income dividends (received in cash).
† Latest discounts based on net asset value as of 6/30/64.
P = premium.

SOURCE: *Financial World,* August 26, 1964, p. 22.

of the common stock ranged from 22 to 29 percent, and a 6.2 percent dilution in such book value would have occurred with the exercise of all warrants. Over the 1956 to 1965 period, the warrants had increased in market value some three times the rate of the common shares, while the latter had grown slightly more rapidly than the DJIA.[2]

Comparing Growth Rates with Stock Averages

Open- and closed-end investment companies have frequently been criticized because their growth rate has been less than that of the popular averages from 1958 to 1965. There are a number of reasons for this gap. First, investment firms to a great extent invest in the large, blue chip companies, which grew at a slower rate over this period than medium- and low-grade securities. In addition, the performance of the investment companies is measured after the payment of management fees, operating expenses, and brokerage fees and transfer taxes.

Open-end investment companies are highly diversified, and as the general level of common stock prices increases, the common stock funds usually increase in value by approximately the same percentage. When an individual fund liquidates much of its holdings prior to a decline in the stock market and reinvests in low-priced stocks, it shows an over-all higher growth rate than a company that remains fully invested during stock market swings. However, few of the mutual funds are able to liquidate substantial amounts of holdings. To whom would they sell their stock—to each other, to pension funds, or to individual investors? Investment companies owned between 6 and 7 percent of the aggregate market value of New York Stock Exchange issues in December 1965 and had been accumulating shares during previous years.

Although some individual investment companies had outstanding growth rates during the early 1960s, others performed less spectacularly. Before an investor commits his money to mutual fund shares, he should study the policies and goals of the company to see whether or not they agree with his own investment philosophy. If he desires to be freed from managing his investment account and prefers a high degree of diversification, an investment in mutual fund shares is desirable. He should not, however, expect the investment company to achieve annual growth rates substantially higher than those obtainable on a widely diversified list of common stocks. Freedom from worry over market fluctuations may be conducive to better health for some individuals, and this may be attainable with mutual fund investments.

The Cost of Owning Investment Company Shares

Load Factor

One who buys open-end investment company shares must pay the ask price for the shares, which is computed each day on the basis of the market value of the investments being held by the fund. In addition, with many

[2] See *Investment Companies,* 1966, pp. 326–327.

companies he must also pay a load factor averaging about 7½ or 8 percent. A few investment companies offer a reduced load factor for large commitments of $10,000, $25,000, or more, but many of the funds do not do so. Assuming that an investment company has $10 million in assets and has one million shares of securities outstanding, the offering price is $10 per share plus a load charge of, say, 8 percent. The investor pays $10.80 for each of the shares acquired, but he pays no odd lot fee for buying less than 100 shares. Assuming that the individual wishes to resell the shares to the company on the following day, and that the market value of the assets has not changed, he receives $10 per share for the securities. Since he is out his load factor, it is unwise to commit funds to this type of investment for a short period of time. If one plans to commit his funds for a longer period, such as one year, two years, or more, it may be profitable to purchase mutual fund shares.

The purchaser of mutual fund shares may buy any number of shares in a lump-sum purchase, thus paying the ask price plus the load charge of 6 to 10 percent; or some companies offer a contractual plan that permits the investor to make monthly installment payments on the contract. The Investment Company Act of 1940 permits mutual funds to assess a load fee not in excess of 9 percent of the total contracted amount and not to exceed 50 percent of the payment within the first year. This *front-end* load contract does absorb a large percentage of the initial year's payments and is therefore undesirable for one seeking to invest for a short period. For example, suppose that an investor entered a $6000 contract to buy mutual fund shares in X company and was assessed a front-end load of 50 percent in the first year, with equal spreading thereafter, as required by the Investment Company Act. He pays $54 per month, and $324 (12 × $27), or one half of his payment, goes as load in the first year, with the balance of $156 in load being distributed over the life of the contract. Thereafter, about $1.48 per month is load and $52.52 is share investment. He may cancel the contract at any time without additional penalty, but the front-end load fee arrangement makes it undesirable to drop out of such a plan before its completion. One attractive feature of the plan is its forced savings tendency because of the cheapness of the load after the first year.

The investor in the closed-end investment company may acquire shares from a securities dealer, paying the ask price, or sell them to the dealer at the bid price. In this way his cost of buying and disposing of the securities is the spread between the dealer's bid and ask prices. When the shares are traded on a registered exchange, the regular brokerage fee and transfer taxes are assessed the customer.

Management Fee

Many investment company funds are not managed by their board of directors but by a special management group hired to advise in the buying and selling of specific securities. The cost range of the management fees for 40 investment companies are reflected in Table 23-5, but ½ of 1 percent per year of the average assets is typical. The management fee for some of the funds was substantially less than this figure in 1965, since in many cases a single management group handles the buying and selling for numerous funds on a fee basis. Rarely is the management fee computed as a percentage of income, but it is usually ⅛ of 1 percent of the average assets during each quarter.

Expenses

In addition to the management fee, salaries must be paid to the corporate directors; costs of preparing annual, interim, and tax reports must be met; and housing and other expenses must be borne. Expenses as a percentage of total assets for selected mutual funds are shown in column 3 of Table 23-5. The operating expenses of the Massachusetts Investment Trust amounted to only 0.18 percent of assets, or 6.1 percent of total income, excluding capital gains; but the expenses of U.S. Science Fund, National Security Growth Stock Series, and other companies were substantially higher. On the average, 18.9 percent of income was absorbed by operating expenses.

Special Tax Provisions for Investment Companies

Chapter 9 outlined the general requirements of the Investment Company Act of 1940 with respect to a registered investment company. The act requires honest and unbiased management and participation in management by security holders (at least two thirds of the directors must be elected by the shareholders). It stipulates that prospectuses must be given to potential purchasers of the shares and that periodic financial statements must be distributed to the shareholders. The amount of investment that may be made by an open-end company in the securities of any one corporation is also limited. For example, an open-end investment company may not acquire more than 10 percent of any class of securities of a corporation and may not invest more than 5 percent of its total assets in a single corporation. This requires some degree of diversification. A closed-end investment company, conversely, is not required to diversify to such an extent. Many closed-end investment companies hold substantial amounts of their total assets in the securities of a very limited number of issuers.

It is advantageous for an investment company to comply with the Revenue Act of 1942, which provides special tax treatment for regulated investment companies. A *regulated investment company* is a domestic corporation that at all times during the year is registered under the Investment Company Act of 1940 as a management company and that satisfies the following prerequisites:

1. At least 90 percent of its gross income is derived from dividends, interest, and gains from the sale or other disposition of securities.

TABLE 23-5 / Management Fees and Expense Ratios

	Range of Management Fees, % of Average Assets	Expenses, As % of Assets	Expenses, As % of Income
Affiliated Fund	.5–.2 of 1%	0.31%	10.0%
American Mutual Fund	.5–.33 of 1%	0.57	19.3
Axe Houghton Fund B	.5–.25 of 1%	0.67	19.2
Boston Fund	.5–.25 of 1%	0.54	15.3
Broad Street Investing Corp.	No set fee	0.19	6.1
Chemical Fund	.5–.2 of 1%	0.41	22.7
Colonial Fund	.5–.375 of 1%	0.48	14.8
Delaware Fund	.5 of 1%	0.56	27.0
Dividend Shares	.5–.19 of 1%	0.46	15.1
Dreyfus Fund	.5 of 1%	0.46	21.4
Eaton & Howard Balanced Fund	.5 of 1%	0.57	15.7
Eaton & Howard Stock Fund	.5 of 1%	0.54	20.7
Fidelity Capital Fund	.5–.4 of 1%	0.50	41.2
Fidelity Fund	.5–.35 of 1%	0.46	17.2
Fidelity Trend Fund	.5–.4 of 1%	0.36	33.3
Financial Industrial Fund	.5–.35 of 1%	0.59	19.6
Fundamental Investors	.5–.2 of 1%	0.46	19.1
Hamilton Funds, Series H-DA	.5–.25 of 1%	0.64	20.3
Incorporated Investors	.5–.35 of 1%	0.55	20.4
Insurance Securities Trust Fund	.5 of 1%	0.45	28.7
Investment Co. of America	.36–.324 of 1%	0.49	19.8
Investors Mutual	.5–.3 of 1%	0.35	9.7
Investors Stock Fund	.5–.3 of 1%	0.38	14.1
Investors Variable Payment Fund	.5–.3 of 1%	0.43	18.2
Keystone Low-Priced Common Stock Fund	.5–.275 of 1%	0.43	25.6
Massachusetts Investors Growth Stock Fund	.25–.05 of 1%	0.34	19.0
Massachusetts Investors Trust	.14–.04 of 1%	0.18	6.1
National Investors Corp.	No set fee	0.16	8.9
National Securities Stock Series	.5 of 1%	0.64	16.8
One William Street Fund	.375–.25 of 1%	0.49	21.2
Price (T. Rowe) Growth Stock Fund	.5–.35 of 1%	0.48	25.3
Puritan Fund	.4 of 1%	0.44	11.8
George Putnam Fund of Boston	.5–.3 of 1%	0.41	13.0
Putnam Growth Fund	.5–.35 of 1%	0.56	29.3
State Street Investment Corp.	.5–.375 of 1%	0.45	20.5
Television-Electronics Fund	.5–.25 of 1%	0.55	23.7
United Accumulative Fund	.5–.35 of 1%	0.41	15.2
United Income Fund	.5–.35 of 1%	0.44	15.3
United Science Fund	.5–.35 of 1%	0.42	25.6
Wellington Fund	.5–.225 of 1%	0.37	10.6
Average		0.45%	18.9%

SOURCE: Standard & Poor's Corporation, "Standard and Poor's Investment Companies," *Industry Surveys* (New York: Standard and Poor's, September 15, 1966), p. I-38.

2. Less than 30 percent of its gross income is derived from the sale of securities held less than three months;

3. Its investments have the requisite diversification (among other things, at least 50 percent of assets must be cash, government securities, or a diversified list of securities);

4. It distributes to its stockholders as taxable dividends at least 90 percent of its net investment income, exclusive of capital gains; and

5. It elects to be treated as a regulated investment company.[3]

To the extent that net investment income is paid out in the form of dividends to the shareholders, the investment company is not liable for the payment of corporate taxes thereon. The income is passed on to the shareholder, who is taxed on his proportionate net investment income allocated into dividend or interest income, short- or long-term capital gains, and short- or long-term capital losses.

An amendment to the Internal Revenue code on January 1, 1957, permitted a regulated investment company to elect to retain long-term capital gains and to pay a 25 percent tax on the same amount for the account of its stockholders. Where this election is made, each shareholder must:

1. Include his share of the capital gain in his federal income tax return.

2. Take credit for the 25 percent tax paid for his account by the company, and

3. Add to the cost basis of his stock 75 percent of his share of the undistributed capital gains.[4]

Security Transactions of Investment Companies

It may be advantageous for the investor to know whether investment companies are accumulating shares of stock in a given company or disposing of the issue. Since investment companies trade in large lots, their purchases frequently create an imbalance between supply and demand, so that the market price of an issue rises. Conversely, when one or more investment companies are distributing an issue, the supply of securities may depress the market price.

In order to determine the securities that are being acquired or liquidated by individual funds, the investor may compare the financial statements of the fund for two different dates or compare the information reported in the prospectus with a less current annual report. In addition, *The Value Line Investment Survey* conducts a quarterly analysis of the holdings of approximately 70 investment companies and reports on the activities of these companies for the past quarter. The special report indicates the number of

---

[3] Standard & Poor's Corporation, "Standard & Poor's Investment Companies," *Industry Surveys* (New York: Standard & Poor's, October 15, 1964), pp. 1–42.

[4] "Standard & Poor's Investment Companies," *Industry Survey*, October 15, 1964, pp. 1–42.

funds holding, buying, and selling individual issues; the number of shares bought, sold, and currently being held; the percentage of the company's stock being held by investment companies; and other data. Similar information is provided by *Barron's*, Arthur Wiesenberger & Company, and the *Statistical Bulletin*. The data are arranged alphabetically by industries and by companies, and an investor may review this material to determine whether investment companies are accumulating or distributing the shares of a specific company or industry. Although the sales have already occurred, and the distribution and/or accumulation has already affected the market value of the securities, the information may indicate that further purchases and/or sales may be forthcoming in the near future.

Summary

An investor who desires (1) freedom from managing his stock portfolio and (2) diversification in security holdings may elect to invest in the shares of an open or closed-end investment company. Before making this decision, however, one should study growth trends of a number of investment companies to see how well they have performed during recent years. Funds that meet the investment objectives of the individual and that have shown satisfactory operating results may be worthwhile investments.

Although a majority of the common shares of investment companies performed less spectacularly than the popular averages from 1958 through 1965, some $2 to $3 billion in annual sales were made in the early 1960s. However, a few open- and closed-end investment companies did show more capital appreciation than the DJIA or Standard & Poor's Average of 500 Stocks during the early 1960s. It is somewhat unfair to contrast the market performance of investment companies with that of the common stock averages, because investment companies must pay a management fee, other operating expenses, and brokerage and transfer taxes, while gains in the popular averages are gross rather than net of expenses.

The investor should not overlook the possibility of investing in debentures or warrants of closed-end investment companies. The debentures, some of which are convertible, and the warrants may offer spectacular market growth during certain periods. Whereas closed-end investment company shares are purchased in the over the counter markets or through registered exchanges, open-end investment company shares are purchased directly from the company through selling agents and are resold to the investment company.

QUESTIONS FOR REVIEW /

1. Indicate the primary differences between a closed-end investment company and an ordinary business corporation.
2. Explain the differences in capitalization and investment policies between open- and closed-end investment companies.

3. Trace the growth of investment companies since 1940.
4. Differentiate between the various investment objectives of investment companies.
5. Would you prefer to purchase investment company shares from a large or small company? Explain, and support your answer with calculations.
6. Contrast the operating performance of the investment companies to that of the popular averages.
7. Describe briefly the various types of costs that must be borne by the owners of mutual fund shares.
8. Outline the special tax provisions that apply to investment companies and to holders of investment company shares.
9. Of what significance is stock trading by investment companies to the investor in listed stocks?
10. Contrast an investment in mutual fund shares with a direct investment in stocks and outline an approach for selecting a worthy investment company.

PROBLEMS /

1. Assume that you have $10,000 which you wish to commit to an investment in the shares of an open- or a closed-end investment company. Through the use of Wiesenberger's *Investment Companies*, analyze a number of these companies and determine three that have shown recent outstanding performances. Discuss their operating objectives and determine the company you prefer as an immediate investment.
2. Apply the dollar cost averaging principle of investment to one of the closed-end investment companies listed in Table 23–4 assuming that you have invested $300 quarterly for the past five years and compute your annual rate of return.

REFERENCES /

Financial World, "A Backward Glance," January 9, 1963; and August 26, 1964. New York: Guenther Publishing Corporation.

Investment Companies. New York: Arthur Wiesenberger & Company, 1965.

New York Stock Exchange, *The Exchange.* New York: The Exchange, January 1964, June, 1965, and January, 1966.

Securities and Exchange Commission, *Statistical Bulletin.* Washington, D.C.: U.S. Government Printing Office, June 1966.

Standard & Poor's Corporation, "Standard and Poor's Investment Companies," *Industry Surveys.* New York: Standard & Poor's, October 15, 1964, and September 15, 1966.

chapter 24 | Other Financial Institutions

Introduction

A knowledge of the relationship between financial institutions and the securities markets is important to an individual stockholder for a number of reasons. First, millions of persons have some indirect interest in common stocks through (1) share ownership in financial institutions, (2) pension fund contributions, or (3) life insurance contracts. Second, financial institutions have in the postwar period become large holders of listed securities, particularly New York Stock Exchange issues. Third, financial institutions were large investors in stocks from 1962 to 1965, while individuals, on balance, were selling their shares. Fourth, the actions of financial institutions, which buy and sell in large blocks, exert a tremendous influence upon stock prices.

Operating policies and performances of insurance companies; noninsured pension funds; nonprofit institutions, such as college endowments; and common trust funds are evaluated in this chapter. Since open- and closed-end investment companies were discussed in the previous chapter, we shall limit our comments concerning these types of institutions to general remarks.

Stock Ownership of Financial Institutions

Although there is no exact count of U.S. citizens who are direct or indirect owners of American securities, the number in 1966 was astronomical. Some 110 million persons owned insurance policies for which the companies maintained reserves invested in real property and various types of securities. More than 20 million were direct owners in equity securities; some 7.8 million owned investment company shares; participants in insured and noninsured pension funds had grown to a large number; and others were indirect owners of securities through common trust funds, mutual savings bank deposits, or investment clubs.

Table 24-1 presents the estimated holdings of New York Stock Exchange stocks by financial institutions for the years 1949 to 1965. At the end of 1965, 20.4 percent of Big Board securities were held by these institutions. The ratio had increased from 12.7 percent of the total in 1949. The largest single type of holder was corporate noninsured pension funds, that is, retirement

TABLE 24-1 /   Estimated Holdings of New York Stock Exchange Stocks by Financial Institutions, 1949 to 1965 (billions of dollars)

Type of Institution	Year End					
	1949	1956	1962	1963	1964	1965
Insurance companies						
Life	$ 1.1	$ 2.3	$ 4.1	$ 4.6	$ 5.3	$ 6.2
Nonlife	1.7	4.5	7.1	8.2	9.5	10.3
Investment companies						
Open-end	1.4	7.1	15.4	18.6	21.8	25.5
Closed-end	1.6	4.0	5.3	5.7	6.6	5.5
Noninsured Pension Funds						
Corporate	0.5	5.3	17.9	22.6	27.5	31.8
Other Private	*	0.4	1.0	1.3	1.6	1.9
State and local government	*	0.2	0.8	1.0	1.5	1.7
Nonprofit institutions						
College and university endowments	1.1	2.4	3.3	4.0	4.6	5.2
Foundations	1.1	4.1	6.7	8.1	9.5	10.5
Other	1.0	3.1	5.0	5.9	6.8	7.7
Common trust funds	*	1.0	1.7	2.4	2.6	2.9
Mutual Savings Banks	0.2	0.2	0.4	0.4	0.4	0.5
Total	$ 9.7	$ 34.6	$ 68.7	$ 82.8	$ 96.8	$109.7
Market value of all NYSE-listed Stocks	$76.3	$219.2	$345.8	$411.3	$474.3	$537.5
Estimated percentage held by all institutions	12.7%	15.8%	19.9%	20.1%	20.4%	20.4%

* Less than $50 million.

SOURCE: New York Stock Exchange, *The Exchange* (New York: The Exchange), selected issues.

funds managed by trustees elected by corporate management and/or labor unions, whose holdings increased by 6000 percent over the 16-year period. The second largest holder was the open-end mutual fund, while nonlife insurance companies, for example, fire and casualty, and foundations approximately tied for third place. At the end of 1965, financial institutions owned New York Stock Exchange issues representing a total market value of about $110 billion.

Figure 24-1 shows that from 1963 to 1965 financial institutions were net purchasers while individuals were net sellers of securities. A substantial portion of the investments made by the institutions flowed into common stocks. Some of the individual sellers, of course, could have become indirect owners of equities, but these statistics do point out that pension funds and

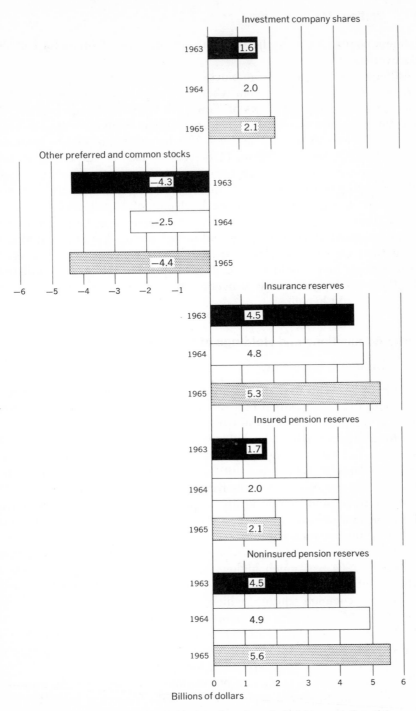

FIGURE 24-1 / Flow of individual savings to selected types of financial institutions, 1963–1965. Compiled from Securities and Exchange Commission, *Statistical Bulletin,* Washington, D.C., U.S. Government Printing Office, July 1966, p. 21.

investment companies were the predominant suppliers of funds for common stocks over the period.

Although ownership of large blocks of securities by financial institutions and their willingness to buy them when they appear at bargain levels does provide some floor for the prices of New York Stock Exchange equities, the annual turnover rate of securities held by mutual funds increased from 21 percent in 1964 to 25 percent in 1965. The turnover rate of life insurance company holdings increased from 11 percent in 1963 to 12 percent in 1964 and to 14 percent in 1965, but the turnover rate for pension funds was quite small, amounting to some 6 percent in 1965. The figures compare to annual turnover rate on the New York Stock Exchange of 15, 14, and 16 percent for 1963, 1964, and 1965, respectively.[1] Of course, if a large number of financial institutions begin to go in and out of the market in attempting to increase their capital gains, such trading could generate wide swings in security prices. Some holders would benefit from the price oscillations while others would lose money. Brokerage firms, because of a larger volume of business, would benefit.

Security Acquisitions and Holdings of Insurance Companies

Life Insurance Companies

Table 24-2 reveals that at the end of 1965 U.S. life insurance companies owned more than $158 billion in assets, with about 44 percent of this total invested in bonds and 6 percent in stocks. An additional 38 percent was committed to mortgages, while the balance was held in other types of assets. From the end of 1963 through year-end 1965, life insurance companies purchased on balance $2 billion in equity securities. Roughly 30 percent of this total was in preferred issues, and the balance was in common stocks. Few railroad stocks were held, public utility acquisitions dominated the preferred stock sector, and industrial and miscellaneous classifications were the most important of the common equities.

For some insurance companies the growth rate of insurance in force from 1959 to 1964 was much higher than the rate of growth of assets or investment income. Stable interest rates from 1960 to 1964 and their small investments in common equities, which normally appreciate in value, made it difficult for life insurance companies to increase their return on investments. The substantial shift from high-cost insurance to group and individual term insurance, induced by lower premiums, also placed some squeeze on revenue growth relative to insurance in force.

Table 24-3, which is an extract of information on selected life insurance companies that are surveyed each year by *Forbes Magazine*, presents a five-year summary of growth rates of admitted assets, insurance in force,

[1] "Higher Turnover—The New Look in Institutional Investing?" *The Exchange* (New York: New York Stock Exchange, May 1966), pp. 11–12.

premium income, and investment income for selected companies. For many of the companies the five-year compounded growth rate of insurance in force was substantially higher than that for admitted assets or for premium income. Although the five-year compounded growth rate in income was substantial for many of the large life insurance companies, only about 20 to 30 percent of total revenue resulted from investment income, while the balance was from premium income.

During the 1950s, life insurance shares were quite popular, and on balance market values increased substantially over the decade. From 1950 to 1955, the market value of insurance shares increased, but from 1955 to 1957 it declined. There was some increase in the market value of the shares from 1958 to 1961, but the market prices of insurance shares were generally at about the same level in early 1965 as in late 1961. A majority of the shares of the companies listed in Table 24-3 were trading at roughly 25 to 30 times annual earnings per share in 1965, while one of these companies, American General, was trading at 42 times earnings. Whether or not the growth rates of these companies will be adequate to offset the tremendous price–earnings ratios is not known, but life insurance companies have been heavy investors in mortgages and fixed-return corporate securities and relatively light investors in equities. A major part of the growth rate in investment income has been facilitated by substantial increases in assets. Life insurance companies were showing a trend toward slightly heavier investments in corporate equities in the mid-1960s than in the past but continued to invest predominantly in fixed-return securities, for example, mortgages, corporate debt, and government issues.

Nonlife Insurance Companies

Table 24-1 indicates that the rate of growth in holdings of New York Stock Exchange stocks from 1949 through 1965 was higher for nonlife than for life insurance companies. Nonlife insurance companies frequently invest a much larger portion of their total assets in common stocks than do life insurance companies. Many nonlife companies invest from 40 to 60 percent of their total assets in equities rather than 5 or 6 percent, which is typical for life insurance companies. Conversely, the total asset holdings of nonlife insurance companies was not increasing nearly as rapidly as was that of life insurance companies. The lower asset holdings of the nonlife companies may be accounted for by the shorter contracts written by these companies, their heavier payouts in benefits, and the low profit margins earned on many of their contracts. For example, the claims paid on automobile liability insurance were in excess of the amount of premiums collected for this type of coverage during the early 1960s. The holdings of New York Stock Exchange common stocks by nonlife insurance companies increased by 505 percent from 1949 to 1965, while the total market value of all New York Stock Exchange securities increased by 605 percent. The nonlife insurance

TABLE 24-2 / Acquisitions and Changes in Security Holdings of U.S. Life Insurance Companies, 1964 to 1965 (in millions of dollars)

Type of Investment		1964 Acquired in Year	1964 Held at Year End	1964 Change in Holdings in Year	1965 Acquired in Year	1965 Held at Year End	1965 Change in Holdings in Year
Bonds							
Government	U.S.	$ 3926	$ 5594	$- 219	$ 3375	$ 5119	$- 475
	Foreign	222	842	+ 28	166	859	+ 17
State, provincial, and local	U.S.	365	3774	- 78	296	3530	- 244
	Foreign	203	1865	+ 164	125	1946	+ 81
Railroad	U.S.	103	3311	- 36	111	3298	- 13
	Foreign	0	16	- 2	0	16	—
Public utility	U.S.	891	16,323	- 121	704	16,122	- 201
	Foreign	49	893	+ 9	64	924	+ 31
Industrial and miscellaneous	U.S.	13,468	33,138	+1925	19,061	35,795	+2657
	Foreign	1171	2207	+ 210	799	2543	+ 336
Total bonds		20,398	67,963	+1880	24701	70,152	+2189
Stocks							
Preferred	Railroad	5	70	+ 6	7	81	+ 11
	Public utility	225	1723	+ 163	302	1995	+ 272
	Ind. & misc.	86	723	+ 32	168	787	+ 64
Common	Railroad	7	46	+ 6	11	62	+ 16
	Public utility	85	1304	+ 153	119	1349	+ 45
	Ind. & misc.	658	4072	+ 443	856	4852	+ 780
Total Stocks		1066	7938	+ 803	1463	9126	+1188

Mortgages						
Farm	1047	4304	+ 512	1149	4823	+ 519
Nonfarm FHA	1879	11,935	+ 775	1784	12,538	+ 603
VA	674	6403	+ 2	553	6286	− 117
Conventional	6833	32,510	+3319	7651	36,366	+3856
Total mortgages	10,433	55,152	+4608	11,137	60,013	+4861
Real Estate						
Company used	145	1335	+ 80	117	1396	+ 61
Investment Residential	8	402	− 5	5	393	− 9
Commercial	261	2707	+ 125	245	2791	+ 84
Other	74	84	+ 9	81	101	+ 17
Total Real Estate	488	4528	+ 209	448	4681	+ 153
Policy loans	1574	7140	+ 485	1702	7678	+ 538
Cash	xxx	1488	+ 22	xxx	1503	+ 15
Other assets	xxx	5261	+ 342	xxx	5731	+ 470
Total assets	$33,959	$149,470	$+8349	$39,451	$158,884	$+9414

SOURCE: Institute of Life Insurance, *Life Insurance Fact Book* (New York: Institute of Life Insurance, 1966), p. 67.

TABLE 24-3 / A Financial Profile of Large Stock Life Insurance Companies on December 31, 1964

Five-Year Summary

Company	Admitted Assets (How much do they have to work with?) 12/31/64 (millions)	5-year Compounded Growth rate	Insurance in Force (How well have their salesmen done?) 12/31/64 (millions)	5-year Compounded Growth rate	Premium Income 1964 (millions)	5-year Compounded Growth rate	Investment Income (How much are their investments earning?) 1964 (millions)	5-year Compounded Growth rate
Multiple Line Companies								
Aetna Life	$5047	5.8%	$32,111	6.9%	$1015.0	6.2%	$210.7	10.3%
Nonlife business	1075	8.8	—	—	566.9	10.8	28.9	13.6
Travelers	3781	3.4	36,721	7.8	979.3	3.8	136.0	4.4
Nonlife business	998	13.0	—	—	572.2	12.7	25.3	14.8
Connecticut General	3043	7.9	15,980	8.7	456.3	6.8	133.4	11.3
Nonlife business	421	7.3	—	—	233.3	8.9	47.9	8.1
American General								
Life business°	384	9.6	2874	12.8	68.2	10.0	14.0	10.2
Nonlife business°	446	4.8	—	—	229.0	3.9	16.1	10.2†
Straight Life Companies								
Lincoln National	1849	5.4	13,593	6.7	279.4	6.6	75.6	7.4
National Life & Accident	1195	7.8	7444	5.8	198.1	5.8	43.5	12.0
Occidental Life°°	1118	8.3	15,078	10.8	294.9	6.5	44.1	9.6
American National	1089	6.1	7619	8.6	157.9	6.7	46.9	13.6
Continental Assurance	1088	10.5	9702	9.4	238.3	8.5	45.6	16.5
Franklin Life	836	9.6	5686	9.6	121.6	5.6	33.1	15.2
Jefferson Standard	780	5.9	2536	5.7	63.1	3.8	39.0	7.3
Pilot†	276	7.2	2710	11.1	65.5	8.4	12.3	8.4
Southwestern Life	753	9.4	3276	10.7	96.3	13.1	30.8	14.3
Life of Virginia	656	6.4	3617	8.5	80.5	4.6	26.7	10.3
Liberty National	482	10.7	3032	12.6	84.9	7.9	20.9	13.3
Kansas City Life	465	3.6	1707	4.4	35.7	1.8	18.7	7.2
Life & Casualty of Tenn.	392	5.8	2526	7.0	60.8	4.7	16.6	11.6

° Four-year compounded rate. °° Largest wholly owned subsidiary of Transamerica Corp. (two-thirds of profits). Stock data applies to Transamerica shares. † Wholly owned subsidiary of Jefferson Standard.

SOURCE: "Life Insurance Stocks: 1965 Reports," Forbes Magazine, May 1, 1965, pp. 22–23.

companies reduced their stock holdings somewhat relative to the total market value of all Big Board issues, in contrast to investment companies, noninsured pension funds, nonprofit institutions, and common trust funds, which increased their holdings.

Experience of TIAA and CREF

The Teachers Insurance and Annuity Association is a nonprofit, legal reserve life insurance and annuity company that was incorporated in New York in 1918 for the advancement of teaching. The TIAA provides annuities and life insurance for the college world at low cost, and more than 150,000 persons, including those employed by over 1000 educational institutions, were enrolled in TIAA retirement plans in 1964.

In 1952, a special act of the New York state legislature provided for the establishment of a College Retirement Equity Fund (CREF), which was organized as a separate, nonprofit corporation and was to be a companion to the TIAA. College teachers may invest none, one fourth, one third, or one half of their retirement payments into the variable annuity plan of CREF, which invests in New York Stock Exchange common shares, with the balance being invested into an annuity plan maintained by TIAA. In 1952, the CREF annuity unit had a value of $10. By the start of the 1964–1965 school year, the annuity unit had increased in value to $26.48, which represented an increase in market value of about 165 percent. This variable annuity plan has become very popular, and roughly 85 percent of the new TIAA enrollees in 1964–1965 were participating in CREF, with about 90 percent of these persons electing to put the maximum amount—50 percent—of their total premium contributions into CREF. The value of the CREF portfolio grew from zero in 1952 to $448 million in December 1964. Each month the CREF investment department invests about $6 million in shares of 77 large companies representative of about 18 industry groupings.

The 25 largest common stock holdings in the CREF portfolio at the end of 1963 and 1964 are listed in Table 24-4. On the latter date, 54,500 shares of International Business Machines were held, with a market value of about $22 million. Blue chip industrial companies and large electric utility companies were widely represented in the list of common stocks held in the portfolio.

Through the principle of dollar cost averaging, the fund has been increasing at a growth rate substantially in excess of the return that would be expected from an investment in fixed-return securities such as government issues, corporate bonds, and mortgages. The administrators of CREF, in addition to the participants in TIAA–CREF, appear to be pleased with the performance of the fund.[2] It is interesting to study some of the operating results of CREF. During 1962, when the stock market suffered a severe

---

[2] See, for example, William C. Greenough, "Is the Variable Annuity Making the Grade in College? The TIAA–CREF Experience," *Pension and Welfare News*, November 1964.

TABLE 24-4 /   The 25 Largest Blocks of Common Stocks in the CREF Portfolio

| | Dec. 31, 1964 | | Dec. 31, 1963 | |
Company	Shares Held	Market Value	Shares Held	Market Value
Intl. Business Machine (1)	54,500a	$ 22,317,750	40,000	$ 20,280,000
Texaco (2)	205,000b	17,963,125	158,000	11,060,000
General Motors (4)	152,000c	14,877,000	108,000	8,491,500
Standard Oil (N.J.) (3)	164,000	14,780,500	123,000	9,348,000
Gulf Oil (8)	201,000	11,758,500	159,000	7,473,000
Monsanto (11)	137,000d	11,747,750	114,000	7,139,250
Shell Oil (14)	196,000	11,662,000	148,000	6,397,500
General Electric (10)	118,000	11,003,500	84,500	7,362,062
Eastman Kodak (7)	75,000b	10,387,500	66,150	7,658,044
Continental Oil (17)	131,000	9,988,750	101,000	6,110,500
American Tel. & Tel. (6)	143,000	9,759,750	55,000	7,658,750
General Foods (5)	107,500	8,667,187	90,500	8,133,687
Caterpillar Tractor	205,500e	8,476,875	93,000	4,464,000
Du Pont (13)	34,500	8,310,188	29,000	6,952,750
Houston L. & P. (19)	154,000	8,046,500	136,000	5,882,000
Corning Glass (9)	39,000	7,839,000	35,500	7,472,750
Texas Utilities (15)	124,500	7,594,500	111,000	6,299,250
Florida P. & L. (18)	96,500	7,321,937	82,000	5,986,000
Proctor & Gamble (16)	89,500	7,294,250	78,500	6,270,187
Virginia E. & P. (20)	148,500	7,202,250	128,500	5,670,062
American Elec. Power (21)	161,000	7,144,375	140,000	5,652,500
Central & South West (22)	139,500	7,114,500	122,000	5,642,500
Merck	138,500f	6,873,062	40,000	4,380,000
Southern Co.	104,500	6,857,813	88,500	4,856,438
Minnesota Mng. & Mfg. (12)	122,000	6,755,750	108,000	6,979,500
Total	3,241,500	$251,744,312	2,439,150	$183,620,230

a—Reflects 25% stock dividend.
b—Reflects 5% stock dividend.
c—Reflects distribution of GM stock owned by DuPont.
d—Reflects 2% stock dividend.
e—Reflects 2 for 1 split.
f—Reflects 3 for 1 split.
Figures in parentheses after names indicate 1963 rank, if any.
SOURCE: *The Exchange,* June 1965, p. 15.

break, the CREF reported a decline in unit value of 14.36 percent. In 1963, a gain of 18.34 percent was reported, while the increase in 1964 was 12.66 percent. By the end of 1964, the fund was holding utility stocks valued at about $73 million, oils valued at $66 million, and chemicals worth about $43 million. Smaller investments were reported for the other industries represented in the fund.[3]

[3] *The Exchange,* June 1965, pp. 14–15.

College and University Endowment Funds

College and university endowment funds increased their holdings of New York Stock Exchange stocks by approximately 300 percent from 1949 to 1965, contrasted to a 605 percent gain for all financial institutions. The probable reason for this substantially smaller growth in investments by college and university endowments is that these funds frequently utilize a part of their investment income to defer operating costs of their institutions. The conservative investment policies followed by the investment officers of many of the university endowment funds, in keeping with state requirements, has contributed to their policy of investing in relatively stable, blue chip issues.

At mid-1965, approximately 54.4 percent of the $980 million in the Harvard University general investment account was in common stock equities. The Yale University investment fund aggregated $457 million at market value and was 61.9 percent committed to common stock investments, and Princeton University held some 73 percent of the endowment fund's investment assets in the form of common stocks. The total market value of the fund at that date was $301 million.

Table 24-5 indicates that the administrators of the investment funds at Harvard, Princeton, and Yale favored petroleum and utility issues. For example, of the 10 leading stock holdings on June 30, 1965, Harvard held Texaco, Gulf Oil, Standard Oil (New Jersey), and Standard Oil of California. Two of the top 10 issues were utilities and included Middle South Utilities and American Telephone and Telegraph. Princeton University holdings included Texaco, Gulf Oil, and Standard Oil (New Jersey). The 4 utility issues included in the top 10 in 1963 had fallen out of the top 10 by 1965. The holdings of Yale, conversely, were more widely distributed by industry than those of the other two universities. For example, only one petroleum company, Standard Oil of Indiana, ranked among the top 10. The fund also held considerable amounts of General Motors, Ford, International Business Machines, International Nickel of Canada, General Electric, and DuPont.[4]

Although not included in Table 24-5, the University of Texas also has a large Permanent University Fund. In the early 1960s, the fund was increasing by substantial amounts. From 1950 to 1964, the cash receipts of the fund ranged from $16 to $37 million per year, and the average annual receipt during the 1959 to 1964 period was about $18 million, a substantial portion of which was invested in the common equities of leading business corporations. Before 1956, no monies were delegated to common equities, but a general election in November 1956 authorized the board of regents of the University of Texas to invest up to 50 percent of the Permanent University Fund in corporate securities. Some 10 percent of the total amount was allo-

---

[4] For a more detailed explanation of the endowment fund holdings of these three universities, see *The Exchange,* January 1966, pp. 14–15.

TABLE 24-5 / Leading Common Stock Holdings of Princeton, Yale, and Harvard at the Close of the Fiscal Year Ended June 30, 1964 and 1965

	1965		1964	
Company	No. of Shares	Market Value	No. of Shares	Market Value
PRINCETON UNIVERSITY				
Texaco	164,937	$12,700,000	154,751	$12,380,000
Xerox	75,655	10,667,000	75,604	8,694,000
Int'l Bus. Machine	20,734	9,496,000	17,113	8,163,000
Louisiana Land & Expl.	161,552	8,078,000	80,776	7,108,000
Standard Oil (N.J.)	96,379	7,516,000	80,821	7,031,000
Gulf Oil	133,960	7,368,000	128,400	7,190,000
Amer. Home Products	82,095	5,582,000	39,408	2,640,000
Bristol Myers	75,307	5,648,000	27,620	1,768,000
General Motors	49,091	4,713,000	38,057	3,349,000
DuPont	19,647	4,617,000	19,115	4,836,000
YALE UNIVERSITY				
Int'l Bus. Machine	24,000	$10,992,000	26,218	$12,505,000
General Motors	109,261	10,489,000	97,011	8,513,000
AT & T	105,000	7,035,000	105,000	7,718,000
General Electric	72,600	6,970,000	70,000	5,583,000
Celanese	80,000	6,240,000	80,000	5,230,000
Standard Oil of Indiana	135,000	6,210,000	85,000	6,736,000
Beneficial Finance	100,000	6,000,000	47,180	2,412,000
Consolidation Coal	125,000	6,000,000	125,000	6,188,000
DuPont	24,500	5,782,000	26,060	6,593,000
Int'l Nickel	65,000	5,460,000	70,000	5,513,000
HARVARD UNIVERSITY				
General Motors	275,604	$26,355,000	142,594	$12,513,000
Texaco	325,361	25,215,477	302,994	24,088,000
Int'l Bus. Machine	54,683	25,044,814	53,776	25,651,000
Gulf Oil	334,352	18,348,000	320,496	17,828,000
Standard Oil (N.J.)	215,537	16,866,000	209,549	18,231,000
Standard Oil Calif.	199,872	13,641,000	199,056	12,714,000
Ford	258,251	13,590,000	172,658	9,065,000
AT & T	199,061	13,412,000	192,242	14,143,000
Middle South Util.	270,837	13,399,000	270,587	12,176,000
Eastman Kodak	112,965	9,009,000	53,933	7,173,000

SOURCE: *The Exchange,* January 1966, p. 15.

cated to investments in corporate bonds and preferred stocks, while 40 percent was earmarked for investment in common equities. The other half was to be devoted to government issues, including U.S. government securities, state of Texas securities, and Texas municipalities. Although assets in the fund were not liquidated and rechanneled in common stock investments, a majority of the new monies that flowed to the Permanent Investment Fund from 1957 to 1965 were invested in common stocks. From 1957, when the fund first began to buy common equities, through August 31, 1964, the Permanent University Fund had invested slightly more than $100 million in common stock equities, which represented a total market value in excess of $140 million on the latter date. In selecting the issues, the fund used the dollar cost averaging method, as outlined in detail below.

The investment policies followed by the Permanent University Fund investment account with regard to standards of quality, price, and diversification were as follows:

Standards as to Quality

*1. Stock must be issued by a company incorporated within the United States.
*2. Except for bank and insurance shares, stock must be listed on a registered security exchange.
*3. Stock must have an unbroken dividend payment record over the preceding ten years prior to purchase.
*4. Not more than 1% of the Permanent University Fund may be invested at any one time in securities issued by any one corporation.
*5. Not more than 5% of the voting stock in any one corporation may be owned by the Permanent University Fund at any one time.
*6. Issuer must be one of the leading corporations in its industry group.
*7. Corporate bonds must be rated "A" or higher by either Moody's or Standard & Poor's. Bonds offered by private placement, by custom not rated, will be considered to carry the same rating as comparable bonds issued by the same company which have been rated "A" or better.

 * Required by provisions of Constitutional Amendment authorizing investments of up to 50% of the Permanent University Fund in corporate securities.

8. The corporation must measure up to the following minimum financial statement ratio standard, these standards applying to initial purchase only—
   a. Bonded Debt to Book Value of Total Investment*
      (1) Public Utilities—not to exceed 55%
      (2) Railroads—not to exceed 45%
      (3) Industrials—not to exceed 30%
   b. Times Bond Service Covered (before income taxes)—
      Public Utilities—average of at least 5 times during past 5 years
      Railroads—average of at least 6 times during past 5 years
      Industrials—average of at least 7 times during past 5 years
   c. Net Profit (after income taxes) to Book Value of Total Investment—
      Public Utilities and Financial Corporations—average of at least 4½% during past 5 years
      Railroads—average of at least 4¾% during past 5 years
      Industrials—average of at least 6½% during past 5 years

 * Total investment is fixed Liabilities plus net worth.

Standards as to Price

As a general rule, corporate bonds and preferred stocks will be purchased to the extent possible at yields to exceed the yield on the longest term Treasury Bond by the following minimum margins—
>   a. Corporate bonds—¼%
>   b. Preferred stocks—½%

Dollar Averaging Principle

Corporate securities are to be purchased on the dollar cost averaging principle, averaging to be based on industry groupings rather than on individual companies, that is—
1. When funds become available, securities are to be purchased without any attempt to appraise the short-term market trend.
2. Percentage allocations to the various industry groups as set out in the policies are to be maintained substantially as approved. However, purchases of stocks within each industry group will be weighted in favor of the companies considered to have better than average long-term investment merit and growth potentials. Size becomes a factor in weighting only when considered in relation to the Constitutional Amendment restriction that not more than 5% of the voting stock of any one corporation may be owned by the Permanent University Fund at any one time.

Broad Diversification Patterns

The broad diversification patterns set out in the policies are as follows—
1. Corporate Bonds and Preferred Stocks—
a. Industrials	15.0%
b. Public Utilities	80.0
c. Railroads (including rail equipment)	2.0
d. Financial Corporations	3.0
2. Common Stocks—
a. Industrials	63.0%
b. Public Utilities	24.5
c. Railroads	2.0
d. Financial Corporations	10.5

Investment of Funds

The provisions of the policies with respect to purchases and sales of corporate and government securities are as follows:
1. As funds become available, the Endowment Office is authorized to purchase corporate and government securities within the policies and programs approved by the Board of Regents.
2. Sales of corporate and government securities, except for sales of temporary investments in Treasury Bills, require prior approval of the Board of Regents.
3. All purchases and sales of corporate and government securities must be reported at the next subsequent meeting of the Board of Regents for ratification and approval.[5]

[5] *Report on Permanent University Fund Investments* (Austin, Texas: University of Texas, 1964), pp. 2 and 3.

Over the 1957 to 1964 period the fund bought only domestic stock issues of registered securities other than bank and insurance company shares. The investment policy requires that not more than 1 percent of the Permanent University Fund be invested in securities issued by one corporation and that not more than 5 percent of the voting stock in any one corporation be owned by the fund. The fund follows a broad diversification pattern and requires that investments be in leading corporations within their industry. Although a majority of the preferred stocks must be representative of public utility companies, some 63 percent of the common stocks must be issued by industrial companies. The railroad issue holdings were relatively unimportant for bonds, preferred stocks, and common stocks.

To aid in the development of a sound investment program and to implement the policies adopted by the board of regents, an investment advisory firm and an investment advisory committee consisting of four senior investment officers of the investment and trust departments of large commercial banks and insurance companies in the state of Texas have been used by the Permanent Fund since 1957. A staff investment committee, consisting of four officers from the University of Texas, was active in making the decision as to which securities to purchase, and in early 1965, the Permanent University Fund was invested in approximately 135 common stock issues representing about 24 different industries. Industry weights had been assigned, but the staff investment committee was authorized to select from approved companies within each industry. The staff investment committee was delegated the responsibility of determining the specific corporate and government securities to be purchased and the timing of such purchases as cash became available for investment. The timing of the sale of securities was delegated to the board of regents of the University of Texas.

It was the intention of the board of regents of the University of Texas to use the dollar cost averaging principle, by industry, but to permit the investment committee complete flexibility in choosing specific companies within the industries for investing. It is not the policy of the university to sell the securities unless they have been dropped from the approved list, but when this occurs, the securities are liquidated as soon as possible. In making specific selections of issues within a specified industry, the investment committee selects only companies that are dominant in their industries and gives additional importance to those that are yielding slightly higher than average dividend yields. From 1957 through August 31, 1964, the fund had invested about $102 million in stocks, representing an aggregate market value on the latter date of about $142 million and producing an annual capital gain in excess of 4 percent plus dividend income. In early 1965, the fund was channeling approximately $1.2 million per month into common stock investments.[6]

[6] The investment policies and procedures followed by the fund are described in order to indicate how the problems of diversification, risk evaluation, and selectivity may be handled. It is not the intention here to criticize these policies nor to recommend them as a specific approach to be followed by other fund managers.

Noninsured Pension Funds

Noninsured pension funds of corporations are rapidly becoming the number one investor in common stocks in the United States. Table 24-1 indicates that corporate noninsured pension fund holdings of New York Stock Exchange issues was only $0.5 billion in 1949 but has grown to $31.8 billion by the end of 1965. On the earlier date, the book value of the assets of private noninsured pension funds, amounted to about $6 billion, but by the end of 1965, the book value had grown to more than $58 billion and the market value was $71 billion (Fig. 24-2). On December 31, 1965, private noninsured pension funds owned common stocks with a total book value of $24 billion and a market value of approximately $39 billion.[7]

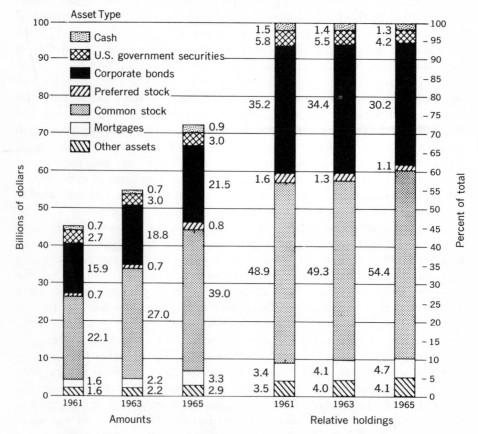

FIGURE 24-2 / Actual and relative distribution of assets for private non-insured pension funds, 1961–1965. From Securities and Exchange Commission, *Statistical Bulletin,* Washington, D.C., U.S. Government Printing Office, June 1966, p. 33.

[7] See, for example, Securities and Exchange Commission, *Statistical Bulletin* (Washington, D.C.: U.S. Government Printing Office, June 1966), p. 33.

Since the investment of pension funds is a long-term proposition, the commitment of assets is a permanent-type investment and not intended as a trading account. Pension fund plans were relatively rare before 1950, but since then they have been increasing in popularity. Figure 24-2 indicates that common stocks were gaining in popularity while corporate bonds were declining slightly in favor. Further growth is anticipated for these plans in the late 1960s and early 1970s.

In 1964, private pension plans covered about 25 million persons, or almost 40 percent of the total working force. In the same year, these retirement plans had annual accumulations of about $6.5 billion and paid out almost $2.75 billion in benefits annually. Thus, almost $4 billion was invested in various types of securities, and to a large degree, these new purchases were common equities. The annual cash inflow by 1980 is forecasted to be about $11 billion a year, and benefits are expected to increase to approximately $9 billion. It is anticipated that private retirement plans will continue to grow and to channel new funds into common stock investments.[8]

In the early 1960s, the value of the common stocks held by welfare and pension plans was growing at an annual rate of about 15 percent. In 1965, private noninsured pension plans had 54.5 percent of their total assets invested in common stocks compared to 48.9 percent in 1961 (Fig. 24-2). Some of the larger plans held almost two thirds of their assets in common stocks, while many of the smaller pension plans have recently begun to diversify their holdings into equities and fixed-return securities rather than investing entirely in the latter.[9]

Common Trust Funds

According to statistics reported in Table 24-1, common trust funds increased their holdings of New York Stock Exchange issues from $1 billion to $2.9 billion from 1956 through 1965. For the period 1955 through 1964, common trust funds grew both in number and in total assets, and according to statistics reported in the *Federal Reserve Bulletin,* 174 commercial banks maintained common trust funds in 1955 compared to 419 in 1964. The number of funds being maintained by these banks increased from 222 to 788 over this time period, the number of participants increased from 87,000 to 228,000, and assets increased from $1.9 billion to $5.9 billion. The average-sized fund fluctuated between $6.3 and $8.4 million and the size of the average account was about $23,000.[10]

A detailed schedule of the asset distribution of common trust funds at

[8] See the President's Committee on Corporate Pension Funds and Other Private Retirement and Welfare Programs, *Public Policy and Private Pension Programs* (Washington, D.C.: U.S. Government Printing Office, 1965), p. vi.

[9] President's Committee, p. vi.

[10] For a more comprehensive analysis of growth and performance of trust funds, see Stanley Silverberg, "Growth and Performance of Common Trust Funds in 1964," *National Banking Review,* March 1965, pp. 363–371.

the end of 1963 and 1964 appears in Table 24-6. Total assets increased from $4.5 to $5.85 billion in 1964, when common stock holdings increased from $2.24 to $2.75 billion. On those dates, common stocks amounted to 49.4 and 47 percent respectively, of the total asset distribution of common trust funds. Corporate and other bonds declined in relative importance, from 24.1 to 23.1 percent, while state and county municipal securities increased from 7.6 to 12.1 percent of the total. Little change was detected in other types of asset distributions.

TABLE 24-6 /   Asset Distribution of Common Trust Funds for 1963 and 1964[1]

Asset	Amount ($ millions) 1963	Amount ($ millions) 1964	Percent of Total 1963	Percent of Total 1964	1963–64 Change Amount ($ millions)	1963–64 Change %
Cash	38.3	40.0	0.8	0.7	1.7	4.4
U.S. government securities[2]						
Under one year	72.1	64.7	1.6	1.1	−7.4	−10.3
All other	427.8	575.8	9.4	9.8	148.0	34.6
State, county, and municipal securities	344.9	705.9	7.6	12.1	361.0	104.7
Corporate and other bonds	1092.8	1353.1	24.1	23.1	260.3	23.8
Mortgages	90.6	132.4	2.0	2.3	41.8	46.1
Preferred stock	221.6	219.2	4.9	3.7	−2.4	−1.1
Common stock	2242.0	2752.1	49.4	47.0	510.1	22.8
Bank and other financial	227.8	247.4	5.0	4.2	19.6	8.6
Utilities	525.3	622.5	11.6	10.6	97.2	18.5
All other	1488.9	1882.2	32.8	32.2	393.3	26.4
Other assets	9.6	11.1	0.2	0.2	1.5	15.6
Total Assets	4539.8	5854.2	100.0	100.0	11,314.4	29.0

[1] These figures were derived from a survey of banks and trust companies operating common trust funds. Data are for the last valuation date in 1964 and 1963.

[2] U.S. government securities include the liabilities of various federal agencies and instrumentalities. Corporate and other bonds include bonds of foreign governments and of the International Bank, corporate mortgage bonds, and privately placed corporate debt other than real estate loans. Mortgages include residential and commercial real estate loans. Other assets include certificates of deposits, other time deposits, and loan shares and ground leases.

SOURCE: Stanley Silverberg, "Growth and Performance of Common Trust Funds in 1964," *National Banking Review,* March 1965, p. 365.

Until April 1963, the comptroller of the currency limited the ceiling on the amount of a single trust account to $100,000. The elimination of that ceiling in April 1963 probably accounted for an increase in the relative importance of the investments in state, county, and municipal securities, since more wealthy individuals began to channel their investments into tax-exempt common trust funds (that is, funds that invest in municipal securities).[11]

The four types of common trust funds are the equity, diversified, fixed-income, and tax-exempt funds. Table 24-7 indicates that in 1964 almost 98 percent of the total assets of equity funds was invested in common stocks, and of this total, the common issues of banks and other financial institutions accounted for 8.6 percent, utility shares aggregated 21.6 percent, and all others totaled 67.6 percent. Small amounts of cash and U.S. government securities were also held by the equity funds. The diversified funds were divided approximately equally between common stocks and all other types of investments, and at the end of 1964, U.S. government securities amounted to about 14 percent of the total, corporate and other bonds accounted for 22 percent, and preferred stocks amounted to 5 percent. The assets of the fixed-

TABLE 24-7 / Distribution of Assets by Type of Common Trust Fund, 1964

Asset	Equity	Diversified	Fixed-Income	Tax-Exempt
Cash	0.6%	0.5%	1.2%	0.8%
U.S. government securities				
Under 1 year	1.1	1.2	1.6	—
All other	0.1	12.6	17.5	—
State, county, and municipal securities	—	0.1	1.5	98.8
Corporate and other bonds	0.1	21.9	63.9	0.4
Mortgages	—	1.7	7.5	—
Preferred stock	0.2	5.1	5.6	—
Common stock	97.8	56.8	0.6	—
Bank and other financial	8.6	5.2	0.1	—
Utilities	21.6	13.0	0.1	—
All other	67.6	38.6	0.4	—
Other assets	0.1	0.1	0.6	—
Total Assets	100.0	100.0	100.0	100.0
Total assets ($ millions)	996.6	3119.4	1042.2	696.1
Number of funds	223	297	202	66
Number of fund participants	50,500	103,800	60,600	13,200
1963				
Total assets ($ millions)	775.0	2764.0	673.7	327.0
Number of funds	191	289	172	41
Number of fund participants	41,800	96,200	46,500	6800

SOURCE: Stanley Silverberg, "Growth and Performance of Common Trust Funds in 1964," *National Banking Review*, March 1965, p. 365.

[11] "Growth and Performance of Common Trust Funds," p. 364.

income common trust funds were devoted primarily to investments in corporate and other bonds, but substantial holdings in U.S. government securities were also maintained. Of the total, 5.6 percent represented preferred issues, with common equities amounting to only 0.6 percent. For the tax-exempt security funds, 98.8 percent of the holdings were in state, county, and municipal securities, while the balance was held in cash.

The size of the fund was influenced substantially by the size of the bank. For example, a bank with less than $100 million in total assets had an average common trust fund of less than $2 million, while a bank with assets above $1 billion had an average trust fund of greater than $20 million. Generally, the larger banks also had more participants in the funds than did the smaller banks.

Equity and diversified common trust funds in 1964 performed somewhat less well than Standard & Poor's Average of 500 Stocks. For the year ended December 31, 1964, Standard & Poor's 500 appreciated 13 percent compared to a median gain of 11.5 percent for common trust equity funds, with a range of 7.7 to 20.4 percent. At the same time, the equity fund was earning an average dividend yield of 3.22 percent. The median capital gain in the diversified funds in 1964 was 6.5 percent, with a range of 1.5 to 17.5 percent. The diversified funds were yielding an average of 3.87 percent during 1964.[12] The performance of the fixed-income and tax-exempt funds, of course, should not be contrasted to that of the stock averages, since these funds are designed for purposes other than capital growth.

Summary

From 1949 to 1965, financial institutions in the United States were important purchasers of common shares, increasing their holdings from 12.7 percent of New York Stock Exchange issues in 1949 to 20.4 percent in 1965. Although life and nonlife insurance companies increased their ownership of common equities, the market values of their holdings did not increase as rapidly as the total market value of all New York Stock Exchange stocks held by all financial institutions. Investment companies, conversely, increased their relative holdings of equity securities over the 16-year period, but common stock holdings of closed-end investment companies did not grow as rapidly as did the total for all financial institutions. Noninsured pension funds, particularly corporate pension funds, grew more rapidly from 1949 to 1965 than did other types of financial institutions. Each year corporate noninsured pension funds channeled some $3.5 to $4 billion into the securities markets, and a large portion of this amount flowed into common equities. Other nonprofit institutions that committed a substantial amount of funds into New York Stock Exchange issues were college and university endowments, foundations, and other nonprofit organizations. Common trust funds and mutual savings banks also channeled new funds into common stock investments.

[12] "Growth and Performance of Common Trust Funds," p. 370.

The investment policies followed by many financial institutions are rather conservative. Often these institutions employ the dollar cost averaging method for investing their common stock funds into a diversified list of American corporations. Investments in petroleum, utility, and office equipment shares were popular in the 1949 to 1965 period.

If past trends prevail, financial institutions will continue to place considerable sums of new money into common equities, largely blue chip issues. Individual investors who are gaining larger indirect interests in common stocks through investment company share ownership or as participants in pension funds are likely to continue to sell securities on balance.

QUESTIONS FOR REVIEW /

1. Contrast the relative growth in holdings of New York Stock Exchange issues by life and nonlife insurance companies.
2. How would you account for the difference in the growth of Big Board holdings by open- and closed-end investment companies?
3. What volume of funds are flowing from corporate noninsured pension funds into common stock investments?
4. How important are college and university endowment funds in channeling monies to the stock market?
5. Contrast the performance of common trust funds to that of the general market.
6. Compare the growth rates of life insurance company (a) assets, (b) insurance in force, (c) premium income, and (d) investment income. What does this comparison reveal about the probable continued growth rate and increase in market value of the common equities of these companies?
7. What industries appear to be well represented in the portfolio of financial institutions?
8. Contrast the asset distribution of common trust equity funds and diversified funds in the United States at the end of 1964. Compare the performance of these funds.
9. What types of investors should use the services of (a) a common trust fund and (b) an open-end investment company?

PROBLEMS /

1. Assuming that the types of financial institutions listed in Table 24–1 continue to purchase and/or sell New York Stock Exchange stocks from 1966 to 1980 in approximately the same amounts that they did from 1949 to 1965, estimate the relative percentage of Big Board stocks owned by financial institutions in 1980. Attempt to project the market value of all New York Stock Exchange issues and the approximate holdings of each of the different types of financial institutions on that date. How much confidence do you have in these projections?
2. For two of the life insurance companies listed in Table 24–3, determine the most recent five-year compounded growth rate of assets, insurance in force, premium income, and investment income. By applying these growth rates as expected future growth rates and taking into account their probable effects

upon earnings per share, determine the appropriate multiple at which the shares of the companies should be traded, assuming that an investor is satisfied with an 8 percent annual return of dividend income and capital appreciation.

3. For some financial institution or endowment fund, determine the 10 largest holdings. Evaluate the market performance of the fund for the past 10 years and attempt to forecast the market performance for the next five years. At current market prices would you recommend that the corporate stock issues continue to be held or be sold? Support your answer with statistical evidence.

4. Assume that you are the senior investment officer of a commercial bank and that you are formulating investment policies for managing an equity common trust fund. You anticipate that $1 million in trust certificates will be issued initially and that an additional $200,000 will be sold each year. Be specific with regard to standards of diversification and quality, accumulation and distribution policies, and so forth. Include a list of industries that you recommend for the portfolio, with a list of specific companies for immediate purchase. (This project may be undertaken on a group basis, with each group composed of 5 to 10 class members. The investment policies may then be compared and modified.)

REFERENCES /

Greenough, William C., "Is the Variable Annuity Making the Grade in College? The TIAA–CREF Experience," *Pension and Welfare News*. New York: Dornost Publishing Company, Inc., November 1964.

Institute of Life Insurance, *Life Insurance Fact Book*. New York: Institute of Life Insurance, 1966.

"Life Insurance Stocks: 1965 Reports," *Forbes Magazine*. New York: Forbes, Inc., May 1, 1965.

"Pension Funds—Number One Investor," *Financial World*. New York: Guenther Publishing Corporation, February 24, 1965.

President's Committee on Corporate Pension Funds and Other Private Retirement and Welfare Programs, *Public Policy and Private Pension Programs*. Washington, D.C.: U.S. Government Printing Office, 1965.

Report on Permanent University Fund Investments. Austin, Texas: University of Texas, 1964.

Silverberg, Stanley, "Growth and Performance of Common Trust Funds in 1964," *National Banking Review*. Washington, D.C.: The Comptroller of the Currency, March 1965.

Appendix

In an attempt to gauge the reliability of certain configurations that appear on vertical bar charts and in order to provide some statistics on the relative moves above and below a pivotal point, 960 weekly range charts[1] were studied for the period from mid-1961 through January 1966. Bullish patterns—inverted head and shoulders, saucer, and rectangle base—and bearish patterns—head and shoulders, inverted saucer, and rectangle top—were classified as to number of occurrences in low-, medium-, and high-priced issues. Stocks below $20 per share were considered low priced, those between $20 and $50 were classified as medium priced, and those trading above $50 were called high priced, and the break out, or completion of a formation, was used in classifying each issue into its price range.

Numerous technicians have suggested that a stock usually moves as far above its pivotal point, that is, the neckline of an inverted head and shoulders or saucer, or above the top of a rectangle, as the depth of the formations below this point. In order to determine the expected values of these relative moves, the depth of each of the above patterns was measured, and the moves above the pivotal points relative to the depths of the patterns that occurred within 90 days and within one year of the break outs were computed and classified into frequency distributions for their respective price categories and patterns. The relative moves that occurred within 90 days of break out were classified into the following categories: below 35; 35–65; 66–99; 100–199; and above 200 percent. The relative moves that occurred within 12 months of break out were classified as follows: below 51; 51–99; 100–199; 200–299; and 300 percent or above. The results are reported in Table A-1 and Figures A-1 to A-5. From a study of the statistics, the following conclusions may be drawn:

1. The inverted head and shoulders formation occurred most frequently with the medium-priced issues, and the relative actual moves of these issues were somewhat greater within 90 days following break out. The greater relative moves occurred within 12 months of break out with the low-priced issues contrasted to medium- and high-priced stocks.

[1] The charts analyzed were those that appeared in *Trendline's Current Market Perspectives* (New York: Trendline Corporation, mid-January, 1965 and 1966).

(*Text continues on page 476.*)

TABLE A-1 / Actual Move as Percentage of Expected Move within 90 Days and One Year of Break Out for Selected Chart Patterns on 960 Weekly Bar Charts Covering Mid-1961 through January 1966

Formation and Price	Number of Occurrences	Relative Occurrences Expressed as Percentages of Expected Move Occurring within 3 Months of Break Out						Relative Occurrences Expressed as Percentages of Expected Move Occurring within 1 Year of Break Out					
		Below 35%	35–65%	66–99%	100–199%	Above 200%	Average*	Below 51%	51–99%	100–199%	200–299%	300 or More	Average*
Inverted head and shoulders													
Stock below 20	21	14.3	33.3	38.9	9.5	4.7	78	4.8	19.0	42.9	19.0	14.3	200
Stock 20–50	78	10.3	29.5	29.5	26.9	3.8	88	9.0	14.1	38.5	25.6	12.8	179
Stock above 50	25	8.0	32.0	28.0	32.0	—	79	8.0	12.0	40.0	28.0	12.0	165
Saucer													
Stock below 20	33	6.1	30.3	36.4	27.2	—	73	3.0	18.2	33.3	30.3	15.2	186
Stock 20–50	144	7.6	27.9	23.6	33.3	7.6	91	6.9	13.2	38.9	26.4	14.6	190
Stock above 50	22	13.6	36.4	13.6	27.3	9.1	90	—	9.1	31.8	45.5	13.6	209
Rectangle base													
Stock below 20	8	—	25.0	12.5	62.5	—	105	12.5	12.5	25.0	12.5	37.5	210
Stock 20–50	10	30.0	10.0	20.0	40.0	—	84	—	—	40.0	40.0	20.0	240
Stock above 50	3	—	—	33.3	66.7	—	93	—	33.3	33.4	—	33.3	203
Head and shoulders													
Stock below 20	7	14.3	14.3	28.6	42.8	—	79	28.6	14.3	57.1	—	—	104
Stock 20–50	93	—	12.9	18.2	66.7	2.2	112	2.2	15.1	68.7	12.9	1.1	126
Stock above 50	41	—	9.8	26.8	48.7	14.7	124	—	12.2	56.1	26.8	4.9	172
Inverted saucer													
Stock below 20	4	—	25.0	25.0	50.0	—	97	—	—	100.0	—	—	118
Stock 20–50	62	—	3.2	27.4	58.1	11.3	127.0	—	19.3	53.2	25.8	1.6	156
Stock above 50	20	5.0	10.0	20.0	35.0	30.0	140.0	5.0	5.0	35.0	40.0	15.0	219
Rectangle top													
Stock below 20	0	—	—	—	—	—	—	—	—	—	—	—	—
Stock 20–50**	2	—	—	—	100.0	—	162	—	—	—	100.0	—	245
Stock above 50	0	—	—	—	—	—	—	—	—	—	—	—	—

* Computed from raw data.   ** Too few to be significant.

SOURCE: *Trendline's Current Market Perspectives* (New York: Trendline Corporation, mid-January, 1965 and 1966).

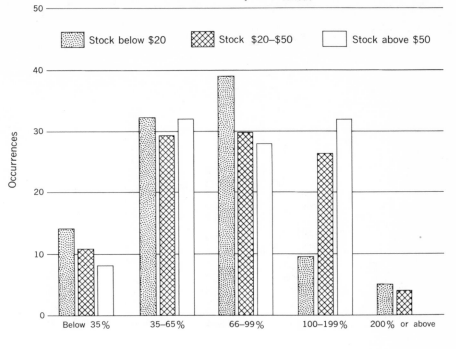

Distribution of Relative Moves within 90 Days of Breakout

Stock below $20   Stock $20–$50   Stock above $50

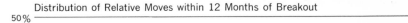

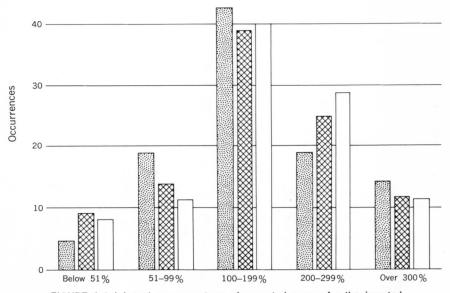

Distribution of Relative Moves within 12 Months of Breakout

FIGURE A-1 / Actual as percentage of expected moves for the inverted head and shoulders occurring on 960 vertical bar charts, 1961–1965. From Table A-1.

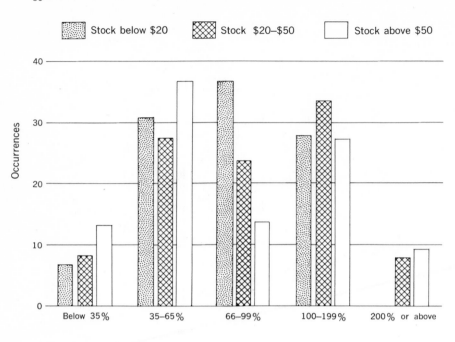

Distribution of Relative Moves within 90 Days of Breakout

Stock below $20   Stock $20–$50   Stock above $50

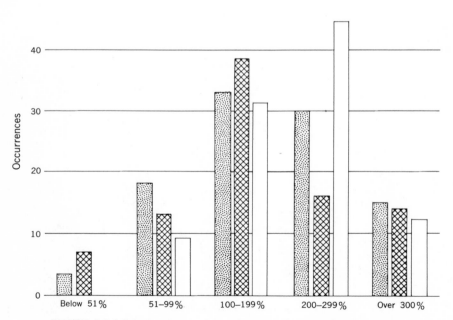

Distribution of Relative Moves within 12 Months of Breakout

FIGURE A-2 / Actual as percentage of expected moves for the saucer
patterns occurring on 960 vertical bar charts, 1961–1965.
From Table A-1.

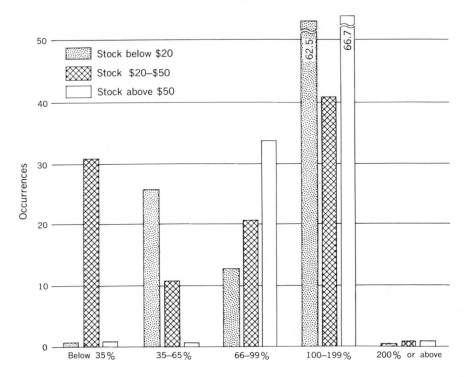

Distribution of Relative Moves within 90 Days of Breakout

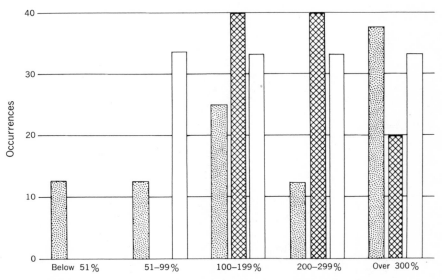

Distribution of Relative Moves within 12 Months of Breakout

FIGURE A-3 / Actual as percentage of expected moves for the rectangle
base formations occurring on 960 vertical bar charts, 1961–
1965. From Table A-1.

Distribution of Relative Moves within 90 Days of Breakout

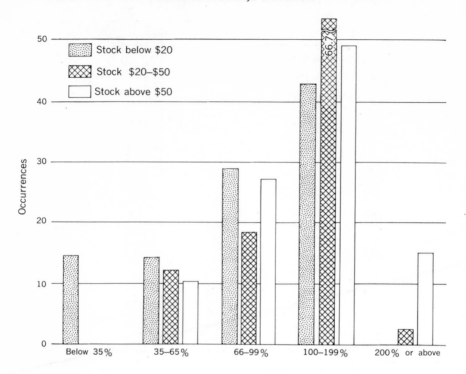

Distribution of Relative Moves within 12 Months of Breakout

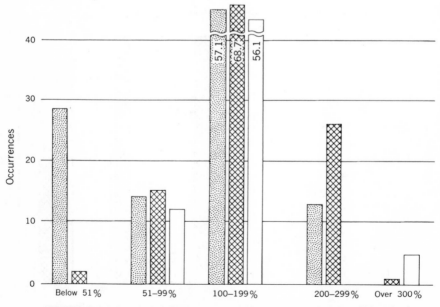

FIGURE A-4 / Actual as percentage of expected moves for the head and shoulders formations appearing on 960 vertical bar charts, 1961–1965. From Table A-1.

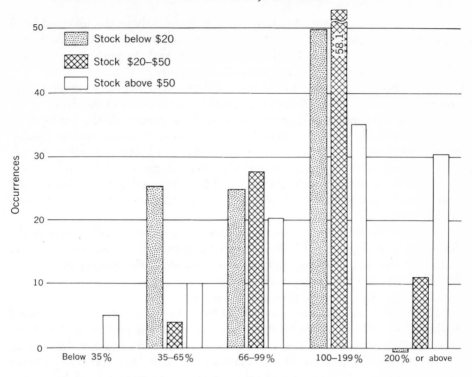

Distribution of Relative Moves within 90 Days of Breakout

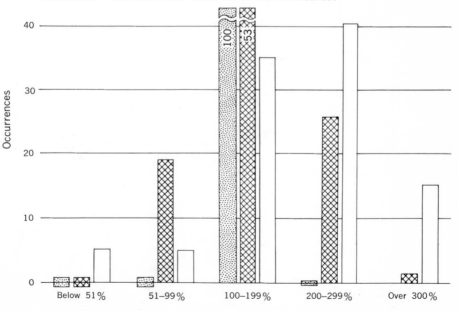

Distribution of Relative Moves within 12 Months of Breakout

FIGURE A-5 / Actual as percentage of expected moves for the inverted saucer formations occurring on 960 vertical bar charts, 1961–1965. From Table A-1.

2. The saucer occurred almost twice as frequently as the inverted head and shoulders, the medium- and high-priced issues were equally preferred over the low-priced issues for the 90-day moves, and the performance of the high-priced stocks was optimum over the 12-month period.

3. Although the rectangle bottom seldom occurred, the average moves from the patterns within 90 days was almost exactly equal to the depth of the rectangles. The low-priced issues were slightly preferred, the high-priced issues ranked intermediate, and the medium-priced issues ranked poorest within 90 days. The latter were optimum for a 12-month holding period.

4. Short sales from a head and shoulders at the break-out point were preferred with the high-priced issues and least favored with the low-priced issues, with about 70 to 80 percent of the 12-month moves achievable within 90 days.

5. The inverted saucers occurred about two thirds as frequently as the head and shoulders, but the moves from the former were more extensive in both time periods. The high-priced issues produced the largest moves, followed by the intermediate-priced issues.

6. Only two rectangle tops were observed.

7. For the bullish formations, about twice the extent of moves occurred within 12 months as within 90 days, which indicates a preference for short-term trading when one disregards transfer costs and income tax differences.

8. Almost 80 percent of the maximum moves from bearish patterns occurred within 90 days and should set the approximate time limit of a short sale.

Index

Index